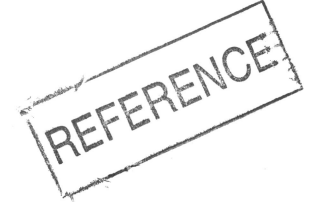

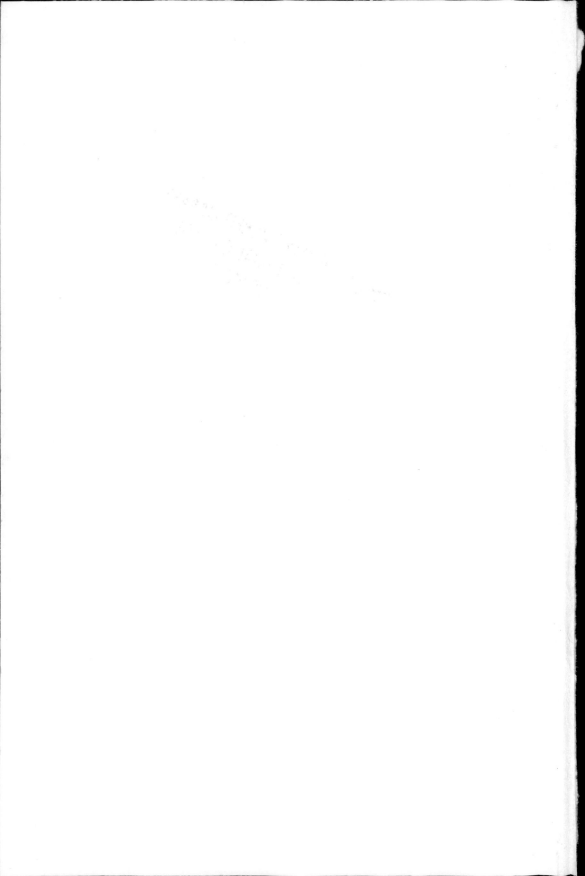

Sport and the Law

Sport and the Law

NEVILLE COX *and* ALEX SCHUSTER

with

CATHRYN COSTELLO

First Law

Published in 2004 by
First Law Limited,
Merchant's Court,
Merchants Quay,
Dublin 8,
Ireland.
www.firstlaw.ie

Typeset by Gough Typesetting Services, Dublin.

ISBN 1–904480–11–X

© Neville Cox and Alex Schuster

A catalogue record for this book
is available from the British Library.

Printed by Judita Press

For my Mother, and in memory of my Father. Thank you.
NC

For Peggy Schuster and in memory of John Schuster.
AS

Foreword

For a subject which is said not to exist, sports law has spawned a remarkable number of books. Now Dr Neville Cox and Alex Schuster have added an essential volume to the sports lawyer's library.

Sports Law in Ireland is both an accurate and a deceptive title. It is accurate because it contains everything that anyone would wish to know about the Irish sporting legal scene. It is deceptive because properly it contains far more than information and analysis on the way in which law impacts upon Gaelic Games. Indeed it could hardly be otherwise for what do they know of Ireland, who only Ireland know?

Fair play is a key value in sport, and so it should be in the field of sports discipline. So Dr Cox gives pride of place to due process. It is interesting to note that the Courts of Ireland take a more pragmatic view than their English equivalents towards identifying the kinds of bodies that are amenable to judicial review and the kind of bodies that are obliged to act fairly, although paradoxically in the extent that private bodies *are* under that duty, by that token it matters less whether they also have that public element which makes them subject to public law procedures and remedies.

It is a sad reflection on the state of contemporary sport that Dr Cox starts his *tour d'horizon* of substantive as distinct from procedural law with the development of contemporary anti doping policy – especially valuable in the year in which the World Anti Doping Agency (WADA) code comes into effect; a second edition may need to examine the extent to which that code has usefully clarified rather than complicated a much disputed area of the law.

He highlights the sad case of Michelle de Bruin, found guilty by a CAS Tribunal (on which I sat) of a doping offence which cast retrospective doubt on (although not formally affecting the result of) her triple Olympic triumph that I had earlier and excitedly observed in the Georgia Tech pool in Atlanta in 1996.

Whether sports law is a distinct subject, it is, of course, on any view also an amalgam of discrete legal rules created for areas of human activity other than sport. So Dr Cox next considers the impact on sport of civil and criminal law: it is important to note in this context that the field of play is not a zone of immunity, or to use Lord Atkin's famous phrase, an Alsatia where the kings writ does not run – something not always appreciated by participants in contact sports.

Dr Cox is not afraid to express views on moral as well as legal principles:

and not only orthodox ones. He asks whether a ban on drugs is not itself more contradictory of the sporting ethos of contest than would be permitting their use. He suggests that boxing not only should be, but, under Irish law is unlawful. He proposes that sporting bodies may have to be more relaxed in future about unisex competitions.

I was glad to note that Irish Courts would regard a reply to a woman's application for a sporting post addressed "Dear Sir" as indicative of sex discrimination, since I failed to impress the English Employment Appeal Tribunal with a similar submission in the case of *Vivien Saunders v Richmond Borough Council*, admittedly a quarter of a century ago when judges were not trained in, still less aware of, the diversity agenda.

Throughout Dr Cox shows an impressive mastery of the periodical literature, and indeed of predecessor volumes on the same subject. The footnotes alone are worth the price. His book will be valuable not only for the litigation, but for the transactional lawyer. Indeed I was able to read tests its utility at an early stage; as a result of which Dr Cox achieves an unusual distinction of having his book cited in a legal opinion while still only in proof stage.

I had the privilege of giving a keynote speech at the first sport law conference to take in Ireland in Dublin in 2002. Dr Cox's book shows that the subject is alive and kicking (not to say running, punching, and the like) in the Republic. I am happy to commend it to large readership.

MICHAEL J. BELOFF QC
President's Lodgings, Trinity College, Oxford
Blackstone Chambers, Temple
Member of the Court of Arbitration for Sport
Chairman, International Cricket Council Code of Conduct Commission
Steward of the Royal Automobile Club
Ethics Commissioner for London 2012 Bid

Preface

The idea for a book of this nature first came to me in Barcelona in May 1999 when seated in the Nou Camp stadium with my colleague Eoin O'Dell. I had watched 90 minutes of the Champions League final between Manchester United and Bayern Munich, during the course of which the former team failed to score (or indeed to look like doing so). It struck me then, that the area of Sports Law was an important one, and moreover, that as more Irish sports showed signs of turning professional, the area was an emerging and growing one. Then Manchester United scored twice to win the final, and the issue of Sports Law temporarily went out of my mind.

Since work on this book commenced some three and a half years ago, the increased impact of the law on sport has been notable. During this time we have witnessed many legal challenges to disciplinary sanctions consequent on positive doping tests. We have seen the ambit of the famous *Bosman* decision expanded, as the EU institutions play an increasing role in regulating the business of sport. We have seen legal actions, both criminal and civil, taken for acts of negligence and brutality connected with the playing of sport. We have seen controversies involving the broadcasting of sport and the marketing of sport. We have seen the emergence of the lucrative 'sports celebrity' who can sell his or her image and name to companies who would use that image and name to sell products. We have seen a revolution in global anti-doping policy. We have seen legal action taken against a leading Irish golf club that violated Irish equality rules. And these are just a few of the many developments that mean that there is a necessity for sport and sportspersons to look to lawyers for assistance.

This book aims to provide practitioners and students alike with an understanding of the current state of interaction between sport and the law. In writing this book, the authors have sought to examine the legal principles underpinning sports law and the opportunities and problems of a legal nature encountered by both the sporting community and practising sports lawyers in their day to day lives. From an Irish perspective, the area is plainly an embryonic one, and many of the developments and precedents to which we refer come from other jurisdictions including the European Union. Nonetheless we suggest that as and when these issues arise in Ireland, it will be these precedents that are used to compliment the existing Irish developments to which reference is made.

There are very many people that we would like to acknowledge who assisted in the writing of this book. We would refer to our colleagues in the Law School in Trinity College Dublin, and in particular to Professor William Binchy, Dr Hilary Delany, Terry Calvani, Paul Coughlan and Estelle Feldman for their generous help. We are delighted to acknowledge the work of other Irish authors in this area, most notably Professor Paul McCutcheon, Jack Anderson and Laura Donnellan, all of the University of Limerick. In addition we would like to thank those students and former students who have helped with research, namely Raymond Ryan, Deirdre O'Brien, Bryan McMahon Jnr, Rachel Casey, Barbara Salmon and especially Judy Goldman. Finally, we express our gratitude to Elizabeth Gleeson and the staff of the Berkeley Library in Trinity College Dublin.

We have received assistance from practitioners and others connected with the day-to-day business of sports law. We would like to thank them, especially Michael Twomey, Keenan Furlong, Gary Rice, Joe Lennon, Joe Christle BL, Mel Christle SC, Stephen Blair-White, Toni Yague, Eric A. Gleeson, Melissa Urquhart and Eoin MacNeill. We would also like to acknowledge the input of staff in the Irish Sports Council, the Office of the Director of Public Prosecutions and the Department of Sport and Tourism, to whom we have spoken, and who have generously provided assistance when asked.

Beyond this jurisdiction, we would like to thank John Shafer, Professor Bob Farrell, Professor Klaus Viewig, Professor John Denvir, Janet Sinder, Julie Gresham and the remarkable Jim Ferstle, all of whom have provided a good deal of help.

We owe a particular debt to the staff at Firstlaw, and especially to Bart Daly and Therese Carrick, for their exemplary professionalism (often in the face of considerable provocation from our side). We would also thank Gilbert Gough for all his work, and for being so good at what he does. Finally, we are enormously grateful to the Hon. Michael Beloff QC for taking time out of his busy schedule to write the foreword to this book.

Lastly, and on a personal note I would like to acknowledge with extreme gratitude the patience and kindness of my mother, my brothers and above all Sharon, Jessica, Jamie and Martha.

This book reflects, as far as we are aware, the law as it stands on June 1, 2004. Whilst this book is designed to give the reader a detailed insight into the current state of the law in this jurisdiction, no liability can be accepted for any errors or omissions contained in or missing from the text. The authors would, however, welcome any comments in respect of the same.

Neville Cox,
Law School, Trinity College Dublin.
June 16, 2004.

Table of Contents

Foreword vii

Preface ix

Table of Cases xxi

Table of Legislation xxxix

Chapter One: Introduction to Sports Law in Ireland 1
INTRODUCTION 1
1.1 SHOULD THE LAW BE INVOLVED IN SPORT? 2
1.2 THE IMPACT OF PROFESSIONALISATION ON SPORT AND THE LAW 4
1.3 "SPORT AND THE LAW" OR "SPORTS LAW"? 5
1.4 WHAT IS A SPORT? 6
1.5 WHO OWNS SPORT? 9
1.6 THE STRUCTURES OF SPORTS GOVERNANCE IN IRELAND
       AND BEYOND 10
       1.6.1 Governmental and quasi governmental control of sport in
               Ireland and the role of the Irish Sports Council 10
       1.6.2 The European Union and sport 11
               1.6.2.1 The development of an EU sports policy 13
       1.6.3 The Council of Europe and Sport 16
1.7 THE INTERNAL GOVERNMENTAL STRUCTURE OF SPORT 18
       1.7.1 The Olympic Movement 18
       1.7.2 The governance of individual sports 19
       1.7.3 The role of arbitration in sport 19
               1.7.3.1 The International Court of Arbitration
                       for Sport 20
               1.7.3.2 Taking a case to CAS 23
1.8 CONCLUSION 25

Chapter Two: Sports Rules and Fair Procedures 27
INTRODUCTION 27
2.1 THE FORM OF CHALLENGES TO DECISIONS OF SPORTING BODIES 29
       2.1.1 Judicial review and the status of sporting bodies 29
       2.1.2 Are sports bodies "public" for judicial review purposes? 32
       2.1.3 Should sports governing bodies be regarded as public
               for the purposes of judicial review? 37

2.2 PRIVATE LAW CHALLENGES TO DECISIONS OF SPORTING BODIES 38
    2.2.1 The doctrine of unreasonable restraint of trade
          and the emergence of competition law 39
          2.2.1.1 The Irish position 42
          2.2.1.2 Denial of access to the profession 44
          2.2.1.3 Suspension as an unreasonable restraint
                  of trade 48
          2.2.1.4 Restrictions on the sportsperson's ability to
                  exploit his or her ability for financial reward 50
          2.2.1.5 The impact of competition law 53
    2.2.2 The constitutional right to earn a livelihood 53
    2.2.3 Breach of contract 55
    2.2.4 Irrationality 56
2.3 FAIR PROCEDURES AND SPORTING BODIES 57
    2.3.1 Creating and applying "fair rules" 59
    2.3.2 Acting intra vires the rules 62
    2.3.3 Fair procedures and disciplinary hearings 73
2.4 THE IMPACT OF THE EUROPEAN CONVENTION ON HUMAN RIGHTS 78
2.5 CONCLUSION 80

Chapter Three: Performance Enhancing Substances and Methods 82
3.1 INTRODUCTION 82
    3.1.1 The history of the problem 82
    3.1.2 The scale of the problem 85
3.2 THE PROHIBITED SUBSTANCES AND METHODS 86
    3.2.1 Prohibited substances 87
          3.2.1.1 Stimulants 88
          2.2.1.2 Narcotic analgesics 89
          2.2.1.3 Cannabinoids 89
          3.2.1.4 Androgenic anabolic agents 89
          3.2.1.5 Masking agents 93
          3.2.1.6 Beta-2 agonists 93
          3.2.1.7 Peptide hormones, mimetics and analogues 94
3.3 PROHIBITED METHODS 95
    3.3.1 Manipulation 95
    3.3.2 Blood doping and erythropoietin 96
3.4 SUBSTANCES PROHIBITED IN PARTICULAR SPORTS 99
    3.4.1 Alcohol 99
    3.4.2 Beta blockers 99
    3.4.3 Diuretics 99
3.5 SHOULD DOPING BE BANNED? 100
    3.5.1 The health of the athlete who uses drugs 100
    3.5.2 Protecting the good name both of sport and of the
          clean athlete 102

3.5.3 A level playing field for all competitors 103
3.5.4 The interests of the "would-be clean athlete" 103
3.5.5 Protecting the ethic of sport 104
3.6 THE MAJOR PLAYERS IN THE FIGHT AGAINST DOPING 105
3.6.1 The impact of the International Olympic
        Committee (IOC) 106
3.6.2 The World Anti-Doping Agency (WADA) 107
3.6.3 The Council Of Europe 109
3.6.4 The impact of the European Union 112
3.6.5 Doping control In Ireland 115
        3.6.5.1 The Michelle Smith case 115
        3.6.5.2 The Irish Sports Council Anti-Doping Unit 119
3.7 FAIR PROCEDURES, THE RIGHTS OF THE ATHLETE AND THE
     APPLICATION OF ANTI-DOPING POLICY 121
3.7.1 Standard of proof 122
3.7.2 Burden of proof and the definition of a doping offence 123
        3.7.2.1 The burden of proof and fault based
                  doping offences 126
        3.7.2.2 The burden of proof and strict liability
                  offences 126
3.7.3 Strict liability doping rules, moral innocence and
        severity of sanction 129
3.7.4 Therapeutic exceptions to anti-doping rules 135
3.7.5 Provisional suspension prior to a hearing 136
3.7.6 Deviations from listed rules and procedures 137
3.7.7 The right to a fair hearing 141
3.8 PRIORITIES FOR THE FUTURE 141
3.8.1 Development of testing and of testing procedures 142
        3.8.1.1 Increasing the extent of testing 142
        3.8.1.2 Protecting the rights of athletes 144
        3.8.1.3 Research into the science of testing 145
        3.8.1.4 Greater accreditation of laboratories 148
3.8.2 Regulation of dietary supplements 148
3.8.3 The threat posed by genetics 151
3.8.4 Harmonization of anti-doping policy and the
        development of WADA 152
3.8.5 The World Anti-Doping Code 153
3.8.6 The Irish Sports Council's Anti-Doping Rules 155
        3.8.6.1 The definition of doping 156
        3.8.6.2 Burden and standard of proof 157
        3.8.6.3 Therapeutic use exemptions 157
        3.8.6.4 Testing 158
        3.8.6.5 Results management 159
        3.8.6.6 Fair procedures and the doping hearing 160

3.8.6.7 Penalties for doping offences 161
3.9 CONCLUSION 163

Chapter Four: Sport and the Criminal Law 165
4.1 INTRODUCTION 165
4.2 WHY IS CONTACT SPORT LAWFUL? 165
  4.2.1 The consent of the participants 165
  4.2.2 The Irish position 167
  4.2.3 The response of the United Kingdom Law
         Commission 168
4.3 THE LEGALITY OF BOXING 169
  4.3.1 Boxing and the criminal law in Ireland 176
  4.3.2 Reform of boxing 176
4.4 PROSECUTING ON-FIELD VIOLENCE 178
  4.4.1 Instances of prosecution for violence on the field
         of play 181
  4.4.2 The inconsistent nature of sports field prosecutions 187
4.5 SHOULD THE CRIMINAL LAW REGULATE THE SPORTS FIELD? 190
  4.5.1 The impact and extent of player consent 191
  4.5.2 Beyond consent – Is it good policy for the criminal law
         to police the field of play? 194

Chapter Five: Civil Liability and Sport 197
5.1 INTRODUCTION 197
5.2 NEGLIGENCE AND CIVIL LIABILITY ON THE FIELD OF PLAY 199
  5.2.1 Duty of care on the sports field 199
  5.2.3 Standard of care 202
  5.2.4 Defences 207
  5.2.5 Vicarious liability 210
5.3 LIABILITY OF SPORTS PARTICIPANTS FOR NEGLIGENCE ON THE
    SPORTS FIELD 211
  5.3.1 Duties of participants in contact sports 211
  5.3.2 Duties of participants in non-contact sports – the
         game of golf 216
  5.3.3 Duties of participants to spectators 221
5.4 DUTIES OF REFEREES 223
5.5 DUTY OF COACHES 230
5.6 DUTIES OF SPORTS TEACHERS AND SCHOOLS 235
  5.6.1 Mandatory participation in school sport 236
  5.6.2 Duties in respect of coaching school sports 237
  5.6.3 Duties in respect of sports equipment in schools 238
  5.6.4 Duties in respect of supervision of school sports 239
    5.6.4.1 Circumstance one: the vulnerability of the
             injured party 241

5.6.4.2 Circumstance two: the nature of the activity 243
5.6.4.3 Circumstance three: the location of the
activity 244
5.6.5 Duties in respect of facilities 245
5.6.6 Litigation avoidance strategies 246
5.6.7 The Irish Sports Council Code of Good Practice for
Children's Sport 247
5.7 DUTIES OF GOVERNING BODIES TO PARTICIPANTS 248
5.8 CONCLUSION: REPLACING THE LAW ON THE SPORTS FIELD –
ALTERNATIVE DISPUTE RESOLUTION AND NO FAULT
INSURANCE 253

Chapter Six: Occupiers, Organisers and Crowd Control 255
INTRODUCTION 255
6.1 THE DUTIES OF OCCUPIERS OF SPORTS STADIA 255
6.1.1 The Occupiers' Liability Act 1995 256
6.1.1.1 Visitors 256
6.1.1.2 Recreational users and trespassers 257
6.1.1.3 Injury resulting from the state of the premises 259
6.1.1.4 Exclusion notices 260
6.1.2 The duty of the occupier to the sporting participant 261
6.1.3 The duty of the occupier to the non-participant –
stadium and crowd safety 265
6.1.3.1 Statutory obligations 266
6.1.3.2 The approach of the courts 268
6.1.3.3 Non-binding recommendations and codes
of practice 269
6.1.4 Best practice for stadium and crowd safety 273
6.1.4.1 Fire safety 273
6.1.4.2 Structural matters 273
6.1.4.3 Crowd management 274
6.1.4.4 Co-Ordination of efforts....................................274
6.1.4.5 Best practice checklists 275
6.2 DUTIES OF ORGANISERS OF SPORTING EVENTS 277
6.2.1 The duty of the organiser to participants 277
6.2.2 The duty of the organiser to non-participants 279
6.3 CASE STUDY – OCCUPIER AND ORGANISER LIABILITY ON THE
GOLF COURSE 283
6.3.1 Unreasonable risks in course design 284
6.3.2 Unreasonable risks in the organisation of a tournament 285
6.3.3 Lightening on the golf course 286
6.4 DUTIES TO PERSONS OUTSIDE THE STADIUM 287
6.4.1 Negligence 288
6.4.2 Nuisance...290

6.5 THE PROBLEM OF SPECTATOR VIOLENCE 293
    6.5.1 The Lansdowne Road riots 294
    6.5.2 The legislative response to spectator violence
          in England 297
    6.5.3 The Council of Europe and spectator violence 300
6.6 CONCLUSION 303

Chapter Seven: The Business of Sport 304
INTRODUCTION 304
7.1 THE RIGHTS INVOLVED 304
7.2 SPORTS BUSINESS AND THE OWNERSHIP OF SPORT 305
7.3 THE SIGNIFICANCE OF INTELLECTUAL PROPERTY RIGHTS 306
7.4 THE IMPACT OF CONTRACT LAW 306
    7.4.1 Employment contracts and sport 307
    7.4.2 The express terms of the employment contract 309
    7.4.3 The implied terms of the employment contract 311
    7.4.4 Termination of contracts of employment in sport 312
    7.4.5 Exclusion clauses 319
    7.4.6 The importance of a written contract 321
7.5 THE RIGHTS OF THE INDIVIDUAL SPORTSPERSON 324
    7.5.1 Image rights agreements 325
    7.5.2 Protecting image rights under the tort of passing off 327
    7.5.3 Protection of image rights beyond the tort of
          passing off 335
    7.5.4 A property right in one's image? 337
7.6 THE RIGHTS OF THE SPORTS CLUB AND THE GOVERNING BODY 338
    7.6.1 The sports club 339
          7.6.1.1 Arsenal FC v. Reed 339
    7.6.2 The governing body 345
    7.6.3 The sportswear company 351
7.7 THE RIGHTS OF THE EVENT ORGANISER 352
    7.7.1 Sponsorship 353
          7.7.1.1 The sponsorship contract 354
7.8 AMBUSH MARKETING 358
    7.8.1 Targeting ambush marketing 360
7.9 BROADCASTING OF SPORTS EVENTS 363
    7.9.1 What are broadcasting rights? 363
    7.9.2 Article 3A of the Television Without Frontiers
          Directive and the protection of "listed" events 366
    7.9.3 The FAI/Sky Television deal, July 2002 370
    7.9.4 The Broadcasting Commission of Ireland Codes
          of Practice 375

Chapter Eight: European Community Law Freedoms and the Business of Sport 377

INTRODUCTION 377

8.1 *WALALRAVE AND KOCH V. UNION CYCLISTE INTERNATIONALE (UCI)* 379

8.2 *DONÀ V. MANTERO* 382

8.3 *UNCTEF V. HEYLENS* 383

8.4 *UNION ROYAL BELGE DES SOCIÈTÈS DE FOOTBALL ASSOCIATION ASBL V. BOSMAN*..385

    8.4.1 UEFA Rules prior to *Bosman* 386

    8.4.2 The facts of Bosman 387

    8.4.3 The judgment of the European Court of Justice in Bosman 388

        8.4.3.1 The application of Article 39 to this case 388

        8.4.3.2 The transfer fee rule 389

        8.4.3.3 The nationality quota rules 390

    8.4.4 Conclusions on the *Bosman* case 392

        8.4.4.1 Introducing the consequences of professionalisation 392

        8.4.4.2 The effects on the football transfer system 393

        8.4.4.3 Application to "in-contract" players 394

        8.4.4.4 Application to domestic transfers 394

        8.4.4.5 Application to non-EU nationals 395

8.5 THE *DELIEGE* AND *LEHTONEN* CASES 398

    8.5.1 *Deliège v. Ligue Francophone de Judo ASBL* 398

    8.5.2 *Lehtonen and Castors Canada dry Namur-Braine v. Fédération Royale des Sociétés de Basketball and Ligue Belge-Belgische Liga* 400

8.6 ALCOHOL ADVERTISING AND FREEDOM TO PROVIDE SERVICES 402

8.7 SPORTS BETTING AND THE FREEDOM TO PROVIDE SERVICES 405

8.8 CONCLUSION 406

Chapter 9: Competition Law and Sport 407

INTRODUCTION 407

9.1 INTRODUCTION TO COMPETITION LAW 409

    9.1.1 Anti-competitive agreements between undertakings..........410

    9.1.2 Abuse of a dominant position 413

        9.1.2.1 Dominance 413

        9.1.2.2 Abuse 414

9.2 COMPETITION LAW AND SPORT 416

    9.2.1 The balance to be drawn 417

        9.2.1.1 Sport as big business...418

        9.2.1.2 Sport as "something special" 418

    9.2.2 Drawing the balance 420

9.2.3 Categories of rules 421
      9.2.3.1 Inherently acceptable "sporting" rules 421
      9.2.3.2 Inherently unacceptable rules 423
      9.2.3.3 Rules in violation of Article 81(1) but
               exempted under Article 81(3) 423
9.2.4 When will the Commission intervene in sport? 424
9.3 EXCESSIVE DOMINATION OF A SPORT BY A GOVERNING BODY 425
      9.3.1 Use of a dominant position to restrict activities
            of competitors 426
      9.3.2 Separating regulatory and commercial dominance 428
9.4 SPONSORSHIP AND EQUIPMENT 429
9.5 TICKETING 430
9.6 SALARY CAPS 433
9.7 STATE AID 434
9.8 OWNERSHIP OF MULTIPLE CLUBS 435
9.9 TRANSFER RULES 437
9.10 TELEVISION AND BROADCASTING 442
      9.10.1 Assessment of markets 443
      9.10.2 Exclusive broadcasting contracts 445
      9.10.3 Maximum possible exploitation of broadcast rights
             and the use of "new technology" 448
      9.10.4 Collective selling of broadcast rights 448
      9.10.5 Collective purchasing 451
      9.10.6 The approach of the European Commission to major
             broadcasting deals 453
             9.10.6.1 The UEFA Broadcasting Rights Deal
                       2003 453
             9.10.6.2 The Sky/FA Premier League Broadcasting
                       Rights Deal 2003 454
9.11 CONCLUSION 456

Chapter Ten: Sport and Equality 457
INTRODUCTION 457
10.1 OVERVIEW OF THE RELATIONSHIP BETWEEN IRISH EQUALITY LAW
      AND SPORT 461
10.2 GENDER DISCRIMINATION IN SPORT 465
      10.2.1 Irish law 465
      10.2.2 The United Kingdom 467
             10.2.2.1 Challenging discrimination 467
             10.2.2.2 Preserving segregation 469
      10.2.3 The United States of America 471
             10.2.3.1 Sport and the American way 471
             10.2.3.2 Title IX – Ensuring equality in a segregated
                       world? 472

10.2.3.3 Title IX – A victim of its own success?...........474
10.2.3.4 The equal protection clause 475
10.3 NATIONALITY, RACE, ETHNICITY AND RELIGION 477
10.3.1 Nationality discrimination in EC and Irish law...............477
10.3.2 Race, ethnicity and membership of the Traveller
Community in EC and Irish law 479
10.3.3 UK Law on race discrimination 480
10.3.4 Religious discrimination...481
10.4 DISABILITY 484
10.5 SEXUAL ORIENTATION 487
10.6 AGE 487
10.7 SPECIAL PROVISIONS IN RELATION TO CLUBS 489
10.8 CONCLUSIONS 492

Index 497

Table of Cases

A (a minor) v. Leeds City Council, unreported Queen's Bench,
March 2, 1999 .... 198, 242
A v. FILA, CAS 2001/A/317 312
Abrahamson v. Law Society [1996] 1 I.R. 403 30
Accolade Limited (Trading as Shelbourne FC v. FAI, unreported,
High Court, O'Sullivan J., February 18, 2002 .... 64 *et seq.*
Adidas v. O'Neills [1983] 1 I.L.R.M. 112, [1983] F.S.R. 76 .... 329, 351, 353
Affiong-Day v. High Performance Sports Ltd [2003] E.W.C.A. Civ. 197,
February 26, 2003 .... 233, 277
Affutu-Nartoy v. Clarke, *The Times*, February 9, 1984 .... 234, 238
AG v. Paperlink [1984] I.L.R.M. 373 54
Agar v. Canning 54 W.W.R. 302 (1965) 203
Agar v. Hyde and Worsley v. Australian Rugby Football Union
[2000] H.C.A. 41 .... 251 *et seq.*
Alcock v. Chief Constable of South Yorkshire [1992] 1 A.C. 310 266
Alexander (A Minor) v. King Edward School Bath Governors, unreported,
Circuit Court, May 9, 2000 239
Alpine Investments v. Minister van Financien, Case C–384/93,
[1995] E.C.R. I–1141 396
Alwyn Treherne v. Amateur Boxing Association of England
[2001] 3 I.S.L.R. 231, [2002] All E.R. (D) 144 55
American Greetings Corporation's Application [1984] R.P.C. 329 340
American Shooting v. Quigley v. Union Internationale de TI.R./International
Shooting Union, CAS 94/129 63
An Agreement Between the FA Premier League and BskyB, re
[2000] E.M.L.R. 78, [1999] U.K.C.L.R. 258. 424
An Bord Trachtala v. Waterford Foods [1994] F.S.R. 316 329
Angus v. British Judo Federation, *The Times*, June 15, 1984 141
Anns v. Merton London Borough Council [1978] A.C. 728 199
Arsenal v. Reed. [2003] All E.R. (EC) 1, [2003]
R.P.C. 144 .... 336, 339 *et seq.*, 346, 402
Article 26 and the Employment Equality Bill 1996, re
[1997] 2 I.R. 321 .... 54, 461
Assicurazioni Generali Spa v. Arab Insurance Group [2002]
E.W.C.A. Civ. 1642 228
Associated Provincial Picture Houses Limited v. Wednesbury Corporation
[1948] 1 K.B. 223 56
Athens v. Canadian Adventure Camps Limited (1977) 17 O.R. 2d 425 ... 328
Attorney General v. Paperlink [1984] I.L.R.M. 373 54

Attorney General's Reference (No. 6 of 1980) [1981] Q.B. 715, [1981]
    2 All E.R. 1057, [1981] 3 W.L.R. 125 166

B v. FINA, CAS 98/211 and B v. International Judo Federation,
    CAS 98/214 .... 76, 123, 126, 141
B v. International Judo Federation, CAS 98/214 .... 127, 132, 141
B v. International Triathlon Union CAS 98/222 .... 123, 127, 138
Bacardi-Martini SAS, Cellier des Dauphins v. Newcastle United Football
    Company Ltd Case C–318/00 (January 21, 2003) 403
Bacon v. White, unreported, Queen's Bench, May 21, 1998 232
BAF v. IAAF [2001] I.S.L.R. 264 124
Baker v. Jones [1954] 2 All E.R. 553 .... 28, 31,58
Baker v. Mid Maine Medical Centre, 499 A. 2d. 464 (1985) 286
Balfour v. Balfour [1919] 2 K.B. 571 28
Bane v. Garda Representative Association [1997] 2 I.R. 449 .... 31, 33
Barfoot v. East Sussex CC, unreported, August 16, 1939 239
Bateson v. Belfast YWCA[1980] N.I. 135 468
Baxter v. FIS, CAS 2002/A/396 125
Baxter v. IOC, CAS 2002/A/376 122
BBC v. British Satellite Broadcasting Limited BBC v. British Satellite
    Broadcasting Limited 364
BBC v. Talksport [2001] F.S.R. 53 .... 364 *et seq.*
Beirne v. Garda Commissioner[1993] I.L.R.M. 1 31
Bellew v. Irish Cement Limited [1948] I.R. 61 .... 288, 290
Bernhard v. International Triathlon Union, CAS 98/222 127
Bidwell v. Parks 218
Bolger v. Osborne [2000] 1 I.L.R.M. 250 .... 29, 33, 56, 72
Bolton v. Jones, Stratton v. Hughes, unreported, Court of Appeal,
    March 17, 1998 279
Bolton v. Stone [1951] A.C. 850 .... 264, 288, 289
Bord na Mona v. John Sisk, unreported, High Court, Blayney J.,
    November 30, 1989 66
Bourque v. Duplechin 334 So. 2d 210 (1976) LA 201
Boy Scouts of America v. Dale 530 US 640 (2000) 492
Brady v. Sunderland Association FC, unreported, Court of Appeal,
    November 17, 1998 .... 198, 230 *et seq.*
Brewer v. Delo [1967] 1 Lloyd's Rep. 488 .... 197, 217 *et seq.*
Bristol-Myers Squibb v. Paranova, Euri -Pharm v. Beiersdorf, MPA Pharma
    v. Rhone-Poulenc [1997] F.S.R. 102 340
British Horseracing Board v. William Hill Ltd[2001] R.P.C. 612 .... 348 *et seq.*
Broadnet Ireland Ltd v. Office of the Director of Telecommunications
    [2000] 2 I.L.R.M. 241 30
Brown v. Lewis(1896) 12 T.L.R. 455 265
Brutus v. Cozens [1973] A.C. 854 298
Buckley v. Tutty [1971] 125 C.L.R. 353 50
Bundesgerichtsof Case IZR 21/98, (July 6, 2000), [2000] European Trade
    Mark Review 325 353
Butcher v. Jessop [1989] S.L.T. 593 181

Byrne v. Dun Laoghaire County Council 20 Ir. L. T. (ns) 16, Circuit Court,
    Smyth P., November 13, 2001) 257

C & A Modes v. C & A (Waterford) Ltd [1976] I.R. 198 329
C v. FINA, CAS 95/141 .... 125, 131
C&A Modes v. C&A Waterford Ltd [1976] I.R. 198 329
Cahill v. West Ham Corporation (81 Sol. J. 630 (1932)) 245
Caldwell v. Maguire [2001] E.W.C.A. Civ. 1054; [2001]
    I.S.L.R. 224 .... 197, 214, 223, 226
Callaghan v. Killarney Race Company Limited [1958]
    I.R. 366 .... 197, 198, 259, 279 *et seq.*
Campbell v. Mirror Group Newspapers[2004] U.K.H.L. 22,
    May 6, 2004 333
Campus Oil v. Minister for Industry and Commerce (No.2)
    [1983] I.R. 88 .... 30, 37, 61
Canadian NOC & Scott v. IOC, CAS 2002/O/373 98
Caparo Industries plc v. Dickman [1990] 2 A.C. 605 200
Cape v. Tennessee Secondary School Athletic Commission,
    424 F Supp 732 (1976) 476
Cape, 563 F2d (6th Cir, 1977) 476
Capitol Raceway Promotions Inc v. Smith, 332 A.2d. 238
    (Mo. App. 1974) 283
Carew Park Amateur Football Club v. FAI, unreported, High Court,
    Barr J., February 19, 1999 229
Carey v. Albany Golf Club, 4 S.R.W.A. 168 (D.C.) 283
Carlton Communications plc v. The Football League [2002]
    E.W.H.C. 1650 (August 1, 2002). .... 323 *et seq.*
Carna Foods Limited v. Eagle Star Insurance (Ireland) Limited
    [1995] 1 I.R. 526 30
Case C–46/02, June 8, 2004 349
Case C–203/02, June 8, 2004 349
Case C–338/02, June 8, 2004 349
Case C–444/02, June 8, 2004 349
Castle v. St Augustine's Links Ltd(1922) 38 T.L.R. 615 289
Castle v. St Augustine's Links, (1922) 38 T.L.R. 615 287
Chittock v. Woodbridge School, *The Times*, July 15, 2002 239
Christie v. Davey [1893] 1 Ch 316 290
Clancy v. IRFU [1995] 1 I.L.R.M. 193 .... 43, 62
Clark v. Bethnal Green Corporation, 55 T.L.R. 519 (1939). 240
Clark v. Welsh, 1975 (4) S.A. 469, 1976 (3) S.A. 484. 217
Cleghorn v. Oldham [1927] 43 T.L.R. 465 .... 197, 217
Coditel v. Cinè Vog Films SA, Case 262/81, [1982] E.C.R. 3381 445
Cohen v. Brown University, 101 F3d 155, 178-179 (1st Cir 1996),
    cert denied 520 US 1186 (1997) 471, 474
Coleman v. Kelly (1951) 85 I.L.T.R 48 280
Collins v. Resto, 746 F. Supp. 360 (SDNY, 1990) 175
Comer v. Governors of St Patrick's Roman Catholic Primary School,
    unreported, Court of Appeal, November 13, 1997 .... 242, 243, 262

Commission v France, Bacardi France SAS v. Television Française TF1,
   Groupe Jean-Clàude Darmon SA Girosport Sarl, Cases C–262/02 and
   C–429/02, Reference CJE/04/15 (March 12, 2004) 404, 456
Commonwealth v. Collberg 119 Mass. 350 (1875) 172
Condon v. Basi [1985] 2 All E.R. 453, [1985]
   1 W.L.R. 866 .... 197, 204, 207, 211 *et seq.*, 223
Conteh v. Onslow Fane, unreported, CA, June 26, 1975 50
Cook v. Doncaster Borough Council, *The Sporting Life*, July 16, 1993 262
Cooke v. FEI, CAS 98/194 138
Cool v. FA, *The Times*, March 24, 1972 50
Cowan v. O'Freaghaile (representing the GAA) and McInerney
   & Sons Ltd [1991] 1 I.R. 389 .... 259, 268 *et seq.*
Cowley v. Heatley, *The Times*, July 24, 1986 38
Cox v. Ireland [1992] 2 I.R. 503 54
Criminal Proceedings against Piergiorgio Gambelli and others, Case
   C–243/01 (March 13, 2003). 405
Cullwick v. FINA, CAS96/149 135
Cunningham v. Reading FC [1991] P.I.Q.R. 141 .... 275, 282, 291
Currie v. Barton, Times Law Reports, February 12, 1988 75

D&F Estates Ltd v. Church Commissioners for England [1988]
   2 All E.R. 992 234
Danish Tennis Federation case, Case Nos IV/F-1/33.055 and 35.759
   [1996] 4 C.M.L.R. 885 .... 354, 429, 430
Davis v. Carew-Pole [1956] 2 All E.R. 524 62
Davis v. Country Club, 381 S.W. 2d. 41 (Tenn, 1991) 287
Davis v. Feasy, unreported, Court of Appeal, May 14, 1998 264
Decker Slaney, April 25, 1999 128
Dekker, Case C–177/88, [1990] E.C.R. I–3941 466
Delaney v. O'Dowd[1997] I.R. L. Log W. 157 (C.C.). 237
Deliege v. Ligue Francophone de Judo et Disciplines Associees ASBL,
   Case C–51 &191/97, [2000] E.C.R. I–2549, [2002]
   2 C.M.L.R. 1574 .... 307, 383, 398 *et seq.*, 416, 437
Denny v. Minister for Social Welfare [1988] 1 I.R. 34 308
Deutscher Handballbund v. Kolpak, Case C–438/00, (May 8, 2003). .... 395 *et seq.*
Devlin v. Roche [2002] 2 I.L.R.M. 192 199
Dewar v. City and Suburban Racecourse [1899] 1 I.R. 345 290
Dibble v. Carmarthern Town, unreported, Queen's Bench, 2001 262
Distribution of Package Tours During the 1990 World Cup (1992)
   O.J. L.326/31, [1994] 5 C.M.L.R. 253 431
DLV v. IAAF (Krabbe II), November 20, 993 140
Dodson v. Arkansas Activities Association, 468 F Supp 394 (1979). 476
Doe v. Dolton Elementary School District No. 48, 649
   F. Supp. 440 ND Ill, 1988 279
Donà v. Mantero C13/76 [1976] E.C.R. 1333, [1976]
   2 C.M.L.R. 578 .... 382, 383, 477
Donaldson v. Irish Motor Racing Club & Thompson, unreported,
   Supreme Court, February 1, 1957. .... 221, 258, 259, 280

Donna v. Mantero [1976] 2 C.M.L.R. 578 12
Donoghue v. Stevenson [1932] A.C. 562 199
Doug Walker v. UK Athletics and IAAF, *Guardian*, July 27, 2000 137
Dougan v. Glasgow Rangers Football Club, *Daily Telegraph*,
    October 24, 1974 265
Douglas v. Hello! [2001] 2 All E.R. 289 333
Doyle v. Kildare County Council & Shackleton [1995] 2 I.R. 424 66
Doyle v. Little, unreported, Circuit Court, August 2, 2002 241
DPP (Traynor) v. Lennon[1999] 2 I.R. 403 145
Duffy v. Midlothian 481 N.E. 2d. (Ill. Ct. App., 1985) 286
Dundalk Interim Co. Ltd T/A Dundalk Football Club v. Eircom League and
    Kilkenny City Football Club[2001] 1 I.R. 434 .... 62 *et seq.*, 66 *et seq.*
Dundee United Football Club v. Scottish Football Association
    [1998] S.L.T. 1244 .... 30, 75
Dunne v. National Maternity Hospital [1989] I.R. 1 .... 207, 234

Eastham v. Newcastle United Football Club [1964] 1 Ch. 413 .... 50 *et seq.*
Edwards v. British Athletic Federation, [1998] 2 C.M.L.R. 363,
    [1997] Eu L.R. 721 .... 49, 385
Elliot v. Saunders, unreported, Queen's Bench,
    June 10, 1994 .... 192, 201, 206, 209 *et seq.*, 253
Ellison v. Rogers. 67 D.L.R. (2d.) 21 (1967). 285
Elvis Presley Enterprises v. Sid Shaw, Elvisly Yours [1999]
    R.P.C. 567 .... 330, 332
Enderby Town Football Club v. Football Association [1971]
    1 Ch. 591 .... 28, 36, 56, 57
Eogan v. University College Dublin [1996] 1 I.R. 390 .... 30, 31
Estate of Fisher v. City of South Portland, No CV-92-714
    (1994 M.E.) 286, 287

F, in re [1990] 2 A.C. 1 175
FA Premier League v. Panini [2002] E.W.H.C. 2779, [2002] All E.R. (D) 260,
    (2002) S.L.J.R. 8 (HC), [2003] E.W.C.A. Civ. 995,
    [2003] All E.R. (D) 201 (July), (CA). 339, 347
Faramus v. Film Artistes' Association [1964] A.C. 925 45
Farrant v. Thames District Council, unreported, Queens' Bench Division,
    June 11, 1996 262
Faulkner v. Talbot [1981] 3 ALL E.R. 468 175
Favia v. Indiana University of Pennsylvania, 7 F3d 332 (3rd Cir 1993). 474
Federal Republic of Germany v. European Parliament and Council of the EU,
    Case C–376/98, [2000] E.C.R. I–2247 357
Feeney v. Lyall [1991] S.L.T. 151 .... 200, 208, 219
Ferguson v. Coolmore, *Sunday Times*, February 1, 2004 .... 321 *et seq.*
Ferguson v. Normand (Procurator Fiscal, Glasgow) [1995] S.C.C.R. 770 186
FIFA 'Denominations Scheme' case, Case No IV/F-1/35.266 429
Fixtures Marketing Limited v. AB Svenska Spel, Gotland City Court [2001]
    European Copyright and Designs Reports 406ff noted at 9(3) Sport
    and the Law Journal (2001) 77 348

Flanagan v. UCD [1988] I.R. 724 .... 58, 76
Fletcher v. Britton v. Bradford City AFC, *The Times*,
      February 24, 1987 265
Fletcher v. Commissioner of Public Works (February 21, 2003)
      [2003] I.E.S.C. 8 200
Flynn v. O'Reilly[1999] 1 I.L.R.M. 458 245
Football Association and Nottinghamshire Football Association v. Bennett,
      unreported, Court of Appeal, July 28, 1978 470
Football League v. Littlewoods Pools Ltd[1959] 2 All E.R. 546 348
Football World Cup, 1998, Case IV/16.888, (2000) O.J. L. 5, ... 424
Foschi, Case No. 77 1900036, April 1, 1996 130
Fowles v. Bedfordshire County Council, *The Times s*, May 22, 1995 (C.A.) 231
Francis v. Cockrell (1870) 5 L.Q.R.B. 501 265
Frazer v. Johnston, (1990) 21 N.S.W.L.R. 89 202
Freedman v. Petty and Greyhound Racing Control Board [1981] V.R. 1001 74
French v. Crosby Links Hotel, unreported, Great Yarmouth County Court,
      May 7, 1982 469
Frost v. Chief Constable of South Yorkshire [1999] 2 A.C. 455 266
Fullam v. Associated Newspapers Limited [1953-54] Ir. Jur. Rep. 79 (H.C.) 230

Gallagher v. Revenue Commissioners [1995] 1 I.R. 55 .... 29, 76
Galvin v. Chief Appeals Officer [1997] 3 I.R. 240 75
Gannon v. Rotherham MBC, *Halsburys Monthly Review* (1991) 91/1717.
Garvey v. Ireland [1981] I.R. 75 55
Gary Mabbut v. John Fashanu, *The Times*, August 14, 1994 189
Gasser v. Stinson, unreported, Queen's Bench,
      June 15, 1988 .... 48 *et seq.*, 54 *et seq.*, 131
Gavin v. Criminal Injuries Compensation Tribunal [1997] 1 I.R. 132 .... 30, 33
Gaynor v. Blackpool FC [2002] 7 C.L. 432 215
General Tyre & Rubber Co v. Firestone Tyre & Rubber Co [1975]
      2 ALL E.R. 173 334
Geoghegan v. Institute of Chartered Accountants [1995] 3 I.R. 86 .... 30 *et seq.*
Georgopoulus v. Beaumont Hospital Board, unreported, Supreme Court,
      June 4, 1997 123
Gibbs v. Barking Corporation, [1936] All E.R. 115 243
Gilchrist v. City of Troy, 495 N.Y.S. 781 (N.Y. App., 1985) 282
Gillon v. Chief Constable of Strathclyde Police, *The Times*,
      November 22, 1996 282
Gilsenan v. Gunning, (1982) 137 D.L.R. (3d) 252 207
GLC v. Farrar [1980] I.C.R. 266 469
Glencar Exploration plc & Andaman Resources plc v. Mayo County
      Council [2002] 1 I.R. 84 .... 200, 227, 234
Glenie v. Slack [2000] E.W.C.A. (Civ.) 145 263
Glolite Ltd v. Jasper Conran Limited, Times Law Reports, 28 January, 1998 322
Glover v. BLN Ltd [1973] I.R. 388 .... 29, 55, 73
Goldfarb v. Williams [1945] I.R. 433 290
Gottrub-Klim e.a. Grovvareforeninger v. Dansk Landbrugs Grovvareselskab
      AmbA, Case C–250/92, [1994] E.C.R.-I 5641 426

Gough v. Chief Constable of the Derbyshire Constabulary [2002]
2 All E.R. 985; [2002] 2 W.L.R. 289 297
Governor of the Peabody Donation Fund v. Sir Lindsay Parkinson & Co. Ltd
[1985] A.C. 210 .... 200, 227
Grange Marketing v. M&Q Products, unreported, High Court,
June 17, 1976 329
Gray v. Leopardstown Golf Centre, unreported, Circuit Court,
July 20, 1999 284
Greally v. Minister for Education (No. 2) [1999] 1 I.R. 1. 54
Greig v. Insole [1978] 1 W.L.R. 302 .... 40, 52, 426
Griffith v. Barbados 279
Grisim v. Tapemark Charity Pro-Am Golf Tournament,
394 N.W. 2d. 261 (Minn. Ct App., 1986) 283, 286
Grove City College v. Bell 465 US 555, 570 (1984) 472

H v. International Motorcycling Federation,
CAS 2000/A/281 .... 123, 124, 131, 132, 138, 141
Haelan Laboratories Inc v. Topps Chewing Gum Inc, 202 F.2d 866
(2d Cir, 1953), 346 US 816, (1953) 328
Haga v. FIM CAS 2000/A/281 138
Hall v. Brooklands Auto Racing Club [1932] All E.R. 208 .... 198, 259, 281
Halliwell v. Panini, unreported, High Court, June 6, 1997 330
Hames v. State, 808 S.W. 2d. 41 (Tenn, 1991)............................... 286, 287
Hamish v. Smailes, unreported Epsom County Court, 1983.................... 199
Hamstra v. British Columbia Rugby Union [1997] 1 S.C.R. 1092......... 225
Hand v. Dublin Corporation [1991] 1 I.R. 409 54
Hanrahan v. Merck Sharpe & Dohme [1988] I.L.R.M. 629 290
Hardwick v. FA. IT Case 2320451/96 468
Harrison v. Shields, unreported, High Court, November 15, 1996......... 239
Harrison v. Vincent [1982] R.T.R. 8 .... 263, 277
Harrods v. Harrodian School of Law, [1996] R.P.C. 697 329
Haughey v. Mr. Justice Moriarty [1999] 3 I.R. 1 75
Haughey, in re [1971] I.R. 217 73
Healy v. Fleming, 19 Ir. L .Times (ns 241 (Circuit Court, Kanturk,
June 2, 2001) 269
Hearn and Matchroom Boxing v. Collins, unreported, High Court,
O'Sullivan J., February 3, 1998 .... 309, 317 *et seq.*
Heaves v. Westmeath County Council (May 2002)
Law Society Gazette 38 258
Hedley Byrne v. Heller[1964] A.C. 465 233
Heintz van Landewyck Sarl v Commission, Joined Cases 209-215 and 218/78,
[1980] E.C.R. 1325 [1981] 3 C.M.L.R. 134 409
Hendry and Others v. World Professional Billiards and Snooker Association
[2002] U.K.C.L.R. 5, [2002] E.C.C. 8, [2002] I.S.L.R. 1,
[2002] Eu LR 770 .... 53, 309, 427
Hennessey v. Pyne [1997] 694 A.2d. 691 287
Hicks v. Chief Constable of South Yorkshire Police [1992]
2 All E.R. 65 266

Hilder v. Associated Portland Cement Manufacturers [1961]
    1 W.L.R. 1434 289
Hill v. Durham County Council, unreported, Court of Appeal,
    January 31, 2000 231
Hofner and Elser v. Macrotron GmBH, Case 41/90, [1991] E.C.R. I –1979
    [1993] 4 C.M.L.R. 306 409
Hogan v. Koala Dundee Pty Ltd, September 23, 1988, 12 I.P.R. 508 329
Hollywood Silver Fox Farm v. Emmet [1936] 2 K.B. 468 290
Horton v. Jackson, unreported, Court of Appeal,
    February 28, 1996 .... 220, 284
Horton v. Tim Donut Ltd (1997) 75 C.P.R. (3d) 451 328
Hosie v. Arbroath FC [1978] S.L.T. 122 291
Hospitality Group Ltd v. FA, unreported, January 24, 1996 431
Hughes v. Garda Commissioner, unreported, High Court, Laffoy,
    July 23, 1996 .... 74, 75
Hunt v. Bell, (1822) 1 Bing 1; 130 E.R. 1 172
Hunter v. Canary Wharf [1997] A.C. 655 290
Hussaney v. Chester City Football Club, IT 2102426/97 (unreported,
    November 21, 1997) 480

IAAF v. Athletic Federation of Nigeria, April 10, 1995 127
IAAF v. Athletics Australia (Capobianco), March 17, 1997 .... 132, 138
IAAF v. Athletics Congress of the US (TAC) 138
IAAF v. Boulami & MAR, CAS 2002/O/401 146
IAAF v. FCA (P & Others v. FINA, CAS 97/180 133
IAAF v. Federazione Italiana di Athletica Leggera, (Bevilacqua case),
    November 25, 1996 132
IAAF v. German Athletic Federation (Krabbe 1),
    February 28, 1992 .... 126, 130, 131
IAAF v. JAAA [2001] I.S.L.R. 260 127
IAAF v. USATF, August 3, 1999 128
IAAF v. USATF, CAS 2002/O/401, [2003]
    International Sports Law Review 61 143
Inspector of Taxes v. Kiernan [1981] I.R. 117 .... 62, 176
International News Service v. Associated Press, 248 US 215 (1919) 328
International Tennis Federation v. K, CAS 99/A/223 .... 123, 138
IPC Magazines v. Black and White Music Corporation
    [1983] F.S.R. 348 329
Irvine v. Talksport [2002] 2 All E.R. 414, [2002] E.W.H.C. 539 (HC),
    [2003] 2 All E.R. 881, [2003]
    1 W.L.R. 1576 (CA). .... 304, 331 *et seq.*, 337, 342, 353, 360
Italia 90, (1992) O.J. L. 326/31 [1994] 5 C.M.L.R. 252 .... 424, 431, 432

Jason Green (A Minor) v. Dublin Corporation, 13 Irish Law Times
    (2001) 212 264
Jenks v. McGranaghan, 285 N.E. 2d. 876 (N.Y., 1972) 217
Johnston v. Chief Constable of the RUC [1986] E.C.R. 1651, Case 222/84,
    [1986] 3 C.M.L.R. 240 384

Johnston v. Cliftonville FC and Irish Football League [1984] 2 N.J.I.B. 9;
    [1984] N.I. 9 50
Johnston v. Frazer [1990] 21 N.S.W.L.R. 89 214
Jones & Ebbw Vale RFC v. Welsh Rugby Union unreported Queen's
    Bench, February 27, 1997, *The Times,* January 6, 1998
    (Court of Appeal) noted at (January/February 1998)
    Sports Law Administration and Practice 10 76
Jones v. Northampton BC, *The Times*, May 2, 1990 262
Jones v. Welsh Rugby Football Union, unreported, High Court,
    February 27, 1997, The Times, January 6, 1998 .... 58, 59
Jordan Grand Prix Limited v. Vodaphone Group Plc[2003] E.W.H.C. 1956
    (Queens Bench, August 4, 2003) 322, 323
Junior Books v. Veitchi [1983] 1 A.C. 520 199

Kabaeva v. FIG, CAS 2002/A/386 .... 124, 129, 132, 138
Kane v. Kennedy, unreported, High Court, March 25, 1999 .... 198, 235, 244
Karpow v. Shave [1975] 2 W.W.R. 159 197
Kaye v. Robertson [1991] F.S.R. 62 333
KB v. NHS, Case C–117/01, January 7, 2004 465
Kearn-Price v. Kent County Council [2002] E.W.C.A. Civ. 193 239
Keck and Mithouard [1993] E.C.R. I–6097, Joined Cases C–267
    and 268/91, [1995] 1 C.M.L.R. 101 396
Keenan v. Shield Insurance [1988] I.R. 89 66
Keighley Football Club v. Cunningham, Times Law Reports,
    May 25, 1960
Kennaway v. Thompson [1980] 3 W.L.R. 361, [1981] Q.B. 88 (CA) 287, 292
Kiely v. Minister for Social Welfare [1977] I.R. 267 58
Kinane v. Turf Club, unreported, High Court, McCracken J.,
    July 27, 2001 .... 37, 62, 77
Klyne v. Bellegarde (1978) 6 W.W.R. 743 282
Knittle v. Miller, 09 P. 2d. 32 (1985) 283
Korda v. ITF [1999] All E.R. (D) 84 55
Krabbe v. DLV, March 28, 1996 Case U (K) 3424/95 .... 130 *et seq.*
Krouse v. Chrysler Canada Ltd (1973) 40 D.L.R. (3d) 15 328

L v. FINA, CAS 95/142 135
Lacey v. Parker, *The Times*, May 15, 1994 291
Lancefort Ltd v. ABP, unreported, High Court, *ex tempore*,
    February 13, 1998 30
Lane v. Eastern Carolina Drivers Assoc., 117 S.E. 2d. 737 (N.C., 1961) 283
Latchford v. Spedeworth International, The Times, October 11, 1983 263
Law v. National Greyhound Racing Club (NGRC) [1983] 1 W.L.R. 1302,
    [1983] 3 All E.R. 300 .... 30, 34 *et seq.,* 78
Laws v. London Chronicle [1959] 2 All E.R. 285. .... 314 *et seq.*
Leakey v. National Trust [1980] 2 W.L.R. 6 290
Leatherland v. Edwards, unreported, Queen's Bench,
    November 28, 1998 213
Leebody v. Ministry of Defence (2001) C.L.Y. 4544 .... 198, 199

Lehtonen and Castors Canada dry Namur-braine v. Federation Royale des
    Societies de basketball and Ligue belge-Belgische Liga
    [2000] E.C.R. I–2681 .... 43, 437
Lehtonen and Castors Canada dry Namur-Braine v. Fédération Royale
    des Sociétés de Basketball and Ligue Belge-Belgische Liga Case
    C–176/96, [2000] E.C.R. I–2681, [2000] 3 C.M.L.R. 409,
    [2001] All E.R. (EC) 97 .... 400 *et seq.*, 416
Leigh & Sillavan v. Aliakmon Shipping Co Ltd [1986] A.C. 785 200
Lennon v. McCarthy, unreported, Supreme Court, July 13, 1976 .... 243, 245
Lester Travers v. City of Frankston[1970] V.R. 2 291
Letang v. Cooper. [1965] 1 Q.B. 232 199
Lewis v. Buckpool Golf Club [1993] S.L.T. 43 .... 218 *et seq.*
Lugosi v. Universal Pictures, 25 Cal 3d 813 (1979) 328
Lunenburg (County) Dist. School Board v. Peircy (1998)
    41 C.C.L.T. (2d) 60 (N.S.C.A.) 244
Lyngstad v. Aanabas Products [1977] F.S.R. 62 329

Macari v. Celtic Football and Athletic Co. Ltd [1999] I.R.L.R. 787,
    (2000) S.L.T. 80 .... 316 *et seq.*
MacCabe v. Westlock [1998] 226 A.R. 1 (Q.B.). 244
MacDonald v. FIFA/SFA, unreported Court of Session, Outer House, 1999 279
Macken v. O'Reilly [1979] I.L.R.M. 79 42
Magic Merchandising v. Lomu, unreported High Court of New Zealand,
    Barker J., March 3, 1997 327
Magill v. Radio Telefís Éireann RTE, Case C–241/91P, [1995] E.C.R. I–743;
    [1995] 4 C.M.L.R. 718 414
Maher v. Irish Permanent [1998] 4 I.R. 302 76
Maigueside Communications Limited v. I.R.T.C. [1998] 4 I.R. 115 30
Malaja v. French Basketball Foundation (2000) 3 (2) *Sports Law Bulletin* 1 395
Marca Mode v. Adidas, ECJ Case C–425/98 (June 22, 2000) 353
Masgio v. Bundesknappschaft, Case C–10/90, [1991] E.C.R. I–1119 389
Matthews v. Irish Coursing Club and Hogan [1993] 1 I.R. 346 .... 33, 57
Maussner v. Atlantic City Country Club, 691 A. 2d. 826 (N.J. Super.
    Ct. App. Div. 1997) 287
May v. Strong [1991] B.P.I.L.S. 2274 198
McAuliffe v. Minister for Social Welfare [1995] 2 I.R. 238 308
McCabe v. Westlock, (1998) 226 A.R. 1 (Q.B.) 237
McCann v. An Bord Pleanála [1997] 1 I.R. 264 75
McComiskey v. McDermott [1974] I.R. 7 .... 197, 201 *et seq.*, 209, 221, 256
McCord v. Swansea City FC, unreported Queen's Bench,
    December 19, 1996 .... 197, 212 *et seq.*
McCullough v. Lewis A May[1947] 2 All E.R. 845 329
McCutcheon v. David MacBrayne [1964] 1 All E.R. 430 .... 353, 364
McDermott v. Sports Management, unreported, Supreme Court,
    January 12, 1988 .... 231, 232, 237
McDonald v. Bord na gCon [1965] I.R. 217 73
McInnes v. Onslow Fane [1978] 3 All E.R. 211; [1978] 1 W.L.R. 1520 .... 28, 48, 49
McNamara v. Duncan [1971] 26 A.L.R. 584 .... 199, 204

McShane Wholesale Fruit and Vegetables Ltd v. Johnston Haulage Company
 Limited [1997] 1 I.L.R.M. 86 (H.C.) 234
McStay v. Assicurazioni Generali [1991] I.L.R.M. 237 66
Meca-Medina & Majcen v. FINA, CAS 99/A/234 127
Merrigan v. Minister for Justice, unreported, High Court, Geoghegan J.,
 January 28, 1998 75
Meskell v. CIE [1973] I.R. 21, Glover v. BLN Ltd [1973] I.R. 75 54
Mètropole Tèlèvision SA, Reti Televisive Italiane SpA, Gestevision Telecinco,
 Joined Cases T–528/93 and T-542-543/93, Antena 3 de Television,
 Case T–546/93, [1996] E.C.R. II–649 452
Milan A.C. and Juventus A.C. v. Topps Italia, Decision of Tribunal de
 Grande Instance of Grenoble 25/3./1998 [1999] *European Trade
 Mark Review* 450 346
Miller v. Commission, Case 19/77, [1978] E.C.R. 13 [1978]
 2 C.M.L.R. 334 410
Miller v. Jackson [1977] Q.B. 966 .... 287, 290 *et seq.*
Minister for Industry & Commerce v. Hales [1967] I.R. 50 176
Mirage Studios v. Counter Feat Clothing[1991] F.S.R. 145 330
Modahl v. British Athletics Federation [2002]
 1 W.L.R. 1192 .... 29, 30, 39, 55, 56, 74, 76, 78, 126, 138
Moloney v. Bolger [2000] I.E.H.C. 63 .... 29, 56
Molumby v. Kearns [1999] I.E.H.C. 86 .... 290, 292
Mooney v. An Post [1998] 4 I.R. 288 .... 29, 39, 75, 312
Moore v. Hampshire County Council, 80 L.G.R. 481 (C.A.),
 November 4, 1981 237
Moran v. O'Sullivan, unreported, High Court, Carroll J.,
 March 18, 2003 .... 33, 71 *et seq.*
Morrell v. Owen, unreported, Queen's Bench, December 14, 1993 .... 198, 233
Mouscron Commission Press Release IP/99/965, December 9, 1999 441
Muehlfelder v. Crystal Woods Golf Club, No. 851-27954,
 (1993) W.L. 456111 Cir. Ct Ill. 286
Mullen v. Hynes, unreported, Supreme Court, November 13, 1972 288
Mulligan v. Doherty, unreported, Supreme Court, May 17, 1966 242
Mullins v. Harnett [1998] 2 I.L.R.M. 304 .... 62, 176
Murphy v. Brentwood District Council [1991] 1 A.C. 398 200
Murphy v. Jackson D.P.I.J. Trinity and Michaelmas Terms 1993
 (H.C.) 146 237
Murphy v. Steeplechase Amusement Co. Inc., 166 NE 173 (1929) 200
Murphy v. Stewart [1973] I.R. 97 54
Murphy v. Turf Club[1989] I.R. 172 33
Murray v. Haringey Arena [1951] 2 All E.R. 320 .... 198, 259, 281
Murtagh Properties v. Cleary [1972] I.R. 330 54

N v. Equestrian Federation, CAS 94/126 131
N, J, W and Y v. FINA, CAS 98/208 .... 123, 129, 133, 138
Nagle v. Feilden [1966] 2 Q.B. 633 .... 44, 45, 47, 53, 467
Narbonzy v. Barnhill, 31 Ill. App. 3rd 212, 334 NE 2nd 255
 (1975) 191

Neal v. Board of Trustees of the California State Universities,
    198 F3d 763,770 (9th Cir 1999) 472
Nettleship v. Weston [1977] 2 Q.B. 691 .... 202, 209
New Zealand Rugby Football Union v. Canterbury International
    Limited 346
Newport Association v. Football Association of Wales (No. 2),
    unreported, April 12, 1995 76
Ngugi v. Kenyan Amateur Athletic Association (KAAA) and IAAF,
    (November 5, 1994, IAAF Tribunal 124, 138
Nice & Safe Attitude v. Piers Flook [1997] F.S.R. 14 330
Noade v. Teague, Queen's Bench, March 1, 2001 [2001] B.N.I.L. No. 143 217
Nordenfelt v. Maxim Nordenfelt Guns and Ammunition Company
    [1894] A.C. 535 .... 40, 49
Norwegian NOC & Others v. IOC, CAS 2002/O/372 98
NWBA v. International Para Olympic Committee, CAS 95/122 .... 131, 137, 139

O'Brien v. Garda Commissioner, unreported, High Court, Kelly J.,
    August 19, 1996 75
O'Coindealbhain v. Mooney, High Court, Barr J., March, 12, 1992 308
O'Donohoe v. O'Baroid & Quirke, High Court, unreported, McCracken J.,
    April 23, 1999 .... 54, 55
O'Hanlon v. ESB [1969] I.R. 75 208
O'Kane v. Campbell [1985] I.R. 115 .... 290, 291
O'Keefe v. An Bord Pleanála [1993] 1 I.R 56
O'Leary v. Medical Council, unreported, Supreme Court, July 25, 1997 123
O'Neills Irish International Sports Co Ltd v. O'Neills Footwear Dryer,
    unreported, High Court, April 30, 1997 .... 336, 351
O'Neills v. Adidas, unreported, Supreme Court, March 25, 1992 351
O'Reilly v. Mackman [1983] 2 A.C. 237, [1982] 3 W.L.R. 1096, [1982]
    3 All E.R. 112434 34
O'Reilly v. Minister for Industry and Commerce, unreported, High Court,
    Carroll J., March 4, 1993 312
O'Reilly v. Nolan & Irish Amateur Boxing Association, unreported,
    Galway Circuit Court, May 2, 2003 201
Oswald v. Township High School District,
    84 Ill App. 3d 723, 406 N.E. 2d, 157 205

P v. S & Cornwall, Case C–13/94 [1996] E.C.R. I–2143 465
Pallante v. Stadiums PTY [1976] V.R. 331 .... 172 *et seq.*
Paracidal Pty v. Herctum Pty Ltd (1983) 4 I.P.R. 201 328
Parochial Church Council of Aston Cantlow v. Wallbank
    [2001] E.W.C.A. Civ. 713 79
Parry v. Clucking, unreported, High Court, March 22, 1990 198
Pawlak v. Doucette & Reinks [1985] 2 W.W.R. 588 232
Payne & Payne v. Maple Leaf Gardens [1949] 1 D.L.R. 369 197
Pearson v. Lightening, unreported, Court of Appeal, April 1, 1998 219
People (DPP) v. McCarthy, unreported, Circuit Court Dublin,
    October 20-22, 1987 181

People (DPP) v. O'Driscoll, Cork Circuit Court, February 10-11, 1993 181
Perriss Wilkins v. UK Athletics, CAS 2003/A/455 125
Pestalozzi v. Philadelphia Plyers, 595 A. 2d. 1269 (Pa. Super. 1991) 282
Petersen v. School District No. 36 (1993) 104 D.L.R. 334 (BCC.A.) 245
Pett v. Greyhound Racing Association [1969] 1 Q.B. 125 75
Petty v. British Judo Association [1981] I.C.R. 660 470
Piddington v. Hastings, *The Times*, March 12, 1932 281
Pitcher. v. Huddersfield Town FC, unreported, Queen's Bench,
    July 17, 2001 .... 197, 214, 226
Pittsburgh Athletic Co v. KQV Broadcasting, 24 F.Supp 490
    (WD Pa 1937) 363
Player & Wills (Irl) Ltd v. Gallagher, unreported, High Court,
    April 30, 1997 329
Poll v. FINA, CAS 2002/A/399 .... 122, 138
Polycell Products Ltd v. O'Carroll, [1959] Ir. Jur. Rep. 34 329
Poplar Housing & Regeneration Community Association Limited v.
    Donoghue[2002] Q.B. 48 79
Potter v. Carlisle and Cliftonville Golf Club [1939] N.I. 114 283
Pourcet and Pistre v. Assurances Generales de France, Joined cases
    159-160/91, [1993] E.C.R. I – 637 409
Price v. Hal Roach Studios, 400 F. Supp. 836 (1975) 328
Priestly v. Stork Margarine Social and Recreational Club, unreported,
    Birkenhead County Court, June 24, 1988 468
Private Research Ltd v. Brosnan [1996] 1 I.L.R.M. 27 329

Questore di Verona v. Zenatti, Case C–67/98, [1999] E.C.R. I–7289 405
Quinn's Supermarket v. Attorney General [1972] IR 1 461
Quirke v. BLE[1988] I.R. 83 .... 33, 58, 75, 124

R (on the application of Amius) v. Secretary of State for Trade and Industry
    and conjoined applicators [2004] All E.R. (D) 238,
    April 26, 2004-09-02 482
R v Football Association, *ex parte* Football League [1993]
    2 All E.R. 225 .... 34, 36
R v. Aitken [1992] W.L.R. 1006 167
R v. Assam (1997) Ont. C.J.P. Lexis, 136, 1997 W.C.B.J. .424117,
    36 W.C.B. (2d) 453 .... 192, 193
R v. Billinghurst [1978] Criminal L.R. 553 183
R v. Birkin (1988) 10 Cr. App. R. 303 184
R v. Bishop (1986) *The Times*, October 12, 1986 184
R v. Blissett, *Independent*, December 4, 1992 183
R v. Bradshaw. (1878) 14 Cox C.C .83 .... 182, 183, 191
R v. Brown [1994] 1 A.C. 212 [1993] 2 All E.R. 75 [1993]
    2 W.L.R. 556 .... 166, 167, 169, 176
R v. Calton [1999] 2 Cr. App. Rep.(s) 64 CA 185
R v. Cantona, *The Times*, 25 March 1995 180
R v. Cey (1989) 48 C.C.C. (3d) 480 193
R v. Coney, (1882) 8 Q.B.D. 534 .... 166, 172, 173

R v. Davies 12 Cr. App. Rep. (s) 308 [1991] Criminal L.R. 7. 185
R v. Disciplinary Committee of the Jockey Club, *ex parte* Aga Khan
    [1993] 1 W.L.R. 909, [1993] 2 All E.R. 853 .... 33–35, 39, 45
R v. Disciplinary Committee of the Jockey Club, *ex parte* Massingberd
    Munday [1993] 2 All E.R. 207 34
R v. Donovan [1934] 2 K.B. 498 166
R v. FA of Wales, *ex parte* Flint Town [1995] 2 All E.R. 87 45
R v. Football Association, *ex parte* Flint Town [1991] C.O.D. 44 34
R v. Football Association Ltd, *ex parte* Football League Ltd [1993]
    2 All E.R. 833 .... 33, 79
R v. Goodwin, (1995) 16 Cr. App. R.(s) 885 184
R v. Hardy, *The Guardian*, 27 July 27, 1994 185
R v. Hargreaves (1831) 5 C. & P. 170 172
R v. Independent Television Commission *ex parte* TV Danmark 1 Ltd
    [2001] 1 W.L.R. 1604 .... 367 *et seq.*
R v. Jockey Club, *ex parte* RAM Racecourses [1993] 2 All E.R. 225 .... 34, 45
R v. Johnson [1986] 8 C.A.R. (5) 343 184
R v. Kamara, *The Times*, April 15, 1988 184
R v. Kirk, Daily Telegraph, October 17, 1995 180
R v. Leyte (1973) 13 C.C.C. (2d) 458 193
R v. Lincoln (1990) 12 Cr App R (s) 250 184
R v. Lloyd [1989] 36 *Criminal Law Review* 513 184
R v. Maki [1970] 14 D.L.R. (3d) 164, R v. Green [1970] 16 D.L.R. (3d) 137 192
R v. Maloney (1976) 28 C.C.C. (2d) 3232 193
R v. McHugh, unreported, High Court, February 20, 199 185
R v. Moore (1898) 14 T.L.R. 229 182
R v. Moss, unreported, Court of Appeal, July 5, 1999 185
R v. Orton (1871) 14 Cox C.C. 226 172
R v. Panel on Mergers and Takeovers, *ex parte* Datafin [1987] Q.B 699,
    [1987] 2 W.L.R. 699, [1987] 1 All E.R. 509 .... 31, 34, 35
R v. Perkins, (1831) 4 C & P 537, 172 E.R. 814 172
R v. Shervill (1989) 11 Cr. App. R 284 .... 184, 185
R v. Southby (1969) *Police Review*, February 9, vol. 77 p. 110 183
R v. St Croix (1979) 7 C.C.C. (2d) 122 193
R v. Watson (1975) 26 C.C.C. (2d) 150 193
R v. Wilson [1997] Q.B. 47 167
R v. Young, (1866) 10 Cox C.C. 371 172
Raducan v. IOC, CAS Ad Hoc. Sydney OG) 2000/011 129
Rafferty v. Bus Éireann [1997] 2 I.R. 424 .... 30, 31, 33
Ralph v. London County Council, King's Bench,
    February 11, 1947 .... 198, 245
Regan v. The Irish Automobile Club[1990] 1 I.R. 278 260
RFU & Nike v. Cotton Traders[2002] 2 All E.R. (d) 417, [2002]
    E.W.H.C. 467 (Ch.). 346
Rice v. Chatterton, *The Times*, June 29, 1977. 468
Richoux v. Herbert, 449n So. 2d. 491 (La. Ct App., 1983) 283
Ridge v. Baldwin [1964] A.C. 40 29
Roberts v. Colorado State University, 998 F2d 824 (10th Cir 1993). 474

Roberts v. United State,s 468 U.S. 609 (1984) 492
Roche v. Kelly [1969] I.R. 100 308
Roddie v. Ski Llandudno Limited, unreported, Court of Appeal,
    July 31, 2000 231
Rogers v. Bugden & Canterbury-Bankstown (1993) A.T.R. 81 198
Rootes v. Shelton [1968] A.L.R. 33 192
Rootes v. Shelton 207
Rosa v. County of Nasseau, 544 N.Y.S. 2d. 652 (N.Y. Ct App. 1989) 282
Rotherham & English Second Division Rugby Limited v. English First
    Division Rugby Ltd [2000] 1 *International Sports Law Review* 33 39
Rotunda Hospital & Mater Misericoridiae Hospital v. Dr. Gleeson,
    ODEI Determin. No. DEE003, 18/04/00 466
Royal Dublin Society v. Yates [1997] I.E.H.C. 144 290
Russell v. Duke of Norfolk [1949] 1 All E.R. 109 3974
Ryan v. Criminal Injuries Compensation Tribunal [1997] 1 I.L.R.M. 194 33
Rylands v. Fletcher, (1868) L.R. 3 H.L. 330 288

S v. FINA, CAS 2000/A/274 129
SA CNL-Sucal NV v. Hag GF AG [1990] 3 C.M.L.R. 571 340
SABEL v. Puma [1997] E.C.R. 1-6191 351
Salomon SA v. Commission, Case T – 123/97, [1999] E.C.R. II–2925 435
Salomon v Salomon & Co [1897] A.C. 22 323
Sandra Gasser case, Decision of Richteramt Bern III of December 22,
    1987, (SJZ 84, (1988) 130
Saunders v. Richmond-Upon Thames BC[1978] I.C.R. 75 466
Scholes v. Beaton and Equestrian Federation of Australia,
    CAS 2003/A/ 477 138
Sea Containers Limited v. Stena Sealink Ports & Stena Sealink Line,
    Commission Decision IV/34.689, (1994) O.J. L. 15/8;
    [1995] 4 C.M.L.R. 84 414
Segal v. Derrick Golf & Winter Club (1977) 76 D.L.R. (3d.) 746 291
Shanahan v. One Pico DEC–S2003-056, June 30, 2003 487
Shankland v. Airdrieonians (1956) S.L.T. 69 315
Shapiro v. Queen's County Jockey Club, 53 N.Y.S. 2d. 135 Court
    (1945) 229
Sheahan v. FBD Insurance, unreported, Kelly J., March 25, 1998 66
Simms v. Leigh[1969] 2 All E.R. 923 264
Singh v. FA & Others, IT 5203593/99 [2002] I.S.L.R 141 480
Sirdar v. Secretary of State for Defence, Case C–273/97, [1999]
    E.C.R. I–7403 466
Smith v. CIE [1991] I.R. 1. 259
Smith v. Jolly, unreported, High Court, O'Hanlon J., May 17-18, 1984 241
Smithkline Beecham v. Antigen Pharmaceuticals, [1999] 2 I.L.R.M. 190 329
Smoldon v. Whitworth (1997) E.L.R. 249, [1997]
    P.I.Q.R. 133 .... 197, 207, 208, 223 *et seq.*, 228
Sotomayor [2001] I.S.L.R. 254 .... 133, 138
Sports & General Press Agency Ltd v. Our Dogs Publishing Company
    Limited [1917] 2 K.B. 125 .... 305, 353, 364

Sports Club Evelyn and Jocelyn v. Inspector of Taxes [2000]
    S.T.C. (SCD) 443 .... 326, 337
Spray v. Mayor Alderman and Burgess of Ellesmere Port [1997]
    E.W.C.A. (Civ.) 2883 287
St Johnstone FC v. Scottish Football Association (1965)
    S.L.T. 171 .... 58, 75
State (Gleeson) v. Minister for Defence [1976] I.R. 280 .... 73, 74
State (Haverty) v. An Bord Pleanála [1987] I.R. 485 76
State v. Burnham 56 Ver. 445 (1884) 172
State v. Forbes (No. 6328-; District Court Mann; July 19, 1975) 193
Stergios Delimitis v. Henninger Brau, Case C–234/89, [1991]
    E.C.R. I – 935; [1992] 5 C.M.L.R. 210 411
Sterling v. Leeds Rugby League Club (2000) Case No IT 1802453/00 480
Stevenage Borough FC v. Football League, *The Times*,
    August 1, 1996, (1997) 9 Admin L.R. 109 .... 41, 44 *et seq.*, 49, 425
Stratton v. Hughes and Others, unreported, Queen's Bench,
    February 28, 1997 202
Stretch v. Romford Football Club Ltd, [1971] E.G.D. 763 292
Sturges v. Bridgman, (1879) 11 Ch. D. 852 292
Sweeney v. Duggan [1997] 2 I.L.R.M. 211 246
Swiss Athletic Federation & Gasser v. IAAF, January 18, 1988 138

Talamax Pty v. Telstra, unreported, Supreme Court of Queensland,
    Byrne J., March 14, 1996 329
Tavaner Routledge v. Trexaplam [1977] R.P.C. 275 329
Taylor v. Bath & NE Somerset District Council, unreported,
    Queen's Bench, January 27, 1999 245
Tetley v. Chitty [1986] 1 All E.R. 663 .... 287, 292
Thornton v. Board of School Trustees of School District No. 57,
    73 D.L.R. 3d 35 (1976) 235, 244
Tibor Balog v. Charleroi Sporting Club, C–264/98, Opinion of
    March 29, 2001 .... 392, 417, 437
Tierney v. An Post [2000] 1 I.R. 536 308
Tolley v. Fry [1931] A.C. 333 336
Tomjanovich v. California Sports Inc, No. H-78-243 (S.D. Tex. 1979) 234
Tomlinson v. Congleton Borough Council [2003] U.K.H.L. 5 [2003]
    All E.R. 1122 263
Trebor Bassett v. FA[1997] F.S.R. 211 .... 345, 346
Twentieth Century Fox v. South Australian Brewing (1996)
    34 I.P.R. 225 329

UCI v. A, CAS 97/175 139
UCI v. M, CAS 98/212 127
UNCTEF V. Heylens, Case 222/86, [1987] E.C.R. 4097 .... 383 *et seq.*
Union Royale Belge des Societes de Football Association ASBL v. Jean Marc
    Bosman, Case C–415/93, [1995] E.C.R. I – 4921; [1996] 1 C.M.L.R. 645;
    [1996] All E.R. (EC) 97 .... 12, 39, 40, 51, 377, 384,
                                    385 *et seq.*, 407, 416, 417, 437, 438, 440, 477

United Brands v. Commission, Case 27/76, [1978] E.C.R. 207;
  [1978] 1 C.M.L.R. 429 413
Unruh v. Webber 98 D.L.R. 4th 294 (Supreme Court, 1992) 203
USA Shooting & Q v. International Shooting Union,
  CAS 94/129 .... 124, 130, 137, 138

V v. FINA, CAS 95/150 125
Van Oppen v. Bedford Charity Trustees [1990] 1 W.L.R. 235 246
Van Oppen v. Clerk to the Bedford Charity Trustees [1989]
  1 All E.R. 273 (Q.B.) [1989] 3 All E.R. 389 (C.A.) 198, 231
Victoria Park Racing & Recreation Grounds v. Taylor
  (1937) 58 C.L.R. 479 .... 304, 352
Vine Products Limited v MacKenzie [1969] R.P.C. 1 345
Volk v. Vervaecke, Case 5/69, [1969] E.C.R. 295 [1969]
  C.M.L.R. 273 410
Vowles v. Evans & WRU [2003] 1 W.L.R. 2607 .... 197, 206, 226, 228, 248

Wainwright v. Home Office[2003] All E.R. (D) 279 333
Walker v. Crystal Palace Football Club [1910] 1 K.B. 87 308
Walker v. IAAF [2001] I.S.L.R. 264 .... 134, 139
Walrave and Koch V Union Cycliste Internationale (UCI) Case 36/74,
  [1974] E.C.R. 1405, [1974] 1 C.M.L.R. 320 .... 379 *et seq.*, 382, 383
Walrave and Koch v. Union Cycliste Internationale
  [1974] E.C.R. 1405 12
Walsh v. Butler [1997] 2 I.L.R.M. 81 62
Walsh v. Red Cross Society [1997] 2 I.R. 479 31
Ward v. Donegal Vocational Committee, D.P.I.J. Hilary and Easter Terms
  1993 (H.C.) 116
Ward v. McMaster [1988] I.R. 337 200
Warnink v. Townsend & Sons Hull Ltd, [1979] A.C. 731 329
Waterford Trademark, re [1984] F.S.R. 390 340
Watson & Bradford City FC v. Gray & Huddersfield Town, unreported,
  Queen's Bench, October 26, 1998 .... 197, 213 *et seq.*, 264
Watson v. British Boxing Board of Control
  [2001] 2 W.L.R. 1256 .... 170, 178, 198, 248 *et seq.*, 278
Watson v. Haines, unreported, Allen J., Supreme Court of New South Wales,
  April 10, 1987 236
Watson v. Prager [1991] 1 W.L.R. 726 .... 45, 53, 53
Wertheim v. United States Tennis Association 252
WH Smith & Son Ltd v. Screensport and the European Broadcasting Union,
  Case IV/32.524, (1991) O.J. L.63/32 [1992] 5 C.M.L.R. 273 447
Wheeler v. Leicester City Council [1985] 1 A.C. 1054, [1985] 2 All E.R. 1106,
  [1985] 3 W.L.R. 335 56
White v. Blackmore[1972] 2 Q.B. 651 260
White v. Mellin [1895] A.C. 154 336
Whitefield v. Barton[1987] S.C.L.R. 259 289
Wilander v. Tobin, [1997] 2 C.M.L.R. 346, [1997] 2 Lloyd's Rep. 296,
  [1997] Eu L.R. 265 .... 48 *et seq.*, 54, 55, 57, 76, 131, 385

Wilkins v. Smith (1976) 73 Law Society Gazette, 938 281
Wilks v. Cheltenham Home Guard Motor Cycle and Light Car Club
    [1971] 2 All E.R. 369 .... 197, 202, 205, 222, 223
Williams and Cardiff RFC v. Pugh, unreported, Queen's Bench,
    July 23, 1997, Court of Appeal, August 1, 1997 53
Williams v. Reason [1988] 1 W.L.R. 96 .... 57, 336
Williams v. Rotherham LEA, Times, August 6, 1998 237
Wilson v. Governors of the Sacred Heart Roman Catholic School
    [1998] 1 F.L.R. 663 243
Wilson v. Racher[1974] I.R.L.R. 114 315
Wimbledon FC v. Football League, FA Arbitration, January 29, 2002 50
Windsurfing Inc v. Tabur Marine [1985] R.P.C. 59 306
Wombles Ltd v. Wombles Skips [1975] F.S.R. 488 329
Woodbridge v. Chittock [2002] E.W.C.A. Civ. 915 240
Woodroffe-Hedley v. Cuthbertson, unreported, Queen's Bench,
    June 20, 1997 .... 198, 232 *et seq.*
Wooldridge v. Sumner [1963] 2 Q.B. 43 .... 197, 205, 221 *et seq.*
Wright v. Cheshire County Council[1952] 2 All E.R. 789 243

Yates v. Chicago National League Ball Club, 595 N.E. 2d. 570 (Ill. 1992) 282
Yuen Kun-Yeu v. AG of Hong Kong [1987] 2 All E.R. 705 200

Zapf v. Muscat 11 B.C.L.R. 3d 296 203
Zockoll Group Limited v. Telecom Éireann [1998] 4 I.R. 287 29

Table of Legislation

IRELAND

Bunreacht na hÉireann

art.26 461

art.40.3 333

art.40.3.1 54

art.40.3.2 54

art.43 54

Anti-Discrimination Pay Act 1974 308

Broadcasting Act 1990

s.4(1) 375, 376

s.4(2) 376

s.16 376

s.6(1) 376

s.7 376

s.20(2) 376

s.23(4) 376

s.23(5) 376

Broadcasting (Major Events Television Coverage) Act 1999 .... 370 *et seq.*

s.1(2) 371

s.1(4) 371

s.2 .... 370, 373

s.2(1)(b) 371

s.2(2)(a) 371

s.2(3) 371

s.3 371

s.4 .... 371, 372

s.5 372

s.6 371

s.7 371

Broadcasting (Major Events Television Coverage) (Amendment) Act 2003 373

s.4 .... 373, 375

s.4(1) 374

s.4(1)(a) 373

s.4(4) 373

s.4(8) 373

s.4(1) 374

s.6 374

s.9 374

Building Control Act 1990 268
Civil Liability Act 1961
    s.34(1)(b) 208
Competition Act 1991 410
Competition Act 2002 .... 410, 413
    s.5 .... 415, 416
    s.4 410
Copyright and Related Rights Act 2000 .... 347, 348
    s.51(2) 364
    Pt V 347
Criminal Justice (Public Order) Act 1994 .... 294, 300, 301
    s.21 .... 276, 293
    s.22 .... 293, 294
    s.166 299
Employment Equality Act 1998 .... 308, 461, 464, 465, 479, 481, 484, 487
    s.2 484
    s.6(2)(h) 477
    s.6(3) 488
    s.7(4) 462, 494
    s.7(4)(a) 462, 467, 485, 488, 489
    s.7(4)(b) 462, 485
    s.15 464
    s.16 .... 484, 485, 488
    s.25(2) 492
    s.33 480
    s.34(3) 488
    s.35(1) 484
    s.37(1) 481, 482
    s.37(2) 478, 479
    s.37(3) 478, 479
    s.37(4) 478, 479
    s.39 464
Equal Status Act 2000 .... 461, 464, 479, 481, 484, 487, 489
    s.5(1) 461
    s.5(2)(f) 467, 478
    s.5(2)(i) 479
    s.5(2)(h) 485, 487
    s.6 462
    s.7 462
    s.7(1) 462
    s.7(2) 462
    s.8 489
    s.9 491
    s.9(a) 489
    s.9(b) 489
    s.9(c) 490
    s.9(d) 490
    s.9(e) 490

Equal Status Act 2000—*contd.*

        s.25(2) 466, 467

        s.37(3) 467

        s.39 464

        Pt VI 485

European Convention on Human Rights Act 2003 79

Fire Services Act 1981 .... 266, 267

Freedom of Information Act 1997 .... 79, 81

Human Rights Act 2000 332

Irish Sports Council Act 1999 .... 10, 119

        s.2 7

Licensing of Indoor Events Act 2003 267

        s.2 267

        s.4(2) 267

        s.5(2) 267

        s.5(4) 267

        s.11 267

        s.12 267

Minimum Notice and Terms of Employment Act 1973

        Sch.1 312

Misuse of Drugs Act 1977 106

Misuse of Drugs Act 1984 106

Non-Fatal Offences Against the Person Act

   1997 .... 167, 168, 169, 176, 188

        s.2 167

        s.3 167

        s.4 .... 167, 176, 188

        s.22 167

Occupiers Liability Act 1995 .... 256 *et seq.*, 265, 269, 279, 280, 284, 287

        s.1 .... 256, 257, 259

        s.2 256

        s.3 256

        s.4 257

        s.4(1) 259

        s.5 .... 260, 321

        s.5(2)(b)(ii) 260

        s.5(2)(c) 260

        s.5(5) 260

Organisation of Working Time Act 1997 308

Parental Leave Act 1998 308

Payment of Wages Act 1991 308

Prohibition of Incitement to Hatred Act 1991 .... 294, 295

Public Health Acts (Amendment) Act 1890

        s.37 267

Registration of Clubs Act 1904–1999 489

Road Traffic Act 1961

        s.13 145

Safety, Health and Welfare at Work Act 1989 .... 268, 308

Sales of Goods and Supply of Services 1980
         s.40(1) 320
Terms of Employment (Information) Act 1994 308
Trade Marks Act 1996
         s.4 340
         s.8 340
         ss 10–12 340
         s.10(4) 327
         s.14 340
         s.14(2) 340
         s.14(3) 341
         s.18 341
         s.20 341
         s.22 341
         s.23 341
         s.47 341
         ss 92–94 341
         s.97 341
Unfair Dismissals Acts 1977–1993 .... 308, 312, 314
Unfair Dismissals Act 1977
         s.6(2) 313
Unfair Dismissals (Amendment) Act 1993 312
         s.5 313

STATUTORY INSTRUMENTS

**Broadcasting (Major Events Television Coverage) Act 1999 (Designation
   of Major Events) Order 2003 (S.I. No. 99 of 2003)** 374
Building Regulations 1991 (S.I. No. 306 of 1991) 268
**Building Regulations (Amendment) Regulations 1994
   (S.I. No. 154 of 1994)** 268
**European Communities (Safeguarding of Employees' Rights on Transfer
   of Undertakings) Regulations 1980 (S.I. No. 306/1980)** 308
**European Communities (Unfair Terms in Consumer Contracts)
   Regulations 1995 (S.I. No. 27 of 1995)** 261, 320, 321
         reg.8 320
**Fire Safety In Places Of Assembly (Ease Of Escape), Regulations 1985
   (S.I. No. 249 of 1985)** 267

ENGLAND

Broadcasting Act 1996 .... 367 *et seq.*
Criminal Procedure (Scotland) Act 1995
         s.12 188
Football Spectators' Act 1989 .... 296, 297
         Pt II 297

Football (Disorder) Act 2002 297
Football (Disorder) (Amendment) Act 2002 297
Human Rights Act 1998 78
Occupiers Liability Act 1957
              s.2 .... 261, 284
Public Order Act 1986
              s.40 298
              sch.1 299
Race Relations Act 1976 .... 480 *et seq.*
              s.39 481
Race Relations Act 2000 480
Sex Discrimination Act 1975 .... 467 *et seq.*, 492
              s.34 492
              s.44 .... 469 *et seq.*
              Pts II–IV 469
Sporting Events (Control of Alcohol) Act 1985 .... 298, 299
Unfair Contract terms Act 1977 .... 261, 319

NEW ZEALAND

Sporting Injuries Insurance Act 1978 254

SOUTH AFRICA

Merchandise Marks Act 1941 361
Trade Practices Act 1976 361

SWITZERLAND

Federal Law on Arbitration
              art.8 22

EUROPEAN CONVENTIONS, DIRECTIVES, REGULATIONS AND TREATIES

Community Trade Mark Regulation (40/94/EEC) 340
Council of Europe Anti-Doping Convention 1989 .... 110 *et seq.*
        art.10 111
        appendix 112
Council of Europe European Convention on Transfrontier Television (ETS: No 132 as amended by the Protocol to the Convention (ETS: NO 171)
        art.9 366
Council Directive 89/552/EEC, as amended by Directive 97/36/EC .... 366 *et seq*
        art.3A 369, 372, 374
        art.3(a)1 367
        art.3(a)3 367
Council Directive 76/207/EEC .... 462 *et seq*
        art.2(2) 466
        art.2(3) 465
Council Directive 92/27EEC
        art.12 114
Council Directive 96/99/EC .... 348 *et seq.*
        para.27 349
        para.47 348
        para.51 349
        para.53 349
        para.59 349
        para.70 350
        para.73 350
        para.75 350
        para.81 350
        para.89 350
        paras 97-99 350
        paras 105ff 350
        paras 125ff 350
        paras 132ff 350
        para.134 351
        para.138 351
        para.152 351
Council Directive 97/36/EC 366
Council Directive 2000/43/EC .... 462 *et seq.*, 479
        art.2(2)(b) 463
        art.2(3) 464
        art.13 465
Council Directive 2000/78/EC .... 462 *et seq.*, 481, 482, 484, 485, 487
        art.2(2)(b) 463
        art.4 488
        art.5 485
        art.6 488

Council Directive 2000/78/EC—*contd.*
art.4(2) 482
Recital 17 485
Council Regulation 1/2003 411
art.16 411
art.11(6) 412
EC Treaty 113, 421, 422
art.12 476
art.39 .... 378, 379, 382, 384, 388 *et seq.*, 392
art.43 .... 378, 406
art.49 .... 115, 377, 384, 399, 403, 404, 406
art.81 .... 115, 378, 384, 392, 395, 399,
408, 410, 412, 414, 417, 422,
425, 426, 433, 437, 445, 450
art.81(1) 423, 424
art.81(3) .... 408, 410 *et seq.*, 423, 424, 433, 446
art.82 .... 115, 378, 384, 395, 399, 408,
411 *et seq.*, 425, 426, 432, 450
art.87 .... 434, 435
art.152 114
art.234 .... 399, 401
European Convention on Human Rights 78
art.6 73
art.8 .... 333, 334
art.10 334

**European Convention on Spectator Violence and Misbehaviour at Sports
Events and in Particular at Football Matches, of 1985** 272
art.2 300
art.3 300
art.3(1)(b) 300
art.4 .... 272, 300
art.5 300
art.6 274
art.8 272
**Parliament and Council Directive, September 23, 2002 [2002]
O.J. L2691** 462
art.1(7) 465
Paris Convention of 1883
art.6 347
Treaty of Amsterdam 398
Treaty of Nice 398
Trade Mark Harmonisation Directive (89/104/EEC) .... 340, 343 *et seq.*

SPORTS' CODES AND RULES

Irish Sports Council Anti-Doping Rules .... 18, 87 *et seq.*, 119 *et seq.*,
141, 154, 155 *et seq.*

art.1.1.1.1 156
art.1.2 155
art.2 157
art.2.1.1 156
art.2.2 156
art.2.3 156
art.2.4 156
art.2.5 156
art.2.6 156
art.2.7 156
art.2.8 157
art.3 157
art.3.1 157
art.3.2.2 157
art.3.2.1 157
art.4 157
art.4.4 157
art.4.4.2 157
art.4.4.3 158
art.4.5 158
art.4.7 158
art.4.8 .... 157, 158
art.4.9 158
art.4.10 158
art.4.12 158
art.5 158
art.5.4 159
art.5.4.4 159
art.5.4.5 159
art.5.6.1 159
art.5.6 159
art.5.6.3 159
art.5.9 159
art.5.7 159
art.6 157
art.7 159
art.7.3 160
art.7.4.3 160
art.7.5 160
art.7.7 160
art.7.8 160
art.7.8.5 160
art.8 160
art.8.2.4 160

Irish Sports Council Anti-Doping Rules—*contd.*
art.8.3 160
art.8.3.7 161
art.8.4.2 161
art.8.4.8 161
art.8.5 161
art.10.1 161
art.10.1.2 161
art.10.2 161
art.10.3 162
art.10.5 161
art.10.5.1 162
art.10.5.2 162
art.10.5.3 162
art.10.6.1 16
art.10.7 161
art.10.8 162
art.10.9 162
art.10.10 162
art.11 161
art.13.2 160
art.13.2.1 162
art.13.3 162
art.13.4.4 162
art.13.8 158
art.13.11 163
art.14 156
art.17 160
Irish Sports Council Code of Good Practice for Children's Sport 247
para.2.6.1 247
para.2.6.2 247
International Olympic Anti-Doping Code 107, 144
World Anti-Doping Code 18, 82, 87, 106, 109, 121, 123, 138,
139, 141, 153 *et seq.*, 155 *et seq.*, 162, 163
art.2.1 139
art.4.1 154
art.4.2 154
art.4.3.1 154
art.4.3.3 144
art.4.5 155
art.8 160
art.18 154
art.19 154
arts 20–22 155

CHAPTER ONE

Introduction to Sports Law in Ireland

INTRODUCTION

For some, the two concepts of sport and law seem like natural enemies.[1] Sport, so this argument goes, is something idealistic and ethereal – something that should be above the crude machinations of the law, and certainly something that should not be sullied by lawyers.[2] The various governing bodies that are in charge either of the playing or indeed of the business of sport should be trusted to make the decisions that are in the best interests of this important social commodity, and should not be beholden to the excessively dogmatic formalities associated with law.

To others, the picture is not so ideal. Sport is seen as a big business, and the businesspeople who make their livings from the activity are regarded as being just as foolish and just as prone to error and corruption as any other businesspeople.[3] The professionalisation of sport has meant that what is at stake is a scenario in which issues pertaining to employment law, tax law, commercial law, tort law and so on are thrown up on a regular basis. And the fact that this particular business is also, for many people, a hobby – both in terms of participation in amateur sport and in terms of viewing and supporting professional sport – does not mean that it is any less reasonable for the law to vindicate the rights of those who are affected by "illegal" actions in the sporting context, than to vindicate those of workers in any other place of employment.

Whichever approach is preferred, the reality is that the law of the land *does* have a role to play in the regulation and governance both of sport itself and also of the actions of individual sportsmen and sportswomen – even if the question of the appropriate limits to such role remains a matter for debate.[4] In

---

[1] See for example, "Cheating Superstars Thrive – Thanks to Their Legal Eagles", *Observer*, August 12, 2001.

[2] Woodhouse, "The Lawyer in Sport: Some Reflections", 4(3) *Sport and the Law Journal* (1996) 14 and by the same author, "The Role of the Lawyer in Sport Today", 1(1) *Sport and the Law Journal* (1993) 1.

[3] Generally see Smith, "The Commercial Exploitation of Sport", 6(2) *Sport and the Law Journal* (1998) 59 and Boon, "Sport Scores in the Business League", 2(3) *Sport and the Law Journal* (1994) 23.

[4] See MacNeill, Furlong and Crowley, "A Game of Two Halves", October 2000, *Gazette*

this book we consider how the relationship between sport and the law has developed and what the most appropriate future is for such development. In this respect an initial caveat should be made, namely that given that the biggest stimulus for legal involvement in sport is undoubtedly professionalisation, and given also that the bulk of Irish sport is still amateur, much of the analysis presented herein relates to developments in other jurisdictions. But it is these developments which, we suggest, will foreshadow likely developments in Ireland as more sports become professional and as more aspects of amateur sport become professionalised.

This first chapter has two major focuses. First, we address certain pressing introductory questions about the relationship between sport and the law, including the impact that the latter has on the former, the reasons why it has such an impact and the level of impact that it *should* properly have. Secondly, we look at some of the basic regulatory structures in sport – both the structures that come from within sport and also the structures that are imposed from without by governmental and quasi-governmental organisations.

1.1 *Should* the Law be Involved in Sport?

There is an ongoing debate as to whether the law should play a role in resolving sports disputes or whether the resolution of contentious issues is best left to the internal disciplinary bodies governing sport. Edward Grayson,[5] for example, has long argued that sports administrators cannot be trusted with the business of self-regulation and hence, that the use of law in this regard will prove advantageous to sport as it seeks to return to the halcyon days of Corinthianism and fair play.[6] In this respect, we might consider the allegations of corruption regularly aimed at sporting bodies, including those that were made, for example in respect of the judging process for the figure skating competitions at the Salt Lake City Winter Olympic Games in 2002.[7] Simon Gardiner, in reply feels

---

of the Law Society of Ireland 12; McCutcheon, "The Rule of Law in Sport", 9(2) *Sports Law Administration and Practice* (2002) 1 and Pittman, "The Interaction of Sport and Law: Where Has It Been, Where is it Now and Where is it Going?", 2(2) *Journal of Legal Aspects of Sport* (1992) 64.

[5] Grayson, *Sport and the Law* (3rd ed., Butterworths, London, 2000), p.111.

[6] See for example, Grayson, "Sport and the Law: A Return to Corinthian Values", 6(1) *Sport and the Law Journal* (1998) 5.

[7] In this instance a Russian pair won the Olympic Pairs Gold medal despite clearly not being as good as their Canadian counterparts, and eventually a Russian crime figure was arrested and accused of being the ringleader of a major conspiracy to "fix" the competition, which also centred on a French judge Marie-Reine Le Gougne, who admitted that she had been pressurised to "vote a certain way" and the President of the French skiing Federation Didier Gailhaguet. See Michaelis, "Skating Hearing Plotlines Come Out Despite Secrecy", *USA Today*, April 19, 2002 and Shipley, "Skating Prepares for Day of Judgement", *Washington Post*, April 28, 2002.

that Grayson is dreaming of a Corinthian model which never properly existed.[8] In his view, sport should, save in extreme circumstances, be allowed to regulate itself – certainly where "on field" action is at stake. Increased use of the law (which may simply be a reaction of moral panic to events on the playing field) merely has the undesired effect of converting what has traditionally been seen as a social relationship into a legal relationship – to the detriment of all involved. It might be argued in reply, that the most sacred of all social relationships – the marriage relationship – is beset by a huge number of differing legal rules, and that this is a good thing. Gardiner accepts this in principle but says that the central question merely alters from whether law should *ever* be involved in sport to when and where it should be so involved – and he believes that it should be involved as little as possible.

What the arguments of both Grayson and Gardiner have in common is that they both focus almost exclusively on the concerns of sport and whether sport will be improved by exclusive self-regulation, or whether it would be preferable for sport's sake to have some form of external control. This is also, arguably the flaw in such arguments, in that the public policy considerations that will determine whether or not the law is to be used in any situation will encompass far more than merely the viewpoint of sport. Clearly, given that sport is generally regarded as a significant social commodity, the interests of sport will be relevant. But so also will the interests of society in preventing unwanted public displays of violence by social role models, or the interests of a seriously injured plaintiff whose livelihood has been removed, or the interests of competitors, consumers or the overall well being of the sports market when faced with anti-competitive practices by a dominant business.

Of greater relevance is the fact that when on field violence or general indiscipline is at issue, the internal sports remedies may well be capable of dealing more effectively with the culprit than the law ever could. To take the example of a professional footballer who has committed a serious foul tackle, that player will almost certainly suffer more if he is faced with a long suspension than if he is fined by a court of law. This is not to say that law has *no* role to play in governing on field activity. There may be cases where an injured party needs the sort of financial compensation that only a court can award, or indeed a situation where public policy demands that the criminal law step in. Equally, as in many areas, it should only intervene where it can be certain that it will be effective in so doing.

Having said this, as we shall see the law – both criminal and civil – is in fact reasonably under-utilized when on field activity is at issue. Where the law is used more regularly is in situations where the rule making procedures of

---

[8] Generally see Gardiner *et al*, *Sports Law* (2nd ed., Cavendish Publishing, 2001) [hereafter Gardiner], *inter alia*, p.652 and Gardiner, "Not Playing the Game: Is it a Crime?" (1993) *Solicitors Journal* 628 at p.629.

governing bodies and clubs are being challenged, or especially where the business of sport – in terms of sponsorship, marketing and so on – is at stake. This is because of the impact of professionalisation of sport – a topic which we will now briefly consider.

1.2   THE IMPACT OF PROFESSIONALISATION ON SPORT AND THE LAW

It is clear that the incidences of legal involvement with sport are on the increase.[9] It tends also to be accepted that the reasons for this are generally related to the "big business" nature of sport. With increased professionalism, and so much money at stake, a top soccer player playing in the English premiership for example can earn tens of thousands of pounds per week. If such a player has his career cut short through what he regards as a reckless and dangerous tackle of an opponent, the amount of money which he will have lost is astronomical. Unsurprisingly he will want redress and in 21st century western society, litigation is the accepted means for gaining such redress. Moreover, with increased professionalisation, sport has become an industry, in which there are intellectual property rights to be protected and exploited, in which anti-competitive practices may thrive, and in which vast sums of money are invested in equipment. Finally, with increased professionalism has come increased power for sports governing bodies to affect the lives and livelihoods of athletes, and with such increased power has come a desire for higher standards of justice in the application of such powers. Thus according to Beloff,

> "If one wishes to make a cogent case against increased involvement of lawyers in sport, one must make a corresponding case against the increase in the power of sports administrators to affect the lives and livelihoods of sports men and women and conversely the increased power of sportsmen and women to dictate terms to sports administrators."[10]

It is arguable that both observers and more particularly, those involved in professional sport have failed to appreciate some of the consequences of professionalisation[11] – of the fact that what is under discussion is a business

---

[9]   Grayson, *Sport and the Law* (3rd ed., Butterworths, London, 2000) [hereafter Grayson] pp. 16ff and 65fff. Also by the same author, 'The Historical Development of Sport and Law", p.3 in Greenfield and Osborn eds, *Law and Sport in Contemporary Society*, (Frank Cass and Co. Ltd, 2000). See also Beloff *et al*, *Sports Law* (Hart Publishing, 1998) [hereafter Beloff], p.6.
[10] Beloff, *op. cit.*, p.6.
[11] See for example, Hemphill, "Amateurism a Thing of the Past", *Salt Lake Tribune*, January 20, 2002 and Engelbrecht and Schimke, "The Social Status of the Sporting Profession", 4(2) *Sport and the Law Journal* (1996) 16.

(albeit a rather unusual and special one). Thus for example, when the Irish soccer manager Mick McCarthy summarily sent his captain Roy Keane home from the World Cup in July 2002 following an outburst from the latter there was much media and public comment on what was perceived as one of the most infamous sporting moments of recent times, but little if any of it suggested that there were employment law issues at play. There was little questioning of whether McCarthy should have had to follow an official FAI disciplinary process and whether this process was a staged one, such that Keane was entitled to a certain number of warnings before a punishment of this severity was imposed. The popular view was that McCarthy was entitled to do what he did because he was the manager of the team. Admittedly there are differences in degree between the nature of the employment relationship arising between a player and his national association and the contractual ties that bind a player and his club. Yet the general notion that an employer may ever summarily dismiss an employee without having recourse to a stated disciplinary procedure sits very uneasily with Irish employment law. One of the themes of this book is that as long as the consequences of professionalisation are *not* fully appreciated the law will find sport to be a fertile ground for *its* business.

1.3   "SPORT AND THE LAW" OR "SPORTS LAW"?

A further question that arises, is whether this discipline should properly be called "sports law" – which implies that it is a specific body of law, like criminal law or contract law – or sport and the law – which suggests merely the application of existing legal principles in the context of sporting dispute.[12] In the terms used by Michael Beloff[13] the question is whether it is an activity led area of law like, for example commercial law, or an area of law upon which the law occasionally touches (like for example gardening). Academic opinion seems to be split on the question,[14] although Beloff[15] argues convincingly that sports law can be seen to exist as a separate "activity led" area of law for a variety of reasons. These range from the fact that, in comparison to many other big businesses, sport is subject to a high degree of self-regulation, to the fact that certain doctrines are starting to emerge on the playing field which are not found elsewhere, to the fact that the courts pay increasing deference to the

---

[12] See for example, Gardiner, "Birth of a Legal Arena: Sport and the Law or Sports Law?", 5(2) *Sport and the Law Journal* (1997) 10.

[13] Beloff, *op. cit.*, p.2.

[14] Gardiner, "Birth of a Legal Arena: Sport and the Law or Sports Law?", 5(2) *Sport and the Law Journal* (1997) 10. See also Weatherill, "Resisting the Pressures of 'Americanisation': The Influence of European Community Law on the 'European Sport Model", p.157 in Greenfield and Osborn, *Law and Sport in Contemporary Society* (Frank Cass, 2000) at p.176 and p.267 in the same book, Foster, "How Can Sport be Regulated?"

[15] Beloff, *op. cit.*, pp.1–5.

decisions of sporting tribunals provided that they stick within certain acceptable guidelines. Nowhere is this more prominent than where the EU institutions deal with sport. Thus as we shall see in Chapter 9, the EU in the application of competition law has created a "sporting exception" to the application of EC competition law, such that a purely sporting rule – even one with economic repercussions – will be deemed not to violate the terms of EC law. The point is also made that "sports law" may be regarded as a specific form of law in that it is international in operation, and by virtue of the nature of sport is not subject to the same geographical limitations as other forms of law.[16]

It is submitted that whereas Beloff's view is perhaps the more appealing, in reality the question is not of huge importance. On one level of abstraction, after all, the totality of law can simply be divided into public and private law, and so called branches of law may be viewed simply as applications of each; thus criminal law is in reality applied public law, and tort applied private law and on a narrower level of abstraction, planning law might simply be regarded as applied administrative law and human rights simply applied public international law. Equally case law from a variety of courts indicates that whereas what we are seeing is simply the application of accepted legal principles to the context of disputes involving sportsmen and women, nonetheless on occasions the courts or the legislature may tweak such accepted principles *because* what is at issue is sport.

Having said this, it should be accepted that simply because a particular plaintiff or defendant in a case happens to be a sportsman, this does not suddenly make the issue a sports law one. Thus we are not concerned in this book with, for example, a situation where a professional sportsperson breaks the law in his private life, or sues for libel or where a company owned by him declares bankruptcy. Our sole concern is with those situations where the law regulates the operation of sport as an activity or as a business.

1.4 WHAT IS A SPORT?[17]

The next introductory question that needs to be addressed is "what is a sport?" – a question which is ultimately a sociological rather than a legal one. Nonetheless for our purposes, the answer to this sociological question is of

---

[16] Beloff, *op. cit.*, p.7ff. Thus during the summer Olympic Games in Atlanta in 1996, the Court of Arbitration which operated during these games was told to apply "general principles of law and rules of law", and indeed apart from some degree of reference to Swiss law, CAS tends to look to principles of equality, sportsmanship and fair play, as well as general principles such as privity of contract, natural justice, proportionality and good faith.

[17] Gardiner, *op. cit.*, p.13ff and by the same author, "Sport: A need for A Legal Definition", 4(2) *Sport and the Law Journal* (1996) 31.

great legal importance in that there are a number of significant benefits in having an activity defined as a sport. First, the activity may receive charitable status or benefit from tax relief or state funding. Secondly, in the context of contact sport, as the House of Lords noted in *R v. Brown* – a celebrated case in which several men were convicted of engaging in sado-masochistic acts[18] – such activity may be deemed to be an exception to the traditional common law rules against consensual assault. So for our purposes, the question is not "what is sport?" but rather 'how does the law determine when it will recognise something as a sport?'

From an Irish perspective sport is defined in two different contexts in section 2 of the Irish Sports Council Act of 1999.[19] Thus recreational sport is defined as "all forms of physical activity which, through casual or organised participation, aim at expressing or improving physical fitness and mental well-being and at forming social relationships" – a definition that echoes the approach of the Council of Europe *European Sports Charter*.[20] Similarly competitive sport is defined as "all forms of physical activity which, through organised participation, aim at expressing or improving physical fitness and at obtaining results in competition at all levels." Equally, these definitions are perhaps rather vague, and for example the definition of recreational sport would seem to cover the types of sexual activities at issue in the *Brown* case.

Using **physical activity** as a touchstone for defining sport is problematic in that there is after all a strong view that certain physical activities simply do not constitute sport – that there is, for example a qualitative difference between the Dublin City Marathon and one individual out for his nightly jog – and indeed that certain non-physical activities (snooker for example) are undoubtedly sports. Similarly, use of the requirement of a **competitive element**, is not satisfactory. Bridge, chess and the like may involve great levels of inter-personal competitive activity and yet it is unlikely that they can be seen as "sports." Finally, it might be argued that the relevant issue is the **level of organisation** involved, but this would mean that for instance individual fitness training or a random game of football between children could not be regarded as a sport, and would commit us to the untenable view that professional sport is more properly "sport" than is its amateur counterpart because of the more sophisticated level of organisation and refereeing involved. The moral of the story appears to be that it is ultimately futile to create a general principle leading to an objective definition of sport.

Yet for the reasons outlined above, some level of objectivity – at least as far as the law is concerned – is necessary. In trying to come to grips with these problems, the UK Law Commission[21] outlined what it saw as an appropriate

---

[18] *R v. Brown* [1993] 2 All E.R. 75. This issue is discussed in detail in Chap.4.
[19] Number 6 of 1999.
[20] See www.coe.int/sport.
[21] Consultation Paper 139 on *Consent in the Criminal Law*, p.177.

recognition scheme for sports, drawing substantially on the list of criteria used by the British Sports Council (UK Sport) in determining whether an activity constitutes a sport namely:

- Physical Skills including an assessment of whether the relevant activity involves or requires physical skills and whether such skills are inherent or can be developed in the individual;

- Physical Effort – including an assessment of the importance of such effort and its relationship within the activity to mechanical or other aids;.

- Accessibility – is the sport available to all sections of the community or is it 'exclusive' on grounds of gender, cost etc;

- Rules and organization – is the activity subject to some organisational structure and are national or international competitions organised in respect of it;

- Strategies and tactics: is the employment of strategies and tactics an important element of successful;

- Essential Purpose: Is physical recreation the essential purpose of the activity, or is it a means to another more basic purpose;

- Physical Challenge – does the activity present a physical and/or mental challenge to the participant whether against himself/herself, others or the environment;

- Risk: does the activity involve some level of risk, is this level acceptable and are there any safeguards in place to minimize this risk for participants;

- Uniqueness: is this a unique activity or is it a variation on an existing activity;

- Other considerations: Are there any other political, moral or other ethical considerations which might prohibit the Sports Council from recognising the activity.[22]

A couple of points should be made in respect of these criteria.[23] First, were it not for the final of these criteria, it is quite arguable that the type of activities

---

[22] Thus in refusing to recognise darts as a sport, the UK Sports Council told the British Darts Organisation that its task was not just to decide what was and was not a sport, but also "sports and governing bodies with which they wish to be associated." This led the British Darts Organisation to conclude that: "They're really saying that they don't want to be identified with fat blokes with fags in their mouth, but that is such an outdated image of the sport." See Duncan, "Darts Swept from the Board", *The Guardian*, February 14, 1996.

[23] Other criteria may also be relevant. Most notably, perhaps, as Gardiner points out in "Sport: A need for A Legal Definition", 4(2) *Sport and the Law Journal* (1996) 31 at 33) the subjective perceptions of the athletes as to what they are doing may be relevant.

outlawed in *R v. Brown*, could be deemed to constitute a lawful sport. Secondly, it is by no means clear why the final of these criteria does not demand the declassification of boxing as a sport. Thirdly, these criteria are sufficiently vague that they could be used to declassify certain sports in the future.[24] Finally, from a legal standpoint, it is the eighth and tenth of these criteria – the degree of risk inherent in the activity and the claims of public policy, which are the most relevant.

1.5 WHO OWNS SPORT?

The final introductory question about the relationship between sport and law concerns the "ownership" of sport.[25] Throughout the book we will consider instances of governing bodies and clubs often at odds with each other over the "rights" to a sporting event. A clear example of a tension in this regard in the recent past concerns the decision of the Football Association of Ireland in 2002 to sell the exclusive live "rights" to all competitive home Irish soccer matches to Sky television, thereby (in the view of many Irish soccer fans) violating the rights of the general public to watch such matches on a free to air basis. The logic was clear – Irish people own Irish sport and should have a stake in its exploitation. A further, perhaps rather far fetched instance of this principle can be found in the comments of Mr. Alan Hunter, a representative of the Irish Football Supporters' Association, in an interview for the RTÉ *Prime Time* programme,[26] to the effect that the potential return of former soccer captain Roy Keane to the Irish team for the 2004–2005 World Cup qualifying campaign was of such seismic importance that it should be put to the people in a referendum. Again the logic (such as it was) was clear – Irish people own Irish soccer and have a right to be part of major decision making processes in respect of the same. Yet it is by no means clear that this view – that sport transcends ownership by any one group – is correct. Indeed, as we shall see in chapter seven, there is a strong argument in Ireland for saying that there is simply no such thing as ownership rights in sporting events.[27]

The point is that on one level there is a great deal of money to be made out of sport, and hence there will be people who will seek to make money from

---

[24] Gardiner, "Sport: A need for A Legal Definition", 4(2) *Sport and the Law Journal* (1996) 31.

[25] See Bitel, "Redefining the Ownership of Sport", 6(3) *Sport and the Law Journal* (1998) 88 and Abramson, "Whose Rights are They Anyway?", 4(3) *Sport and the Law Journal* (1996) 100. Generally see Chap.7 of this book.

[26] RTÉ, April 13, 2004.

[27] Generally, see Wise, "A 'Property Right' in a Sports Event: Views of Different Jurisdictions", 5(3) *Sport and the Law Journal* (1996) 63 and Abramson, "Whose Rights are they Anyway?", 5(3) *Sport and the Law Journal* (1996) 13.

the exploitation of what are loosely termed the rights in a sporting event or a sports club. On another level, however, it may be that sport as a national or a regional possession simply transcends ownership, and hence that any money made out of a sporting event or out of sport must be held in trust for that sport by those charged with its governance. How one answers the question "who owns sport?" therefore will determine one's overall attitude to sport and indeed to the proper role of law in its regulation.

These then are some basic introductory questions in respect of the relationship between sport and law. For the rest of this chapter we will consider the structure of authority by which sport in Ireland is governed.

1.6   THE STRUCTURES OF SPORTS GOVERNANCE IN IRELAND AND BEYOND

From the outset it is convenient to distinguish between governmental or quasi-governmental regulation of sport, and non-governmental control.

1.6.1 Governmental and quasi governmental control of sport in Ireland and the role of the Irish Sports Council

Ministerial responsibility for sport falls in Ireland to the Department of Tourism, Sport and Recreation. The Department and Minister are assisted in this regard by the work of the Irish Sports Council created pursuant to the Irish Sports Council Act of 1999. This body, which is perhaps best associated in the public consciousness with the twin objectives of providing funding for sports bodies and spearheading the fight against doping in sport, was established with the aims of furthering the development of sport (both recreational and competitive) and assisting athletes in the pursuit of excellence within competitive sport.

The contemporary approach of the Irish Sports Council is outlined in its 2003 document *Sport for Life*, which sets out its objectives and strategies for the three-year period 2003–2005 and replaces the previous strategy document *A New Era for Sport* which had been in existence since 2000.[28] Both these documents seek to implement the pillars of the overall Sports Council strategy, namely increased participation in sport, development of sporting performance and the promotion of sporting excellence. Under the terms of this document, the Council sees its mission as "To plan, lead and coordinate the sustainable development of competitive and recreational sport in Ireland."[29] In this respect it speaks of the role of sport in breaking down barriers[30] (and there is a major

---

[28] Both these documents are available at www.irishsportscouncil.ie.
[29] *Sport For Life*, p.1.
[30] *Ibid.*, p.14.

focus on increasing ease of access to sport for young people[31]) and in promoting health[32] (including the health of children increasingly open to the risk of obesity[33]). Moreover it recognises that there is an immense interest in sport in Ireland, and hence that the ideal would be to channel this interest into increased participation in sport.[34] On this basis it sees the objectives of the Sports Council over the relevant three-year period as being:

• To create an evidence based understanding of sports participation through research;

• To build capability in individuals from a young age through physical education and coaching;

• To build capacity in organisations to develop a sustainable framework for sports participation and performance;

• To maintain the foundations laid in the first three years, consolidating for example the existing Local Sports Partnerships and the High Performance Strategy.[35]

For our purposes, the most significant work of the Sports Council is in its creation and operation of a "state of the art" anti-doping programme. This is considered in detail in Chapter Three.

1.6.2 The European Union and sport

Much has been written about the evolving role of the EU in respect of sport, and in particular about the possible evolution of a specific "sports policy" within the EU framework.[36] Whereas this book will consider various contexts

---

[31] *Ibid.,* p.10.
[32] *Ibid.*, p.3.
[33] *Ibid.*, p.2.
[34] *Ibid.*, p.13.
[35] *Ibid.*, p.3 and p.18ff.
[36] See for example Parrish, *Sports Law and Policy in the European Union* (Manchester University Press, 2003), Gardiner *et al*, *op. cit.*, p. 172ff, Beloff *et al*, *op. cit.*, pp.36, 69ff and 108ff, Lewis & Taylor, *op. cit.*, p.307, Miller, "The EC Commission Final Report on the Impact of European Community Activities on Sport", 2(2) *Sport and the Law Journal* (1994) 8, Parrish, "Reconciling Conflicting Approaches to Sport in the European Union", p.21 in Caiger & Gardiner eds., *Professional Sport in the European Union: Regulation and Re-regulation*, (TMC Asser Press, 2000), Parrish, "Steering a Middle Course in European Union Sports Policy", 2 (2) *Sports Law Bulletin* (1998) 12, Parrish, "A Path to A Sports Policy in the European Union", 1(1) *Sports Law Bulletin* (1998) 10, Weatherill, "The Helsinki Report on Sport" (2000) *European Law Review* 282, Parrish, "Sport and the Intergovernmental Conference", 5(1) *Sport and the Law Journal* (1997) 31, Parrish, "The Amsterdam Treaty: Declaring an Interest in Sport",

in which EC law impacts on sport – notably in the areas of competition law and in the protection of free movement of workers within the community and union – it is not intended now to provide any more than a cursory overview of the general policy of the EU in respect of sport. For a fuller and indeed an excellent analysis in this regard we recommend Dr Richard Parrish's text *Sports Law and Policy in the European Union.*[37]

The decision of the European Court of Justice in *Union Royal Belge des Sociètès de Football Association ASBL v. Bosman*,[38] is undoubtedly the most high profile occasion on which sport has come into conflict with EU law.[39] This was not only because of the impact of the decision on the transfer system within European football, but also because it represented an announcement to a very broad section of the population of the EU (i.e. those who participate in or who follow sport) that whenever sport operates as a business, it is subject to the constraints of (the still predominantly economic focussed) EU law – both hard law and soft law.

Equally, however, and despite the fact that there has never been any provision enacted into an EU treaty exempting sport from the operation of EC law, the institutions of the EU have always operated with great respect for sport, viewing it as a social commodity that has importance throughout the Community.[40] Particularly, they have accepted that a Community based sports

---

5(2) *Sport and the Law Journal* (1997) 23, Parrish, "The Path to a Sports policy in the European Union", 2(1) *Sports Law Bulletin* (1998) 10, "Football's View of the Future of European Sports Policy", 6(1) *Sports Law Bulletin* (2003) 7, Weatherill, "Resisting the Pressures of 'Americanization': The Influence of European Community Law on the 'European Sport Model", p.157 in Greenfield and Osborn, *Law and Sport in Contemporary Society* (Frank Cass, 2000), Vieweg, "The Restrictions of European Law", p.85 in Caiger & Gardiner eds. *Professional Sport in the European Union: Regulation and Re-regulation* (TMC Asser Press, 2000) and Blanpain, *The Legal Status of Sportsmen and Sportswomen under International, European and Belgian National and Regional Law* (Kluwer Law International, 2003).

[37] (Manchester University Press, 2003). Parrish sees EU sports policy as operating in three phases; the pre-*Bosman* phase, the phase from *Bosman* to the 1996 Intergovernmental Conference and the Declaration on Sport attached to the Amsterdam Treaty and the phase following this declaration. Foster, on the other hand inserts another phase (between the second and third of those suggested by Parrish) where there was an increase in the level of Commission involvement with sport. See Foster, "Can Sport be Regulated by Europe?", pp.44–45 in Caiger & Gardiner eds. *Professional Sport in the European Union: Regulation and Re-regulation* (TMC Asser Press, 2000).

[38] Case 415/93 [1995] E.C.R. I–4921, [1996] 1 C.M.L.R. 645.

[39] It was far from the first occasion of such involvement, however. See Case 36/74, *Walrave and Koch v. Union Cycliste Internationale* [1974] E.C.R. 1405, Case–13/76, *Dona v. Mantero* [1976] 2 C.M.L.R. 578. See also "The European Community and Sport", COM2/92.

[40] See "The Developments and Prospects for Community Action in the Field of Sport", EC Commission, (1998), available at www.europa.eu.int. See also Gardiner *et al*, *op. cit.*, p.177.

policy would be inappropriate in light of the fact that the primary regulatory authority for sport should rightly remain the prerogative of sports governing bodies.[41] Moreover, whereas it is accepted that there will be aspects of general EC law that will apply to sporting bodies – for example competition law – and that such bodies must act in accordance with such laws,[42] nonetheless, even in these circumstances the institutions show enormous deference both to the special characteristics of sport and also the needs of sport. Thus it may be argued that the (somewhat undefined) EC policy as regards sport, involves affording sports bodies a considerable benefit of the doubt as regards the application of hard EC law. This is not to say that the EC law will have no significant role in governing sport – it will and does – but it is fair to say that the extent of the application of the same is far more limited than might be expected given that what is at stake is a multi-billion Euro industry.

1.6.2.1 The development of an EU sports policy

At the time of the creation of the Amsterdam Treaty in 1996, there was some pressure on the drafters of the Treaty to include a specific article on sport, however in the event, a declaration on sport was attached to the treaty and reads as follows:

> The conference emphasises the social significance of sport, in particular its role in forging identities and bringing people together. The conference therefore calls on the bodies of the EU to listen to sports associations when important questions affecting sport are at issue. In this connection, special consideration should be given to the particular characteristics of amateur sport'.

The precise impact of this clause is uncertain, although it arguably does little more than reinforce the notion that law should apply only leniently in this area, as outlined above.[43] Following the Amsterdam declaration, the European Commission published the *European Model of Sport Consultation Document*,[44] an attempt to determine, through consultation with relevant parties, the essential characteristics of sport in Europe. The document invited the submission of

---

[41] See *The Helsinki Report on Sport* (COM (1999)) 644 (10 December 1999), para.4.

[42] *Ibid.*

[43] Certainly it is a far cry from the rumoured possibility at the time that, in the wake of *Bosman* the Amsterdam treaty would contain a clause exempting sport from the application of EC law. See Weatherill, "Resisting the Pressures of 'Americanization': The Influence of European Community Law on the 'European Sport Model'", p.157 in Greenfield and Osborn, *Law and Sport in Contemporary Society* (Frank Cass, 2000), p.163.

[44] See Gardiner *et al, op. cit.*, p.177ff and Lewis & Taylor, *op. cit.*, p.314.

views on three major areas, namely the organisation of sport in Europe, the relationship between sport and television broadcasting, and sport and social policy.[45] The conclusions that emerged from the process were contained in the Helsinki Report on Sport.[46]

The *Helsinki Report* was aimed at safeguarding current sports structures and on maintaining the current social importance of sport within Europe – the two issues that had been identified to the Commission as worthy of concern by the Vienna meeting of the European Council in 1998.[47] The Helsinki Declaration took as its ethical basis a concern that certain developments in sport – violence in stadia, doping, commercialisation and the like – were weakening the important social and educational functions of sport.[48] Thus the Report called for a re-enhancement of the educational and social role of sport. This would be achieved through use of existing Community programmes to deal with "exclusion, inequalities, racism and xenophobia" and also to combat the violence that occasionally occurs at sporting events.[49] In particular it would be the objective of the Commission that Member States and community institutions would work together to deal with the issue of doping in sport.[50]

Such ethical concerns do not, however, operate in a vacuum. The Report went on to require that the moves to maintain the social importance of sport would instead operate in the context of a recognition that community policies *would* apply to sport, but equally that such application would ideally involve "… greater consultation between the various protagonists (sporting movement, Member States and European Community) at each level," a process which would "… lead to the clarification, at each level, of the legal framework for sports operators."[51] Thus the Report concluded by tentatively suggesting certain areas that would not come under EC competition rules, certain areas that would in principle be prohibited thereby, and certain practices likely to be covered by but also exempted from the application of the competition rules.[52] We shall

---

[45] See Lewis & Taylor *op. cit.*, p.314 for the view that the document is open to the criticism that it focused too much on commercially elite sports such as Formula One motor sport and football. Generally see Blanpain, *The Legal Status of Sportsmen and Sportswomen under International, European and Belgian National and Regional Law* (Kluwer Law International, 2003), p.2ff.

[46] *Report from the Commission to the European Council with a View to Safeguarding Current Sports Structures and Maintaining the Social Function of Sport Within the Community Framework*, ['The *Helsinki Report'*] COM (1999) 644 Final, December 10, 1999. Generally see Weatherill, "The Helsinki Report on Sport", [2000] 25 *European Law Review* 282 [hereafter Weatherill] and Parrish, "The Helsinki Report on Sport: A Partnership Approach to Sport", 3(3) *Sports Law Bulletin* (2000) 16.

[47] Weatherill, *op. cit.*, at 285 and Lewis & Taylor, *op. cit.*, p.314.

[48] The *Helsinki Report*, pp.1–4.

[49] *Ibid.*, para.3.1.

[50] *Ibid.*, para.3.2.

[51] *Ibid.*, para.4.2.

[52] *Ibid.*, para.4.2.1ff

consider the nature of such rules in chapter nine. Finally and in conclusion, the report stressed the need for a new movement for sport in Europe, with all groups – sporting and political – working in the same direction in order to encourage the promotion of sport in Europe.

It is not clear precisely what the point of the declaration was, largely because the sentiments expressed therein constitute, it is submitted, little more than platitudes and indeed rather obvious ones at that. Ultimately the report could be summarized in two sentences. First, sport is generally a "good thing" in Europe and the EU would like it to keep it this way, *inter alia*, by dealing with bad things in sport. Secondly, sport will, on occasion be affected by EC law, but only in a watered down fashion. So much was obvious at the time of the declaration (in that it represented the existing approach of the institutions), and it says a lot both for lawyers and politicians that it could take ten pages for them to make these points.

Of more practical relevance is the adoption in December 2002 of a "Declaration on the Specific Characteristics of Sport," annexed to the Nice Treaty of that year.[53] The Declaration clearly envisages that sport has "social, educational and cultural functions," which combine to make sport "special"[54] – a significant concession in light of the impact that the designation of sport (the industry as well as the hobby) as "special" might have on the future application of hard EC law to this area. Moreover, this concession was further bolstered by the statement in the Declaration that fundamental and primary responsibility for the organisation and regulation of sport rests with the governing bodies.[55] The Declaration stresses the role of sport as an instrument for promoting social cohesion and equality, and seeks to promote the value of amateur participation, of disabled sport and of voluntary services in and to sport.[56] Beyond this, it encourages governing bodies and even public authorities to take necessary measures to preserve the training capacities of clubs in order to prepare young people to take part in high-level sport.[57] Equally, it also speaks of the concerns that young people would be protected, both from threats to their physical and emotional well-being,[58] and also from the risk of commercial exploitation.[59] Finally, the Declaration refers to three aspects of the business of sport that have attracted the interest of the commission both before and since the Nice Treaty, namely the ownership by one party of a stake

---

[53] Parrish, "The Road to Nice", 4(2) *Sports Law Bulletin* (2001) 15. Generally see Gardiner *et al*, *op. cit.*, p.184, Lewis & Taylor, *op. cit.*, p.315 and Blanpain, *The Legal Status of Sportsmen and Sportswomen under International, European and Belgian National and Regional Law* (Kluwer Law International, 2003), p.41.

[54] Para.1 of the Declaration.

[55] Para.7.

[56] Paras 2–6.

[57] Para.11.

[58] Para.12.

[59] Para.13.

in more than one club[60] (a possibility that poses a threat to the perception of fair competition), the sale of broadcasting rights[61] and the transfer systems in sport, and particularly in football.[62]

As Parrish notes, the declaration has the potential to be of intense importance to sport, in that it allows governing bodies (provided that they are acting reasonably) to determine the extent to which the EU will get involved in sport. In short, it allows sport to play the dominant role in the construction of a sports policy for Europe. Thus at the time of going to print, news is emerging that the place of sport within the European Union is to be recognised within the terms of the Article III–182 of the European Constitution.[63]

On a day-to-day level, EC law has in practice influenced many areas of sport, and in particular of the business of sport, and similarly, many different facets of the EU are involved with sport. Indeed of the 24 Directorate Generals in the EU it is estimated that twenty will deal on a regular basis with sports related issues. Most importantly the Sports Unit within the Directorate-General of Education and Culture is responsible for encouraging cooperation within the Commission and with other institutions including national and international federations on sport-related issues. Moreover since 1991 an annual European Sports Forum is organised by the European Commission and the Member State holding the presidency, and aims to bring together every year all those involved in European sport: those responsible in the European institutions (Commission, Parliament, Council), in the sporting movement (national and international federations), the media, the sports industries, the public authorities of the Member States, universities and all the partners of the world of sport. In addition various ad hoc meetings will occur, as, for example, that between Commissioner Reding and the Sports Federation in April 2000. Further impact on sport is made by the Parliament's Committee on Culture, Youth, Education and the Media, and since 1992 a cross-party group of MEPs has met regularly to examine the implications of developments in the Union on sport.

Finally, it is notable that the Parliament declared 2004 to be the European Year of Education Through Sport – a project intended to tie in with the Athens Olympic Games.

1.6.3 The Council of Europe and Sport

In subsequent chapters we will also consider the impact of the Council of Europe on specific areas of sports law – notably in the areas of spectator safety and opposition to doping. For present purposes, it is intended to give a brief

---

[60] Para.14.
[61] Para.15.
[62] Para.16. For an analysis of how the EU institutions have sought to realise these ambitions, see Lewis & Taylor , *op. cit.*, p.317ff.
[63] Parrish, "The Road to Nice", 4(2) *Sports Law Bulletin* (2001) 15.

overview of the role of this organisation in the area of sport.[64] Equally it should be stressed from the outset that nothing of any immediate practical impact is likely to emerge from the Council of Europe "laws" in this respect. Instead a good deal of well meaning aspirational statements, that seek to generate consensus, have emanated from the Council of Europe, and this emphasis on consensus has effectively precluded the attainment of anything worthwhile in practice.

Since 1999, sport has been the focus of the restructured Directorate on Sport and Youth. Consistent with its general 'human rights based' approach to diverse issues in society, the Council of Europe sees its role in sport as (a) furthering democracy through the promotion of sport for all as a means of improving the quality of life, (b) facilitating social integration and contributing to social cohesion, particularly among young people and (c) fostering tolerance through sport and dealing with manifestations of xenophobia and racism therein. In so doing, the Council of Europe regards sport as important for the example it sets, for the part it plays in society and for the contribution it makes to the health of the population. To this end, the Council has adopted a number of initiatives aimed at furthering the development of sports itself, and especially of these qualities within it. In 1975 the Sport for All Charter was adopted with the aim of helping to democratise sport and was replaced in 1993 by the European Sports Charter (an update of the 1975 Charter), backed up by the Code of Sports Ethics. Moreover these documents have been overseen since 1992 by the work of the Committee for the Development of Sport (CDDS).[65]

In addition, the Council has produced two major conventions. First there is the Anti-Doping Convention (1989) (which will be considered in Chapter III) and, to back this up "Europack," or the "Clean Sports Guide," an education and information pack (produced in co-operation with the European Union), available for schools and sports organisations. Secondly, and in response, *inter alia*, to the Heysel stadium tragedy in 1985, the Council drew up the European Convention on Spectator Violence and Misbehaviour at Sports Events. We consider this document in chapter six.

Finally, the Council of Europe has also undertaken work in the areas of sustainable development and sport, (calling on all sectors of the sports world to take measures to establish a harmonious relationship between sport and the environment), and encouraging tolerance and fair play in sport. In respect of all of these charters the CDDS has developed a monitoring programme to assess whether the requirements of these conventions and charters are being fulfilled in member states; for example whether the "check list" of some 70 requirements to be fulfilled in the staging of major sports events are being fulfilled. Moreover, apart from the creation of conventions the Directorate

---

[64] Generally see Gardiner, *op. cit.*, pp.173–4.
[65] Generally see www.coe.int/sport.

organises a variety of conferences and meetings and the Parliamentary Assembly and Committee of Sports Ministers have produced resolutions on themes ranging from xenophobia in sport to measures to combat use of drugs.

Looking to the future, and with the increase in its membership following the break-up of the former Soviet Union, the CDDS has set up a mutual assistance programme known as SPRINT (Sports Reform Innovation and Training) to help new members reform their sports structures. The programme covers a variety of issues ranging from legislation on sport to sports funding to the development of sport on democratic lines, to emphasising the role of sport in education, with special programmes being set up in certain Balkan countries following the cessation of hostilities.[66]

1.7 THE INTERNAL GOVERNMENTAL STRUCTURE OF SPORT

There are three main strands of governing structure within sport. The first is the worldwide Olympic movement, the second is the more general structure of sports governing bodies on a national, international and regional basis and the third (operating in tandem with the increasingly important role of domestic dispute resolution panels) is the International Court of Arbitration for Sport.

1.7.1 The Olympic Movement

In global terms the International Olympic Committee (IOC) is as powerful as any sporting organization in the world, despite the fact that its jurisdiction only directly covers the Summer and Winter Olympic Games, each held every two years. Thus for example a swimmer who would normally operate under the control of FINA (the world swimming body) will be bound by IOC rules when he or she competes at the Olympic Games. The impact of the Olympic Movement is partially due to the moral and social significance of the Olympic Games, and partially due to the revenue that smaller sports (which are not financially independent) can hope to achieve from their share in the advertising and television revenue earned by the Games. Thus in 2003 when IOC President Jacques Rogge warned International Sports Federations that failure to sign up to the new World Anti-Doping Code could lead to them facing expulsion from the Olympic Games, he was making as potent a threat as was the Irish Sports Council in 2004 when it made Sports Council funding conditional on sports bodies signing up to the new Irish anti-doping rules.

---

[66] In Bosnia and Herzegovina, the organizers of a programme on sport for the rehabilitation of those disabled through war have trained sports leaders and held summer camps attended by children from all parts of the country. In Kosovo, and Albania, sports programmes for refugee children have been promoted.

Each Member State that belongs to the IOC has, in turn, its own National Olympic Committee. The Olympic Council of Ireland came into existence in 1923. Ireland was given formal recognition as an independent nation in the Olympic Movement at the IOC session in Paris in 1924 and it was at the Paris Games that Ireland made its first appearance in an Olympic Games as an independent nation.

1.7.2 The governance of individual sports

Secondly, there is the "non-Olympic" governance of sport by sport. Thus each sport is governed internationally by an International Federation (e.g. FIFA, the international governing body for soccer) regionally by a regional body (e.g. UEFA, the European soccer governing body) and domestically by a National Governing Body (e.g. the FAI, the Irish soccer governing body). In general the domestic body will be affiliated to and bound by the rules of the European and thence of the international governing body. In Ireland the majority of these bodies are non-statutory in nature (although most would be in receipt of Sports Council funding), and their precise legal form differs from body to body, with some existing as limited liability companies and some existing as charities. Clearly it is important to be aware of the status of any such body before issuing a challenge to its rules.

1.7.3 The role of arbitration in sport

Recourse to arbitration rather than the law courts is something to which sports bodies both international and domestic are well used.[67] Such a way of

---

[67] See for example, Gardiner, *op. cit.*, p.251ff, Lewis & Taylor, *Sports Law and Practice*, (Butterworths LexisNexis, London, 2003) [hereafter Lewis & Taylor], p. 259ff, Kaufman, "Issues in International Sports Arbitration" (1995) *Boston University International Law Journal* 527, Mack, *"Reynolds v. IAAF*: The Need for an Independent Tribunal in International Athletic Disputes", 10 *Connecticut Journal of International Law* (Spring 1995) 653, Haslip, "A Consideration of the Need for A National Dispute Resolution System for National Sport Organisations in Canada", 11 *Marquette Sports Law Journal* (Spring 2001) 245, Ansley, "International Athletic Dispute Resolution", 12 *Arizona Journal of International and Comparative Law* (Spring 1995) 277, Nafziger, "Arbitration of Rights and Obligations in the International Sports Arena", 35 *Valparaiso University Law Review* (Spring 2001) 357, Straubel, "Arbitrating Sports Disputes: A World View", 35 *Valparaiso University Law Review* (Spring 2001) 353, Blackshaw, "Resolving Sports Disputes by ADR", 142 No 6581 *New Law Journal* 1753, Doyle, "The ANZSLA Dispute Resolution Service", 3(3) *Sport and the Law Journal* (1995) 38 and Pigden, "Players' Courts: Sport's Answer to Alternative Dispute Resolution?", 5(3) *Sport and the Law Journal* (1997) 14.

proceeding after all is less time-consuming and less expensive than litigation. Moreover, in Grayson's view, there may be another benefit attaching to recourse to arbitration:

> "...because of the incompetence of National Governing Sports Bodies and their legal advisers, there is a movement towards exclusion of the jurisdiction of the courts against them, in favour of arbitration and away from the courts."

Whether or not this is true, however, it must be accepted that such arbitration will only be appropriate in some circumstances, generally those involving a dispute between an individual and a sports governing body.[68] Most governing bodies and international federations will now have an arbitration clause within their rules, and, from an Irish perspective, the presence of such an arbitration clause within the rules of the governing body (which, as we shall see, also constitutes the terms of the contract between the governing body and the individual) will almost certainly represent a bar to litigation. Thus far, Ireland has not followed the approach of the United Kingdom in creating a sports disputes resolution panel.[69] Equally, in the following chapters, a number of high profile sports arbitrations in Ireland are discussed. Of greater relevance, in terms of arbitration in sport is the work of the Court of Arbitration for Sport, which will be considered next.

1.7.3.1 The International Court of Arbitration for Sport[70]

The Court of Arbitration for Sport (CAS) is becoming increasingly important internationally both in the resolution of sporting disputes, and also in the development of a species of sports law.[71] CAS was originally founded in 1983 as the official court of arbitration of the IOC,[72] but faced significant early

---

[68] Wodehouse, "The Role of the Lawyer in Sport Today", 1(1) *Sport and the Law Journal* (1993) 1 at 3. See also, however, Schalley, "Eliminate Violence from Sports Through Arbitration Not the Civil Courts", 8 *Sports Lawyers Journal* (Spring 2001) 181.

[69] See for example, "The Sports Dispute Resolution Panel", 5(2) *Sports Law Administration and Practice* (1998) 1 and Beloff, "Finding out the Facts: The Role of the Sports Disciplinary Tribunal", 2 (2) *International Sports Law Review* (2002) 35.

[70] See Woodhouse, "The Role of the Lawyer in Sport Today", 1(1) *Sport and the Law Journal* (1993) 1 at 2–3, Grayson, *op. cit.*, p.385 and Beloff, *op. cit.*, p.260ff. A wealth of information in respect of CAS can be found at www.tas-cas.org.

[71] See Polvino, "Arbitration as preventative Medicine for Olympic Ailments", 8 *Emory International Law Review* (Spring 1994) 434, McLaren, "The Court of Arbitration for Sport: An Independent Arena for the World's Sports Disputes", 35 *Valparaiso University Law Review* (Spring 2001) 379, Beloff, "International Sports Arbitration", paper presented at an Irish Centre for European Law conference on Sports Law, April 26, 2002.

[72] This was the brain child of Juan Antonio Samaranch, and was originally chaired by HE

criticism because of a perception that it was connected too closely with the IOC. This came to a head in a case taken against the Swiss Equestrian Federation by an individual rider, which came before CAS.[73] After the latter body had delivered its decision in relation to this matter, its findings were subsequently appealed to the Swiss Federal Tribunal.[74] The Federal Tribunal recognized CAS as a true court of arbitration independent from the Equestrian Federation, but also criticized the extent of the connection between CAS and the IOC (in terms of funding, appointment powers and the power of the IOC to amend the statute of the CAS), and concluded that there was a need for the CAS to become more independent of the IOC.

So in 1993, following an International Conference on Law and Sport in Lausanne, the International Council of Arbitration in Sport was created to promote arbitration in sport and to take responsibility for the running and maintenance (including financial maintenance) of the CAS, with special responsibility for ensuring the maintenance of the independent status of CAS.[75] To support this change the Statutes and Procedural Regulations of CAS were fundamentally overhauled, and a new Code of Sports Related Arbitration came into effect on November 22, 1994. This "new" court arguably still has excessive connections to the IOC, but in theory functions as an independent body – a requirement stressed in the preamble to the Paris agreement. It operates on the basis of consent, such that individual athletes agree, either on the basis of an ad-hoc contract, or, more usually on the basis of a standard clause within the statutes and regulations of a domestic governing body or an international federation (or via a term affiliating the domestic federation to its international governing body), that should a dispute arise between them, then it will be resolved exclusively by reference to arbitration before the CAS. Moreover, participants in the Olympic Games are required to sign up to a similar clause. It would be contrary to public policy and arguably unconstitutional for such agreement to oust the jurisdiction of the courts absolutely from such matters; however, it is equally clear that once a matter has been set down for arbitration that the courts will be very reluctant to overturn it. Finally under Article R27 of the code, CAS has jurisdiction only to rule on issues connected to sport. In any event, CAS has never decided that it has lacked jurisdiction on this basis.

Since the overhaul of CAS in 1993, the court sits in divisions with an ordinary arbitration division (which looks at for example, contractual issues

---

Judge Kèba Mbaye, a judge of the International Court of Justice in the Hague. See CAS/TAS at XXIV. The statutes of CAS were officially ratified by the IOC in 1983 and came into force on June 30, 1984.

[73] *TAS 92/63 G v. FEI*, p.115. See Beloff, *op. cit.*, p.261.

[74] Published in the *Recueil Officiel des Arrets du Tribunal Fédéral* 119 II 271.

[75] These changes were endorsed by all the major sporting federations through their summer and winter associations, the IOC and the Association of National Olympic Committees in Paris on June 22, 1994 under a document known as the Paris Agreement.

between parties) and an appeals arbitration division (which hears appeals by athletes against decisions of sports federations in circumstances where such procedure is provided for under the statutes of the relevant organisation). The vast bulk of this latter type of hearing involves doping cases, and will be considered in Chapter III. Equally CAS has provided an important lead in many different areas of sports law.[76] Thus for example in an Irish context, in January 2002 CAS struck down a ruling of the International Hockey Federation's Disciplinary Commission which had required the Irish women's hockey team to requalify for the 2002 Hockey World Cup after an improperly conducted penalty shoot out between Ireland and Lithuania in the qualifying tournament in September 2001.[77]

CAS has 150 arbitrators appointed by the international federations, national Olympic committees and the IOC president, and representing 37 countries. It is based in Lausanne in Switzerland but since 1996 it has also had permanent branches in Denver (USA) and Sydney (Australia). Finally, there are *ad hoc* divisions, which give immediate (within 24 hours) arbitration decisions in the context of major sporting events – as for example occurred during the Atlanta (1996) and Sydney (2000) Summer Olympic Games and the Negano (1998) and Salt Lake City (2002) Winter Olympic Games.

Recourse to CAS may be had by any individual or legal entity with the capacity and power to agree to arbitration including athletes, clubs, federations, organising committees, sponsors or manufacturers of sports goods or TV organizations.

CAS is regarded as providing a large number of advantages for the resolution of disputes in the sporting context. First, such disputes will often be international in nature, and CAS provides a single unified jurisdiction to deal with such disputes, founded on a single and easily comprehensible Code of Sports Arbitration. Secondly, in the context of ordinary arbitration, it is generally up to the parties themselves to choose the relevant law, which will be applied in their case. Moreover, the procedural rules, which apply, are generally simple and flexible, and the overall procedure is not hampered by excessive formalities. Such procedural rules are drawn up in such a way as to be fully integrated into the framework established by Article 12 of the Swiss Federal Law on Private Arbitration. Finally, and perhaps most importantly, the jurists appointed to be CAS judges are selected both for their legal pedigrees and also for their interest in and knowledge of sport. Hence the arbitration procedure is specifically sports oriented, and the arbitrators will have an empathy with the concerns of all relevant parties.

---

[76] See Fitchen, "The Court of Arbitration's Appellate Doping Cases: Analysis and Evaluation", 5(2) *Sports Law Bulletin* 10.
[77] See Hannigan, "Irish Score Emphatic Win at CAS Appeal", *Irish Times*, February 1, 2002.

Such a system as CAS has the potential to be very effective indeed, providing as it does a unified system of resolution of sports disputes. Issues are decided "pursuant to the Olympic charter, the applicable regulations, general principles of law and the rules of law, the application of which it deems appropriate." Essentially this means that CAS will look to the internal regulations of the relevant federation and thence to general rules of law and principles of fair procedures. It is possible for parties to a dispute to specify a particular legal system, which they would wish to govern their dispute, but should there be no such specification, and some legal order must be applied, the CAS will apply rules of Swiss law. The major problem with CAS (apart from its continued identification as an organ of the IOC) is that certain sporting federations (most notably FIFA (the soccer governing body)) do not recognize CAS and hence have their own rules and appeals procedures.[78] Nonetheless, in the view of Michael Beloff – himself a judge of this court – CAS "... represents the best hope for future harmonization of international sports dispute resolution." Equally, he argues that a specific code of rules applicable both to domestic and international sporting disputes should be created as should a national sports dispute resolution forum in each country with a mandatory right of appeal to CAS.

One final point should be made. As Reeb notes, the CAS is still seen as a relatively new player in the international sports arena. It has evolved radically since its inception in 1981 – largely in the direction of securing independence from the IOC. Indeed given the fact that the IOC has been involved in several scandals, not least the allegations of bribery and corruption following the award to Salt Lake City of the rights to host the 2002 Winter Olympic Games, this is of huge importance. Nonetheless, the CAS is clearly still evolving – most notably in Reeb's view through the ad-hoc divisions, and the increasing numbers of cases submitted to it bear testimony to this fact.

1.7.3.2 Taking a case to CAS

Procedurally, cases are taken to CAS in the following fashion. In the case of ordinary arbitration, an application is sent to the court office of CAS, the contents of which are outlined in Article R 38 of the CAS code. This is not a detailed statement of claim, but briefly describes the relevant legal issue, and sets out in detail what the claimant wants. It will be accompanied by a copy of the relevant arbitration clause or arbitration agreement. The court office checks to ensure that CAS has jurisdiction to address the issue, and this being the case, it forwards the application to the opposing body setting out relevant time

---

[78] Interestingly UEFA – The European governing body for soccer – does recognise CAS. It is of great significance that the IAAF has comparatively recently signed up to the authority of CAS. See Reeb, "The IAAF to Recognise the Court of Arbitration for Sport", 4 *International Sports Law Review* (2001) 246.

limits including for the appointment of arbitrators and to present an answer. If this latter option is taken, such answer will include a brief description of the case for the defence and, if appropriate, a statement that the competence of CAS is questioned and any counter-claim. Moreover, once the overall procedure is activated, either party may seek interim relief from CAS.

Following these exchanges, parties are summoned to a hearing for the taking of evidence and oral pleadings. Under the CAS code, it is within the rules to be represented at such hearing by a person of choice, and not necessarily a lawyer. Generally the issue will be heard by a panel of three judges, with either side selecting one arbitrator from the CAS list and the two selected arbitrators choosing a President from the CAS panel. In exceptional circumstances, either where both parties agree or where CAS deems it appropriate, a single arbitrator may be appointed. Arbitrators must be completely independent and not have previously been involved with the case. The case will be heard according to the law of any jurisdiction agreed on by the parties, or, if there is no such agreement then, by default, it is heard according to Swiss law. In principle the final decision and any award, which is made, is communicated to the parties some weeks later.

Any award made will be in the form of a majority verdict, or where this is not possible, a verdict from the President of the panel. Such decision is in writing and states the reasons underpinning the award. The award is final and binding as soon as it is communicated by the court office of CAS. Appeals are possible on very limited grounds to the Swiss Federal Tribunal.[79] Refusal to execute any such award may be challenged in national courts, most easily in countries, which are signatories to the New York Convention. The ordinary procedure lasts between six and ten months, although in circumstances of urgency, interim measures may be ordered. Costs of the ordinary procedure are met by the parties, who will be responsible for the fees of the arbitrators (calculated on a fixed scale of charges) and a share of the CAS costs. Finally, decisions generated by the ordinary procedure are confidential.

In terms of the appeals procedure, an applicant must first ensure that all internal remedies have been exhausted. He must then lodge a brief statement of appeal with the court office, attaching the contested decision and the operative provisions of the statutes of the relevant sport body. Such appeal must be lodged within 21 days of the communication of the impugned decision.

---

[79] Such grounds would include, incompetence, irregular formation of the arbitration panel, awards beyond jurisdiction, lack of a decision on a major point within the application, violation of the rights of one party, incompatibility with public order, lack of equal treatment. Such appeals must be lodged within 30 days of the verdict. Generally see Baddley, "The Protection of the Personal Rights of Athletes: Concept, Application and Function of Such a Protection in Swiss Civil Law", 6(1) *Sport and the Law Journal* (1998) 19.

No less than ten days later,[80] the appellant should submit a statement of the case, outlining the facts and the legal arguments giving rise to the appeal, accompanied by all the exhibits and other evidence to be relied on, at which point CAS will invite the other side to submit an answer within 20 days. Again, after the process has been activated, either party may apply for interim relief, including suspension of the impugned decision. Here the appeal is heard according to the rules of the federation or sports body whose decision is challenged, or where necessary the law of the land in which the federation is domiciled. Decisions from the appeal procedure are not confidential. The appeal procedure is free, save for an initial court office fee of Sfr 500.

Finally, the IOC as well as any international or domestic federations may request an advisory opinion from CAS on any legal issue. Such opinions may be published, but do not constitute an arbitral award nor do they have any binding force.

1.8   CONCLUSION

This then represents the manner in which the governance of Irish sport is structured and the ideological context in which any legal involvement with sport must operate. In the following chapters, we consider the nature of such legal involvement in a wide variety of areas. As has been mentioned, our focus in this book is purely on those laws that affect the operation of sport or are peculiar to sportspeople. Thus we do not consider contexts in which individual sportspeople, clubs or governing bodies have interacted in incidental fashion with the law. So for example no analysis is made of the issue of child abuse in Irish sport,[81] on the basis that this is a stand alone crime, although some analysis is made of the Sports Council *Code of Ethics and Good Practice in Children's Sport*, on the basis that this gives guidelines to those involved in the organisation of children's sport as to how to ensure that a culture of abuse cannot develop.

In chapter two we assess the nature of challenges to the rules of governing bodies on grounds related to fair procedures. In Chapter three, we consider the nature and development of contemporary anti-doping policy. Chapters four and five analyse the contexts in which foul play or bad training can generate either criminal or civil liability for participants and related parties. In chapter six we assess the responsibilities of the organizers of sporting events and the occupiers of stadia in which sporting events take place. In chapter seven, we

---

[80] If no such statement is forthcoming within ten days the appellant is taken to have withdrawn his appeal.

[81] Generally on this see MacKay, "Sport Faces Up to Its Final Taboo", *Guardian*, October 27, 2001, Gray, "Swimming and Child Protection", 4(5) *Sports Law Administration and Practice* (September/October 1997) 1 and Williams, "Child Protection in Sport", 8(1) *Sport and The Law Journal* (2000) 8.

consider the legal protections available to those who would exploit the financial possibilities of sport – and in particular the contractual and intellectual property rights of governing bodies, clubs and individuals. In chapters eight and nine we assess aspects of the development of EU policy in this area, looking at how the 'free movement' rules – the cornerstones of the internal market – have radically transformed the economics of professional sport in Europe, and at how EC competition law has impacted on other aspects of the business of sport. In chapter ten we look at the issue of equality within sport, and at how recent Irish legislation has altered the position of clubs and individual participants.

CHAPTER TWO

Sports Rules and Fair Procedures

INTRODUCTION

The governance of sport, no less than the playing of sport is dominated by rules.[1] There are playing rules, safety rules, disciplinary rules, and administration rules, created both by sports clubs and sports governing bodies, and enforced by either an on field arbiter or referee or an official disciplinary body. Moreover, such rules will necessarily impact on the interests and potentially the careers of individual sports persons and sports teams.

The nature of this impact is also the reason why a sports body may be subject to legal obligations in the creation and enforcement of the rules of sport. Thus as we shall see in Chapter Five, both sports governing bodies and on field referees have on occasion been held civilly liable where their negligence in the creation or application of the safety rules of sport have led to participants being harmed. In this chapter, however, we focus on situations where a sportsperson's interests are injured by reason of the application of what may be termed the administrative rules (as distinct from the safety or playing rules[2]) of sport.

---

[1] See generally Gardiner *et al*, *Sports Law* (2nd ed., Cavendish, 2001) [hereafter Gardiner], Chap.5, Beloff, *Sports Law* (Hart Publishing, 1998) [hereafter Beloff], Chaps 3 and 7, McCutcheon, "Sports Discipline, Natural Justice and Strict Liability" (1999) *Anglo-American Law Review* 37, McCutcheon "Judicial Review of Sporting Bodies; Recent Irish Experiences", 3 (3) *Sport and the Law Journal* (1995) 20, McArdle, *From Boot Money to Bosman: Football, Society and the Law* (Cavendish, 2000), Chap.9, Greenfield and Osborn, *Law and Sport in Contemporary Society* (Frank Cass Publishers, 2000) [hereafter Greenfield & Osborn, Chaps 5 and 7], Cox, "Sports Governing Bodies and Fair Procedures, Recent Irish Developments", 10 (2) *Sport and the Law Journal* (2002) 162, McCutcheon "Judicial Scrutiny of Sports Administration" (1995) 13 *Irish Law Times* 171, and McCutcheon, "The Rule of Law in Sport", 9 (3) *Sports Law Administration and Practice* (July, 2002) 1.

[2] Thus if a player is sent off for a dangerous tackle in a soccer match and is then suspended for four games, the legal challenge that might arise will be to the application of the suspension rule by the governing body and not with the application of the playing rule by the referee. On the other hand in the John Boland case (considered below at p.60), a challenge was partially based on the claim that the referee had incorrectly applied the playing rules of the sport. It is highly unlikely, however, save in the most egregious

Before we proceed with this analysis, two introductory points should be made. First, the majority of controversial cases involving sports governing bodies will relate to use of banned substances and methods by athletes, and may end up before the Court of Arbitration for Sport. These cases will, however, be considered separately in Chapter Three. Secondly, whereas increasingly, the rules of sports clubs that come under most scrutiny are those relating to its membership policy and particularly whether such policy satisfies requirements of equality law, these will be considered in Chapter Ten.

The administrative rules of sports bodies that have been successfully challenged in the courts (despite the traditional practice of the courts to defer to the sports body when the application of sports rules is at issue),[3] may be divided into three broad categories, namely those pertaining to **admission to sporting bodies**, **suspension and expulsion from them**, and **forfeiture within them**.[4] Our focus in this chapter is threefold;

– First, what must such bodies do to ensure that their rules in respect of such matters are legally valid?

– Secondly, in what circumstances may the enforcement of such rules be subject to legal challenge, and

– Thirdly what is the correct procedure for making such a challenge and specifically should it be taken by way of judicial review or plenary summons?[5]

It is with the final of these issues that our analysis will commence.

---

circumstances (for example if a referee in a rugby match deemed the team that scored fewer points to be the winner) that a court would sustain a challenge to a referee's decision in respect of a playing rule. Thus in 1999, in *Carew Park Amateur Football Club v. FAI* (unreported, High Court, Barr J., February 19, 1999), a challenge to a decision of a referee failed with the judge commenting that unless he did "something appalling" the referee's decision was sacrosanct. Equally the judge made no order as to costs, because of what he termed the "vacillation" of the referee. See "Referee's Word Final Says Judge", *Irish Times*, February 20, 1999. See also March/April 1999, "Sports Law Administration and Practice", p.2.

3   This was the approach taken by Lord Denning in *Enderby Town Football Club v. Football Association* [1971] 1 Ch. 591. See also *Balfour v. Balfour* [1919] 2 K.B. 571, and generally Beloff, "Pitch, Pool, Rink ... Court? Judicial Review in the Sporting World" (1989) *Public Law* 95. See also Farrell, "The Dutch Cup Final 1991 and its Aftermath", 2 (1) *Sport and the Law Journal* (1994) 18 and Corrigan "The Ref is Right, Right?", *Observer*, February 25, 1990. On the other hand the courts will not permit sports bodies to exclude their role as interpreters of the law. See *Baker v. Jones* [1954] 2 All E.R. 553, 558.

4   *McInnes v. Onslow Fane* [1978] 3 All E.R. 211.

5   See for example, Jeacock, "Unincorporated Associations in Litigation: A Note", 3 (3) *Sport and the Law Journal* (1995) 24.

2.1 THE FORM OF CHALLENGES TO DECISIONS OF SPORTING BODIES

The manner in which decisions of sports bodies are challenged will depend largely on the nature of that body, the relationship between it and the claimant and the type of decision being made. Thus for example, a claim against a private decision taken by a private club or governing body or, more problematically, by an international federation, might, depending on the circumstances, proceed on the basis of the common law doctrine of restraint of trade, as a competition law action, by way of a constitutional challenge relating to the right to earn a livelihood, or in the form of a breach of contract action. If the body is an incorporated one moreover, a challenge could also be brought under the rules of company law. However, if it could be established that the body in question was a *public* one and the impugned decision public in nature, then the claimant could proceed by way of the very different legal vehicle of judicial review under the European Convention on Human Rights. Our first question then, is whether and when decisions of sports bodies may be subject to judicial review.

2.1.1 Judicial review and the status of sporting bodies

The benefits of a judicial review action over a challenge brought by way of plenary summons are perhaps more theoretical than real, particularly in the Irish context, where even private contracts will be subject to both an implied right to fair procedures and natural and constitutional justice,[6] and the constitutional right to earn a livelihood. Furthermore, Irish courts have even been prepared to set aside decisions of private bodies on the (traditionally public law) basis that such decisions were irrational.[7] This is not to say, however, that judicial review offers *no* benefits over the private remedy,[8] and we will now consider such benefits.

---

[6] See *Mooney v. An Post* [1998] 4 I.R. 288 at 298 for the view that:
 "Society is not divided into two classes one of whom – office holders – is entitled to the protection of the principles of natural and constitutional justice and the other of whom – employees is not. Dismissal from one's employment for alleged misconduct with possible loss of pension rights and damage to one's good name may, in modern society be disastrous for any citizen. These are circumstances in which any citizen, however, humble, may be entitled to the protection of natural and constitutional justice."
 See also *Glover v. BLN Ltd* [1973] I.R. 388 and *Gallagher v. Revenue Commissioners* [1995] 1 I.R. 55. See McCutcheon, pp.123–124 in Greenfield & Osborn, *Law and Sport in Contemporary Society* (Frank Cass Publishers, 2000) [hereafter Greenfield & Osborn]. In the UK see *Ridge v. Baldwin* [1964] A.C. 40 and *Modahl v. British Athletic Federation* [2002] 1 W.L.R. 1192.
[7] *Bolger v. Osborne* [2000] 1 I.L.R.M. 250, *Moloney v. Bolger* [2000] I.E.H.C. 63, *Zockoll Group Limited v. Telecom Éireann* [1998] 4 I.R. 287 at 318.
[8] See Parpworth, "Guarding the Game", pp.71–73 in Greenfield & Osborn, for the view

First, judicial review may be the *only* procedure available to an applicant who does not have a contract with the relevant governing body – for example a supporter, or indeed an athlete whose circumstances do not display a sufficient contractual nexus with the relevant governing body.[9] Secondly, by reason of the "court management" of public actions, they will almost inevitably be more expeditious[10] than their private law counterparts.[11] Thirdly, under Order 84 of the Rules of the Superior Courts, it is arguably easier to get a stay on proceedings than it is to get interlocutory relief in the course of a private action,[12] a factor that will become extremely important where one is challenging a suspension that prohibits one from competing in a major upcoming sporting event. Fourthly, in judicial review actions the applicant is entitled to depend upon the doctrine of legitimate expectations,[13] whereas in private actions he or she is left to rely on the more nebulous doctrine of promissory estoppel. Fifthly, it is possible that the obligation to give reasons for a decision only applies to public bodies.[14] Sixthly, an applicant in a judicial review case might benefit from the fact that under the doctrine of *ultra vires*, a public body is absolutely prohibited from acting outside of its delineated powers – although

---

that there are also downsides to taking a judicial review action, not least the short limitation period and the fact that one has to seek leave to bring a judicial review action. The same point was made by the court in *Law v. National Greyhound Racing Club* [1983] 3 All E.R. 300. Moreover as a basic requirement an applicant seeking to make a judicial review application must have exhausted all internal remedies. Indeed in this light Pannick ("Judicial Review of Sporting Bodies" [1997] J.R. 150 at p.153 [hereafter Pannick]) suggests that a sports body should in fact welcome being subject to judicial review. As he puts it:

> "We are, after all talking of a jurisdiction with very short time-limits for bringing claims, no automatic discovery, affidavit evidence (so that sports officials do not need to give oral evidence) a power in the court to refuse relief for discretionary reasons, a reluctance to intervene in relation to the merits of decisions and very limited circumstances in which damages can be awarded."

9   See Pannick, *op. cit.*, p.152. See also *Modahl v. BAF* [2002] 1 W.L.R. 1192 and Farrell, "*Diane Modahl v. The Law of Contract*", 9 (1) *Sport and the Law Journal* (2001) 110.

10 *Rafferty v. Bus Éireann* [1997] 2 I.R. 424, *Geoghegan v. Institute of Chartered Accountants* [1995] 3 I.R. 86. See also on this point Beloff, *Sports Law*, 602 and Catherine Bond, "Sporting Bodies and Judicial Review", 1 *Sport and the Law Journal* (1993) 7.

11 Moreover the limitation periods for public and private actions are different. See McCutcheon, pp.123–124, in Greenfield & Osborn.

12 Compare the test in *Campus Oil v. Minister for Industry and Commerce* [1983] I.R. 82 with the approach in *Lancefort Ltd v. ABP*, unreported, High Court *ex tempore*, February 13, 1998. See also *Broadnet Ireland Ltd v. Office of the Director of Telecommunications* [2000] 2 I.L.R.M. 241.

13 *Eogan v. University College Dublin* [1996] 1 I.R. 390 and *Abrahamson v. Law Society* [1996] 1 I.R. 403.

14 *Gavin v. Criminal Injuries Compensation Tribunal* [1997] 1 I.R. 132, *Maigueside Communications Limited v. I.R.T.C.* [1998] 4 I.R. 115, *Carna Foods Limited v. Eagle Star Insurance (Ireland) Limited* [1995] 1 I.R. 526. In the sporting context, see *Dundee United v. Scottish Football Association* [1988] S.L.T. 1244.

this will almost certainly also apply to a private body acting outside the terms of a contract.[15] Finally, as Beloff[16] notes:

> "... the characterization of a judicial right as one arising in public law, or it may be, in private law can – perversely some would say – actually influence the substantive content of the right asserted and may thereby determine the result of the case."[17]

If a decision of a sports body is to be challenged by judicial review, then two criteria must be fulfilled, namely the body must itself be a public one, and so also must the impugned action that it takes. In this light, we can assume that individual sports *clubs* are "private" entities and hence challenges to their decisions will be in the form of contractual claims instituted by way of plenary summons. The situation is perhaps less clear-cut when we are dealing with challenges to decisions of sports governing bodies.[18]

Traditionally, in both Ireland and the UK, the starting point for determining whether a body was a public one or not, was analysis of the source of its power. Thus a decision made pursuant to statute or by a body created by statute was seen as a public law one, challengeable via judicial review proceedings.[19] In recent years however in both the UK[20] and Ireland, the view that *only* a statutory body could be deemed to be a public one for these purposes has been firmly rejected. In *Beirne v. Garda Commissioner*,[21] it was held that the exercise even of a non-statutory power could be reviewed if it was of such a *nature* that it might ordinarily be seen as coming within the public domain. In such circumstances, it could only be excluded from judicial review if it could be shown that its power derived exclusively from an individual contract made in private law. More pertinently still in *Geoghegan v. Institute of Chartered*

---

[15] *Rafferty v. Bus Éireann* [1997] 2 I.R. 424, *Eogan v. UCD* [1996] 1 I.R. 390, *Baker v. Jones* [1954] 2 All E.R. 553.

[16] Beloff, *op. cit.*, p.226

[17] See also Pannick, *op. cit.*, p.152 for the view that it is simply inappropriate that decisions of sporting bodies that are in breach of rules of fair procedures should be challenged by way of the fiction of an implied contractual term.

[18] Generally see Hogan and Morgan, *Administrative Law in Ireland* (3rd ed., Round Hall, 1998), Chap.13.

[19] See for example *Eogan v. University College Dublin* [1996] 1 I.R. 390, *Bane v. Garda Representative Association* [1997] 2 I.R. 449, *Walsh v. Red Cross Society* [1997] 2 I.R. 479. Parpworth (at p.80 in Greenfield & Osborn) argues that the reason why there is so much uncertainty as to whether judicial review would lie in such situations is because judicial review traditionally attaches to governmental activity yet there is no certainty as to what the proper ambit of governmental activity actually is.

[20] *R v. Panel on Mergers and Takeovers, ex parte Datafin* [1987] Q.B 699, [1987] 2 W.L.R. 699, [1987] 1 All E.R. 509.

[21] [1993] I.L.R.M. 1.

Accountants in Ireland[22] (a challenge to a decision of a domestic tribunal whose power was contractually based), the court recognised the public nature of the source of the body's powers (founded on royal charter), the public nature of its activities, and the fact that had it not been for its existence, government would have had to have taken responsibility for such actions.[23] Moreover, it noted that the relationship between the Institute and its members was consensual only in name, in that a contract with the body had to be signed in order for an individual to practice as a chartered accountant. On this basis, the court found that the power being exercised was, fundamentally a public law one with a virtual statutory effect for members.

This decision has been followed,[24] such that it can now be asserted that, as a matter of Irish law, if a body is operating in the public domain and if its relationship with its members is more monopolistic than (genuinely) consensual in nature, its decisions may be judicially reviewed even where the source of its power is non-statutory.[25] Equally, it should be stressed that all public bodies will also make decisions that are private in nature, and such private actions must still be challenged by plenary summons.

2.1.2 Are sports bodies "public" for judicial review purposes?

Ireland has conflicting authority on the question of whether decisions of sporting bodies may be judicially reviewed.[26] In *Murphy v. Turf Club*[27] the High Court ruled against this possibility because of the consensual nature of the relationship between the parties. Conversely in *Quirke v. BLE*[28] – a challenge to a decision

---

[22] [1995] 3 I.R. 86.

[23] In the sporting context in *R v. Football Association Ltd ex parte Football League Ltd.* [1993] 2 All E.R. 833, Rose J. argued that if the Football Association were not in place it would not be government who would be responsible for the running of soccer – rather it would probably be some television company. In *R v. Disciplinary Committee of the Jockey Club, ex parte Aga Khan* [1993] 1 W.L.R. 909, Bingham M.R. held that in the absence of the Jockey Club, government would have to take responsibility for horse racing, but the rest of the court rejected this. Beloff & Kerr, "Why *Aga Khan* is Wrong" [1996] *Judicial Review* 30 at 31 argue, however, that the correct question is whether government would intervene if *no one else did.*

[24] See for example, *Bane v. Garda Representative Association*, above, *Rafferty v. Bus Éireann* [1997] 2 I.R. 424, *Bolger v. Osborne* [2000] 1 I.L.R.M. 250, *Ryan v. Criminal Injuries Compensation Tribunal* [1997] 1 I.L.R.M. 194, *Gavin v. Criminal Injuries Compensation Tribunal* [1997] 1 I.R. 132.

[25] See Beloff, *op. cit.*, p.226 for the view that the proper test in this regard should not be whether the decision maker is a public body or whether the nature of the decision is public or not, but whether "public rights" are at issue.

[26] McCutcheon, "Judicial Control of Sporting Bodies; Recent Irish Experiences" (1995) 3(2) *Sport and the Law Journal* 20.

[27] [1989] I.R. 172.

[28] [1988] I.R. 83.

of the Irish Athletics Federation to suspend an athlete for failing to provide a urine sample – the court did allow a judicial review application to proceed, with little comment on the manner by which the case was proceeding. Unusually, Barr J. who presided over both cases did not refer to the latter in deciding the former. A judicial review action was also taken in *Matthews v. Irish Coursing Club*,[29] but as McCutcheon points out, this decision may be distinguished from the other two in that in this case the respondent body derived its powers from statute.

The issue also came up for discussion in *Bolger v. Osborne* – a challenge to a decision of the Jockey Club suspending both a jockey and a trainer on the grounds that a horse did not run on its merits. The case was taken by way of plenary summons in that being a claim that principles of natural and constitutional justice were being violated there was little need to proceed via judicial review. Hence Macken J's comments on this issue are at best *obiter dicta*. Nonetheless they are instructive. Counsel for the plaintiff had argued that although he was proceeding via plenary summons he was in fact entitled to take a judicial review in this case particularly (albeit not exclusively) because the Irish Turf Club had been placed on a statutory footing since 1994. Macken J. seemed to accept this proposition holding that because of both the 1994 Act *and* decisions like *Geoghegan v. Institute of Chartered Accountants,* it was possible that judicial review did now lie against the Turf Club (and by extension other sporting bodies) and hence that the decision in *Murphy v. Turf Club* on this point no longer stood. The exact impact of this holding is unclear, and particularly whether it would apply to all sports bodies or only those that have a statutory basis.[30] Hence in Ireland the question of whether sporting bodies may be the subject of judicial review actions remains open. It is further submitted that a particularly significant question mark hangs over the status of the GAA – a body that quite apart from receiving government funding is so closely linked with the Irish nation and is in charge of an activity which is so close to the hearts of such a large number of Irish people that it may in principle be regarded as a public body, albeit one that makes both public and private decisions.

In England, on the other hand, there is a body of authority in which the possibility of decisions of sports governing bodies being subject to judicial review has been rejected, although the Court of Appeal or House of Lords

---

[29] [1993] 1 I.R. 346.

[30] The recent case of *Moran v. O'Sullivan*, unreported, High Court, Carroll J., March 18, 2003 (considered below at p.71) involved a challenge to a decision of the statutory body Horseracing Ireland taken by way of judicial review. The case involved a challenge to a suspension on one horse imposed by racing stewards, and whereas there was little doubt that the body was public in nature in this case, it is perhaps questionable whether the decision was a sufficiently public one to justify a judicial review action.

have never expressly confirmed this stance. In the first of these cases, *Law v. National Greyhound Racing Club (NGRC)*,[31] it was held that any claim against a decision of this body would have to be via a private law challenge – a principle upheld in a number of subsequent cases, namely *R v. Disciplinary Committee of the Jockey Club, ex parte Massingberd Munday*,[32] *R v. Jockey Club, ex parte RAM Racecourses*,[33] *R v. Disciplinary Committee of the Jockey Club, ex parte Aga Khan*[34] and *R v Football Association ex parte Football League*.[35]

Of these cases, the first was the most important, in that the precedent it set was the basis for the decisions in the later cases. Indeed, in *R v. Disciplinary Committee of the Jockey Club, ex parte Massingberd Munday*, the Court of Appeal accepted that some of the powers of the Jockey club did operate in the public domain, and at least two of the judges would have been prepared to ground an action in judicial review had it not been for the precedent set in *Law v. National Greyhound Racing Club*. Equally it is arguable for three reasons that there was no need for such a slavish adherence to precedent.

First, of all the above decisions, *Law v. NGRC* is the only one that occurred before the *ex parte Datafin* restatement of the rules in respect of judicial review in England.[36] Indeed in the *R v. Jockey Club, ex parte RAM Racecourses* case, the court accepted that the precedent in *Law v. NGRC* could have been overruled in light of the ruling in *ex parte Datafin*, and concluded that certain powers of the Jockey Club – licensing for example – could have been subject to judicial review.[37] Secondly, the nature of the powers of many sporting bodies is

---

[31] [1983] 1 W.L.R. 1302, [1983] 3 All E.R. 300.

[32] [1993] 2 All E.R. 207.

[33] [1993] 2 All E.R. 225.

[34] [1993] 1 W.L.R. 909, [1993] 2 All E.R. 853. See Moore, *Sports Law and Litigation* (2nd ed., Welwyn Garden City CLT Professional, 2000) [hereafter Moore] pp.136–137. See also Beloff & Kerr, "Why *Aga Khan* is Wrong" [1996] *Judicial Review* 30.

[35] [1993] 2 All E.R. 225. See also *R v. Football Association ex parte Flint Town* [1991] C.O.D. 44 For analysis see Lewis & Taylor, *op. cit.*, p.123 *et seq.*, Beloff, *op. cit.*, pp.606–608, Griffith Jones, *Law and the Business of Sport* (Butterworths, London, 1997) [hereafter Griffith Jones], p.54ff, Moore, *op. cit.*, p.134, McArdle, *Football Society and the Law* (Cavendish, 2001) [hereafter McArdle], p.173, Bond, "Sporting Bodies and Judicial Review" (1993) 1 *Sport and the Law Journal* 7 at 7–9, and Parpworth, *Guarding the Game*, p.80. Other cases in which the English courts have refused to accept the possibility that a ports governing body could be amenable to judicial review include *R v. FA of Wales, ex parte Flint Town,* and *R v. Eastern Counties Rugby Union ex parte Basildon Rugby Club.* See Parpworth, *op. cit.* (1993), pp.78–79.

[36] See Pannick, p.152. See Moore, p.133 for the view that even post the *ex parte Datafin* the UK courts are not keen to interfere with decisions of sporting bodies, and p.138 for a criticism of the courts failure to apply the significance of the *Datafin* judgement in these cases.

[37] See for example the partial dissent of Simon Brown J. For a general criticism of this decision see Beloff, p.228–229. Beloff points out that the procedural exclusivity rule in the UK founded in the much criticized decision in *O'Reilly v. Mackman* [1983] 2 A.C. 237, [1982] 3 W.L.R. 1096, [1982] 3 All E.R. 1124 is at the root of the problem. This

indistinguishable from those exercised by the Panel on Mergers and Takeovers,[38] which were the subject of the *ex parte Datafin* case. Finally, the powers of the Jockey Club (set up by Royal charter), and the Football Association in the latter cases were entirely unlike those of the Greyhound Club in *Law v. NGRC*. At the time, of 107 greyhound racing clubs in the UK only 48 were licensed by the NGRC, hence there was no suggestion of monopolistic control of greyhound racing by the NGRC. In the context of horse racing and football, on the other hand, there was virtually absolute control of all major events by the relevant governing bodies.[39]

This leads on to perhaps the most salient criticism of the three Jockey club and the FA cases, namely that because the jurisdiction which the governing bodies were exercising was monopolistic rather than properly consensual in nature, (in that anyone wishing to compete professionally in such sports was as a matter of fact bound to accept that jurisdiction),[40] and operated in the public domain, they fulfilled the criteria for being regarded (at least in principle) as public bodies. In *R v. Disciplinary Committee of the Jockey Club, ex parte Aga Khan* Farquharson J. had ruled that because no one was forcing the applicant to engage with the Jockey Club – he could after all, simply abstain from the sport – the jurisdiction which it enjoyed *was* consensual in nature. Such an approach is, however, entirely unrealistic in the context of professional sport, where a person's capacity to practice a trade is at issue.

Nor indeed was this conclusion actually necessary in the context of the facts of any of these cases,[41] where the *decisions* that were at stake were undoubtedly private and not public – a fact, indeed, which was at the heart of the *ratio* of the decisions.[42] It would have been perfectly legitimate to conclude that whereas in this instance a judicial review did not lie, because the impugned

---

rule does not exist currently in Ireland but for general consideration see O'Dell, "Contract Law", p.179ff in Byrne and Binchy, *Annual Review of Irish Law 1998* (Roundhall Sweet & Maxwell, 1999).

[38] As Bond, 1 *Sport and the Law Journal* (1993) 7, points out the panel in question was not based on statutory or prerogative or common law powers but was indirectly supported by statute and had a duty to act judicially.

[39] McArdle, *op. cit.*, pp.183–186.

[40] Thus Parpworth, "Guarding the Game", p.71 in Greenfield and Osborne, asks "Can it really be said that the submission to jurisdiction is consensual when in truth an individual has no other alternative if he wishes to ride own or train racehorses in the UK?" See also Beloff & Kerr, "Why *Aga Khan* is Wrong", 1 [1996] *Judicial Review* 30.

[41] Pannick, "Judicial review of Sporting Bodies" [1997] J.R. 152.

[42] On the other hand Beloff & Kerr ("Why *Aga Khan* is Wrong"), conclude that in this case "... the right the applicant seeks to enforce bears many of the hallmarks of a public law right." For a suggestion that in Ireland too many cases involving merely private rights are brought by way of judicial review see O'Dell, "Contract Law" in Byrne and Binchy, *Annual Review of Irish Law 1998* (Roundhall Sweet & Maxwell, Dublin, 2000), p.179ff, and by the same author, p.116 in *Annual Review of Irish Law 1999* (Roundhall Sweet & Maxwell, Dublin, 2000).

action was private in nature, equally the Jockey Club itself was a public body, (precisely because the relationship between the parties was *not* based on consent in any meaningful way)[43] and hence its *public* decisions could be subject to judicial review. This indeed had been the conclusion of Lord Denning many years earlier in *Enderby Town FC v. FA*,[44] where he concluded that whereas the rules of governing bodies such as the FA were presented as forming part of a private *inter partes* contract, in reality this was a fiction and such rules amounted to a quasi legislative code.

In *R v. Football Association ex parte Football League*[45] – a challenge to the creation by the FA of a new Premier League for soccer in England – the court held that despite the FA's absolute power to govern football in the UK, it could not be seen as a public body for judicial review purposes. Readily discernible in the decision is a fear that extension of the ambit of judicial review to bodies, which while they possess a monopoly of control in an area nonetheless operate on the basis of contractual relationships with their members, could lead to the judicial review procedure becoming overused.[46] It is arguable, however, that allowing such public policy considerations to override the interests of someone whose rights have been affected by a body with monopolistic powers to govern something as public as sport, and who for some reason has no standing to take a breach of contract action against the body, is simply unfair.[47]

Nonetheless, in practice in the UK, it may be argued that without a House of Lords decision overruling *Law v NGRC*, a would be litigant, challenging a decision of a sporting body should be advised to proceed by way of plenary summons.[48] From an Irish perspective, we would note that the benefits of

---

[43] This was the tenor of Bingham M.R.'s judgment in the case. Beloff, *op. cit.*, pp.226–229, criticizes this decision both for what he sees as a misapplication of the decision in *ex parte Datafin* and because the logic would suggest that any behaviour, even that subject to licensing authority was not a subject for judicial review unless there was some degree of statutory control. The decision is also arguably open to criticism for the court's apparent failure to appreciate the public nature of the powers of the Jockey Club in this case.

[44] [1971] 1 Ch. 591.

[45] [1993] 2 All E.R. 853.

[46] For criticism of the intellectually unsatisfying nature of this approach see Beloff, "Pitch, Pool, Rink ... Court? Judicial review in the Sporting World" [1989] *Public Law* 95 at 110. Beloff points out that if leave to seek judicial review was granted in such situations, it would mean that sports bodies would feel it incumbent upon themselves to improve their standards, thereby potentially reducing the threat of excessive litigation. In any event, Gardiner, *op. cit.*, p.122, argues that since the creation of the UK Task Force on Football (1995) it may be more legitimate to regard the FA as a public body.

[47] As Moore, *op. cit.*, p.138, concludes, "... as a matter of justice and fairness it is difficult to see why an aggrieved party should be in a worse position simply because he has no privity of contract with his governing body and the consensual issue is missing".

[48] It has been noted that in countries like New Zealand, Australia and indeed Scotland judicial review has been held to lie against sporting bodies, but it should be mentioned

proceeding by way of judicial review rather than plenary summons are not hugely significant. Thus in *Kinane v. Turf Club*[49] the plaintiff, proceeding by the 'private route' against a body which was clearly public in source and nature, sought and obtained an interim injunction against a suspension incurred for careless riding as easily as he would have got a stay on proceedings had he proceeded by way of judicial review. Indeed the logic of this decision – that the athlete stands to lose more from being suspended than a governing body does from having such suspension lifted – however questionable, has widespread application, and would arguably justify the granting of an *interlocutory* injunction under the rules in *Campus Oil v. Minister For Industry and Commerce (No. 2)*[50] in all but the most unusual cases. Moreover, as we have seen, the standards of fair procedures demanded of governing bodies will be essentially the same irrespective of whether they are challenged on a public law or a private law basis. In other words there is little to gain and much to lose by attempting to bring a challenge by way of judicial review and accordingly, we would submit that unless the relevant governing body is a statutory one, and the issue in question plainly public in nature, an Irish litigant should simply proceed by way of plenary summons.

2.1.3 Should sports governing bodies be regarded as public for the purposes of judicial review?

The question remains whether judicial review *should*, as a matter of principle, be available to applicants in cases involving Irish sports governing bodies. It is submitted that the professionalisation of sport, in tandem with the developments in Irish rules pertaining to judicial review outlined above, means that in principle it should. Sport is after all an inherently public thing, and as we saw in the previous chapter, its operation especially at professional level is generally completely dominated by the relevant governing body. As Stewart put it,[51]

"A striking feature of modern sport is the degree to which national and

---

that in these countries there is no hard and fast distinction between public and private bodies. See Gardiner, *op. cit.*, p.210, Griffith Jones, *op. cit.*, p.52ff. See also Stewart, "Judicial Control of Sporting Bodies in Scotland", 3 (3) *Sport and the Law* Journal (1995) 45, Beloff & Kerr, "Judicial Control of Sporting Bodies; the Commonwealth Jurisprudence", 3 (1) *Sport and the Law Journal* (1996) 5 and Parpworth, "Sports Governing Bodies and the Principles of Natural Justice; An Australian Perspective", 4 (2) *Sport and the Law Journal* (1997) 5.

[49] Unreported, High Court, McCracken J., July 27, 2001, considered below, p.77.
[50] [1983] I.R. 88.
[51] Stewart, "Restraint of Trade in Sport", 6 (3) *Sport and the Law Journal* (1999) 41 at 42.

> international governing bodies control all activities in their own sport.
> ... If you don't do what they say you don't play. No contract is needed.
> There just isn't any other practical way of organizing leagues and teams
> and obtaining referees for properly competitive amateur or professional
> games. The possibility of rival competitions or associations operating
> outside the established structure of national and international ...
> associations is fanciful."[52]

Equally, whatever about the public status of sports governing bodies, many if
not most decisions and actions of such bodies particularly where it is in dispute
with an individual athlete will only involve private rights, and in such
circumstances the appropriate means of challenge is also private in nature.[53]

2.2 PRIVATE LAW CHALLENGES TO DECISIONS OF SPORTING BODIES

Beyond a judicial review action, there are four principal grounds for challenging
a decision or an action made by a club or governing body in the process of the
enforcement of its rules namely;

– The action or decision constitutes a breach of contract.

– The action or decision constitutes an unreasonable restraint of trade or is
  anti-competitive.

– The action or decision violates the applicant's constitutional right to earn a
  livelihood.

– The decision was clearly irrational (in the sense of being unsupported by
  any evidence before the decision maker).

Equally, courts are traditionally loath to substitute their own decisions for those
of a sports body set up for the purposes of making decisions in respect of the
rules by which its sport is governed.[54] Rather they require that one of these
four criteria is clearly shown to have been met before they will be prepared to
intervene.

The link between these grounds for challenge is that they all address
situations where the decision or action or the process by which it is made is

---

[52] See Parpworth, p.84, in Greenfield & Osborn, *op. cit.*, for the view that sports bodies
now exercise so much power that it might be possible to control their powers under
competition law.

[53] Thus Beloff & Kerr, "Why *Aga Khan* is Wrong", conclude that because of its impact on
consensuality, market dominance ought to be seen as an indication of a body exercising
public law functions. For a similar conclusion see Pannick, *op. cit.*, at 153.

[54] See also *Cowley v. Heatley*, *The Times*, July 24, 1986. See Griffith Jones, *op. cit.*, p.64.

unfair. Thus to be actionable a restraint of trade must be "unreasonable," and in assessing whether an action is anti-competitive, regard will be had to whether it generates some public benefit. Similarly, it is only where a restriction on the applicant's constitutional right to earn a livelihood is unjustified or disproportionate that it will be struck down.[55] Finally, the most obvious reasons why a determination of a governing body will be found to be in breach of a contract with its members will be either that the governing body unfairly acted outside of the terms of the contract, or alternatively that the impugned action breached the implied term in the contract guaranteeing fair procedures and natural and constitutional justice in the performance thereof.[56] Indeed such perceived "unfairness" will also be at the heart of a judicial review action. Accordingly, following a brief consideration of the nature of the four grounds for challenge mentioned above, we will focus on the basic requirements of fair procedures that will bind sporting bodies.

2.2.1 The doctrine of unreasonable restraint of trade and the emergence of competition law

Prior to the famous *Bosman* case[57] in which the European Court of Justice said that professional sportspersons benefited from the protection afforded under the EC Treaty to the free movement of workers and the freedom of European citizens to provide services, the doctrine of unreasonable restraint of trade provided the most useful legal vehicle for sportspersons who claimed that their capacity to follow their chosen career was being restricted by some body – be it a club, a governing body or any other entity.[58] The doctrine has

---

[55] For a comparable British case see *Colgan v. The Kennel Club* [2001] W.L. 1171941, [2002] *International Sports Law Review* 187. For comment see Stone, "A Question of Proportionality", 10 (4) *Sports Law Administration and Practice* (2003) 1.

[56] *Stevenage Borough FC v. Football League, The Times*, August 1, 1996 (1997) 9 Admin L.R. 109. For analysis see Alderson, "Admission Criteria", 4(3) *Sport and the Law Journal* (1996) 107, and Stewart, "Stevenage Borough FC v. The Football League", 4 (3) *Sport and the Law Journal* (1996) 110, and Bailey, "Conditions of Entry", May/June 1997 *Sports Law Administration and Practice* 11. See also *Rotherham and English Second Division Rugby Limited v. English First Division Rugby Ltd.* [2000] 1 *International Sports Law Review*, 33, Modahl *v. British Athletics Federation* [2002] 1 W.L.R. 1192, *Mooney v. An Post, op. cit., Russell v. Duke of Norfolk* [1949] 1 All E.R. 109, *R v. Disciplinary Committee of the Jockey Club, ex parte Aga Khan, op. cit.*

[57] *Union Royale Belge des Societes de Football association ASBL v Jean-Marc Bosman*, Case C–415/93 [1995] E.C.R. I–04921.

[58] See generally Lewis & Taylor, p.173, Griffith-Jones, p.42, Grayson, p.391, Steele, "The Doctrine of Restraint of Trade – How has it Contributed to the Development of Sports Law?", 3(3) *Sport and the Law Journal* (1995), 5, Stewart, "Restraint of Trade in Sport", 6(3) *Sport and the Law Journal* (1998), p.41, Farrell, "Transfer Fees and Restraint of Trade", 5(3) *Sport and the Law Journal* (1997) 54.

survived, although it is arguable that the impact of the doctrine for sportspersons either has been or shortly will be overtaken by National and European Competition law (considered in Chapter Nine) as well as the *Bosman* line of cases (considered in Chapter Eight).[59] Nonetheless, because of its impact on the development of sports law, it merits some detailed consideration.

The doctrine, which is rooted in public policy, declares that all restraints which prevent an individual from carrying on his trade are contrary to public policy and void unless they are justified – and hence reasonable.[60] In this respect, the issue of when a restraint of trade may be regarded as justified is a significant one, raising questions not unlike those addressed by the doctrine of proportionality as it is known to Irish constitutional law. Thus the courts have stated that:

> "It is a sufficient justification and indeed it is the only justification, if the restriction is reasonable – reasonable that is, in reference to the interests of the parties concerned and reasonable in reference to the interest of the public, so framed and so guarded as to afford adequate protection to the party in whose favour it is imposed, while at the same time it is in no way injurious to the public."[61]

In order for a restraint of trade action to be successful, a number of hurdles must be crossed.[62]

• First the impugned action must be shown to constitute a restraint on the applicant's ability to carry out his or her trade (at which point the onus is on the person attacking it).[63] Such restraints are *prima facie* invalid unless they can be shown not to be unreasonable in the sense of their impact both on the parties involved and on the public generally.

• Secondly, if the measure is shown to be *prima facie* in restraint of trade, the person supporting the rule must show that it is justified having regard to the interests of the parties in the case (in which case the onus of proof is on the person justifying the measure). What is "reasonable' in any context (and the standard by which reasonableness can be gauged) remains a matter of

---

[59] For an excellent evaluation on this point see Lucey, "Regulating Post-Employment Relationships: The Restraint of Trade Doctrine Versus the Competition Act 2002", 25 *Dublin University Law Journal* (2003), p.124.

[60] *Nordenfelt v. Maxim Nordenfelt Guns and Ammunition Company* [1894] AC 535. See generally Lewis & Taylor, p.174, Steele, "The Doctrine of Restraint of Trade – How has it Contributed to the Development of Sports Law?", 3(3) *Sport and the Law Journal* (1995) 5.

[61] *Nordenfelt v. Maxim Nordenfelt Guns and Ammunition Company* [1894] A.C. 535 at 565.

[62] Lewis & Taylor, pp.175ff.

[63] See for example, *Greig v. Insole* [1978] 1 W.L.R. 302.

uncertainty, although it seems clear that for a measure to be deemed to be reasonable it must follow a legitimate objective and be proportionate thereto.[64] Moreover, it is clear that something can be reasonable in one era but unreasonable in a later era, and vice versa.[65]

- Finally, if the party supporting the rule manages to display that it *is* justified, *inter partes*, then the person challenging the rule may still seek to have it struck down by demonstrating that it is unreasonable having regard to the public interest.[66]

Equally, the doctrine does not exist as a device for challenging a decision of a governing body or club merely on the basis that it goes against a particular sportsperson or sports body. In other words it is a specific doctrine that exists for a specific purpose. Moreover, in applying the doctrine to sport, the courts are prepared to defer to what they perceive as the greater knowledge and experience of the governing bodies, and also tend to endorse the proposition that the more self-regulating sport can be, the better.[67] Thus it is far more likely that a successful challenge on restraint of trade grounds will be taken in respect of a new rule imposed by a governing body than in respect of the application of an existing rule.[68]

As far as professional sport is concerned, the doctrine - which potentially has very widespread application[69] – has, in practice, been raised in three sets of circumstances; first, where a sportsperson is being denied access to the profession, secondly where, as a result of disciplinary action he or she is being denied the possibility of engaging in his or her profession (for example where a sportsperson is suspended for two years from all sport for a positive doping offence) and thirdly, and perhaps most amorphously, where the rules of a governing body, or an existing agreement with a club prevent the sportsperson from exploiting his or her abilities to the greatest extent possible.[70] We will shortly consider these three sets of scenarios in turn, as they have applied,

---

[64] Lewis & Taylor, p.852.

[65] Stewart, "Restraint of Trade in Sport", 6(3) *Sport and the Law Journal* (1998) 41 at 44.

[66] In *Stevenage Borough v. Football League, Times*, August 1, 1996 Carnwath J. suggested that where sporting bodies were concerned, the second stage of this test might be omitted, such that the only relevant concern would be whether the decision was reasonable as regards the public interest.

[67] Stewart, "Restraint of Trade in Sport", 6(3) *Sport and the Law Journal* (1998) 41 at 43.

[68] *ibid.*, p.49.

[69] See for example Farrell, "Transfer Fees and Restraint of Trade", 5(3) *Sport and the Law Journal* (1997) 54 and by the same author, "Salary Caps and Restraint of Trade", 5(1) *Sport and the Law Journal* (1997) 53.

[70] See Steele, "The Doctrine of Restraint of Trade – How has it Contributed to the Development of Sports Law?", 3(3) *Sport and the Law Journal* (1995) 5 at 6ff for the view that the doctrine has also been important for sport in that it has helped to raise the profile of sport as a business.

most notably in England. Before this, however, we will look at the rather brief analysis afforded by the Irish courts to the issue of restraint of trade in sport.

2.2.1.1 The Irish position

In Ireland, the impact of this doctrine to sport has been limited – both because of the amateur nature of the majority of Irish sport, and also because there may be more effective constitutional (or competition law) remedies available to an Irish citizen in such circumstances. The major Irish restraint of trade case in this area is *Macken v. O'Reilly*,[71] a case which involved a challenge by well known Irish show jumper Eddie Macken to a requirement of the Irish equestrian federation preventing Irish show jumpers from riding non-Irish bred horses. He claimed that in as much as this rule prevented him from pursuing his career to its utmost potential (in that no matter how good a rider, his success will depend *inter alia* on his horse, and the pool from which he could select an ideal horse for himself was being severely restricted) it amounted to an unreasonable restraint of trade.

It is submitted that there is no doubt that the rule in this case *did* constitute a restraint of trade, hence the only really significant question was whether it was justifiable and thus reasonable. The federation argued that the rule was necessary to safeguard the future of the Irish horse breeding industry, and that it was its duty to support such industry by such a rule and hence that the rule was *intra vires* and reasonable. At first instance, the High Court held that the defendants had not discharged the onus of proving that the rule was reasonable and so struck down the rule. On appeal, the Supreme Court accepted the defendant's claim, holding that whereas the rule was against the private interests of the applicant this was more than offset by the public policy justifications in its favour.

There are perhaps two problems with this logic; first, the Supreme Court did not give sufficient consideration to the argument that the rule represented a disproportionate response to a perceived problem. Secondly, as Clark has noted, there is no provision in the doctrine, where a rule has been held to be unreasonable *inter partes* for it then to be saved by reference to its reasonableness as a matter of public interest.[72] Such prioritization of the public interest over the private needs of the parties would have been more appropriate had this been a judicial review action.[73] Moreover, it is submitted that it would

---

[71] [1979] I.L.R.M. 79. See Lucey, "Regulating Post-Employment Relationships: The Restraint of Trade Doctrine Versus the Competition Act 2002", 25 *Dublin University law Journal* (2003), p.124 at 126.

[72] See Clark, *Contract Law* (4th ed., Round Hall Sweet Maxwell, 1998), p.91.

[73] See Lucey, "Regulating Post-Employment Relationships: The Restraint of Trade Doctrine Versus the Competition Act 2002", 25 *Dublin University law Journal* (2003), p.124 at

be very difficult for the rule to be upheld under the microscope of either national or European competition law.

In *Clancy v. IRFU*[74] the former Irish rugby player Tom Clancy challenged an IRFU player mobility rule, which provided that if a player played for his club three times or more and then registered for another club for the following season he would not be allowed to play in a league match for his new club until after 31 December in the same year – a rule which applied both prospectively and retrospectively. The court *per* Morris J, upheld the rule, largely on the basis that the IRFU rules also provided for an internal appeal in such situations, and therefore that the impact of the rule was not disproportionate to its objective.[75] Equally, it is perhaps questionable, following the decision of the European Court of Justice in *Lehtonen and Castors Canada dry Namur-Braine v. Fédération Royale des Sociétés de Basketball and Ligue Belge-Belgische Liga*[76] (considered later in Chapter Eight), whether such a rule would withstand scrutiny under EC law.[77]

Finally, at the time of going to print an Irish case is ongoing in which the legitimacy of one aspect of the new FIFA transfer rules (considered in Chapter Nine) is being challenged. The plaintiff in the case is Alan Cawley, a 23 year old former Leeds United and Sheffield Wednesday player. Having returned from England, Mr. Cawley played for two seasons at UCD, and when his contract expired (and UCD were relegated from the Eircom Premier League), Cawley was approached by Shelbourne FC – one of the top League of Ireland clubs – and offered €500 per week to play for them. Cawley wished to play for Shelbourne but, because he was 23, under FAI rules (which derived from the FIFA rules) UCD were entitled to compensation for training him. The UCD club demanded €50,000, which was later reduced by an FAI tribunal to €20,000. Shelbourne refused to pay this figure and repudiated its agreement with Cawley.[78] As a result, Cawley issued High Court proceedings against the refusal of the National League to register him as a player, claiming that the imposition of the €20,000 fee which now, effectively accompanied him wherever he sought work constituted a severe restraint on trade and a breach of EU law.[79] In late

---

127 for the view that reliance on public interest concerns within restraint of trade analysis may provide a framework by which the doctrine of restraint of trade may be allowed to operate harmoniously with competition policy.

[74] [1995] 1 I.L.R.M. 193.

[75] As McCutcheon points out ("Judicial Control of Sporting Bodies; Recent Irish Experiences", 3 (2) *Sport and the Law Journal* (1995) 20 at 23), on the other hand, the court felt that the appeal procedure was itself flawed. This will be considered later in the section on fair procedures.

[76] Case C–176/96 [2000] E.C.R. I–2681.

[77] See McArdle, *From Boot Money to Bosman: Football, Society and the Law* (Cavendish, 2001), p.54.

[78] See "Club Disputes Fee for ex-UCD Player", *Irish Times*, April 15, 2004.

[79] Malone, "Cawley Plans Test Case", *Irish Times*, April 9, 2004.

April 2004 an interim deal was reached with the FAI allowing Cawley to register
with Shelbourne pending a full hearing of the action which will take place in
the autumn of 2004 and which has the capacity to throw the validity of the
new transfer system into jeopardy. The outcome is awaited with interest.

2.2.1.2 Denial of access to the profession

The first category of restraint of trade case then, involves the situation where
a club or more usually governing body is denying a sportsperson some form of
membership in circumstances where participation in that sport at a professional
level is conditional on such membership. What is involved here is complex,
mainly because of the fact that the courts are naturally reluctant to compel a
private body to accept a member whom they do not wish to accept and, as we
have seen, in Ireland and England the courts have generally classified sports
governing bodies as being private in nature despite their monopolistic control
over an entire profession.

In *Nagle v. Feilden*,[80] a female horse trainer was refused a trainer's license
by the jockey club by reason of her gender and claimed that such rules amounted
to an unreasonable restraint of trade. The High Court had struck out her claim,
which had originally been based on an alleged contract between Mrs. Nagle
and the Jockey Club. Lord Denning, however, returned the matter for trial on
a different basis – holding that restraint of trade rules can apply outside of
contractual relationships to cases where the rules of the governing body amount
to a quasi legislative code in an area.[81] As far as Lord Denning was concerned,
what was important in a case of this nature was not the presence or absence of
a written contract, but rather the right to work in a context where the governing
body essentially licensed that right.[82] In respect of such matters, said Lord
Denning, the governing body must act reasonably (in the sense of not acting
arbitrarily or capriciously).[83]

It may perhaps be said of Lord Denning that he was generally more
concerned with getting the right result than with ensuring the correct application
of legal principle in order to reach that result. Thus there is a certain amount of
controversy as to whether this may properly be seen as being a restraint of
trade case at all, given that there was not a contract in place between the plaintiff
and the defendant.[84] Equally, it is submitted that there is no good principle of

---

[80] [1966] 2 Q.B. 633. For analysis see Stewart *"Stevenage Borough FC v. The Football
League"*, 4(3) *Sport and the Law Journal* (1996) 110 at 115ff.

[81] The matter never actually proceeded to trial but was instead settled. See Stewart
"Stevenage Borough FC v. The Football League", 4(3) *Sport and the Law Journal* (1996)
110 at 116.

[82] See *Pharmaceutical Society of Great Britain v. Dickson* [1970] A.C. 403. See also Stewart,
"Restraint of Trade in Sport", 6(3) *Sport and the Law Journal* (1998) 41.

[83] 1966] 2 Q.B. 633. at 647.

[84] See Griffith Jones, p.66 and especially Stewart, "Restraint of Trade in Sport", 6(3) *Sport*

law excluding the doctrine of restraint of trade from situations where the rules of a body are restrictive of membership in an unreasonable fashion.[85] Moreover, the reluctance to apply the doctrine to the issue of membership of sports organisations derives from an over-emphasis on the "private' nature of sports governing bodies. Nonetheless, it would perhaps have been more satisfactory if the case could have been heard on a judicial review basis. Indeed from an Irish perspective, were such a case to arise today, there is little doubt that the plaintiff would be able to obtain relief on either constitutional or competition law grounds.

Admission rules were also considered in *Newport Association Football Club v. Football Association of Wales Limited.*[86] Here, the Welsh FA had a rule in place that hindered Welsh clubs from joining the more lucrative English football leagues. The Welsh FA argued that this was no more than was reasonable to protect the interests of the future of Welsh soccer. The court, however, disagreed, holding that the FA had gone beyond what was reasonably necessary to achieve these objectives and hence that the decision constituted an unreasonable restraint of trade.[87] Moreover, the court held that in such a case, the court could offer the applicant declaratory and injunctive relief, despite the argument that in as much as a contract in unlawful restraint of trade is simply void and unenforceable there should be no further cause of action arising out of it.

The law was less favourable to the applicant in the important if rather confusing case of *Stevenage Borough v. Football League.*[88] In this case the applicant club had finished at the top of the Football Conference in England, and should thus have been promoted to the Football League and Torquay FC

---

and the Law Journal (1998) 41 at 117ff. For judicial comment on the validity of *Nagle v. Feilden* see *inter alia Watson v. Prager* [1991] 1 W.L.R. 726, in which it was seen as a proper restraint of trade case and *R v. Jockey Club ex parte RAM Racecourses* [1993] 2 All E.R. 225 and *R v. Disciplinary Committee of the Jockey Club ex parte Aga Khan* [1993] 1 W.L.R. 909, in which it was seen as falling outside the scope of the restraint of trade doctrine.

[85] *Faramus v. Film Artistes Association* [1964] A.C. 925. See Lewis & Taylor, p.177 for the view that the doctrine applies not merely to the governing body's rules but also to its decisions and actions.

[86] [1995] 2 All ER 87. See Lewis & Taylor, p.181, Steele, "The Doctrine of Restraint of Trade – How has it Contributed to the Development of Sports Law?", 3(3) *Sport and the Law Journal* (1995) 5 at 9, Stewart, "Restraint of Trade in Sport", 6(3) *Sport and the Law Journal* (1998) 41 at 42ff.

[87] See also *R v. Football Association of Wales, ex parte Flint Town United Football Club* [1991] C.O.D. 44.

[88] [1997] 9 Admin LR 109. For comment see Alderson, "Admission Criteria: *Stevenage Borough FC v. The Football League*", 4(3) *Sport and the Law Journal* (1996) 107, Steele, "The Doctrine of Restraint of Trade – How has it Contributed to the Development of Sports Law?", 3(3) *Sport and the Law Journal* (1995) 5 at 9 and Stewart "*Stevenage Borough FC v. The Football League*", 4(3) *Sport and the Law Journal* (1996) 110.

relegated to the conference. FA rules required, however that promoted clubs enjoyed a certain financial status (their audited accounts needed to show a net surplus) and that their grounds has a certain seating capacity (there needed to be a ground capacity of 6,000 with 1,000 seats) *at the end of the December previous to the date on which they were promoted.* At that time Stevenage did not meet the terms of these rules,[89] and hence the following April when Stevenage finished top of the conference, the Football League refused to admit Stevenage and instead, Torquay retained its place. Stevenage challenged the admission rules, pointing out that many existing clubs within the lower regions of the Football League would not enjoy the financial status required of newly promoted clubs, and arguing that the requirements were unreasonable, were not necessary to protect the interests of the Football League, and moreover, that the December deadline was unreasonably early for clubs that found themselves in the position of Stevenage Borough during the 1995–96 season.[90]

Both the High Court and the Court of Appeal refused to exercise their discretion to grant the relief sought, citing what they saw as undue delay on the part of Stevenage, which had waited until the end of the season in which it won promotion before challenging the rules of the league. The High Court held rather that such a claim should have been brought at the beginning of the 1995-196 season.[91] The Court of Appeal affirmed this conclusion, holding that if it were to find for Stevenage FC at this juncture it would cause unreasonable hardship to Torquay FC. This conclusion seems somewhat strange. It is surely unlikely that a team would challenge a rule of the football league simply in anticipation of possible promotion to such league.[92] Indeed there is an argument that they would not have adequate standing to make such challenge.[93]

Importantly from our perspective, both the High Court and Court of Appeal

---

[89] Stevenage had expected to meet the December 1995 deadline, but there had been problems attaining local authority permission. Nonetheless there was no question but that the stadium would be ready for the 1996–1997 season. See Alderson, "Admission Criteria; *Stevenage Borough FC v. The Football League*, 4(3) *Sport and the Law Journal* (1996) 107 at 108.

[90] As the trial judge Carnwath J. noted, there had never previously been a case where a private organization like the football league was forced to admit a member against its will. Stewart, "*Stevenage Borough FC v. The Football League*", 4(3) *Sport and the Law Journal* (1996) 110 at 111. This is perhaps to ignore the inherently "public" nature of the business of professional soccer in the UK and the monopolistic control exercised by the Football League.

[91] Alderson, "Admission Criteria; *Stevenage Borough FC v. The Football League*, 4(3) *Sport and the Law Journal* (1996) 107 at 109.

[92] The Stevenage manager, Paul Fairclough argued that "If you go on holiday in July you don't pack your suitcase in December". See Alderson, "Admission Criteria; *Stevenage Borough FC v. The Football League*, 4(3) *Sport and the Law Journal* (1996) 107 at 108.

[93] For criticism see Moore, pp.134–136.

engaged in some analysis of the application of the restraint of trade doctrine to this case. The High Court, was not concerned with the fact that what was at stake was an alleged restraint of trade inherent in the admission rules of a private body. In what may be seen as a somewhat unorthodox application of the doctrine,[94] it accepted that the requirement that the club carry out ground improvements before being certain of promotion and the relevant financial criteria were "open to objection" as being in restraint of trade. Nonetheless Carnwath J. did not find that they had been shown to have been sufficiently objectionable that they could be deemed to violate the doctrine – given that case-law does seem to indicate that where admission issues are at stake, the body refusing admission must be shown to have acted in an "arbitrary or capricious manner".[95] What was unusual was that Carnwath J. noted that the powers exercised by the football league were exercised in the public interest, and felt that, on this basis, the "reasonableness' test (in terms of justifying any restraint of trade) could itself assess merely whether the decision was reasonable *as a matter of public interest* and could safely ignore the question whether it was justifiable *inter partes*. Apart from going against usual application of the doctrine, this approach of analyzing the issue on a fundamentally public law basis, leads, it is submitted to the logical conclusion that because of the public nature of sports bodies' decisions, the appropriate remedy for a challenge thereto is by way of judicial review.[96] As Lewis & Taylor point out, restraint of trade is usually regarded as a private law concept, and hence public law and public interest considerations that would arise in a judicial review action are less appropriate in this context.[97]

On appeal, the Court of Appeal noted Carnwath J.'s comments but neither endorsed nor rejected them, merely stating that it was essentially being asked to interfere with the self-regulation powers of a sports governing body, and to do so retrospectively by striking down an existing governing body rule – something that it would frankly be reluctant to do.[98] The Court of Appeal further held that the perceived delay on the part of Stevenage Borough in bringing the case militated against the exercise by the court of a discretionary power in its favour.

It should be noted that the challenge of Stevenage Borough was also brought on competition law grounds. The case was, however, decided before the new competition law dispensation in England, and therefore the challenge was brought under EC Competition law principles. Because of this fact, it was incumbent on the applicants to demonstrate that their case had some cross-

---

[94] See Lewis & Taylor, p.183.

[95] *Nagle v. Feilden* [1966] 2 Q.B. 633. See Stewart, "*Stevenage Borough FC v. The Football League*", 4(3) *Sport and the Law Journal* (1996) 110 at 111.

[96] Griffith-Jones, p.49.

[97] Lewis & Taylor, p.185.

[98] Alderson, "Admission Criteria: *Stevenage Borough FC v. The Football League*", 4(3) *Sport and the Law Journal* (1996) 107 at 109.

border element to it. They attempted to do so by claiming that if Stevenage Borough was granted membership of the Football League it might soon (through promotion) wind its way up to the Premiership, and might eventually finish high enough in the premiership that it might qualify for a European competition such as the UEFA cup or the UEFA Champions' League. The court rejected this claim – largely on the basis that the possibility of such an occurrence was simply too remote, given Stevanage's lowly status as a conference side.[99] Equally, it is entirely arguable that were the case to arise today, then a claim should be brought under the *new* UK Competition legislation, where there would be no need for Stevenage to display a cross border element to their case.

Finally, as we consider admission rules, it is necessary to look at *McInnes v. Onslow-Fane and Others.*[100] The plaintiff in this case (who, over time had had a number of licenses revoked by the BBBC) was refused a manager's license by the BBBC (without which he could not operate as a boxing manager in the UK), without any reasons being given for the refusal. The court *per* Megarry VC held that there were various different categories of case in which challenges could be made to decisions of governing bodies, which would demand different levels of fairness on the part of those governing bodies. Whereas sports governing bodies might be subject to requirements of natural justice in dealing with applications for membership, these requirements would be applied with considerably more stringency in forfeiture or disciplinary cases, especially where one of the parties had a legitimate expectation in respect of the matter. There is, however, a suggestion in the case that if there is no evidence offered as to why the applicant is unsuitable for membership then this is itself, strong evidence that the rejection of his application is unreasonable. On the other hand, the court also stressed that it would be reluctant to review the honest decision of a body charged with governing a sport, where the issue of applications to gain admission to membership of that body were at issue.

2.2.1.3 Suspension as an unreasonable restraint of trade

The second major category of restraint cases are those involving disciplinary matters.[101] As the English courts in *Gasser v. Stinson*[102] and *Wilander v. ITF*[103]

---

[99] Stewart, *"Stevenage Borough FC v. The Football League"*, 4(3) *Sport and the Law Journal* (1996) 110 at 112.
[100] [1978] 1 W.L.R. 1520. See Stewart, "Restraint of Trade in Sport", 6(3) *Sport and the Law Journal* (1998) 41.
[101] Steele, "The Doctrine of Restraint of Trade – How has it Contributed to the Development of Sports Law?", 3(3) *Sport and the Law Journal* (1995) 5 at 10. See also Cox, "Legalisation of Drug use in Sport" [2002] *International Sports Law Review* 77.
[102] Unreported, Queen's Bench, June 15, 1988.
[103] [1997] 2 Lloyd's Rep. 293.

noted, all rules restricting a professional sportsperson from playing – even the "red card' in soccer – are prima facie in restraint of trade.[104] It is virtually inconceivable in the absence of proof of *mala fides*, that a court would set aside the decision of a referee on these grounds. Thus where such challenges have been made, they have tended to focus on the rules of the governing body, be it the rules governing disciplinary processes or the rules providing for punishments in the event of a finding of a disciplinary offence. The question, once again, is whether such rules are reasonable, both as regards the individual whose trade is being restrained, and as regards the public generally.[105] It is possible to find in the case law a general trend to give the benefit of any doubts to the governing body, such that an honest decision thereof will only be overturned in extreme circumstances.[106]

In *Wilander v. Tobin and ITF*,[107] certain drug testing rules of the International Tennis Federation were challenged as *unreasonable* restraints of trade on the grounds *inter alia* that they reversed certain burdens of proof and provided for mandatory sentencing.[108] The Court of Appeal while admitting its concern with any rules that reversed burdens of proof – the presumption of innocence being such a cornerstone of English criminal law - still found these rules to be legally valid because of the level of procedural safeguards in place to protect the athlete, particularly the fact that testing would take place at an IOC accredited laboratory. Perhaps more importantly, in *Gasser v. Stinson*,[109] Scott J upheld the IAAF doping rules, concluding that whereas they constituted a restraint of trade, they were justified by the need of sport to be able to formulate a tough and effective anti-doping policy. It is arguably a criticism of these cases, however, given the level of the restraint of trade which would arise if someone was suspended for two years following a doping offence, that insufficient analysis was made both of whether the anti-doping rules were justified in professional sport, and also, given the stringency described in

---

[104] It is interesting that in *Gasser v. Stinson* Scott J allowed the amateur athlete plaintiff to invoke the doctrine or restraint of trade on the basis of the degree of sponsorship that Ms. Gasser was likely to attract. See Griffith Jones, p.47. On the other hand in *Edwards v. BAF* [1998] 2 C.M.L.R. 363, the court doubted whether the plaintiff – an amateur athlete – could invoke the doctrine of restraint of trade.

[105] *Nordenfeld v. Maxim Nordenfeld* [1894] A.C. 535.

[106] *Stevenage Borough FC v. Football League, McInnes v. Onslow Fane* (both *supra*), *Cowley v. Heatley, Times*, July 24, 1986. Stewart (Stewart, "Restraint of Trade in Sport", 6(3) *Sport and the Law Journal* (1998) 41 at 49) says that as a matter of practice, restraint of trade will be likely to fail in most cases when used to challenge disciplinary decisions of sporting bodies.

[107] Unreported, Queen's Bench, March 19, 1996 (See Lewis & Taylor, p.180).

[108] They were also later challenged as being in violation of EU law. See 4 (2) *Sport and the Law Journal* (1996) 81. The Court of Appeal eventually held that despite the absence of an internal system of appeal, such rules were proportionate as there were other avenues of redress, including for example recourse to the courts. [1997] EuLR 265 at 274–275.

[109] Unreported, Queen's Bench, June 15, 1988.

Chapter Three, whether they represent a proportionate response to the supposed needs of anti-doping policy.[110]

On the other hand in *Conteh v. Onslow Fane*,[111] the court of appeal did grant an injunction to restrain the BBBC from engaging in disciplinary proceedings against a boxer pending a court determination of an action taken by him against a former manager, during the course of which the issues at stake in the disciplinary proceedings would be largely determined. In other words, the injunction was granted to prevent duplicity of actions. On this basis Stewart[112] concludes that whereas the notion of restraint of trade is perhaps not hugely likely to succeed in simple challenges to the application of existing disciplinary rules of governing bodies, it is more likely to be successfully invoked against something of an *ad hoc* reaction by a sporting authority to an action which they dislike, and especially where there is any suggestion of discrimination in the application rules

2.2.1.4 *Restrictions on the sportsperson's ability to exploit his or her ability for financial reward*

The third category of case in which the doctrine has had an impact is where the applicant rather than being denied admission to a profession or being suspended or banned from engaging in the profession, is merely having a restriction placed on his capacity fully to earn money and otherwise to fulfill himself within the profession. Thus in *Johnston v. Cliftonville FC and Irish Football League*,[113] the applicant successfully obtained a declaration from the Northern Irish High Court that the IFL rules were invalid insofar as they imposed a cap on the amount of money that he could earn from the sport in terms of wages and bonuses.[114]

Arguably the most famous restraint of trade case in British sports law is that of *Eastham v. Newcastle United Football Club*.[115] At issue was an FA

---

[110] See Cox, "Legalisation of Drug use in Sport" [2002] *International Sports Law Review* 77.

[111] Unreported, CA, June 26 1975.

[112] Stewart, "Restraint of Trade in Sport", 6 (3) *Sport and the Law Journal*, 41 at 49.

[113] [1984] 2 N.J.I.B. 9; [1984] N.I. 9.

[114] In *Wimbledon FC v. Football League* (FA Arbitration, January 29, 2002, see Lewis & Taylor, p.174) the FA arbitration panel held that a rule that prevented Wimbledon FC from moving out of the area from which it took its name to Milton Keynes was in restraint of trade, with the view being expressed that Wimbledon's need to find a new home in which to play its matches far outweighed any arguments in support of the rule.

[115] Lewis & Taylor, pp.850ff [1964] 1 Ch. 413. See Griffith Jones at 41ff, Steele, "The Doctrine of Restraint of Trade – How has it Contributed to the Development of Sports Law?", 3(3) *Sport and the Law Journal* (1995) 5 at 6ff, Stewart, "Restraint of Trade in Sport", 6(3) *Sport and the Law Journal* (1998) 41 at 44ff, Farrell, "Transfer Fees and Restraint of Trade", 5(3) *Sport and the Law Journal* (1997) 54. Similarly see *Cook v. FA, Times*, March 24, 1972, *Buckley v. Tutty* [1971] 125 C.L.R. 353.

rule, known as the "retain and transfer' rule whereby a club could hang on to its players even after their contracts had expired until it decided to negotiate their transfer with another club. If a player was retained in this fashion, he was prevented from joining another club anywhere in the world. All he could do was to re-sign for the club, (on an offer made on its terms) and if he *failed* to re-sign, he would get no wages. This essentially meant that a club could prevent a former player from playing in the football league indefinitely, which, to state the case in business terms, meant that his pursuit of his career was dramatically stymied.

The plaintiff in this case was an international footballer who wished to transfer from Newcastle United to Arsenal, but, owing to the fact that Newcastle did not want to sell him, he was placed on the list of retained players under the retain and transfer procedure. The plaintiff claimed that this rule constituted an unreasonable restraint of trade, in that it effectively prevented him from engaging in his career in England without the consent of his club. Indeed his counsel said that the transfer system effectively regarded football players as chattels. In agreeing the court granted a declaratory judgement not only against Newcastle United, with whom the plaintiff had a contract, but also against the FA and the Football League, with whom he did not.[116] Interestingly, however, Wilberforce J's concern was exclusively with the retention aspect of the rules, which, given that they operated with no maximum period and completely halted a player's capacity to "better' himself, by pursuing his career with a different club, quite clearly restrained his capacity to engage in trade, and, (it may be incontrovertibly argued), did so in a fashion that the defendant bodies had been unable to justify.

On the other hand, and in an interesting precursor to the *Bosman* ruling, Wilberforce J. did not find the transfer aspect of the rules to be objectionable. He accepted that the transfer system would restrict the capacity of a player to pursue his trade (in that he could only move when another club was prepared to pay for him to do so), but he felt that the system could be justified in the interest of ensuring that poorer clubs would get some needed revenue in return for a successful player.[117] Importantly, however, Wilberforce J. struck down the *combined* retain and transfer ruling, noting that the system as it stood was inherently "employer focused', and represented a significant imbalance of power between employers (clubs) and employees (players). As a result, the

---

[116] See Grayson, "The Ralph Banks Road to *Bosman* via *Eastham, Greig v. Insole* and Beyond", 3 (2) *Sport and the Law Journal* (1995) 19.

[117] Wilberforce J was less receptive to the arguments of the FA and the other defendants as to the importance of the "retain" rules for the governance of English soccer. Indeed he made the point that however important the rules appeared (from the employer's perspective), this would not prevent the courts from assessing whether they were justified bearing mind the impact on the employee. See Stewart, "Restraint of Trade in Sport", 6(3) *Sport and the Law Journal* (1998) 41 at 45.

FA modified its rules, such that whereas a player was free to leave his club at the end of his contract, equally the club could still charge a fee for him.[118]

More recently, in *Greig v. Insole*,[119] a private sports promoting company (World Series Cricket Pty Ltd) under the management of Kerry Packer, engaged 34 of the world's top cricketers to play in a series of test matches that would take place. Such a move struck at the heart of the hitherto accepted rule that official cricket matches (for which there is a reasonably limited television audience) would involve national teams competing against each other in fixtures organised by the international cricket governing body (ICC) and the relevant domestic federations. In an attempt to bolster their control of the sport the ICC and the English Test and County Cricket Board (TCCB) made a rule that anyone competing in such unofficial matches would be disqualified from playing in official test matches (and in England, in county matches). Three well known international players challenged these rules claiming that they were made *ultra vires* and constituted an unreasonable restraint of trade.

The court accepted that such rules were clearly prima facie in restraint of trade, in that they restricted the ability of these players to exploit their abilities for financial gain. Slade J. also found, (despite the arguments from the defendant bodies that the "rival test series' represented a threat to the economic survival of world cricket), that this restraint of trade was not justified. This was because the impact on the players was substantial (especially as the ban on their ability to play *county* cricket represented an overall threat to their livelihoods) and also because the threat to cricket generally and in England in particular was not as great as the defendants made it out to be. It was possible that Australian cricket might be affected by the current proposed series, in that the matches were to take place in Australia but it would not have such an impact in England. It was also possible that if the notion of this unofficial series and others like it were to become popular, that there might be a more significant threat to cricket – and the judge suggested that a prospective ban on *future* players signing up to the unofficial tour might be acceptable. But the retrospective ban on players who had already signed up to the tour was a clear and unreasonable restraint of trade.

Finally, it should be noted that the doctrine is not confined to cases in which a player is challenging a governing body. In *Watson v. Prager*,[120] the boxer Michael Watson, whom we will encounter in more tragic circumstances

---

[118] Farrell, "Transfer Fees and Restraint of Trade", 5(3) *Sport and the Law Journal* (1997) 54 at 55.

[119] [1978] 1 W.L.R. 302. See Lewis & Taylor, p.179, Steele, "The Doctrine of Restraint of Trade – How has it Contributed to the Development of Sports Law?", 3(3) *Sport and the Law Journal* (1995) 5 at 7, Stewart, "Restraint of Trade in Sport", 6(3) *Sport and the Law Journal* (1998) 41 at 45.

[120] [1990] 1 WLR 726. See Steele, "The Doctrine of Restraint of Trade – How has it Contributed to the Development of Sports Law?", 3(3) *Sport and the Law Journal* (1995) 5 at 8.

in Chapter Five, successfully sued his former manager Mickey Duff in respect of the contract between the two. Duff was obliged under the terms of the contract *inter alia* to arrange matches for Watson on terms as favourable as possible for Watson, and Watson was obliged not to enter into agreements with any other parties without obtaining Duff's consent. This contract was extended (as provided under its own terms) as Watson became more successful. Watson claimed, however, that Duff was actually the promoter of the fights in which Watson took part, and therefore there was a clear conflict of interests as regards Duff's obligation to get fights for Watson on terms most favourable to the latter. Scott J. felt that this dual obligation, which would inevitably work against Watson's financial interests was thereby in unreasonable restraint of trade and was void.

2.2.1.5 The impact of competition law

It is arguable that in as much as competition law provides applicants with a straightforward remedy to deal with anti-competitive practices (that are also in restraint of trade) without having to deal with any of the uncertainties imposed on the restraint of trade doctrine by its development in the courts, that this therefore should be the preferred approach of an applicant in such circumstances in the future. Indeed it is notable that in a number of recent sports cases in England, the court appeared either to prefer to deal with such matters on a competition law basis, or alternatively to regard the competition law and restraint of trade issues to be so similar as to be effectively indivisible.[121] The nature of competition law challenges to such rules is considered in Chapter Nine.

2.2.2 The constitutional right to earn a livelihood

In Ireland a professional sportsperson or indeed an amateur who is indirectly earning money from sport, (for instance through sponsorship or image rights) and who has had his or her career ended or interrupted by a governing body or club, (typically where [s]he has been suspended as the result of a disciplinary process, or where the governing body that has exclusive control of the operation of professional competition in a sport does not permit him or her to compete in its competitions[122]) may seek to challenge the decision or action of the relevant

---

[121] *Williams and Cardiff RFC v. Pugh*, unreported Queen's Bench, July 23, 1997, unreported, Court of Appeal, August 1, 1997, *Hendry and Others v. World Professional Billiards and Snooker Association* [2002] Eu LR 770, [2002] *International Sports Law Review*, 1. See Harris, "Abusive Sports Governing Bodies", *Competition Law Journal* (2002), p.2.

[122] In England this kind of situation has been dealt with by the doctrine of restraint of trade. See *Nagle v. Feilden* [1966] 2 Q.B. 633.

body on the basis that it represents an unjustified violation of his or her constitutional right to work and earn a livelihood.

The protection within the Irish constitution of a right to work and earn a livelihood is of uncertain pedigree, with different judges regarding the right as an unspecified one contained within Article 40.3.1 of the Constitution, or alternatively as an aspect of the right to private property within Article 40.3.2 and Article 43.[123] Importantly in the present context, however, all Irish constitutional rights apply both against the state and also against private bodies and private persons,[124] including, obviously, sports governing bodies.

The right is neither absolute,[125] not does it entitle one to a particular means of earning a livelihood.[126] Rather it may be restricted in the common good, provided that such restriction is proportionate to the objective sought to be achieved.[127] In practice in a sporting context this would seem to mean for example that an athlete who was suspended by the relevant sports body for drug taking, could not claim that the strict liability nature of the governing body's anti-doping policy violated his right to earn a livelihood, in that this kind of policy would undoubtedly be justified by the public interest in ridding sport of drugs.[128] On the other hand, if an athlete accused of doping was subjected to disciplinary sanction in circumstances where there was insufficient protection afforded to his rights, or where the investigation into his case was procedurally flawed, he could potentially succeed in such a claim.[129]

An athlete may also seek to invoke other constitutional rights against the exercise by a club or governing body of its administration rules – notably the right to freedom of association. In *O'Donohoe v. O'Baroid & Quirke*,[130] the plaintiff was a young Gaelic Football player, who wished to transfer from a small team in Clonmel to a larger team in the village with whom he would be able to play more senior club football. The local GAA board, who alone had authority to sanction such transfers, refused to do so on the basis that the Tipperary board had some years previously adopted a rule (ostensibly aimed at protecting junior clubs from a mass exodus of young players) permitting

---

[123] *Murtagh Properties v. Cleary* [1972] I.R. 330, *Murphy v. Stewart* [1973] I.R. 97, *Attorney General v. Paperlink* [1984] I.L.R.M. 373, *Article 26 and the Employment Equality Bill, 1996, Re* [1997] 2 I.R. 321.

[124] *Meskell v. CIE* [1973] I.R. 21, *Glover v. BLN Ltd.* [1973] I.R. 75.

[125] *Article 26 and the Employment Equality Bill, 1996, Re* [1997] 2 I.R. 321, *Hand v. Dublin Corporation* [1991] 1 I.R. 409.

[126] *AG v. Paperlink* [1984] I.L.R.M. 373, *Greally v. Minister for Education (No.2)* [1999] 1 I.R. 1.

[127] *Cox v. Ireland* [1992] 2 I.R. 503.

[128] For a similar conclusion in the English courts, see *Gasser v. Stinson, op. cit.* and *Wilander v. Tobin* [1997] 2 Lloyd's Rep. 293.

[129] As we shall see in the next chapter, this is also the approach taken in matters of this kind by the Court of Arbitration for Sport.

[130] High Court, unreported, McCracken J., April 23, 1999.

clubs in Clonmel to opt out of the transfer market for what was ultimately an uncertain duration. Counsel for the plaintiff claimed that the rule in question violated the plaintiff's constitutional right to freedom of association. The court rejected this argument largely on the grounds that the club which the applicant wished to join was not prepared to accept him, if doing so would violate the rules of the local GAA board.[131]

2.2.3 Breach of contract

If an athlete is in a contractual relationship with the body making the impugned decision or action, then there are two possible grounds for challenging the decision on a breach of contract basis. First, where the body does not act in accordance with its rules, then it is simply breaching the contract and relief may be sought on this basis. Secondly where the body acts unfairly, then it violates an implied term in the contract guaranteeing fair procedures.[132]

For this reason, it is plainly a pivotal question as to whether the person challenging the decision of a sporting body is in a contractual relationship with that body. In *Modahl v. British Athletic Federation*,[133] the appellant had been a member of a particular British athletics club. The club was affiliated to the British Athletics Federation (BAF), which was in turn affiliated to the International Amateur Athletics Federation (IAAF). The appellant had tested positive for testosterone and had been banned for four years by a disciplinary panel appointed by the respondent, but this suspension was lifted on appeal to a BAF appeal panel. She now sued claiming damages for breach of contract, on the basis of an allegation that the original disciplinary panel had been biased against her.

In the High Court, Douglas Brown J. rejected her claim, *inter alia,* on the basis of his conclusion that there was no contract between her and the respondents, deriving from the affiliation of her club to the BAF.[134] On appeal, she claimed that the requisite contractual nexus could be found in three separate factors, namely her membership of an affiliated club, her participation in an athletics meeting for which BAF permission was necessary, and/or her voluntary submission to BAF rules. The Court of Appeal accepted that over a period of many years she had accepted that if she entered athletic meetings under the

---

[131] Generally on this point see *Alwyn Treherne v. Amateur Boxing Association of England* [2001] 3 I.S.L.R. 231, [2002] All E.R. (D) 144.

[132] *Glover v. BLN Ltd.* [1973] I.R. 75, *Garvey v. Ireland* [1981] I.R. 75.

[133] [2002] 1 W.L.R. 1192.

[134] *Modahl v. British Athletic Federation*, Queens Bench, December 14, 2000. See Farrell, "Diane Modahl v. The Law of Contract", 9 (1) *Sport and the Law Journal* (2001) 100, Stoner, "Contractual Harmony", 8 (4) *Sports Law Administration and Practice* (August 2001) 1. This appeared to go against the line of authority in *Korda v. ITF* [1999] All E.R. (D) 84.

auspices of the defendant she would be subject to its rules. It also accepted that the respondent accepted responsibility to administer those rules fairly. Hence it could be inferred from all three of the factors submitted by Ms Modahl that she and the respondent were involved in a contractual relationship, with the BAF rules constituting the terms thereof. There is, however, an implication in *Modahl* that there is no guarantee (in different circumstances) that a contract between athlete A and organisation C would always be found simply because A is a member of Club B and club B is affiliated to organisation C.

Equally in the Irish context there is less need to find such a contractual link, in that any such claim could be framed as one based on an alleged breach of the athlete's constitutional right to earn a livelihood. Moreover, as the Court of Appeal noted in *Modahl*, even if no contract of employment was found, it retained the right to grant injunctive and declaratory relief where a person's right to work was at issue.[135] Finally, the courts may simply assume jurisdiction of the case on the basis of the athlete's consensual submission to the authority of the governing body.[136]

Having said all this it should, however, be noted that because the relationship between the governing body and the athlete *is* typically regarded as contractual in nature, the courts are reluctant to intrude in, or review the operation of such a relationship. The preferred view of the courts is that matters arising in the relationship between the sports body and the athlete should be resolved ideally by internal procedures and not by recourse to the courts.[137]

2.2.4 Irrationality

In both *Bolger v. Osborne* and *Moloney v. Bolger*, the High Court made it clear that whether an action proceeds via judicial review or plenary summons, a challenge on the merits of the decision (rather than the decision making procedure) will be sustained if the decision was irrational in the sense of being unsupported by evidence before the decision maker.[138] Thus the court will not strike down a decision on its merits simply because it feels that it is bad, or

---

[135] Generally see Stoner, "Modahl – The Last Word?", 9 (1) *Sports Law Administration and Practice* (February 2002) 1.

[136] *Gasser v. Stinson*, unreported, Queen's Bench 15 June, 1988.

[137] *Enderby Town Football Club v. FA* [1971] 1 Ch. 591, *Calvin v. Carr* [1980] A.C. 574.

[138] This is the standard laid down in *O'Keeffe v. An Bord Pleanála* [1993] 1 I.R. 39. For the English perspective see Beloff, p.184. Thus in *Wheeler v. Leicester City Council* [1985] 1 A.C. 1054, [1985] 2 All E.R. 1106, [1985] 3 W.L.R. 335 (see Griffith Jones, *op. cit.*, p.50ff) the respondents were deemed to have acted unreasonably (under the standard in *Associated Provincial Picture Houses Limited v. Wednesbury Corporation* [1948] 1 K.B. 223) in refusing to allow Leicester RFC to use its facilities on the basis that three of its players had gone on tour in South Africa during the apartheid related ban on such sports tours.

that it would have made a different decision on the evidence as presented. Experience in other areas of public law where courts recognize the superiority of the knowledge of the governing body, indicates that it the onus of proving such irrationality is a very heavy one indeed.[139] Nonetheless it may well be that in respect of disciplinary issues, because so much is at stake, a decision may be challenged on its merits in cases where there are significant discrepancies in the evidence supporting it – as for example in doping cases where there are major problems with the chain of custody of the impugned sample.[140]

As has been mentioned, the most important element of all these challenges is the fact that the sporting body is alleged to have acted otherwise than in accordance with fair procedures. For the rest of this chapter we will consider what this entails.

2.3 Fair Procedures and Sporting Bodies

As an introductory point it should again be noted that the courts both in Ireland and in England are highly reluctant to strike down decisions of sporting bodies, for want of fair procedures, essentially on the basis that governing bodies are reckoned to be expert in the governance of their sports and also that it makes sense as a matter of social policy to allow sport to be self-regulating.[141] This way of thinking was famously encapsulated by Lord Denning in *Enderby Town Football Club v. Football Association*,[142] in his aphorism that "justice can often be done better by a good layman than a bad lawyer."[143] So, for example in *Gasser v. Stinson* and *Wilander and Novacek v. Tobin*,[144] courts in England declined to rule that anti-doping rules that operated on a strict liability basis were unfair, (despite the fact that the judges had obvious misgivings about the consequences of such rules) on the basis that they were necessary if sport was to forge the kind of anti-doping policy that it wished.

On the other hand, the law does retain some measure of control over the

---

[139] It is also clear that a decision can be reviewed on its merits for adversely affecting the rights of a third party. See *Matthews v. Irish Coursing Club and Hogan* [1993] 1 I.R. 346.

[140] See for instance *Modahl v. British Athletic Federation,* Queen's Bench, June 28, 1996 and more generally, Grayson, "Drugs in Sport – Chains of Custody", Vol.145 No.6670 *New Law Journal* (January 20, 1995) 44.

[141] See for example *Williams v. Reason* [1988] 1 W.L.R. 96.

[142] [1971] Ch. 591, [1971] 1 All E.R. 215.

[143] As McCutcheon points out (Greenfield and Osborn, *op. cit.*, p.115), Lord Denning qualified this comment by saying that it applied: "Where no points of law are likely to arise." Generally see Woodhouse, 1 *Sport and the Law Journal* (1993) 1 at 2–3, Beloff, *op. cit.*, p.222ff.

[144] For analysis see Moore, *op. cit.*, p.137.

actions of governing bodies,[145] requiring that where the operation of a rule is
likely to have significant consequences for that athlete (most obviously where
his sport is also his career), then the relevant body in creating and applying the
rule should afford him an appropriate standard of fair procedures. From the
law's perspective, the sports body may be the expert in the area of governing
sport but this does not make it an expert in the area of fair procedures, especially
given that there is a risk that its exclusive agenda will be to protect its own
interests. This, however, by itself is not good enough, for as McCutcheon
points out:[146]

> "Where serious disciplinary matters are involved, the fundamental dictates
> of justice demand scrupulous adherence to the highest standard of
> procedural and substantive fairness."

There is no set level of fair procedures to which all athletes are entitled. Rather
it will vary from case to case depending on the impact of the impugned decision
on the person affected thereby.[147] Thus in *Quirke v. Bord Luthchleas na
hÉireann (BLE)*[148] where an athlete was facing a suspension from competitive
athletics for a period which would cover the then forthcoming Olympic Games
in Seoul in the summer of 1988, the High Court ruled that the highest standards
of fair procedures would have to be in place, to the point where it would be
necessary for the governing body to act judicially, because the athlete was
having a lifetime's ambitions put in jeopardy.[149] On the other hand, where a
decision in respect of an athlete does not constitute a punishment, or where
the consequences are not particularly onerous, the governing body has more
discretion in respect of it.[150] In the Irish context, where most sport is amateur,
this will mean that the standards required are not particularly excessive (though
this is not to devalue the importance of pride and passion in a sporting context),
however the logical corollary of this is that as sport becomes increasingly
professionalised, and hence as more and more is at stake, higher standards of
fair procedures will be demanded.[151]

---

[145] *Baker v. Jones* [1954] 2 All E.R. 553, *St Johnstone FC v. Scottish Football Association*
[1965] S.L.T. 171.
[146] Greenfield and Osborn, *op. cit.*, pp.116–117.
[147] *Flanagan v. UCD* [1988] I.R. 724. See Griffith Jones *op. cit.*, P.65.
[148] [1988] I.R. 83.
[149] Greenfield and Osborn, *op. cit.*, p.119. See also *Kiely v. Minister for Social Welfare*
[1977] I.R. 267 at 281, for the conclusion that whereas quasi-judicial tribunals may on
occasion depart from strict courtroom procedure in respect of, for example, rules of
evidence, they may not act in such a way as to imperil a fair hearing or fair result.
[150] See McCutcheon, "Judicial Review of Sporting Bodies: Recent Irish Experiences", 3
(2) Sport *and the Law Journal* (1995) 20 at 23. This was essentially the logic of the
court in *Quirke v. BLE*, where the court was concerned that the relevant suspension was
a punishment in itself rather than an interim measure pending a hearing.
[151] This was the conclusion of Ebsworth J. in *Jones v. Welsh Rugby Football Union*,

From the point of view of a governing body or club, there are three broad areas of activity in which fair procedures should be observed, namely;

– in the creation of rules,

– in the application of rules,

– in the operation of a disciplinary process conducted pursuant to such rules.[152]

In reality, what is demanded in respect of these three areas can be boiled down to two requirements, namely that the rules of a governing body (or a club) should be inherently fair and should provide for basic procedural fairness, and that the governing body or club adhere strictly to such rules and such procedural guarantees in its relationship with sportsmen and women. If these two criteria are met, then the prevailing judicial attitude is that sporting matters should be left to sporting bodies.[153]

2.3.1 Creating and applying "fair rules"

Some rules, particularly disciplinary rules of sports governing bodies may be regarded as intuitively unfair. Criticism in this respect has been particularly levelled at the anti-doping rules of certain federations, and especially those rules that operate on a reverse burden or strict liability basis – essentially providing that an offence is committed once a banned substance is found in an athlete's system, with individual moral innocence merely serving to mitigate punishment – which can lead to a situation where an athlete may lose his or her livelihood despite being entirely morally innocent in respect of the issue.[154] Beloff regards such rules as justified on the basis that because it is still incumbent on the governing body to prove the presence of the impugned substance in the body, the burden of proof has not been completely reversed in such cases.[155] Moreover, because governing bodies disciplinary tribunals and CAS are inevitably more inquisitorial than adversarial the impact of burdens and standards of proof may be more illusory than real.[156] These issues will be discussed in detail in Chapter Three.

---

unreported, High Court, February 27, 1997, *The Times*, January 6, 1998 (CA affirming). For comment see Rose and Albertini, "*Jones v. The Welsh Rugby Union*, New Law for the New Era", 5 (1) *Sport and the Law Journal* (1997) 20.

[152] For a comprehensive fleshing out of these requirements see Wearmouth, "No Winners on the Greasy Pole? Ethical and Legal Frameworks of Evaluating Disciplinary Processes in Sport", 3 (3) Sport *and the Law Journal* (1995) [hereafter Wearmouth], 33ff.

[153] McArdle, *Football Society and the Law*, 173 at 178–179.

[154] See McCutcheon, "Sports Discipline, Natural Justice and Strict Liability" (1999) *Anglo-American Law Review* 37.

[155] Beloff, *op. cit.*, p.176ff.

[156] *Ibid.*, pp.188–189.

Other sports rules that cause concern are those that provide for mandatory penalties,[157] and those that require an athlete expressly to waive his or her right to fair procedures.[158] Particularly of concern are rules that create an offence of "bringing the game into disrepute" – a provision that is so open textured that it can afford virtually unlimited powers to a governing body to control the actions (public and potentially private) of sportspersons, and particularly to quash any criticism that the individual sportsperson may have of the body or any of its employees, notably its referees.[159] Use of this rule in this latter manner may be of questionable validity under Article 10 of the European Convention on Human Rights. Finally, as regards specific clubs, there is an obvious concern with rules of membership that are discriminatory in nature – a concern that will be addressed in a later chapter.

A recent example of an arguably unfair rule being the subject of legal challenge arose in September 2002, when the High Court granted an interlocutory injunction temporarily lifting a ban imposed on a Tipperary minor hurler, John Boland.[160] During a club match on August 14, 2002, Mr. Boland had been involved in what was termed "some jostling" behind the referee's back for which he and three other players were dismissed from the field of play – a sanction which would in turn typically lead to the local GAA board suspending the offending player for four weeks. In this case, however, the facts were rather unusual. According to the referee's report on the match, he had in fact meant only to issue yellow cards to the offending players (and indeed this was objectively the appropriate penalty for behaviour of this nature) and he was about to correct himself, when he was struck in the back by the team coach of one of the clubs. In the ensuing chaos, the match was abandoned. When the North Tipperary county board reviewed the case on August 26, it accepted the referee's report and decided that the four players (wrongly) sent off in the game would receive no suspension. However, on August 27, a board member received a press release from the GAA president Sean McCague (issued on August 21 in response to a number of high profile cases where

---

[157] McCutcheon, pp.122–123 in Greenfield & Osborn, *op. cit.*

[158] See *ibid.*, for the view that in such circumstances, the response of the courts is generally to interpret such clauses as strictly as possible, giving all the benefit of the doubt to the athlete and generally reducing their impact, or to strike down such clauses as being in unreasonable restraint of trade. McCutcheon, "Judicial Control of Sporting Bodies; Recent Irish Experiences", *op. cit.*, pp.21–22 further argues that because of the constitutional impact in Ireland, any attempt to require an athlete to waive constitutional rights, both to fair procedures and to freedom of association in this area would face enormous problems. See *Murphy v. Stewart* [1973] I.R. 97. See also Beloff, *op. cit.*, p.201 for the view that such clauses might well be void as being in violation of public policy.

[159] Bitel, "Disciplinary Proceedings from the Point of View of the Individual", 3(3) *Sport and the Law Journal* (1995) 7, Lewis & Taylor, *op. cit.*, pp.61–62.

[160] See "All-Ireland Minor Final Ban on Hurler Lifted" and "Tipperary Minor Wins Court Battle", both *Irish Times*, September 7, 2002.

county boards overruled referees decisions in club games so that players would be available to play inter-county games[161]) ruling that in future cases the County board could not depart from the rule that a straight red card merited a four week suspension simply on the basis of a referee's report.[162] Indeed the only context in which such rule could be overlooked was where exculpatory video evidence was presented to the relevant board. On that basis Mr. Boland's red card was reinstated and he was suspended for the prescribed four-week period.

Mr. Boland sought an interlocutory injunction in the High Court alleging that the offence of which he was guilty was not a 'sending off' offence under the rules of hurling, and that in any event the application of the rules in his case ran contrary to natural and constitutional justice. At the crux of the case was the fact that his suspension covered the date of the All-Ireland minor hurling final – an enormously prestigious game in which he would otherwise have played.[163] Finlay-Geoghegan J. granting the interlocutory injunction sought, stressed that this was not a case where a court was interfering with a decision made on the field of play, but rather one that concerned the application of administrative rules by the GAA. Given that all that was at stake was an interlocutory injunction, and given that the balance of convenience in the case clearly favoured the player who would otherwise have been prevented from playing in the most important match of his career thus far, all that the applicant had to show was a stateable case,[164] and as far as the court was concerned this had been made out. The interlocutory injunction having been granted, the player was allowed to play in the minor final, and unsurprisingly, at this point the action against the GAA was dropped.

Had the matter proceeded to trial, however, it is submitted that the player would have had a strong case to argue. What was relevant was not the fact that he had been sent off in the match, (nor was this a challenge to such an on-field decision) but rather that the GAA president (albeit for good reasons) had issued a decree that was unfair, both because it was deemed to have retrospective effect and also because it failed to accommodate a situation where a referee might make a fundamental error and later wish to remedy the same. In other words, the unfairness of the rule in question was manifested poignantly in the situation that it created in this case.[165]

---

[161] See "McCague Right to see Red Over Cards", *Irish Times*, September 4, 2002.

[162] See Moran, "McCague Steps in over Minor Red", *Irish Times*, August 29, 2002.

[163] See Moran, "Minor to Miss Final as Red is Revisited", *Irish Times*, September 3, 2002.

[164] *Campus Oil v. Minister for Industry and Energy (No.2)* [1983] I.R. 88.

[165] See Moran, "GAA to tackle anomalies in Disciplinary Procedures", *Irish Times*, October 22, 2002 and O'Riordan, "Tipperary calls for Suspension Review", *Irish Times*, December 12, 2002.

2.3.2 Acting *intra vires* the rules

There are two basic reasons why it is vital that a club or governing body does
not act *ultra vires* the rules that it has created for itself. First, because such
rules are incorporated into the terms of the contract between the club or body
and its members, and to act outside such rules therefore is *prima facie* a breach
of contract, or, if the body is to be regarded as a public one, it is a *prima facie*
ground for seeking judicial review of such decision. Secondly, it is a requirement
of fair procedures that a body act *intra vires* its rules.[166] In other words, as a
matter of due process, the relevant rules should be adhered to absolutely, and
any failure to do so, will ground an action whether in judicial review or for
breach of contract. Thus in *Clancy v. Irish Rugby Football Union (I.R.F.U.)*,[167]
the decision of the defendant organisation to deem a rugby player to be
temporarily ineligible to play for his new club – a decision made under the
terms of a perfectly fair and legitimate transfer rule – was set aside because in
applying this rule in this instance, the defendant body had not followed the
appropriate procedures listed therein.[168] Similarly in *Kinane v. Irish Turf
Club*,[169] a two-day suspension on a jockey by the Turf Club was struck down
on the grounds that in hearing an appeal in relation to the imposition of such
suspension, the Appeals and Referrals Committee of the Turf Club had not
followed the procedure it had agreed with the plaintiff.

It is obvious therefore, that the rules of governing bodies should be created
with as much foresight as is possible so that there are no lacunae that would
require the body to act outside the terms of the said rules, and ideally no
ambiguities that would require governing bodies to get involved in the tortuous
business of interpretation.[170] Moreover, if there *is* uncertainty then *all* such
rules should be construed as narrowly as possible, and if there *is* a gap in the
rules, then a position consistent with fair procedures and the presumption of
innocence should be followed.[171]

Application of this principle is seen in a number of recent Irish cases,
including a trilogy of cases involving the registration policy of the Football
Association of Ireland.[172] *Dundalk Interim Co. Ltd t/a Dundalk Football Club*

---

[166] See e.g., *Davis v. Carew-Pole* [1956] 2 All E.R. 524. See also Beloff, "Pitch, Pool,
Rink Court", p.98.

[167] [1995] 1 I.L.R.M. 193. See McCutcheon, "Judicial Scrutiny of Sports Administration"
(1995) 13 *Irish Law Times*, 171.

[168] See also *Walsh v. Butler* [1997] 2 I.L.R.M. 81.

[169] Unreported, High Court, McCracken J., August 22, 2001, considered below, p.77.

[170] McCutcheon in Greenfield & Osborn, *op. cit.*, at 121.

[171] This approach is consistent with the requirement at Irish Law that all penal and tax
statutes be interpreted as narrowly as possible in order to avoid uncertain imposition of
fresh liability in either area. See *Inspector of Taxes v. Kiernan* [1981] I.R. 117, *Mullins
v. Harnett* [1998] 2 I.L.R.M. 304.

[172] Generally see Cox, "Sports Governing Bodies and Fair Procedures – Recent Irish
Developments", 10 (2) *Sport and the Law Journal* 162 [hereafter Cox].

v. Eircom League and Kilkenny City Football Club[173] involved a soccer match between Kilkenny City and Limerick FC in the first division of the Eircom National soccer league, which Kilkenny won. As a result, Kilkenny finished in third place in the first division of the Eircom league (thereby qualifying for play-offs to the premier division) with Dundalk a further point adrift in fourth place, and out of the qualifying positions. Kilkenny had, however, played an individual called Fran Carter on that day, who (it was argued) was not properly registered to play with Kilkenny, in that his manager and not he had signed his (Carter's) name on the registration form. After an enquiry into this by officers of the Eircom league it was decided that there had been a breach of rule 16a of the Eircom League rules, section ii of which provides that a player is properly registered when he has signed a registration form, and section vi of which provides that 'any club playing an unregistered player or players in any match under the jurisdiction of the league ... *will* forfeit three points per match in which a non-registered player plays' (emphasis added). Accordingly Kilkenny were docked three points, thereby elevating Dundalk into the play off positions.

When Kilkenny City issued a summons, however, to challenge the decision, it was decided to refer the matter to arbitration. The arbitrator concluded that the Kilkenny/Limerick match should be replayed. Kilkenny won the replay and hence suffered no loss for the alleged misdemeanour. Dundalk Football Club then issued High Court proceedings challenging the decision of the FAI (the governing body under whose auspices the Eircom league is run) to send the matter to arbitration. In the High Court, Finnegan J. held that the rules of the Eircom League provided for a mandatory penalty to be applied in such cases and that it had no jurisdiction to act outside of the rules or to transfer the matter to arbitration.[174] In explicit terms the judge ruled that:

> "The penalty for a breach of Rule 16 in terms of the forfeiture of three points is mandatory and there is no discretion in the management committee or the honorary officers in relation to the same. The rules contain no provision for the reference of disputes to arbitration. Again there is no provision for matches to be replayed in the event of a breach of Rule 16 as an alternative to the forfeiture of three points. In these circumstances if the honorary officers were correct in finding that Kilkenny played a non-registered player then it was mandatory that

---

[173] [2001] 1 I.R. 434.

[174] An analogous situation arose in *American Shooting v. Quigley v. Union Internationale de TI.R./International Shooting Union*, CAS 94/129 (see Beloff, *op. cit.*, p.181) where the CAS struck down a strict liability test applied by the UIT not because such test was itself invalid but because according to the UIT rules, the relevant offence was the taking of drugs with the *aim* of improving performance – which implies malicious intention. Hence the rules did not provide for strict liability, and the application of such a test was thereby invalid.

Kilkenny should forfeit three points; the reference to arbitration and the carrying out of the direction of the arbitrator to replay the match are outside the rules and are nullities. The rules of the league represent a contract between the league, and one club playing in it cannot adversely affect the rights under the rules of another club."[175]

The principle of this decision is therefore plain; a governing body and by extension a club, once it has created its rules must follow them – rather than seek to replace these rules with an ad hoc resolution of an issue based on its view of what is fair.

The same principle was at issue in the next case, *Accolade Limited (Trading as Shelbourne FC v. FAI.*[176] The case involved a dispute between the two Irish soccer clubs who were at the top of the premier division of the Eircom League in 2001–2002 (Shelbourne FC and St Patrick's Athletic FC), of which only one could win the league and therefore qualify to compete in the initial stages of the European Champion's League and gain an enormous financial windfall from doing so. One of St Patrick's Athletics' players – Paul Marney – had been a product of an internal club youth programme and had played for and been registered with the club during the 2000–2001 season. In September 2001, however, it transpired that he had not been registered properly for the 2001–2002 season,[177] ostensibly because St Patrick's Athletic sent an appropriately signed and witnessed registration form by *ordinary* as distinct from *registered* post (and under Rule 33 of the FAI rule book the requirement is that such forms be sent by registered post) to the FAI in respect of Mr. Marney, but that form was lost in the post.[178] In any event, Mr. Marney had played in three games for St Patrick's Athletic as an unregistered player, and after a hearing into the matter, Eircom League officers found a breach of Rule 16 (a) of the Eircom league rules and decided to fine the club £1,000 but not to deduct nine league points from it (as was required under the rules) on the basis that the non-registration in question was inadvertent.[179] On appeal by Shelbourne FC, the FAI appeal board decided it had no option but to apply strictly the provisions of Rule 16(vi) and to deduct nine points from St Patrick's

---

[175] In the event Finnegan J. held in favour of Kilkenny City, concluding that the player in question was properly registered at the time of the decision on the grounds that, at common law, it is possible for one's agent to sign one's name and for that signature to have legal validity.
[176] Unreported, High Court, O'Sullivan J., February 18, 2002. See Cox, *op. cit.*, p.166.
[177] See "Dolan may Face Points Deduction", *Irish Times*, September 6, 2001.
[178] St Patrick's Athletic officials had a receipt from a Dublin Post-Office which it was accepted (albeit not without some controversy) was issued in respect of Mr Marney's form which had itself been sent by unregistered post.
[179] See "St Patrick's Athletic Escape with all the Points", *Irish Times*, September 7, 2001

for playing an unregistered player for three matches.[180] St Patrick's Athletic requested that this decision be placed before the FAI's board of management, and on October 8, 2001 it was decided by a 10–9 majority of representatives of 19 of the 21 Eircom League teams present, "in the spirit of football" to transfer the matter to arbitration and to be bound by any decision of the arbitrator.[181]

The arbitrator, Mr Liam Reidy SC (also chairman of Kilkenny City FC), decided to restore to St Patrick's the nine points deducted, and instead to impose a twelve hundred pound fine.[182] He was influenced in this, by the anecdotal evidence before him of widespread violation (admitted by the FAI) of registration rules, concluding that "... if all the provisions of Rule 16 and Rule 33 were to be interpreted strictly ... there are many ineligible players ... participating in the league." Moreover, he saw the present violation as a particularly innocuous one. Of most significance, however, is the fact that he did not accept that the imposition of the nine point deduction was a mandatory step under the words of rule 16. Instead in his view,

> "The rules of the Eircom league are not a penal code. They must be interpreted in the context of a sporting organisation with the aims and objects to which that organisation aspires. It is my view that reposed in the league itself is the entitlement and duty to do justice in any given situation.
>
> There are many instances in which a penalty such as has been imposed would be warranted where there has been a deliberate attempt to breach the provisions of rule 16. We are not dealing with such an instance here. There cannot be a more innocuous or technical breach of the provisions of Rule 16 than in this instance. The question therefore, is whether the league has discretion to impose a penalty other than in accordance with Rule 16 (a)(vi).
>
> As I have stated I believe that there are exceptional circumstances in which there is reposed in the league through its officers the entitlement and duty to impose a discretionary penalty. I believe that that was what was done by the league officers when this matter came before them in the instance and I believe they were right."

Various aspects of the decision of the arbitrator were challenged in High Court

---

[180] See "Administrators must Follow the Rules", *Irish Times*, September 18, 2001 and "League Leaders Lose Nine Points", *Irish Times*, September 26, 2001.

[181] It was clear that the FAI regarded only the Eircom league and St Patrick's and not Shelbourne FC to be parties to the arbitration, despite the claim of Shelbourne that it should also be involved.

[182] See "Marney Affair Makes a Mockery of the Rule Book", *Irish Times*, January 8, 2002, "Fury at Tolka as St Patrick's Get Points", *Irish Times*, January 8, 2002.

proceedings,[183] although it seems that the exclusive concern of the court was the validity of the decision of the arbitrator rather than the more questionable validity of the decision to refer the matter to arbitration. In as much as the focus was on the actual arbitration decision, O'Sullivan J. of the Irish High Court had no difficulty in concluding that "there is ... no question of a fundamental error on the face, or indeed otherwise, of this arbitration award." After all, Shelbourne FC while not a party to the arbitration (which was between St Patrick's Athletic and the Eircom League), had been invited by the arbitrator to make submissions on the case yet had declined to do so. Moreover, Irish case law is absolutely clear on the point that an arbitrator's decision will only be interfered with in the rarest of circumstances, particularly when challenged by a party to the arbitration process.[184]

Somewhat surprisingly, the court gave no more than perfunctory attention to the question of whether the matter should have been submitted for arbitration at all, in light of the mandatory character of Rule 16, and the decision in the *Dundalk* case. It is true that Rule 28 of the FAI rulebook contains a general arbitration clause, in line with the requirements of FIFA and consistent with many sports governing bodies. This clause applies, however, "... in the event of any differences or disputes under these rules." In the instant case, however, there was no dispute in the proper meaning of the term. Parties were agreed that the player was not properly registered and most importantly, the penalty prescribed under the terms of Rule 16 could not have been clearer. As such, there was simply no justification for the activation of the Rule 28 (FAI) procedure. Counsel for the plaintiff had submitted that:

> "The relevant rule (Rule 16 (Eircom League) provided for an automatic and mandatory forfeiture of nine points. There was no discretion to abate these. The decision and appeals proceedings were not amenable to subsequent arbitration, nor can the defendant dilute the clear mandatory effect of rule 16(b)(6) of the Eircom League's rules by itself or by conferring unlimited jurisdiction on an arbitrator."

This was of course the conclusion reached in *Dundalk*. Yet this pivotal point was not dealt with in this case. It seems that counsel for the plaintiff did not refer to the *Dundalk* case. On the other hand, counsel for the defence referred to the case, but sought to distinguish it on the grounds that whereas the former case involved a decision to refer the matter to arbitration without any

---

[183] See "Shelbourne take Marney case to Court", *Irish Times*, February 6, 2002.
[184] S.38 of the Arbitration Act 1954. Generally, see *Keenan v. Shield Insurance* [1988] I.R. 89, *Doyle v. Kildare County Council & Shackleton* [1995] 2 I.R. 424, *Bord na Mona v. John Sisk*, unreported, High Court, Blayney J., November 30, 1989, *Sheahan v. FBD Insurance*, unreported, High Court, Kelly J., March 25, 1998, *McStay v. Assicurazioni Generali* [1991] I.L.R.M. 237.

consultation with the other parties who were affected (that is to say the other clubs in the Eircom league), here the decision to refer to arbitration was taken by an admittedly very narrow majority at a meeting at which all but one of the Eircom league clubs were represented. Thus "... in the terms of the resolution of 8 October 2001, the very thing that was referred to arbitration was that the league and the participating members were sympathetic to the plight of St Patrick's Athletic ...".

It is submitted however, that this is simply not sufficient as a ground for distinction. Had the decision been taken at that meeting to amend Rule 16 and had all the relevant parties been present and the appropriate procedure complied with then, in as much as the rules of the governing body amount to contractual terms with the various member clubs of the governing body, this would have amounted to no more than the amendment of such terms via a procedure provided for in the contract. But that is not what happened. Rather an express term of the contract was breached, without the consent of all (or even a majority) of the parties to that contract. The arbitrator had deemed the actions of the Eircom League to be valid, concluding that "... reposed in the League itself is the entitlement and duty to do justice in any given situation." With respect this is simply an inaccurate conclusion. As Finnegan J. recognised in *Dundalk*, the rules are drafted in such a fashion that no such discretion could possibly exist. Nor should the fact that the rule was habitually breached be a reason now for an arbitrator to decide that, 'in the spirit of football' it should be deemed to be something discretionary.

It is an inescapable conclusion that the decision to refer the matter to arbitration, and thereby to ignore the terms of the rule, constituted a clear breach of contract, and also impinged on requirements of fair procedures and natural and constitutional justice.[185] It may be argued that such rigid requirements of fair procedures may perhaps be relaxed in a case of this nature, involving what is at best a semi-professional sport, where, apart from pride and glory, not a great deal is at stake. Again, however, this argument should be resisted both because it is wrong to denigrate concepts like pride and glory in a sporting arena, and also because as we have seen, in financial terms a great deal was at stake in that the winners of this domestic league would qualify to compete in the European Champions league.

The extent of the problems which this episode created, and the reason why acting *intra vires* one's rules is so tied up with fair procedures became evident in March 2002, when it emerged that St Patrick's Athletic had in fact fielded *another* unregistered player – Charles Mbabazi Livingstone – for the first five games of the season.[186] In a rigid application of Rule 16, the Eircom League

---

[185] See "A Long Season of One Fiasco after Another", *Irish Times*, March 20, 2002, and "Rule Book Flaws Begin to Register", *Irish Times*, March 26, 2002.
[186] Malone, "St Patrick's Look Set to be Docked Fifteen Points", *Irish Times*, March 20, 2002.

docked St Patrick's Athletic fifteen points.[187] This time, however, when St Patrick's Athletic appealed this decision, the appeal was rejected, despite the fact that St Patrick's Athletic officials pointed out that many clubs within the league also had unregistered players playing for them, and that having inspected various documents at Eircom league headquarters, 28 of the 40 registrations forms considered did not comply with the organisation's rules.[188] Roy Dooney, the Eircom League commissioner admitted that the registration rules were regularly flouted, but argued that the other breaches to which St Patrick's Athletic referred were largely technical and minor in nature.[189] Equally, he admitted that he had been aware since the previous September that there was a problem with Livingstone's registration yet had done nothing about it, despite the fact that, during the Marney dispute, the reason why most club representatives felt that St Patrick's Athletic should be dealt with in lenient fashion was because their breach of the rules was accidental in nature and hence that they were merely the victims of ill fortune.[190]

Even more importantly, from a St Patrick's Athletic point of view, it was clear that they were not the only club in breach of registration rules. Indeed Roy Dooney admitted *"There are other forms that I am aware of that are not correctly filled in. It's not hugely widespread but there would be other clubs who would probably be facing points deduction."*[191] Moreover, in both the arbitration report of Liam Reidy and also the decision of the High Court in the *Accolade* case, it is clear that great significance was attached to the fact that minor breaches of the registration rules were widespread, and that if Rule 16 were to be applied rigidly, then the final league table would be farcical in nature, with (possibly) the winning team finishing on a minus number of points! Responding to the news of the fifteen-point deduction St Patrick's Athletic officials therefore accepted the legitimacy of the decision, but demanded that all other breaches of registration rules would be similarly punished.[192] The Eircom league refused, claiming that the other cases to which St Patrick's Athletic referred did not merit the same punishment as it had incurred.[193]

There are two problems with this conclusion. First, as a matter of fact the problems with the registration of Mbabazi Livingstone were themselves technical and minor. At the date when he should have been registered, the FAI had a copy of his contract with St Patrick's Athletic in their offices (it was discussing his registration with FIFA) and in as much as registration is essentially a procedure for ensuring that players are properly linked to clubs,

---

[187] Malone, 'St Pat's Lose 15 Points in Crushing Blow", *Irish Times* March 23, 2002.
[188] See Malone, "Dooney Defends Inquiry", *Irish Times*, March 28, 2002.
[189] Malone, "St Patrick's Look to be Docked Fifteen Points", *Irish Times*, March 20, 2002.
[190] This is borne out both in the arbitrator's report and in the High Court judgment.
[191] Malone, "St Patrick's Look to be Docked Fifteen Points", *Irish Times*, March 20, 2002.
[192] See "St Patrick's to Study the Options", *Irish Times*, April 12, 2002.
[193] Malone, "St Patrick's Claims are Rejected", *Irish Times*, April 24, 2002.

they had clear proof of such link and hence the absence of a specific registration form was something of a technicality. Moreover, such registration forms can cover two years of a player's contract, and it seems that the player's contract in this case was supposed to run until the end of the 2001–2002 season, but owing to a typographical error it referred to the end of the 2000–2001 season.[194] Secondly and more importantly, St Patrick's Athletic were undoubtedly being treated unequally as against the other clubs in the league whose players were not properly registered, in as much as they were the only team against whom the terms of Rule 16 were being strictly enforced. It might be argued that because the cumulative effect of the two controversies, St Patrick's Athletic crossed a threshold of liability that other clubs did not cross, but there is no provision in the Eircom League or FAI rulebook justifying such an approach in such circumstances. The Marney/Mbabazi Livingstone saga is therefore, graphically illustrative of the reason why the requirement that governing bodies do adhere rigidly to the standards laid down in rule books is such an indispensable element of the guarantee of fair procedures; the alternative leaves open the possibility of an approach which is at best unequal and arbitrary and at worst a facility for favouritism and bias.[195]

A similar problem concerning application of rules arose within the GAA in November 2002 and concerned a Dublin club championship quarterfinal match between Raheny and Na Fianna.[196] The latter club won the game, but it transpired that during the game, as well as the five substitutes permitted it had also used a "blood substitute" – that is a temporary substitute replacing a player who was receiving treatment for a blood wound.[197] Moreover, under the rules of Gaelic Football, the penalty for using more than five substitutes is forfeiture

---

[194] See Doyle, "When the National League becomes an Irish Stew", *Irish Times*, April 26, 2002.

[195] In the event and after some novel suggestions as to how the league would be decided (including the possibility of a two-legged match between Shelbourne and St Patrick's Athletic to decide the title ("Rivals may make peace and play for the title", *Irish Times*, March 29, 2002, and "Play off plan looks dead in water", *Irish Times*, March, 30, 2002)) and the right to play in the European Champion's league was won by Shelbourne, who finished six points clear of their nearest rivals Shamrock Rovers, but crucially only ten points clear of St Patrick's Athletic. Finally, at the same time, it appeared that the outcome of the Eircom League first (i.e. sub-premier) division might also be decided in the High Court, this time as Dublin City objected to being docked three points for playing an unregistered player, Noel Hunt.

[196] See generally, Humphries, "Dublin Clubs Farce Embarrasses Everyone", *Irish Times*, November 4, 2002, Fee, "An Audit of Fair Procedures within the GAA", 7 T.C.L.R. (2004), 135

[197] This error of judgement was all the more surprising given that Na Fianna had used too many substitutes the previous year in the Leinster Championships, and had only avoided forfeiting that championship game when their opponents, Sarsfields of Kildare generously offered Na Fianna a replay. See "Oops I did it Again", *Irish Times*, 28 October 28, 2002.

of the relevant match. Application of this rule to the situation where five regular substitutes plus a blood substitute are used had produced controversy earlier in the year in the context of the Munster Football Championship final replay between Cork and Tipperary, when Cork had used a blood replacement as a sixth substitute. In that instance, the Munster Council had decided incorrectly that the GAA rules (specifically rule 109) did not proscribe any penalty for such a situation. Equally the Games Administration Committee, the GAA central council and the GAA President all subsequently intimated that this was a misapplication of the rules, and that where a blood substitute was used as a sixth substitute, then save in a limited number of permitted exceptional circumstances, the club in question should forfeit the relevant match.[198]

On this basis the Dublin County Board awarded the game to Raheny under the explicit terms of Rule 109(b)(i).[199] In response, Na Fianna having obtained an interim injunction preventing the Dublin semi-final taking place[200] sought an interlocutory injunction pending a full hearing into the question of whether the Dublin county board had acted *ultra vires* its powers and in violation of rules of fair procedures.[201] The situation was fraught, not least because the tightly scheduled time frame of the Leinster Championship meant that, as the Dublin county board had insisted that the matter could only be resolved at a full hearing rather than on the submission of affidavits to the High Court, should the injunction have been granted pending such full hearing, Dublin would have had no representative team in the Leinster club championships.[202]

In the event, the High Court refused to grant the interlocutory injunction sought.[203] The court appeared to accept the contention put forward by Na Fianna (and rejected by the Games Administration Committee) that the blood substitute rule was "a matter of interpretation" Of more significance for the court, however, was the fact that Rule 151(f) prohibits "... appeal to any court

---

[198] See "Blood Rule makes for a Clear Cut Case", *Irish Times*, November 6, 2002.

[199] The rule provides that "A team exceeding the number of substitutes permitted ... shall be subject to a penalty of forfeiture of the game to opposing team." Moreover under Rule 1.5 of the GAA rules of control there are "blood rule" exceptions to the normal rule that a side is allowed no more than five substitutes but none of these exceptions covered the present case.

[200] See "Na Fianna gets High Court Injunction to Stop Next Round Match", *Irish Times*, November 2, 2002.

[201] See O'Sullivan, "Na Fianna go to High Court as Appeal Fails", *Irish Times*, November 2, 2002, "Court hears GAA Club's Application to Stop Match", *Irish Times*, November 8, 2002.

[202] See Moran, "Exchange of Letters Fails to Resolve Na Fianna Dispute", *Irish Times*, November 7, 2002, "Court to Decide on Na Fianna Issue Today", *Irish Times*, November 8, 2002 and "'Na Fianna under Pressure to Drop Case", *Irish Times*, November 5, 2002.

[203] See Moran, "Judgment Restores Home Rule", *Irish Times*, November 9, 2002 and "Disciplinary Committee Facing into Busy Winter", *Irish Times*, November 15, 2002.

of law or … any outside body on any matter." Plainly as a matter of Irish law, such provision taken literally is invalid. Equally the court felt that unless the decision of the GAA or any sub-body thereof was in violation of constitutional rights or natural or constitutional justice, then resolution of disputes should occur within the internal GAA structure.

On one level, there is nothing new in this statement. As we have seen the standard judicial line is that when sport is at issue then as far as possible disputes should be resolved by sports bodies that have been put in charge of its regulations. On another level, however, in this case it is arguable that had the Dublin County Board (as a representative of the GAA) acted otherwise than in accordance with fair procedures, then it was breaching the contractual terms of its relationship with Na Fianna, and therefore the latter should have been entitled to legal recourse irrespective of the fact that what was at issue was sport. It may also be argued that the nature of the GAA is such that it could legitimately be the target of a judicial review action. It is almost certain that in this instance, the decision of the Dublin county board was perfectly fair, in that the earlier decision of the Munster Council was plainly flawed, nor could it be regarded as setting a precedent of general application. Equally the case is indicative once again of the importance of governing bodies having clear rules that allow no variation in interpretation, and applying such rules strictly and consistently.

It is also vital that a sports federation's rules clearly cover all the situations that they are intended to cover, such that there is no need for them to be stretched or strained to achieve a desired result. In *Moran v. O'Sullivan*,[204] the applicants were members of a horse racing syndicate, which owned the well-known racehorse *David's Lad*. The horse had been suspended for 42 days from March 4, 2003, following a decision of stewards at Leopardstown racecourse that the horse had not been allowed to run on its merits in a race on February 23, 2003. The significance of the ban lay in the fact that it covered the date of the English Grand National for which David's Lad was second favourite.[205] On March 6 the owners of the horse sought and obtained an interlocutory injunction lifting the suspension.[206] However, following an appeal by the Turf Club, on March 10 the High Court lifted part of the injunction thereby ensuring that the horse was prevented from running at Cheltenham on March 13, 2003.[207] Thereafter, the applicants having obtained leave, sought a judicial review of the decision

---

[204] Unreported, High Court, Carroll J., March 18, 2003.

[205] See "David's Lad to Miss National", *Irish Times*, February 24, 2003 and O'Connor, "Martin to Appeal David's Lad ban", *Irish Times*, February 25, 2003

[206] See "David's Lad back in Business", *Irish Times*, March 7, 2003.

[207] See "Ban on Horse Running at Cheltenham Upheld", *Irish Times*, March 12, 2003. In the case, the horse's trainer had admitted that it was not essential that the horse run at Cheltenham, and hence the balance of convenience in the case appeared to favour the suspension.

to suspend the horse *inter alia* on the grounds that it was *ultra vires* the powers of the stewards to penalise the owner of a horse for an infraction of this nature.[208]

A similar claim had been made in *Bolger v. Osborne*,[209] where a trainer (who it was accepted had been guilty of no misconduct) successfully challenged the imposition of a penalty on him in circumstances where his jockey had not ridden his horse on its merits. The claim was upheld on the grounds that at the time the rules of the Turf Club did not allow a trainer to be held vicariously liable for the actions of a jockey. Since that case the Turf Club rules had been amended such that Rule 148 (i) now provides that:

> "A trainer shall be responsible (except where otherwise provided for in these rules) for everything connected with the running of a horse trained by him/her and shall be liable for any sanction available to the stewards unless the trainer provides a satisfactory explanation."

The applicants in *Moran v. O'Sullivan*, however, argued that whereas the rules now provided for liability to attach to the *trainer*, they did not make a similar provision in respect of the *owner* of the horse. Yet the financial reality of the situation was that it would be the owner who would in practice suffer most should the horse be banned. Therefore because any suspension of the horse would have the effect of imposing liability on the owner, the decision to suspend the horse should be regarded as being *ultra vires* the powers of the stewards under these rules.

Carroll J. rejected these arguments. She noted that (unlike in the case where a trainer was suspended) there was no question of the applicants' livelihood being at stake here – a fact which presumably indicated that there was less need for the highest standards of fair procedures to be protected. Moreover, she recognised that the practice of not running a horse on its merits constituted a threat to racing itself as a sport, and also to those involved in the betting industry. She was also swayed by the fact that "It would make a nonsense of a rule designed to keep racing fair if a horse could not be suspended unless the owner had been at fault in some way" – a fact which, while accurate, was scarcely relevant if the rules did not provide for the power to order such suspension in the absence of such fault. She concluded, however that in fact the rules did provide for the legitimacy of such sanction. Everyone connected with racing knew of the existence of the rule penalizing the failure to run a horse on its merits. Moreover,

> "In my opinion, the disqualification of a horse ... is not a punishment imposed on the owner, but is a consequence arising out of the actions of

---

[208] See "Owners of Suspended Horse seek Legal Redress", *Irish Times*, March 14, 2003.
[209] [2001] I.L.R.M. 250.

the trainer and or jockey which necessarily arise in the interests of ensuring that races are run fairly and properly."

It is submitted that this conclusion is perhaps somewhat questionable. After all, although the applicants' livelihoods were certainly not at stake, nonetheless they did stand to lose a good deal if the suspension was upheld (in that David's Lad stood a realistic chance of winning one of the most famous horse races in the world). In such circumstances, the prize money would go neither to the jockey nor the trainer but to the owner, and indeed the value of the horse would rise inestimably. As such it is arguably legitimate to regard the suspension of the horse as primarily hurting the owner. Moreover, it is undoubtedly the case that the rules of the Turf Club[210] do not provide for vicarious liability to attach to the owner for the actions of jockey or trainer. Carroll J. was correct in her view that requiring fault on the part of an owner (who may never see the horse train or run, and who may have no part in creating race tactics) in order to suspend a horse would create ludicrous results for the sport. Equally that is a reason for the Turf Club to amend its rules and not for the High Court to permit it to act outside the terms of its existing rules and hence in breach of its contract with persons with whom it was involved.

2.3.3 Fair procedures and disciplinary hearings

The basic requirements of natural and constitutional justice as far as hearings of this nature are concerned are of course contained in the twin maxims *audi alterem partem* and *nemo iudex in causa sua*[211] but are strengthened by the Irish constitutional guarantee of fair procedures[212] as well as Article 6 of the European Convention on Human Rights. The manner in which these principles are to receive specific application in Ireland is explained in the case *Haughey, in re*[213] where the court accepted that depending on the circumstances, someone facing a disciplinary hearing might be entitled to:

– the right to be furnished with a copy of any evidence, which reflected on the good name of the applicant,

---

[210] The Supreme Court upheld the decision of the High Court on appeal. See "One Last Throw of the dice for David's Lad", *Irish Times*, March 27, 2003, "David's Lad's Owners Face Final Hurdle", *Irish Times*, March 28, 2003, O'Connor, "David's Lad out of Favour", *Irish Times*, March 19, 2003 and "Final Blow for David's Lad", *Irish Times*, March 29, 2003.

[211] Generally see Hogan & Morgan, *Administrative Law in Ireland* (3rd ed., Round Hall Sweet & Maxwell, Dublin 1998), Chaps 10 and 11, Nicholson, "Does Speedy Disposal Mean Rough Justice?", April 2003, *Sports Law Administration and Practice* 12.

[212] *McDonald v. Bord na gCon* [1965] I.R. 217, *Glover v. BLN* [1973] I.R. 388 and *State (Gleeson) v. Minister for Defence* [1976] I.R. 280.

[213] [1971] I.R. 217.

– the right to cross examine – and indeed generally to have legal representation,

– the right to give rebutting evidence,

– the right to address (if necessary by counsel) the relevant body in his defence.

Once again, we should stress that the level of fair procedures to which an athlete is entitled will primarily depend on the severity of the consequences of such decision for him. Thus, in *Russell v. Duke of Norfolk*,[214] Lord Denning concluded that because of the essentially monopolistic rights which the Jockey Club had in this area (and indeed irrespective of the fact that the relationship between the parties was based on private contract), common justice required that if someone was to lose his livelihood, there would have to be a proper hearing in advance of this, and the rules of the club or governing body should provide for the same. Such considerations apply not just within the civil courts but also at hearings of the Court of Arbitration for Sport, but given that the bulk of cases heard by CAS relate to the issue of doping, the procedural requirements within that court will be considered in the next chapter.

Whereas the precise requirements of any disciplinary hearing will depend on the facts of the case,[215] equally some basic procedural requirement will apply in all cases. Thus the disciplinary panel would have to be properly constituted in accordance with the rules of the federation,[216] and should be independent from the party alleging the wrongdoing.[217] It is also obviously vital that there be no taint of bias within such hearing.[218] The athlete is entitled to be given notice of the issue at stake, the nature of the alleged misdemeanour for which he is being disciplined,[219] and the gravity of the decision that has

---

[214] [1949] 1 All E.R. 109. See also Grayson, *op. cit.*, p.391.

[215] Griffith-Jones, *op. cit.*, p.65. See also Raj Parker, "Disciplinary Proceedings from the Governing Body Point of View", 3 (3) *Sport and the Law Journal* (1995) 3 and Bitel, "Disciplinary Procedures from the Point of View of the Individual", 3 (3) Sport *and the Law Journal* (1995) 7.

[216] Beloff, p.176. Beloff further points out that a decision of such disciplinary panel will be stuck down it involves a misunderstanding or misapplication of the rules of the federation. See *ibid.*, p.179.

[217] Thus in November 2002, Paraic Duffy, Chairperson of the GAA Games Administration Committee admitted that there might be a legal difficulty with the system whereby the GAC fulfilled all functions in the process leading to suspension on video evidence, including evidence gathering, prosecuting and deciding the case. See Moran, "Disciplinary Committee Facing into Busy Winter", *Irish Times*, November 15, 2002.

[218] *Modahl v. British Athletics Federation* [2001] E.W.C.A. 1447, [2002] 1 W.L.R. 1192, *Freedman v. Petty and Greyhound Racing Control Board* [1981] V.R. 1001. It is perhaps arguable that the composition of the GAA games administration committee, where each member is a representative of a club, a county and a province is not conducive to a clear absence of bias.

[219] *State (Gleeson) v. Minister for Defence* [1976] I.R. 280, *Hughes v. Garda Commissioner*,

been taken,[220] so that he has ample opportunity to prepare a defence for himself.[221] It may also be necessary – depending on the severity of the case and the possibility of appeal – that the applicant be given reasons for the relevant decision.[222] Moreover, if the breach of the disciplinary rules of a federation also generates proceedings at criminal law, it would be inappropriate to hold the internal tribunal before the criminal proceedings are finished on the grounds that one's defence to the sports panel might violate the privilege against self-incrimination at the criminal trial.[223]

It is not clear whether an applicant has a right to an oral hearing.[224] This would seem to depend on the nature of the case, whether the issue involves any disputed issues of fact, and whether the rules of the governing body provide for an appeal. It seems clear that whether or not such oral hearing is permitted the applicant is entitled as a matter of natural justice, to be present[225] and to make representations outlining his side of the story,[226] and that the relevant body must consider such representations.[227] Depending on the gravity of the issue, rules of natural justice may also require that the applicant be entitled to

---

unreported, High Court, Laffoy J., July 23, 1996, *Keighley Football Club v. Cunningham*, Times Law Reports, May 25, 1960, *St Johnstone Football Club Ltd v. Scottish Football Association* [1965] S.L.T. 171. On the other hand see *Currie v. Barton*, Times Law Reports, February 12, 1988, for the view that lesser standards are required in the context of amateur sport.

[220] *Quirke v. BLE* [1988] I.R. 83.

[221] *O'Brien v. Garda Commissioner*, unreported, High Court, Kelly J. August 19, 1996.

[222] See *Dundee United Football Club v. Scottish Football Association* [1998] S.L.T. 1244 for the view that:
> "...the existence of a right of appeal is a factor strongly indicative of an obligation on the decision maker to give reasons for his decision. Whether or not there is a duty to give reasons will depend on the particular circumstances of the decision being made."

See Beloff, *op. cit.*, p.202. The question of whether reasons must be given for a decision is also relevant as it impinges on the sports body's potential obligations under the Freedom of Information Act.

[223] McCutcheon, p.123 in Greenfield & Osborn, *op. cit.*

[224] *Galvin v. Chief Appeals Officer* [1997] 3 I.R. 240, *Mooney v. An Post* [1998] 4 I.R. 288, *McCann v. An Bord Pleanála* [1997] 1 I.R. 264, *Pett v. Greyhound Racing Association* [1969] 1 Q.B. 125. As Beloff notes (p.210) if the rules of sporting associations do not provide for costs, the disciplinary body may not make an order in this regard, and hence each party will have to bear his own costs.

[225] In *Moran v. O'Sullivan*, unreported, High Court, Carroll J., March 18, 2003 (the *David's Lad* case referred to above), the court held that there was no need for the relevant racehorse owners to be present at the stewards' enquiry, both because the stewards' punishment would not directly impact on the owners and also because the trainer could be regarded as the agent of the owner, entitled to make representations on the latter's behalf.

[226] *Haughey v. Mr. Justice Moriarty* [1999] 3 I.R. 1.

[227] *Merrigan v. Minister for Justice*, unreported, High Court, Geoghegan J., January 28, 1998.

legal representation,[228] and to cross examine witnesses.[229] This arose in the significant case of *Jones & Ebbw Vale RFC v. Welsh Rugby Union*,[230] where (admittedly in the context of an application for an interim injunction where the court was merely looking for *prima facie* evidence of possible unfairness) the court *per* Ebsworth J. found that a decision of a disciplinary panel to suspend a particular rugby player, bore the hallmarks of being in breach of fair procedures because the relevant player (who had a stammer) was not entitled to legal representation, to be present at the hearing and (thereby) to cross examine witnesses.[231]

Following such a hearing, it may well be (again depending on the facts of the case) that the application of fair procedures will require that there be provision for an appeal,[232] and if so that the appeal board should be independent from the body that made the original decision.[233] Indeed as the Court of Appeal noted in *Modahl v. British Athletic Federation*,[234] (and as the Court of Arbitration for Sport has regularly pointed out[235]) a properly constituted appeal hearing can have the useful effect of curing any defects that may have existed at the initial stage of the disciplinary process.

Finally, it is also important that where there is an agreed procedure for conducting a hearing or an appeal, then that procedure should be adhered to.

---

[228] *Flanagan v. UCD* [1988] I.R. 724, *Gallagher v. Revenue Commissioners* [1991] 2 I.R. 370, *Maher v. Irish Permanent* [1998] 4 I.R. 302.

[229] *Gallagher v. Revenue Commissioners* [1995] 1 I.R. 65, *State (Haverty) v. An Bord Pleanála* [1987] I.R. 485.

[230] Unreported, Queen's Bench, February 27, 1997, *Times* January 6, 1998 (Court of Appeal) noted at (January/February 1998) *Sports Law Administration and Practice* 10.

[231] See Beloff, *op. cit.*, pp.194–195 for a criticism of this case that it implies that it is invalid to operate an inquisitorial system of justice unless it has within it some elements of the adversarial system. See Gardiner, p.237ff, Moore, p.14ff and Griffith Jones, p.59ff. More generally see Stoner, "Sports Disciplinary Matters: An Analysis of Evidential Requirements" (February 2003) *Sports Law Administration and Practice* 13.

[232] Beloff, *op. cit.*, p.210, says that procedural fairness rules do not necessarily require an appeal. See for example the conclusions of the Court of Appeal in *Wilander v. Tobin* [1997] Eu. L.R. 265. Nevertheless it will be remembered that in *Clancy v. I.R.F.U.*, one of the reasons why the player mobility rules in question were upheld was because of the possibility of an internal appeal, although the actual appeal procedure was deemed invalid. As with other areas of public law, however, it may well be that the defect at the first stage subsists at the appeal stage (as for example where there is an error of law with which the appeal body is not competent to deal), and hence that the right of appeal is illusory.

[233] Thus in *Newport Association v. Football Association of Wales (No.2)*, unreported, Queen's Bench, April 12, 1995, one of the reasons why the decision was deemed to be in violation of standards of fair procedures was because the rules provided for a right of appeal but the appeal from the decision of the Welsh FA was to be heard by a Welsh FA Commission. For analysis see Parpworth, "Guarding the Game", p.71 in Greenfield, *op. cit.*, p.78.

[234] [2002] 1 W.L.R. 1192.

[235] See *B v. FINA*, CAS 98/211 and *B v. International Judo Federation*, CAS 98/214.

In *Kinane v. Turf Club*,[236] the champion jockey Michael Kinane had been suspended for two days for careless riding at Leopardstown, which suspension would have prohibited him from competing in the highly prestigious King George VI and Queen Elizabeth Diamond Stakes horserace at Ascot.[237] As such he appealed the decision of the Leopardstown Stewards before the Appeals and Referrals Committee of the Turf Club (Ireland's horseracing governing body).[238] It was agreed between all parties that, in the event of the committee upholding the decision of the stewards, it would hear representations from counsel for Mr. Kinane in respect of the penalty to be imposed, but in fact after hearing evidence in respect of the race and adjourning for deliberation, the committee announced that both the Leopardstown stewards' decision *and* the two-day ban imposed would stand.

Counsel for Mr. Kinane, Ercus Stewart SC, objected that he had not (as agreed) been afforded an opportunity to make representations in respect of the penalty to be imposed, and after taking legal advice, the committee allowed him to make submissions on the penalty imposed. Mr. Stewart argued, however, that it would be impossible at this point for the committee to come to a different conclusion and hence sought an adjournment without a decision to allow a newly constituted committee to hear the appeal. The three-man committee again deliberated in private and returned to inform the plaintiff that they had made their decision and were sticking to it.[239] The plaintiff then sought and obtained both an interim injunction in the High Court restraining the implementation of this decision and also a declaration that the decision of the appeal committee was null and void and in breach of principles of natural and constitutional justice.[240] The ban was therefore temporarily lifted, and Mr. Kinane competed in and won the King George VI and Queen Elizabeth Diamond Stakes on another Aidan O'Brien trained horse, Galileo. The turf club subsequently agreed to a permanent injunction being granted against the decision, a declaration that the decision of the committee was null and void and to pay damages to the plaintiff and the costs of the proceedings.[241] Finally on August 27, a newly convened appeals and referrals committee upheld the finding of the stewards and a two-day ban was finally imposed on Mick Kinane, although obviously not covering the date of any major race meeting.[242]

---

[236] Unreported, High Court, July 27, 2001. See Cox, *op. cit.*, pp.165–166 and Cox & Costello, "Sports Law" in Byrne & Binchy eds., *Annual Review of Irish Law 2001* (Roundhall Sweet & Maxwell, 2002), p.45.

[237] See "Kinane May Miss Ascot Over Ban", *Irish Times*, July 19, 2001.

[238] See "Kinane Lodges Appeal", *Irish Times*, July 21, 2001.

[239] See "Decision on Kinane Today", *Irish Times*, 26 July, 2001 and "Kinane Misses Galileo Ride as Appeal Fails", *Irish Times*, July 27, 2001.

[240] See "Kinane's Fate Remains Uncertain", *Irish Times*, July 27, 2001.

[241] "High Court Rules in Favour of Kinane", *Irish Times*, August 22, 2001.

[242] "Kinane's 2 Day Ban is Finally Enforced", *Irish Times*, August 27, 2001, and "Kinane Issue is Finally Resolved", *Irish Times*, August 28, 2001.

It is true that because what was at issue was an interlocutory injunction, and therefore all that was necessary was for the applicant to make out a stateable case, the decision may not be particularly forceful as a precedent. Nonetheless it is indicative of the fact that, both by failing to allow the applicant to address the panel on the sole point of real significance in the case, and especially by failing to follow agreed procedures, the panel simply did not vindicate the interests of the applicant and its decision was therefore inconsistent with requirements of fair procedures.

Finally, although it seems clear that there is no duty either contractual or otherwise for the disciplinary body to reach the "right" result,[243] nonetheless, even if the procedure followed has been appropriate, the merits of the decision itself – including the question of whether the penalty was disproportionate to the offence[244] and whether the decision was irrational – may in extreme circumstances ground a legal action.

2.4 THE IMPACT OF THE EUROPEAN CONVENTION ON HUMAN RIGHTS

One final, somewhat brief point should be made. In the United Kingdom, sports lawyers have made much about the potential impact in sport of incorporation of the European Convention on Human Rights via the Human Rights Act of 1998.[245] It is questionable, however, given that the act only applies to "public bodies," whether the Human Rights Act could apply in circumstances where an athlete was challenging a decision of a sports governing body for want of fair procedures. Parliament left the definition of "public bodies" as a matter for judicial discretion, and on one level of course, it may be argued that the courts have already excluded sports governing bodies from such definition in cases like *Law v. NGRC*, thereby meaning that the Human Rights Act has no

---

[243] *Modahl v. British Athletic Federation* [2002] 1 W.L.R. 1192, *Colgan v. Kennel Club* [2002] *International Sports Law Review* 187. See Stoner, "A Question of Proportionality", 10 (4) *Sports Law Administration and Practice* (August 2003) 1.

[244] Lewis & Taylor, *op. cit.*, p.157. See Wearmouth, *op. cit.*, p.34. See *Colgan v. Kennel Club* [2002] *International Sports Law Review*, 187. For comment see Stone, "A Question of Proportionality", 10 (4) *Sports Law Administration and Practice* (2003) 1.

[245] See, *inter alia*, Lewis & Taylor, *op. cit.*, pp.127 *et seq*. Lloyd, "Sports Disciplinary Proceedings and the Human Rights Act", (8)2 *Sport and the Law Journal* (2000) 61, Cairns, "Introducing the Human Rights Act", 8 (3) *Sport and the Law Journal* (1998) 60, Valeck, "The Human Rights Act – The Impact on Sports Governing Bodies", 8 (3) *Sport and the Law Journal* (2000) 71, Bitel, "Human Rights Act", 8 (3) *Sport and the Law Journal* (2000) 72, Boyes, "Regulating Sport after the Human Rights Act 1998" (2001) 151 *New Law Journal* 444, Lask, "The Potential Impact of the Human Rights Act 1998 on the Law Relating to Sport" [2000] *International Sports Law Review* 48 and Anderson, Mulcahy & Reindorf, "Independent and Impartial? The Potential Impact of the Human Rights Act 1998 on Sports Tribunals" [2000] *International Sports Law Review* 65.

application in cases of this nature.[246] McArdle, however, feels that this may not necessarily be the case.[247] He notes that one of the obvious concerns of the courts in a succession of judicial review cases, (most notably the *R v. Football League ex parte Football Association* case), was the fact that it constituted good policy not to allow the judicial review procedure (which is supposed to be specific and expeditious) to become clogged up by claims which might just as easily be processed via a plenary summons for breach of contract. On the other hand, commentators are increasingly calling for some effective external control of sporting bodies in light of their ever-increasing powers to impact on a person's livelihood.[248] The Human Rights Act provides the means for such control and the policy reasons for excluding the judicial review procedure in such cases are absent. After all, the court's point in *Football League* was that a perfectly effective alternative route was available for a sportsperson who felt that he or she had been unfairly treated by a governing body. If, however, a *Human Rights* claim is at issue, then no alternative is available to such sportsman if sports bodies are not deemed to be "public" for such purposes. Thus McArdle concludes that simply because a body is not deemed to be public for judicial review purposes does not *per se* prevent it from being public for other purposes. Indeed the conclusion of the Court of Appeal in *Poplar Housing & Regeneration Community Association Limited v. Donoghue*,[249] to the effect that the nature of the functions exercised by the body would be determinative in deciding whether or not it was a public one for the purposes of the Human Rights act rather leaves this question open.

This is of significance in Ireland but for somewhat different reasons. Since January 1, 2004 the European Convention on Human Rights has been incorporated into domestic law,[250] yet the position in respect of fair procedures is unlikely to change very much, because the constitutional protections in respect of both the right to earn a livelihood and the right to natural and constitutional justice apply against both public and private bodies. The classification of a sports body as public or private may however, be important in Ireland beyond application of the judicial review procedure, in determining whether an individual can gain access to records and documentations of sporting bodies under the Freedom of Information Act. Developments in this regard are awaited.

---

[246] Beloff, *op. cit.*, p.232. See also McArdle, *Football Society and the Law* (Cavendish, 2000), pp.178–179.

[247] See McArdle, "Judicial review, Public Authorities and Disciplinary Powers of Sports Authorities" (1999) *Cambrian Law* Review 30 at 35–39.

[248] See for example McCutcheon, *op. cit.*, pp.117ff in Greenfield & Osborn.

[249] [2002] Q.B. 48. See also *Parochial Church Council of Aston Cantlow v. Wallbank* [2001] E.W.C.A. Civ. 713.

[250] European Convention on Human Rights Act 2003.

2.5 CONCLUSION

As McArdle points out[251] it is probably not all that difficult for sports bodies to ensure that their rules remain immune from legal challenge. A sensible pre-planned policy coupled with carefully drafted rules that are comprehensive and clear and leave little or no need for interpretation should do the trick. In this respect Beloff argues that it would be well for legal advice to be taken in respect of the following matters:[252]

– The drafting of rules, constitutions etc (and Bitel suggests that it is important that three important factors should be borne in mind when drafting such rules, namely (1) to avoid the pursuit of untenable aims, (2) to involve sports participants at all stages of discussion and drafting of such rules and (3) to remember that such rules can be changed).[253]

– The composition of adjudication bodies.

– The conduct of disciplinary hearings, including the question of how discretion is to be exercised.

– The role of the adjudication body in determining issues as fundamental as guilt and innocence.

– Behaviour of the relevant body after the impugned action has occurred but before legal proceedings commence.

– The likelihood of success or failure in any proceedings, which may occur.

– The need to have a lawyer as a member of a disciplinary panel.

– The drawing up of a framework document outlining how procedures operate and thereby ensuring that they are in accordance with fair procedures.

Beyond this, care should be taken in the handling of such matters; for example all correspondence should be recorded[254] and all procedures should be followed with as much precision as is possible,[255] having regard to such matters as

---

[251] McArdle, "Judicial Review, Public Authorities and Disciplinary Powers of Sports Authorities" (1999) *Cambrian Law Review* 30 at 33–34.

[252] Beloff, p.211.

[253] Bitel, "Disciplinary Procedures from the Point of View of the Individual", 3 (3) *Sport and the Law Journal* (1995) 7 at 9.

[254] See Wearmouth, *op. cit.*, p.33 for the view that, such recording be conducted by a person independent of the relevant body.

[255] For similar checklists see Gardiner, *op. cit.*, p.2139. McArdle, "Judicial Review, Public Authorities and Disciplinary Powers of Sports Authorities" (1999) *Cambrian Law Review* 30 argues (pp.33–34) that because most sports governing bodies *will* employ good lawyers to draft their rules, they are unlikely to run into any overly significant problems and yet may be able to reserve a good deal of discretion for themselves.

privilege and confidentiality and the possible application of the Freedom of Information Act. Finally, as was witnessed in the Na Fianna case, whereas the High Court will retain a supervisory jurisdiction over disputes of this nature, equally an arbitration clause is a useful device for asserting the primacy of the sports body in sports matters, and for keeping disputes of this kind out of the courts.[256]

In an era in which the administrative rules of sports bodies are increasingly being challenged before civil courts, the lessons for sports governing bodies and by extension for clubs is clear. Rules and procedures do matter, and it is no longer good enough for a sports body to operate on and *ad hoc* basis or to seek to exclude the law in favour of trying to find a "sporting solution to a sporting problem." On the other hand if the basic standards mentioned above are followed then the ongoing deference shown by the courts to sporting organisations in the administration of their rules, should mean that it is not overly difficult for a sports body to stay out of the courts.[257]

---

[256] See Morton-Hooper, "The Right to a Fair Hearing", 9 (3) *Sport and the Law Journal* (2001) 155.

[257] At the time of going to print, the GAA has become involved in a new controversy, as a Longford player, Dave Barden, obtained a High Court interlocutory injunction in May 2004, preventing the GAA from imposing any sanction on him arising out a match in April 2004 during which Barden was sent off, pending a full hearing of his action against the GAA authorities. Mr Barden claims that the GAA had no jurisdiction to impose a sanction on him because the match in which he was sent off was not a properly constituted competition under GAA rules. See "GAA Player Initiates Court Action over Red Card Incident", *Irish Times*, May 11, 2004 and "Court Order for Banned Footballer", *Irish Times*, May 15, 2004.

CHAPTER THREE

Performance Enhancing Substances and Methods

3.1 INTRODUCTION

As we have seen in the previous chapter, sports governing bodies are required to act in accordance with basic standards of fair procedures, especially when they are engaged in disciplinary action against an athlete. The context in which such disciplinary action receives most prominence, is where an athlete is being suspended or permanently banned for using performance-enhancing drugs. Much has been written about the approach taken by sports bodies and indeed national governments to the issue of doping in sport. It is arguable, however, that many of the problems traditionally associated with this area will be ameliorated to a significant extent by a comparatively recent movement within sport to ensure that all agencies enforcing anti-doping policy are operating from the same rulebook – namely the World Anti-Doping Agency (WADA) *World Anti-Doping Code*. Equally some problems will remain, and in this chapter we consider both the evolution and the current state of global anti-doping policy, focusing in particular on the circumstances in which such policy attracts the attention of sports lawyers.

3.1.1 The history of the problem

Two recent events have brought the issue of doping in sport into particular international focus. In 1988, the world looked on in awe as Canadian superstar sprinter Ben Johnson broke the world 100-metre record in a time of 9.79 seconds, to win the Olympic title. The sun had barely set on this remarkable event, however, when International Olympic Committee officials announced that he had tested positive for a banned steroid Stanozolol, and would be stripped of his medal.[1] This was shocking for sports fans, not because the

---

[1] For analysis see de Pencier, "Law and Athlete Drug Testing in Canada", Vol. 4 (1) *Marquette Sports Law Journal* 259 [hereafter de Pencier], Goodbody, "Stanazolol or Sabotage", *The Times*, September 23, 2003, Slot and Goodbody, "Cock-up or Conspiracy? The Reasons Why that Positive Test makes no Sense", *The Times*, September 22, 2003. 13 years later on August 7, 2001, Canada was forced to relive the experience when, at

notion of doping was new to sport (it wasn't) but because it was presumed by many to have been the preserve of forces on the eastern side of the Iron Curtain. As a direct result of the incident, a Canadian Commission of Inquiry into the use of Banned Drugs and Practices intended to increase athletic performance was set up, under the Chairmanship of Judge Dubin.[2] This inquiry, which ran from November 1988 through September 1989, implicated large proportions of the entire Canadian set up in the Johnson scandal and also indicated the extent of drug use in sport at the time. Evidence was heard from 122 witnesses, and by the end of the inquiry, 48 athletes, including Ben Johnson admitted to using banned substances over a protracted period of time.[3] The clear implication of the report was that drug use at the upper levels of sport was utterly rife, and it is arguably from this period that we can see the beginnings of the first period of intense anti-doping effort within sporting and governmental circles

Just as shocking were the events surrounding the 1998 Tour de France cycling race – arguably the greatest annual sporting event in the world – where a doping scandal, which seemed to run deep within the cycling world[4] and would result in significant criminal prosecution for those involved – was uncovered.[5] On July 18, 1998, the leading FESTINA team, (whose sponsor

---

the World Athletics Championships held in Edmonton Canada, National 100 metres champion, Venolyn Clarke also tested positive for Stanozolol, with authorities admitting that she had not been tested for nine years.

[2] See *Commission of Inquiry into the Use of Drugs and Banned Practices Intended to Increase Athletic Performance* (Canadian Govt Publishing Centre, 1988) For analysis see de Pencier, "Law and athlete drug testing in Canada", Vol. 4 (1) *Marquette Sports Law Journal* 259. See also Moriarty, Fairall and Galasso, "The Canadian Commission of Enquiry into the use of Drugs and Banned Practices intended to increase athletic performance", *Journal of Legal Aspects of Sport*, Vol. 2 (1) (1992) 23.

[3] Johnson did however continue to protest that he was innocent of the offence for which he was banned. McArdle, "Say it ain't so Mo", p.91 in O'Leary ed. *Drugs and Doping in Sport* (Cavendish, England, 2001) concludes that "Johnson, a cocksure but semi-literate immigrant had the misfortune to come along just as the IOC decided that it needed to make an example of someone with a high profile. The Ben Johnson affair was nothing more than the high-tech lynching of an uppity black".

[4] See 1 (4) *Sports Law Bulletin* (1998), p.5, and also "Tour of Shame", *Irish Times*, August 3, 1998 and Tom Humphries, "Drug Fiascos Force us to Dethrone Naked Emperors", *Irish Times*, August 1, 1998.

[5] A criminal trial of 10 defendants connected with the FESTINA team indicted under a 1998 French statute criminalizing the supply of sporting drugs took place from October 2000. On December 22, 2000 the French court handed down a somewhat anti-climatic decision in which it sentenced both Bruno Roussel, the FESTINA trainer, to a one year suspended prison term and fined him 50,000f and Willy Voet, the team physiotherapist, to a 10 month suspended term and fined him 30,000f, for supplying the banned substance EPO. However, it acquitted the 'star defendant' Richard Virenque of the accusation of assisting in the supply of such substances. Interestingly the International Cycling Union, the French cycling Federation and the Tour de France organisers had asked that they be awarded a symbolic one franc compensation for damage to their reputation, which claim was rejected by the court who said that the 'passivity' of these bodies was to blame for the proliferation of drugs in cycling.

was heavily involved with the organisation of the tour) including the darling of the French public Richard Virenque, world champion Laurent Brochard and two time Tour of Spain winner Alex Zulle, was formally expelled from the tour after large quantities of the banned substance rEPO (as well as growth hormones, testosterone, corticoids and amphetamines) were found in team luggage. Bruno Roussel the team manager admitted that there was widespread doping in cycling but argued that it was necessary to enable riders to cope with the otherwise impossible conditions and that it was strictly controlled.

Later in the tour, more cyclists (including those from the ONCE team whose doctor, Nicolas Terrados was charged with drug offences under France's 1989 drugs act) dropped out because of increased drugs scrutiny, bringing the number of teams competing in the tour down to 15 from 21. On police orders, riders were required to undergo medical tests and had their luggage searched. Various riders including Belgium's Eddy Planckaert and France's Armen Meier admitted to using drugs. President of the International Cycling Union Hein Verbruggen admitted that whereas he did not know the number of cyclists who were implicated, it could be as high as 40% of all riders in the tour. The impact on French sport, and on public perception of cycling generally was enormous. Thus, on the initiative of the French Minister for Youth and Sport Marie-George Buffet, a new French criminal law was passed criminalising the supply of sports drugs.

Beyond French sport, the controversy led, for instance, to the Italian Minister for Sport Giovanna Melandrini setting up a similar investigation into drug use in Italian sport, especially cycling and soccer.[6] Most importantly the IOC convened a World Conference on Doping in February 1999, allegedly bringing together everyone involved directly or indirectly in the fight against doping[7] which itself led to the creation of the World Anti-Doping Agency (WADA).[8]

Yet doping in sport is not a new phenomenon. Indeed there is evidence that it has been around for as long as sport has been around[9] with the earliest reports of such activities dating from the third century BC.[10] Doping, as it is understood in contemporary terms, however, first came onto the scene in the

---

[6]   In Italy if an athlete tests positive for banned substance he may receive up to a two-year prison sentence. For analysis see 1 (6) *Sports Law Bulletin* (1998) 12.

[7]   For analysis see 2 (1) *Sports Law Bulletin* (1999) 1.

[8]   The declaration provided for greater education of athletes, continued responsibility for the IOC, International Federations, the National Olympic Committees and the CAS, and reinforced collaboration between sports organisations and public authorities.

[9]   See Houlihan, *Dying to Win* (Council of Europe Publishing, 1999) [hereafter Houlihan], p.33. Such reports date from the sixth century BC, when Gladiators used stimulants when fighting in the Circus Maximus, through to the third century BC, when Greek athletes used stimulants at the Olympic Games and the Middle Ages in preparation for jousts. See the Council of Europe "Europack" on sport without doping [hereafter Europack] at http://culture.coe.int/sp/Europack/CSGectionBModule3.html.

[10] Houlihan, *op. cit.*, p.33.

nineteenth century. Reports from this era suggest that both heroin and morphine were used to assist sports performance with the former being prominent in horse racing and the latter in endurance sports such as boxing. After World War II, when a nation's sporting prowess was seen to reflect its overall international status, the use of drugs in sport became considerably more common. Thus in the 1960s until the fall of the Berlin wall, East Germany (and probably other countries)[11] operated a state sponsored doping programme, compelling very young boys and girls to take pills, (including athletes who would become world famous like Olympic long jump champion Heike Drechsler) – which unbeknownst to these children contained anabolic steroids – thereby ensuring that East Germany was a force on the world sporting stage while causing many of these young athletes irreparable physical and mental harm.[12]

Since this time drug use in sport has escalated with more sophisticated drugs being developed to "beat the testers."[13] The Ben Johnson affair and the scandal surrounding Tour de France 1998, are merely high profile incidences of a problem that is ongoing and increasing.

3.1.2 The scale of the problem

It is virtually impossible to assess the true contemporary scale of the problem, because of the undoubted reality that the science of detecting drugs is some years and a large amount of money behind the science of using drugs.[14] A British Medical Association Report from May 2002 warned that anabolic steroid

---

[11] There is strong evidence of a similar programme within the Soviet Union. See Rae Brooks, "Former Sports Scientist Reveals Soviet Steroids Programme for Athletes", *Salt Lake Tribune*, September 1, 2003.

[12] See Ungerleider, *Faust's Gold; Inside the East German Doping Machine* (St Martin's Press, 2001), Panek, "Tarnished Gold", *Women's Sport and Fitness*, May/June, 1999, Rae Brooks, "East German Athletes Struggle with Legacy of Forced Doping", *Salt Lake Tribune*, April 7, 2002, Meyer, "Harvey took on East German Sporting Machine", *Denver Post*, October 21, 2001. In November 2002, the German Bundestag approved a compensation package of Stg£1.3 million for the 500–100 athletes who suffered damage as a result of the East German programme, however it appears that many affected athletes will not be able to bring claims as vital evidence relating to their cases has been destroyed. Moreover, in criminal trials, the two men at the heart of the doping programme, Manfred Ewald and Dr Manfred Hoeppner were sentenced to 22 months and 18 months respectively in prison for what the judge referred to as a 'system of state order crime'. See Florence, "Little Blue Pills Produce Sports Horror Story", *The Star Phoenix*, December 2, 2002, Cleaver, "Marxism, Medals and Misery", *The Observer*, March 2, 2003. Finally, in March 2003, a Frankfurt Court of Appeal ruled that East German athletes who were victims of state organised doping could sue the German Olympic Committee for damages.

[13] See Hemphill, "Para Olympics not Immune to Scandal", *Salt Lake Tribune*, March 13, 2002.

[14] See Mottram, "Prevalence of Drug Misuse in Sport", pp.357–378 in Mottram *Drugs in Sport* (3rd ed., Routledge, New York & London, 2003).

use was widespread among athletes from body builders in gyms to athletes at world championship level,[15] with up to 150,000 recreational users of such substances in Britain alone. In 2002, American baseball was rocked by allegations from former baseball greats Jose Canseco and Ken Caminiti that 50%-85% of major league baseball players use anabolic steroids, prompting the development of a 'steroid policy' within major league baseball.[16] In Canada, a recent study Commissioned by the Quebec sports ministry found that 26% of the 3,573 young athletes surveyed admitted to using one or more drugs on the IOC banned list – although less than 1% of the group admitted to using steroids.[17] Certainly it seems that banned substances are easily available to athletes,[18] and that there is a large industry for so-called "drug gurus" employed by cheating athletes to provide them with effective and non-traceable performance enhancing drugs.[19]

3.2 THE PROHIBITED SUBSTANCES AND METHODS[20]

Contrary to some public perception, there is no single list of banned substances automatically applicable to the whole of sport. Rather each sporting federation will have its own list of banned substances, tailored to meet the particular concerns of that sport.[21] Thus for example, use of beta-blockers – which

---

[15] See King, "Doping Widespread in Sports", *Express News*, October 23, 2002. As we shall see use of legal supplements is even more rife.

[16] See Kuc, "An Anabolic Edge", *Chicago Tribune*, June 11, 2002, Fry, "For Players' Sake Ban Steroids", *St Petersburg Times*, June 1, 2002, Callahan, "Steroids; Blame the Players", *Boston Herald*, June 1, 2002, Buckley, "A Sad Died-in-the-Wool Attitude; Condoning Steroids Deadly", *Boston Herald*, June 1, 2002, Antonen, "Caminiti's Claim Spurs Steroid Talk", *USA Today*, May 30, 2002, Bodley, "Senate Steps up Heat on MLB Drug Testing", *USA Today*, June 18, 2002, "A Dopey Policy", *Sports Illustrated*, 16 September, 2002, Shipley, "Stimulants are a Major League Hit", *Washington Post*, March 2, 2003, Knapp, "It's Time for Baseball to follow IOC's Lead", *San Francisco Chronicle*, February 21, 2003.

[17] "More than one in Four Young Quebec Athletes used Banned Drugs: Report", *Canadian Press*, November 2, 2002. From a British perspective see also Firn, "Drugs in Sport Report Warns of Mini Epidemic of Heart and Liver Disease caused by taking Anabolic Steroids", *Financial Times*, April 17, 2002. In 2002 Justin Wadsworth an American cross-country skier suggested that 40-50% of athletes in his sport used drugs of some kind. See Robertson, "The Longest Race", *Miami Herald*, January 29, 2002.

[18] Sherman, "Steroids used by Athletes Easy to Obtain, Paper Finds", *Knight Rider News Service*, August 11, 2002.

[19] See Bamberger and Yaeger, "The Use of Performance Enhancing Drugs is Common", p.15 in Dudley ed. *Drugs and Sports* (Greenhaven Press, San Diego, 2001) [hereafter Dudley] and Shipley, "Drug Testers have Designs on New Steroid", *Washington Post*, March 8, 2003.

[20] Houlihan, *op. cit.*, pp.35 and 82.

[21] *Ibid.*, p.57.

regulate the heart – is of no concern to the authorities dealing with track and field athletics but is absolutely banned by snooker and archery federations, and is of increasing concern to the world golfing authorities.[22]

Increasingly, however this supposed lack of uniformity is illusionary in that the rules of most federations have long integrated around the efforts of the International Olympic Committee, and hence the IOC 'banned list' has been the blueprint adopted by sports federations and tailored to meet their needs, even though this list only has practical application for the specific duration of the Summer and Winter Olympic Games. Currently sports federations are under increasing pressure to adopt the WADA "banned list" which itself represents one of the international standards envisaged under the new World Anti-Doping Code, and is brought into force for Irish sport under the terms of the Irish Sports Council Anti-Doping Rules, which are considered below. Therefore, in considering the types of drugs that are banned in sport, we will focus on this list, the most recent variant of which came into effect on January 1, 2004.

3.2.1 Prohibited substances

The list makes nine sub-divisions of prohibited substances,[23] banning; (1) Stimulants, (2) Narcotics, (3) Cannabinoids (4) Anabolic Agents, (5) Peptide Hormones, (6) Beta-2 Agonists (7) Agents with anti-oestrogenic activity, (8) Masking agents including Diuretics[24] and (9) Glucocorticosteroids. Of these only substances (4), (5). (6), (7) and (8) above are prohibited both in and out of competition with the rest only being subject to "in-competition" testing. We will now consider the most significant substances covered by the list.

Before we do so, however, one important point should be made. In respect of all these categories of banned substances, the WADA list mentions particular substances that are banned and concludes with the line "… and related [in the sense of having related pharmacological actions or chemical structure] substances." This reflects the undoubted fact that whatever efforts are made to restrict doping methods, the science of cheating is working harder to produce new, non-detectable forms of performance enhancing drugs, and sports authorities do not want to leave potential loopholes for cheats. Equally, as we

---

[22] In December 2000 top Australian golfer Craig Parry controversially claimed that several top players had used beta-blockers to calm nerves. (Indeed three-time major winner Nick Price had admitted using beta-blockers for this reason). Possibly as a reaction and possibly as a move to further the claims of golf that it should be re-introduced as an Olympic sport in 2008, the Royal and Ancient Golf Club, the governing body for golf, announced that it would introduce a doping programme.

[23] For analysis of the history of use of different drugs see Houlihan, *op. cit.*, p.35.

[24] For an interesting account of the effects of such drugs see Knapp, "Up Close Tale of 8 Months on Drugs", *San Francisco Chronicle*, October 23, 2003.

shall see later this may be simply too vague a term to use to ground a disciplinary procedure which might cost an athlete his or her career. Thus in 1996 at the Atlanta summer Olympic games, Russian athletes tested positive for Bromantan, which was not on the banned list but was deemed to be a "related substance," and this positive test was overturned by the ad-hoc CAS panel at those games, on the grounds that a positive finding in such circumstances would not adequately vindicate the rights of the athletes involved.[25]

3.2.1.1 Stimulants[26]

The common link between all the banned stimulants is that they operate to stimulate the body's central nervous system, allegedly provoking increased alertness, stamina, competitiveness and aggression. Equally, they may have the downside of leading the body to believe that it has an unrealistic pain threshold, causing the athlete to push him or herself beyond his or her natural limits and potentially to suffer a heart attack. Apart from the most widely used stimulants – amphetamines[27] – there are also stimulants like modafinil – allegedly the current stimulant of choice among high profile athletes.[28] In January 2004, both caffeine and also pseudo-ephedrine – a substance found in over the counter cold remedies – were taken off the banned list.[29] Finally, cocaine appears on the list (even though it is fundamentally a recreational drug with little if any known performance-enhancing properties), largely because it is felt that apart from any harmful consequences to the user, the presence of such substances in the sporting life tarnishes the image of sport generally.[30] Amphetamines were extremely popular in the period prior to the 1970s but their popularity has waned because they are now so easily traced in the body system.

---

[25] See Foster, "The Discourses of Doping; Law and Regulation in the War against Drugs", p.191 in O'Leary, *op. cit.*

[26] *Ibid.*, p.8. See also the *Dubin Report*, p.115 and George, "Central Nervous System Stimulants", p.63 in Mottram ed., *Drugs in Sport* (3rd ed., Routledge, New York & London, 2003).

[27] Houlihan, *op. cit.*, p.58.

[28] Rowbottom, "Modafinil is Drug of Choice says IAAF Chief", *Independent*, October 28, 2003, Rowbottom, "IAAF confirms at least Six Athletes Tested Positive for Banned Stimulant", *The Independent*, October 29, 2003.

[29] See Goodbody, "Tea and Coffee Back on the Menu for World's Athletes", *The Times*, September 25, 2003.

[30] See Welch, "A snort and a Puff: Recreational Drugs and Discipline in Professional Sport", p.75 in O'Leary and Hann, "The Persecution We Call Drug Testing", *The Guardian*, October 15, 2003.

2.2.1.2 Narcotic analgesics[31]

Included in this category are substances such as heroin, methadone, morphine and pethidine. These operate to reduce feelings of pain and enable an athlete either to carry on despite being in considerable pain or to be de-sensitised to feelings of pain when participating in contact sports where the risk of pain is high, with the obvious risk that an athlete may play through pain and exacerbate an existing injury.

2.2.1.3 Cannabinoids

Cannabinoids are neither performance enhancing nor harmful to the health of the user. Indeed the probability is that such substances are banned because their use by sporting heroes can be seen to tarnish the image and good name of sport.[32] Equally, some celebrated cases arise in respect of them, including that of snooker player Ronnie O'Sullivan who was stripped of his 1998 Irish Masters' title for using cannabis,[33] and in February 1998, that of Canadian snowboarding champion Ross Rebagliati who had his gold medal taken away at the Winter Olympics in Nagano following a positive test for marijuana.[34]

3.2.1.4 Androgenic anabolic agents[35]

These substances have been around for over one hundred years, and received widespread use during the Second World War, where they were given to German

---

[31] Houlihan, *op. cit.*, p.65. See also the *Dubin Report, op. cit.*, p.115.

[32] Gardiner, *op. cit.*, p.197, argues that whereas the National Governing Bodies have been fairly consistent when actual cheating is at issue that are far less consistent when dealing with the use of recreational drugs and possible threats to the integrity of sport. See also Welch, "A Snort and a Puff: Recreational Drugs and Discipline in Professional Sport", p.75 in O'Leary, *op. cit.*

[33] See "O'Sullivan Fails Test", *Irish Times*, May 16, 1998.

[34] The medal was, however reinstated a day later at the behest of the CAS because of technical irregularities in respect of the rules (at the time neither the IOC nor the Skiing federation banned marijuana), leading to an IOC decision to strengthen the rules in respect of recreational drugs in advance of the Sydney Olympics. See "IOC acts after Nagano incident", *Irish Times*, April 28, 1998. See also Beloff, "Drugs, Laws and Versapaks", p.39 in O'Leary, *op. cit.*, p.42, and Rae Brooks, "Arbitrator Recalls 'Slam Dunk' Ruling", *Salt Lake Tribune*, January 25, 2001.

[35] See Houlihan, p.66. See also Thurston, "Chemical Warfare: Battling Steroids in Athletics" 1 (1) *Marquette Sports Law Journal* (1990) 93 [hereafter Thurston], p.100 for a list of the major benefits of steroid use. Generally see Lowther, "A fine body of Law: The New Status of Anabolic Steroids", 6 (3) *Sports Law Journal* (1998), p.53 and James Wright "Anabolic Androgenic Steroids", p.53 in Tricjer and Cook, *Athletes at Risk* (Dubrinque IA, WC Brown, 1990) and George, "Androgenic anabolic steroids", p.189 in Mottram, ed., *Drugs in Sport* (3rd ed., Routledge, New York & London, 2003).

soldiers to increase their aggression levels. It is known that they have been used as performance enhancers in sport since the 1950s, notably on a state sponsored basis in the former East Germany.[36] Within the banned list, they are divided into two classes, namely anabolic androgenic steroids such as stanozolol, clostebol and the increasingly prominent nandrolone,[37] and Beta-2 agonists such as clenbuterol and formoterol. Of these two categories, the former is by far the more significant.

As their title suggests, these steroids are both androgenic (having the capacity to develop male characteristics) and anabolic (having the capacity to build muscle tissue), and they operate by causing nitrogen retention in the body, leading to the production of protein in the muscle cells and hence an increase in lean muscle mass, and a greater explosive energy. On the downside, the potential side effects of such steroids are frightening.[38] Psychologically they are associated with heightened aggression and what is termed "roid rage,"

---

[36] Houlihan records that by the time of the 1956 World Games in Moscow, Soviet athletes use of steroids was so great that they had to be catheterised, because their prostate glands had swelled so much that they were physically incapable of urinating naturally. Houlihan, p.45.

[37] Since the late 1990s increasing number of sports-persons have tested positive for Nandrolone or nandrolone metabolites or markers, including athletes Linford Christie, Doug Walker, tennis player Petr Korda and soccer players Frank de Boer, Edgar Davids and Fernando Couto. This is surprising in that Nandrolone has been detectable for years. (See 2 (1) *Sports Law Bulletin* (1999) 5 for analysis of the case of British athlete Doug Walker who tested positive for Nandrolone in January 1999). See also Kerr, "Doped or Duped? The Nandrolone Jurisprudence" [2001] *International Sports Law Review* 97 and "Nandrolone: What is it and who takes it", *Irish Times*, March 4, 2003. It has been suggested that the reason for the increasing prominence may be that the metabolites found in the sports person's system which appear to be derived from Nandrolone may in fact derive from two newer substances namely 19-Norandrostenedione and 19 Norandrostenediol. Both substances are widely available and until recently were not banned. The IOC banned both on January 31, 1999 and the IAAF took the same step in August 1999. Alternatively it has been suggested that dietary substances may influence the production of Nandrolone in the body although this suggestion has been disputed. In February 2001, new (IOC funded) research from a laboratory in cologne concluded that contaminated food supplements on general sale can give the metabolic impression of Nandrolone in the system at a level many hundreds of times greater than that which is acceptable.

[38] See Thurston, *op. cit.*, p.105. See especially Goldman and Katz, *Death in the Locker Room* (Elite Sports Medicine Publications, 1992), and the Dubin Report at 544. See Kuc, "A substance that enhances athletic performance can cause Severe Physical Harm; an Anabolic Edge", *Chicago Tribune*, June 11, 2002, Firn, "Drugs in Sport Report Warns of Mini Epidemic of Heart and Liver Disease Caused by Taking Anabolic Steroids", *Financial Times*, April 17, 2002, Manning, "Build Muscles, Shrink Careers. Using Anabolic Steroids Means Risking Health and Even Life", *USA Today*, July 8, 2002, Fry, "For Players' Sake, Ban Steroids", *St Petersburg Times*, June 1, 2002, Stamford, "You can Detect the Signs of Anabolic Steroid Use", *Courier Journal*, November 14, 2003, Taylor, "Live and Learn", *Sports Illustrated*, October 27, 2003, and Posnanski, "Steroids Just Feel Too Good", *Kansas City Star*, November 19, 2003.

as well as with athletes pushing themselves beyond natural limits.[39] Physically, because the body is artificially having testosterone pumped into it, it will decrease its natural production thereof leading in men to baldness, decreases in testicle size, growth of breasts, reduced sex drive and increased blood pressure leading to heart problems. There may also be risk of jaundice, cancer and liver damage. In women, steroids have been shown to lead to increased male characteristics including body hair and development of Adam's apples, as well as infertility and foetal abnormality. Finally, the fact that some athletes are using in excess of one hundred times the recommended dose – at which level testing becomes unsafe – means that the full effects of steroids on athletes are uncertain.[40]

The most pertinent example of these risks coming to fruition is in the case of the victims of the East German state sponsored doping regime.[41] Of all the tales of hardship arising from these sorry events, the most notable is perhaps the case of Heidi Krieger a former East German European shot-putt champion who had been given steroids as part of the state sponsored doping policy operating in pre-unification East Germany. Her psychology and physiology had become so masculinised (both physically and in the sense that she started to have transsexual feelings) that she had to have two operations to complete the process of turning into a man, which process was begun by the physicians who proscribed steroids for her.[42]

Steroids became detectable from the mid 1970s, at which point they were added to the IOC list of banned substances. Testing proper began in 1976 at the Montreal Olympic games, but the relevant tests (immunoassay) were not developed enough to catch any more than a handful of athletes.[43] By 1983, two new testing procedures, the Gas Chromatography and Mass Spectrometry

---

[39] Houlihan, *op. cit.*, p.69.

[40] Thurston, *op. cit.*, p.109.

[41] Rae Brooks, "East German Athletes Struggle with Legacy of Forced Doping", *Salt Lake Tribune*, April 7, 2002, Coonan, "Fund Plan for Doping Victims", *Guardian*, October 18, 2001. Other athletes like European Swimming Champion sought to take civil action against the German Olympic Committee claiming that she was doped during the communist regime. It should be noted that such litigation is not confined to the situation in the former East Germany. Thus in 2001, Erich Kaiter an American, sued the US cycling federation and his former coach and team trainer, claiming that his former coach gave him anabolic steroids and amphetamines without his knowledge, causing him to suffer from Crohn's colitis. See McPhee, "Ex racer sues coach for doping", *Denver Post*, 21 December, 2001.

[42] See O'Leary at 1 (2) *Sports Law Bulletin* (1998) 6. See also Grayson and Ionnadis, "Drugs, Health and Sporting Values", p.245 in O'Leary, and Florence, "Little Blue Pills Produce Sports Horror Story", *The Star Phoenix*, December 2, 2002. In November 2003 the IOC announced that athletes who had undergone sex change operations would be permitted to compete in the Olympics with the IOC medical director saying that "We will have no discrimination. The IOC will respect Human Rights."

[43] At the 1976 Olympics only eight out of 275 athletes tested positive.

tests were in place and were proving far more reliable.[44] Equally, after the Ben Johnson scandal, athletes tended to turn to the newer drugs like Human Growth Hormone (hGH) and Erythropoietin (rEPO) (both of which will be considered later) as well as specially created 'designer steroids' that are more effective, more expensive and virtually impossible to trace. Thus O'Leary notes that currently hGH is seen as the "rich man's drug," with the listed steroids seen as the cheap alternative.[45] Indeed it may be argued that if an international athlete tests positive for a listed steroid today, this indicates that [s]he has been incredibly careless, incredibly stupid or, incredibly, innocent in the sense that the positive showing derives from (most usually) a supplement which [s]he has ingested that contains metabolites of a banned substance.[46]

Operating in tandem with, or as a replacement for steroids, is simple administration of testosterone itself. This is a major area of concern because it is so difficult to trace. The traditional approach to testing focuses on the fact that as the body produces testosterone, it also produces a substance called epitestosterone. Normally the ratio between the two substances is 1:1. Equally, it is possible that an athlete may have an unusually high natural level of testosterone. In order to avoid the risk of legal challenge therefore, the IOC rule is that if the ratio in a particular competitor is greater than 6:1, then this denotes a positive finding, unless there is some evidence that the unusual ratio is due to a pre-existing physiological or pathological condition.[47] Moreover, in the event of a positive test for testosterone, the relevant medical authority must conduct an investigation before the sample is declared positive to discount this possibility. These problems may, however, disappear in the near future in

---

[44] Hence at the 1983 Pan-American games in Venezuela, 19 athletes from ten countries tested positive for steroids, with many more withdrawing form the games for fear of the new testing procedures. In May 1987, 34 people were indicted by US drug enforcement agencies on 110 counts of conspiracy to manufacture, distribute and smuggle huge quantities of anabolic steroids. Indeed by the late 1980s, as many as 70% of all positive results in the IOC laboratories were for anabolic steroids.

[45] O'Leary, 1 (2) *Sports Law Bulletin* (1998) 6. It has also been suggested that the economics of the situation will mean that whereas positive drug tests will fall where athletes from first world countries are concerned, athletes from poorer countries may continue to test positive for steroids. See also Houlihan, *op. cit.*, p.47ff. for analysis of the fact that even in the 1990s high profile athletes like Butch Reynolds, Katrin Krabbe and latterly Linford Christie and Merlene Ottey have tested positive for steroids. See also Moore, *op. cit.*, p.114. Thus when Canadian sprinter Venolyn Clarke tested positive at the 2001 world athletic championships, commentators suggested that what was extraordinary about her case was not that she tested positive but rather that she tested positive for such an outdated substance. See Taylor, "Drug Dilemma", *Calgary Sun*, August 10, 2001.

[46] See Kindred, "Steroid Testing Catches Only the Stupid Ones", *The Sporting News*, August 15, 2002.

[47] For claims that the t/e ratio is too high see Bamberger and Yaeger, "The Use of Performance Enhancing Drugs is Common", p.18 in Dudley, ed., *Drugs and Sports* (Greenhaven Press, San Diego, 2001).

that latest testing mechanisms are able to detect the exogenous administration of testosterone. Equally it is notable that since 2003, the WADA/IOC banned list includes a new category of substances with anti-oestrogenic impact. Finally, substances like androstenedione and dehydroepiandrosterone are banned. These are precursors to the natural production of testosterone, and are freely available in the United States as dietary supplements

3.2.1.5 Masking agents[48]

These include, but are not restricted to, diuretics which will affect the kidneys by increasing the rate at which urine is formed, and hence the secretion of other drugs from the body, thereby speeding up what is known as a clearance time.[49] The effects of diuretics are not easy to monitor, because they are generally used in conjunction with other drugs, but they may well lead to dehydration, muscle fatigue and cramps in the latter stages of competition.[50] Diuretics have been popular since the 1980s, with perhaps the most notable example of their use being that by the cyclist and 1988 Tour de France winner Pedro Delgado, who tested positive for a diuretic (probenecid) which was shortly afterwards added to the list of banned substances.[51]

3.2.1.6 Beta-2 agonists

These include salbutamol,[52] salmeterol and terbutaline, which are permitted by inhaler to prevent or treat asthma, or exercise induced asthma, provided that the relevant medial authority is informed in writing by the team doctor of this complaint.[53] Medically necessary substances of this kind are the subject of a new WADA international standard in respect of Therapeutic Use Exemptions, considered below.

---

[48] *Dubin Report*, p.116 and Houlihan, *op. cit.*, p.72.

[49] For the clearance time for particular drugs, see Bamberger and Yaeger, pp.14–15 in Dudley, ed., *Drugs and Sports* (Greenhaven Press, San Diego, 2001).

[50] Houlihan, p.73.

[51] *Ibid.*, p.50.

[52] In July 2002, sprinter Kim Collins won the gold medal in the 100 metres at the Commonwealth Games, tested positive for Salbutamol, but was exonerated when he told officials that he was an asthmatic but that his national organisation had forgotten to pass his documentation on to the competition organisers. See Mitchell, "President takes a Deep Breath over Asthma Controversy", *The Observer*, August 4, 2002.

[53] See Armstrong and Chester, "IOC regulations in relation to drugs used in the treatment of respiratory tract disorders", p.102 in Mottram, ed., *Drugs in Sport* (3rd ed., Routledge, New York & London, 2003). Recently those at the forefront of opposition to doping have feared that the immunity afforded to persons using asthma medication has been abused. Generally 1% of the population suffer from asthma, yet 6% of athletes competing at the Sydney Olympic Games claimed to be entitled to use asthma medication. Indeed some 30–40% of the Australian swimming team claimed such relief.

3.2.1.7 *Peptide hormones, mimetics and analogues*[54]

Human Chorionic Gondatrophin (hCG) is naturally produced in the placenta during pregnancy and stimulates the production of progesterone. When injected into men it has the effect of stimulating cells within the testes to produce testosterone and epitestosterone in equal amounts, thereby ensuring that the ratio between the two is kept below the IOC threshold, and hence making it very difficult to detect. For this reason the substance was added to the IOC list of banned substances. Similar in effect is Adrenocoticotrophic hormone (ACTH),[55] or its derivative tetracosactrin, which stimulates a rise in blood cortisol and corticosterone concentration and is used to reduce lethargy and produce positive effects on mood during training and competition. Furthermore, the IOC deems insulin to be a prohibited substance unless it is used to treat diabetes and a doctor testifies to this fact.[56] Moreover, written certification of insulin dependency must be obtained from an endocrinologist or team physician.[57]

Perhaps the two most notable substances in this class are Erythropoietin (EPO), (which will be dealt with in the next section) and Human Growth Hormone. This last substance is released from the pituitary gland and controls the natural growth of almost every body system. It stimulates nitrogen retention, breaks down fat and converts it to energy and stimulates the production of somattomedins, which are the molecules that facilitate growth. Hence it can be used to increase height (for basketball players) and muscle growth, but probably not strength. Human Growth Hormone is reckoned to be the current drug of choice especially for sprinters, not least because at the time of writing, it is virtually impossible to detect.[58] Equally, its overall efficacy may be more imaginary than real, and it is also enormously expensive.[59]

---

[54] *Ibid.*, p.73. See also George, "Peptide and glycoprotein hormones and sport", p.189 in Mottram, ed., *Drugs in Sport* (3rd ed., Routledge, New York & London, 2003).

[55] *Ibid.*, p.74.

[56] Insulin has been on the banned list since 1998, however anecdotal reports suggest that it is becoming increasingly popular amongst athletes today, and if administered incorrectly is entirely likely to lead to fatal results. See Bamberger and Yaeger, p.19 in Dudley, ed., *Drugs and Sports* (Greenhaven Press, San Diego, 2001).

[57] Dr Harm Kuipers, a member of the IOC medical Commission suggested at a conference in Madrid on November 13, 2002 that insulin might be removed from the banned list in 2004 on the grounds that it did not have performance enhancing properties and was in fact being used by athletes simply because it was on the banned list and therefore was assumed to have performance enhancing properties, despite the fact that it could lead to sever hypoglycaemia in users. Dr Kuipers suggested that substances like caffeine, heroin, morphine, glucocorticoids, pseudo-ephedrine and cannabis were all likely to be removed from the banned list as the IOC sought to move to a situation where only drugs that were both harmful to the health of the user *and* performance enhancing would be banned.

[58] See the *Dubin Report*, p.118. The downside of hGH is uncertain but will link in with downside of the over-secretion of naturally produced growth hormone, i.e. overgrowth

3.3 Prohibited Methods[60]

The list refers to three forms of prohibited methods namely:

1. Enhancement of Oxygen transfer by blood doping or the administration of products that enhance the uptake, transport or delivery of oxygen.

2. Pharmacological, chemical and physical manipulation.[61]

3. Gene Doping – defined as the non-therapeutic use of genes, genetic elements and/or cells that have the capacity to enhance athletic performance.

The last of these three prohibited methods will be dealt with in detail later in this chapter.

3.3.1 Manipulation

Manipulation is regarded as particularly heinous in that a dual infringement appears to be involved – the athlete is undermining the system, and is doing so in all probability because he or she has taken a banned substance to begin with. From an Irish standpoint, Michelle Smith (as she then was) was banned by FINA after it found that she had manipulated a sample.[62] Methods of manipulating samples include substitution of another person's urine, retention of pre-doping urine and then reintroduction thereof into one's system by a catheter in time for the test, use of a drug to prevent renal excretion, alterations of testosterone and epitestosterone or – as appears to have been the case in the Michelle Smith affair – trying to manipulate the sample through dilution with whiskey or any masking agent.

---

of soft tissue in e.g. forehead, jaw and fingers and coronary artery disease. It may also cause diabetes, arthritis or cancer. See Dudley, *op. cit.*, p.10. Moreover, in May 2001, it was announced that quantities of hGH found in Europe were infected with CJD – the human variant of mad cow disease. Given that hGH was reckoned to be the drug of choice among cheating athletes at Sydney 2000, the potential consequences are ominous.

[59] Duchaine, *Underground Steroid Handbook II* (Venice California, HLR Technical Books, 1989).

[60] Houlihan, *op. cit.*, p.76.

[61] *Ibid.*, p.78.

[62] See *inter alia*, Kimmage, "Awaiting the Sting", *Sunday Independent*, May 2, 1999 and Humphries, "One Minute out of Sight" and "At Least Four to Six Minutes", *Irish Times*, May 4, 1999.

3.3.2 Blood doping and erythropoietin[63]

Up until about ten years ago, blood doping (defined as *"The administration of blood, red blood cells and/or related blood products to an athlete which may be preceded by withdrawal of blood from the athlete who continues to train in such a blood depleted state."*) was reckoned to be as common as any procedure for breaking the anti-doping rules. The manner in which it operates is as follows.[64] The presence of oxygen in the muscles (generated by red blood cells) gives rise to capacity for endurance. Hence, the higher one's red blood cell count, the more endurance one will have. So the athlete will have about a litre of blood removed from his body or from that of a compatible donor, and from that litre of blood the red blood cells are scientifically separated from the plasma. The athlete's natural resistance will ensure that in time his body's blood level will return to normal, but then the original blood taken from the athlete and now in the form of pure red blood cells will be re-introduced into his system. Hence his oxygen level increases, and he has generally greater endurance and also the capacity to use more oxygen during intense exercise.[65] This procedure has been shown to be particularly useful for athletes with an existing high level of fitness and for those engaging in endurance sports.

A major criticism of the ban on blood doping, is the fact that much the same effect can be achieved by the perfectly legal procedure of high altitude training,[66] in that because there is less oxygen at higher altitude, the body compensates by pumping more oxygen into the blood stream, in a natural procedure called Erythropoiesis. Equally, it is not possible to train at a high level of intensity at high altitude. This is the reason why many top athletes train at low altitude but sleep or sit in tents or huts that have nitrogen artificially pumped into them.[67] This training method is known as hypoxia, and whereas

---

[63] Houlihan, *op. cit.*, p.76. See also the *Dubin Report*, p.120 and Armstrong and Reilly, "Blood Boosting and Sport", p.205 in Mottram, ed., *Drugs in Sport* (3rd ed., Routledge, New York & London, 2003).

[64] See Sawka *et al*, "The Use of Blood Doping as an Ergogenic Aid", Med. Sci. Sports Exerc., June 28, 1996, p.R1,

[65] Controlled studies suggest that an athlete having recourse to blood doping will have 5%–30% greater endurance levels. See Jones and Perdoe, "Blood Doping a Literature Review", 23 *British Journal of Sports Medicine* (1989) 84.

[66] See Floria, "Hypoxia: An Altitude about Training", *Sweat Magazine*, November 11, 2002.

[67] See Meyer, "Preparation for Salt Lake Games Moves in-House", *Denver Post*, July, 7, 2001, DeSimone, "Drug Talk Hits a Higher Level", *Chicago Tribune*, July 28, 2002, Rae Brooks, "The Science of Speed", *Salt Lake Tribune*, January 6, 2002, Rae Brooks, "Speed Skaters Turn to Hyperoxic Training", *Salt Lake Tribune*, October 15, 2001 Sivakkumaran, "Controversial Oxygen Machine on its Way Here", *The Straits Time (Singapore)*, November 18, 2002, Norcross, "Top Athletes Gain Edge by Spending their Nights in Altitude Tents", *San Diego Union-Tribune*, September 17, 2001, Hart, "Captain Snooze", *Sunday Telegraph*, April 22, 2002, Maffly, "Controversy Arises in Norway

it is currently perfectly legal as far as sport is concerned, equally WADA regards it with increasing suspicion.[68]

Recognition of the efficacy of this procedure led, in 1984, to the development of the production of synthetic Erythropoietin (rEPO), which has figured on the IOC banned list since 1990. This substance is allegedly dangerous to the health of athletes taking the drug[69] and is a major contemporary concern for anti-doping rules.[70]

Up until 2000, the drug was almost impossible to trace, but with the Sydney Olympics in mind, the WADA and the IOC adopted a combined blood/urine test for rEPO in August 2000.[71] In fact the test proved somewhat less than effective, in that whereas the blood testing showed up nine positive cases of EPO use, the urine testing failed to do so, and for legal reasons, the IOC was advised that no athlete could be deemed to have failed such test.[72] As a result since 2000, intense research was undertaken for the purposes of developing a

---

Over Use of Hypobaric Tents", *Salt Lake Tribune*, August 26, 2001, Haight, "Skating, Skiing on Thin Air – Literally", *The Oregonian*, December 20, 2001, Chin, "Getting High: Finland Athletes get an Altitude", *St Paul Pioneer Press*, January 24, 2002, Berger, "Air conditioning a hot topic", *Rocky Mountain News*, February 2, 2002, De Simone, "Drug Talk Hits a Higher Level", *Chicago Tribune*, July 28, 2002.

[68] Both the IOC president Jaques Rogge and the WADA Chairman Dick Pound have spoken in opposition to such tents. On the other hand Frank Shorter, head of the US anti-doping agency (USADA) has spoken in favour of such tents, comparing their use to travelling to train at altitude. Maher, "Tent Users Dream of Gold in Their Sleep", *American Statesman*, February 12, 2002.

[69] Excessive use of EPO can lead to thickening of blood leading to heart attacks and strokes. It is estimated that since 1990 some 20 cyclists have died as a result of using this product. In July 2002 former Australian middle distance runner Ron Clarke argued that because rEPO has precisely the same effect as high altitude training, it should be permitted where there is no risk to user athletes. See Fordyce, "Cram Hits Back in Drugs Row", *BBC Sports Online*, July 3, 2002. It is notable that Paula Radcliffe who is a long time critic of EPO use actually adopts a similar line in principle to Clarke in that she sees use of nitrogen tents as merely a means of levelling the playing field viz a viz athletes living at a higher altitude level. See Clarey, "If Doping is Banned, Should Sleeping in Altitude Tents be Allowed", *International Herald Tribune*, December 7, 2001.

[70] For an excellent evaluation of the development of EPO see Ferstle, "Blood is Thicker" *Athletics Weekly*, September 12, 2001. See also "Drugs and Doping: Blood Doping and Recombinant Human Erythropoietin", p.130 in Mellonm ed., *Sports Medicine Secrets* (Philadelphia, Hanley and Belfus, 1994), Pfitzinger, "EPO: Illegal and Deadly", *Running Times*, November, 1998.

[71] The immediate impact of the introduction of this test was that China, a country concerning which numerous allegations of state sponsored doping programmes have been made, withdrew in the region of thirty athletes from its Olympic team. The move was made, according to Mr Liu Jianyong of the Chinese Olympic Committee in order to "protect the health of the athletes and uphold the fairness of the Olympic Games.", See Watterson, "Chinese Squad Decimated by EPO Tests", *Irish Times*, September 6, 2000.

[72] For the purposes of this test, the blood sample merely indicates the possibility of the presence of EPO – the urine test is that which proves the issue conclusively.

urine only test for EPO.[73] Indeed this was at the centre of controversy in July and August 2001, where Russian distance runner Olga Yegorova tested positive for EPO in France and was banned from competing at the World Championships in Edmonton in Canada, only to have her ban controversially lifted some days later when it was discovered that the French were using a non-validated urine only test, thereby rendering her positive test unsafe and unsatisfactory.[74] As we shall see CAS has recently accepted the legitimacy of a urine only test for EPO.[75]

Linked with EPO is a new stamina-boosting drug called Darbepoetin, sold under the brand name Aranesp. This drug is ten times more powerful than EPO and requires injections once every two weeks rather than every other day – as is the case with EPO. It was found to have been used by cyclists during the 2001 Giro d'Italia, and in February 2002, three of the most successful cross country skiers at the 2002 winter Olympic Games – Johann Muehlegg, Larissa Lazutina, and Olga Danilova – were expelled from the games and suspended for testing positive for this substance – which although it was so new that it was not on the IOC banned list, nonetheless constituted a 'related substance' to EPO.[76] Other new substances which appear to be prevalent but which are not on the IOC list include perflurocarbon (PFC) which has huge oxygen carrying capacity and is as yet undetectable, and the use of which constitutes a banned method,[77] DynEPO, a blood boosting hormone that is cultivated using human rather than animal cells and which in tests appears identical to the EPO naturally produced in the human body, thereby proving undetectable under the EPO blood-urine test, Perftoran a substance that allows

---

[73] On July 10, 2001, the IOC announced that as a result of research in a Russian laboratory, in tandem with similar research in laboratories in Barcelona, Paris, Sydney and Japan, a new urine only test for EPO would be validated in a matter of weeks.

[74] See Ferstle, "Controversy over Yegorova EPO", *Runners World Daily*, September 13, 2001, Patrick, "IOC's Most Trying Test", *USA Today*, August 2, 2001. At the same time another controversy arose in respect of EPO. In April 2001 UCI – the international cycling federation announced that it would be reverting to a urine only test (with pre-race blood tests being used to determine who would be urine tested) based on a search for percentage of young red blood cells in the athlete's system. See Fotheringham, "Test in Sight for EPO but what Comes Next", *Guardian*, March 26, 2001. One rider, Bo Hamburger tested positive for EPO on this test, but on August 11, 2001, the Danish Doping Board said that the new test was not validated and hence that Mr Hamburger's positive test could not stand.

[75] *IAAF v. Boulami & MAR*, CAS 2002/O/401.

[76] See Smith, "Busted: Nordic Skiers Stripped of Medals; Tests Show Use of New Substance that is Similar to EPO", *Salt Lake Tribune*, February 25, 2002. Interestingly it seems that these athletes were so confident of not testing positive for this substance that they took the drugs on the eve of the games. Originally they were only stripped of one gold medal each, but in a decision of CAS on December 18, 2003, they were stripped of all their medals from the entire games. See *Canadian NOC & Scott v. IOC*, CAS 2002/O/373 and *Norwegian NOC & Others v. IOC*, CAS 2002/O/372.

[77] Houlihan, p.145 in O'Leary, *op. cit.*

the blood to carry 20% more oxygen than normal blood, hydroxyethyl starch (HES) the plasma volume expander used by members of the Finnish cross-country ski team at the 2001 world championships, and Repoxygen, an anti-anemia drug which encourages natural production of EPO.

3.4 SUBSTANCES PROHIBITED IN PARTICULAR SPORTS[78]

3.4.1 Alcohol

Alcohol is prohibited by the aeronautic, archery, automobile, billiards and boules federations. It is only prohibited on an 'in-competition' basis, and is tested for using either breath or blood analysis.

3.4.2 Beta blockers

These are substances that reduce the heart rate, the degree of contraction of blood vessels around the heart and systemic arterial blood pressure. They are mainly used in sports such as shooting, golf, archery and snooker when a very steady arm is necessary (but they are shown to have a deleterious effect on stamina and hence are useless in endurance sports). The major federations to be concerned with Beta-blockers are the modern pentathlon federation, the Archery federation, and the snooker and billiards federation. Again they are only prohibited on an 'in-competition' basis

3.4.3 Diuretics

As we have seen, diuretics are prohibited in all sports when they operate as masking agents. They are also, however, effective in furthering weight loss, and hence they are specifically prohibited both in and out of competition, in sports where weight loss can enhance performance such as body building, boxing, wrestling, rowing and certain martial arts. No Therapeutic Use Exemptions may be granted for use of diuretics.

---

[78] Houlihan, *op. cit.*, p.78. See also Reilly, "Alcohol, Anti-anxiety Drugs and Sport", p.256 in Mottram ed., *Drugs in Sport* (3rd ed., Routledge, New York & London, 2003).

3.5 SHOULD DOPING BE BANNED?[79]

There is a significant argument that despite the almost universal condemnation of doping in sport, nonetheless it should still be permitted.[80] This argument has particular resonance within professional sport, where in principle any restriction on the use of technology to improve one's performance constitutes a restraint of trade, and any such restriction that is not consistently applied and rationally underpinned constitutes an unreasonable restraint of trade or an anti-competitive practice.[81] In assessing the merits of this argument it is therefore necessary to consider the traditional justifications offered for anti-doping policy.

3.5.1 The health of the athlete who uses drugs

First it is argued that drugs are harmful to users and should therefore be banned.[82] In 1998, the then President of the IOC argued both that the IOC list

---

[79] See, *inter alia*, Gardiner, *op. cit.*, pp.163–164, Houlihan, *op. cit.*, pp.107ff, Cox, "Legalisation of Drug Use in Sport" [2002] *International Sports Law Review* 77, Cox, "Victory with Honour or Victory at All Costs" (2000) *Dublin University Law Journal* 19, Verokken, "Drug Use and Abuse in Sport", p.29 in Mottram ed., *Drugs in Sport* (3rd ed., Rutledge, London/New York, 2003) WM Brown, "Paternalism, Drugs and the Nature of Sports", XI *Journal of the Philosophy of Sport* (1985) 14, W. Fraleigh, "Performance Enhancing Drugs in Sport: The Ethical Issue", Vol. XI *Journal of the Philosophy of Sport* (1985), p.23, Simon, "Good Competition and Drug Enhanced Performance", XI *Journal of the Philosophy of Sport* (1985) 16 [hereafter Simon], Simon, "Responses to Brown & Fraleigh", XI *Journal of the Philosophy of Sport* (1985) 30, Brown, "Responses to Simon and Fraleigh", XI *Journal of the Philosophy of Sport* (1985) 33, Brown, "Ethics, Drugs and Sport", VII *Journal of the Philosophy of Sport* (1980) 15, Lavin, "Sports and Drugs, Are the Current Bans Justified?", XIV *Journal of the Philosophy of Sport* (1987) 34 [hereafter Lavin], Vernacchia, "Ethical Issues of Drug Use in Sport", p.33 in Tricker & Cook, *Athletes at Risk* (Dubrinque IA, WC Brown, 1990) and Marazzo, "Athletes and Drug Testing; Why do We Care if Athletes Inhale?", Vol. 8 *Marquette Sports Law Journal* (1997) 75.

[80] See Kolata, "The Impropriety of Taking Performance Enhancing Drugs is Debatable", p.42 in Dudley, Herhold, "Let's Get Real", *Mercury News*, October 23, 2003, Antonucci, "We have to have Standards", *Mercury News*, October 23, 2003, Ratto, "Drugs: Do We Really Care?", *San Francisco Chronicle*, October 25, 2003, Cashmore, "Stop Testing and Legalise the Lot", *The Observer*, October 26, 2003, Bee, "Moral Majority are out of Touch with the Real Issues", *Guardian*, November 10, 2003, Kravitz, "Losing battle Still Worth the Fight", *Indianapolis Star*, November 19, 2003.

[81] See Cox, "Legalisation of Drug use in Sport" [2002] I.S.L.R. 77. Thus it has been noted that in many other professions, 'workers' use performance enhancing substances – most notably caffeine. See Dudley, *op. cit.*, p.9.

[82] See Goldman & Klatz, *Death in the Locker Room* (Chicago Elie Sports Medicine, 1992). See also Houlihan, *op. cit.*, p.66, and Thurston, "Chemical Warfare: Battling Steroids in Athletics", 1 (1) *Marquette Sports Law Journal* 93 [hereafter Thurston] 100, for a list of the major benefits of steroid use. Generally see Lowther, "A Fine Body of Law: The

of banned substances should be reduced and also that the only substances that should be banned are those that are harmful to the health of the users.[83] The difficulty with this justification, however, is that it could be used to target far more aspects of sport than drug use. From the food supplements that seem to permeate modern sport, to the training regimes of athletes, to the nature of contact sport, we see threats to the welfare of the athlete.[84] If the governing bodies of sport were genuinely and consistently concerned with athletes' health, then all these things should also be banned – in other words sport itself should be banned as a health hazard. Moreover, the reason why, for example boxing is not banned, is because respect is afforded to the liberty of the athlete to decide for him or herself whether or not he wishes to harm him or herself[85] – a logic that could apply equally in the context of drug use.

Finally, it should be noted that drug use in sport is rampant even though it is banned; in other words the restraint of trade that is involved in anti-doping policy is actually ineffective in achieving its desired objectives. Indeed it may even be counter productive in that it is argued that if drug use was permitted it could be effected openly and safely, thereby alleviating many risks that drug users currently face.[86]

New Status of Anabolic Steroids", 6 (3) *Sports Law Journal* (1998) 53 and James Wright, "Anabolic Androgenic Steroids", p.53 in Tricjer and Cook, *Athletes at Risk* (Dubrinque IA, WC Brown, 1990). Malliarakis, "Doping Robs Athletic Success of its Legitimacy", *Deserest News*, February 18, 2002, Arie & Campbell, "Deaths of Italian Footballers fuel doping fears in Britain", *Observer*, January 19, 2003, Abt, "After a Rider's Sudden Death, More Questions on Doping", *International Herald Tribune*, January 2, 2003.

[83] See *Sports Law Bulletin*, 1 (4) (1998) 5. See also "Some Drugs Okay says IOC Chief Samaranch", *Irish Times*, July 27, 1998. Reaction both within and outside the IOC, however, was one of criticism for these comments. See, *inter alia*, Watterson, "Drip, Drip of Drug Revelations Continues", *Irish Times*, August 1, 1998, and by the same author, "IOC Didn't Move Against Drugs Due to Conscience", *Irish Times,* August 21, 1998. Indeed, the IOC's own Prince Alexandre de Merode head of the medical Commission, said that he was "appalled", by the comments of the IOC chief. See "Samaranch Under Renewed Fire", *Irish Times*, August 18, 1998. On the other hand Grayson and Ionnadis (at p.248 in O'Leary, *op. cit.*) welcomed such comments. Finally in July 2002, former middle distance runner Ron Clarke, a revered sporting figure in Australia told the Australian Associated Press that athletes should be free to use all performance enhancing drugs that were not user-harmful.

[84] There is an ongoing investigation in Italy into the inordinately high incidences of Motor Neurone Disease among footballers. See Fotheringham, "FA to Probe Link between Football and Nerve Disease", *The Guardian*, January 21, 2003.

[85] See Cox, "Victory with Honour or Victory at all Costs", 22 (2000) *Dublin University Law Journal* 19 at p.37, Lypsyte, "Athletes have the Right to Accept the Risks and Benefits of Performance Enhancing Drugs", p.59 in Dudley and Brown, "Paternalism, Drugs and the Nature of Sports", (1984) *Journal of the Philosophy of Sport* 14. Generally see Mill, *On Liberty, and Other Essays* (ed., Himmelfarb, Penguin, 1985), Feinberg, *Harm to Self* (Oxford University Press, 1986), Ten, "Paternalism and Morality", (1971) *Ratio* 56 and G. Dworkin, "Paternalism", p.107 in Wassestrom, ed., *Morality and the Law* (Wadsworth, California, 1971).

[86] Thus O'Leary ("Doping Solutions and the Problem with Problems", p.267 in O'Leary,

3.5.2 Protecting the good name both of sport and of the clean athlete

Secondly, it is argued both that drug use gives sport a bad name[87] and also that 'clean' athletes who perform some remarkable feat are tarred with the 'cheater's brush' such that it is assumed that they too must be using drugs.[88] Indeed this has led some athletes to insist that they be tested following competitions.[89] It has also resulted in situations where certain athletes have alleged that fellow competitors are using drugs – allegations which, if false are dreadfully insidious,[90] and which have prompted the IAAF to introduce compulsory athlete licences by which competitors are prevented from making such unsubstantiated comments. Linked with this it is argued that the allegations that drug use is widespread in sports reduces the capacity of sport to attract lucrative sponsorship deals.[91]

In response it may be argued that it is the fact that drugs are banned that creates the stigma attaching to them, and hence that their legalisation, by removing the stigma would also remove the threat to the good name of sport. It should be remembered that in the year that Americans were vilifying Michelle Smith for having allegedly manipulated a sample in order to disguise the presence of the banned anabolic agent androstenedione, they were also cheering baseball legend Mark McGwire who openly admitted using androstenedione (which was banned by FINA but not by the baseball federation), and it is estimated that as a result of McGwire's endorsement of the product, sales increased by more than 1000%.[92] Moreover, it is arguable that for many people

---

op. cit.) says, "Once competitors could openly use doping, then the terrible side-effects of some drugs could be prevented by their effective administration by medical staff."

[87] See "Even a Suspicion of Drugs Destroys Trust", *International Herald Tribune*, April 3, 2002, Barnes, "Ben Johnson and the Legacy of Suspicion", *Daily Telegraph*, November 2, 2002, O'Connor, "Suspicion is sucking the life out of fair play", *The Journal News*, November 27, 2002, Dyer, Owen and Buckley, "Football Doping Probe Threatens to Disfigure the Beautiful Game", *Financial Times*, May 29, 2002.

[88] See McKay, "Much Tested Radcliffe Rebuffs Drug Smear", *Guardian*, August 8, 2002.

[89] See Litke, "Radcliffe Distances Herself from Drugs", *Associated Press*, October 15, 2002.

[90] See Rowbottom, "Holmes Refuses to Apologise for Ceplak Slur", *Independent*, August 10, 2002, McKay, "Holmes in Trouble over Drug Smears", *Guardian*, August 10, 2002.

[91] A 1999 survey by the Healthy Competition Foundation found that 71% of the American public would be less likely to watch the Olympics if they know athletes are using drugs. See McCaffrey, "The United States Must Spearhead Reforms to Eradicate Drugs in Sports", p.71 in Dudley, *op. cit.*, but see also Briggs, "Doping Scandals Haven't Diminished Sports' Popularity", *Denver Post*, November 16, 2003. For suggestion that this may be a reason why the IOC is not fully committed to anti-doping policy and may even have covered up positive tests see Dudley, *op. cit.*, pp.8–9. A number of athletes, including CJ Hunter and Merlene Ottey claim that the IAAF promised to cover up their positive drugs tests in advance of major competitions if the athletes feigned injury and withdrew from these competitions. The IAAF denies these claims.

[92] Dudley, *op. cit.*, p.10.

watching professional sport, what is important is the sight of people or teams winning, and the manner in which they achieve this is rather less important. Thus Charles Yesalis, commenting on the controversy concerning steroid use in baseball said that:

> "Baseball is no longer a sport but a multi-million dollar business. You can argue that the owners think steroids are good for baseball because people hit more home runs and that increases the players' salaries and it increases the TV viewing audience and it increases the attendance in stadiums."[93]

3.5.3 A level playing field for all competitors

Thirdly it is argued that it is necessary to ban drugs in order that sport may be played on a metaphorical level playing field. This is a rather questionable argument. First, sportspersons at all levels are not equal. Some are richer (and hence have access to better facilities) than others; some appear to be genetically more able; some live at higher altitude; and if sport was serious about combating inequalities then it would have to deal with these factors too.[94] More to the point, the absence of a level playing field stems from the ban on drugs not from their "decriminalisation". After all, at the moment drugs are banned yet we know that their use is widespread – so the ban does nothing to level playing fields. The only way that this could be achieved is if drug use was permitted and if efforts were made to distribute drugs to as many athletes as wished to use them.

3.5.4 The interests of the "would-be clean athlete"

It is also argued that drugs should be banned in order to protect the interests of "innocent" athletes who would ideally prefer not to use drugs yet who believe that if they do *not* do so, (and thereby expose themselves to the concomitant risks outlined above) then they do not stand a chance of winning because everyone else in the starting line up may be being assisted by drugs,[95] and

---

[93] Kuc, "An Anabolic Edge", *Chicago Tribune*, June 11, 2002, see also Jenkins, "Steroids all the Rage – but Signify Little', *San Francisco Chronicle*, June 17, 2002.

[94] Thus as we have seen Paula Radcliffe justifies the use of altitude tents, and Ron Clarke justified the legalisation of drug use on the grounds that it was necessary in order to level the playing field as regards athletes who live at low altitude. See Clarey, "If Doping is Banned, Should Sleeping in Altitude Tents be Allowed", *International Herald Tribune*, December 7, 2001.

[95] See Olivier, "Banning Performance Enhancing Drugs is Justified", p.62 in Dudley, *op. cit.*

hence years of dedicated training will be wasted. Alternatively, it might be said that when young would-be athletes see their heroes using drugs then they will inexorably be drawn to the same path.

Again there are a number of responses to this. First, even though drug use in sport *is* currently banned, this pressure is still on the innocent athlete, because it can still be assumed that at least some of one's fellow athletes will be using drugs. In other words, the situation would not change if drug use was permitted. Secondly, no one is forcing the innocent athlete to use drugs. It is always possible to compete cleanly. Obviously for a clean athlete who has trained day in and day out for years, it is galling to be beaten by someone suspected of using drugs, yet justifying the prohibition of drugs on this basis smacks of a 'have your cake and eat it' approach to professionalisation. On the one level the innocent athlete is obsessed by being the best, on the other, he is refusing to accept that it may be necessary to do unpalatable things to be the best. Yet in other highly competitive careers, it is necessary to do things that one may regard as ethically suspect to succeed in ones career (working excessive hours, sacrificing time with one's family) and some of these things may not be conducive to the good health of the worker. Indeed it may be argued that the claim of many who would oppose drug use in professional sport, while approving of the concept of professionalisation of sport, rings hollow and seems to be premised on a misunderstanding of the precise consequences of turning a much loved pastime into a business.

3.5.5 Protecting the ethic of sport

Finally, it is argued that drugs are banned, because drug use is a form of cheating and ultimately it is as simple as that. This is perhaps a more convincing explanation for the rule yet it is also flawed. Cheating suggests that some ethical or other fundamental norm going to the heart of the raison d'etre of the activity is being struck at. Yet it is not quite clear what ethic is being protected by anti-doping policy.[96] There is no ethic prohibiting the use of technology in sport (or saying that sport is only about the athletes' natural abilities). Indeed modern sport is replete with technology for those who can afford it – from vitamin supplements, to body suits in swimming,[97] to nitrogen huts,[98] to

---

[96] See Cashmore, "Stop Testing and Legalise the Lot", *The Observer*, October 26, 2003, Mitchell, Campbell and Donegan, "Saints or Monsters? What kind of Athletics Stars Do we Want?", *Observer*, October 26, 2003.

[97] See Kolata, "The Impropriety of Taking Performance Enhancing Drugs is Debatable", p.42 in Dudley, *op. cit.*

[98] See DeSimone, "Drug Talk Hits a Higher Level", *Chicago Tribune*, July 28, 2002, Rae Brooks, "The Science of Speed", *Salt Lake Tribune*, January 6, 2002, Sivakkumaran, "Controversial Oxygen Machine on its Way Here", *The Straits Time (Singapore)*,

oxidisation cylinders,[99] to graphite shafted golf clubs. Nor is there an ethic prohibiting the ingestion of chemical compounds for most athletes use food supplements and energy drinks.[100] Finally there can be no ethic that prohibits the secretive use of technology/ingestion of chemical compounds, in that many athletes have secret dietary schemes designed to ensure that they and only they have the best chance of winning.

Those who would seek to maintain a Corinthian ethic along any of these lines for professional sport have failed to appreciate the impact of professionalisation. Professional athletes somewhat crassly stress the win at all costs mentality, yet they are right to do so. Sport is a business and the only dominant ethic is to be the best at all costs. In this light and paradoxical as it may seem, it may be the prohibition rather than the use of drugs in sport that strikes at the dominant ethic thereof.[101]

3.6 THE MAJOR PLAYERS IN THE FIGHT AGAINST DOPING

Many different bodies are involved in the fight against doping. Within sport, the various international sporting federations and national governing bodies as well as the IOC and the World Anti-Doping Agency (WADA) have anti-doping policies and rules, governing, *inter alia*, the question of what constitutes a doping offence, the procedures involved in testing, provision for disciplinary hearings and how they are to be conducted, and relevant sanctions.[102] Outside sport, National Governments have developed specific anti doping agencies (for example the anti-doping unit of the Irish Sports Council), and supra-national

---

November 18, 2002, Clarey, "If Doping is Banned Should Sleeping in Altitude Tents be Allowed?", *International Herald Tribune*, December 7, 2001. Thus Tom Steitz, coach of the US Nordic combined team at the Salt Lake City Winter Olympic Games in 2002 commented that "I have a hard time trying to see the distinction between a pill somebody might swallow or a nasal spray somebody might use and a 200,000 dollar house where every breath of air has been artificially altered.", On the other hand Frank Shorter of the USADA defended such tents on the basis of their availability to all and concluded that "as long as it's not pharmacology but it's lifestyle, I don't see a problem with it.", See Meyer, "Preparation for Salt Lake Games Moves In-House", *Denver Post*, July, 7, 2001.

[99] See Hart, "Captain Snooze – David Beckham has been told to lie back and think of England", *Sunday Telegraph*, April 22, 2002.

[100] In October 2001, Naoko Takahashi who became the first woman to run the marathon in under two hours and twenty minutes announced that as part of her training regime she imbibed the juice extracted from giant killer hornets – a beverage not banned by the IOC/WADA but which was shown to reduce muscle fatigue and improve the body's efficiency by increasing metabolism and reducing the build up in the muscles of lactic acid.

[101] See Beloff, "Drugs, Laws and Versapaks", pp.46–47 in O'Leary, *op. cit.*

[102] See Houlihan, "The World Anti-Doping Agency: Prospects for success", p.125 in O'Leary.

organisations such as the Council of Europe and the EU have concerned themselves with the issue. Finally, in certain countries, the criminal law of the land steps in to proscribe use and/or supply of performance enhancing substances.[103] In the pre-WADA era, the absence of harmonization of the efforts of the respective bodies, and the degree of suspicion with which the sporting bodies regard the governmental bodies and vice versa was a matter of concern.[104]

We now consider the impact of the most important bodies involved in the implementation of anti-doping policy and in doing so, seek to present the picture of the current state of the fight against doping. Since March 2003, the major force in this area has been the World Anti-Doping Code, which will be considered later.

3.6.1 The impact of the International Olympic Committee (IOC)

The IOC has historically been at the forefront of opposition to doping,[105] even if its precise practical impact is confined to the duration of the summer and winter Olympic Games.[106] Since the 1960s its Medical Commission has been effective in testing athletes for banned substances (starting at the Winter Games

---

[103] See Lowther, "Criminal Law Regulation of Performance Enhancing Drugs: Welcome Formalisation of Knee Jerk Response", p.225 *ibid.* It is expected that Ireland will shortly follow the approach taken by English law and add performance-enhancing substances to its list of controlled drugs in sch.4 of the Misuse of Drugs Act 1977 and 1984.

[104] See Houlihan, "The World Anti-doping Agency Prospects for Success", p.125 in O'Leary, *op. cit.*

[105] See Boyes, "The IOC Transnational Doping Policy and Globalisation", p.167 in O'Leary, *op. cit.*

[106] In *H v. FINA*, CAS 98/218, CAS confirmed that outside of Olympic competition, the rules of the IOC medical and now anti-doping code, only bind an international federation to the extent to which they have been voluntarily accepted. Thus in November 2001 Latvian Bobsledder Sandis Prusis was banned by the International Bobsled Federation for three months having tested positive for a banned substance. This comparatively minor sentence (based on the fact that the athlete claimed that his positive showing stemmed from his use of a lawful nutritional substance) was inconsistent with IOC policy. Hence when the athlete attempted to compete in the Salt Lake City Olympic games in 2002, the IOC refused to accept him. CAS rejected the IOC decision, on the basis that the IOC had no jurisdiction in the case, as Prusis did not test positive during an Olympic event. This being the case he had a legitimate expectation that having served his FIBD penalty he would be accepted for future competitions. Thus the IOC decision effectively infringed the rule against double jeopardy. *Prusis v. IOC*, CAS OG 02/001. See Shipley, "Jovanovic's Suspension Extended to Two Years", *Washington Post*, February 8, 2002. See also *IAAF v. Federazione Italiana di Athletica Leggera* (*Bevilacqua case*), November 25, 1996, p.143 in Tarasti, *Legal Solutions in International Doping Cases* (SEP Editrice, 2000) [hereafter Tarasti].

in Grenoble, 1968 and more extensively at the Summer Olympics in Mexico of the same year) during Olympic events as well as in extending the list of banned substances.[107] In addition, in 1983, the IOC, at the behest of the IAAF introduced a laboratory accreditation process. At present throughout the world there are 27 such accredited laboratories, however, the IOC role in the accreditation of laboratories may in time be superseded by that of WADA.

By the mid 1980s with the increasingly public proliferation especially of steroids, a new impetus was added to the campaign against drugs with the creation by the IOC, the Canadian government the Council of Europe, the European Sports conference and the United States Olympic Committee of the *International Olympic Charter Against Doping in Sport* replaced in 1995 by the *IOC Medical Code* and in January 2000 by the *IOC Anti-Doping Code*. This last code, whose application is obligatory for all members of the Olympic family, seeks to balance the competing needs of anti-doping policy and those of the athlete who tests positive and as a result faces the loss of his or her livelihood, while providing harmonized rules in respect of testing, sanctions, systems of appeal and so on.

Moreover it also provides for the role of an Independent anti-doping agency as the centralised body, charged with galvanising and harmonising the various different approaches to anti-doping policy within the various institutions. This body is WADA.

3.6.2 The World Anti-Doping Agency (WADA)

The Lausanne declaration in 1999 foresaw the creation of an international anti-doping agency. As a result the World Anti-Doping Agency was set up in Lausanne on November 10, 1999 under the initiative of the IOC. The organisation was set up to promote and co-ordinate the fight against doping, reflecting the ongoing concern with the need for harmonisation in this area

According to Article 4 of its Constitutive Instrument of Foundation, WADA has eight objectives namely,

1. (In co-operation with intergovernmental organisations, governments, public authorities, sporting organisations including the IOC) to promote and co-ordinate the fight against doping in sport.

2. To reinforce at international level ethical principles for the practice of doping-free sport and to help to protect the health of athletes.

3. To establish, adapt and where necessary modify the list of banned substances. To this end the WADA will publish a new list of banned substances every year to come into effect on January 1 of each calendar year.

---

[107] See Houlihan, *op. cit.*, p.132.

4. To encourage, support, co-ordinate and where necessary undertake, in full
    co-operation with the relevant public and private bodies and sporting
    organisations the organisation of unannounced out of competition
    testing.[108] The impact of this cannot be overstated. It is highly unlikely
    that a 'cheating' athlete, aware of his clearance time (that is the length of
    time that it takes the drugs that he is using to clear his system) would be
    foolish enough to put himself in the position where he might test positive
    during a competition (especially given that if he clears a couple of weeks
    before a competition, he will still gain the benefit of the drugs he has
    used), and therefore an anti-doping policy that does not test out of
    competition is doomed to fail. Indeed one of the big successes for the
    WADA in its inaugural year was the impact of its pre-competition testing
    procedure prior to the Sydney Olympics.[109]

5. To develop, harmonise and unify scientific, sampling and technical
    standards, including the homologation of laboratories, and to create a
    reference laboratory.[110]

6. To harmonise rules, disciplinary procedures, sanctions etc. while taking
    into account the rights of athletes. In this respect, one of the measures
    adopted by WADA in February 2002 at the Salt Lake City winter Olympic
    games is the "anti-doping passport." This would be an official personal
    register for any athlete (linked to an internet based database) to demonstrate
    that (s)he was available for testing throughout the previous year and had a
    clean record.

7. To devise and develop anti-doping education and prevention programmes
    at international level.[111]

8. To promote and co-ordinate research into the fight against doping.

---

[108] To this end, WADA determines annually the number of unannounced out-of-competition
tests it will finance, conducts such tests of its own volition and especially works in
harmony with sporting organisations who are also engaged in such testing. The focus of
such controls primarily are those athletes eligible for or striving to be eligible for
competition at international level.

[109] Some 2043 tests were undertaken prior to the Sydney Games, involving 27 Olympic
sports

[110] In this context WADA will develop a certification procedure for doping control officers,
a procedure for the accreditation of doping laboratories, protocols for the analysis of
prohibited substances and methods and standards for equipment, techniques, methods,
recruitment and training of staff, the provision of annual statistics on the number of
tests performed worldwide and standards for the protection of personal rights and data
protection.

[111] To this end, WADA improves anti-doping information and education programmes,
provides assistance to sporting organisations, national anti-doping agencies etc. and
organises conferences seminars and workshops.

As we shall see many of these objectives are realised within the WADA Anti-Doping Code.

The agency was incorporated in 1999 as a foundation governed by Swiss law and supervised by Swiss Federal Authorities, and in its own words is guided by "the highest ethical principles." It is composed of a Foundation Board, and Executive Committee and five working committees. The Foundation Board is the supreme decision making body of the WADA, but it delegates to the Executive Committee the actual management and running of the Agency, the performance of its activities and the administration of its assets. Moreover, the five working committees exist to accomplish specific tasks. In all these matters it is to co-operate with intergovernmental organisations, governments, public authorities and other public and private bodies fighting against doping in sport including the IOC, International Sports Federations, NOCs and athletes.[112] Importantly WADA is merely a testing *agency* working with and for sporting federations and through the medium of appointed testing companies. Equally, it created for the first time, the office of an independent observer to observe and report on all aspects of doping control operations in a neutral and unbiased manner – a role which first became effective at the Sydney Olympic Games in 2000 and has since been used at many other major sporting events.

3.6.3 The Council Of Europe

If the IOC has provided the bulk of the momentum for anti-doping policy within the Sports world, it is the Council of Europe which, since the mid 1960s has been at the forefront of political moves in this area. In 1981, the Council of Europe Committee for the Development of Sport was asked by its panel of doping experts to prepare a Convention on doping in sport. The CDDS decided, for political reasons, not to go for the option of a binding Convention, but rather to consolidate all its pre-existing work into a non-binding recommendation then known as the European Anti-Doping Charter.[113] By 1989 the charter had received the support of the IOC, UNESCO, the EC, the WHO, the General Association of International Sports Federations and the Association of European National Olympic Committees. Moreover, by 1988 both Canada and the USA had been admitted as observers in the CDDS work on doping.[114] Finally, in 1989, the Charter was re-designated as a binding Anti-Doping

---

[112] Indeed at the moment the WADA board includes representatives from the EU, the Council of Europe, the Supreme Council for Sport in Africa and the Olympic Movement.
[113] This was adopted in 1984 as Recommendation No. R (84) 19.
[114] Also in 1988 (June, 21) the Committee of Ministers adopted Recommendation No. R (88) 12 on the institution of no warning out of competition testing.

Convention,[115] thereby affording public authorities the opportunity to express a general responsibility for active participation in the work of forging anti-doping policy, at a time when the Ben Johnson scandal as well as similar stories during the 1988 Tour de France had brought the issue of doping firmly onto the global legal agenda. It was hoped that the Convention would provide a clear framework by which such policy could be enforced free from procedural problems.

Houlihan points out that the designation of the document as a Convention coincided with two significant factors.[116] First, the Dubin Inquiry into Drug Taking demonstrated very clearly that the problem of drug abuse in sport was absolutely rife, and involved occasional collusion between athletes, team officials and representatives of National Sports bodies in such doping. This led to the beginnings of national anti-doping policy in countries like Canada, America, Australia and eventually Britain. Secondly this period marked the fall of communism. As we have seen, secret service files from the former East Germany reveal a three decade history of a state sponsored policy of giving athletes performance enhancing substances, often without these athletes being aware of the nature of these substances.[117] With the fall of communism, newly independent states were required to rebuild sporting organisations often with little or no state support. The Council of Europe saw this as an opportunity to provide support on issues pertaining to infrastructure, and in doing so to stress a strong anti-doping ethic for such countries. Indeed Houlihan points out that for many states, membership of the Council of Europe was made conditional on their signing up to the European Cultural Convention and the Anti-Doping Convention.[118] Equally, it seems clear that, owing to lack of resources, many former Eastern European states do not have an effective anti-doping programme.

The Convention requires that parties co-ordinate the policies and actions of their government departments, including if necessary the transfer to a designated sports authority of the power and responsibility for implementing the Convention. It requires such governments to further the concerns of anti-doping policy both in negative terms – by means of regulation/legislation/administrative measures,[119] by making the effective implementation of anti-

---

[115] Council of Europe ETS no. 135 Anti-Doping Convention, Strasbourg November 16, 1989.

[116] Houlihan, *op. cit.*, pp.145–146.

[117] See Paterson, "Stasi helped make a star out of Witt", *Sunday Telegraph,* May 5, 2002. The exposure of the East German doping story was largely the result of the courageous efforts of molecular biologist Werner Franke and his wife Brigitte Berendonk – a former track and field athlete, whose father an East German doctor defected from East Germany for fear that his athletic daughter would fall into the hands of the East German doping machine.

[118] Houlihan, *op. cit.*, p.140.

[119] The explanatory report suggests (para.53) that such measures include strict control of

doping policy by relevant sports organisations a criterion for grant of public subsidies to such organisations, and indeed by stopping funding for sports men and women who have been caught doping – and by positive means – by assisting sports organisations to finance doping controls and indeed by encouraging and possibly facilitating the carrying out thereof, by devising and implementing educational programmes and information campaigns stressing the dangers to health inherent in doping and the impact which it has on the ethical values of sport and by promoting research into the area. The Convention also requires parties either to establish laboratories for testing which would be accredited by the monitoring group set up under Article 10 of the Convention, or to assist sports organisations to gain access to such laboratories on the territory of another party.

The Convention also calls on national governments to work *with* sports organisations to further the implementation of the treaty. Thus, governments shall work with sports organisations to introduce out of competition testing,[120] to negotiate with foreign sports organisations to allow its nationals to be tested on their territory, to promote active participation by athletes in the fight against doping, to clarify and harmonise rules in respect of eligibility to take part in sporting events following a positive doping test and to study scientific training methods and devise guidelines to protect sportsmen and sportswomen of all ages appropriate to each sport.

Enforcement of the Convention falls to a monitoring group set up under Article 10 thereof. It has responsibility, *inter alia*, for reviewing the provisions of the Convention, including the list of banned substances and practices and the criteria for accreditation of laboratories. Essentially, its job is to ensure that the Convention is working and that any improvements that need to be made are being made. The monitoring group has worked with the EU, UNESCO and the WHO and has America, China and Australia as ratifiers or as parties to any relevant discussion.

In September 2000, the Committee of Ministers of the Council of Europe produced recommendation 2000/16 on common core principles to be introduced into domestic legislation to combat the traffic in doping agents. This recommendation called on Governments of the Member States of the Council of Europe to adopt suitable legislation to deter and punish (if necessary by imprisonment) individuals and legal persons involved in the production, manufacture, transport, import or export, storage, offer, supply or any form of traffic in doping agents. According to the appendix to the recommendation, relevant laws would include criminal law, medical laws, customs laws, public

---

medical ethics, collaboration between police, customs, veterinary services and public health inspectors, control of private gymnasiums and fitness centres, co-operation between police and customs authorities and sports organisations, inspection of sports teams luggage at border points etc.

[120] This is basically a replication of Recommendation No. R (88) 12.

health law, law relating to the protection of children, laws concerning professionals and any other laws.

The appendix also called for a harmonisation of efforts, *inter alia*, by having recourse to the definitions adopted by the monitoring group in the appendix to the anti-doping Convention. It called for appropriate information and warnings about medicine and its effects as a doping agent to be clearly printed on all labels. Finally it called for increased co-operation between police forces in various Member States for the purpose of co-ordinating efforts.

3.6.4 The impact of the European Union

The bulk of European Union anti-doping policy has been forged in the period since 1998.[121] This is arguably for two reasons. First, the original economic based objectives of the EU have only been expanded in recent years (and particularly since the Treaty on European Union of 1992) to cover issues like the non-economic aspects of sport. Secondly the Tour de France scandal in 1998 gave a new impetus in this area. It is true, however, that there was some Community legislation in force in this area before 1998. Thus in 1990, the Council (of Ministers) published a resolution on Community action to combat use of drugs particularly within sport.[122] This resolution invited the Commission to draft and circulate a code of conduct to combat the use of drugs in sport, denouncing such behaviour as both unsporting and as contravening rules in respect of health protection. It also invited the Commission to propose to Council, measures of community interest in respect of areas such as education and information on doping, study of the most common drug-use practices and of drug-testing methods, co-operation between laboratories and research into the effects of drug taking on health within the Community biomedical research framework programme.

Since 1998, the EU has started to get increasingly involved in the fight against doping. Thus for instance, in 1998 and 1999 the Hardop Project was jointly carried out under its auspices and those of the IOC with a view to identifying the essential research needed to combat doping in sport. The report from this project concluded that a major problem affecting the fight against

---

[121] For analysis of EU activities in the area see http://www.europa.eu.int/comm/sport/index_en.html. See also more generally, Weatherill, "Resisting the Pressures of "Americanisation", the influence of European Community Law on the European Sports Model", p.155 in Greenfield and Osborn (eds.), *Law and Sport in Contemporary Society* (Frank Cass and Co. Ltd, 2000).

[122] Resolution of the Council and of representatives of the Governments of Member States, meeting within the Council of December 3, 1990 on Community Action to combat the use of drugs, including the abuse of medicinal products, particularly within sport. Official Journal NO C 329, 31/12/1990 P. 0004–0005.

doping was absence of co-operation and harmonisation,[123] and that there was a need for a centralised body to co-ordinate research and technology and to form a centralised policy on the accreditation of laboratories. That centralised body would work with the courts, police, public authorities and sporting federations and would promote co-operation between them, and would move to increase education and the dissemination of information on the topic. Also at this time the EU together with the IOC, and operating as part of the BIOMED 2 medical research programme under the fourth research and technological development framework programme (1994–1998) funded the $1.8m GH2000 project, aimed at identifying detection methods for rEPO and hGH.

Since this time, various EU bodies have become involved in the anti-doping movement. Thus in 1999 the European Group on Ethics, following a request by the Commission, adopted an opinion on the Ethical Aspects arising from Doping in Sport calling, *inter alia*, for police and judicial co-operation to combat doping under the third pillar of the EU treaty. Also in 1999, the Commission adopted a Community support plan to combat doping in sport.[124] This plan, again influenced by the setting up of the WADA focused on:

- Conducting a significant analysis of the reasons behind the proliferation of doping (including the over commercialisation of sport), bearing in mind the conclusions of the European Ethics Group considered above.

- Helping to establish WADA.

- Ensuring greater mobilisation of the Community instruments with a view to supplementing the action already started by Member States, international organisations and sports associations in the furtherance of research into substances, detection methods and the impact which doping has for health,[125] education, vocational training and youth programmes in the service of information and training, awareness-raising and prevention.[126]

- Making the most of Police and Judicial co-operation programmes.

---

[123] European Commission Research DG – Standards, Measurements and Testing Programme "Harmonising the ways and means of fighting against doping in sport", (HARDOP) – final report on project SMT4 – 199806530.

[124] The European Parliament had also adopted a resolution in which it called on the Commission to take into account the real dimension of the doping problem and to propose measures at Community level with a view to better co-ordination and complementarity between national and European measures and actions. O.J. C. 98, 09/04/1999.

[125] In September 2000, the European Commission selected fifteen projects to receive €2.5 million between them and which would include information campaigns, research and conferences aimed at increasing harmonisation in the fight against doping.

[126] In 2001, the European Commission started to fund a European anti-doping e-learning project.

- Reinforcing the rules in respect of information on medicaments.[127]

The Commission also promised to work with the Council of Europe in this area (and indeed to see whether, on the basis of Article 300 of the EU Treaty the Community could accede to the European Anti-Doping Convention), and to publish a report on the results of Community and National anti-doping measures as well as trends in doping practices.

In its response to the Commission report, the European Parliament in 2000 made two further suggestions, namely that the Commission make full use of its powers under Article 12 of Council Directive 92/27EEC to explore the feasibility of putting a "traffic light" logo on all medicinal products indicating whether they contained banned substances. Moreover, it called on the Commission under Article 152 of the EC Treaty to include in its information campaigns, information on the possible harmful effects of "near doping products" as well as discouraging leading sports shops, gymnasia, etc. from selling these products.

From this point on, the annual discussions of EU Sports ministers in respect of this topic have been predominantly concerned with the development of WADA and the most appropriate role for the EU in this area and with the need for a harmonization of the anti-doping efforts of Member States. The former has become something of a fraught issue. The EU formerly had a seat on the WADA board, but after continuous wrangling about EU funding of WADA, the EU sports Commissioner withdrew her seat on the WADA board in March 2002, to prepare a different plan of action against doping – and specifically one that would overcome the differences in the approaches taken by the various Member States (and in particular to the issue of punishment for persons caught using banned substances) so that the EU could speak with a unified voice on the subject.

EC law was invoked in the English High Court in *Edwards v. The British Athletic Federation and IAAF*.[128] Here the applicant was a British athlete who had been banned for four years by the IAAF for a doping offence. Two German athletes who had committed similar offences and had been similarly sanctioned by the IAAF had had the final two years of the suspension lifted by the German courts who held that this amounted to a disproportionate sanction. Edwards therefore argued that the final two years of his suspension should be similarly lifted, and that if they were not, this would amount to unlawful discrimination

---

[127] Thus for example, Council Directive 92/27/EEC of March 31, 1992 lays down certain conditions concerning labelling of medical products. The Commission suggests here that it could be universally used to indicate whether a particular pharmaceutical product contained a banned substance.

[128] [1998] 2 C.M.L.R. 363, 141 S.J.L.B. 154. See Stoner, "Rules of Sporting Conduct Unfettered by European Law", July/August (1997) *Sports Law Administration and Practice* 6.

against him by the IAAF, contrary to the terms of the EU Treaty. Lightman J., however, concluded that Community law only applied to sport where sport was an economic activity and that it did not apply in the imposition of rules relating to cheating, which were of sporting relevance only.

Finally, in May 2002, the European Commission rejected a complaint taken against the IOC by two swimmers who had tested positive for banned substances and following an unsuccessful appeal to CAS, had been banned for four years by FINA. The swimmers claim was that the rules of the IOC and FINA regarding the definition of doping, the threshold for defining the presence of a banned substance in the body as constituting doping, and the requirement of recourse to CAS restricted competition under the terms of Articles 81 and 82 of the EC Treaty, and unjustifiably restricted the freedom of swimmers to provide services under Article 49 of the Treaty. Mario Monti, the Competition Commissioner stated that the Commission would not be prepared to take the place of sporting bodies when it comes to drawing up rules for competition or deciding how best to enforce anti-doping policy.[129]

3.6.5 Doping control In Ireland

3.6.5.1 The Michelle Smith case[130]

From an Irish perspective, undoubtedly the most significant incident involving doping concerned the swimmer Michelle de Bruin. Michelle Smith as she then was had been a leading Irish swimmer for some years, although she had never made an outstanding impact on the world stage. She briefly retired following the Barcelona Olympics in 1992, the same year in which she met her future coach and husband Erik de Bruin – at one stage the world number two in discus, but who was serving a four year ban for taking banned substances.[131] When she stepped back into the pool in 1993, looking considerably more muscular than before,[132] she smashed twenty-three Irish records in the space of twelve months. What made this particularly surprising was the fact that her incredible improvement happened at an age when her career might

---

[129] See Cox, "Sports Law", in Byrne & Binchy, eds, *Annual Review of Irish Law 2002* (Round Hall, Dublin 2003).

[130] Galuzzi, *op. cit.*, p.95ff. See also, Paul Howard, "Silver Ladies", *Sunday Tribune*, May 2, 1999, Johnny Watterson, "No Mercy from Abroad", *Irish Times*, June 9, 1999.

[131] For analysis see Tom Humphries, "The Man behind the Woman", *Irish Times*, June 8, 1999.

[132] Former Irish national coach Peter Banks commented in 1996 that: "I wish they could pull out a picture of her five years ago because no one would recognise her. I can't imagine how she has gained the muscle mass she has and still swims the 100,000 metres a week she is supposedly swimming". See "De Bruin in Words", *Irish Times*, June 8, 1999.

have been seen as coming to an end.[133] In 1994, she finished fifth in the World Championship, and in 1995 she became the first Irish woman to win a European swimming title, taking two golds and a silver. In 1996, the year in which she married de Bruin, she reached even higher than this, winning three gold medals and one bronze at the Atlanta Olympic Games. Finally, in 1997 she won two gold and two silver medals at the European Championships in Seville.

Question marks surrounded her vastly improved levels of performance. At Atlanta, there was widespread suggestion that she must have been using banned substances, an allegation that she refuted, claiming that her improved performances were the result of an improved training regime[134] and that she had been tested regularly over a number of years and no traces of banned substances had ever been found.[135] Equally, her relationship with the FINA anti-doping authorities was not always the happiest.[136] In April of 1996, for instance, she was required to fill out a standard form announcing where her training facilities would be for the Olympics and simply wrote that she did not know. In 1996 and again in January 1997, FINA complained to her that she had not been available for a random doping test in both 1995 and October 1996, and indeed that the details which she had provided to them in respect of her training schedule in 1997 were overly vague. On February 3, 1997 she narrowly missed another random test, thereby rendering her technically eligible for a ban (as she had received the warning in January 1997). The FINA executive meeting in Lausanne on 23 February 1997, discussed seriously the possibility of imposing such a ban on her, and, in accordance with FINA rules, of stripping the Olympic champion of all medals won and records set over the previous twelve months. It was decided, however, that because she had missed the February 1997 test by as little as one hour, a legal challenge to the validity of imposing such a ban could well be successful. Finally in early January 1998, she *again* missed a random test, but instead of it being registered as such, the International Tests and Doping Management testers were instructed to try again two days later.

And so, on January 10, 1998, Michelle Smith was given an unannounced, out of.competition test.[137] The test, performed by Al and Kay Guy was a

---

[133] The average age of the previous ten Olympic Gold Medallists in the 400 metre free-style was 16.9 years. Michelle de Bruin at the time was 26. Humphries comments that 'Only a nation as broadly ignorant of the science of swimming as we Irish were could have swallowed it all without question.' See "Time to Tackle Tainted Legacy", *Irish Times*, Wednesday, June 9, 1999.

[134] American Pierre La Fontaine, her coach in 1988 and 1990 regarded Michelle Smith as the toughest trainer with whom he had ever worked.

[135] See John Dowling, "De Bruin "Praised for Being Helpful in Anti-dope Checks", *Irish Independent*, May, 4, 1999.

[136] See Tom Humphries, "High-risk Strategy Costs Dear", *Irish Times*, June 8, 1999.

[137] For analysis see Paul Kimmage, "Awaiting the Sting", *Sunday Independent*, May 2, 1999.

matter of substantial controversy, with the testers and Ms. Smith offering radically different versions of events.[138] The latter said that at the very most she would have been out of the testers sight for a very few moments. The former alleged that Ms. Smith "disappeared" for anything up to six minutes. The latter alleged that she provided the sample in clear view of Ms. Guy. Ms Guy on the other hand said that her view of Ms Smith was partially obscured by the latter's fleece top which was not pulled up high enough. Ms. Smith further alleged that when the testers called to collect the sample, she had urinated very recently hence there was an inevitable wait before she could be ready to provide the necessary 70ml sample. Indeed even here there was some controversy as to whether Ms de Bruin had to urinate on two or three occasions before the sample could be provided.

What is clear is that following one of the samples being provided, both Mr. and Mrs Guy smelt what they described as a "sweet whiskey type smell."[139] Having sealed and verified the samples in Ms Smith's presence (who suggested that at this point the sample was out of her sight for a minute or so), they took the sample home, and because it was the weekend and the sample could not be transferred to the laboratory in Barcelona until the next Monday, it was stored in the family refrigerator for the weekend before being sent to Barcelona by courier on the Monday. There were some minor procedural anomalies in respect of the movement of the sample from Kilkenny where the test occurred to Barcelona but, according to FINA and the scientist who would ultimately test the sample in Barcelona, Dr Jordi Segura, there was nothing that would objectively affect the veracity of the test.

On April 27, Ms Smith was informed that her A test showed "unequivocal signs of adulteration." The content of alcohol in her urine (higher than 100mg/ml) was in no way compatible with human consumption and her sample showed a very high whiskey content. Giving evidence before the Court of Arbitration for Sport, when the case was appealed to it, Dr Segura said that manipulation of a sample by dilution with whiskey would be in the interest of a hypothetical cheating athlete. Moreover its low specific gravity (0.983 g/ml) was also compatible with physical manipulation.[140] Her B sample, tested on May 21, 1998, showed similar results. As a result, on August 6 1998 she was banned

---

[138] See Tom Humphries, "One Minute Out of Sight" and "At Least Four to Six Minutes", *Irish Times*, May 4, 1999.

[139] For analysis see, *inter alia*, John Dowling, "Testers tell of Whiskey Smell in Swimmer's Sample", *Irish Independent*, May 4, 1999.

[140] Originally there was a degree of controversy in that the specific gravity recorded by the Guys at the time of the test was different to that recorded in the laboratory, which according to the defence indicated that the two urine samples were different. Dr Segura, however, explained that the different types of test used in Kilkenny and Barcelona would explain the differentiation. Indeed he had tested the B sample in Barcelona using *both* methods and the same differential was found. See Tom Humphries, "FINA Ascribe Motive and Opportunity", *Irish Times*, May 4, 1999.

for four years by FINA for violation of Rule DC 1.2 (b) (taking advantage of a banned procedure and Rule DC 3.1 (b) (interfering with a testing procedure).

At the time when the original testing of the sample occurred, in January 1998, Dr Segura identified within Ms Smith's diluted sample, a drug which was a precursor to testosterone, that is, one designed to promote the growth of testosterone in the body.[141] Later, however, in February 1998, owing to scientific development of a new variant of mass spectrometry analysis of urine called isotope radio mass spectrometry he was able to identify that the relevant substance was in fact androstenedione – a substance which, he alleged was on the banned list at the time of the test. Equally, having taken advice from the IOC who suggested that the new test itself would not be enough to support a case for discovery of the banned substance, FINA decided not to proceed with any charge of using this substance (although it was legal to use such a test to discover supporting evidence). Equally, this finding suggested a motivation for Ms de Bruin to manipulate the sample, especially as, in Dr Segura's view, the relevant substance had probably been ingested in the period ten to twelve hours before the sample was given.

In September 1998, Ms de Bruin lodged an appeal with CAS. Among other things, she alleged that the burden of proof lay on FINA to exclude all possibilities other than that the sample had been manipulated by her, that the procedures which had been followed by both the testers and later the laboratory were riddled with inaccuracies and anomalies and that the relevant bottles were susceptible to tampering – an allegation which FINA rejected as hearsay.[142] She argued that the possibility of a conspiracy against her involving FINA and possibly Mr and Mrs Guy could not be ruled out, but in any event that it was not her duty to prove this. She had protested her innocence and it was up to FINA to demonstrate clearly how the sample had been manipulated – something which, she argued, they had been unable to do. FINA in response argued that the appellant was wrong in her view of the burden of proof in a case of this nature, and that, in any event the only reasonable possibility was that the sample given by Ms de Bruin in January 1998 was that which was tested in Barcelona, that that sample had been interfered with, and that the only person with the motive and the opportunity for such interference was Ms de Bruin.

---

[141] In fact three of her samples from November 1997 to March 1998 had shown evidence of this precursor. Dr Segura said that in as much as the alcohol had diluted the sample, the concentration of the banned substance in it could be at double the recorded level. See Humphries, "Banned Substance Evident, Court Hears", *Irish Times*, May 4, 1999.

[142] At the CAS hearing, Monica Bonfanti, a representative of the University of Lausanne laboratory reported that following extensive tests on such canisters, it was impossible to tamper with such canisters without leaving a mark on them. See John Dowling, "Trials Show Bottles Could not be Opened Undetected", *Irish Independent*, May 5, 1999.

After a two-day hearing on May 3 and 4, 1999 – the first ever CAS hearing to be heard in public – her appeal was rejected and the four-year ban upheld.[143] The Court decided that the burden of proof did not lie on FINA to eliminate all possibilities other than manipulation of the sample by the applicant. It concluded that Ms. De Bruin had not demonstrated that the samples which were tested were not hers or that a third party had manipulated the samples. Indeed based on the facts of the case and the evidence before them, the arbitrators were of the opinion that the appellant was the only person who had the motive and the opportunity to manipulate the sample.

The case was, however, not quite finished. In June 1997, LEN the European swimming Governing Body, on instruction from FINA as to the application of the latter's rules, announced that it would not be stripping Michelle de Bruin of the medals which she won at the Seville European Championships in 1997.[144] Also, in October 1999, Swim Ireland (the governing body for swimming in Ireland) announced that it would not try to remove the thirty two Irish records held by de Bruin from the Irish record books. This was largely because Michelle de Bruin had threatened them with legal action if they tried to do so, describing Swim Ireland's actions as "atrociously vindictive."[145]

3.6.5.2 *The Irish Sports Council Anti-Doping Unit*

In 1999, the Irish Sports Council Act[146] came into force at the behest of the Minister for Sports and Tourism.[147] Under section 18 of the Act, an Anti-Doping committee was set up to further the development of anti-doping policy within the Council. This committee has nine members drawn from a variety of backgrounds including medicine, pharmacy, law, science and administration as well as four specialist advisers.

In November, 1999 the Council launched its National Anti-Doping

---

[143] *B v. FINA*, CAS 98/211. See Humphries, "Finding Motive made Appeal Uphill Struggle", and "De Bruin's reputation in Shreds", *Irish Times*, June 8, 1999. Johnny Watterson, "Acceptance of Guilt", *Irish Times,* June 9, 1999 and John Dowling, "Agonizing Wait for de Bruin as Verdict Reserved", *Irish Independent*, May, 5, 1999. For reaction to the decision internationally, see Watterson, "No Mercy from Abroad", *Irish Times*, June, 9, 1999.

[144] See Watterson, "De Bruin to Keep Medals won in Seville", *Irish Times*, June, 18, 1999.

[145] See Watterson, "Move Vindictive says de Bruin", *Irish Times*, October 14, 1999.

[146] Act No. 6 of 1999.

[147] The President signed the Irish Sports Council Act on May 18, and the body began to operate as an executive agency on July 1, 1999. At its formal launch on June 30, 1999 the Minister for Tourism, Sport and Recreation described the role of the Council as being:

"'… to plan and support the future development of Irish sport in conjunction with the various sports organisations and through them the thousands of volunteers who have been sport's lifeblood in Ireland for generations."

programme. Within the programme, the ISC works with and for the national governing bodies who sign up to the programme, by coordinating their anti-doping policies, and testing athletes according to the rules of the sport in which they operate.[148] The ISC cannot force sports bodies to come on board, although it has linked the distribution of grants to the anti-doping regulations. In 2001, in two major developments the FAI and the GAA signed up to the ISC programme,[149] although there has been a certain amount of discontent within the GAA in respect of the same[150] and in particular with the notion that the amateur GAA players should be subjected to the rigorous standards expected of professional athletes,[151] in ensuring that routine medicines that are ingested do not contain banned substances.[152] Equally, the ISC has sought to enhance and facilitate the anti-doping policies of governing bodies through, for instance, the publication of a model sample form, a model whereabouts form and indeed a model anti-doping policy and a doping control officers handbook. All of these documents may be accessed through the ISC web page.[153]

The programme has expanded significantly since its inception. Thus in 2001, it carried out 693 tests (well in excess of the targeted figure of 608 tests), of which 50% were out of competition and 53 took place overseas. Of these tests there were four positives (as compared to 12 in 2000) – a statistic roughly commensurate with international experience.[154] In 2003, 957 tests were carried out by the Sports Council in 36 sports of which some 60% were "out of competition" tests. In addition there were 48 tests for alcohol. It is estimated that some 86% of senior athletes in Ireland have now been tested at some time.

According to John Treacy, Chief Executive of the Irish Sports Council, the new testing regime forms part of the Sports Council's three-strand approach

---

[148] For example, it provides NGBs with a list of responsibilities with regards to competition testing, including a statement of appropriate procedures, the nature of a proper doping control station and the relevant equipment which is needed.

[149] See Duggan, "Four Tested for Drugs,", *Irish Times*, September 10, 2001.

[150] See O'Riordan, "GAA go to War on Drug Tests", *Irish Times*, May 8, 2002, and by the same author, "Tracey Defends Drug Tests", *Irish Times*, May 9, 2002 and "Bosses Naïve about Drug Issue", *Irish Times*, May 10, 2002 and Breheny, "GAA has to Stand by Assets in Doping War", *Irish Independent*, May 29, 2002. In December 2002, the GAA announced that it would be participating fully in the ISC anti-doping programme.

[151] In fact 95% of ISC tests are carried out on amateur athletes.

[152] Thus, for instance, the Dublin GAA manager Tommy Lyons remarked:
   "The idea that a lad can be classed as a drugs cheat because he takes something in all innocence to cure a cold or a cough is unacceptable. It's all very fine having lists and guidelines, but everyone knows that mammy is the first doctor in any house. Are all the mammies of Ireland supposed to be clued into what's in a cough bottle just because the Sports Council thinks GAA players should be drug tested?"
   See Breheny, "GAA set to Boycott Drug Tests", *Irish Independent*, May 8, 2002.

[153] www.irishsportscouncil.ie

[154] See Watterson, "Rotten Apples Still Spoiling the Barrel", *Irish Times*, March 27, 2001.

to anti-doping – testing, education and research, and the Sports Council also operates an effective anti-doping education programme. Thus, in July 2002, in association with the Monthly Index of Medical Specialties Ireland (MIMS Ireland) and Eirpharm.com – the Irish Pharmacy and Health website – the Council launched the Anti-doping initiative for Medical Professionals – the first of its kind in Europe. This programme seeks, through the use of symbols to provide information to doctors as to the status of medications in sport, thereby enabling them to proscribe medication for athletes in confidence that this will not fall foul of a doping test. Given that a large number of athletes who fail doping tests allege that their positive tests are the result of innocent ingestion of banned substances contained in routine medical substances, this is an important development

Arguably the single greatest contribution of the ISC to anti-doping policy, albeit one whose effects are as yet uncertain, is in the creation of the *Irish Anti-Doping Rules*, which are effective from June 1, 2004. All sports bodies who wish to receive sports council grants are obliged to sign up to these rules, hence they will almost certainly comprise the single anti-doping code operative across the whole of Irish sport. They are considered in detail at the end of this chapter.

3.7 Fair Procedures, The Rights of the Athlete and the Application of Anti-Doping Policy

Since the coming into being of WADA then, there have been consistent movements to harmonise the anti-doping policies of the various agencies with an interest in the matter, culminating in the creation of the new World Anti-Doping Code. Equally, WADA has used the opportunity not merely to harmonise anti-doping rules, but to do so at a high level, by requiring governing bodies and international federations to sign up to rules that are extremely severe, and indeed are far stricter than those that individual federations had previously used. In this respect it may be said of WADA that it works zealously with one single objective in mind, namely to combat doping in sport by requiring all federations to subscribe to *its* view of how doping should be combated.

The problem with this approach is that this cannot be the single objective of a legitimate anti-doping policy, in that the interests of the athlete accused of a doping offence must also be accommodated. There is after all a great deal at stake for such an athlete in that [s]he may face a suspension that will effectively end his or her career. As a matter of law, this means that he or she is entitled to a high level of fair procedures in respect of any action taken against him or her. As we shall see, both the WADA code and the Irish Rules have taken account of this fact, and contain significant safeguards for the rights of the athlete. In order to understand, however, precisely what these safeguards are likely to entail in practice, it is necessary to consider the approach taken by civil courts and in particular by CAS in its interpretation of the rules of sports bodies. Such analysis demonstrates not only the basic standards of fairness to which athletes are entitled, but also the major areas in which application of the new rules are likely to cause controversy.

Traditionally, the particular areas for concern within the rules of different federations include:

– The definition of a doping offence.

– The burden and standard of proof in doping cases.

– The strict liability nature of anti-doping rules and the level of sanction in doping cases.

– Lawful exceptions to anti-doping rules.

– The legality of suspension prior to a hearing.

– Deviations from agreed procedures.

– The fairness of the disciplinary hearing itself.

In this respect and in a throw back to chapter two of this book it is well to remember the three basic principles of fairness to which all sports bodies should subscribe namely that the rules should be fair, that they should be strictly applied, and that any disciplinary hearing should be conducted fairly, having regard to the seriousness of the matter.

3.7.1 Standard of proof

The first question concerns the standard to which a doping offence must be proven. It can be accepted that disciplinary actions against athletes are not the same as criminal proceedings – if for no other reason than that sports governing bodies do not have the same investigatory powers as the state does in criminal proceedings. Therefore, it is arguable that it is unnecessary for the standard of proof in such proceedings to be at the level of the criminal standard of proof beyond reasonable doubt.[155] Equally, the fact that such disciplinary proceedings may put a premature end to the athlete's career means that a great deal is at stake, and hence that the standard of proof should be set at a high threshold, and possibly at a higher threshold than the civil standard of balance of probabilities.[156]

Different federations take different approaches to this issue. Thus under

---

[155] *Poll v. FINA*, CAS 2002/A/399 and *Baxter v. IOC*, CAS 2002/A/376.

[156] Generally on this point see Soek, "The Fundamental Rights of Athletes in Doping Trials", p.58 in O'Leary and Donnellan, "Fair Procedures in Doping Cases" (June 2003) *Sports Law Administration and Practice* 12.

rule 59 the IAAF requires that a doping offence be proved beyond reasonable doubt. Other federations do not go as far as this and where the rules are silent on this point, or where an inadequate standard of proof is required, CAS has consistently said that the appropriate standard is located somewhere between the civil and criminal standard, such that proof must be to the comfortable satisfaction of the court bearing in mind the seriousness of the allegation made.[157] Thus in *International Tennis Federation v. K*,[158] where CAS was dealing with the potential suspension of a professional tennis player, the court held that the seriousness of the issue was such that the 'balance of probabilities' test would have to be applied unusually strictly. As we shall see, this is the approach adopted in the new World Anti-Doping Code. Moreover, the practice is to allow the athlete the benefit of all but the most fanciful doubts.[159]

This approach is consistent with the view of the Irish Supreme Court, which has consistently endorsed the notion that in all civil matters, a standard of proof on the balance of probabilities will satisfy requirements of natural and constitutional justice, provided that such standard is sufficiently flexible that it can be applied bearing in mind the severity of the consequences for the subject of the action.[160] In the final analysis, however, such rules are contractual arrangements between the athlete and the federation, and more controversy is likely to arise in the interpretation of such rules than in the question of whether they are empirically fair.

Finally, it seems clear that where a federation has proven to the relevant standard that a doping offence has occurred and the athlete is permitted to offer evidence of moral non-culpability in mitigation of sanction, then he or she will be required to demonstrate such innocence on the balance of probabilities.[161]

3.7.2 Burden of proof and the definition of a doping offence

The question of burden of proof is equally difficult and is linked inextricably with the fact that the elements of the offence of doping differ from federation to federation. Put another way, it is plain that the burden of proving a doping offence lies with the relevant sports governing body, but the definition of a doping offence changes from governing body to governing body. There are,

---

[157] *B v. FINA*, CAS 98/211, *B v. International Triathlon Union*, CAS 98/222, *H v. International Motorcycling Federation*, CAS 2000/A/281 and *Kabaeva v. FIG* (CAS 2002/A/386).

[158] CAS 99A/223.

[159] See Beloff, "Drugs, Laws and Versapaks", p.51 in O'Leary, *op. cit.*

[160] *Georgopoulus v. Beaumont Hospital Board*, unreported, Supreme Court, June 4, 1997, *O'Leary v. Medical Council*, unreported, Supreme Court, July 25, 1997.

[161] *N, J, Y, and W v. FINA*, CAS 98/208.

however, four major classes of doping offence – and again it depends on the rules of the particular federation as to what precisely is prohibited:

(a) Intentionally taking a drug with the aim of improving performance.

(b) Having a prohibited substance in one's system.

(c) Manipulating a sample.

(d) Evading doping control.

The burden is on the governing body to prove the substance of whichever of these classes of offence it proscribes within its rules, and in this context it seems that the athlete will enjoy a presumption of innocence.[162]

It should be obvious that it is relatively easy to prove (d) above unless there is a random test that an athlete may have missed accidentally.[163] It should also be obvious that in the case of (b) above, the intention of the athlete who ingests the banned substance is irrelevant, and that it is therefore considerably easier for an International Federation to prove (b) than to prove (a) which requires proof of culpability on the part of the athlete (as also in practice does (c)). CAS has repeatedly said that even the strictest approach – (b) – is legitimate in the interests of the effective functioning of anti-doping policy. However, it has also held that it is incumbent on a governing body to be clear about what is prohibited within its rules. Thus in *US Shooting & Q v. International Shooting Union*,[164] the relevant governing body felt that its rules provided for an offence of strict liability, however the rule itself provided that the banned substance be taken 'with the aim of improving performance' which, according to CAS meant that the offence was a fault based one. CAS insisted that as these rules are strict in nature, the governing bodies must start by being strict with themselves, and that athletes are entitled to be governed by predictable rules.[165] Moreover, CAS has held that where there *are* uncertainties and ambiguities in a federation's

---

[162] *H v. International Motorcycling Federation*, CAS 2000/A/281.

[163] See for instance *Ngugi v. Kenyan Amateur Athletic Association (KAAA) and IAAF* (November 5, 1994, IAAF Arbitration Tribunal), p.133 in Tarasti. From an Irish perspective see *Quirke v. BLE* [1988] I.R. 83.

[164] CAS 94/129.

[165] In *H v. International Motorcycling Federation*, CAS 2000/A/281, the FIM rules forbade "use", of certain substances, but CAS refused to interpret this word so strictly that it would render the offence a fault based one. Similarly in the case of Walker (*BAF v. IAAF* [2001] I.S.L.R. 264) the former IAAF arbitration panel refused to interpret IAAF "help-notes for athletes" that refer to the "taking" of a banned substance and IAAF rules that refer to the substance "entering" the athlete's body as meaning that the IAAF rules were fault liability based. Rather it found that a reading of the totality of such rules indicated that they create an offence of strict liability. On the other hand in *Kabaeva v. FIG*, CAS 2002/A/386, a rule that specified sanctions where an athlete was "guilty of doping" was interpreted by CAS as including an element of fault.

rules, then these rules should be interpreted according to the *contra preferentem* rule of interpretation – that is to say that they should be given the interpretation that is most favourable to the athlete and least favourable to the governing body relying on them.[166]

CAS was more tolerant of problems inherent in the wording of governing body rules in *V v. FINA*.[167] Here a coach had been banned for one year (a period that included the 1996 summer Olympic games) for providing one of his swimmers with a headache tablet that unbeknown to him contained a banned substance, but in such low dosage that it had no performing enhancing qualities. The coach argued that whereas FINA applies strict liability rules for swimmers the position for coaches is different. Thus Rule 4.17.6 of the FINA rules, provides that 'If a person including a coach…is found to have helped or advised a competitor in misuse or is in knowledge of such misuse without reporting to FINA, that person will be suspended up to life …''. The appellant here argued that this implied a requirement of fault on the part of the coach. CAS, accepting that the rules could potentially have been drafted more clearly, opted, however, to read all the FINA rules on doping conjunctively and harmoniously, and to imply a general strict liability standard across the board.

Finally, in *C v. FINA*,[168] CAS suggested that the precise nature of a federation's anti-doping policy would depend not just on its rules, but also potentially on the manner in which such rules had been interpreted in the past. Here a swimmer was banned for two years having allegedly ingested a capsule given to her by her coach, which unknown to either, contained a banned substance. She challenged the decision to ban her, claiming that it was patently unfair. CAS accepted FINA's argument that strict liability rules were an indispensable element of the fight against doping, and whereas it would have preferred that the athlete be allowed to adduce evidence of non-culpability in mitigation of sanction (an issue that will be returned to later), nonetheless it recognised that if a federation's rules precluded such possibility then it (CAS) had no jurisdiction to dispense with such rules. Equally, CAS noted that the seeming rigidity of the FINA rules was offset by the fact that in the *V v. FINA* case mentioned above, FINA had been prepared to accept evidence of non-culpability on the part of R – the swimmer coached by V – and to exonerate her on this basis. The implication was that FINA did not appear to regard its rules as immutable, and on this basis, neither would CAS.

---

[166] *Perriss Wilkins v. UK Athletics*, CAS 2003/A/455.
[167] CAS 95/150. See also *Baxter v. FIS*, CAS 2002/A/396. For comment see Caldow, Nicholson and MacLeod, "The Implementation of Sanctioning Powers" (November 2002) *Sports Law Administration & Practice* 8.
[168] CAS 95/141.

3.7.2.1 *The burden of proof and fault based doping offences*

If a doping offence is fault based in nature, then plainly the burden of proof on the governing body includes proving that the athlete is morally culpable, in respect of the offence with which [s]he is charged. Thus for instance, whereas the IAAF rules are strict liability in nature as regards the presence of a banned substance in an athlete's tissue or fluids, they are not so as regards a situation where an athlete "uses or takes advantage of a prohibited technique."[169] In *Krabbe 1*,[170] three East German athletes had been subjected to an out of competition test at their training camp in South Africa, organised under the auspices of the German Athletics Federation (DLV). All three samples tested negative, but it was also shown that the three samples all contained the same person's urine, indicating strongly that the samples had been manipulated. Equally there was no evidence as to who had manipulated the samples or how it had been done. The IAAF panel, (which recognised that the responsibility for such testing lay with the DLV which was itself subject to the constitutional demands of German Law) had certain reservations about the DLV conclusions. Equally it accepted that it was a reasonable conclusion that the doping offence under the DLV/IAAF rules was not made out, because the offence required the relevant governing body to prove that the person facing disciplinary action was the person responsible for the offence.

On the other hand in *B v. FINA*,[171] CAS rejected the contention of the appellant that the burden of proof lay on FINA to eliminate all possibilities other than manipulation of the sample by the applicant – including for example the somewhat fanciful possibility that the testers in the case had themselves manipulated the sample, being biased against her.[172]

3.7.2.2 *The burden of proof and strict liability offences*

In the case of a strict liability doping offence – that is to say where the offence exists in having a prohibited substance in one's system – the governing body may still face some difficulty in proving that the offence has taken place. This is for two reasons: first, the athlete may claim that what appears to show up as a banned substance in his or her system is in fact a lawful substance with the same or similar metabolites as the banned substance (a conceptually different case to that where an athlete claims he innocently ingested a banned substance contained in for instance a cough medicine or a dietary supplement). Secondly, some of the banned substances and their metabolites (for instance testosterone

---

[169] Rule 55.2 (ii). See on this *B v. FINA*, CAS 98/211.
[170] *IAAF v. German Athletic Federation*, February 28, 1992, p.125 in Tarasti, *op. cit.*
[171] CAS 98/211.
[172] A similar allegation was rejected by the English Court of Appeal in *Modahl v. British Athletic Federation* [2002] 1 W.L.R. 1192.

or nandrolone)[173] may be produced naturally in the body, and hence the athlete may claim that what appears to be a positive showing for these substances is in fact the result of excessively high *natural* production thereof. In both cases, the burden of proof on the governing body extends to the requirement that it disprove these contentions to the relevant standard.

To take the first of the above situations, in *IAAF v. Athletic Federation of Nigeria*,[174] the athlete had tested positive for the substance 19-norandrosterone – a metabolite of the banned substance nandrolone. Equally, 19-norandrosterone is also a metabolite of the contraceptive pill Norilyn (which the athlete claimed to be using), and the athlete claimed that it was *this* substance that triggered her positive test. The IAAF panel accepted that a doping offence had not been proved to the requisite standard. Equally there was significant scientific evidence here supporting this contention – notably the fact that there was no clear indication of the presence of 19-noretiocholanolone – another nandrolone metabolite that is not a metabolite of Norilyn.

As regards the second of the above situations – a number of athletes have claimed that their positive results, typically for nandrolone or testosterone, are the result of unusually high natural production of the said substances. The arbitration panels have tended to concede this possibility and to require that the federations do the same.[175] In the *Merlene Ottey* case,[176] the IAAF arbitration panel noted that whereas the IAAF rules made provision for the possibility that an athlete might have unusually high natural levels of testosterone in his or her system they made no such concession in the case of nandrolone despite the scientific possibility of high natural production of its metabolites. Accordingly, and in order to remedy this lacuna, the IAAF panel read into the rules a requirement that the burden of proof on the IAAF in nandrolone cases required it to prove beyond reasonable doubt that the level of nandrolone in a sample so exceeded what might be termed "normal" levels that it was not consistent with natural endogenous production – as existed for instance within IOC guidelines. This is not to say that under IAAF rules the burden of disproving natural production lay with the IAAF where there were excessively high levels of nandrolone found. Rather it required that such rules have some threshold requirement in terms of the level of nandrolone within

---

[173] Such metabolites are known as 19-norandrosterone and 19-noretiocholanolone, and some studies have shown that natural production of these metabolites may run close to the IOC threshold of 2ng/ml for men and 5 ng/ml for women (the higher threshold for women being explained by the fact that there may be increased natural production of such substances during pregnancy).

[174] April 10, 1995, p.135 in Tarasti.

[175] *Bernhard v. International Triathlon Union*, CAS 98/222, *UCI v. Mason*, CAS 98/212 and *Meca-Medina & Majcen v. FINA*, CAS 99/A/234. Generally see Kerr, "Doped or Duped? The Nandrolone Jurisprudence" (2001) *International Sports Law Review* 97.

[176] *IAAF v. JAAA* [2001] I.S.L.R. 260.

the sample, before a positive test could be deemed to have occurred – as for example is the case when a positive showing for testosterone is concerned.

Similarly in *B v. International Triathlon Union*,[177] CAS said that the severity of strict liability anti-doping rules meant that they would have to be applied strictly, such that it would have to be incontrovertibly demonstrated that any positive test undoubtedly denoted the presence of the banned substance. Thus when dealing with small quantities of nandrolone in the human system (in this case 2ng/ml), which recent scientific evidence suggested might be naturally produced,[178] the governing body would have to take significant steps to disprove the natural production of the substance (for example by requiring the athlete to undergo scientific tests to assess the likelihood of natural production of the substance) and could not simply rely on a presumption of external application thereof.

On the other hand in *Decker Slaney*[179] – a case that would eventually end up before the American Supreme Court – the athlete in question contended that her positive test for testosterone might have been the result of a number of factors, including bacteriological deterioration, her age, her menstrual cycle, the fact that she had consumed half a bottle of wine 24 hours before the test, and her use of birth control pills. Again the arbitration panel rejected these contentions as not constituting a reasonable doubt as to her guilt. Equally in this case, (wherein there was a good deal of acrimony between the United states governing body for track and field athletics (USATF) and the IAAF), the IAAF panel interpreted its rules as meaning that it was required to prove beyond reasonable doubt that a doping offence had occurred (that is that the T/E ratio was greater than 6:1), and then that the athlete was required to prove that such excessive levels were the result of a pathological or psychological condition. Here, given that Ms Decker Slaney refused to appear and to be cross-examined, or indeed to produce medical evidence to support her claim, it was impossible for her claim to be upheld.

Perhaps most unusually, in the *Denis Mitchell* case,[180] the athlete had tested positive for testosterone, but contended that the positive results might have stemmed from his use of the legal supplements Symbitropin and Triboxin. Alternatively he mentioned that the night before the test, he had driven a good deal, had drunk eight beers and had had sex several times with his girlfriend and suggested that these factors had combined to increase his testosterone levels to the point at which they were above the 6:1 IAAF testosterone/ epitestosterone ratio. Again the arbitration panel required that the burden of proving that high testosterone levels were the result of psychological or

---

[177] CAS 98/222.

[178] See on this point also *UCI v. M*, CAS 98/212, *B v. FIJ*, CAS 98/214.

[179] April 25, 1999, p.155 in Tarasti, *op. cit.*

[180] *IAAF v. USATF*, August 3, 1999, p.165 in Tarasti, *op. cit.*

pathological condition lay with the applicant,[181] and in this case he had not satisfied the burden of proof required of him.

It should also be noted that recently developed testing mechanisms – for example Longitudinal Hormonal Study (LHS) and Isotopic Ratio Measurement Test (IRMS) – can indicate not just the presence of excessive testosterone (as was formerly the case with the old T/E ratio test) but also exogenous administration of testosterone. Unsurprisingly in *S v. FINA*,[182] CAS held that where such a test indicated exogenous application of the substance there was no need to allow the athlete to produce evidence of a physiological or pathological condition leading to heightened natural testosterone production, as would be the case when using the T/E test which indicates the presence thereof. Moreover, according to CAS the IRMS test and the T/E test were both methods of garnering evidence and accordingly could stand in isolation from each other.

Finally, on the question of burden of proof, it should be noted that CAS has dealt with the difficulties posed by a situation where there is inconsistency between the A and the B sample of an athlete. It is clear that a negative B sample will displace a positive A sample. In *N, J, W and Y v. FINA*,[183] however, the swimmers in question claimed that where the B sample contained significantly less of a banned substance than the A sample, then it should become the focus of the doping investigation. CAS accepted that a negative B sample would outweigh a positive A sample but rejected the notion that a positive B sample could outweigh a positive A sample.

3.7.3 Strict liability doping rules, moral innocence and severity of sanction

It is an ongoing if somewhat misstated criticism of doping rules that operate to a strict liability standard that they are, quite simply, unfair.[184] The notion, after all that an athlete like Romanian gymnast Andrea Raducan who tested positive for a banned stimulant after she took a cold remedy that had been given to her by her team doctor should be branded a drugs cheat is intuitively repulsive.[185]

---

[181] The contention that the burden of disproving natural production lay with the governing body was rejected in *Ottey* [2001] I.S.L.R. 260.

[182] CAS 2000/A/274.

[183] CAS 98/208.

[184] Generally on the validity of such rules see Beloff, "Drugs, Laws and Versapaks", p.39 in O'Leary and Wise, "Strict Liability Rules of Sports Governing Bodies", 146 *New Law Journal* No. 6755 (2 August, 1996) 1161 [hereafter Wise], Donnellan, "Strict Liability in Drug Cases" (December 2002), *Sports Law Administration and Practice* 13.

[185] See Ginn, "Common Medicines can be Costly", *St Petersburg Times*, February 3, 2002. The disqualification was upheld by CAS. See *Raducan v. IOC*, CAS (Ad Hoc. Sydney OG) 2000/011. See also *Kabaeva v. FIG* (CAS 2002/A/386). Generally see Dyer &

On the other hand it may be argued that if the sports governing body were to be required to prove not only the presence of a substance but also its intentional (or possibly negligent) ingestion, then this would mean that the fight against doping would be seriously undermined, in that it is entirely impossible to prove beyond reasonable doubt that (for example) an athlete did not have a drink of water spiked by another athlete etc. The counter argument, however, is that in applying anti-doping rules, governing bodies have power to impose sanctions that are greater than those imposed in the courts for most criminal offences, in that a two year suspension, for example, can signal the end of the career of a very high-earning athlete. In these circumstances, just as the criminal courts could never do away with the presumption of innocence, on the basis that those accused of crimes might lie in the witness box, so also it is simply not good enough for the governing bodies to claim to be incapable of determining the probative value of evidence. If governing bodies are to punish in quasi-judicial fashion, then they should be expected to act judicially when presented with conflicting testimony.

Once again, the stock response to this is to say that what is at issue is not the application of law, but merely the operation of the rules of governing bodies to which athletes have consented as a matter of contract. Under these contractual rules, athletes and team doctors are merely being required to be responsible and hence to ensure that any substances that they ingest or prescribe do not contain banned substances.[186] Equally, as we have seen, such rules are not consensually adopted contractual clauses, but rather because of the highly unusual and monopolistic control enjoyed by governing bodies over a section of industry, they amount to a quasi legislative code, and hence may be regarded as "pseudo-criminal law."

The response of national courts to this issue is informative. In the USA the American Arbitration Arbitral Tribunal in the *Foschi Case*,[187] held that the FINA rules, which imposed a strict liability standard, were in violation of standards of fair procedures. Similarly in Switzerland in the *Sandra Gasser* case[188] the IAAF strict liability standard was rejected on the grounds that the IAAF did not give sufficient credence to the athlete's allegation that she had not intentionally taken the banned substance and indeed that her test had been sabotaged. In Germany in the *Krabbe* case, it was held that, on the facts Ms.

Owen, "Drugs Tests May Condemn the Innocent and Miss the Cheats", *Financial Times*, May 30, 2002.

[186] See Branswell, "Over the counter nightmare: Olympic Athletes Given Lists of What They Can and Can't Consume for Things Such as Colds", *Vancouver Sun*, January 31, 2002. Thus in *USA Shooting v. Quigley*, CAS 94/129, CAS would have been prepared to uphold the disqualification of an athlete who had been given a cough mixture by a hotel doctor where the latter reassured the former that the cough mixture contained no banned substances.

[187] *Foschi*, Case No. 77 1900036, April 1, 1996.

[188] Decision of Richteramt Bern III of December 22, 1987 (SJZ 84 (1988)).

Krabbe had intentionally ingested the banned substance, but had she not, her ban would have been deemed to have been invalid.[189] On the other hand, in both *Gasser v. Stinson*,[190] and *Wilander v. ITF*[191] the UK courts took the view that whereas strict liability rules did pose concerns, nonetheless, because sports bodies were ostensibly the experts in running sport, therefore deference should be paid to their concerns that in the absence of any strict liability rules, it would be virtually impossible to operate a coherent anti-doping policy. Finally, the Council of Europe Anti-Doping Convention requires that in applying the rules relating to banned substances, the relevant authorities must support principles of natural justice and protection of fundamental rights.[192] Wise interprets this as meaning that strict liability rules are in violation of the terms of the Convention,[193] although given that such rules were in place in 1989 and yet the Convention is silent on the specific point, this is unlikely to be so.

CAS, in its role as an arbiter working within the parameters of the rules of governing bodies rather than as a critic of them has consistently accepted the legitimacy of strict liability rules. Thus in *NWBA v. International Para Olympic Committee*,[194] it concluded that an athlete was strictly liable for using a painkiller even when a component of the painkiller rather than the painkiller itself contained a banned substance. The court concluded that whereas the athlete under investigation was not a cheat in the sense of being morally culpable, nonetheless he had failed to keep his body free of banned substances and that was enough.

In order to mitigate the severity of such rules, however, CAS has favoured the approach that when the governing body has satisfied the burden of proving the presence of a banned substance in the athlete's system, it should then afford the opportunity[195] to the athlete to prove that he was morally innocent in respect of the issue.[196] If he does so, then the governing body should bear this in mind when deciding on sanction. Thus, where an athlete tests positive during a competition, then he or she should be automatically disqualified from the same

---

[189] Decision of Oberlandesgericht Munchen *Krabbe v. DLV*, March 28, 1996 Case U (K) 3424/95.

[190] Unreported, Queen's Bench, June 15, 1998.

[191] [1997] 2 Lloyd's Rep. 293.

[192] Art.7 of the Anti-Doping Convention.

[193] Wise, *op. cit.*, p.1164.

[194] CAS 95/122.

[195] Thus in *N v. Equestrian Federation*, CAS 94/126, a positive test on a horse was overturned on the basis that the relevant urine samples had been destroyed before the end of the judicial process, hence he did not have the relevant evidence necessary to demonstrate his moral innocence.

[196] See for example *C v. FINA*, CAS 95/141, *H v. International Motorcycling Federation*, CAS 2000/A/281 CAS requires the athlete to "… provide counter evidence which allows it to be established with near certainty that he has not committed a fault." See generally McLaren, "Doping Sanctions, What Penalty?" (2002) *International Sports Law Review* 23.

and should forfeit any medals won or records set – on the grounds that, whatever his intentions, he still gained an unfair advantage over his opponents.[197] However, any further sanction (for instance suspension) should be proportionate to his or her moral culpability in the matter.[198] Indeed in recent cases, CAS has indicated that where an international federation has 'fixed tariff' rules that do not permit moral culpability to be taken into account when assessing sanction, then it would be prepared to modify the same where circumstances demanded this.[199]

The potential leniency of this approach is, however limited by the fact that CAS and indeed the former IAAF arbitration panel in interpreting governing body rules, do expect professional athletes to be responsible for what they consume and to ensure that it does not contain a banned substance.[200] In other words a suspension will only be reduced where there is neither fault nor significant negligence on the part of the athlete. Furthermore, the significance of the fact that the burden of proving innocence rests with the applicant should not be underestimated. In the *Bevilacqua* case,[201] the implication was that this rationale applied particularly where pills or medicine were at issue. However in other cases most notably *Capobianco*,[202] the IAAF panel intimated that this degree of strictness will also apply in the context of an athlete innocently ingesting food that contains a banned substance. In this case, the IAAF panel rejected the athlete's contention that his positive test for the banned steroid stanozolol might have been the result of eating meat from animals which had been injected with steroids by unscrupulous farmers. Even though such a suggestion was remotely possible, (and the panel accepted this point) it was concluded that in this case and on the basis of the scientific evidence

---

[197] On the other hand (and again depending on the rules of the governing body) if the governing body rules do not provide for disqualification following an *out of competition* test, then CAS will not allow such disqualification to occur. *B v. International Judo Federation* CAS 99/A/230.

[198] *H v. International Motorcycling Federation*, CAS 2000/A/281 and *Kabaeva v. FIG* (CAS 2002/A/386).

[199] *B v. International Judo Federation*, CAS 98/214, *Kabaeva v. FIG* (CAS 2002/A/386) and *A v. FILA*, CAS 2001/A/317.

[200] *Kabaeva v. FIG* (CAS 2002/A/386). See Gray, "Doping Control, the National Governing Body Perspective", p.11 in O'Leary, *op. cit.*, for the view that there is a need for greater education of athletes in this regard. Thus in February 2002, CAS increased a suspension imposed on US bobsledder Pavle Jovanovic from nine months to two years, essentially on the grounds that he had not done enough to investigate the contents of a dietary supplement. See Shipley, "Jovanovic's Suspension Extended to Two Years", *Washington Post*, February 8, 2002, Henderson & Meyer, "Court Increases Sledder's Suspension", *Denver Post*, February 8, 2002 and Temkin, "US Sledder Loses Gamble", *Chicago Tribune*, February 8, 2002.

[201] *IAAF v. Federazione Italiana di Athletica Leggera* (*Bevilacqua case*), November 25, 1996, p.143 in Tarasti, *op. cit.*

[202] *IAAF v. Athletics Australia*, March 17, 1997, p.147 in Tarasti *op. cit.*

before the court, the athlete had not proven his innocence on the balance of probabilities. Finally, in *P & Others v. FINA*,[203] three Russian swimmers tested positive for a banned substance, and claimed that a fourth Russian athlete T had spiked their food out of malice. T herself admitted that she had done so, having been the subject of an unsuccessful criminal prosecution and a successful if undefended civil action. CAS, however, accepted the view of the FINA panel that the swimmers had not proven their moral innocence to the standard required, in that they had not disproven the not improbable theory that T was sacrificing herself for the good of her teammates.[204]

The possibility of innocent ingestion of banned substances attracted a good deal of public attention in the late 1990s and beyond, as many high profile sportspersons tested positive for the banned substance nandrolone. This was surprising, given both the calibre of the athletes under discussion and also the sports in which they competed (especially soccer).[205] A number of explanations have been offered for such positive tests, ranging from the natural production of nandrolone metabolites within the body, to the fact that the athlete may have eaten contaminated meat.[206] The most common explanation, however, is that the positive tests were the result of the athlete using lawful dietary supplements.[207] Use of such supplements is plainly widespread in sport, and there is increasing scientific argument that some may metabolise as banned substances.[208] Indeed, many sports bodies have urged athletes not to use dietary

---

[203] CAS 97/180.

[204] In the *Sotomayor* case *IAAF v. FCA* [2001] I.S.L.R. 254 where the contention that the sample given by the Cuban high-jumper in question which tested positive for cocaine had been manipulated (and in a speech President Castro suggested that there had been anti-Cuban machinations at foot) and that had Mr. Sotomayor ingested that much cocaine he would have been unable to have jumped, was rejected. In *N. J. W. and Y. v. FINA*, CAS 98/208, CAS rejected the claim of the defendants – four Chinese swimmers – that the popular world view was that doping was endemic within Chinese sport and hence that they were suffering discrimination within FINA.

[205] See Agnew, "Juventus Faces Tough Questions Over Doping Allegations", *Irish Times*, February 1, 2002. Equally it is argued that drug testing in football is notoriously lax, and is epitomised both by FIFA's reluctance to get involved with the WADA movement, and also with the comparatively minimal sanctions for doping offences in soccer as compared to other sports. See Campbell, "Hidden scandal of Drug Cheats who Shame English Football", *Observer*, March 31, 2002, Agnew, "Football Accused of Serious Foul Play", *Irish Times*, April 23, 2001. In February, 2002, FIFA launched its own anti-doping campaign.

[206] See Morris, "Guest Vows All-out Fight to Clear Name: Cattlemen Scoff at Claim Steak Possible Source of Banned Drug", *Calgary Herald*, July 31, 2002.

[207] In similar vein in *N.J. W. & Y. v. FINA*, CAS 98/208, the swimmers unsuccessfully attempted to blame their positive showing for the banned substance Triamterene on their ingestion of the lawful food supplement Actovegin.

[208] See Mick Hayley, "What's Really in those Nutritional Substances?", *Vancouver Sun*, July 31, 2002, Gillon, "Sports Supplement Contains Banned Steroid", *Glasgow Herald*, July 23, 2002, Korobanik, "Lyons has had to Learn the Hard Way you can Never be too

supplements both because they may contain banned substances and also because they may otherwise lead to positive tests.[209] Governing bodies and indeed CAS have not accepted these excuses as justifying the reduction of sanction, stating that athletes are supposed to be responsible for what enters their systems, particularly in the case of dietary supplements where there are known risks that they may contain banned substances.

This issue arose in *Walker v. IAAF*.[210] Here British athlete Douglas Walker had tested positive for two substances, 19-Norandrosterone (19 NA) and 19 Norethlocholanolone (19 NE) – both of which are metabolites of nandrolone. Mr Walker claimed that a study from Aberdeen University indicated that it was possible that a combination of use of legal supplements and vigorous exercise, exacerbated by stress and dehydration could lead to the natural production of 19-NA in an athlete's body fluids. The IAAF noted, however, that the Aberdeen study was flawed and indeed that other studies had produced different results. Hence in this case, Mr. Walker had not satisfied the burden of disproving the case made by the IAAF. Equally the arbitration panel concluded that it was possible that at some time in the future a study like the Aberdeen one would be of such scientific legitimacy that it might be determinative in a case of this nature.

Careful with Supplements", *Edmonton Journal*, July 8, 2002, Barron, "Olympians Weigh Drug-Test Gamble", *Houston Chronicle*, February 6, 2002, Meyer, "Supplements Under Suspicion", *Denver Post*, February 6, 2002, Rowbottom, "Research Casts Doubt on Nandrolone Testing", *Independent,* January 30, 2001, Malone, "Male Stars Given Food for Thought on Steroids", *Australian Daily Telegraph*, January 22, 2002, Spector, "Marion Jones Hires Technician to Analyse Substances to Make Sure They Don't Contain Banned Substances", *Edmonton Journal*, 25 May, 2001, Cheater, "No Excuses for Using Drugs: Inquiry", *Toronto Sun*, November 26, , 2001, O'Riordan, "Drugs Survey Shock for GAA", *Irish Times*, May 21, 2002 and Agnew, "Doping Controversy may Harbour Some Hard Truths", *Irish Times*, December 4, 2001. See also the "Nandrolone Review", a Report to UK Sport, January, 2000, available on the UK sport website at www.uksportgov.uk.

[209] In an IOC study of 634 nutritional supplements, 14.8% would have led to a positive test and a further 10.4% would have led to borderline results. See www.olympic.org/uk/news/publications/press_uk.asp?release=266. Of the countries examined, it is notable that in the UK nearly 19% of substances examined would have returned positive tests. See Goodbody, "Research Confirms Fears Over Steroid", *The Times*, September 20, 2001. Unsurprisingly the IOC has consistently warned athletes of the dangers of using nutritional supplements. See Mackay, "IOC Warns, Diet Supplements Can Cause Positive Drug Tests", *Guardian*, December 13, 2000, Meyer, "IOC Again Warns Against Supplements", *Denver Post*, April 5, 2002, Smith, "Panel Agrees, Olympians Should Avoid Supplements", *Salt Lake Tribune*, January 30, 2002 Other groups to urge athletes not to use supplements include the Australian Olympic Committee, the British Triathlon Association, the Dutch Government, Dr Enrico Castellacci, president of the Italian soccer doctors association. Similarly in February 2003 UK Sport issued a "nandrolone alert.", See www.uksport.gov.uk/template.asp?id=1326.

[210] [2001] I.S.L.R. 264.

3.7.4 Therapeutic exceptions to anti-doping rules

The IOC/WADA banned list refers to certain substances, which may be used for medical reasons. As we have seen, most recent versions of the IOC/WADA list have attempted to tighten the procedures by which use of such substances can be permitted. Nonetheless these therapeutic exceptions can create difficulties, typically in respect of the procedure with which an athlete must comply if he is to avail of the same.

In *L v. FINA*,[211] the swimmer in question had tested positive for the substance salbutamol. This substance is not, however, absolutely banned by FINA, but may be used by inhaler if this is required as a matter of medical necessity. Hence in order to prove that a doping offence had been committed, FINA would have to prove more than simple presence of the substance, but also that it was not used as a matter of medical necessity. In this case, the swimmer in question had not mentioned use by inhaler of salbutamol in his doping test form. On this basis FINA determined that a doping offence had occurred and suspended the swimmer for two years. On appeal to CAS, however, it was held that whereas failure to declare use of Salbutamol on a doping test form might raise serious doubts as to whether such use was necessary for medical purposes, nonetheless it by itself did not indicate that a doping offence had occurred. Such doubts as might exist could be resolved by clear indications as to the medical necessity for such use, and in this case, the swimmer and his national federation had produced significant amounts of information indicating that the substance was being used by inhaler and for the treatment of asthma. Most importantly, his doctor had provided prior notification to the federation that L was using salbutamol by inhalation. Hence in the view of CAS no offence had been committed.[212] On the other hand in *Cullwick v. FINA*,[213] a New Zealand water polo player tested positive for salbutamol (again inhaled for medical reasons). Here, however, there had been no prior notification to the relevant authorities of this use – on the basis that on a literal reading of the rules, the athlete believed that use by inhaler for medical purposes was in fact legal. CAS, however, took a purposive rather than literal interpretation of the rules, and held that failure to notify in advance meant that a doping offence *had* been committed. Equally, it found a mere technical breach of the rules, and ordered that the two-year sanction on Mr. Cullwick be lifted.[214]

---

[211] CAS 95/142.

[212] On the other hand, CAS refused to uphold the damages claim brought by L against FINA on the basis that it had not acted in bad faith.

[213] 96/149.

[214] In this case, CAS also favoured the application of the doctrine of *Lex Mitior*, that is that a disciplinary tribunal should apply current sanctions to a case where they were less severe than those which existed at the time the offence was committed.

More recently at the Commonwealth Games in August 2002, 100 metres champion Kim Collins tested positive for salbutamol. Under WADA rules, in order for use of such substance to be permitted, the games organisers should be informed in advance of the athlete's condition and the need to use the substance. This had not happened in this case, however, Commonwealth Games officials allowed Collins to keep his medal on the grounds that his claim that he used the substance for medical reasons was patently true, and it was felt that it would be unfair to punish him for the negligence of team officials who had failed to submit the requisite forms.[215] However, fair this result may have been, it is plainly inconsistent with the more draconian approaches to doping taken by the IOC on other occasions.[216]

In the summer of 2003 Irish rugby international Frankie Sheahan tested positive for salbutamol. His medical records show that he suffers from exercise-induced asthma and he uses the substance Ventolin, (which contains salbutamol) to treat this complaint. At a Heineken European Cup match, he failed to fill in the doping form given to him properly (and thereby to indicate that he used a substance that contained salbutamol). He thus tested positive for salbutamol and was banned for two years by the ERC.[217] The appeal body of the ERC, upheld the finding that there had been a breach of anti-doping rules, but accepted that it was the result of administrative oversight, and while criticizing both Sheahan and the Munster rugby organization for the same, replaced the original two year ban with a three month suspension (which left Sheahan free to take part in the rugby World Cup in October/November 2003) and fined the player €5,000.[218]

3.7.5 Provisional suspension prior to a hearing

A major question mark hangs over the legitimacy of a situation where an athlete who tests positive for a banned substance is then suspended from competing pending a hearing or appeal of the matter.[219] This is of particular significance

---

[215] See MacKay, "Collins Escapes Ban Despite Positive Test", *Guardian*, August 2, 2002, Rowbottom, "Collins Keeps Gold Despite Positive Test", *Independent*, August 2, 2002.

[216] See Hayward, "Lenience Leaves Door Ajar For Real Cheats", *Daily Telegraph*, August 2, 2002. See also *Australian Olympic Committee & Australian Handball Federation v. A*, CAS (Oceania) A3, A4/99, where an asthmatic had been openly taking asthma related medication for ten years, yet because of problems within the AHF was not informed of a change in AOC policy that required him to give express notification of this fact to the AOC and AHF. Here CAS accepted that he had, technically committed a doping offence but found no culpability and refused to apply a sanction. See also *AOC & ABUA v. E*, CAS (Oceania) A 2/99.

[217] See Watterson, "Process That Leaves Grounds For Appeal", *Irish Times*, July 12, 2003.

[218] "Appeal Tribunal Ruling", *Irish Times*, September 3, 2003.

[219] See Gray, "Doping Control the National Governing Body Perspective", p.21 in O'Leary

where the period of suspension covers the date of a major sporting event in which the athlete would otherwise compete. There are again two ways of looking at this kind of case. On the one hand, arguments can be made from the standpoint of the other athletes in the race, who may unjustly lose medals and glory if he is cheating, or more poignantly (because it is possible to rectify the position of the "other athletes" by giving them medals they should have won) from the standpoint of an athlete who missed out on attending because the cheating athlete took his place. On the other hand of course arguments can be made from the standpoint of an athlete who is *wrongly* accused of an offence and who is not permitted to take part in such major sporting event as a result.

In *Doug Walker v. UK Athletics and IAAF*,[220] Hallet J seemed to afford prominence to this latter concern when he granted an interim injunction to the plaintiff athlete, lifting a provisional suspension pending a full hearing by IAAF because the loss otherwise to the athlete would have been so enormous.

3.7.6 Deviations from listed rules and procedures

Apart from having fair rules and procedures that are also clear and comprehensible,[221] the governing body MUST stick precisely to the terms of such rules and procedures, be they procedures relating to "chain of custody" (that is the process by which a sample is taken, stored, transported and eventually tested) or procedures relating to the disciplinary process. Thus as we have seen in *USA Shooting & Quigley v. International Shooting Union* an international federation operated a strict liability regime despite the fact that its own rules did not authorize it to do so, and as a result CAS struck down one of its decisions. Similarly in the *Rebagliati* case, where the athlete in question tested positive for marijuana, CAS struck down the disqualification, because on the proper interpretation of IOC rules, the use of marijuana was treated as doping only if there was an agreement between the IOC and the relevant sports federations to that effect, and there was no such agreement in this case.[222]

---

ed., *op. cit.* Gray notes that some governing bodies retain a discretion as to whether or not to suspend which is problematic in that it may lead to allegations of favouritism.

[220] *Guardian*, July 27, 2000.

[221] Thus in *NWPA v. IPC*, CAS refused to grant the IPC its costs because its rules on doping were not sufficiently clear, for example on the question of the definition of doping.

[222] See Beloff, "Drugs, Laws and Versapaks", p.39 in O'Leary, *op. cit.*, p.42. In similar vein in March 2003, the French Rugby Federation was unable to punish prop Pieter de Villiers who had tested positive for cocaine and ecstasy on the basis that the FFR did not have authority to engage in out of competition testing for such substances without permission from the French sports ministry. De Villiers was, however suspended for bringing the game into disrepute. See Rees, "De Villiers Faces New Ban Threat", *Guardian*, March 6, 2003 and Jenkins, "Cocaine Farce –French Star Free to Play Despite Positive Test", *Daily Telegraph*, March 7, 2003

It is true that the WADA code and the Irish rules seek to ensure that minor breaches of procedure cannot be used to set aside positive tests where these minor breaches do not cast genuine doubt on the validity of the overall finding. It is perhaps questionable whether such rules would stand up to scrutiny under Irish rules in respect of fair procedures – especially in light of the fact that the code also creates a presumption that IOC laboratories are operating properly. Equally, both CAS and the former IAAF arbitration panel have consistently upheld the validity of such rules.[223]

Nonetheless, it remains of pivotal importance that governing bodies do not act in a manner unauthorized by their rules, especially where this impacts negatively on the athlete. Thus in *Cooke v. FEI*,[224] the applicant's horse tested positive for a banned substance in a urine test but negative for the same substance in a blood test. CAS overturned the penalty imposed on the applicant, because she was not told of the negative blood test and hence given the right to demand analysis of the B sample, despite the fact that the urine test was the more important test, and hence tended to indicate the correct result. CAS however noted that the rules as laid down by the FEI required that this procedure be followed. Indeed CAS has repeatedly stressed that it is a fundamental right of an athlete in a doping trial to be present when his or her B-sample is being analysed.[225]

Because governing bodies are required to stick precisely to the rules which they set up for themselves, it is vital that all elements of the doping rules of sports bodies be as precisely drafted as possible. Somewhat paradoxically, however, such rules should also seek to afford a broad discretion to governing bodies in the enforcement of their rules. The moral of the story is that in drafting its rules the sports governing body should be absolutely clear as to what it wants and should then draft accordingly. Thus for example, it is vital that it does not just ban the use of drugs but should also ban supply, nor should it

---

[223] *Poll v. FINA*, CAS 2002/A/399, *Haga v. FIM* CAS 2000/A/281, *USA Shooting & Q v. International Shooting Union*, CAS 94/129, *N, J, W and Y v. FINA*, CAS 98/208, *B v. International Triathlon Union*, CAS 98/222, *International Tennis Federation v. K*, CAS 99/A/223, *H v. International Motorcycling Federation*, CAS 2000/A/281, *Swiss Athletic Federation & Gasser v. IAAF*, January 18, 1988, p.117 in Tarasti, *op. cit., IAAF v. Athletics Congress of the US (TAC)*, p.121 in Tarasti, *op. cit., Ngugi v. Kenyan Athletic Association (KAAA) and IAAF*, p.133 in Tarasti, *op. cit., IAAF v. Athletics Australia*, March 17, 1997, p.147 in Tarasti, *op. cit., Sotomayor* [2001] I.S.L.R. 254. On the other hand in the *Modahl* case, the IAAF recognised that the problems with procedures were so enormous that they did in fact cast doubt on the overall validity of the finding. See McArdle, "Say it Ain't So Mo", p.94ff in O'Leary, *op. cit.*

[224] CAS 98/194.

[225] *Scholes v. Beaton and Equestrian Federation of Australia,* CAS 2003/A/ 477. See also *Kabaeva v. FIG* (CAS 2002/A/386) where the failure of the governing body to notify the athlete as to when the B-sample would be analysed, thereby preventing her from being present on the occasion, represented a grave violation of her rights and would result in the test being struck down.

merely ban the prohibited substance in its final form but also its metabolites and markers.[226] Relevant issues pertaining to burden and standard of proof, and any presumptions that the governing body wishes to create (for instance the presumption that a test conducted in an IOC accredited laboratory is valid) should be inserted. The rules should also provide specifically for out of competition testing and should not, for instance refer to testing of "the competitor", as this implies that testing will be performed only on people who are in the process of competing. Moreover, there should be clear specification as to the consequences of a positive test – for example whether, if one member of a team tests positive, the whole team should be disqualified or should face further sanction.[227] Finally, the precise consequences of breaches by the testers of the chain of custody rules or other procedural rules should be made clear. As we shall see, the WADA code is absolutely clear on these points and should provide a blueprint for the future.

One particular area where rules are not drafted precisely is within the banned list itself where certain prohibited substances are listed within particular sections, and it is then provided that the prohibition also applies to "other related substances." The problems inherent in the retention of vague discretionary powers by the governing body is evident in *Walker v. IAAF*.[228] Here the athlete had tested positive for 19-Norandresterone (19-NA) – a metabolite of nandrolone. The athlete argued that whereas 19 NA is a metabolite of nandrolone it is also a metabolite of 19-norandrostenediol and 19-norandrosetenedione – neither of which substances were banned at the time of test. Accordingly, it could not be conclusively proven that his positive showing was the result of nandrolone use, and hence, that he had committed a doping offence. The IAAF panel noted that on the IAAF banned list the prohibited substances are prefaced by the expression "e.g.". So for example it provides that stimulants are banned, *e.g. amphetamines....* Use of "e.g." indicated clearly that the list was not exhaustive. Indeed the list specifically bans 'chemically or pharmacologically related compounds of the banned substances." Despite opposition from UK Athletics, the IAAF panel held that the two substances above were related compounds of Nandrolone, and were deemed to be banned substances despite not appearing on the list.[229] Similarly in *UCI v. A*,[230] a cyclist tested positive for the substance Bromantan at various events between April and June 1997. Bromantan had appeared on the UCI "banned list" in

[226] See Article 2.1 of the World Anti-Doping Code. See also Gray, "Doping Control, the National Governing Body Perspective", p.15–16 in O'Leary, *op. cit.*

[227] See *NWBA v. International Para Olympic Committee*, CAS 95/122.

[228] [2001] I.S.L.R. 264.

[229] This is not dissimilar to the decision of the IAAF panel in *Krabbe I*, to uphold a German federation decision to ban three German athletes for use of the substance Clenbuterol, not because it was on the banned list – it was not – but because such use brought the sport into disrepute and constituted unsportsmanlike conduct.

[230] CAS 97/175.

May 1997, but not on previous lists, hence the cyclist claimed that his positive tests before the May 1997 list was published should be struck down. CAS however, held that it was patently obvious within sport (and for instance by reference to the IOC banned list) that Bromantan was regarded as a banned substance and the cyclist could not be regarded as not having committed an offence simply because UCI only updated its list once annually.

It is submitted that even with the deference traditionally shown by the civil courts towards sports bodies, there is a real problem in a situation where athletes' livelihoods may be taken from them on the basis of vague guidelines of this nature.[231] As we saw in Chapter Two, the more that is at stake, the higher the standards of fair procedures must be. For an athlete facing two years suspension there is sufficient at stake that these vague rules could be challenged on the basis either of breach of contract or of a violation of the constitutional right to earn a livelihood.

An interesting example of this in practice is seen in the case *Krabbe II*.[232] Here East German athlete Katrin Krabbe and two fellow athletes tested positive in 1992 for the banned steroid clenbuterol – a drug that she in fact admitted using, as it was contained in a medical substance called spiropent. The steroid was not, however, on the German Federation's list of banned substances, hence she could not be penalised in respect of its use (indeed at the time the DLV rules did not incorporate those of the IAAF). Instead, she was banned by the German athletics federation for one year, for "unsportsmanlike conduct." In 1993, however, the IAAF added a further two year ban for unsportsmanlike conduct likely to bring the sport into disrepute, and rejected the notion that the IAAF was required to act in accordance with German law in the interpretation of its own rules. In 2001 a Munich court ordered that the IAAF pay Ms Krabbe compensation for loss of earnings, essentially on the basis that she had been punished twice for the same offence. The case settled in 2002, when the IAAF agreed to pay Ms Krabbe an undisclosed sum.[233]

---

[231] See on this, Foster, "The Discourses of Doping: Law and Regulation in the War against Drugs", p.181 in O'Leary, *op. cit.*

[232] *DLV v. IAAF*, 20.11.1993, p.129 in Tarasti, *op. cit.*

[233] See MacKay, "Krabbe Strikes Gold Again", *Observer*, May 5, 2002. Equally in 2002 a German court ruled that former Olympic champion Dieter Baumann was not entitled to compensation having been suspended by the IAAF for testing positive for nandrolone (in circumstances where he claimed that his toothpaste had been spiked) despite the fact that the German federation had acquitted him of the charges. Finally, in December 2003, Kenyan athlete John Ngugi announced that he would be suing Athletics Kenya for $2m for loss of revenue following his suspension by the IAAF in 1993.

3.7.7 The right to a fair hearing

The Council of Europe anti-doping Convention requires that all suspected athletes be afforded, *inter alia*, the right to a fair hearing. This is a call to governments, however, and it is not clear to what extent federations are bound by this. Nonetheless the *Krabbe* case indicates that a domestic body is bound by the law of the land and that an international governing body must respect this fact. So what are the essential elements of a 'fair hearing' in the context of a doping offence? We have already considered the nature of the rules pertaining to burden and standard of proof in such hearings. Beyond this, it is true that the rules of evidence in such cases are much more relaxed than in criminal cases. Essentially if something is both reliable and probative it may be admitted provided that there is not fundamental unfairness to an accused. So for instance expert evidence may be admitted in writing and without being subject to cross-examination.

On the other hand, it is undoubtedly true as we saw in chapter two, that fair procedures will require an athlete to be informed of the charges against him or her, to be afforded adequate time to prepare his or her defence, and to be permitted either to appear himself or to have legal representation and to submit evidence and call and cross-examine witnesses.[234] Thus for example in *Angus v. British Judo Federation*,[235] the fact that an accused was precluded from defending himself, led to a successful action for breach of fair procedures. An athlete will also have a right to appeal the decision of the governing body to an independent appeal body. In this respect, CAS has consistently noted that its own appeal system allows for a full re-hearing of all relevant facts, and hence has the effect of curing any defects in the original hearing.[236] As we shall see, the new WADA code and the Irish Rules are explicit in affording these protections to athletes.

3.8 PRIORITIES FOR THE FUTURE

Much has been achieved in the area of anti-doping policy in the last three decades, and it is probably true that the gulf between the "cheats" and the testers is not quite as stark as it was in the early 1980s. Equally, there are a number of important priorities for the future as far as anti-doping organisations are concerned.

---

[234] *H v. International Motorcycling Federation*, CAS 2000/A/281.
[235] *Times*, June 15, 1984.
[236] *B v. FINA*, CAS 98/211. See also *B v. International Judo Federation*, CAS 98/214.

3.8.1 Development of testing and of testing procedures

If there is to be a serious attempt to deal with the issue of doping in sport, the top priority is still to ensure that the nature of testing and of the testing process is developed.[237] Essentially this involves four separate concerns:

– Increasing the extent of Testing.

– Protecting the constitutional rights of athletes.

– Research into the science of testing.

– Greater IOC accreditation of laboratories.

3.8.1.1 Increasing the extent of testing

One of the chief concerns of the movement to harmonise anti-doping policy is that all sports federations (and all countries) should routinely test athletes both in and more importantly out of competition, and especially for drugs like EPO.[238] This is where bodies like WADA and the Irish Sports Council are particularly useful, in that they will organise drug testing for those sports federations that desire this. Currently competitors in the various sports to have signed up to the ISC anti-doping programme are required to sign a "whereabouts form" indicating where they will be on all dates for the foreseeable future. As such, they are subject to random out of competition testing, both in and out of Ireland.[239] Moreover, WADA has introduced a "passports for athletes" scheme, whereby athletes are given a paper passport which will highlight the statistics as to how often they have been tested, and the fact that their tests have shown up as negatives. It is hoped that this scheme will be fully operational by the time of the Athens Olympic Games in 2004. It is also being suggested by the Chairman of WADA that coaches may be punished if their athletes are found guilty of doping.[240]

---

[237] Generally on the issue of testing see Verokken and Mottram, "Doping Control in Sport", p.307 in Mottram, ed., *Drugs in Sport* (3rd ed., Routledge, New York & London, 2003).

[238] See Walsh, "One Small Step on the Road to Redemption", *Sunday Times*, 8 October, 2001, "Swim Dope Tests Approved", *Daily Telegraph*, 28 February, 2002. Moreover in November 2002, FINA announced that any swimmers setting world records would be subject to automatic EPO testing. See also "ITF Holding Off On EPO Blood Tests", *Associated Press*, July 4, 2002. Generally see Powell, "Anti-Doping Net Tightening in Athens Build-up", *Times*, August 31, 2003.

[239] Equally, UK Sport for instance found that more than one in ten out of competition tests on top-class athletes could not be carried out because officials could not find the athletes sought. See Bond, "UK Sports Annual Report", *Evening Standard*, September 5, 2002.

[240] Rawling, "Managers, Agents an Coaches Should Be Hit Too", *Guardian*, October 27, 2003.

On a global level, it is undoubtedly true that even with the creation of the US Anti-Doping Agency – responsible for drug tests year round that are administered to American athletes in the Olympics and Pan-American Games[242] – there is a need for a more serious attitude to the impropriety of doping within American sport.[242] The attitude of American sport to anti-doping policy is indicated by the fact that the major American sports – baseball, basketball, football and hockey – have a comparatively under-developed anti-doping policy,[243] and also by the fact that the USOC knowingly allowed an athlete who had tested positive for a banned substance to travel to the Sydney Olympic Games in 2000.[244] It had apparently done this on a number of occasions in the past, often with high profile athletes, most notably in the case of Carl Lewis who tested positive for stimulants in the US Olympic trials in the summer of 1988, but was allowed to travel to the Olympics where he won the 100 and 200 metres titles – the former in default after Ben Johnson's disqualification. Another notable incident involved the American 400 metre runner Jerome Young who tested positive for steroids in 1999 yet who was allowed to compete in the 2000 Olympic games, where he was a member of the gold medal winning 4x400 metres relay team.[245]

More recently, however, the USATF and USADA have become far more proactive in their efforts, such that the USATF has been at the forefront of moves to introduce a lifetime ban for all doping offences[246] – a move which the head of WADA claimed was "unenforceable."[247]

---

[241] See King, "Agency Hoping to Stop Doping", *San Antonio Express-News*, January 13, 2002, Benedetti and Bunting, "There's a new Sheriff in Town: A Review of the USADA" [2003] *International Sports Law Review* 19.

[242] See McCaffrey, "The US must Spearhead Reforms to Eradicate Drugs in Sport", p.67 in Dudley, "Drug Czar Rips US Inaction", *Chicago Tribune*, November 19, 2003.

[243] See Seligman, "Commentary: Drug Solution is Simple if Rules Followed", *The Columbian*, 24 June, 2002.

[244] See Goodbody and Powell, "US Accused of Drugs Cover up", *Times*, March 5, 2001. In January 2003, CAS upheld the decision of the USATF not to reveal the name of the impugned athlete. Equally CAS determined that in general IAAF rules allowed the governing body to demand disclosure of the names of athletes who test positive. See *IAAF v. USATF*, CAS 2002/O/401 [2003] *International Sports Law Review*, 61. See also MacKay, "American Drug Positive to Stay Secret", *Guardian*, January 11, 2003, Mitchell, "Hypocrisy at the Heart of the Affair", *Observer*, October 19, 2003.

[245] See Patrick, "New Twist To Long Standing Doping Case", *USA Today*, September 25, 2003, MacKay, "Young Move puts US golds in Danger", *Guardian*, September 26, 2003, Chadband, "US Accused of Cover Up", *Evening Standard*, 27 August, 2003, Walker, "Olympic Drug Testing Programme called Whitewashing", *Milwaukee Journal Sentinel*, September 26, 2003, "Feeble Testing, penalties won't stop steroid scourge", *USA Today*, December 8, 2003.

[246] See Meyer, "Lifetime Ban Urged For Steroid Abuse", *Denver Post*, October 24, 2003, Harasta, "Track adopts zero tolerance policy", *Dallas Morning News*, October 22, 2003, Powell, "US Imposes Life Bans in Crackdown on Drugs", *Times*, December 8, 2003, Crumpacker, "Track Body OKs Lifetime-Ban Legislation", *San Francisco Chronicle*,

3.8.1.2 *Protecting the rights of athletes*

We have already considered the question of the rights of athletes in the context of disciplinary hearings into alleged doping offences. From an Irish perspective, there may, however, also be constitutional problems with testing methods, and in particular with the current EPO test, which is mandatory and which involves blood testing.[248] Such a test, it may be argued, has the potential to violate constitutional rights to bodily integrity and privacy.[249] Blood, unlike urine is not a waste product. The taking of blood is an invasive, painful and potentially traumatic procedure. Moreover, it will affect the oxygen carrying capacity of any athlete, and indeed poses a risk of infection. Now it might be argued that athletes, by reason of their choice of career implicitly consent to such testing, or indeed that the interests of sport are such, that limited intrusion into the constitutional rights of athletes might be justified.[250] This, however, poses the question of whether it is reasonable to require someone who wishes to pursue a career to waive constitutional rights to this degree.

Nor is the procedure for urine testing immune from constitutional concern. According to the IOC anti-doping code, a competitor is called into the consulting area where there may also be present a representative of the IOC Medical Commission, the doping control medical officer, the doping control technical officer, a representative of the relevant International Federation and an interpreter. The competitor is required to urinate into a collection vessel under the observation of the Doping Control officer (who must be the same

---

December 8, 2003, Mackay, "Get Tough on Drugs or Quit", *Observer*, October 19, 2003.

[247] McKay, "Pound Piles Pressure on US Federation", *Guardian*, December 9, 2003, Heath, "Proposed ban of Steroid Users gets Mixed Reviews", *Washington Post*, December 9, 2003.

[248] Generally see Rigozzi, Kaufmann-Kohler and Malinverni, "Doping and Fundamental Rights of Athletes" [2003] *International Sports Law Review* 39, Donnellan, "The Right to Privacy and Drug Testing" (November 2002) *Sports Law Administration and Practice* 11.

[249] See, *inter alia*, Beloff & Beloff, "Blood Sports – Blood Testing, the Common Law and the Human Rights Act, 1998", 2 *International Sports Law Review* (2000) 43, Saler, "Non-Constitutional Privacy Based Challenges to NCAA Drug Testing", 2 *Sports Lawyers Journal* (1995) 303, Charles Palmer, "'Drugs v. Privacy; the New Game in Sports", 2 (2) *Marquette Sports Law Journal* 175, Crowley, "Student Athletics and Drug Testing", Vol. 6 *Marquette Sports Law Journal* 95 and M. Ciccolella, "Right to Privacy Challenges to NCAA Drug Testing", *Journal of Legal Aspects of Sport*, Vol. 2 (1992) 46–55.

[250] An analogy might be drawn with the situation in America where the Federal Supreme Court has upheld the constitutionality of random drug testing for high school students. See Stout, "Court Approves Random Drug Tests for Many Students", *New York Times*, July 20, 2002, "Editorial – Drug Tests in Schools", *Washington Post*, July 1, 2002. For the Canadian perspective, including a statement by the privacy Commissioner that such testing might violate constitutional rights to privacy see de Pencier, p.281ff.

gender as the athlete), ensuring that any clothing preventing the direct observation of the urination is removed. [S]he is then required to pour two thirds of the contents into another vessel and one third into yet another and then close the bottles checking that there has been no leakage. In all these stages there may be acute embarrassment for the athlete.[251] The question is whether either of these embarrassing procedures cross the constitutional line and violate rights of the individual athlete required to submit to them.

The most significant Irish case for gauging the constitutionality of these testing procedures is that of *DPP (Traynor) v. Lennon*.[252] Here the plaintiff was arrested under the 1961 Road Traffic Act, section 13 of which provided that in such circumstances, the arrested person would have the choice of providing a urine sample or allowing a doctor to take a blood sample. She originally chose to give a urine sample but when directed to a cubicle in the corner of a room in which a male doctor and a male Garda would be present she opted to take a blood test instead. In court proceedings she claimed that her right to a real choice as to the nature of the test that she would take had been violated. The Supreme Court took the view that the plaintiff's right to a choice of which procedure to follow would only have been violated had the circumstances in which she was required to give the test been so excessively or unnecessarily intrusive on her dignity that they would violate reasonable standards of modesty. Murphy J. felt that the giving of blood or urine in any circumstances was bound to generate embarrassment and related problems, and whereas such factors should be eliminated as far as possible, they could never be fully eradicated. The implication for the WADA/Irish Sports Council procedures would seem to be that provided that all reasonable steps are taken to reduce as far as possible the level of embarrassment involved, the procedure will remain constitutionally sound.

3.8.1.3 Research into the science of testing

To reiterate a point already made, and indeed to quote the opinion of Jacques Rogge the president of the IOC, the fight against doping is being lost, in that most athletes using drugs are not being caught for so doing.[253] Human Growth Hormone after all has been around sport since 1982, yet there is at the time of

---

[251] See Barnes, "Appliance of Science that Just Takes the Pee", *Times*, August 31, 2003 for the view that "The anti-drugs enforcement seems to me to be nearly as bad as the drugs. It is an horrific invasion of privacy that specialises in a bullying, hectoring, quasi fascist treatment of its victims."

[252] [1999] 2 I.R. 403.

[253] See McAuley, "Drug Testing for Athletes Must Be Improved", p.45, Cyphers, "Mandatory Drugs Fest in Sports", p.55 and Matt Barnard, "Drug Use in Sport is Not Eradicable", p.80 all in Dudley, *op. cit.*

writing no efficient test for hGH.[254] Similarly EPO has been around for fifteen years, yet the blood/urine test used to detect EPO can only detect if the substance has been used in the days immediately before the test, and the efficacy of the stand alone urine test is still a matter of some concern – as was manifested in the embarrassing events involving Olga Yegorova in 2001, whose "positive" test was rightly struck down on the basis that the efficacy of the testing procedure was not established, and hence to have sanctioned her on its basis would have been fundamentally unfair.[255] On the other hand, in November 2003, CAS upheld a suspension of a Moroccan athlete who had tested positive for r-EPO on a urine only test, and in doing so, upheld the legitimacy of the test itself.[256]

As we have seen, developments in the science of testing have made it easier to detect both use of the listed steroids and also exogenous administration of testosterone. Nonetheless considerably more research (and more funding for such research) is needed into existing methods of testing, and also into the means for establishing effective tests for the newer drugs and the designer steroids.[257]

In this last respect, a major development occurred in October 2003 with the discovery by the USADA both of the existence of and a test for a designer steroid tetrahydrogestrinone (THG). It is perhaps an exaggeration, however, to say that this represents a major success for the anti-doping authorities in the world. In fact the discovery was made in most unusual circumstances.[258] Early in the summer of 2003 the USADA received a message from someone representing himself as a high profile athletics coach[259] who provided the

---

[254] In October 2003, WADA announced that it was confident that a test for hGH would be in place by the time of the 2004 Olympic Games.

[255] See Monti, "Scientist Casts Doubt on French EPO Test", *Race Results Weekly*, August 2, 2001.

[256] *IAAF v. Boulami & MAR,* CAS 2002/O/401.

[257] See Schanzer, Geyer, Gotzmann and Mareck-Engelke, *Recent advances in doping analysis* (Cologne: Sport & Buch Straus, 1999), McKay, "Doping Initiative is Halted By Lack Of Funds", *Guardian*, March 5, 2003.

[258] See Shipley, "USADA: Elite Athletes Using 'Designer' Steroid'", *Washington Post*, October 17, 2003, Rosen, "New Drug Scandal Surfaces in Track", *Atlanta Journal*, October 17, 2003, Patrick, "Designer Drug Test Flags US Track Stars", *USA Today*, October 17, 2003, Williams, "Bay Lab linked to Huge Steroid Bust", *San Francisco Chronicle*, October 16, 2003, Hersh, "Steroid 'Conspiracy' Said To Involve Athletes", *Chicago Tribune*, October 17, 2003, Parrish and Trivett, "Agency reveals doping scandal", *Rocky Mountain News*, October 17, 2003, MacKay, "New Drug Scandal Shakes Sport", *Guardian*, October 18, 2003, Mackay, "Get Set for Biggest Dope Scandal Ever", *Guardian*, October 18, 2003, Morris, "Diet Expert Under Spotlight", *Guardian*, October 18, 2003, Fainaru-Wada, "Raid Uncovered Suspected Steroids", *San Francisco Chronicle*, October 19, 2003.

[259] Warner, "Drugs Scandal Sparks Hunt For The Supergrass", *Evening Standard*, October 24, 2003, MacKay, "Francis fits the bill in whistleblower whodunit", *Observer*, October

association with both the names of athletes who, he said were using a particular designer steroid, and also a used syringe containing some of this substance, which is chemically related to Gestrinone – a banned substance. Using this, Dr Don Catlin with the staff of the IOC laboratory at UCLA[260] was able to identify the designer steroid (which would not have shown up on normal WADA/IOC tests) and to develop a test for it. As a result a number of high profile athletes tested positive for THG,[261] and a range of samples that had been taken at previous sporting events and had been frozen and stored were retested.[262] It was also reported that the IAAF were prepared to offer British sprinter Dwain Chambers a deal, whereby his penalty for testing positive for THG would be reduced if he gave them information about his case.[263] In the event, however, Chambers received a two-year ban from all sport, and a lifetime Olympic ban. Moreover a major investigation (ongoing at the time of writing) was launched into the company at the centre of controversy (Balco Laboratories) and its president Victor Conte. Nonetheless, given both the unique nature of the coming to light of THG, and also the fact that there are probably dozens more designer steroids available to athletes, these events may not be the huge development in anti-doping policy that has been suggested.[264]

26, 2003, Crumpacker, "Searching For A Mystery Man", *San Francisco Chronicle*, December 7, 2003.

[260] Meyer, "UCLA Drug Lab at Heart of Scandal", *Denver Post*, October 19, 2003 and Hall, "Lab Sleuths Tracked Clue to Doping Drug", *San Francisco Chronicle*, October 26, 2003.

[261] Bialik & Fry, "Probe of THG use by Athletes Includes Some Very Big Names", *Wall Street Journal*, October 21, 2003, MacKay, "UK's Top Sprinter In Positive Drug Test", *Guardian*, October 22, 2003, Powell, "Top Stars Face Designer Steroid Probe", *Times*, October 22, 2003, Goodbody, "Doping Expert Predicts Further Revelations Among Sports Elit", *Times*, October 22, 2003.

[262] Powell, "Drugs Scandal Threatens To Overturn Paris Medals Table", *Times*, October 18, 2003, McKay, "New Paris THG Tests Yield A Positive", *Guardian*, November 22, 2003, Warner, "Hunt On For THG cheats", *Evening Standard*, October 21, 2003, Powell, Lord and Goodbody, "IOC Unable To Endorse Re-Testing Of Old Samples", *Times*, October 26, 2003, Meyer, "Doping War Broadens", *Denver Post*, October 26, 2003, Rae Brooks, "Urine Samples May Be Retested", *Salt Lake Tribune*, October 29, 2003, Meyer, "Samples From Salt Lake May Be Tested Again", *Denver Post*, October 30, 2003, Rowbottom, "Retesting of World Championship Samples Reveals More THG Abuse", *Independent*, November 22, 2003. The legality of retesting a sample that had already been tested and found to be negative is perhaps uncertain.

[263] Rowbottom, "Rogge Offers Chambers Drugs 'Plea Bargain'", *Independent*, 28 November, 2003, Stevens, "Plea Bargain Storm Rages Over Chambers", *Guardian*, November 28, 2003.

[264] Sheridan, "Major Doping Scandal Puts Sports At A Crossroads", *Philadelphia Inquirer*, October 22, 2003, Emmons, "Discovery of Designer Drug likely to spur labs to create successor", *Mercury News*, October 22, 2003, Barnes, "Time to stop this shocked reaction to the inevitable", *Times*, October 22, 2003, Ferstle, "Exposure Risks New Batch Of Cheats", *Guardian*, October 24, 2003, Mitchell, "Drugs Code Is Cracked: Let's Start Anew", *Observer*, October 26, 2003, Rae Brooks, "Scientists Scurry To Find The Latest

3.8.1.4 Greater accreditation of laboratories

Most federations use the IOC accredited laboratories whether their rules provide for this or not. This is another issue which has been taken over by the WADA, which has undertaken to standardise laboratories (as the IOC did before it) and indeed to create a reference laboratory, and indeed since January 1, 2004 the 31 laboratories operate under the direction of WADA. Nonetheless the fact remains that it costs a good deal to run an accredited laboratory and hence the likelihood is that the bulk will continue to be located in Australia, North America and Europe.

3.8.2 Regulation of dietary supplements

Billions of dollars are spent annually on dietary and nutritional supplements that are, for the most part both lawful[265] and not prohibited within sport.[266] Moreover, it is clear that many young athletes use such substances.[267] For the purposes of sports bodies this poses two problems. First, as we have seen, sport will almost certainly have to accept the argument that athletes testing positive for banned substances and in particular for nandrolone often do so because of having ingested supplements which contain nandrolone metabolites or which themselves metabolise as such, and it will have to assess whether

---

Drugs – And Ways To Test For Them", *Salt Lake Tribune*, November 18, 2003, Bialik and Fry, "A Growing Drug Scandal Brings Sport To Crossroads", *Wall Street Journal*, November 18, 2003, O'Connor, "Sports Should Put Their Weight Behind Stopping Steroid Use", *USA Today*, November 18, 2003

[265] In the United States, under the Supplement Act of 1994, FDA approval is not needed for a supplement if it is not claimed that it will treat, cure or prevent disease.

[266] In America in 2001, $17.7 billion was spent on food supplements. See Meyer, "Added Danger", *Denver* Post, September 15, 2002, O'Brien, "Calculating the Long Term Cost of Drugs", *Irish Times*, October 25, 2003, Olson, "The Shifting Stimulant Debate", *Omaha World Herald*, November 5, 2002.

[267] According to the American Sports Medicine Institute, approximately 11% of all high school,, college and professional athletes in the US use drugs or supplements. This amounts to approximately one million people aged between 12 and 17. Moreover, the vast majority of professional sprinters and cyclists use creatine. See Kroichek, "A problem from pros to preps", *San Francisco Chronicle*, December 18, 2003. Halasz and DeBrosse, "Supplementing Strength: Many Teenage Athletes Are Buying Unregulated Dietary Supplements", *Dayton Daily News*, October 23, 2002, Meyer, "Added Danger: Popularity Of Sports Supplements Grows Among Young Athletes", *Denver Post*, September 15, 2002, Speaker, "The Next War On Drugs? Teens and Supplements", *Wilmington Morning Star*, August 30, 2002, Murray, "Ban on Ephedra Should Affect Many", *Fort Lauderdale Sun-Sentinel*, July 8, 2002, Hayes, "Supplements Becoming A Major Concern", *The Sporting News*, August 21, 2001, Deardorff and Dougherty, "Supplements Lure Athletes", *Chicago Tribune*, August 20, 2001, Smith, "Supplement Oversight", *Salt Lake Tribune*, May 21, 2001 and Simms, "Fourth of Males taking Creatine", *Wisconsin State Journal*, June 10, 2002.

this fact should serve to mitigate any sanction incurred by such athletes. Secondly, it is clear that many of these substances pose significant dangers to the health of users,[268] or – as for instance in the case of the increasingly popular supplement creatine[269] – the safety of such substances (especially for people with existing kidney problems) is uncertain.[270] In as much as those involved

---

[268] See Ruskin and Goldsmith, "A Tragic Loss" (June 2003) *Sports Law Administration and Practice* 9, Olson, "The shifting Stimulant debate", *Omaha World Herald*, November 5, 2002, Wesskopf, "Doctors Warn of Ephedrine", *Fort Worth Star Telegram*, August 2, 2002, "Institute of Medicine Lays Groundwork For Study Of Safety Of Dietary Supplements", *White House Bulletin*, July 24, 2002, Landman, "Supplemental Danger", *St Petersburg Times*, August 15, 2002, Gonzalez, "Learning Supplements", *Hartford Courant*, June 26, 2002, Torassa, "New Diet Pill – New Health Risks' *San Francisco Chronicle*, July 22, 2002, Navarro, "Cracking Down On Ephedrine, Dangers of Supplement Revealed", *Miami Herald*, July 22, 2002, Gonzalez, "Report Points Out Dangers of Supplements", *Hartford Courant*, May 21, 2001, "A Deadly Diet Aid?' *People Magazine*, June 24, 2002, Munn, "Bitter Pills to Swallow", *The Daily Oklahoman*, August 29, 2001, Meyer, "Andro Is Creating Major Health Concerns", *Denver Post*, 15 September, 2002, McDougal, "Ban Protein Bars – Swim Star Warns Young Athletes", *Daily Telegraph (Sydney)*, January, 9, 2003, Jill Spitznass, "Don't take ?", *Portland Tribune*, January 14, 2003.

[269] See MacLaren, "Creatine", p.286 *et seq.* in Mottram *Drugs in Sport* (3rd ed., Routledge, London and New York, 2003).

[270] See O'Riordan, "Study Links Creatine to Cancer Risk", *Irish Times*, January 24, 2001. On March 14, 2001, the Irish Sports Council issued a formal warning to athletes about the potential dangers of using creatine. See generally, Lapp, "Students Use Creatine for Immediate Effects, Wonder About Long-Term", *Daily Orange*, March 26, 2001, Smith, "Supplements; Some From Utah Firms Get Conflicting Messages From IOC", *Salt Lake Tribune*, February 26, 2001, Thomas, "Specialists Say Creatine Report Is Not Correct", *Omaha World Herald*, May 23, 2001, Gugliotta, "Dietary Supplement Makers Flex Muscle", *Washington Post,* December 25, 2000, Deardorff and Dougherty, "Supplements Lure Athletes", *Chicago Tribune*, August 20, 2001, Hayes, "Supplements Becoming A Major Concern", *The Sporting News*, August 21, 2001, Munn, "Bitter Pills to Swallow", *The Daily Oklahoman*, August 29, 2001, "No Signs of Danger", *San Francisco Chronicle*, January 17, 2002 and Cyphers and O'Keefe, "Supplements Losing", *Daily News*, April 7, 2002. In America the focus has predominantly been on the stimulant ephedrine/ephedra, which was banned by the NFL in September 2001 because of perceived health risks. See Cole, "2001 Booklet Warned of Ephedra's Dangers' *Miami Herald*, March 14, 2003. But see also, Thomas, "Specialists say Creatine Reports is not Correct", *Omaha World-Herald*, May 25, 2001, Levesque, "Ephedra Reaction Entirely Too Rash", *Seattle Post*, March 13, 2003. See also generally, Samson, "Coaches Owe It To Kids To Keep Up On Supplements", *Kansas City Star*, January 31, 2003, Meyer, "Added Danger: Popularity Of Sports Supplements Grows Among Young Athletes", *Denver Post*, September 15, 2002, Jaroff, "Ephedra: Who's Telling the Truth?", *Time*, August 22, 2002, Meyer, "Enhancers take Chances", *Denver Post*, August 19, 2001, Hu, "Bringing Ephedra's Risk To Light", *Houston Chronicle*, February 24, 2003, Hopper, "Pressure Mounts To Remove Ephedra From Market", *Houston Chronicle*, 24 February, 2003, "Get Ephedra Off The Shelves", *LA Times*, 21 February, 2003, Antonen, "Questions of Substance", *USA Today*, February 21, 2003, Bondy, "Battle of the Bulge turning Deadly", *NY Daily News*, 20 February, 2003, Paige, "Ephedra Takes Toll On

in the fight against doping cite the health of the athlete as a key reason to ban drugs, it is surely inconsistent not to target the very widespread and very powerful food supplement industry.[271]

Moreover, there is no reason not to do so. It is not the case that all substances on the banned list are more performance enhancing or more dangerous for the user than all substances not on the list. Indeed it is notable that in the United States the NFL has a stricter policy in respect of dietary supplements that contain steroids than in respect of recreational drugs such as marijuana or cocaine.[272] Moreover as was mentioned earlier, the substances on the banned list are stigmatised simply by virtue of their being on the list, rather than because they are somehow inherently evil. It has been argued before that if WADA wishes to present a logical and reasonable justification for its anti-doping policy,

---

Users", *Denver Post*, February 21, 2003. Other substances such as the "red bull", energy drink have also caused controversy over potential health risks and have been the subject of civil actions in the US. See "Athlete's Widow Sues Energy Drink, Supplement Makers", *The Deseret News*, August 26, 2002. In Ireland, a jury at the inquest into the death of a young basketball player who had collapsed having drunk red bull recommended that the safety of stimulant drinks be investigated, and the body conducting the investigation concluded that such drinks should carry safety warnings. See Donnellan, "Jury Calls For Research Into Stimulant Drinks", *Irish Times*, November 15, 2000 and O'Connor, "Food Safety Group Advises That Stimulant Drinks Carry Warnings", *Irish Times*, March 19, 2002.

[271] See Verroken and Mottram, "Doping Control in Sport", pp.350–351 in Mottram ed., *Drugs in Sport* (3rd ed., Routledge, New York & London, 2003).

[272] This is largely a response to the deaths in 2001 of football players Korey Stringer, Rashidi Wheeler and Eraste Austin, and in 2003 of Steve Bechler which were speculatively linked to their use of the supplement ephedra. See Lightly, "As Part of Any Settlement, NU Coaches Must Go", *Chicago Tribune*, February, 5, 2003. Indeed in 2002 the US Justice department launched a criminal investigation into the affairs of Metabolife – a leading seller of remedies containing ephedra – for the purposes of determining whether it lied when it said that it had never been notified of any serious health effects of the substance. See Ruskin & Goldsmith, "A Tragic Loss", June 2003, *Sports Law Administration*, p.9, Jaroff, "Ephedra: Who's Telling The Truth", *Time*, August 22, 2002, Deardorff, "Metabolife calls for banning sale of supplements to minors", *Chicago Tribune*, August 23, 2002, O'Keefe, "New Blow-up over Ephedra", *New York Daily News*, August 26, 2002, Kemper, "US Investigates Metabolife over Ephedrine Concerns", *LA Times*, August 16, 2002, Cyphers and O'Keefe, "Supplements Losing", *New York Daily News*, April 7, 2002. LaMar, "Senate Passes Bill Outlawing Certain Diet Supplements For Minors", *Contra Costa Times*, May 24, 2002, Eichner, "NFL Ban On Ephedra Is Overdue", *The Daily Oklahoman*, September 14, 2001, Sheinin, "Union Stays Quiet On Ephedra", *Washington Post*, February 21, 2003, Salladay, "New Bill would Outlaw Ephedra", *San Francisco Chronicle*, February 21, 2003, Rubin, "House Committee Wants More Info On Ephedra", *USA Today*, March 14, 2003. Equally, it should be noted that sports federations in the United States have been notoriously slow to ban substances that all international federations and the IOC ban. Thus for example the supplement ephedrine was, until recently permitted within American sport but was on the IOC banned list. See Bodley, "Baseball Must Act Now To Prevent Further Deaths", *USA Today*, March 14, 2003.

then it must explain more clearly and more consistently why certain substances are present on its banned list. The nature of many nutritional supplements is such that it will also have to explain the absence of many such substances from the same list.

3.8.3 The threat posed by genetics

Most of the more modern prohibited substances – Human Growth Hormone, EPO and so on – are genetically engineered. In its January 2003 "banned list," however, the IOC and WADA recognised the new potential of genetics for sport, when its banned list included for the first time genetic manipulation as a prohibited method.[273] This is very much an unknown quantity, in terms of its existence as a means of enhancing performance, in terms of its likely effectiveness, in terms of whether it can be detected outside of taking a muscle biopsy, (an undoubtedly unconstitutional action from an Irish standpoint) and indeed in terms of how it is likely to operate. (It can also be questioned whether such a practice should figure on the IOC list, but this will not be dealt with).

The basis of the threat from genetics is as follows. Scientific developments in the construction of the human genome map have led to the development of what is known as "gene therapy." This involves new genetic information being packaged into a tiny virus and injected into the body as a means of curing or preventing disease such as muscular dystrophy and cancer. It is feared that such developments will be used either to manipulate genes (in both born humans and indeed potentially in embryos) that are scientifically regarded as enhancing athletic ability,[274] or to suppress the activity of certain genes that restrict performance, thereby potentially creating a "super athlete."[275] Scientists are uncertain as to whether such genetic manipulation may have already happened, or if not, when it is likely to start to occur, with some suggesting that it may be

---

[273] See Goodbody, "World Sport Clamps Down Quickly On Latest Doping Threat", *Times*, October 1, 2002, "Spare Parts Will Not Be Allowed", *Irish Times*, October 2, 2002.

[274] See O'Connell, "Do Genes Play A Role In Sport?", *Times*, May 13, 2002, Radford, "Sprinters Get Genetic Head Start", *Guardian*, August 28, 2003.

[275] See Dyer & Firn, "Gene Doping Threatens To Transform Sport", *Financial Times*, May 31, 2002, Garreau, "The Next Generation, Biotechnology May Make Superhero Fantasy A Reality", *Washington Post*, April, 26, 2002, Maher, "Following The Gene Map; Scientific Advances Could Spawn More Doping By Athletes", *American Statesman*, January, 29, 2002, King, "High Tech Cheating A Threat", *San Antonio Express News*, October 26, 2002, Purgavie, "Of Mice and Supermen", *Sunday Telegraph (Sydney)*, November 10, 2002, Stroh, "Scientists Concerned About 'Gene Doping'" *Baltimore Sun*, February 12, 2002, Clarey, "Chilling New World", *International Herald Tribune*, January 26, 2001, Miah, "Genetics, Privacy ands Athlete's Rights", 2001 *Sports Law Bulletin*, p.10, Miah, "The Use Of Genetic Information In Sport" at www.austlii.edu.au/au/other/alrc/publications/issues/26/.

a reality by the 2004 Athens Olympics, and others suggesting that the 2012 Olympics may be a more realistic date for such advances to occur and still others suggesting that it may already have happened.[276] Nonetheless, by reason of its (admittedly uncertain) capacity to affect sport, its regulation must be a top priority for the future. In October 2003, representatives of WADA announced that it was close to unveiling tests that will detect gene doping, but at the time of writing no such tests have been scientifically approved.

3.8.4 Harmonisation of anti-doping policy and the development of WADA

It is widely argued that WADA represents the best chance for success in the fight against doping, providing as it does an independent and unified front against doping across sport.[277] Its primary responsibility remains to further the harmonization of anti-doping policy among all the partners against doping, in matters such as the definition of doping, the banned list, the procedures for anti-doping investigations and disciplinary tribunals and sanctions.[278] Moreover, it exists to galvanise anti-doping policy by making the harmonised rules as strict as possible.[279]

The future success of WADA is likely to be determined by a number of factors. First there is the question of its membership. Ultimately if WADA is to represent the common face of anti-doping policy, then plainly there is a need that as many bodies engaged in the fight against doping sign up to WADA as is possible. Much has been achieved in this respect. At the end of 2002, FIFA signed a memorandum of understanding with WADA (while maintaining its traditional independence in respect of its anti-doping programme). At the same time, FIFA also signed up to the jurisdiction of CAS such that CAS will

---

[276] This suggestion was mooted by Dr Johann Olav Koss of the WADA. See Entine, "The Gene Genie Is Out Of The Bottle, Doping's Next Wave Is Already On Us", *Guardian*, December 1, 2001.

[277] Thus its independence was asserted in symbolic form in 2001, with the decision that its permanent headquarters would be in Montreal, rather than in Lausanne – the seat of the IOC. See Spencer, "Drug Cheats May Be Winning The War – But Not For Long: World Anti-Doping Agency Will Be On Site", *Edmonton Journal* (22 July, 2002) and Pound, "The World Anti-Doping Agency: An Experiment In International Law" [2002] *International Sports Law Review* 53.

[278] On the question of sanction, see *UCI v. C & FCI*, CAS 98/213, where CAS amended a FCI suspension of a cyclist for six months on the grounds that the said six months were "dead", as far as cyclists were concerned in that they were not part of the cycling season. CAS postponed the period of suspension until a "live", period of the year, but blamed UCI for the fact that its rules in respect of sanctions were not harmonised with those of other governing bodies in that it provided for minimum sanctions of less than 12 months.

[279] See Vrijman, "Harmonisation, A Bridge Too Far", p.147 in O'Leary, *op. cit.*

be the final arbiter of any disputes at FIFA or its member confederations.[280]
Moreover at a meeting of the International Inter-governmental Consultative
Group on Anti-Doping in Moscow in December 2002, more than forty countries
signed a memorandum of common principles to fight doping in sport.[281] In
November 2002, the US Government and WADA agreed on the expansion of
co-operation in the fight against doping. In January 2003, the former Russian
Prime Minister, Mikhail Kasyanov issued a decree for Russia to join WADA.
At the same time, however, the European Union has recently distanced itself
from the agency. This leads on to a related issue namely the question of funding
for WADA on both a long and a short term basis (currently in the region of
twelve million pounds annually) – something that has caused significant
acrimony, notably between WADA and the European Commission. At present
WADA is funded equally by the IOC on the one hand and World Governments
on the other. In October 2003, Dick Pound, Chairman of WADA suggested
that countries that did not meet their obligations to fund WADA would not
have their national anthems played if their athletes won gold at the 2004
Olympic Games in Athens.[282]

3.8.5 The World Anti-Doping Code

Above all, WADA may stand or fall on the success of its innovative anti-
doping measures such as the athlete passport, its e-learning interactive
programme for athletes, coaches and trainers, and especially the new anti-
doping programme comprising the world anti-doping code, prescribed
international standards and the development of models of best practice. The
anti-doping code was presented and accepted at a conference in March, 2003,[283]

---

[280] In August 2001, the IAAF constitution was amended to allow CAS to operate as its
international arbitration court. See Reeb, "The IAAF to recognise the jurisdiction of
the Court of Arbitration for Sport" [2001] *International Sports Law Review* 246.

[281] See "Countries Get Together To Pound Drug Cheats Into Submission", *Daily Telegraph
(Sydney)*, December 12, 2002.

[282] In December 2003 the IOC executive board informed the committees supporting the
bids of New York and Rio de Janeiro to host the 2012 Summer Olympic games that
their bids would be unsuccessful if America and Brazil did not pay their dues to WADA.
Shortly afterwards, the US paid its 2003 dues to WADA.

[283] See Stoner, "World Harmonization of Anti-Doping Policy", April 2003 *Sports Law
Administration and Practice*, p.14, Shipley, "Nations Agree To Uniform Drug Code",
Washington Post, March 6, 2003, Powers, "Global Policy Adopted on Anti-Doping
Reforms", *Boston Globe*, March 6, 2003, Parrish, "Historic New Anti-Doping Code",
Rocky Mountain News, March 6, 2003, "The Need For A World-Anti-Doping Code",
January February 2002, *Sports Law Bulletin*, p.2, Caborn, "Back The Code, Beat The
Cheats And Believe Again", *Guardian*, November 7, 2003. 65 sports federations and
73 national governments gave their support to the new WADA code, as did the USADA.

after WADA had considered a large number of comments in respect of earlier drafts *inter alia* from governments,[284] International Federations and the IOC. It is hoped that the code will be fully operational in time for the Athens Olympic Games in 2004 and incorporated into national legal systems by the 2006 Winter Games. Equally the heads of two of the largest federations namely FIFA and the International Cycling Union refused to attend the summit (although FIFA has signalled its support for the code), and the new rules do not apply to the major American sports, save where they are involved in the Olympic games.[285] The Chairman of WADA, Mr. Dick Pound and the IOC President, Mr. Jacques Rogge have warned sporting federations that their Olympic status will depend on their signing up to the code,[286] and that their chances of hosting international sporting events would be similarly affected.[287]

Apart from encouraging greater efforts in the areas of education and research,[288] the main impact of the code is to provide an element of standardization across the sporting world for some of the central elements of anti-doping policy. We will consider the nature of such standardization shortly when we analyse the Irish Sports Council Anti-Doping Rules, enacted pursuant to the WADA code. Beyond this the code seeks the development of models of best practice, and of international standards on matters such as laboratories, testing, Therapeutic Use Exemptions, and the list of banned substances.

In this last respect WADA commits to publishing an updated list at least annually[289] of substances that are prohibited at all times (that is to say both in and out of competition).[290] Interestingly, the code creates criteria for deciding whether or not a substance should be included on the banned list,[291] namely:

– if it enhances or has the potential to enhance sport performance,

– if its use represents an actual or potential threat to the health of the athlete,

– if its use violates the spirit of sport.

WADA requires that the substance in question fulfil at least two of the above

---

[284] For the UK sport reaction see www.uksport.gov.uk/images/uploaded/Code3response.pdf.
[285] Goodbody, "Dope Code Must Embrace All Bodies If Chaos Is To Be Avoided", *Times*, 7 March, 2003, Shipley, "Olympic Policy Concerns NBA Players", *Washington Post*, March 7, 2003, "Who's A Dope?", *New York Daily News*, March 12, 2003.
[286] Bierley, "It's Just A Drug Check Mate", *Guardian*, October 15, 2003.
[287] See Goodbody, "Rogge in Olympic Threat to Football", *Times*, March 4, 2003, Mackay, "Football Risks Exclusion Over Drugs' *Guardian*, March 4, 2003, McKay, "US Dope Delay Puts New York at Risk", *Guardian*, November 19, 2003. See also Art.23.5 of the code.
[288] Arts 18 & 19.
[289] Art.4.1.
[290] Art.4.2.
[291] Art.4.3.1.

criteria if it is to be placed on the banned list. The code makes it clear, however, that it is WADA that decides whether or not a substance meets these requirements. In other words, an athlete cannot challenge the banned list on the basis that a particular substance does not meet the relevant criteria.[292] Alternatively, WADA is prepared to place a substance on the banned list if it can be shown to have the potential to act as a masking agent for other banned substances.[293] Finally, WADA in consultation with other parties commits to establishing a monitoring programme in respect of substances that are not as yet on the banned list, but whose use is a matter of concern.[294]

Importantly the code also clarifies matters pertaining to the allocation of responsibility for doping control. Thus testing *within an event* is the responsibility of the body organising the event, whereas out of competition testing may be initiated by WADA, the relevant federation (or the IOC if an Olympic event is in progress), the athlete's national anti-doping organisation or the anti-doping organisation of the country where the athlete is located. Results management, hearings and sanctions shall be the responsibility of the anti-doping organisation that initiated and directed sample collection, save where the national anti-doping organisation of a country tests an athlete who is not a resident of the country, in which case the matter is referred to the relevant international federation.[295] The Sports Council Anti-Doping Rules outline how this is to take shape within the context of Irish Sport and it is to these rules that we now turn.

3.8.6 The Irish Sports Council's Anti-Doping Rules

In January 2004, in a major development, and pursuant to the signing by the Minister for Sport of the Copenhagen declaration on Anti-Doping in Sport in April 2003, the Irish Sports Council published the Irish Anti-Doping Rules, which will govern the conditions under which sport is played in Ireland. All Irish governing bodies in receipt of government grants are required to sign up to these rules. The essential function of the rules is to incorporate the terms of the WADA code (and the international standards and models of best practice adopted by WADA in support of the code) and to ensure that they govern the totality of organised sport in Ireland. In this respect, the introduction to the anti-doping rules classifies such rules as being akin to the competition rules by which competitors in an event agree to be bound. The rules must be accepted by participants as a condition of participation in sport[296] and as a result of

---

[292] Art.4.3.3.
[293] Art.4.3.2.
[294] Art. 4.5.
[295] Generally on this see Arts 20–22.
[296] Art.1.2.

their contractual relationship with the relevant governing body.[297] The Sports Council intends for the rules to be adopted by National Governing bodies, and indeed adoption of the rules is a pre-requisite to receiving financial assistance from the government or the Sports Council.[298] Much of what is in the Irish anti-doping rules simply replicates the terms of the WADA code, and indeed there are further links with WADA, for example in the obligation that all results, Therapeutic Use Exemptions and testing should be communicated to WADA as well as the athlete's governing body.[299]

3.8.6.1 *The definition of doping*

The rules adopt a multi-faceted definition of doping akin to that contained in the WADA code, drafted in clear terms and covering every conceivable situation. Thus a doping offence is committed whenever any of the following can be demonstrated:

– Presence of a prohibited substance, its metabolites or markers in an athlete's bodily specimen (and the code insists that it is the athlete's personal duty to ensure that no prohibited substance enters his or her body).[300]

– Use or attempted use of a prohibited substance.[301]

– Refusing or failing to submit to or evading a sample collection.[302]

– Violating applicable requirements regarding out of competition testing including failure to provide reliable information as to the athlete's whereabouts.[303]

– Tampering or attempting to tamper with any part of doping control.[304]

– Possession of prohibited substances or methods, save where it can be established that the substances in question were permitted for therapeutic reasons.[305]

– Trafficking in any prohibited substance or method.[306]

---

[297] Art.1.1.1.
[298] *Ibid.*
[299] Art.14.
[300] Art.2.1.1.
[301] Art.2.2.
[302] Art.2.3.
[303] Art.2.4.
[304] Art.2.5.
[305] Art.2.6.
[306] Art.2.7.

– Administration or attempted administration of a prohibited substance or method to any athlete.[307]

– Assisting, encouraging, aiding, abetting, concealing, covering up, or any other type of complicity … involving a breach [or attempted breach] of the rules.[308]

3.8.6.2 Burden and standard of proof

The Irish rules also adopt the WADA code approaches to questions of burden and standard of proof,[309] and in doing so also adopt and incorporate the WADA prohibited list[310] as well as the WADA International standard for laboratories.[311] It is stressed that the anti-doping organisation has the burden of establishing that a violation of an anti-doping rule has occurred, and must prove that allegation "to the comfortable satisfaction of the court" – a standard between the traditional criminal and civil standards of proof.[312] The Rules also create a quasi-legislative presumption that WADA-accredited laboratories have conducted sample analysis and custodial procedure in accordance with international standards of best practice. Whereas departures from international standards that do not cause an adverse analytical finding do not invalidate test results,[313] if the athlete proves that such departure *has* occurred, then the burden shifts back to the anti-doping organisation to establish that the departure does not cast doubt on the analytical finding.[314]

3.8.6.3 Therapeutic use exemptions

The Irish rules also adopt the WADA international standard for Therapeutic use exemptions (TUE).[315] Thus athletes with a documented condition who require to use a prohibited substance must obtain a TUE either from the Sports Council or from the relevant international federation[316] *prior to* competing in any sporting event – although provision is made for retrospective approval of a TUE in exceptional or emergency circumstances.[317] If the athlete is granted a TUE by the international federation, then he or she must inform the Sports

---

[307] Art.2.8.
[308] Art.2.
[309] Art.3.
[310] Art.4.
[311] Art.6.
[312] Art.3.1.
[313] Art.3.2.2.
[314] Art.3.2.1.
[315] Art.4.4.
[316] Art.4.4.2.
[317] Art.4.8.

Council of this fact.[318] Finally, if the athlete is competing in an international event, then he or she must obtain a TUE from the international federation irrespective of whether or not he or she has previously obtained one from the Sports Council.[319] The rules provide that the Sports Council shall appoint a committee of not less than three physicians to consider requests for TUEs.[320] A TUE shall only be granted where:

• The athlete would suffer a significant impairment to health if he or she was unable to avail of the prohibited substance or method.

• The therapeutic use thereof would not provide performance enhancing benefits over and above those that would derive from a return to a state of normal health. Thus the use of a prohibited substance or method to boost below normal levels of endogenous hormones is not regarded as an acceptable therapeutic intervention.

• There is no reasonable therapeutic alternative to the use of the prohibited substance or method.

• The need to use the prohibited substance or method is not the consequence of prior non-therapeutic use of the same.[321]

In order to avail of a TUE, the athlete must comply with strict rules regarding the submission of supporting medical evidence to the Sports Council,[322] although provision is made for an abbreviated procedure in the case of prohibited substances that are acknowledged as being frequently used to treat medical complaints (the beta-2 agonists formoterol, salbutamol, salmeterol and terbutaline ingested by inhalation, and glucocorticosteroids by non-systemic routes).[323] The grant of any such TUEs is subject to review by WADA[324] and the athlete may appeal (to CAS) both a decision not to grant him or her the TUE, or the decision by WADA to reverse a TUE that had been granted to him.[325]

3.8.6.4 Testing

The rules also adopt the WADA provisions in respect of testing, providing for a rigorous programme of testing both in and out of competition.[326] The Irish

---

[318] Art.4.4.3.
[319] Art.4.5.
[320] Art.4.7.
[321] Art.4.8.
[322] Art.4.9.
[323] Art.4.10.
[324] Art.4.12.
[325] Art.13.8.
[326] Art.5.

Sports Council is obliged under the rules to identify a registered testing pool (subject to revision from time to time) of athletes to be tested.[327] Athletes who have been informed that they are in this pool, are obliged to fill out quarterly reports specifying their location for the next period (and such information may be altered as the need arises). Failure to provide such a report after receipt of two formal warnings from the sports council in the previous eighteen months constitutes a doping offence.[328] Should an athlete prove unavailable for testing on three occasions in an 18 month period, [s]he will be considered to have committed a violation of the anti-doping rules.[329] In terms of the selection of athletes to be tested, at international events, the international organisation which is the ruling body for the event shall determine the number of tests to be taken,[330] but in all other cases, including national events, international events where the Sports Council is responsible for testing, out of competition testing and target testing, the decision as to which athletes are to be tested rests with the Sports Council.[331] The Sports Council may also select athletes or teams for target testing, provided that this is done for legitimate doping control purposes.[332] Testing of minors may only take place with the consent of a person with legal responsibility for such minor, but such consent is a condition precedent to the participation of the minor in sport.[333] Finally the rules provide that no liability for inconvenience or loss resulting from the testing process shall arise and no cause of action shall accrue[334] – although plainly the rules do not have the power to oust the jurisdiction of the courts. Thus for example, if owing to the negligence of the testers an athlete suffered a serious injury (for example in the context of the extraction of a blood sample) then the testing body and in all probability the governing body would be liable for such injury.

3.8.6.5 Results management

The Sports Council takes responsibility for results management of all tests conducted under its auspices.[335] Having determined, in the case of a positive A sample, that there is no applicable TUE governing the case, and that the International Standard for Testing has been complied with, the Sports Council is obliged to inform the athlete (and the relevant governing body) of the fact of the positive finding and of his right to request analysis of the B sample and to

---

[327] Art.5.4.
[328] Art.5.4.4.
[329] Art.5.4.5.
[330] Art.5.6.1.
[331] Art.5.6.
[332] Art.5.6.3.
[333] Art.5.9.
[334] Art.5.7.
[335] Art.7.

be present when such analysis is undertaken.[336] If the B sample is negative then the entire test is to be considered negative.[337] The Sports Council may also engage in any further follow up analysis required by the WADA code.[338] Interestingly the Irish rules provide both for provisional suspension of financial support, potentially from the point at which the A sample tests positive,[339] and also for provisional suspension of the athlete from all competitive sport.[340] If the athlete is suspended then the hearing into the matter should take place as soon as possible in order to avoid what is termed "substantial prejudice to the athlete".[341]

3.8.6.6 *Fair procedures and the doping hearing*

The Irish Rules provide a significant fleshing out to the relatively bare right to a fair hearing envisaged under Article 8 of the WADA code. The Irish Sports Council is required to appoint an Irish Sport Anti-Doping Disciplinary Panel consisting of a chair, two vice chairs (lawyers of not less than ten years standing) three medical experts with relevant experience, and three sports administrators, who will preside over disciplinary hearings and can essentially determine all issues arising from any matters referred to it pursuant to the rules, including the consequences of violation thereof.[342] Decisions of the panel may be appealed to the Court of Arbitration for Sport.[343] The rules provide for principles for a fair hearing namely:[344]

– A timely hearing (it is envisaged that the hearing process should be completed within three months of the completion of the results management process). Moreover there is an absolute time limit of eight years from the date of a violation in which to bring an action.[345]

– A fair and impartial panel.

– The right to be represented by counsel and where appropriate to have an interpreter.

– The right to be informed of the alleged violation and the resulting consequences.

---

[336] Art.7.3.
[337] Art.7.4.3.
[338] Art.7.5.
[339] Art.7.7.
[340] Art.7.8. This may be appealed under Art.13.2.
[341] Art.7.8.5.
[342] Art.8.
[343] Art.8.2.4.
[344] Art.8.3.
[345] Art.17.

– The right to present evidence and to summon witnesses.

– The right where necessary to an interpreter.

– A timely, written and reasoned decision.

The Sports Council has the right to join proceedings[346] (which shall be confidential and held in private),[347] and it, the relevant International Federation and WADA have the right to attend such hearings. Equally the obligations on the Disciplinary Panel are not as onerous as those that would apply in a court room. Thus for example the hearing panel may receive evidence (including hearsay evidence) as it thinks fit.[348] Decisions of the hearing panel shall be in the form of one brief, reasoned opinion with no dissenting decisions produced.[349] Finally the rules make provision for circumstances where, by reason of an agreement with the Sports Council (which may be rescinded) determination of a doping matter is transferred to the disciplinary panel of a National Governing Body.

3.8.6.7 Penalties for doping offences

In line with the WADA code, the Irish rules provide that in the event of a positive test, all the athlete's results in an event in which the violation occurs will be disqualified,[350] as shall all results obtained from the date of the production of the positive sample through the commencement of any period of suspension.[351] Beyond this, the athlete will also receive a two year ban for a first offence and a lifetime ban for a second offence,[352] subject to the possibility of his or her being able to present exceptional mitigating evidence, which can lead to a reduction in sanction.[353] The period of ineligibility starts

---

[346] Art.8.3.7.

[347] Art.8.4.2.

[348] Art.8.4.8.

[349] Art.8.5.

[350] Art.10.1. See also Art.10.1.2 for the consequences of a single unintentional and non-negligent violation in one competition on the athlete's results in other competitions in the same event. In a team event, if more than one member of a team is notified of a possible anti-doping violation than the entire team is subject to target testing for the event, and if more than one member is found to have committed a violation then the team may be subject to disqualification or other disciplinary action. Generally see Art.11.

[351] Art.10.7.

[352] Art.10.2. Specific rules exist where there have been multiple violations of the rules, for example where the athlete tests positive for more than one banned substance at the same time. Art.10.6.1.

[353] Art.10.5. The penalties for trafficking in drugs or administration thereof are four years suspension for a first offence. Moreover if, for example a coach is found to have committed a doping offence involving a minor then this shall attract a lifetime ban.

on the date of the hearing decision and any period of provisional suspension shall be credited against the total period of ineligibility.[354] Importantly this means that an athlete is suspended from *all* sporting competitions organised by any governing body that has signed up to the code.[355] The athlete must submit to reinstatement testing as a condition to regaining eligibility.[356]

Like the WADA code, the Irish rules provide that the banned list may identify specified substances which, are particularly susceptible to unintentional or innocent use,[357] and where an athlete can show that such a substance has been used with no intention to enhance performance, then for a first offence he can receive anything from a warning and a reprimand to a one year ban, for a second offence he will receive a two year ban, and for a third offence he shall receive a lifetime ban.[358] Moreover, in the context of most doping offences (excluding manipulation of a sample and trafficking in drugs) if the athlete can demonstrate that [s]he bears no fault or negligence in respect of a doping offence then the otherwise applicable period of ineligibility shall be eliminated,[359] and if [s]he can demonstrate that [s]he bears no significant fault or negligence then the period of suspension can be reduced, yet must not be less than half of the minimum period of ineligibility otherwise applicable. It is also specifically provided that where the offence involves the presence of a banned substance in an athlete's system, then the athlete must demonstrate how the substance entered his system.[360] Finally the rules provide for the reduction of a suspension where the athlete has provided assistance to an anti-doping organisation which assists the latter in discovering or establishing an anti-doping violation by another party.[361]

The rules also provide for the creation of an Anti-Doping Appeal Panel, comprising two legal practitioners of not less than ten years standing, two medical practitioners of not less than ten years standing and two members each of whom is either a sports administrator or an athlete.[362] This body has power to hear and determine all appeals arising out of the above process. The rules provide that decisions of this body are only to be appealed to CAS,[363] even where there have been flaws in procedures, provided only that a miscarriage of justice has not occurred.[364] The procedures before the appeal

---

[354] Art.10.8.
[355] Art.10.9.
[356] Art.10.10.
[357] The January 2004 "banned list", lists certain substances that are unusually prone to innocent ingestion. See p.9 of the list.
[358] Art.10.3.
[359] Art.10.5.1.
[360] Art.10.5.2.
[361] Art.10.5.3.
[362] Art.13.3.
[363] Art.13.2.1.
[364] Art.13.4.4.

body are similar to those before the original disciplinary panel, and seek to provide a high level of protection for the athlete and to ensure that, as far as possible, issues of this nature are kept out of the civil courts.[365]

The rules give the Sports Council a greatly increased power not just to organise the testing procedure of governing bodies, but now effectively to determine the totality of anti-doping policy in Ireland, or more accurately to ensure that such policy is brought into line with the approach of WADA. There will no doubt, be pitfalls ahead, not least the fact that the WADA rules are undoubtedly designed for professional or near professional sport, where it is reasonable to demand that athletes should be able to provide detailed 'whereabouts' information, and to take responsibility for everything that goes into their systems. As we have seen, even before the Rules came into operation (June 1, 2004) representatives of the GAA argued that such an approach was neither feasible nor reasonable in the context of amateur sport. Nonetheless, from the lawyer's point of view the rules are admirable in their clarity and in the thorough manner in which they reconcile the competing claims of the individual athlete and the anti-doping movement.

3.9 CONCLUSION

However meritorious the approach taken by WADA to the issue is, it is, nonetheless open to criticism. In particular, the wisdom of requiring mandatory sentences for doping offences is open to question. The point is that there *are* technical breaches of the rules, and there are some infringements of anti-doping policy which, by reason of the moral innocence of an athlete who negligently ingests a banned substance, are less serious (and less of a threat to the whole crusade against drugs) than others. Yet the mandatory rules require that all of these offences be treated identically, and ultimately prohibit the use of common sense in dealing with doping cases. They may also result in situations where two year suspensions for essentially minor offences are struck down either by CAS or by the civil courts on the grounds that they are disproportionate, bearing in mind the impact that they may have on the athlete's earning potential. Indeed the fact that in the wake of the THG controversy in October 2003, the IAAF mooted the possibility of re-introducing four year bans, represents an admission that simply standardizing penalties defeats the important purpose of allowing governing bodies to distinguish different cases and to strike with particular ferocity at particularly flagrant and pernicious breaches of the rules.

The harmonization that was required from WADA was a harmonization of attitude among the various bodies fighting doping, not a rule requiring an

---

[365] Art.13.11.

identical response to each and every doping case. It is true that the rules allow the athlete to plead moral innocence *in exceptional circumstances* in mitigation of sanction. Quite apart from the difficulties of proof that this presents for the athlete, however, this concession does not answer the charge that the new WADA rules prevent governing bodies from dealing with a case according to basic intuitive views of fairness. The principal rule, whereby any doping infraction leads to a two-year suspension will undoubtedly inform the overall approach of governing bodies in this area, and athletes who commit minor breaches of the rules *will* be over-penalised. Harmonization of sanctions in this fashion is arguably counter-productive and leads to the charge against WADA and its Chairman that they are now more concerned with the success of its code and with people buying into its view of how anti-doping policy should proceed than with a genuine and focused endeavour to stop drug use in sport. It may be this that will prove its undoing.

CHAPTER FOUR
Sport and the Criminal Law

4.1 INTRODUCTION

Two conceptually different questions present themselves in any analysis of the relationship between the criminal law and sport. The first is whether and why contact sports (and especially the sport of boxing) should be lawful, given that they involve actions that would ordinarily attract criminal liability. The second is whether, assuming that a particular sport *is* lawful, the criminal law should have any concern with activity that occurs on the field of play, and if so, when it should become involved. These two broad questions form the basis of this chapter. It should, however, be noted that our focus in this chapter is exclusively on criminal liability of participants for acts committed on the field of play. We will consider the potential criminal liability of supporters in a later chapter.

4.2 WHY IS CONTACT SPORT LAWFUL?

As most people know, ordinarily if one person were to grab another person around the waist and force him to the ground, this would be considered a criminal offence – especially where the said action caused the other real harm. Yet if such action occurs during a rugby match, it is something to be lauded. In simple terms then, the rules of most contact sports seem to permit and encourage uncivilized behaviour, and remarkably the law of the land allows them to do so, provided only that the sport in question is recognised as lawfully constituted.[1]

4.2.1 The consent of the participants

The most intuitively logical reason why this should be the case is that the parties participating in contact sports may be taken to have consented to the normal assaults and batteries associated with such activities. In fact, however,

---

[1] As Beloff, *et al*, *Sports Law* (Hart Publishing, 1999) notes (p.106) some activities that have in the past been regarded as sports are inherently illegal such as bear baiting, prize fighting and gladiatorial fights to the death.

as a matter of consistent legal principle this does not explain the privileged position of sport at law, in that in both Ireland and England, the consent of a victim to an assault that causes significant harm is no defence to a prosecution brought against the person who occasioned the assault. Thus in *R v. Brown*,[2] a criminal prosecution for assault against a group of homosexual men who engaged in sadomasochistic activities was upheld irrespective of the consent of such men to any harm suffered.

The lawfulness of sport is instead one of a number of historically recognised exceptions to this basic legal principle.[3] Thus in *Attorney General's Reference (No. 6 of 1980)*, Lord Lane had held that nothing in his decision was intended to cast doubt on the:

> "accepted legality of properly conducted games and sports, lawful chastisements or correction, reasonable surgical interference, dangerous exhibitions etc."[4]

Similar comments were made by the judges in *R v. Brown*,[5] with Lord Jauncey commenting that the legality of organised sport derived from its organisational structure and the presence of a referee at sporting contests,[6] and especially from the fact that there is a public interest in permitting lawfully constituted sport to be played.[7]

There are three difficulties with this proposition, certainly as it was stated in *R v. Brown*. First, on the facts of the case itself, it may be difficult for those

---

[2] [1994] 1 A.C. 212 [1993] 2 All E.R. 75 [1993] 2 W.L.R. 556. This decision involved a restatement of the principle laid down in *Attorney General's Reference (No. 6 of 1980)* [1981] Q.B. 715, [1981] 2 All E.R. 1057, [1981] 3 W.L.R. 125, which was itself based on the earlier decision in *R v. Donovan* [1934] 2 K.B. 498 and indeed *R v. Coney*, (1882) 8 Q.B.D. 534. Generally on this issue see Williams, "Consent and Public Policy" [1962] *Criminal Law Review* 74. See also McCutcheon, "Sports Violence, Consent and the Criminal Law" [1994] *Northern Ireland Legal Quarterly* 267 [hereafter McCutcheon] 269.

[3] United Kingdom Law Commission, *Consultation Paper 134 on Criminal Law – Consent and Offences Against The Person'*, p.4. See analysis at 3 (2) *Sport and the Law Journal* (1994) 1.

[4] [1981] Q.B. 715 at 719.

[5] See especially the comments of Lord Mustill, pp.592–593.

[6] *Ibid.*, p.567.

[7] See Law Commission, *Consultation Paper 134 on Criminal Law – Consent and Offences Against The Person*, p.22ff. Similar conclusions were reached by the Irish Law Reform Commission in its 1997 *Report on Non-Fatal Offences against the Person*, p.272. For analysis see Anderson, "Citius, Altius, Fortius? A Study Of Criminal Violence in Sport", 11 *Marquette Sports Law Review* (Fall 2000) 87 [hereafter Anderson], p.104ff. Sir Michael Foster, *Crown Law* (3rd ed., Clarendon Press, Oxford, 1792), p.260 explained the legality of sport on the grounds that it was a 'manly diversion' which tended to give strength, skill and activity and may fit people for defence public as well as personal in times of need'.

who are interested in sexual freedom but not in sport, to see why the latter invokes a public interest sufficient to justify setting aside a general principle of law while the former does not.[8] Indeed the validity of the principle in *Brown* is arguably undermined by the fact that their Lordships were so obviously disgusted by what they saw as "evil" activities that they did not address the question whether liberal principles could nonetheless justify the legality thereof. Secondly, in *Brown*, the decision was based both on a paternalistic concern with the well being of the men involved and also on a public policy concern with preventing the spread of what was termed "a cult of violence." These are both worthy aims, yet they could apply with greater rigour to all contact sport and particularly to boxing. After all a boxing match may result in serious injury to participants, and, being held in public and engaged in by social role models, this intentional infliction of injury has surely greater potential to cause social problems than have the private sexual acts of uncelebrated men.[9] Finally a more fundamental question may have to be addressed as to *why*, even if sport *per se* is of social utility, it is necessary to permit the more violent and anti-social sports (and aspects of sport) to ensure that that social utility is maintained.

4.2.2 The Irish position

In Ireland, the statutory position in respect of assault is now outlined in sections 2–4 of the Non-Fatal Offences against the Person Act 1997. Under section 2 of this Act, absence of consent is a definitional element of assault. Moreover, in as much as section 3 deals with the offence of "assault causing harm" it can be assumed that absence of consent is an essential element of this crime. Of greater concern is section four, which criminalises the act of "causing serious harm" (defined as 'injury which creates a substantial risk of death, or which causes serious disfigurement or substantial loss or impairment of the mobility of the body as a whole or of the function of any bodily member or organ). There is no reference in section 4 to the presence or absence of consent in such cases, but it is likely that consent is not a defence to such action, especially given that section 22 of the Act, which provides that "the provisions of the act

---

8 See for example the comments of McArdle describing the decision as "… little more than an exercise in queer bashing" (McArdle, *From Boot Money to Bosman; Football, Society and the Law* (Cavendish, 2001) [hereafter McArdle], p.146). It is submitted that this is not necessarily fair. While the Law Lords in this case made no attempt to disguise their disgust at the nature of the actions, their concern was primarily with the violence involved and the question whether the law could validly permit such violence. Arguably a better criticism of general UK policy in this area is the fact that other violent behaviour *has* been permitted on the basis of consent, including setting fire to a man as part of military initiation ceremonies (*R v. Aitken* [1992] W.L.R. 1006) and the branding of a man's initials in his wife's buttocks as a "loving" gesture (*R v. Wilson* [1997] Q.B. 47).

9 McArdle, *Football Society and the Law, op. cit.*, 92

have effect subject to any enactment or rule of law providing a defence or providing lawful authority justification or excuse for an act or omission," was envisaged as preserving the basic common law rule that consent not be an absolute defence to all forms of assault.[10] It is probable therefore that the 1997 Act alters the old common law position, only to the extent that whereas previously one could not consent to assaults causing simple bodily harm, now one can consent to assaults save those which will create a serious risk of maiming or indeed death.[11]

The 1997 Act was to a large extent based on the recommendations of the Law Reform Commission in its 1997 Report on Non-Fatal Offences against the Person. Two recommendations of the Commission that were *not* adopted are, however, relevant for present purposes. First, it recommended that where an act causing serious bodily injury was concerned, consent to such action should not amount to a defence, save where the harm was inflicted with the purpose of benefiting another person, or in pursuance of a socially beneficial function or activity, or where it occurs in specific situations – for example where a lawful sport is being played according to its rules. Secondly the Commission recommended that there be a specific statutory provision absolving persons who cause serious harm to others during the course of and in accordance with the rules of any bona fide sporting activity. The 1997 Act did not incorporate this recommendation, although as McCutcheon and McAuley note,[12] section 22 of the Act may ensure that the existing common law rules whereby assaults arising out of participation within the rules of lawful sports were not the subject of criminal prosecution will be retained.

4.2.3 The response of the United Kingdom Law Commission

The UK Law Commission had also dealt with this issue in two Consultation Papers.[13] While approving of the general principle that absence of consent

---

[10] McAuley & McCutcheon, *Criminal Liability* (Round Hall Sweet & Maxwell, Dublin, 2000), p.533. See Brian Foley, "Consensual Assault – Just what is the Law?", 5 *Trinity College Law Review* (2002) 266.

[11] This is arguably in line with the holdings of Lord Slynn and Lord Mustill in *R v. Brown*, and with the recommendations of the UK Law Commission.

[12] McAuley & McCutcheon, *Criminal Liability* (Round Hall, Sweet & Maxwell, Dublin, 2000), p.533.

[13] Consultation Papers 134 and 139 on *Criminal Law – Consent and Offences Against The Person*. For comment see Farrell, "Violence in Sport and Consent to Injury", 2 (1) *Sport and the Law Journal* (1994) 1, Gardiner, "The Law and the Sports Field" (1994) *Criminal Law Review* 513, Singh, "Consent to Violence in Sport", 2 (3) *Sport and the Law Journal* (1994) 7 and "The Law Commission Consultation Paper No. 134 on Criminal Law – Consent And Offences Against The Person: A Response To The Issues For Sports And Games By The Central Council Of Physical Recreation", 2 (3) *Sport and the Law Journal* (1994) 1.

need not be a constituent element of the crime of assault,[14] it recommended that this should only apply where the action in question caused 'seriously disabling injury'[15] – an approach which as we have seen was adopted in recent Irish legislation. It then went on to apply this approach to sport. First, it noted that sport generally could be justified in the public interest and that in as much as bodily contact and unpredictability are essential elements of sport, these kinds of 'assaults and batteries' could be justified in the public interest.[16] Equally, the Commission insisted that not *all* serious assaults occurring on the field of play should be lawful, concluding that intentional or reckless infliction of injury should remain criminal offences. Importantly, it also recommended that in as much as the status of an activity as a "lawfully recognized sport" afforded that activity significant immunity under criminal law there was a need to create a scheme for recognition of sport, and especially for emerging forms of martial arts.

In general the legality of most contact sports is not difficult to understand, if for no other reason than because the injuries that result from activity within the rules of the game are typically unintentional and incidental side effects of participation. Far more difficult to justify is the continued legal validity of the sport of boxing, where the essence of the sport and the inherent objective of participants is the occasioning of assaults and where a prime way to win the contest is to cause serious harm to one's opponent.

4.3 THE LEGALITY OF BOXING

It may be strongly argued as a matter of principle that boxing should be classified as an unlawful activity even under the terms of the Irish Non-Fatal Offences Against the Person Act of 1997.[17] The House of Lords after all justified the criminalisation of the activities of the defendants in *R v. Brown*[18]

---

[14] For comment see Farrell, "Consent to Violence in Sport and the Law Commission – Part Two", 4 (1) *Sports Law Journal* (1996) 3.
[15] Consultation Paper 139, p.46.
[16] For a criticism of this conclusion on the basis that the only reason why such deeply uncivilized behaviour has been socially accepted is because of the impact of a male dominated sports culture which tolerates such behaviour to the detriment of society see Hazel Hartley, "Hard Men – Soft on Sport", 6(2) *Sport and the Law Journal* (1998) 37.
[17] See Farrell, at 2 (1) *Sport and the Law Journal* (1994) 1 at 5ff, Parpworth, "Boxing and Prize Fighting, the Indistinguishable Distinguished", (4) 1 *Sport and the Law Journal* (1996) 5 for the view that "...the inevitable conclusion is that the apparent immunity of boxing from the sanction of the law defies rational explanation." See also Anderson, "Citius, Altius, Fortius? A Study of Criminal Violence in Sport", 11 *Marquette Sports Law Review* (Fall 2000) 87.
[18] See Flannery & O'Brien, "Mandatory HIV Testing of Professional Boxers: An Unconstitutional Effort to Regulate a Sport that Needs to be Regulated", 31 *University of California Davis Law Review* (1998) 409 at 426.

by reference both to a paternalistic concern with the well being of the participants and also a societal concern with the immoral nature of the action, and particularly its capacity to generate a cult of violence. Yet boxing provokes identical concerns.

First, the activity of boxing is dangerous for the participant, and hence the medical profession has been at the forefront of the movement calling for its abolition.[19] It is true that, in terms of fatalities, boxing is far from being the most dangerous lawful sport in the world.[20] Nonetheless the statistics hide the crucial fact that whereas boxing accounts for limited instances of brain trauma – the drastic injury that results in immediate death – medical studies do suggest that it will lead to significant instances of chronic brain damage.[21] This is the type of injury which manifests itself some years after the boxer's career may be over and leads to the boxer becoming significantly mentally handicapped in a manner also known as punch drunk syndrome. Nor is this surprising. Medical studies again indicate that the impact of a punch in a heavyweight contest is the equivalent of that caused by a mallet travelling at 20miles per hour.

Secondly, the activity may be regarded as anti-social, in that protagonists know[22] that its very objective involves the (immoral) act of *intentionally* hurting another person[23] – one ground for distinguishing it from other contact sports.[24]

---

[19] [1959] 1 *The Lancet* 1185 (June 6, 1959). Such calls have been made *inter alia* by medical associations in the US, Canada, Britain and Australia and by the World Medical Association. See Flannery & O'Brien, "Mandatory HIV Testing Of Professional Boxers: An Unconstitutional Effort To Regulate A Sport That Needs To Be Regulated", 31 *University of California Davis Law Review* (1998) 409 at p.436. See also Rosen, "In the Aftermath of McClellan, Isn't It Time For The Sport Of Boxing To Protect Its Participants?", 5 *Seton Hall Journal of Sports Law* (1995) 611.

[20] In response to the Law Commission Paper 134, the British Boxing Board of Control had argued that there were objectively very few fatalities in boxing and that the safety precautions to assist boxers were second to none. See Paper 139 at pp.166–167. This was before the decision in *Watson v. British Boxing Board of Control* [2001] 2 W.L.R. 1256 in which the Court of Appeal found the BBBC safety precautions to be hugely defective.

[21] Rosen, "In the Aftermath Of McClellan Isn't It Time For The Sport Of Boxing To Protect Its Participants?", 5 *Seton Hall Journal of Sports Law* (1995) 611 at pp.620–625.

[22] See Grayson, "Boxing Clever", 142 *New Law Journal* (No. 6535) January 17, 1992, 48 for the view that such awareness is itself a justification for the criminalisation of boxing.

[23] See Greenfield and Osborn, "A Gauntlet for the Glove: The Challenge to English Boxing Contracts", 6 *Marquette Sports Law Journal* (1995) 153 for the view that professional boxing is undoubtedly a contentious sport, primarily because the objective of each bout is to inflict physical injury on the other party and clearly outside of the ring such an activity would be unlawful and could attract both civil and criminal sanctions.

[24] Thus Forman, "Boxing in The Legal Arena", 3 *Sports Lawyers Journal* (1996) p.75 notes that:

> "While many contact sports permit aggressive physical contact throughout the contest … scoring goals or points is the main objective rather than the physical suppression

Moreover, as mentioned, it occurs in public and hence has a far greater chance of generating a cult of violence than the private activities in *Brown*, especially given that the participants may well be social heroes and role models.[25] Finally, it may be argued that because of the above factors there is little public benefit in its legality – and certainly far less than exists in other contact sports where the infliction of injury is not an objective of the activity. It may, of course be argued that boxing itself provides certain public benefits, not least in the fact that in many places it is seen as an "inner-city" sport providing an acceptable focus for young persons who might otherwise turn to crime,[26] and indeed those in favour of the sport have argued for its continued legality on simple civil liberties grounds.[27] Equally it is questionable whether any such benefits outweigh the social detriments of the activity.

The United Kingdom Law Commission plainly felt that boxing *should* continue to be legal, but accepted that it was entirely anomalous that this should be the case, given that under both UK law and also the thrust of its own proposals, the intentional or reckless infliction of significant physical harm should be a crime irrespective of the consent thereto of the "victim."[28] This anomaly becomes even more pronounced when one considers the difference between lawful and unlawful sporting fights.

---

of the other athletes. Conversely fighting is the sport of boxing and a boxer can win a match only through sustaining superior physical domination over his opponent."
See also McElroy, "Current and Proposed Federal Regulation of Professional Boxing", 9 *Seton Hall Journal of Sports Law* (1999) 463 and Forman, "Boxing in the Legal Arena", 3 *Sports Lawyers Journal* (1996) 75.

[25] See Rains, "Sports Violence a Matter of Societal Concern", 55 Notre Dame L. Rev. (198) 796 and Nelson, "Sports Violence; Too Late for the Carrots – Bring on the Big Stick", 74 *Iowa L. Rev.* (1989) 681, for the view that because big sport stars are such heroes, their violence glorifies violence. See also Hanson and Dernis, "Revisiting Excessive Violence in the Professional Sports Arena", 6 *Seton Hall Journal of Sports Law* (1996) 127.

[26] See e.g. Rosen, "Exposing Illegality in Sports; The Limits of the Law", 6 (3) *Sport and the Law Journal* (1998) 36.

[27] This was the basis on which the House of Lords declined in 1995 to give a second reading to a bill designed to make boxing illegal. See for example the comments of Baroness Trumpington, *Hansard* (HL) April 5, 1995, vol. 563 Col. 306. See also Parpworth, "Parliament and the Boxing Bill", 4 (1) *Sport and the Law Journal* (1996) 24 and Grayson, "Boxing Clever", 142 *New Law Journal* (No. 6535), January 17, 1992, 48. There was also a view that the bill was so vaguely drafted that it could lead to the criminalisation of amateur boxing. Equally it was felt that the utmost in safety measures should be applied to boxing. See also Farrell, at 2 (1) *Sport and the Law Journal* (1994) 1 at 5ff. For analysis of attempts in America to have boxing banned see Howard, "Regulating the Sport of boxing – congress throws the first punch with the Professional Boxing Safety Act", 7 *Seton Hall Journal of Sports Law* (1997) p.104, Anderson, "The Punch that Landed: The Professional Boxing Safety Act of 1996", 9 *Marquette Sports Law Journal* (1998) 191 and McElroy, "Current and Proposed Federal Regulation of Professional Boxing", 9 *Seton Hall Journal of Sports Law* (1999) 463.

[28] See *Consultation Paper 134 on Criminal Law – Consent and Offences Against The Person* 134 at p.27.

In the nineteenth century in *R v. Coney*,[29] it was held that assaults occurring during bare knuckle prize fighting could be the subject of criminal prosecution, irrespective of the consent of participants.[30] Moreover, depending on the circumstances, those present at such contests could be guilty of aiding and abetting a crime, and of affray, riot and unlawful assembly.[31] Various reasons were offered for the 'unlawful' status of the activity, ranging from the threat to public peace caused by a riotous crowd,[32] to the mental state of the fighters who, it was felt were acting out of anger and in a manner calculated to harm opponents, to the dangerous weapons used – namely the bare fists of the fighters.[33] Nor was the consent of the participants relevant for as Stephen J. concluded:

"... the consent of the person who sustains the injury is no defence ... if the injury is of such a nature or is inflicted under such circumstances that its infliction is injurious to the public as well as the person injured. But the injuries given and received in prize fights are injurious to the public both because it is against the public interest that the lives and health of the combatants should be endangered by blows and because prize fights are disorderly exhibitions, mischievous on many grounds."

The court in *R v. Coney* was keen to distinguish prize-fighting from other lawful forms of sport, including boxing, although the precise distinction between the two activities is not absolutely clear.[34] Thus in *R v. Hargreaves*,[35] the activity involved was variously referred to as prize fighting, a pugilistic contest and a boxing match. The distinction seems to be centered on the

---

[29] (1882) 8 Q.B.D 534. For an analysis of the facts of the case see Anderson, p.87ff.

[30] For analysis see Osborough, "Sport, Freedom and the Criminal Law", p.37 in Whelan, ed., *Law and Liberty in Ireland* (Oaktree Press, Dublin, 1992), p.51ff and Williams, "Consent and Public Policy" [1962] *Criminal Law Review* 74 at p.79ff.

[31] In *Pallante v. Stadiums PTY* [1976] V.R. 331, McInerney J. made the point that there was not a specific offence of prize fighting at common law any more than there was a specific offence of duelling.

[32] Thus Lord Coleridge said that: "The brutalizing effects of prize fights are chiefly due to the crowd who resort to them."

[33] See Williams, "Consent and Public Policy" [1962] *Criminal Law Review* 74 at p.79ff.

[34] Parpworth, "Boxing and Prize Fighting, The Indistinguishable Distinguished", (4) 1 *Sport and the Law Journal* (1996) 5. For 19th century case law dealing with the distinction see *Hunt v. Bell* (1822) 1 Bing 1; 130 E.R. 1, *R v. Perkins* (1831) 4 C & P 537, 172 E.R. 814, *R v. Young* (1866) 10 Cox C.C. 371, *R v. Orton* (1871) 14 Cox C.C. 226, and also *R v. Coney* and *Pallante v. Stadiums PTY* [1976] V.R. 331. For analysis of the history of such case law see Grayson, "Boxing Clever", 142 *New Law Journal* (No. 6535) January 17, 1992, 48 and Anderson, *op. cit.*, p.87ff. From an American perspective, see *Commonwealth v. Collberg* 119 Mass. 350 (1875) and *State v. Burnham* 56 Ver. 445 (1884).

[35] (1831) 5 C. & P. 170.

organisation of the contest, with prize fights being (a) bare knuckle contests and (b) of unlimited duration. Moreover, in *Coney*, the court was also undoubtedly concerned with the nature of the crowd that would typically attend prize-fights. The similarities between the two activities are, however, more striking than the differences between them. Both are violent and generate a substantial risk of injury to the parties; in both cases the infliction of such injury is an almost inevitable concomitant of the functioning of the sport; both involve public displays of violence with all the unsavoury side-effects which this involves, and both are consensual.[36] Indeed, as McCutcheon points out, if *R v. Coney* is still good law, then it is presumably legitimate to suggest that if the factors which were present in that case and which concerned the court - intention to cause serious harm, likelihood of serious injury to participants, anger and hostility, threat to public order and so on – are present in any sport (and most obviously in boxing) then there is no reason why such activities should not be illegal whether or not they are within the rules of sport.[37]

The question of whether boxing should be unlawful has never been directly addressed in English or Irish courts. It was however the focus of the decision of the Supreme Court of Victoria in the important case *Pallante v. Stadiums PTY Ltd.*[38] Here the plaintiff sought to recover damages from various parties for injuries sustained during a lawful boxing match. As part of the defence submission it was contended that the boxing match in question was a prize-fight and that in any event boxing should be unlawful in as much as it involved the striking of blows that were either likely or intended to cause serious harm.

McInerney J. felt bound by the traditional common-law principle that one may not consent to an assault that is intended or likely to cause serious bodily harm – a principle which, as we have seen, seems to militate against the legality of boxing. Counsel for the defence, after all, had argued that in as much as the objective of a boxing match is to subject one's opponent 'to such prolonged and sustained blows' that either the opponent's trainer will throw in the towel or the referee will award him the fight on points, or most effectively of all that he will knock his opponent out, plainly the intention of the parties is to inflict serious bodily injury on his opponent. McInerney J., agreed concluding that:

"... the case law on the matter cannot be taken as affirming that boxing

---

[36] See Williams, "Consent and Public Policy" [1962] *Criminal Law Review* 74 at p.80, for the view that the basis for the decision in *Coney* was a paternalistic concern with the health of the participants. See Anderson, *op. cit.*, p.92 for the view that; "At first instance, it would seem to supporters of the sports of boxing and martial arts that ... [the holding in *Coney*] ... renders their sports illegal."

[37] McCutcheon, *op. cit.*, 267 at p.272. It is notable that in Sweden and Norway professional boxing is banned. See Flannery & O'Brien, "Mandatory HIV Testing Of Professional Boxers: An Unconstitutional Effort To Regulate A Sport That Needs To Be Regulated", 31 *University of California Davis Law Review* (1998) 409 at p.436.

[38] [1976] V.R. 331.

is only lawful so long as there is no intention to inflict blows causing actual physical harm, for it is virtually impossible for boxing to take place without the infliction of some physical harm. It is a form of sport or pastime in which the striking of blows capable of inflicting physical harm is not only inevitable but, indeed, envisaged."

Nonetheless, McInerney J. felt that the legality of the sport could still be salvaged by a more in depth analysis of the motivations as distinct from the intentions of individual boxers:

"If the encounter is conducted either from its inception or is not from some point in its course by either, or both of, the contestants, in a spirit of anger or a hostile spirit and with the predominant intention of inflicting substantial bodily harm so as to disable or otherwise physically subdue the opponent it may be an assault on the part of the contestant or contestants so animated, even though each contestant may have consented to the infliction of blows on himself and whether or not that encounter is for reward, in public or in private, bare fisted or in gloves. It may be an assault, at all events, from the time when the element of hostility becomes the predominant motive. On the other hand, boxing is not an unlawful and criminal activity so long as, whether for reward or not, it is engaged in by a contestant as a boxing sport or contest, not from motive of personal animosity, or at all events not predominantly from that motive, but predominantly as an exercise of boxing skill and physical condition in accordance with rules and in conditions the object of which is to ensure that the infliction of bodily injury is kept within reasonable bounds, so as to preclude or reduce, so far as is practicable, the risk of either contestant incurring serious bodily injury, and to ensure that victory shall be achieved in accordance with the rules by the person demonstrating the greater skill as a boxer."

This conclusion – that boxing may be seen as lawful because boxers while intending to hit their opponents do not do so in a spirit of hostility – is far from satisfactory. In the first place, McInerney J. had previously concluded that whereas quite often in a boxing match the boxers will initially entertain no sentiment of anger or hostility towards each other, equally at a certain point in the match the character thereof might change and an atmosphere of hostility takeover, wherein blows are very much struck in anger. Yet he did not take this point to its logical conclusion by holding that at the point where such hostility enters the frame, previously legitimate activities would suddenly become criminal offences. Secondly, and even bearing in mind the fact that organisers of professional fights will try to hype up an upcoming bout as much as possible, three is still evidence that in fact it is far from true to say that all boxing matches commence in the absence of a spirit of hostility or anger.[39] Witness for example Mike Tyson's message to Lennox Lewis in June 2000 that:

> "I want to eat your heart. I want to eat your children. He (Lewis) is no match for me when I am right. I want to rip his heart out and feed it to him."[40]

More to the point, as a matter of general legal principle, hostility is not a central element of unlawful violence,[41] nor indeed is motivation (why a person committed an act) as distinct from intention (the conscious decision to commit the act) relevant to the question of whether an action is lawful. Thus McCutcheon sees McInerney J.'s reasoning as "admirable in its efforts," but concludes that "it is difficult to be convinced by it."[42]

As such we are still left with the difficult question of whether and if so how the ongoing legality of boxing can be justified. The UK Law Commission simply saw boxing as an anomalous case and concluded that:[43]

> "The only explanation of injury and death continuing to be caused in boxing with complete impunity, at least as far as the criminal law is concerned, is that the immunity of boxing from the reach of the criminal law is now so firmly embedded in the law that only special legislation can change the position."[44]

---

[39] Parpworth indeed argues that in all boxing matches the intention is the same and is criminal. See Parpworth at 4 (1) *Sport and the Law Journal* (1996) 5.

[40] See Rawling, "Appetite For The Ugly Is Unsated", *Irish Times*, June 26, 2000. Lennox Lewis himself was less than dignified, referring to challenger Hasim Rahman as "a piece of meat that I'll play with" in April 2001, some days before Rahman defeated him. See Rawling, "Shabby Arrogance To Cost Lewis", *Irish Times*, Monday, April 23, 2001. An even more extraordinary controversy arose in January 2002, when, at a press conference to publicise an upcoming boxing match between Lewis and Tyson, a brawl broke out between the two, during which Tyson is alleged to have bitten Lewis's foot. See Oliver Burkeman, "New York Melee Puts Bout in Doubt", *Irish Times*, January 23, 2002.

[41] *Faulkner v. Talbot* [1981] 3 ALL E.R. 468, *F, in re* [1990] 2 A.C. 1.

[42] McCutcheon, *op. cit.*, p.279.

[43] Report 134, p.28.

[44] Equally, it is questionable whether punches thrown by boxers in a "boxing setting" but outside of the legitimate contours of the specific contest could be subject to criminal prosecution. This would include, for instance pre-fight brawls, the situation where boxers continue to throw punches after the bell sounds for the end of a round, and most notoriously the instance where Mike Tyson bit off part of the ear of an opponent during a world heavyweight boxing match. For a case in point see "Tyson May Appeal Record British Fine", *Irish Times*, August 23, 2000. See also *Collins v. Resto*, 746 F. Supp. 360 (SDNY, 1990) a case where the defendant boxer was held criminally liable for injuries inflicted on an opponent during a match on the grounds that he had removed the interior padding from his gloves before the fight thereby exacerbating the seriousness of the injuries suffered by his opponent. See Forman, "Boxing in the Legal Arena", 3 *Sports Lawyers' Journal* (1996) 75.

This comment echoes the viewpoint of Lord Mustill in *R v. Brown*, to the effect that it was impossible to do what McInerney J. had attempted in *Pallante* and come up with an intellectually satisfying justification for the continued legality of boxing. Rather it was necessary simply to regard boxing as "...another special situation, which for the time being stands outside the ordinary law of violence because society chooses to tolerate it."[45] Equally, the focus then shifts to the question of why public displays of aggression and fighting where there is real risk of intentionally inflicted serious injury occurring in a sport riddled with corruption should be regarded as justified in the public interest.[46]

4.3.1 Boxing and the criminal law in Ireland

In Ireland there is no specific statutory statement as to the lawfulness of boxing. Under the Non-Fatal Offences against the Person Act 1997 as we have seen, consent is a defence to assault and therefore to assault causing harm. It is not, however, a defence to causing serious harm and given that many boxing matches *do* result in serious harm to competitors it may be suggested that this may lead to liability under section 4 of the Act. Even if this is possible in theory, however, it is inconceivable that in practice the courts would give this interpretation to the Act, if for no other reason than that Irish courts require penal statutes to be interpreted strictly to avoid unclear imposition of fresh criminal liability,[47] and the historic legality of boxing would mean that if it were to be criminalized that this would have to be clearly and unambiguously stated under statute.[48] Thus it remains as an anomalous exception to the general rule.

4.3.2 Reform of boxing

More generally, it is argued that in any event, any attempts in any jurisdiction to ban boxing would be counter-productive as far as participants' health is concerned, as it would simply drive the sport underground making it more

---

[45] Such justification is also supported by what was a central point of the judgment of McInerney J. in *Pallante* – namely that boxing has sufficient internal safeguards as to minimize the risk to boxers in fighting. See generally Osborough 'Sport Freedom and the Criminal law', p.61 in Whelan, ed., *Law and Liberty in Ireland, op. cit.* See also Rosen, "Exposing Illegality in Sports: The Limits of the Law", 6 (3) *Sport and the Law Journal* (1998) 36.

[46] See Williams, "Consent and Public Policy" [1962] *Criminal Law Review* 74 at p.159.

[47] *Minister for Industry & Commerce v. Hales* [1967] I.R. 50, *Inspector of Taxes v. Kiernan* [1981] I.R. 117, *Mullins v. Harnett* [1998] 2 I.L.R.M. 304.

[48] For a similar conclusion from a UK perspective see Farrell, "Consent to Violence in Sport and the Law Commission – Part Two", 4 (1) *Sport and the Law Journal* (1996) 8.

difficult to regulate.[49] Hence it would be preferable instead to reform the rules of boxing in order to make the sport safer.[50] From the end of the Nineteenth Century, boxing attempted to reform itself through the introduction of the Queensbury rules which *inter alia* prohibited bare-knuckle fighting, wrestling, striking below the belt, hitting an opponent while he was on the ground and fights of unlimited duration. In *Pallante*, McInerney J cited various factors, which in his view explained the reductions in prosecutions and indeed the change in judicial attitude to boxing. These included the introduction of a fixed number of rounds of fixed duration, the use of more scientifically designed boxing gloves, the power of a referee to stop a fight and of a trainer to throw in the towel, the presence of legally qualified medical practitioners at the ringside and the insistence on a medical examination before the fight and public regulation and control over the behaviour of spectators.[51]

New and innovative reforms are frequently mooted. Among such reforms,[52] there are calls for increased padding in gloves and on the floor (on the basis that studies indicate that boxers have died from acute brain trauma caused by hitting the floor too hard), or the utilization of headgear by professional boxers. Other commentators reject such suggestions. Thus it is argued that increased padding in gloves will in fact lull boxers into a false sense of security and encourage them to hit harder. Indeed it has been suggested that in fact it would be safer to ban boxing gloves, as this would mean that boxers would have a concern with protecting their knuckles and as a result boxing would become a more defensively oriented sport. Moreover, the call for boxers to use headgear has also been disputed both because such headgear may slip thereby obscuring the boxers vision and leaving him susceptible to unexpected punches and also because use of headgear increases the circumference of the target thereby increasing the spinning motion of the head and smashing the brain against it with even greater ferocity. Alternatively it has been suggested that boxers should use thumbless gloves, on the basis that studies indicate that detached retina injuries tend to be caused by the mobile thumb when traditional boxing gloves are used.

---

[49] On this point see Grayson, "Boxing Clever", 142 *New Law Journal* (No. 6535) January 17, 1992, 48.

[50] Rosen, "In the Aftermath of McClellan, Isn't It Time For the Sport of Boxing to Protect its Participants?", 5 *Seton Hall Journal of Sports Law* (1995) 611 at p.612.

[51] Various reforms of professional boxing have been attempted in the United States. For comment see Howard, "Regulating the Sport of Boxing – Congress throws the First Punch with the Professional Boxing Safety Act", 7 *Seton Hall Journal of Sports Law* (1997) 104, Rosen, "In the Aftermath of McClellan, Isn't It Time for the Sport of Boxing to Protect its Participants?", 5 *Seton Hall Journal of Sports Law* (1995) 611 at pp.625–633, Anderson, "The Punch that Landed: The Professional Boxing Safety Act of 1996", 9 *Marquette Sports Law Journal* (1998) 191.

[52] Rosen, "In the Aftermath of McClellan, Isn't It Time for rhe Sport Of Boxing to Protect its Participants?", 5 *Seton Hall Journal of Sports Law* (1995) 611 at p.615.

Other suggested reforms include the creation of an office to keep a centralised record of the boxers medical condition such that boxers would be issued with 'passports' outlining their physical condition and no boxer who is not in a fit condition to fight would be allowed into the ring. It has also been suggested that a special national boxing commission should be introduced in all jurisdictions where boxing is legal, to oversee all fights, with any fights *not* authorized by it being illegal. There are calls for increased requirements of education and training for referees, ringside doctors and personnel as well as a requirement that ambulance and medical personnel be continuously present at all boxing matches – a requirement which has taken on a new urgency since the decision of the Court of Appeal in *Watson v. British Boxing Board of Control*,[53] discussed later in this book. It has also been suggested that there should be a sixteen year career limit for boxers, (as studies show that chronic brain damage is directly related to the number of fights undertaken by a boxer) and that the duration of boxing matches should be limited. Finally it has been suggested that boxers should be wired for electronic scoring, thereby obviating the need for violent blows.[54] Ultimately some such reform is necessary for, as Grayson comments:[55]

> "So long as medical risks persist, boxing will always be battling in a shifting social and moral climate for its existence. If it can harness the progress of medical science to a concurrent regulatory framework with strict enforcement procedures, it should survive, controlled, alongside the Anglo-Saxon adversarial court process with which it shares the ideal of fair play common to both sport and the law."

4.4 PROSECUTING ON-FIELD VIOLENCE

The events surrounding the publication in the summer of 2002 of the autobiography of Roy Keane, one time Manchester United and Ireland soccer captain, in which he seemed to indicate that he had on one occasion intentionally

---

[53] [2001] 2 W.L.R. 1256.

[54] See Rosen, "In the Aftermath of McClellan, Isn't it Time for the Sport of Boxing to Protect its Participants?", 5 *Seton Hall Journal of Sports Law*, (1995) 611 and Flannery & O'Brien, "Mandatory HIV Testing Of Professional Boxers: An Unconstitutional Effort to Regulate a Sport that Needs to be Regulated", 31 *University of California Davis Law Review* (1998) 409 at pp.496–497. In the US many of these suggested reforms were introduced under the terms of the Professional Boxing Safety Act of 1996 as was the requirement that all boxers carry health insurance to cover the cost of treatment for injuries sustained. See Anderson, "The Punch That Landed", 9 *Marquette Sports Law Journal* (1998), p.191 and McElroy, "Current and Proposed Federal Regulation of Professional Boxing", 9 *Seton Hall Journal of Sports Law* (1966), 463 at 505.

[55] Grayson, "Boxing Clever", 142 *New Law Journal* (No. 6535), January 17, 1992, 48.

injured another player generated a limited public debate on the question of prosecuting on-field violence.[56] Thus Bob Russell MP, Liberal Democrat representative for Colchester, announced that he had written to the Greater Manchester Police calling on them to institute a criminal prosecution for assault against Roy Keane.[57] Mr Russell argued that the fact that a particular action occurred on a sports field should not of itself render it immune from the operation of the criminal law.[58] This is the second major question that must be addressed in this chapter, namely (notwithstanding the fact that contact sport is lawful), whether and when actions on the field of play should be the subject of criminal prosecutions.

In principle in both Ireland and England, foul play may also be a crime – although it is fair to say that *most* foul play (including violent foul play) is not prosecuted. The police are, however, clear that they have authority over what goes on on the sports field. Thus Anderson reports that during a minor hurling game in April 1999, things had got so out of hand on the field, and so manifestly beyond the control of the match referee, that a uniformed Garda who happened to be in the vicinity went on to the field and spoke to some of the players, informing them that in his view an assault had already happened and that it was his duty to step in. At this point the match was abandoned.[59] Similarly in

---

[56] See *Keane, The Autobiography*, (Michael Joseph, Penguin Books, 2002) p.231. For analysis see Cox, "Civil Liability for Foul Play in Sport", 54 (4) *Northern Ireland Legal Quarterly* (2003) 351.

[57] It seems unlikely that a successful criminal prosecution could have been launched against Keane. The actual tackle on Haaland was a bad one, but crucially it did occur during an on-the-ball incident, and was not unlike many other fouls that occur in an English soccer season. Nor indeed was the harm that was caused particularly serious – indeed Haaland played on for the remainder of the match in question after Roy Keane had been sent off. It may be argued that Keane's autobiography contains an incriminating statement of malicious intent but in fact this is not true. Nowhere in the book does Keane actually admit intending to injure Haaland ("I hit him hard" is not the same as "I set out to injure him"). Most importantly, at the FA disciplinary hearing into the matter Eamon Dunphy had claimed that he had used poetic license to make Keane's intention in the matter seem more dramatic than it was, and whereas the FA correctly decided that as author of the book, Keane had to take responsibility for its contents, it is a long way from that to proving Keane's intention for the purposes of a criminal action. In traditional criminal law terminology, Dunphy's claim would surely constitute a reasonable doubt as to Keane's state of mind in that moment.

[58] See Brennan, "Keane's Book Tackles First Day Sales Record", *Irish Examiner*, August 28, 2002 and "Keane may face criminal enquiry over tackle", *Times*, August 14, 2002. In fact it emerged that police had already questioned Keane in respect of the incident at the time but decided that there was not strong enough evidence to prosecute him. See "New Questions For Keane", *Times*, August 28, 2002.

[59] See Anderson, "Violence, Sport and the Law: An Application to Gaelic Games", 7 (2) *Sport and the Law Journal* (1999) 51, and by the same author "Citius, Altius, Fortius; A Study of Criminal Violence in Sport", 11 Marq. Sports L. Rev. (Fall, 2000) 87 [hereafter Anderson] and Lennon, "Violence, Sport and the Law", 7 (3) *Sport and the Law Journal* (1999) 41.

England in February 2000 in a bad tempered Nationwide League Division One game between Wolverhampton Wanderers and Nottingham Forest, it was reported that police came into both dressing rooms at half time and issued warnings to the effect that the playing field was also their jurisdiction and that they would enforce law and order on it.[60] More recently in March 2002, an English Nationwide League division one game between Sheffield United and West Bromwich Albion was abandoned after three Sheffield United players were sent off and two more were unable to continue because of injury. One player, Patrick Suffo had been sent off for head butting an opponent (Derek McInnes) causing him head injuries that required four stitches. Police approached the injured player after the game and asked if he wished them to bring a criminal action against Suffo. McInnes decided, however, that in the interests of football as a whole he would support no such action.[61]

Nor is such police involvement restricted to situations where one player injures another. In *R v. Kirk*,[62] a Scottish soccer player was successfully prosecuted in a criminal action for angrily kicking the ball into the crowd thereby injuring a young girl. In a more high profile case in January 2002, Liverpool FC player Jamie Carragher was given an official police warning for throwing a coin (which had been thrown at him) back into a crowd thereby injuring a spectator during a heated FA cup fourth round tie against Arsenal.[63] In March 2003, a Liverpool FC player El Hadji Diouf appeared to spit at the crowd in a match between Liverpool and Glasgow Celtic, and having pleaded guilty in September 2003 at Glasgow Sheriff Court to assault under prosecution was fined €5,000.[64] Most famously, in 1995 Manchester United player Eric Cantona was convicted and sentenced to perform 120 hours of community service for an incident in which he kicked an opposing supporter, kung-fu style, in the chest when walking off the pitch in a match between Manchester United and Crystal Palace.[65]

---

[60] See "Sports Law Current Survey" 8(1) *Sport and the Law Journal* (2000) 19.

[61] See "Reprieve for Suffo as United Await Fate", *Times*, March 21, 2002.

[62] *Daily Telegraph*, October 17, 1995. See Gardiner et al, *Sports Law* (2nd ed., Cavendish, 2001), p.756.

[63] See Thorpe, "Carragher May Face Charges", *Irish Times*, January 29, 2002 and "Carragher Saved From Lengthy Ban By Swift Apology", *Times*, January 31, 2002.

[64] See Chiesa, "Liverpool Player Faces Charge After Spitting Claims", *The Glasgow Herald*, March 14, 2003, "Ashamed Diouf Left To Regret Spitting Image", *Times* March 15, 2003, Fifield, "Diouf Gets Two Game Sentence", *Irish Times*, March 19, 2003. In fact in November 2002, English police had earlier investigated claims that Diouf had spat at West Ham fans while warming up for a game. See "Spitting Image", *Irish Times*, March 15, 2003.

[65] *R v. Cantona*, *Times*, March 25, 1995. See Lewis & Taylor, *op. cit.*, p.1086. See also "Sent off Cantona Attacks Fan After Taunts From Crowd", *Times*, January 26, 1995; "Cantona Tells How Fans Abuse Drove Him To Violence", *Times*, March 24, 1995 and "Probation Chief Cries Foul Over Cantona Sentence", *Times*, April 26, 1996.

Nonetheless, the relationship between the criminal law and sport is an uncertain one and poses certain fundamental problems. For the purposes of this chapter, these issues will be dealt with by reference to three questions:

– When is sports field violence the subject of criminal prosecution?

– What factors will influence the decision whether or not to prosecute?

– *Should* the criminal law have any such involvement?

4.4.1 Instances of prosecution for violence on the field of play

Irish case law is rather thin on the ground on this topic.[66] Equally Anderson argues that with the advent of professionalisation, sport in general and Gaelic Games in particular, has witnessed more strategic violence and hence there is a greater need for the law to intervene.[67] In 1987 in *People (DPP) v. McCarthy*,[68] a footballer who had kicked an opponent on the ground, and then punched another opponent who came to assist the original victim, (fracturing his jaw) was convicted and fined £50, having paid the victim £5,000 compensation prior to sentencing. In *People (DPP) v. O'Driscoll*,[69] a fracas occurred at a bowling contest involving a competitor, his son and a rival supporter. The spectator suffered serious facial injuries as a result, but the son of the competitor (who was also the accused) claimed that the dispute concerned a bet and that the victim had initiated the force. The accused was acquitted by direction. McCutcheon records that between 1987 and 1992 four other cases were referred to the Director of Public Prosecutions, but no prosecution was directed in three of them and in the fourth the case was dropped by the prosecution. In February 1998, Terry Murphy was convicted of assault during a North Dublin u–21 final for punching an opponent and breaking his jaw, in circumstances where such action could have led to violence among the already hostile sets of rival supporters.[70] In 1999 a GAA player who assaulted another

---

[66] For analysis see Anderson, "Violence, Sport and the Law: An Application to Gaelic Games", 7 (2) *Sport and the Law Journal* (1999) 51 and McCutcheon pp.271ff.
[67] For a reply, see Lennon, "Violence, Sport and the Law", 7 (3) *Sport and the Law Journal* (1999) 41.
[68] Circuit Court Dublin, October 20–22, 1987. See McCutcheon, *op. cit.*, p.271.
[69] Cork Circuit Court, February 10–11, 1993.
[70] Anderson, "Violence, Sport and the Law: An Application to Gaelic Games", 7 (2) *Sport and the Law Journal* (1999) 51. See also 'Sentence on GAA Player Adjourned", *Irish Times*, February 19, 1998. This is similar to an interesting prosecution in Scotland taken in the case *Butcher v. Jessop* [1989] S.L.T. 593. This case concerned an 'old firm' soccer match between Glasgow Celtic and Glasgow Rangers, a match which annually excites enormous passions on both soccer and sectarian lines, with the two clubs representing respectively the Catholic and Protestant allegiances in the city. During the match a group of players became involved in a goalmouth fight. Because of the history of sectarianism

in an off-the-ball incident causing him to suffer brain damage was sentenced to nine months in prison. This sentence was suspended in October 2000 when the Circuit Court was informed that the victim had been compensated to the tune of IR£46,000 from a combination of the GAA's disability and loss of earnings schemes and also a contribution of IR£17,000 from the defendant.[71] In March 2003, Judge Raymond Groarke of the Circuit Court directed a number of people involved with the GAA to give evidence in the District Court in relation to an ongoing police investigation into an incident during a Gaelic Football match where one player is alleged to have assaulted another.[72] Finally in March 2004, a hurling club selector, John Burke was sentenced to four months in prison at Athenry District Court for assaulting a player on an opposing team with a hurley, during a Galway City League final match in February 2003. The injured player sustained a gash to the top of his head requiring nine stitches, after the defendant knocked his protective helmet off by repeatedly hitting him with a hurley.[73] Following an appeal to the Circuit Court, during the course of which Judge Kenny was highly critical of what he perceived as a failure on the part of the GAA to discipline players and officials who bring the game into disrepute, the defendant's sentence was reduced to 200 hours of community service.[74]

In England, the first recorded case in which a criminal prosecution was taken in respect of an on-field assault is that of *R v. Bradshaw*.[75] In this case, during a football game the accused jumped in the air and struck an opponent in the stomach with his knee. The latter subsequently died of a ruptured intestine. The defendant was acquitted on the evidence, but Bramwell L.J. directed the jury that the act would be unlawful if it was intended to cause serious harm, and that no rules of sport could make lawful that which the law of the land deemed unlawful.[76] Similarly, in *R v. Moore*[77] the deceased and the accused were playing on opposing teams in a soccer match. The deceased ran past the accused, who chased him towards the goal. As the deceased ran forward, the accused jumped up and kicked him in the back pushing him into the knees of onrushing goalkeeper. Some days later the victim died from internal

---

in these games and the threat that such behaviour might cause a serious breach of the peace they were bound over to keep the peace.

[71] See Cox & Costello, "Sports Law' in Byrne & Binchy, *Annual Review of Irish Law 2001* (Round Hall Sweet & Maxwell, Dublin, 2002).

[72] See Keogh, "Judge critical of GAA in attack inquiry", *Irish Times*, March 20, 2003.

[73] See Healy, "Judge Told of Hurley Attack on Player by Selector", *Irish Times*, April 29, 2004.

[74] See Healy, "GAA Man to do Public Service in Lieu of Jail For Attack with Hurley", *Irish Times*, May 19, 2004.

[75] (1878) 14 Cox C.C .83.

[76] See Anderson, *op. cit.*, p.95 and "Prosecuting Sports Field Violence a British Perspective", 7 (2) J.L.A.S. (1997), 81

[77] (1898) 14 T.L.R. 229

injuries. The accused was convicted of manslaughter.[78] Hawkins J summing up said that the rules of football were "quite immaterial," nor did it matter whether what the accused had done was within the rules of the game (a point which had also been made in *Bradshaw*). Football was known to be a rough contact sport, and hence persons who played it had to exercise the necessary care to ensure that they did not cause harm to any other person.[79] If a person intentionally or recklessly used force that was likely to injure another, and if as a result the other person died then the crime of manslaughter had been made out.[80]

From the end of the nineteenth century until the 1970s there was a dearth of prosecutions for on-field assaults. The change, which has seen a steady flow of prosecutions since then is attributed by McCutcheon to a judicial appreciation both of the seriousness and quantum of injuries that might be involved, and also of the economic consequences of such injuries.[81] In light of these factors, the courts have been prepared to use the criminal law to impose standards on sport, penalizing even commonplace infractions of the rules of the game, where violence resulted in serious harm. Thus in *R v. Billinghurst*,[82] (the first ever prosecution for a sports field assault causing mere injury rather than death) a player who had punched an opponent during a rugby game breaking his jaw, was found guilty of assault, despite testimony from former Welsh rugby international Mervyn Davies that punching is a common occurrence in rugby.[83] On the other hand in *R v. Blissett*,[84] where, during an English Nationwide League soccer match the defendant and victim had jumped for a ball and in the course of challenge, the victim had suffered a fractured cheekbone and eye socket and was no longer able to play competitive football, the defendant was acquitted of assault largely on the basis of the evidence of Graham Kelly, then FA chief executive, who said that this kind of challenge would occur on average 50 times a game.[85]

---

[78] See Anderson *op. cit.*, p.95 and McArdle, *op. cit.*, p.155.

[79] In subsequent case law, the fact that a sport is known to be rough was used as an argument *against* prosecution, on the basis that participants can be taken to have consented to known risks.

[80] *R v. Southby* (1969) *Police Review*, February 9, vol. 77 p.110, 120 *New Law Journal* 413. See Grayson, *Sport and the Law* (3rd ed., Butterworths, London, 2000) [hereafter Grayson] p.260. The accused was convicted for manslaughter following the death of an opponent whom he had struck in violation of the rules of the game.

[81] McCutcheon, "Sports Violence, Consent and the Criminal Law" [1994] N.I.L.Q. 267 [hereafter McCutcheon], p.270.

[82] [1978] Criminal L.R. 553. For analysis see Grayson, "Keeping Sport Alive", 140 *New Law Journal* (January 12, 1990) 12.

[83] For an analysis of the comparative lack of criminal prosecutions for behaviour on the rugby field see Duff, "A Hooligan's Game – Played by Gentlemen", 2 (3) *Sport and the Law Journal* (1994) 13

[84] *Independent*, December 4, 1992. See Gardiner et al, *Sports Law*, p.662.

[85] McArdle, p.154. See Grayson and Bond, "Making Foul Play A Crime", 137 *Solicitors Journal* (1993) 693 for the view that this evidence should have been excluded.

Since this time, there has been a number of recorded convictions, typically for off the ball incidents ranging from punching,[86] to biting an opponent's ear,[87] to hitting an opponent in the tunnel after a match,[88] to kicking the face of an opponent while the latter was lying on the ground.[89] Traditionally, sentencing in such cases was comparatively lenient. Thus in *R v. Birkin*,[90] the accused ran after and struck an opponent who had tackled him in an amateur soccer match, breaking his jaw. Following a guilty plea to a charge of assault occasioning actual bodily harm, he was sentenced to eight months in prison reduced on appeal to six months. In the same vein, in *R v. Shervill*,[91] the accused kicked an opponent causing injury. He pleaded guilty to unlawful wounding and was sentenced to six months in prison reduced by Court of Appeal to two months.[92] Finally, in *R v. Lincoln*,[93] during a soccer match, the victim stood in front of the defendant as the latter was taking a throw in. After the throw in had been taken, the defendant ran up to the victim, said, "no one

---

[86] See Anderson, *op. cit.*, p.98 and Grayson, "Keeping Sport Alive", 140 *New Law Journal* (January 12, 1990) 12. In *R v. Bishop* (1986) *Times*, October 12, 1986, a Welsh rugby international punched an opponent in an off the ball incident when the latter was on the ground, causing concussion. He was convicted of assault and sentenced to a month in prison, later reduced to a 12 month suspended sentence. See Grayson, *op. cit.*, p.262 and by the same author "Keeping Sport Alive", 140 *New Law Journal* (January 12, 1990) 12 and "The Day Sport Dies", 138 *New Law Journal* (January 8, 1988) 9. It should be noted that in *R v. Venna* [1975] 3 All E.R. 788, it was held that recklessness was a sufficient mens rea for the crime of assault.

[87] In *R v. Johnson* [1986] 8 C.A.R. (5) 343, the accused bit an opponent's ear during a rugby tackle, was found guilty of inflicting grievous bodily harm with intent contrary to s. 18 of the Offences against the Person Act 1861, and was sentenced to six months in prison, with Lord Lane commenting that violence on the sports field needed discouraging just as much as any other kind of violence. See Grayson, *op. cit.*, p.262, Gardiner, "The Law and the Sports Field" [1994] Criminal L.R. 513 and Anderson, *op. cit.*, p.99.

[88] In 1988 in *R v. Kamara*, a professional soccer player who pleaded guilty to breaking an opponent's jaw in a tunnel after a match was fined £1,200 sterling, *Times*, April 15, 1988. See Anderson *op. cit.*, p.99 and Grayson, *op. cit.*, p.263.

[89] In *R v. Lloyd* a player who kicked an opponent in the face while the latter was lying on the ground was sentenced to 18 months in prison, which was roughly what he would have got for a similar action in a non-sporting context. Lord Lane commented that whereas forceful contact was allowed by the rules of rugby union, the game was not a licence for thuggery: [1989] 36 *Criminal Law Review* 513.

[90] (1988) 10 Cr. App. R. 303.

[91] (1989) 11 Cr. App. R. 284.

[92] See also *R v. Goodwin*, (1995) 16 Cr. App. R.(s) 885. Here a rugby player elbowed an opponent in the face as the latter tried to run past him, fracturing his cheekbone, palate and molars. He had his sentence of six months in prison reduced to four months, with the court taking cognisance of the fact that having been banned from playing rugby league for 14 months, the defendant's career had suffered significant harm.

[93] (1990) 12 Cr App R (s) 250

does that to me," and punched him in the face, breaking his jaw in two places. He was sentenced to four months imprisonment but this was reduced on appeal to 28 days.[94]

More recently, it seems that the courts in England are moving away from the lenient approach to sentencing in cases of sports field violence. In *R v. Chapman*,[95] the defendant's brother had been involved in a scuffle with the victim and as the victim lay on the ground, the defendant gave him a kick in the head and caused a wound requiring five stitches, for which he was sentenced to eighteen months in prison. In *R v. Davies*,[96] the victim had collided with a team-mate of the defendant during a soccer match and had given away a free kick. While he was waiting for the free kick to be taken the defendant ran up to him and punched him in the face fracturing his cheekbone. His sentence of six months in prison was upheld by the Court of Appeal, which distinguished the apparent leniency in *Shervill* from the stringency in this case on the grounds that this was an unprovoked and intentional assault of an "off-the-ball" nature.[97] In *R v. McHugh*,[98] the defendant was sentenced to the arguably excessive period of three years in prison for kicking an opponent in the face as he got up from the ground, after both had jumped for a high ball in the penalty area during an amateur football game in Oxford. In *R v. Moss*,[99] the defendant was convicted of punching an opponent in the eye causing extensive damage following a ruck in a rugby match and was sentenced to eight months in prison, despite the fact that a pre-sentence report had said that a non-custodial sentence would be more than enough, that he had no previous convictions for violence and that it was extremely unlikely that he would re-offend.[100] And in *R v. Calton*,[101] a schoolboy rugby player was sentenced to one year's detention (reduced on appeal to three months) in a youth offender's institution for kicking a sixteen year old opponent in the face "with all his might," knocking him out and breaking his jaw.

Finally in a tragic case in Northern Ireland, a seventeen year old youth

---

[94] McArdle, *op. cit.*, p.154.

[95] Grayson, *op. cit.*, p.263.

[96] 12 Cr. App. Rep. (s) 308 [1991] Criminal L.R. 7.

[97] See Anderson, *op. cit.*, p.108. On the other hand in *R v. Hardy*, *Guardian*, July 27, 1994, a brawl developed between players during a game of rugby union. The defendant hit the victim who fell to the ground and banged his head on the frosty ground, dying two years later. The defendant claimed that his action was merely a reaction to the fact that he was being hit at the time and he was acquitted on the grounds of self-defence. See McArdle, *op. cit.*, p.155.

[98] Unreported, High Court, February 20, 1998. See 1 (2) *Sports Law Bulletin* (1998) 3.

[99] Unreported, Court of Appeal, July 5, 1999. See 2 (4) *Sports Law Bulletin* (1999) 2.

[100] See also 2 (1) Sports Law Journal (1994) 24 for analysis of the case of Ian Russell, a Royal Navy Training Instructor, who was court-martialled for punching an opponent in a rugby match, and was given four months detention and reduced in rank to able seaman.

[101] [1999] 2 Cr. App. Rep.(s) 64 CA. See 1 (5) *Sports Law Bulletin* (1998) 3.

punched another during a soccer match. As a result of what was described as a million to one chance, the victim died, owing to a burst artery that caused a brain haemorrhage. The defendant was charged with murder, but in March 2002 this charge was replaced with one of manslaughter to which he pleaded guilty and for which he was given twelve months probation having agreed to carry out seventy hours community service.[102]

Most of these cases involve amateur sportsmen and hence are not particularly high profile. The major exception is the case of *Ferguson v. Normand* (Procurator Fiscal, Glasgow).[103] This involved professional soccer player Duncan Ferguson then of Glasgow Rangers Football Club. In a match between Glasgow Rangers and Raith Rovers on April 16, 1994, following a contested challenge for the ball, Ferguson grabbed an opponent, John McStay, and head butted him, causing him injury. On the basis of the gravity of the offence and also the fact that the accused had a number of previous convictions he was sentenced to three months in prison. The sentence was upheld on appeal. The comments of Lord Justice Hope are worth quoting at length:

> "The court has no wish to intervene in physical contact sports such as professional football. It is well aware that contests in physical fitness, strength and agility and some measure of aggression are part of the game, both for player and spectator. But when acts are done which go well beyond what can be regarded as normal physical contact and an assault is committed, the court has a duty to condemn and punish such conduct. It has to be made clear both to players and to the public that such criminal acts cannot be tolerated on the field of play any more than they can be tolerated in any other place in this country. A footballer who assaults another player on the football field is not entitled to expect leniency from the court just because the incident occurred in the course of a football match...On the contrary, one of the factors which may indicate the gravity of the offence is the fact that the assault has been committed in public before so many spectators. This fact becomes all the more important where the player is a public figure and the incident occurs during a game which has such a high profile as a league match in the Scottish Premier Division. These are fixtures which set the standard of conduct throughout the country and any sentence for an assault committed in these circumstances must reflect the need to deter others from engaging in similar acts of criminal violence."

---

[102] See Manley, "Teen Faces Charge of Murdering Footballer", *Irish News*, October 14, 2000, McIntyre, "Fatal Punch was a Million-to-One Tragedy", *Irish News*, October 23, 2000, "Man is Freed After Football Pitch Death", *Irish News*, February 15, 2003, and "Footballer's Blow Killed Goalkeeper", *Irish Times*, February 15, 2003.

[103] [1995] S.C.C.R. 770. For comment see Duff, "Own Goal", 4 (1) *Sport and the Law Journal* (1996) 12 and by the same author "The Road to Consistency", 4 (1) *Sport and the Law Journal* (1996) 15.

4.4.2 The inconsistent nature of sports field prosecutions

The above analysis is indicative of the fact that in both Ireland and England – and despite the occasional instances of prosecution – the vast majority of incidents of on field violence are not the subject of police investigation. The explanation for this appears to be part theoretical – the view that the sports field is not really the domain of the criminal law – and part practical – in that there are considerable practical impediments to successful prosecution for such actions. In truth there are simply no hard and fast rules by which either the player or the police can gauge whether a particular action on the field of play which violates the rules of the game is also a criminal offence. As McCutcheon points out:[104]

> "... Despite the volume of sports violence cases the law still remains vague. In particular, the point at which force becomes criminal has not been clearly identified, nor has the question of the participants' consent been satisfactorily resolved."

In its Report on Non-Fatal Offences against the Person, the Irish Law Reform Commission concluded that whereas use of criminal law to deal with on-pitch violence would be very much a last resort, equally:[105]

> "It is clearly desirable that criminal liability should continue to attach to acts of violence committed in the course of sporting activities and the Commission would accordingly not recommend that any general exemption be extended to persons engaged in contact sports, where the victim does not consent (expressly or impliedly) to the infliction of the injury."

Moreover it recommended[106] that the possibility should remain open that those who had aided and abetted the commission of an offence on the playing field (coaches, managers etc) should also be liable to face criminal prosecution. On the other hand, the Commission was not in favour of a law, which created specific penalties for sporting violence, in the light of "the amateur status of contact sports in Ireland." Rather "... the criminal law may be enforced when the rules of any sporting activity are broken." Beyond this, the Commission accepted that the general criminal law was arguably an inappropriate mechanism for dealing with offences on the field and particularly for forcing changes in the rules of violent and aggressive sports.

---

[104] See McCutcheon, *op. cit.*, p.275.
[105] Law Reform Commission, *Report on Non Fatal Offences Against the Person* (1997) 272.
[106] *Ibid.*, p.273

In its *Consultation Paper*,[107] the United Kingdom Law Commission proposed that no action within the rules of a lawful sport should ground a criminal prosecution for assault.[108] Intentional or reckless violations of the safety rules (as distinct from merely the playing rules)[109] of the game, which caused serious harm (of the type defined in section 4 of the Irish Non-Fatal Offences Against the Person Act 1997), *could* ground an assault charge but such action would not be deemed to be reckless unless the player in question was aware of a risk of a seriously disabling injury and the risk was not a reasonable one for him or her to take, having regard to all the circumstances of the case,[110] including his or her level of playing experience and the consent of the other participants to the risks inherent in participating in a dangerous sport.[111] If these criteria were not satisfied then the matter should be left up to the sporting body, exercising its own disciplinary powers.[112]

Perhaps most helpfully, in July 1996 the Lord Advocate in Scotland issued instructions to Chief Constables under section 12 of the Criminal Procedure (Scotland) Act 1995, advising them as to the circumstances in which they should be prepared to take action on the sports field (while insisting).[113] The report started by saying that primary responsibility for dealing with on field violence belonged to players, coaches, managers, sports disciplinary bodies and referees. It also advised that the fact that a defendant's actions are within the rules of the game is persuasive, if not conclusive, evidence of his legal innocence.[114] Beyond this, the inference is that that prosecutions should generally only be taken where the participant goes well beyond what can be regarded as normal physical contact within the relevant sport, and especially

---

[107] See *Law Commission Consultation Papers* 134 and 139 on *Consent and Offences Against the Person*. For comment see "The Revisiting of Consent" [1996] *Criminal Law Review* 73 and Farrell, at 2 (1) *Sport and the Law Journal* (1994) 134 at pp.1 & 5ff.

[108] See *Consultation Paper 139*, p.1763.

[109] The distinction between playing and safety rules of sport was made in *Nabronzy v. Barnhill*, 31 Ill. App. 3rd 212, 334 NE 2nd 255 (1975). See also Ormerod, "Second Law Commission Consultation Paper on Consent" [1996] *Criminal Law Review* 694 at p.704.

[110] *Consultation Paper 134*, p.66.

[111] *Consultation Paper 139*, p.163.

[112] Moreover, any immunity afforded to the playing of sport should apply equally to situations where one is practising for a sport.

[113] See Beloff, Kerr and Demitrou, *Sports Law* (Hart Publishers, 1998) [hereafter Beloff], p.130, Gardiner and James, "Touchlines and Guidelines: The Lord Advocate's Response to Sports Field Violence" [1997] *Criminal Law* Review 41, Miller, "Criminal Law and Sport in Scotland: The Lord Advocate's Instructions of 10 July 1996 to Chief Constables", 4 (2) *Sport and the Law Journal* (1996) 40 and "Prosecuting Sports Field Violence, a British Perspective", 7 (2) *Journal of Legal Aspects of Sport* (Spring 1997),81.

[114] See also on this point Williams, "Consent and Public Policy" [1962] *Criminal Law Review* 74 at pp.80–81.

where the violence occurs in a dead ball situation, or in circumstances likely to provoke a violent or disorderly reaction[115] – roughly the type of situations in which prosecutions had been initiated for on field activities since the days of *R v. Bradshaw*.[116]

The above recommendations while helpful, still do not provide any concrete guide for knowing as a matter of certainty whether a specific incidence of violent foul play will be prosecuted. In truth this is because certainty in this regard is precluded by the significant practical difficulties involved in bringing such a prosecution,[117] which themselves stem from a widely held belief (which will be considered shortly) that the law should not really be concerned with what happens on the field of play.[118] Thus there is a shortage of police complaints in respect of sports violence, and especially a shortage of complaints from injured individuals, many of whom feel that the interests of the sport will be better served by allowing the matter to be resolved internally. Evidence suggests that players don't like giving evidence against each other[119] – both for reasons of loyalty and for fear of being seen as a whiner or a sneak – and that when evidence *is* given, it will generally be split along team lines.[120] Indeed in Ireland, in one specific instance it was necessary for the police to seek a court order requiring the GAA to comply with an investigation into an alleged assault on the field. Giving evidence, one official claimed that it was GAA policy not to comply with such investigations unless directed to do so by the court.[121]

Even if criminal proceedings *are* brought, it may, furthermore, be impossible to prove what will be the determinative issue in proceedings involving on the ball incidents, namely the intention of the person who caused the harm.[122]

---

[115] This was the major focus of the prosecution in *Butcher v. Jessop* [1989] S.L.T. 593.

[116] For criticism of the guidelines on the grounds that there may be certain violent behaviour that is in violation of the rules of the game while in conformity with its playing culture see Gardiner and James, "Touchlines and Guidelines: The Lord Advocate's Response to Sports Field Violence" [1997] *Criminal Law* Review 41.

[117] See "Prosecuting Sports Field Violence, a British Perspective", 7(2) *Journal of Legal Aspects of Sport*, (Spring 1997) 81 and James, "The Prosecutor's Dilemma", 3 (3) *Sport and The Law Journal* (1995) 60.

[118] As Osborough notes, "…[the criminal law will be] … too blunt an instrument to punish wrongdoing … [and] … may turn out to be strangely unproductive – prosecutions may not be brought, juries may not convict, sentences may be merely nominal. See Osborough, "Sport Freedom and the Criminal Law", p.61 in Whelan, ed., *Law and Liberty in Ireland* (Oaktree Press, Dublin 1992).

[119] This was witnessed in the case of *Gary Mabbut v. John Fashanu, The Times*, August 14, 1994.

[120] For analysis of the pervasiveness of this concept in Irish case law, see Anderson, *op. cit.*, p.103. See also "GAA Referee and Linesman Criticism in Assault Case", *Irish Times*, June 26, 1997 and "GAA Footballer Loses claim for Damages Against Garda", *Irish Times*, November 14, 1997.

[121] See Keogh, "Judge Critical of GAA in Attack Inquiry", *Irish Times*, March 20, 2003.

[122] See Trichka, "Violence in Sport: Criminal Assault or Part of the Game", 3 (2) *Journal*

Finally from a police perspective there is a real question as to whether prosecution of someone for causing what may be a minor injury, recklessly inflicted in the course of the playing of sport, is in the public interest,[123] or whether police should concentrate more on catching "real criminals" and less on dealing with a couple of overgrown schoolboys who are fighting each other, and who should more properly seek recourse against each other through the disciplinary wings of the relevant sports governing body, or if necessary through the law of torts.[124] It is these practicalities more than any other factors that render the incidences of criminal prosecution for on field violence haphazard in appearance.

4.5 *SHOULD* THE CRIMINAL LAW REGULATE THE SPORTS FIELD?

As we have mentioned, many of the practical difficulties in bringing such prosecutions derive from a popular belief that sport can and should regulate itself and that therefore, if the impugned action bears any relationship whatsoever to the game as it is being played (and for instance one *may* validly conclude that an off-the-ball fight in a rugby match is related to the game) then the actor should be punished by the sporting body, but that it is not properly a matter for the criminal law. This viewpoint will now be evaluated.[125]

---

of Legal Aspects of Sport (1993) 88 at p.91 and Hanson and Dernis, "Revisiting Excessive Violence in the Professional Sports Arena: Changes in the Past Twenty Years?", Vol. 6 *Seton Hall Journal of Sports Law* (1996)127 at p.140. See also McCutcheon, *op. cit.*, p.271 for the view that a prosecutor will be hard pushed to convince a jury that the force used was criminal in nature.

[123] It has however, been argued that there is a stronger public interest in prosecuting high profile cases because of the role-model status of those involved. See Hanson and Dernis, "Revisiting Excessive Violence in the Professional Sports Arena: Changes in the Past Twenty Years?", Vol. 6 *Seton Hall Journal of Sports Law* (1996) 127, Rains, "Sports Violence a Matter of Societal Concern", 55 Notre Dame L. Rev. (1998) 796 and Nelson, "Sports Violence: Too Late For the Carrots – Bring on the Big Stick", 74 Iowa L. Rev. (1989) 681. This was of course the logic applied in the *Duncan Ferguson* case.

[124] See Hanson and Dernis, "Revisiting Excessive Violence in the Professional Sports Arena: Changes in the Past Twenty Years?", 6 *Seton Hall Journal of Sports Law* (1996) 127 at p.142.

[125] See Osborough, "Sport Freedom and the Criminal Law", p.57 in Whelan, ed., *Law and Liberty in Ireland*, for the view that:

"The question [whether the criminal law has a role on the sports field] is arguably more fundamental than it sounds, not least because of the role that sport has come to enjoy in the lives of players and perhaps more importantly in the lives of spectators as well. How indiscipline and violence, whether gratuitous or otherwise are regarded, and how they are actually dealt with may thus constitute a matter of great moment and rather more so than people in the past have been prepared to accept."

4.5.1 The impact and extent of player consent

Once again, the most intuitively obvious ground for opposing the criminalisation of foul play is that by voluntarily participating in sport, a player implicitly consents to injuries suffered in the course of sport - including injuries caused by other participants. Thus it is argued, that such consent renders the activity one which, in the words of the *Wolfenden Committee Report into Homosexual Behaviour and Prostitution*, is "… not the law's business."[126] The problem with this argument is twofold. First, as we have seen, from an Irish perspective, the consent of an injured party does not render lawful an action that causes serious harm (as defined in section 4 of the 1997 Non-Fatal Offences Against the Person Act). Secondly, it is far from clear to what exactly one consents when one walks out onto the field of play.

Some have suggested that one consents only to activity within the rules of the game (which activity is in practice immune from criminal prosecution anyway).[127] This approach creates problems, however, both because the rule in *R v. Bradshaw*[128] allows such activity to be the subject of criminal prosecution, and also because it renders many technical violations of the rules criminal while affording legal protection to the actions of the player who deliberately attempts to injure another while sticking within the rules of the game.[129] Moreover, as McCutcheon argues, allowing the rules of the game (and hence a private body) to determine the legality of an action would fly in the face of the rule of law.[130] Finally, it is difficult to ignore the reality that in practice, players *do* consent to more than merely contact within the rules of the game; it is simply unclear how much more.

The second approach to the question of consent is to say that one can consent to the risk of injury, but not to the risk of that kind of serious injury which is criminally (intentionally or recklessly) inflicted. The problem with this as we have seen is that it poses significant evidential problems, as prosecution counsel must prove beyond reasonable doubt the *mens rea* of a sportsman in what is potentially a split second situation. Indeed, it can be argued that the real reason why Bob Russell MP called for Roy Keane to face criminal charges for the alleged assault on Alfe Inge Haaland was because Keane had removed this evidential difficulty from the equation by admitting

---

[126] C.M.D. 247 (1957).

[127] See McCutcheon, *op. cit.*, p.274 for the suggestion that if sport is lawful, then logically activity within its rules should also be lawful.

[128] (1878) 14 Cox C.C. 83. See "Prosecuting Sports Field Violence: A British Perspective", 7 (2) *Journal of Legal Aspects of Sport* (1997) 81.

[129] McCutcheon, *op. cit.*, pp.273–280. From the American logic in *Narbonzy v. Barnhill*, 31 Ill. App. 3rd 212, 334 NE 2nd 255 (1975) it might be argued that a participant does not consent to harm arising from a breach of safety rules but does consent to routine breaches of playing rules. See McArdle, *op. cit.*, p.165.

[130] McCutcheon, *op. cit.*, p.273.

in his autobiography that his action was at best reckless and at worst intentional. In 1994, the UK Central Council of Physical Recreation (CCPR) had, however, criticized this approach, arguing that certain intentional actions *within the rules of sport* – the short pitched delivery of a very fast bowler or the intentionally debilitating tackle of a rugby player, both aimed at "softening up" one's opponent for example – may very well cause serious harm, yet it is difficult to conclude that they should be seen as criminal, if for no other reason than because such intimidating tactics are part and parcel of these sports, and more importantly are known to be so by consenting participants.[131]

A third approach to consent is to say that a player consents not just to assaults that are within the rules of the game, but also to those that come within the 'playing culture" of the sport – defined in *Rootes v. Shelton*[132] as the "rules, customs or conventions of a sport' – an approach that has the undoubted advantage of fitting in with what is probably the injured player's perception of the situation.[133] Gardiner argues that those actions which violate the rules of sport while keeping within its playing culture should be met by penalties both within the game and by the relevant sports governing body, but should not attract criminal sanction.[134] It is only when an action violates both the rules and the playing culture of the game, such that there is no question of consent on the part of the injured party[135] – typically a violent off-the-ball incident – that the criminal law should be used.[136] Thus Canadian courts have concluded that by reason of the traditional violence in ice-hockey, one may be taken to have consented to being hit in the face during a match,[137] but not to being subject to attacks which are unprovoked and violent and not related to the play.[138]

---

[131] See Radley, "A Study of Consent to Violence in Sport with Particular Reference to the Law Commission Paper No. 134", 3 (3) *Sport and The Law Journal* (1995) 57 at p.52 and Anderson, *op. cit.*, p.87.

[132] [1968] A.L.R. 33. The playing culture is also defined in *Elliott v. Saunders*, unreported, Queen's Bench, June 10, 1994 as "... a frequent or familiar infraction of the rules of a game that can fall within the ordinary risks of the game accepted by all the participants."

[133] See Hanson and Dernis, "Revisiting Excessive Violence in the Professional Sports Arena: Changes in the Past Twenty Years?", 6 *Seton Hall Journal of Sports Law* (1996) 127 at p.134 and Forman, "Boxing in the Legal Arena", 3 *Sports Lawyers Journal* (1996) 75 at p.83.

[134] Gardiner and James, "Touchlines and Guidelines: The Lord Advocate's Response to Sports Field Violence" [1997] *Criminal Law* Review 41.

[135] Forman, "Boxing in the Legal Arena", 3 *Sports Lawyers Journal* (1996) 75.

[136] See also Gardiner, "Not Playing the Game; is it a Crime?", *Solicitor's Journal* (July 2, 1993) 68, Gardiner, "Juridification of the Football Field: Strategies for Giving Law the Elbow", 5 *Marquette University Law Review* (1994–95) 188 at p.200ff, Gardiner, "The Law and the Sports Field" [1994] *Criminal Law Review* 513 and McArdle, *op. cit.*, p.156.

[137] *R v. Maki* [1970] 14 D.L.R. (3d) 164, *R v. Green* [1970] 16 D.L.R. (3d) 137. Generally see Barnes, *op. cit.*, pp.255–269.

[138] *R v. Aussem*, 1997 Ont. C.J.P. Lexis, 136, 1997 W.C.B.J. 424117, 36 W.C.B. (2d) 453,

While this approach has obvious merits, it leaves a good deal to the perception of the prosecuting authorities as to what the playing culture of sport actually entails and hence as to the extent of the implicit consent of the participants.[139] As with the view that one consents to actions within the rules of the game, this approach is also at variance with legal principle in that it enables a private body, by determining the playing culture of sport, thereby to determine the content of the criminal law. Moreover it is unclear whether this formula only applies to negligent or reckless actions that violate the rules of the game but are within the playing culture – for example an accidental high tackle in rugby – or whether it would also apply to such breaches when they are *intentional* – as for example when a rugby player stamps on another at a ruck (a fairly habitual if dangerous infraction of a sport's safety rules). It should also be asked why the playing culture of a particularly violent sport (like for instance ice-hockey in the USA or Canada)[140]) should be able to afford legal immunity to something, which, however regularly it occurs, is fundamentally illegal and uncivilised and may lead to public disturbances – like for instance a mass brawl of players.[141]

A more convincing if less concrete method of determining both whether there *is* consent on the part of the victim of an assault and also whether that consent should exonerate the "assaulter," comes from Beloff[142] who calls for simple application of a common sense analysis of the situation, having regard to factors like the nature of the sport, the type of injury and the manner in which it was inflicted.[143] Once again, this leaves a good deal up to judicial

---

R v. Leyte (1973) 13 C.C.C. (2d) 458, *R v. Watson* (1975) 26 C.C.C. (2d) 150, *R v. Maloney* (1976) 28 C.C.C. (2d) 3232 *R v. St Croix* (1979) 7 C.C.C. (2d) 122. See reports at 1 (4) *Sport and the Law Bulletin* (1998) 14. Generally see McCutcheon, *op. cit.*, p.274ff.

[139] Thus the CCPR in its submission to the Law Commission commented that: "If the courts are to decide whether an activity is lawful by means of objective criteria and not by means of the rules of a particular game then there is also a danger that the offending player would not be tried by reference to what was acceptable to his sport, but by reference to the opinions on the sport in question by a judge and a jury who may never have played the sport." See Anderson, *op. cit.*, p.102.

[140] *State v. Forbes* (No. 6328; District Court Mann; July 19, 1975) discussed by Trichka, "Violence in Sport", 3 (2) *Journal of Legal Aspects of Sport* (1993) 88. This can be compared, however, to the Canadian case *R v. Assam* (1997) Ont. C.J.P. Lexis, 136, 1997 W.C.B.J. .424117, 36 W.C.B. (2d) 453. Generally see Barnes, *Sports and the Law in Canada* (3rd ed., Butterworths, Toronto and Vancouver, 1996) [hereafter Barnes], pp.251–319.

[141] See *Law Commission Consultation Paper 134*, p.66.

[142] Beloff, *op. cit.*, p.130. See also McArdle, *op. cit.*, p.156 and Williams, "Consent and Public Policy" [1962] *Criminal Law Review* 74 at p.81.

[143] This is not unlike the approach followed in the Canadian case of *R v. Cey* (1989) 48 C.C.C. (3d) 480 where it was concluded that analysis of the efficacy of consent should be assessed by reference to certain objective criteria including the nature of the game, the nature of the act and the surrounding circumstances, the degree of force used, the

discretion, and moreover, it does not sit easily with legal principle but the nature of the issue means that any other approach will inevitably lead to results that appear arbitrary and inconsistent in nature.

Arguably the best way for determining the extent of legally effective consent in this area is to return to first principles. As we have seen the only reason why contact sport is legal at all is because it represents an exception to general rules of law justified by public policy interests. It stands to reason therefore that the extent of the legality of such sport (and hence the effectiveness of player consent) should also be subject to a public policy control. Put another way the extent to which a player's consent becomes legally relevant hinges on the question whether it makes good public policy sense to afford legal significance to such consent. In this respect, it can be argued that in as much as sport is a good thing as far as public policy is concerned, so also is wholehearted and sporting participation in sport. On the other hand public policy frowns on violent actions that are neither within the rules of the game nor consistent with wholehearted participation therein in that they bear no relation to the spirit of the game. Perhaps the best test of the legality of an action on the sports field is to assess which of these two categories it falls into, and hence whether it is supported by public policy or not.[144]

4.5.2 Beyond consent – Is it good policy for the criminal law to police the field of play?

Of the leading English writers on the subject, Simon Gardiner tends to the view that the criminal law should only be applied as a matter of last resort in extreme cases – generally where there is no question of consent on the part of the injured party. On the other hand, Edward Grayson has consistently argued that some legal involvement in the sports field is a good thing *for sport* – apart from any other social benefits that it might provide. Indeed Grayson would favour not just criminal prosecution of participants for on field violence, but also of coaches who consistently select habitually violent players or worse, who encourage acts of violence as a team tactic.[145]

Grayson argues that the involvement of the criminal law in sport is necessary

---

degree of risk of injury and the state of mind of the accused. For criticism see Gardiner and James, "Touchlines and Guidelines: The Lord Advocate's Response to Sports Field Violence" [1997] *Criminal Law Review* 41 and Gardiner, "Juridification of the Football Field: Strategies for Giving Law the Elbow", 5 *Marquette University Law Review* (1994–95) 188 at p.204.

[144] For a similar suggestion in respect of civil liability for sports violence see Cox, "Civil Liability for Foul Play in Sport", 54 *Northern Ireland Legal Quarterly* (Winter 2003) 351.

[145] Grayson, "The Day Sport Dies", 138 *New Law Journal* (1988) 9.

for two reasons.[146] First, because sports administrators have simply not dealt with the issue of player violence in sport,[147] (and indeed Gardiner himself argued that "if internal disciplinary mechanisms fail to deter such conduct, the criminal law may be an appropriate though limited tool"),[148] and secondly because the notion that a general immunity from the application of criminal law should extend to someone simply by virtue of the fact that he is on the playing field flies in the face of established practice and authority which plainly require that it is the courts alone who can compensate victims. Thus he endorses the conclusion of the Criminal Injuries Compensation Board to the effect that it is in the best interests of everyone that people who commit what are in reality criminal offences (being intentionally or recklessly harmful) on the sports field should face prosecution.[149]

On balance it is submitted that of the respective theories of Grayson and Gardiner, the former is the preferable one. Whether we are dealing with professional or amateur sport, the fact remains that the criminal law does retain jurisdiction over people's behaviour in order to ensure that public order is upheld, that victims of crime are compensated and that perpetrators of crime are punished. This is not to say that it should not only be used as a matter of last resort – it should. Nonetheless in cases of serious assault – where serious injury is inflicted, there should not be an immunity either legal or indeed cultural afforded to the perpetrators simply because their actions are committed in a sporting context. To afford such immunity would neither be beneficial for society nor for sport. As a *New Law Journal* editorial put it:[150]

"Unfortunately for far too long violence on the pitch or in the arena has been tolerated as something, which should be dealt with by domestic tribunals. The boxer who hits the referee is suspended by his association, the rugby player who stamps on an opponent is banned for a few matches; nothing worse. Very rarely is there a prosecution – Cantona is about the only example we can conjure up – for even the most blatant examples of violence. We have said before that this does not set a standard of conduct for supporters to follow. If a rugby player can break the jaw of an opponent in full view of the television cameras and receive only a suspension, why

---

[146] Grayson and Bond, "Making Foul Play a Crime", 137 *Solicitor's Journal* (1993) 693.
[147] See Law Reform Commission, *Report on Non-Fatal Offences Against The Person*, (1997) 274. See also Hechter, "The Criminal Law and Violence in Sports" (1977) *Criminal Law Quarterly* 425.
[148] Gardiner, "Juridification of the Football Field: Strategies for Giving Law the Elbow", 5 *Marquette University Law Review* (1994–95) 188 at p.201.
[149] Grayson, "The Day Sport Dies", 138 *New Law Journal* (1988) 9. See also by the same author, "Foul Play", 141 *New Law Journal* (May 31, 1991) 742 and "Keeping Sport Alive", 140 *New Law Journal* (January 12, 1990) 12.
[150] 149 No.6887, *New Law Journal* (May 7, 1999) 665.

should a pub lout be prosecuted and not simply banned from the *Horse and Hound* for the rest of the month? The criminal law should not be suspended simply because someone is wearing a red and blue shirt and boots with studs as opposed to metal toecaps."

CHAPTER FIVE

Civil Liability and Sport

5.1 INTRODUCTION

In the last chapter we considered the relationship between the criminal law and the sports field. In this chapter,[1] we assess the role played by the law of torts in regulating the on field actions of a variety of persons engaged in sport, including players,[2] clubs,[3] referees,[4] spectators,[5] coaches[6] and sports

---

[1] Generally see Cox, "Civil Liability for Foul Play in Sport", 55 (4) *Northern Ireland Legal Quarterly* (Winter, 2003) p.351 [hereafter Cox], Kevan, Adamson and Cottrell, *Sports Personal Injury: Law and Practice* (Sweet & Maxwell, London, 2002) [hereafter Kevan *et al*], Beloff *et al*, *Sports Law* (Hart Publishing, 1998), p.111ff, Gardiner & Felix, "*Elliott v. Saunders*: Drama in Court 14", 2 (2) *Sport and the Law Bulletin* (1999) 1, Duff, "Civil Actions and Sporting Injuries", May 13, 1994 *New Law Journal*, 639, McCutcheon, "Sports Violence, Consent and the Criminal Law" [1994] *Northern Ireland Legal Quarterly*, 267 at p.283. McArdle, *Football, Society and the Law* (Cavendish, 2000), pp.260–270, Griffith Jones, *Law and The Business of Sport* (Butterworths, 1996) at Chapter 1, Barnes, p.269ff, Gardiner, *et al*, *Sports Law* (2nd ed., Cavendish, London, 2001) at p.693ff, and Moore, *Sports Law and Litigation* (2nd ed., CLT Professional Publishing, 2000), Chap.5.

[2] See *Brewer v. Delo* [1967] 1 Lloyd's Rep. 488, *Cleghorn v. Oldham* (1927) 43 T.L.R. 465, *Wooldridge v. Sumner* [1963] 2 Q.B. 43, *McComiskey v. McDermott* [1974] I.R. 75, *Condon v. Basi* [1985] 2 All E.R. 453, *Caldwell v. Maguire* [2001] E.W.C.A. Civ. 1054; [2001] I.S.L.R. 224, *Pitcher. v. Huddersfield Town FC*, Unreported, Queen's Bench, July 17, 2001. For American analysis see Laing, "Liability of Contact Sports Participants", 66 *Wisconsin Law Review* (1994) 12 and Lazaroff, "Tort and Sports; Participant Liability for Injuries Sustained During Competition", 7 *University of Miami Entertainment and Sports Law Review* (1990) 191.

[3] *Watson & Bradford City FC v. Gray & Huddersfield Town*, unreported, Queen's Bench, October 26, 1998, *McCord v. Swansea City FC*, unreported Queen's Bench, December 19, 1996.

[4] *Smoldon v. Whitworth*, unreported, Court of Appeal, December 17, 1996, *Vowles v. Evans & WRU* [2003] 1 W.L.R. 1607. See Bellamy, "Who would be a Referee? The Developing Legal Liability of Sports Referees" [2004] *International Sports Law Review* 9. For an example of an a situation in which a referee would surely have had a good cause of action see Murphy, "Referee Assaulted After Kerry Senior Club Game", *Irish Times*, September 8, 2003.

[5] *Callaghan v. Killarney Race Company Limited* [1958] I.R. 366, *Wooldridge v. Sumner* [1963] 2 Q.B. 43, *Wilks v. Cheltenham Home Guard Motor Cycle and Light Car Club* [1971] 2 All E.R. 369, *Payne & Payne v. Maple Leaf Gardens* [1949] 1 D.L.R. 369, *Karpow v. Shave* [1975] 2 W.W.R. 159.

[6] See Gardiner, "Should Coaches Take Care", 1 (1) *Sport and the Law Journal* (1993) 11.

teachers.[7] In the next chapter we shall assess the liability under tort law and statute of those hosting and organising sporting events.[8]

As with criminal prosecutions, there are remarkably few civil actions arising out of the playing of sport, for various reasons, most notably the fact that from the standpoint of many players, the traditional attitude has been that it was somehow unsporting to litigate in respect of an injury suffered in sport,[9] and also the fact that public policy concerns connected with the playing of sport mean that the fallibility of its exponents will be factored into any legal determination of what constitutes reasonable behaviour on the sports field.[10] Equally, just as the criminal law will be used to deal with those assaults which exceed the limits of toleration,[11] so also the civil law will step in where there have been trespasses to the person, or acts of negligence or nuisance leading to significant harm.[12] Very few such cases are taken on a trespass basis,[13]

---

[7] *Woodroffe-Hedley v. Cuthbertson*, unreported, Queen's Bench, June 20, 1997, *Morrell v. Owen* (see 1 (2) *Sport and the Law Journal* (1995) 5), *Brady v. Sunderland Association FC*, unreported, Court of Appeal, November 17, 1998, *Kane v. Kennedy*, unreported, High Court, March 25, 1999, *Ralph v. London County Council*, King's Bench, February 11, 1947, *Van Oppen v. Clerk to the Bedford Charity Trustees* [1989] 3 All E.R. 389, *A (a minor) v. Leeds City Council*, unreported Queen's Bench, March 2, 1999 (see 2 (3) *Sports Law Bulletin* (1999) 5).

[8] *Callaghan v. Killarney Race Company* Limited [1958] I.R. 366, Watson *v. BBBC* [2001] 2 W.L.R. 1256, *Murray v. Harringay Arena* [1951] 2 All E.R. 320, *Hall v. Brooklands Auto Racing Club* [1932] All E.R. 208.

[9] One view as to why there are not more civil actions arising out of sport is that "… legal action by a player. does not sit comfortably with the notion of sportsmanship." See Pickford, "Playing Dangerous Games" (1998) 6 *Tort Law Review* 221 at p.222.

[10] See Griffith-Jones, *Law and the Business of Sport* (Butterworths, London, 1997) [hereafter Griffith-Jones] at pp.3–4. Thus in the Canadian case *Agar v. Canning* (1965) 54 W.W.R. 302 (at 304) it was concluded that: "The conduct of a player in the heat of the game is instinctive and unpremeditated and should not be judged by standards suited to polite intercourse."

[11] See Beloff, *op. cit.* at p.130, Gardiner and James, "Touchlines and Guidelines: The Lord Advocate's Response to Sports Field Violence" [1997] *Criminal Law* Review 41, Miller, "Criminal Law and Sport in Scotland: The Lord Advocate's Instructions of 10 July 1996 to Chief Constables", 4 (2) *Sport and the Law* Journal (1996) 40 and "Prosecuting Sports Field Violence, a British Perspective", 7 (2) *Journal of Legal Aspects of Sport* (Spring 1997) 81, Anderson, "Violence, Sport and the Law: An Application to Gaelic Games", 7 (2) *Sport and the Law Journal* (1999) 51.

[12] Felix, "Sports Injuries and Civil Liability", 1 (1) *Sports Law Bulletin* (1998) 8.

[13] In *May v. Strong* [1991] B.P.I.L.S. 2274, the plaintiff was injured in a football match by a very late tackle from behind by the defendant. The court found that the recklessness of the defendant was so great that it amounted to an assault. See also *Rogers v. Bugden & Canterbury-Bankstown* (1993) A.T.R. 81. On the other hand, in *Parry v. Clucking*, unreported, High Court, March 22, 1990, where during a competitive local derby football match a player had committed a blatant foul on an opponent causing significant harm to the latter, the court felt that there was no doubt but that in tackling his opponent, the defendant had deliberately "gone for man and ball" and had set out to cause injury, yet the case was decided in negligence. See also *Leebody v. Ministry of Defence* (2001)

largely because of the rule at English law,[14] (which is now possibly replicated at Irish law)[15] that a trespass must be committed intentionally, and the consequent evidentiary problems that this rule poses for a plaintiff in a sports case.[16] Accordingly, it is an area dominated by the tort of negligence.

5.2 NEGLIGENCE AND CIVIL LIABILITY ON THE FIELD OF PLAY

Analysis on a negligence model throws up three important primary questions.

– First, in a sporting situation what duties of care arise, and what is the scope of these duties?

– Secondly, what is the standard of care to be expected in any such situation?

– Thirdly, what defences will be available to a sportsperson who falls below the requisite standard of care

5.2.1 Duty of care on the sports field

The concept of duty of care is, at its root, a legal device for restricting the extent of the liability which A may owe to B in any situation, by limiting both the number of persons to whom A owes a duty, and also the extent of the obligations that A owes to such persons.[17] In England, the tendency to approach questions of duty of care by reference to broad conceptual statements of principle[18] has been eschewed in favour of a more pragmatic incrementalist approach, whereby new categories of duty are assessed by analogy with existing

---

C.L.Y. 4544, *Hamish v. Smailes*, unreported, Epsom County Court, 1983 and in Australia *McNamara v. Duncan* [1971] 26 A.L.R. 584. Generally see Grayson, *Sport and the Law* (3rd ed., Butterworths, London, 2000), 279.

[14] *Letang v. Cooper.* [1965] 1 Q.B. 232.

[15] In Ireland the rule in *Letang v. Cooper* recently received some degree of judicial endorsement in the Irish High and Supreme Courts; *Devlin v. Roche* [2002] 2 I.L.R.M. 192. For analysis see Byrne & Binchy, *Annual Review of Irish Law 2001* (Roundhall Sweet & Maxwell, Dublin, 2002) at p.435.

[16] See Kevan, "Sports Injury Cases: Footballers, Referees and Schools" (2001) *Journal of Personal Injury Litigation* 138 at p.140. See however, *Lewis v. Brookshaw*, 120 *New Law Journal* (1970) 413. See McMahon & Binchy, *Law of Torts* (3rd ed., Butterworths, Dublin, 2000) [hereafter McMahon & Binchy] at Chap.22, McArdle, *op. cit.* at p.163 and Felix, "Sports Injuries and Civil Liability", 1 (1) *Sports Law Bulletin* (1998) 8.

[17] McMahon & Binchy, *op. cit.* at p.115.

[18] *Donoghue v. Stevenson* [1932] A.C. 562 *Anns v. Merton London Borough Council* [1978] A.C. 728, *Junior Books v. Veitchi* [1983] 1 A.C. 520. For analysis see Jones, *Textbook on Torts* (7th ed., Blackstone Press, 2001) at p.31ff, McMahon & Binchy, *op. cit.* at Chap.6 and Lunney & Oliphant, *Tort Law* (Oxford University Press, 2000), Chap.3.

categories.[19] In Ireland, on the other hand, the courts traditionally preferred a "general principle" approach to the question, [20] focusing on broad concepts of proximity and foreseeability as the building blocks of the duty of care – although recent developments seem to have altered this trend.[21]

On this basis, we may conclude that whereas all persons involved with sport owe and are owed duties of care, such duties will necessarily be restricted, *inter alia*, by reference to the extent to which one person may be taken to have assumed certain risks inherent in the game. In this respect we may further conclude that the relationship between participants in sport is based on a mutual assumption of the risks that are inherent to that sport. Thus if one player accidentally injures another while engaging in activity within the rules of a lawfully constituted sport (as for example where a rugby player tackles an opponent and accidentally breaks the latter's leg), there would be no question of his being sued,[22] because the injured party's participation in and thus assumption of the inherent risks of the game will mean that the tackler has no duty of care not to tackle his opponent. Alternatively, we may say that the tackler's actions, being within the rules of a lawful sport, are thereby perfectly reasonable – an argument which touches on the issue of standard of care, and which will be addressed shortly.[23] Nor is this the same as saying that the consent of the injured party is a defence in a tort action on which the tackler may rely (although it is). Rather it is a reason why the tackler is not in breach of any duty of care owed to an opponent in the first place.[24] Thus for example in

---

[19] *Governor of the Peabody Donation Fund v. Sir Lindsay Parkinson & Co Ltd* [1985] A.C. 210, *Leigh & Sillavan v. Aliakmon Shipping Co Ltd* [1986] A.C. 785, *Yuen Kun-Yeu v. AG of Hong Kong* [1987] 2 All E.R. 705, *Caparo Industries plc v. Dickman* [1990] 2 A.C. 605, *Murphy v. Brentwood District Council* [1991] 1 A.C. 398.

[20] The judgment that had provided the lead for virtually all subsequent case law in this area is that of McCarthy J. in the Supreme Court in *Ward v. McMaster* [1988] I.R. 337.

[21] In *Glencar Exploration plc & Andaman Resources plc v. Mayo County Council* [2002] 1 I.R. 84, Keane C.J. held that the judgement of McCarthy J. in *Ward v. McMaster* did not represent the position in respect of duty of care at Irish law, and suggested that an incrementalist approach of the kind favoured in the English courts should be adopted in Ireland. See Byrne & Binchy, *Annual Review of Irish Law 2001* (Roundhall Sweet & Maxwell, Dublin, 2002) at p.554ff. This approach was given some degree of support in *Fletcher v. Commissioner of Public Works* (February 21, 2003) [2003] I.E.S.C. 8; [2003] 1 I.R. 465.

[22] See for example *Feeney v. Lyall* [1991] S.L.T. 151, for the view that a golfer who drove the ball straight down the fairway was not in breach of duty to another golfer who had wandered onto the wrong fairway and was invisible to the defendant when playing his shot.

[23] For the view that issues pertaining to assumption or risk should be addressed by the language of standard rather than duty of care see Fleming, *The Law of Torts* (9th ed., LBC Information Services, Sydney, 1998), p.117.

[24] See Griffith-Jones, *op. cit.* at p.7 and, from an Australian perspective, Yeo, "Accepted Inherent Risks Among Sporting Participants", 9 *Tort Law Review* (2001) 114. See also *Murphy v. Steeplechase Amusement Co. Inc.*, 166 NE 173 (1929).

O'Reilly v. Nolan & Irish Amateur Boxing Association,[25] – a case in which one boxer sued *inter alia* his opponent for injuries caused during a boxing match – Judge Kenny in the Circuit Court rejected the claim, pointing out that in all sporting contests, and especially in a boxing match there was a risk that injury might occur. It would, he held, be very difficult to prove that such injuries derived from the negligence (or trespass) of the defendant and not the normal operation of the contest in question. Indeed in this respect, Judge Kenny further intimated that claims of this kind would be more appropriately resolved within the sports organisation structure than in the courts.

As we saw in the last chapter, it is, however, far from clear as to what precisely any player consents in any moment – and therefore precisely what risks [s]he may be taken to have assumed – particularly in a split second moment of a fast moving contact sport.[26] Specifically, there is uncertainty as to whether [s]he only consents to activity within the rules of the game, or whether [s]he also consents to activity, which, whereas it violates the rules of the game nonetheless is sufficiently common that it may be seen as coming within what has been defined in the last chapter as the "playing culture" thereof.[27] As far as civil liability is concerned, the English courts have tended to adopt a variant of the "playing culture" approach to consent, although this has led to somewhat unpredictable results. Thus in *Elliott v. Saunders,*[28] the court concluded that frequent or familiar infractions of the rules of a game were among the ordinary risks of the game accepted by all the participants, and hence that players owed each other no duty not to cause such infractions,[29] but that a player could not be taken to have consented to harmful actions from an opponent that are reckless or intentional, nor indeed those that are simply negligent in the face of a particularly obvious risk.[30]

In Ireland, the Supreme Court took this logic one step further in the case of *McComiskey v. McDermott,*[31] and created an individuated duty of care for

---

[25] Unreported, Galway Circuit Court, May 2, 2003. See "Boxer who Suffered Broken Jaw in the Ring Fails in Compensation Claim", *Connaught Tribune,* May 7, 2003.
[26] Yeo, "Accepted Inherent Risks Among Sporting Participants" (2001) *Tort Law Review* 114 and by the same author, "Determining Consent in Body Contact Sports" (1998) 6 *Tort Law Review* 199.
[27] See Yeo, "Accepted Inherent Risks Among Sporting Participants" (2001) 9 *Tort Law Review* 114, for the view that the only rules to whose violation one may be taken to have consented are playing rules. See also Cox, *op. cit.* at p.373 for the view that one may be taken to have consented to all rule violations save intentional infractions of safety rules underpinned by a motive unconnected to the playing of the sport.
[28] Unreported, Queen's Bench, June 10, 1994.
[29] McArdle, *op. cit.* at p.156.
[30] See *Bourque v. Duplechin* 334 So. 2d 210 (1976) LA, for the view that: "A participant does not assume the risk from fellow players acting in an unexpected or unsportsmanlike way with a reckless lack of concern for others participating." See also Drowatzky, "Assumption of Risk in Sport", 2 (1) *Journal of Legal Aspects of Sport* (1992) 92.
[31] [1974] I.R. 75

participants in sporting events.[32] At issue in this case was the question of whether a rally driver owed a duty of care to a co-participating passenger in the car, following an accident in which the plaintiff was injured. Here the driver had been driving in difficult circumstances consistent with a rally driving competition, along a muddy and narrow course – admittedly on a public road – at an average speed of thirty-five miles per hour. He turned a corner at speed and spotted an obstruction on the laneway ahead and downhill from where he then was. Realising that he could not stop he drove his car into a ditch, where it overturned causing injury to the plaintiff.[33] The plaintiff's claim in the case (which was accepted by Walsh J.) was that the driver owed the same duty to the plaintiff navigator as to any other driver on the road,[34] and whereas the consent to participation of the plaintiff in this case might be a defence to the claim under section 34 of the Civil Liability Act 1961, it could not affect the scope of the duty in the case.[35] Griffin and Henchy JJ. in the majority however, accepted the defendant's claim that, in all the circumstances of the event, this was not the correct test to apply but rather that:[36]

> "... The duty of care owed by the defendant to the plaintiff was to drive as carefully as a reasonably careful competitive rally-driver would be expected to drive in the prevailing circumstances."

It is not clear whether this analysis was peculiar to the sport in question, or whether a similarly tailored duty of care would apply for participants in all sports, or possibly all fast moving sports.[37]

5.2.3 Standard of care

The more usual way of explaining why most incidents where injury occurs on the sports field will not lead to civil liability, is to say that the action of the person causing the injury is not unreasonable. In other words, whereas he may owe a duty to the person whom he has injured, nonetheless he has not breached the standard of care. Irish courts tend not to differentiate particularly clearly

---

[32] McMahon & Binchy, *op. cit.*, pp.136–137. A similar test was created by Edmund Davies L.J. in *Wilks v. Cheltenham Home Guard Motor Cycle and Light Car Club* [1971] 2 All E.R. 369, when he referred to "a reasonable man of the sporting world".

[33] For a similar case in England, see *Stratton v. Hughes and Others*, unreported, Queen's Bench, February 28, 1997.

[34] On this see *Nettleship v. Weston* [1977] 2 Q.B. 691.

[35] [1974] I.R. 75 at 82.

[36] *Ibid.* at p.89.

[37] In *Frazer v. Johnston* (1990) 21 N.S.W.L.R. 89 at 94 the New South Wales Court of Appeal (in assessing standard of care) sad that the defendant in this case was required to act as would "... the reasonable man riding as a licensed jockey in a horse race".

between issues of duty and issues of standard of care, and in the sports situation, exactly the same factors that apply in respect of duty will apply in respect of standard. Thus the action of the sports person is reasonable in that he is pursuing a lawful activity that has known and inherent risks, and his opponent by voluntarily engaging in such activity has implicitly assumed such risks.[38]

In this respect, a somewhat academic question arises as to how the concerns of sport may be factored into standard of care analysis. Typically at Irish law, one is required to fulfil one's duty to another person by acting as would a reasonable person *in the circumstances* of the particular case.[39] In Canada[40] (or, uniquely in America in Wisconsin), where a similar approach is followed, the courts in practice have regard to a range of relevant circumstances[41] including:

– The sport involved – including the question of whether it is a contact or a non contact sport.

– The rules and regulations of that sport.

– The generally accepted customs and practices of the sport, including types of contact and level of violence generally accepted.

– Risks inherent in the game and those outside anticipation and the extent to which players may be taken to have assumed the same.

– Presence of protective equipment or uniforms.

– Facts and circumstances of the particular case, including the ages and physical attributes of the participants, as well as whether the accident is caused in the heat of the moment or in a quiet passage of play.

---

[38] See Felix, "The Standard of Care in Sport", 4 (1) *Sport and the Law Journal* (1996) 32, Toczek, "A Case of Foul Play", *New Law Journal* Vol. 152, No.7035, p.868 (June 7, 2002).

[39] Thus the court in *McComiskey* held (*per* Henchy J. at p.89) that, "the law of negligence lays down that the standard of care is that which is to be expected from a reasonably careful man in the circumstances. Because the particular circumstances dictate the degree of care required, decisions in other cases are frequently of little guidance."

[40] *Agar v. Canning* 54 W.W.R. 302 (1965), *Unruh v. Webber* 98 D.L.R. 4th 294 (Supreme Court, 1992) here the court said that the standard of care involved asking 'what would a reasonable competitor in his place do or not do?' In *Zapf v. Muscat* 11 B.C.L.R. 3d 296, the defendant was found liable in circumstances where he was deemed to be "at best careless and at worst reckless." See Moore, "Has Hockey been checked from Behind North of the Border?", 5 *Sports Lawyers' Journal* (1998) 1 (at p.20) for the view that the standard of care in these cases is deliberately set at a low level because of the presence of mandatory insurance but that such decisions represent a major threat to the future of Canadian amateur ice hockey.

[41] Yeo, "Accepted Inherent Risks Among Sporting Participants" at p.119. See also Beloff, *op. cit.* at p.114. Moore, "Has Hockey been checked from behind North of the Border?", 5 *Sports Lawyers' Journal* (1998) 1.

– Participants' respective skills.

– Participants' knowledge of the rules and customs.

– The costs and availability of precautions.[42]

Moreover, the notion of reasonableness may change over time, such that a tackle for example in a soccer match, which was perfectly normal twenty years ago might be regarded as grossly unreasonable today.[43]

   In England, the first application of this general tort standard to litigation involving two participants arose in the case of *Condon v. Basi*.[44] Here the plaintiff and defendant were on opposing teams in a soccer match. After 62 minutes the defendant attempted to tackle the plaintiff by sliding in from a distance of about three or four yards with his boot studs showing about 12–18 inches off the ground. This slide tackle was late, that is to say after the plaintiff had passed the ball, and as a result of it the plaintiff's leg was broken, and he sued the defendant for negligence. In a remarkably short judgement finding for the plaintiff, the Court of Appeal *per* Donaldson MR concluded that the player was required to act reasonably in circumstances that included the passion, speed and competitivity of an unpredictable contact sport, and that his conduct should be assessed, *inter alia*, by reference to the egregiousness of the breach of the safety rules of the sport that was involved.[45] Moreover, the court also suggested that the standard of care to be expected from a sports person would depend on the level at which the game was played, with "… a higher degree of care required of a player in a first division football match then of a player in a local league football match."[46] It has been suggested that this involves no more than application of the common law principle that the more skill a person possesses the higher the degree of care that can reasonably be expected of him.[47] Equally this conclusion ignores the fact that the skill of a footballer is not measured by his ability to avoid making rash challenges – something in respect of which all footballers of all levels should be competent. Moreover, as we shall see in our analysis of the rules pertaining to civil liability on the golf course, there is an argument that in fact the more skilled a player, the less foreseeable is the risk of his fouling an opponent during a challenge, and the

---

[42] Moore argues (*ibid.*,p. 24) that the drawbacks of this test include excessive verdicts, increased litigation and a chilling effect on participation in sport.

[43] Lewis & Taylor, *Sports Law and Practice* (Lexis Nexis, London, 2003), p.1031.

[44] [1985] 2 All E.R. 453, [1985] 1 W.L.R. 866. For analysis see McEwan, "Playing the Game; Negligence in Sport", 130 *Solicitors Journal* (1986) 581.

[45] See also *McNamara v. Duncan* [1979] 26 A.L.R. 584 at p.588.

[46] Alistair Duff, "Reasonable Care v. Reckless Disregard", 7 (1) *Sport and the Law Journal* (1999) 44. Generally see Pickford, "Playing Dangerous Games" (1998) 6 *Tort Law Review* 221.

[47] See Yeo, "Accepted Inherent Risks Among Sporting Participants" (2001) *Tort Law Review*, p.123.

duty of care to be expected of him will therefore be less than that expected of a lesser player. In any event, this distinction has been rejected in subsequent case law.

An alternative method of factoring the nature of sport into standard of care assessment is to apply a modified standard of care when dealing with such cases, and specifically to impose liability only where the sports person has acted with reckless disregard for the safety of another.[48] This is the standard of care used in sports cases in all but one American state, and had at one stage been used in English courts in actions taken by spectators against sports participants.[49] It is argued that it represents an appropriate balance between the legitimate claim of the severely injured plaintiff and the needs of competitive contact sport, which is fast and furious and often replete with split second acts of negligence.[50]

In the application of this test, recklessness tends to be assessed by reference to a range of factors, similar to those used when assessing whether the impugned action is reasonable in the circumstances, including whether the actions are part of the game, whether the incident occurred during the game and the manner in which play evolved, the rules of the sport and the interpretation of such rules.[51] Because of the similarity in the type of factors under consideration within the two tests, in practice the two tests will tend to deliver the same results.[52] Hence we are left with a frankly rather unimportant question as to whether the existing standard of care should be moulded to fit the reality of sport, or a new standard of care created specifically for sport. As we shall see the most recent decisions from the English courts merge the two, by saying that whereas one must act reasonably in the circumstances, nonetheless in practice, if one participant is to be found liable for injury caused to another, then as a matter of evidence, he will have to be shown to have acted recklessly.

Generally, in assessing whether a particular action or practice is reasonable in the circumstances, Irish courts have isolated a number of factors that are

---

[48] Felix, "The Standard of Care in Sport", 4 (1) *Sport and the Law Journal* (1996) 32, Alistair Duff, "Reasonable Care v. Reckless Disregard", 7 (1) *Sport and the Law Journal* (1999) 44, Duff, "Reasonable Care v. Reckless Disregard Revisited", 10 (2) *Sport and the Law Journal* (2002) 160 Narol, "Sports Participation Litigation; the Emerging Reckless Disregard Standard", 1 *Seton Hall Journal of Sports Law* (1991) 29, McArdle, *op. cit.* at p.162, and Felix, "Sports Injuries and Civil Liability", 1 (1) *Sports Law Bulletin* (1998) 8. This standard was also applied in English cases involving liability of participants for injuries to spectators.

[49] See *Wooldridge v. Sumner* [1963] 2 Q.B. 43, *Wilks v. Cheltenham Home Guard Motor Cycle and Light Car Club* [1971] 2 All E.R. 369.

[50] See *Oswald v. Township High School District*, 84 Ill App. 3d 723, 406 N.E 2d, 157. See McArdle, *op. cit.* at p.163

[51] Hanson and Dernis, "Revisiting Excessive Violence in the Professional Sporting Arena, Changes in the Past Twenty Years", 6 *Seton Hall Journal of Sports Law* (1996) 127.

[52] Narol, "Sports Participant's Litigation; The Emerging Reckless Disregard Standard", 1 *Seton Hall Journal of Sports Law* (1991) 29.

relevant, namely:[53]

- The probability of an accident, with the courts concluding that the higher the risk of an accident, the higher the standard of care that would be required.

- The gravity of the threatened injury, with again a higher standard required in a situation where the risk to any victim would be greater.

- The social utility of the defendant's behaviour, with the courts being prepared to require arguably a lower standard in a situation where the impugned action had a high degree of social utility.

- The cost of eliminating the risk. Thus if a situation is reasonably socially useful and the cost of eliminating the risk would be prohibitive, the courts will favour the action.

Application of these factors to the sporting situation, however, provides no clear answer to the question of when an action that causes injury may validly be regarded as unreasonable. Plainly the activity *is* one (particularly where we are dealing with a contact sport) where the probability of an accident – indeed a serious accident leading to grave injury – is high. On the other hand, the activity has undoubted social utility, and the unpredictable nature of competitive sport where there are inherent risks means that the cost of eliminating such risks would be enormous in social terms, for it would involve the complete dismantling of all contact sports and some non-contact sports.[54] In practice, however, and without prejudice to the fact that such cases will be decided very much on their specific facts, a number of rules of thumb used by the courts in assessing reasonableness have emerged from case law.

- First the courts will take into account the extent to which a player or referee had time to make a considered decision in respect of the impugned action. Thus courts will very rarely deem a split second error of judgement by *a player* in a fast moving contact sport to constitute negligence. On the other hand in *Vowles v. Evans*,[55] the Court of Appeal imposed liability on a referee in respect of a decision taken during a break in play, while holding that very different considerations would have arisen had the decision been taken during a passage of play.

- Secondly the courts assess the question of whether a plaintiff has acted

---

[53] See McMahon & Binchy, *op. cit.*, p.154ff.
[54] Gardiner and Felix, "*Elliott v. Saunders*: Drama in Court 14", 2 (2) *Sport and the Law Journal* (1994) 1 at 3 for the view that: "The appeal of contact sports ... comes from their unrestrained qualities, unpredictability, exploitation and sheer physicality. The involvement of the law and courts put these all at risk and would create a climate where players would shy away from physical contact."
[55] [2003] E.W.C.A. Civ. 318, [2003] All E.R. (D) 134.

reasonably towards a defendant by reference to the extent to which the latter can reasonably be expected to have been within the contemplation of the former. Thus the level of care expected of a referee towards a player is high – in that part of the job of the former is to apply rules aimed at protecting the latter,[56] the level of care expected of a player towards another player is less – as the primary concern of a player is with success in the playing of sport – and the level of care owed by a player to a spectator is less still, on the grounds that a spectator is removed from the immediate playing of the game and hence is likely to be outside the zone of contemplation of the player.

– Finally the fact that a player is playing within the rules or customs of the game (including for example the custom in golf that if your golf ball is heading for another player you warn them through shouting out "Fore!")[57] or the fact that a referee is applying the rules of the game properly, or the fact that a coach or teacher is adhering to a policy based on best practice will be strongly persuasive evidence either that he or she owed no duty to his fellow participants not to engage in a particular action or else that he or she was not in breach of any duty that might arise.[58] Thus as Beloff notes:[59]

> "The clear implication from *Condon v. Basi* is that in the case of contact sports such as football and rugby, it will be almost impossible to establish liability unless the actions of the defendants are outside the rules of the game. Indeed the Court of Appeal appeared to be saying that a breach of the rules is virtually a necessary, albeit not a sufficient requirement for liability to attach. ... Not every foul will constitute a tort; but something short of a foul will not do so."[60]

5.2.4 Defences

The two primary defences that might arise where someone is being sued for

---

[56] See *Smoldon v. Whitworth* (1997) E.L.R. 249, [1997] P.I.Q.R. 133.

[57] Lunney, "A Golfer Is Not A Gentleman", 6 (2) *Sport and the Law Journal* (1998) 4.

[58] In *Rootes v. Shelton* (at p.34) Barwick C.J. argued that adherence to the rules would be merely one circumstance to be considered in assessing both whether a duty of care existed in the circumstances and also whether the standard of care had been breached.

[59] See Beloff, *op. cit.*, at p.114 and Griffith-Jones, *op. cit.* at p.11. See also Yeo, *op. cit.*, "Accepted Inherent Risks Among Sporting Participants" at p.126, and *Gilsenan v. Gunning* (1982) 137 D.L.R. (3d) 252 for a conclusion in a skiing case that there was no negligence in the circumstances because the action was within what was deemed to be the "Customs of the Slopes."

[60] This approach is consistent with the Irish approach to medical negligence where the fact that a practice is widespread will suggest that it is also reasonable unless it was patently otherwise. See *Dunne v. National Maternity Hospital* [1989] I.R. 91 and generally McMahon & Binchy, *op. cit.*, p.363ff.

negligence on the sports field are those of contributory negligence and voluntary assumption of risk.

From an Irish perspective the impact on the sports field of the revised doctrine of contributory negligence under section 34 of the Civil Liability Act 1961 is as yet somewhat untested.[61] Equally, a distinction should be made between contributory negligence and simple assumption of risk. Thus whereas one assumes the risks inherent in participation in a dangerous sport, such participation does not render one negligent. In other words, if one participant in a sporting event is found to be negligent, he will not be able to claim that the simple participation of the injured party constituted contributory negligence.[62] Something more is required, in the shape of a negligent act by the injured party that actually helped to bring about the injury in question. Thus, for instance, the fact that a golfer is voluntarily present on a golf course will not constitute contributory negligence where another player negligently drives his ball and injures him, unless the injured party had been standing on the wrong fairway or in the line of play or had not paid due attention to what was going on around him.[63]

The defence of *volenti non fit injuria* – essentially a claim that the plaintiff consented to the infliction of the harm that he suffered – also underwent fundamental reconstruction in Ireland under the terms of the Civil Liability Act 1961, such that it may now be of virtually no value in a sporting context.[64] Under section 34 (1)(b) of the Act, the defence of *volenti* will only apply where the plaintiff agreed to waive his legal rights in respect of the act that caused the harm complained of. Moreover according to Walsh J. in *O'Hanlon v. ESB*,[65] such agreement involves,

> "Some sort of intercourse or communication between the plaintiff and the defendants from which it could reasonably be inferred that the plaintiff had assured the defendants that he waived any right of action he might have in respect of the negligence of the defendants."

Again this must be distinguished from simple assumption of risk, although there is an obvious link between the two concepts. Thus where there has been a negligent action by the defendant that causes harm, the plaintiff cannot be taken to have assumed the risk thereof by reason of his voluntary participation in the game, insofar as an opponent's negligence is not an inherent risk of the

---

[61] See McCaskey & Biedzynski, "A Guide to the Legal Liability of Coaches for a Sports Participant's Injuries", 6 *Seton Hall Journal of Sports Law* (1996) 7 at p.52.
[62] *Smoldon v. Whitworth* (1997) E.L.R. 249, [1997] P.I.Q.R. 133.
[63] *Feeney v. Lyall* [1991] S.L.T. 156 at 159. See Beloff, *op. cit.* at p.122.
[64] Yeo, *op. cit.*, "Accepted Inherent Risks Among Sporting Participants" at p.117.
[65] [1969] I.R. 75 at 91–2.

game.[66] Equally, neither will the plaintiff's participation in the sport in question activate the defence of *volenti*, unless there has been some express agreement that this should be the case.[67] Put simply, if a plaintiff is injured as a result of the nature of the game, then the person causing the harm is not negligent in the first place, and if he is injured as a result of the defendant's negligence, then absent express agreement, the volenti defence will not apply. The relative uselessness of the defence in this context has meant that many teams and coaches in the United States, for example, attempt to require players to sign releases (surrender for consideration of a right to sue), disclaimers (disavowal of future responsibility of the defendant) or other exculpatory agreements (where one party expressly agrees to accept a risk of harm arising from another's conduct). Equally such clauses have inevitably attracted suspicion on the part of those asked to sign them.[68]

In *McComiskey v. McDermott*, the car in which the parties were driving had a notice in its window which read "all passengers travel at their own risk." It was claimed that, because the plaintiff had voluntarily become a passenger in the car aware of this notice, the doctrine of *volenti non fit injuria* should apply. This suggestion was, however, rejected on the basis that the plaintiff was aware that when the car had been bought, the sign was already in it.[69] Nonetheless Griffin J. intimated that in an appropriate case, getting into a car where there was such a sign on the dashboard might entitle a defendant to invoke the *volenti* exception.[70] Nonetheless, it is submitted that the impact of the *volenti* doctrine on the sports field will be very limited[71] both in Ireland and also in England.[72]

---

[66] See Duff, "Reasonable Care v. Reckless Disregard", 7 (1) *Sport and the Law Journal* (1999) 44.

[67] For the view that the general reluctance of injured players to litigate may stem from a misunderstanding of the *volenti* doctrine see Duff, "Civil Actions and Sporting Injuries" (May 13, 1994) New *Law Journal* 639 and Grayson, *op. cit.* at p.30. See from a US viewpoint Drowatzky, "Assumption of Risk in Sport", 2 (1) *Journal of Legal Aspects of Sport* (1992) 92.

[68] See McCaskey & Biedzynski, "A Guide to the Legal Liability of Coaches for a Sports Participant's Injuries", 6 *Seton Hall Journal of Sports Law* (1996) 7 at 54, Vahrenwald, "Should Athletes sign waiver of liability forms?", 8 (5) *Entertainment Law Review* [1997] 158 and McArdle, *op. cit.*, p.165. Indeed in *Bacon v. White*, unreported Queen's Bench, May 21, 1988, the fact that a pupil had signed a contractual clause excluding liability was held not to defeat his claim.

[69] [1974] I.R. 75 at 87.

[70] *Ibid.*, p.94.

[71] Beloff, *op. cit.*, pp.122–124, Gardiner and Felix, "*Elliott v. Saunders*: Drama in Court 14", 2 (2) *Sport and the Law Journal* (1994) 3, Duff, "Reasonable Care versus Reckless Disregard", 7 (1) *Sport and the Law Journal* (1999) 44, McCaskey & Biedzynski, "A Guide to the Legal Liability of Coaches for a Sports Participant's Injuries", 6 *Seton Hall Journal of Sports Law* (1996) 7.

[72] (1997) E.L.R. 249 at 267. Generally see *Nettleship v. Weston* on this point.

5.2.5 Vicarious liability

Because clubs, or governing bodies or schools for example, will tend to have more resources than players or teachers or coaches, and indeed will in all probability have insurance policies covering such situations, they may be the more appropriate defendants in any action of this nature.[73] Equally, vicarious liability only applies in situations where the employee acts in the furtherance of his employment,[74] and it is likely that this will not cover instances where injury is intentionally inflicted in a manner that is utterly inconsistent with the playing of the game.[75] This may pose tactical problems for a club or governing body, who will face the choice between accepting vicarious liability for the negligence of an employee on the one hand and refusing such vicarious liability by claiming that the impugned action was intentional, thereby opening up their employee to the possibility both of a large bill for damages and also, possibly criminal liability on the other.[76]

Similarly it may well be the case that in the professional context, one participant may owe a duty of care not just to his opponent but also to that opponent's club. Thus in *Watson v. Gray*,[77] the defendant was sued not only by the player whose career was interrupted but also by his club, who claimed a violation of the tort of unlawful interference with contract. Equally in this case the plaintiff club accepted that in order to make out this particular tort, it would have to establish recklessness on the part of the defendant rather than mere negligence and its failure to do so resulted in its case failing.[78]

---

[73] Gardiner and Felix, "*Elliott v. Saunders*: Drama in Court 14", 2 (2) *Sport and the Law Journal* (1994) 3, Kevan *et al*, *op. cit.*, at p.13ff, Beloff, *op. cit.* at pp.128–129.

[74] *McCready v. Securicor* [1991] N.I. 229.

[75] *Watson & Bradford City FC v. Gray and Huddersfield Town*, unreported, Queen's Bench, October 26, 1998. Generally see Duff, "Civil Actions and Sporting Injuries" (May 13, 1994) *New Law Journal* 639 at 640.

[76] For analysis of this issue in the context of a potential legal action involving premiership soccer players Roy Keane and Alfe Inge Haaland and their employers Manchester United and Manchester City, see Cox at p.366 and Taylor, "Can't Get Roy Out Of His Head", *Guardian*, December 13, 2003.

[77] Unreported, Queen's Bench, October 26, 1998. See case note at 1 (6) *Sports Law Bulletin* (1998) 3 and also 2 (1) *Sports Law Bulletin* (1995) 5. See also Levinson, "Foul! Tackling the Problem of Violence in Sport" (November/December 1998) *Sports Law Administration and Practice* 7.

[78] See Kevan, "Sports Injury Cases: Footballers, Referees and Schools" (2001) *Journal of Personal Injury Litigation* 13 at pp.142–143.

5.3. Liability of Sports Participants for Negligence on the Sports Field

All sorts of persons connected with the playing of sport therefore will owe duties of care to each other requiring them to act reasonably in the circumstances.[79] What follows is an examination of the various relationships involved and the nature of the duties that arise. Specifically we will consider:

– The duties of one participant in contact and non-contact sport to fellow participants.

– The duties of participants to spectators.

– The duties of referees to players.

– The duties of coaches and school teachers to players.

– The duties of governing bodies to players.

There are of course other types of duty that arise – notably those of organisers of sporting events and occupiers of sports stadia, but these will be considered in the next chapter.

5.3.1 Duties of participants in contact sports[80]

Following *Condon v. Basi* the next major English case involving inter-participant duties is *Elliott v. Saunders*.[81] During a major English soccer match, Paul Elliott then of Chelsea FC, and Dean Saunders then of Liverpool FC, were challenging for a fifty-fifty ball on the halfway line. Elliott dived in with a flying tackle, hoping to divert the ball away, and a split second later, Saunders, in his attempt to intercept the ball, caught Elliott on the side of his knee, severing the latter's cruciate ligaments and ending his career. Elliott claimed that Saunders deliberately stamped on him, and Saunders claimed that it was Elliott's tackle that was dangerous and that he was merely acting in self defence.

---

[79] See Grayson, *op. cit.* at p.190 for the view that: "School teachers, club coaches and both amateur and professional players ... education authorities, clubs, governing bodies and promoters and entrepreneurs are subject to identical responsibilities ... and all are subject to liability under the criminal law."

[80] Generally see Kevan, Adamson and Cottrell, *Sports Personal Injury: Law and Practice* (Sweet & Maxwell, London, 2002), Chap.3, Gardiner *et al*, *Sports Law* (2nd ed., Cavendish, London, 2001) at p.694ff and Griffith Jones, *Law and The Business of Sport* (Butterworths, 1997), Chap.1.

[81] Unreported, Queen's Bench, June 10, 1994. See Gardiner *et al*, *Sports Law* (2nd ed., Cavendish, London, 2001) at p.699, Gardiner & Felix, "*Elliott v. Saunders*, Drama in Court 14", 2 (2) *Sports Law Journal* (1994) 3, and Felix, "The Standard of Care in Sport", 4 (1) *Sport and the Law Journal* (1996) 32.

The case is illustrative of the difficulty in establishing liability in respect of a split second incident occurring during the playing of a fast moving sport. A great deal of video evidence (rejected by Drake J. as being too two dimensional), and competing expert testimony was presented to the court, however, as far as the judge was concerned, the determinative factor was that the match referee had responded to the incident by giving a free kick *against Elliott*. Drake J. was simply unprepared to override the referee's decision on the basis of the additional evidence presented before him in the court. Equally, he rejected the proposition, suggested in *Condon v. Basi*, that the standard of care would be different at different levels of sport, concluding that the question of whether a particular foul gave rise to liability was a matter to be decided in all the circumstances of a particular case.[82] Most importantly, it was stressed that a simple mistake by a player, even one that caused serious injury would not ground liability. Rather the action would have to be so outrageously negligent that it blatantly exposed the opponent to the risk of injury. The court resisted the temptation to elevate the threshold of standard of care to the level of reckless disregard for the safety of another. As a matter of evidence, however, the strong likelihood is that absent a finding that in practice the player acted recklessly, there would not even be a finding of negligence.

A radically different approach was taken by the English High Court in *McCord v. Swansea Football Club*,[83] where a professional footballer recovered damages (for the first time in an English court) in respect of injury sustained in an "on-the-ball" incident. Here the plaintiff (a 24 year old professional soccer player with Stockport County) and the second named defendant were involved in a fifty-fifty ball situation; the plaintiff got to the ball a fraction sooner than the second named defendant (measured at one fiftieth of a second) and struck it, whereupon the second defendant's right foot struck the plaintiff's right calf breaking both his bones, causing him considerable pain and ending his career. The court was once again subjected to a good deal of conflicting testimony from experts, witnesses and players, and video evidence, which again was resisted. Kennedy J. found as a matter of fact that the plaintiff had been guilty of a "serious mistake or misjudgment."[84] This in itself is uncontroversial. More significantly the court concluded as a matter of law that that even when allowance was made for the nature of the sport at issue, by making a mistake of this nature, the defendant was also negligent.

Kennedy J. was keen to point out that this was an exceptional case and that most injuries caused by foul play on a sports field would not be the subject of successful litigation – although the force of such a proposition was somewhat

---

[82] Unreported, Queen's Bench, June 10, 1994 at p.5 of the transcript.

[83] Unreported, Queen's Bench, December 19, 1996. For analysis see note at 5 (1) *Sport and the Law Journal* (1997) 5 and Kitson, "On-Field Litigation" (March/April 1997) *Sports Law Administration and Practice* 7.

[84] *Ibid*. at p.10 of the transcript.

undermined by the fact that he had previously accepted that as a matter of fact mistakes of this kind occurred routinely on sports fields, even though they did not always result in injury of this nature.[85] The move away from the approach in *Elliott v. Saunders* is thus obvious. Where the court in the latter case required (in essence) an act of recklessness on the part of the defendant if there was to be a finding of negligence, the court in *McCord v. Swansea* was prepared to make such a finding in respect of a mistake that occurred so regularly that it could be regarded as inherent in the game.

This change in approach was continued in *Watson v. Gray*,[86] where the High Court, *per* Hooper J., in a judgment upheld by the Court of Appeal, again imposed liability for a late tackle during a soccer match. Here the plaintiff had been tackled by the defendant and had suffered a "career interrupting" though not a "career ending" injury. The tackle in question was a split second late, but was nonetheless seen as dangerous being "forceful and high." As a result of the tackle the defendant was 'yellow carded', but giving testimony afterwards, the referee in the game accepted that he should have been sent off. The court (which was more amenable to the use of video evidence than it had been in the above cases) found that the defendant *had* acted negligently and imposed liability as a result. Interestingly, however, in dismissing the action brought against the defendant by the plaintiff's employers, the court also concluded that the tackle that had injured the plaintiff could not be seen as being *excessively* negligent.

Liability was also imposed for a simple breach of safety rules in *Leatherland v. Edwards*,[87] a case involving uni-hockey (a game played on a small tarmac pitch at a very fast pace, and with a fundamental rule that the ball should not rise above the ground and that sticks should not go above waist height). In this case the plaintiff was hit in the eye by the defendant's stick when the latter raised it dangerously high. The defence claimed that whereas the action was a violation of the rules of the game it did not amount to negligence in the legal sense. The court disagreed and found that there had been a serious and dangerous breach of a safety rule of the sport, in a situation where it was reasonably foreseeable that such a breach would cause serious injury.

More recently, however, the courts appear to have moved back closer to

---

[85] *Ibid.*
[86] Unreported, Queen's Bench, October 26, 1998. See Jan Levinson, "Foul! Tackling the Problem of Violence in Sport" (November/December 1998) *Sports Law Administration and Practice* 7. This principle was further carried through in *Riddle v. Thaler* (See 1 (1) *Sports Law Bulletin* (1998) 3.) where the defendant – a former Great Britain rugby league scrum half – was ordered to pay in excess of £4,000 in damages and £20,000 in costs for breaking the jaw of an opponent while tackling him in a manner which would not be particularly unusual in rugby matches (he had been acquitted on a criminal charge).
[87] Unreported, Queen's Bench, October 28, 1998. See 2 (1) *Sports Law Bulletin* (1999) 5.

the position taken in *Elliott v. Saunders*. In *Caldwell v. Maguire & Fitzgerald*,[88] the appellant was former professional jockey Peter Caldwell who had been injured while riding in a two-mile novice hurdle race at Hexham. The two defendants plus a fourth jockey, Derek Byrne, had been leading the field after the second last hurdle of the race. Approaching a left hand bend, the two defendants took a line that allowed no room for Mr. Byrne's horse – behaviour that would typically constitute careless racing. In order to avoid a collision, Mr. Byrne's horse veered sharply to the right and into the line taken by Peter Caldwell's horse. As a result, Mr. Caldwell was brought to the ground and suffered a career ending injury.

The Court of Appeal accepted that the activities of the defendants constituted careless riding[89] – indeed they had been suspended for three days following a stewards' inquiry. It refused to conclude, however, that such carelessness could of itself generate legal liability, approving the conclusion of the High Court judge, that in order to establish breach of duty, the plaintiff would essentially have to show reckless disregard on the part of the defendants, (with such reference to the notion of *reckless* disregard representing not a statement of legal principle, but merely an indication of the practicalities of the evidential burden in the case).[90]

The Court of Appeal took a contrary view to that adopted in the *McCord* and *Watson* cases, concluding that it was not possible to characterise as negligence, "momentary carelessness," "error of judgement," "oversight" or "a lapse which any participant might be guilty of in the context of a race of this kind." Indeed where the court in *McCord* used the regularity of the occurrence of such an incident as a reason why other players should not stand in some sort of moral judgment over the defendant in the case, here the court regarded such regularity of occurrence as indicating that such incidents were a constituent element of "all the circumstances of the case" from which both the duty and the standard of care might be judged. Thus Judge L.J. concluded that "accidents and the risk of injury, sometimes catastrophic, both to horses and jockeys are an inevitable concomitant of every horse race" and the mere fact that horse is ridden in the breach of the rules of racing does not *per se* establish liability.

A similar logic was adopted in *Pitcher v. Huddersfield Town Football Club*.[91] Here, during a professional soccer match, the plaintiff and the second named defendant were running together for a ball, towards the first named defendants team goal, with the plaintiff slightly in front of and to the left of the defendant. The plaintiff passed the ball and a split second later (measured at

---

[88] [2001] E.W.C.A. Civ. 1054, [2001] *International Sports Law Review* 224. For a similar case in Australia see *Johnston v. Frazer* (1990) 21 N.S.W.L.R. 89.
[89] *Ibid.* at para.33.
[90] *Ibid.* at para.11.
[91] Unreported, Queen's Bench, July 17, 2001.

0.2 of a second) the defendant "lunged" at him with his left leg and struck him on the outside of his right knee, causing an injury so serous that he could no longer play professional football. Once again, the court heard evidence from a wide range of expert witnesses, but here it refused to find the defendant liable, concluding that:[92]

> "Mistimed tackles do occur; players do make contact with other players without reaching the ball. If they do and the referee sees it, it will lead to a free kick. The rules are designed to discourage late tackles. They are, however, a common feature of the game and they do not lead automatically to a sending off. There must be something more [to generate legal liability] … I am satisfied this was not something more; this was a misjudged attempt to get to the ball … I am not prepared to say on the balance of probabilities that this tackle was anything more than an error of judgement nor am I prepared to find that [the defendant] was guilty of negligence."

At present then, the approach taken in *Caldwell v. Maguire* represents the manner in which the English courts balance the operation of tort law with the specific concerns of sport.[93] Should an equivalent case arise in Ireland, it is desirable that such an approach is taken. The mistakes and misjudgments that generated civil liability in *McCord v. Swansea* and *Watson v. Gray* occur so routinely in various different kinds of sport that they may properly be regarded as inherent risks of the game, assumed by the plaintiff and therefore not properly the subject of a civil action. Imposing liability in respect of such acts would impose so onerous a duty on participants in unpredictable contact sports that the essence of those sports would be lost. Indeed it has been argued that from an Irish standpoint, the civil law should only step in where the defendant has intentionally breached a safety rule of sport motivated by concerns outside the simple playing of the sport (for example where, in effecting a tackle in a soccer match, the evidence indicates that the tackler "took man and ball"), and that in such circumstances the plaintiff should proceed by way of the tort of battery and not the tort of negligence.[94] There is indeed some limited Irish authority that this is in fact the position at Irish law.[95] This is also the blueprint that we

---

[92] *Ibid.* at p.22 of the transcript.

[93] In *Gaynor v. Blackpool FC* [2002] 7 C.L. 432, a county court imposed liability on a player for a reckless tackle that broke the plaintiff's leg. The court expressly followed the precedent in *Caldwell v. Maguire*, but it is submitted that its decision sits uneasily with that precedent, and may be of limited legal authority. See Ryan, "Winner all Right? Liability in Tort for Injury in Sport", 6 *Trinity College Law Review* (2003) 155.

[94] See Cox, *op. cit.* at p.373ff.

[95] In *Brady v. McMahon* (Decision of the Master of the High Court, December 12, 2002) in the context of an application for discovery in a civil action for an injury occasioned on the field of play, the Master of the High Court appeared to endorse this approach holding that:

have suggested as appropriate in determining when the *criminal* law should regulate actions on the field of play.

5.3.2 Duties of participants in non-contact sports – the game of golf

In theory a participant in a non-contact sport also owes a duty to fellow participants to act reasonably in the circumstances. In non-contact sports, however, the general rule of thumb that one will not be deemed to be negligent unless one has breached the rules of the game is more difficult to sustain. Nowhere is this more evident than in respect of the game of golf[96] – largely because unlike contact sports where there are playing rules and safety rules and violation of the latter rather than the former is virtually a pre-requisite to legal liability, in golf the rules of the game are exclusively playing rules. It may be suggested that this is for two reasons. First, because the safety norms of golf are contained in a detailed code of etiquette attached to the rules, and secondly, because the nature of the game is such that rules of themselves are not capable of securing the safety of players. It is impossible for any golfer, no matter how good, to be 100% certain of the precise direction in which his or her (lethally hard) golf ball will travel in when struck. Thus the fact that this hazardous activity is played in a relatively confined space typically with people within the distance that one might hit a ball right or left of a given target, means that virtually every time any golfer plays a shot (provided that he is not alone on the course) there is a risk of injury to another person. Minimizing the risks involved requires such a careful application of experience and common sense in any situation, that the imposition of blunt instruments like rules would be pointless.[97]

The golf course also poses particular conceptual problems as far as the law of torts is concerned. After all, the fact that players are engaged in an activity that carries omnipresent risks of injury should typically mean that they owe an onerous duty in respect of such activity. Yet the fact that all participants voluntarily take part in an activity of this nature would also suggest that they may be taken to have assumed the inherent risks of the same. The response of

---

"In cases involving sporting injuries, I would suggest that the man in the street would judge that all players know and accept the risk of sporting injuries up to and including so-called professional fouls. ... The same cannot be said of an on pitch *assault* (emphasis added), Of course the assaulter is liable."

The precise impact of this decision remains uncertain, especially as the Master did not refer to any decided case law in making his decision. For analysis see Cox, "Sports Law" in Byrne & Binchy, *Annual Review of Irish Law 2002* (Round Hall Sweet & Maxwell, Dublin, 2003).

[96] See for example, Williamson, "Some Legal Aspects of Golf", 3 (1) *Sports Law Journal* (1995) 9. and Lunney, "A Golfer is Not a Gentleman", 6 (2) *Sport and the Law Journal* (1998) 4.

[97] Generally see Murdoch, "Tigerland", *Law Society Gazette* (May 2003), 8.

the law has been to say that a player will never be negligent in respect of an error, however grievous in the playing of the shot *per se*.[98] Rather for liability to arise there must be some separate negligent behaviour connected with the shot. Such negligence will tend to exist in three categories of circumstances:

- First where a player played his shot when he ought not to have done because of the risk to players in the immediate vicinity, which his shot presented.

- Secondly where a player played his shot without exercising due care and attention to what was going on around him at the time.[99]

- Third where a player failed to alert persons in the vicinity either before playing or when the ball was in flight, to the fact that they were in danger.[100]

When then will a player's conduct be deemed to have fallen into any of these categories of negligence? Plainly the issue cannot turn on the foreseeability of risk alone, in that as we have said, in theory every time any player hits a shot then there is a risk of injury to others, yet if players were required to wait until there was no other player in the vicinity before playing their shots then the game would taken even longer than it currently does. In America, the approach of the courts has been to look to what is termed the "foreseeable zone of danger" posed by any shot, such that if another participant is within that zone, then at the very least, the player is obliged to warn him or her (in advance) of his intention to hit the ball.[101] The problem with this approach, however, is that because *all* golfers of whatever level of ability are capable of bizarre errors, the entire course is ultimately a foreseeable zone of danger.

A preferable approach, therefore, involves close analysis of the specific circumstances of any individual shot to see whether, in those circumstances, the risk of injury to others was not just foreseeable, but also sufficiently significant that the shot should not have been played at all or the player should have issued a warning to people around him.[102] Thus in *Brewer v. Delo*,[103] the

---

[98] *Clark v. Welsh*, 1975 (4) S.A. 469, 1976 (3) S.A. 484.

[99] In *Cleghorn v. Oldham* [1927] 43 T.L.R. 465, the defendant golfer was taking a practice swing on the tee when he accidentally struck his caddie causing injury. The court held that there was negligence in the circumstances.

[100] Lunney, "A Golfer is Not a Gentleman", 6 (2) *Sport and the Law Journal* (1998) 16.

[101] *Jenks v. McGranaghan*, 285 N.E. 2d. 876 (N.Y., 1972). See for example, Vieira, "Fore May be Just Par for the Course", 4 *Seton Hall Journal of Sports Law* (1994) 181, Tonner, Sawyer & Hypes, "Legal Issues in Golf; A 25 year Litigation History", 9(2) *Journal of Legal Aspects of Sport* (1999) 125–149, Lang, "Lawsuits on the Links", 72 (6) *New York State Bar Association Journal* (2000) 4.

[102] In *Noade v. Teague*, Queen's Bench 1 March, 2001 [2001] B.N.I.L. No. 143 (noted at 9 (3) *Sport and the Law Journal* (2001) 49), a low handicap golfer whose shot had hit off a decorative stone some five yards from the tee and had rebounded hitting the plaintiff was found not to have acted negligently in teeing up his shot in line with the stones. An expert witness and professional golfer called for the defence claimed that whereas it would have been dangerous to have lined up the ball in this fashion if the stones were two yards from the tee, the risk of the danger in this case could legitimately be overlooked.

defendant was found not to have been negligent in playing a shot without shouting a warning to the plaintiff who was standing some two hundred yards away, on the grounds that a reasonable person would not foresee that the action of driving the ball in such circumstances could cause harm. Similarly in *Ellison v. Rogers*,[104] the defendant golfer was described as a "persistent slicer," that is to say that his shots inevitably went to the right of his intended target. The plaintiff was playing an adjoining hole to the left of that which the defendant was playing. Expecting his usual slice, the defendant drove off the tee, without warning the plaintiff, but inexplicably he hooked the ball (causing it to turn sharply to the left of the intended line of play), and it struck the plaintiff in the eye. The plaintiff lost his action for negligence, with the court concluding that because it was unknown for the defendant to hook the ball, therefore the (admittedly foreseeable) foreseeable risk to the plaintiff was sufficiently remote that it could legitimately be ignored.

The most important factor in determining whether a golfer acted reasonably in playing a particular shot with or without giving warning to persons in the vicinity, is whether it could reasonably be anticipated that he would be able to play the shot safely. This is not to say that "the worse the golfer the higher the risk that he or she will cause injury," as has been suggested.[105] Some "bad golfers" after all pose no risk to others on the course in that they are unable to hit the ball long distances (or indeed at all). The pivotal issue is instead whether the golfer in question would normally be expected to play the shot in such a manner that there is no risk of his or her ball causing injury to another.[106] Most obviously this will relate to his or her tendency to hit the ball straight, in that a golfer who is incapable of hitting the ball straight will clearly pose a graver threat to other golfers in the vicinity than a golfer who hits the ball straight 99% of the time. It is true that both golfers may on any particular occasion make an error and hit the ball right or left injuring another golfer, but for the "wild" golfer, the fact that he habitually does so means that the risk in his case is not merely foreseeable but also sufficiently pressing that he will be under a duty either to wait or to warn.

In *Lewis v. Buckpool Golf Club*,[107] a golfer of very limited ability stood on the fifth tee of his course, and despite seeing another player in the vicinity, decided to drive the ball.[108] He mis-hit the ball, "shanking" it at an angle of

---

[103] [1967] 1 Lloyd's Rep. 488.
[104] (1967) D.L.R. 2152.
[105] *Lewis v. Buckpool* [1993] S.L.T. 43.
[106] In *Bolton v. Stone* [1951] 1 All E.R. 1078, the House of Lords ruled that a foreseeable risk could be ignored if it was also sufficiently unlikely to come to fruition.
[107] [1993] S.L.T. 43. See Beloff, *op. cit.* at p.115 and Griffith Jones, *op. cit.* at p.13. For a similar case, see *Bidwell v. Parks*, reported at p.279 in Grayson, *op. cit.*
[108] Beloff, *op. cit.* at p.115, Williamson, "Some Legal Aspects of Golf", 3 (1) *Sport and the Law Journal* (1995) 9.

thirty degrees, and it hit the other player who was injured as a result. The court held that injury to the other golfer was something that a reasonable golfer would have in his contemplation. Moreover, according to the court, the fact that the defendant did not foresee the damage that might be caused was irrelevant, because his lack of ability meant that he should have foreseen it as something that was not trivial enough to be legitimately ignored.[109]

Similarly in *Pearson v. Lightening*,[110] the defendant golfer had shanked his drive into rough to the right of his fairway[111] The plaintiff was playing another hole that ran parallel to, but was played in the opposite direction to the hole the defendant was playing, and he had driven his ball into rough on the right of *his* fairway. Accordingly the two were standing reasonably close to each other (approximately ninety yards apart). There was a bush about thirty yards from the defendant and in his direct line to the green. He attempted to hit the ball over the bush – a shot of no little difficulty given that he was not a good player and his ball was lying in long grass. The ball deflected off the top of the bush and hit the plaintiff (despite the warning shout from the defendant) who was seriously injured. In giving judgement for the plaintiff, the Court of Appeal held that given the difficulty of the shot, the proximity of the plaintiff and the lack of golfing expertise of the defendant, the defendant owed a duty to the plaintiff in the playing of the shot and had been negligent in the circumstances.

On the other hand, in *Feeney v. Lyall*,[112] the defendant was a good golfer who routinely drove the ball straight and in excess of 300 yards. On this occasion his drive hit another player who had wandered onto the wrong fairway and was hidden from the defendant's view about 275 yards down the course. The court found the golfer not to be negligent in that the plaintiff was not visible from the tee and the shot was a perfectly reasonable one for a golfer of this level to play.[113] Interestingly, the court also said that if there *had* been negligence, then it would also have found 25% contributory negligence on the part of the plaintiff.[114]

---

[109] The plaintiff also sued the club for negligent construction of the course but was unsuccessful in his action. Williamson, *op. cit.* at p.11 suggests that if the plaintiff golfer had been aware of how bad the other golfer was, yet took no steps to protect himself, this might have amounted to contributory negligence.

[110] Unreported, Court of Appeal, April 1, 1998. See note in 1 (3) *Sports Law Bulletin* (1998) 3.

[111] Lunney, "A Golfer is Not a Gentleman", 6 (2) *Sport and the Law Journal* (1998) 4. See also a report in (May/June 1998) *Sports Law Administration and Practice* 12.

[112] [1991] S.L.T. 156. See Beloff, *op. cit.*, p.115.

[113] Williamson, "Some Legal Aspects of Golf", 3 (1) *Sport and the Law Journal* (1995) 9.

[114] Beloff, p.122. See also "A Golfer is Not a Gentleman", 6 (2) *Sport and the Law Journal* (1998) 4. Lunney suggests that (pp. 11–12) liability may or may not arise in a situation where a slow group of golfers call through another group and a member of the former, unaware of this development is hit by the ball of a member of the latter.

The conclusion therefore is that golfers should be aware of their limitations and prepared to take necessary remedial actions where such limitations pose pressing (rather than merely foreseeable) risks to other golfers. Such remedial actions include delaying one's shot until other players are no longer in the vicinity, alerting them before playing, or shouting a warning when one's ball is in flight and heading in their direction. Which of these measures should be taken is a question to be answered by the application of that kind of experience and common sense, which prioritises the well being of others.

This approach generates two major practical difficulties. First, if golfers (and especially bad or "wild" golfers) were required to wait over every shot until anyone within range of a spectacularly mis-hit shot of which the golfer was capable had moved, then a round of golf could take days rather than hours to complete and the enjoyment connected with the game could be severely limited.[115] Secondly, as Williamson notes this legal requirement is unrealistic for it:

> "… involves a degree of self-assessment and I would suggest, self-criticism which is well above the ability of the average golfer, the man who is consistently saying to himself despite being many shots over par, "If I merely finish with 5s I will break one hundred"… [such a golfer] is unlikely to have in immediate contemplation hitting someone substantially out of the intended line of fire."[116]

Beyond acting within one's limitations, it may also be concluded that if a golfer acts in clear breach of a rule of etiquette designed to protect other players (as distinct from a rule of etiquette concerned with courtesy), he is in breach of a duty owed to them. This occurs most obviously where he plays his shot before other golfers ahead of him and on the same hole are out of his range. Thus for example in *Horton v. Jackson*,[117] the defendant golfer played a shot off a tee without looking up to check his intended line of play. Another golfer had overshot the green of a hole in the vicinity of that played by the defendant and hence was directly in the line of the defendant's ball (and about twenty five yards from the defendant) when the latter played his shot. He was seriously injured when struck by the defendant's ball, and recovered some £24,000 in damages, on the grounds that by playing without looking up to check his intended line of play the defendant had violated a safety rule of etiquette and accordingly had acted negligently.

Finally, it may be possible that an individual golfer owes a duty of care to a party who is in a geographical area *adjoining* the golf course, and who is

---

[115] "A Golfer is Not a Gentleman", 6 (2) *Sport and the Law Journal* (1998) 4.

[116] Williamson, *op. cit.* at p.11.

[117] February 28, 1996. See Lunney, "A Golfer is Not a Gentleman", 6 (2) *Sport and the Law Journal* (1998) 4 at 10.

injured either in person or in property by a golf ball that is hit out of bounds.[118] Plainly in such a case the plaintiff passer-by cannot be taken to have assumed the risks of the game in the same way as someone on the golf course. Equally as we shall see in the next chapter, in such circumstances, the proper defendant to a negligence action will generally be the golf club (rather than the individual golfer) and in respect of a defective course design.[119]

5.3.3 Duties of participants to spectators[120]

The majority of claims taken by spectators injured during the course of a sporting event will be against the organiser(s) of the events or the occupier of the premises in which it occurred and these shall be considered in the next chapter. We shall now briefly consider the extent of the duty of a player to a spectator.

In Ireland, the issue was discussed in *Donaldson v. Irish Motor Racing Club & Thompson*.[121] During a motor race at the Curragh road racing circuit, (organised by the first defendant), the driver of one of the cars attempted to pass another car, and swerved off the track and into the crowd killing a number of spectators. The plaintiff – a relative of one of the dead spectators – sued both the organisers and the owner of the car – the latter in respect of the alleged negligence of the driver. The Supreme Court rejected the possibility of negligence on the part of the *organisers* but accepted that it was possible that a jury might deem the action of the *driver* to be negligent and hence allowed the matter to proceed to trial. Indeed the court seemed to attach little significance to the fact that the incident arose during a sporting fixture, appearing to regard the driver in question as if he were simply any road user. Admittedly, however, the court was merely looking to whether there had been a prima facie breach of duty in this case. Moreover, the decision in *McComiskey v. McDermott* indicates clearly that at Irish law, a car race *is* regarded as presenting unique circumstances as far as duty and standard of care is concerned.

---

[118] *Lamond v. Glasgow Corporation* [1968] S.L.T. 291.
[119] In January 2001, a Turkish national was struck by a golf ball while sitting on a wooden bench, which was ten yards to the right of the 18th tee of Greenore Golf Club, Co. Louth. The case settled with Mr. Sahin being awarded IR£250,000 in damages. Significantly, the judge in the case divided liability on a 50–50 basis between the defendant golfer and the golf club. As a result of the decision, the Golfing Union of Ireland issued a recommendation that all its members carry a personal injury insurance policy. See Cox & Costello, *Sports Law*, at p.551 in Byrne and Binchy ed. *Annual Review of Irish Law 2001* (Roundhall Sweet & Maxwell, Dublin, 2002).
[120] See for instance Fitzgerald, "The Liability of Professional Athletes and Team Owners to Spectators", 3 (1) *Journal of Legal Aspects of Sport* (1993) 2.
[121] See McMahon & Binchy, *Casebook on the Irish Law of Torts*, First Edition (Professional Books, 1983) 220.

A fuller analysis of the relevant issues was given in the English case of *Wooldridge v. Sumner*.[122] Here, during a horse show, an experienced rider was galloping his horse around a corner of the competition arena. About two feet away from the edge of the competition arena there were some tubs and beyond this there were some benches. Surrounding the arena and behind the tubs and benches was a cinder track. A film cameraman was standing about twenty five yards from the corner, beside one of the benches, despite having been told by one of the stewards to move out of the competition arena. The rider brought his horse too fast into the corner, it went behind the tubs and collided with the plaintiff who was injured. The plaintiff sued the owner of the horse for negligence (not being a paying spectator he had no contract based action), and was successful at first instance. On appeal, the decision was reversed. Lord Diplock pointed out that a spectator attending a game or competition assumes the risks inherent in the same, including the risk of errors of judgement on the part of participants, and therefore such errors of judgement will not *per se* ground liability. Rather the action of the defendant would have to be unreasonable and in assessing reasonableness Lord Diplock held that a jury should look to all the circumstances of the case and assess whether the participant acted with reckless disregard for the safety of the spectator.[123] If not, then there could be no finding that the defendant was in breach of any duty of care owed to the plaintiff.

There are two possible interpretations of the significance of Lord Diplock's use of the terminology of reckless disregard in *Wooldridge v. Sumner*. The first is to say that, because of the nature of the situation, the standard of care is intentionally lowered. This approach was followed by Lord Denning in the later case of *Wilks v. Cheltenham Home Guard Motor Cycle and Light Car Club*.[124] Here the plaintiffs, spectators at a motor cycle scramble, were lined along the spectator's rope. The course was bordered by what was termed a "wrecking rope" to stop motor cycles crashing into the crowd. Beyond this, there was a stretch of "no-man's land" and beyond this, the spectators' rope. The defendant was driving at some 25–30mph and suddenly and inexplicably lost control and veered to one side, crashed through the ropes and landed in the crowd injuring spectators. He was sued in negligence, however the court rejected this claim. Lord Denning held that a plaintiff spectator would have to show reckless disregard on the part of the participant to recover, and that in this case the defendant's speed in the context of a competitive race could not be regarded as excessive.[125]

---

[122] [1963] 2 Q.B. 43. See Goodhart "The Sportsman's Charter" (1962) 78 *Law Quarterly Review* 490.

[123] *Ibid.* at p.57. See Beloff, *op. cit.* at pp.116–117. As Beloff puts it, "There is in short a difference between a Carling colliding with a spectator and a Cantona kicking one."

[124] [1971] 2 All E.R. 369.

[125] *Ibid.* at p.371.

The second possible interpretation of the notion of reckless disregard as it was used in *Wooldridge v. Sumner* is to say that whereas the standard of care is the same as in other cases – with the participant being required to act reasonably in the circumstances – the nature of the circumstances under consideration are such that in the absence of recklessness the conduct would be deemed to be reasonable.[126] Thus, recklessness is used, not as a statement of the standard of care, but as an evidentiary test – the approach endorsed by the Court of Appeal in *Caldwell v. Maguire & Fitzgerald.* This was also the approach used by Edmund Davies and Phillimore L.JJ. in *Wilks v. Cheltenham Home Guard Motor Cycle and Light Car Club*, with the former stating that it was incumbent on the spectator to "exercise such degree of care as may be expected in all the circumstances"[127] and the latter saying of *Wooldridge v. Sumner* that:

> "It is, however, important to remember that the test remains simply that of negligence and that whether or not the competitor was negligent must be viewed against all the circumstances."[128]

It is not clear, therefore whether a 'reckless disregard' test for cases of spectator/participant litigation survived the decision in *Wilks* in as much as a majority of the court in *Wooldridge* seemed to move away from it.[129] No reference was made to either *Wooldridge* or *Wilks* in the seminal decision in *Condon v. Basi.* Equally in *Smoldon v. Whitworth*, the Court of Appeal did seem to indicate that a reckless disregard test *did* apply when assessing the standard of care required of a participant in respect of a spectator, on the grounds that a participant would be less immediately concerned with a spectator than he (or indeed a referee) would be with another participant, and hence his responsibility to the spectator would be reduced accordingly.[130]

5.4 DUTIES OF REFEREES

The question of whether and to what extent referees owe a duty of care to players was addressed for the first time in England in the well-known case *Smoldon v. Whitworth & Nolan.*[131] Here, the plaintiff was playing in an under

---

[126] Griffith-Jones at p.6.

[127] *Ibid.* at p.374.

[128] *Ibid.* at p.376.

[129] Generally see Pickford, "Playing Dangerous Games" (1998) 6 *Tort Law Review*, 221.

[130] (1997) E.L.R. 115, at p.122E–G.

[131] (1997) E.L.R. 249, [1997] P.I.Q.R. 133. For comment see Bailey, "Referees and the Law" (January/February, 1997) *Sports Law Administration and Practice* 10, McArdle, *Football, Society and the Law*, 166 and Pickford, "Playing Dangerous Games" (1998) 6 *Tort Law Review* 221 at p.225 *et seq.* See also Beloff, *op. cit.* at p.117 and Felix, "The Liability of Officials", 1 (2) *Sports Law Bulletin* (1998) 8, Greenfield & Osborn, "The Referee's Fear of a Penalty" (1996) 12 P.N. 63 and Bellamy, "Who would be a Referee?

19 "colts" rugby match in 1991 refereed by the second named defendant. According to testimony from various witnesses, the match in question had been played at a very fast pace and had been enormously physical, with one player from each side having already been sent off before the incident involving the plaintiff occurred. The plaintiff was a front row forward (the hooker) for one team and with ten minutes left to play in the match, the scrum collapsed and the plaintiff suffered a broken neck. He then sued, *inter alia*, the referee of the match, alleging that his injuries were caused by the latter's negligent refereeing of the game.

At the centre of the claim was an allegation that the referee had no control of the game, and particularly of the scrums, nor was he applying the normal International Rugby Board standards for proper scrummaging, which state that in order to prevent front rows from "charging," each scrum should commence using a procedure known as CTPE – that is to say that each side would crouch, then the prop forwards on each side would touch their opposite numbers on the shoulder, then they would pause and only then would they engage. The referee's failure to control the scrums was obvious, in that the scrum had previously collapsed some 20 or 25 times during the game.[132] Moreover, the linesman had directed the referee's attention to the fact that there had been punching in the scrum which would indicate that front row forwards were not bound properly – a recipe for a collapsing scrum – yet the referee had done nothing about this, claiming that he was unable to see the perpetrator of the acts. Indeed in the incident in which Mr. Smoldon was injured the scrum had collapsed twice and had to be re-set three times before the tragic occurrence.

Both the High Court and the Court of Appeal concluded that the referee owed a duty of care to the players (a point accepted by counsel for the defence) in that it was part of his job to enforce the safety rules of sport that were designed to protect players. In fulfilling that duty the referee was required to act reasonably in the circumstances (and the Court of Appeal explicitly rejected the adoption of a "reckless disregard" test for such cases), but one of the circumstances of such a case was the fact that the referee was employed *inter alia* to protect the players, and therefore their well being should have been more to the forefront of *his* mind than of that of a player who was primarily preoccupied with playing the game.[133]

Equally, Curtis J. in the High Court and Bingham L.C.J. in the Court of Appeal stressed that a very high threshold had to be crossed before negligence on the part of the match referee could be established. Thus it was recognised

---

The Developing Legal Liability of Referees" [2004] *International Sports Law Review* 9.

[132] Expert evidence before the court suggested that the maximum number of scrums, which should collapse in a properly refereed game, was about six.

[133] (1997) E.L.R. 249 at p.257.

that rugby was a fast game in which split second decisions would have to be made, and that it also made good public policy not to reach a decision that would constitute a disincentive to people to undertake the already unenviable task of refereeing. In the instant case, however, there was evidence of the requisite level of serious negligence on the part of the referee, as was apparent most obviously from his failure to apply the CTPE procedure, and to take measures to control what was going on in the front row,[134] which failure caused the plaintiff's injury.

The referee pleaded the defence of *volenti* – claiming that by voluntarily playing in the front row, the plaintiff had implicitly consented to injury of this nature. The Court of Appeal held, however, that whereas a player implicitly consented to the risk of injury inherent in the game of rugby, one did not consent to negligence on the part of the referee.[135] The Court of Appeal also rejected the possibility that there might have been contributory negligence on the part of the plaintiff, on the grounds that there was no evidence of the plaintiff behaving in a manner likely to collapse the scrum and thereby to cause injury.[136]

Both the High Court and the Court of Appeal reiterated that the ruling in this case should not be used as authority for the proposition that referees would be liable for injuries occurring as a result of violations of the rules in matches under their control. In the High Court, Curtis J. stated that: "No responsible player and no responsible referee has anything to fear"[137] and in the Court of Appeal, Bingham L.C.J. concluded that:[138]

> "[Curtis J.] did not intend to open the door to a plethora of claims by players against referees and it would be deplorable if that were the result. In our view that result should not follow provided all concerned appreciate how difficult it is for any plaintiff to establish that a referee failed to exercise such care and skill as was reasonably to be expected in the circumstances of a hotly contested game of rugby football."[139]

McArdle on the other hand says that the decision in *Smoldon* has: "... the potential to create a massive new area of liability for officials and in all

---

[134] It was further suggested that in the circumstances, the referee should have considered ending the match prematurely.

[135] (1997) E.L.R. 249 at p.267.

[136] In the event Ben Smoldon eventually reached a STG £1.95 million settlement with the RFU. See 2 (4) *Sports Law Bulletin* (1999) 4.

[137] Unreported, April 19, 1996 at p.5. See for example the Canadian Case *Hamstra v. British Columbia Rugby Union* [1997] 1 S.C.R. 1092, where there had been an injury to a player as a result of a collapsed scrum and yet the jury was discharged.

[138] (1997) E.L.R. 249 at P.268.

[139] Interestingly the Court of Appeal did intimate that it would be beneficial if all players, as a matter of course, were to be insured against the risk of catastrophic injury.

probability coaches as well."[140] He asks whether, for example a referee who refused to dismiss a player who was being unduly violent from the field of play would be liable in tort to anyone on the field whom that player subsequently injured, or whether a referee who allows a game to be played on an unplayable pitch might be liable for injury suffered by participants as a result of the nature of the playing surface.[141] These are questions that remain to be answered. For present purposes it should be noted that the level of negligence on the part of the referee in the *Smoldon* case *was* enormous, nor is there anything in that ruling to suggest that a referee could be found to be liable in tort for simple errors or misjudgments.[142] Indeed the ruling in *Smoldon* is fully consistent with that given in respect of participant liability in *Caldwell v. Maguire & Fitzgerald* and *Pitcher v. Huddersfield Town.*

In *Vowles v. Evans & WRFU,*[143] the claimant was playing as hooker in an amateur rugby game in Wales. After about 32 minutes of the game the loose head prop on the claimant's team was injured, and had to leave the field of play. The claimant's team had no experienced or trained front row forward to take his place, and so the referee discussed options with the two captains including the option of having non-contested scrums – an option which both captains rejected, because of uncertainty as to whether, if the option of non-contested scrums were taken, league points would be awarded to the winning team in the game.[144] The referee also asked the claimant's team captain whether his team had any appropriate replacement, and eventually a back row forward, "J" who had never trained in the front row but who had played prop in some low level games announced that he "would give it a go." The referee did not impose a requirement of non-contested scrums but told both packs that he wanted them to be sensible. In the 85th minute, during a scrum where the two front rows failed to engage properly, the claimant suffered a dislocated neck resulting in permanent incomplete tetraplegia. He sued, *inter alia,* the referee and his employer (the Welsh rugby union) for negligence, with the WRU

---

[140] McArdle, *op. cit.* at pp.267–268. See also Graves, "Teachers may refuse to Take Up Whistle", *Daily Telegraph*, December 18, 1996.

[141] As a result of an out of court settlement with the RFU, Ben Smoldon received nearly two million pounds. See 2 (4) *Sports Law Bulletin* (1999) 3, and also see Levinson, "Foul! Tackling the Problem of Violence in Sport" (November/December 1998) *Sports Law Administration and Practice* 7.

[142] See Griffith-Jones, *op. cit.,* at pp.23–25 for the view that: "Referees may take comfort from the fact that, if they know the laws of their game and simply seek to apply them in a reasonable manner, then they should have little to fear."

[143] [2002] All E.R. (D) 210 (Q.B.), [2003] All E.R. (D) 134 (C.A.), noted by James, 5 (1) *Sports Law Bulletin* (2002) 1.

[144] In the High Court, Morland J. criticised the coach and captain of the claimant's team for allowing considerations of points to override considerations of player safety; [2002] All E.R. (D) 210 (Q.B.) at para.87.

accepting that if the referee was deemed to have acted negligently, it would be vicariously liable for that negligence.

In both the High Court and the Court of Appeal it was held that the referee owed a duty to amateur rugby players – a slight extension from *Smoldon v. Whitworth* where counsel for the defence had conceded merely that a referee owed a duty to colts players. The policy considerations inherent in not imposing onerous obligations on an amateur referee which might amount to a disincentive to other potential referees had been stressed by counsel for the appellant, but the Court of Appeal ruled that there was no good reason to distinguish between colts' rugby and amateur adult rugby, in that in both cases, players were entitled to rely on the referee's application of safety rules for their own safety. On the other hand, the Court of Appeal did accept the possibility that – as a matter of policy and in light of the requirement in English tort law that in order for a duty of care to be recognised in any situation it should *inter alia* be just and reasonable to do so[145] – the extent to which the defendants were insured against claims of this nature was a relevant factor in deciding whether or not to impose liability.

The Court of Appeal held that whereas referees would rarely be found to be liable for injuries suffered during matches under their control,[146] in this case the referee had acted negligently, *not in his control of the game* but in his failure to follow the clear and unambiguous rules of the game by requiring that if either team was unable to field three trained front row forwards, scrums would be non-contested. Thus under Law 3 (12) of the WRU laws, it is specifically provided that: "*Where there is no other front row forward available due to a sequence of players ordered off or injured or both then the game will continue with non-contestable scrummages. ...*" In other words, this safety rule of the game imposed a clear and unambiguous responsibility on a referee to take a particular cause of action,[147] and here the referee had not followed this course of action having neither taken sufficient steps to determine "J's" level of front row experience nor demanded non-contested scrums.[148]

---

[145] *Governors of the Peabody Donation Fund v. Parkinson* [1985] A.C. 210 at 240. The "just and reasonable" requirement for determining duty of care was expressly endorsed by Keane C.J. in *Glencar Explorations & Andaman Resources plc v. Mayo County Council* [2002] 1 I.L.R.M. 481. See Byrne and Binchy, "Tort Law" at p.565ff in *Annual Review of Irish Law 2001* (Roundhall Sweet & Maxwell, Dublin, 2002).

[146] Moreover, it was suggested that where, for example a referee failed to turn up and hence a volunteer from the crowd refereed the match, the standard of care to be expected would be less than that to be expected from a more qualified official such as the defendant in this case. *Ibid.* at para.28.

[147] The requirement that a referee order uncontested scrummages where there was not sufficient qualified front row players available was also made in a 1997 Referee's Manual published by the English Rugby Football Union.

[148] The Court of Appeal said that if the referee had asked the captain whether any of his players had front row experience and the captain had misled him on this point, then he could not have been faulted. Here however, he had simply not done enough to ascertain

Of pivotal importance for the Court of Appeal was the fact that the referee's decisions both to allow 'J' to play in the front row without ascertaining his level of experience, and also not to order non-contested scrums, was not made in the split second rush of a game, but rather during a break in play. In other words the circumstances of this case were conducive to the making of good decisions, and hence his negligent decision was less reasonable than it would have been had it been made on a split second basis during a moment of play. Indeed the Court of Appeal expressly stated that had the latter been the case then very different considerations might apply.[149]

Perhaps the aspect of the decision of Morland J. in the High Court most open to criticism is his conclusion that the decision by the referee to allow "J" to play in the front row was, as a matter of fact, the cause of the claimant's injuries.[150] Morland J. had referred to testimony from players, which intimated that "J" was not as good a scrummager as the player whom he had replaced, that the claimant's scrum had been in a certain amount of trouble since the replacement, and also that the actual injury to the claimant occurred because the two packs failed to engage properly in the last scrum of the match. As against this, however, it could be argued that "J" had been playing in the front row for an hour before the injury occurred, and whereas there were problems with the scrum (which might also be attributed to the fact that the wet and muddy state of the pitch made scrummaging difficult) there does not appear to have been anything to suggest that J. was not doing a reasonable job, nor that another player would necessarily have done a better one *simply by virtue of having front row experience* Especially there is no evidence to suggest that the mistimed engagement of the front rows in the fateful scrum was caused by J. (rather than the other props) or that it was the result not of the nature of the game (where scrums regularly do not engage properly) but of some defect in J's technique that was so basic that any player of front row experience would necessarily not have made the same mistake. Proof of causation in this case should have involved demonstrating not only that J. was not an experienced scrummager, but also that the incident in question was the direct result of this inexperience. The Court of Appeal upheld the High Court's finding of facts, but with significant reference to the principle that appellate court should only overturn findings of fact of lower courts in extreme circumstances.[151]

Arguably the best way to categorise the *Vowles* case is to say that it, like *Smoldon*, involves a referee acting negligently by not applying a clear and unambiguous safety rule. The moral of the story for referees therefore is simple.

J.'s playing experience in the front row – although it is notable that "J" himself had intimated that he had some limited playing experience in the front row at a junior level. *Ibid*. at para.34.

[149] *Ibid*. at para.31.

[150] [2002] All E.R. (D) 210 (Q.B.), at para.74.

[151] *Assicurazioni Generali Spa v. Arab Insurance Group* [2002] E.W.C.A. Civ. 1642.

It is vital that they familiarize themselves with such safety rules and apply them strictly and irrespective of the impact on the playing of the game. Doing so will almost certainly amount to a shield against liability.

It is unusual to see a situation where a referee's decision in respect of a *playing rule* (as distinct from a safety rule) is the subject of legal challenge. Nor is this surprising. As long as sports use human referees then they must accept that mistakes will be made in the manner in which that contest is umpired. In *Carew Park Amateur Football Club v. FAI*,[152] a challenge was made to a decision of a referee during an FAI Junior Cup Match to disallow a goal scored by the Carew team. The referee had in fact disallowed the goal, then changed his mind and allowed it following protest from the Carew players, and then disallowed it again following protest from members of the opposing team, Mungret Regional. To make matters worse, Munget Regional went on to win the match 1–0 and progressed to the next round of the cup. Following an unsuccessful challenge within the FAI system, the Carew Club applied to the High Court seeking, *inter alia*, a replay of the match. Barr J. while sympathising with the plaintiffs, said that the view of the law was that the decision of a referee, whether right or wrong would not be struck down by a court unless the referee did "sornething appalling". The alternative was what the judge termed "a hopeless degree of anarchy". Interestingly, however, the judge made no order for costs in light of what he saw as the "vacillation" of the referee.[153]

A more unusual claim against a referee was made in 1997.[154] In the final minutes of the second period of extra time in an FA Cup 5th Round replay between Leicester City FC and Chelsea FC, the referee Mike Reed awarded a controversial penalty kick to Chelsea who duly scored and proceeded to the Sixth Round. One supporter sued for £140 in damages claiming that the referee owed a duty of care to supporters to referee a match fairly and that failure to do so here caused the plaintiff trauma, shock and distress meaning that he could not attend work for two days. Unsurprisingly the court rejected this claim holding that a referee owed no duty of care to spectators (and by extension to players or teams) always to make the right decision.[155]

Finally a referee will himself or herself be owed certain duties by players, clubs coaches or even spectators. Thus there is no good reason why a referee

---

[152] Unreported, High Court, Barr J., February 19, 1999.

[153] See "Referee's Word Final Says Judge", *Irish Times*, February 20, 1999 (March/April 1999), *Sports Law Administration and Practice* 2.

[154] See Coward & Blain, "Who's the Defendant in the Black?", 5 (2) *Sport and the Law Journal* (1996) 5.

[155] The American approach is to suggest that in the absence of corruption, fraud or bad faith, no action against decisions of sports officials would be sustained. See *Shapiro v. Queen's County Jockey Club*, 53 N.Y.S. 2d. 135 Court (1945). See also Shlomi Feiner, "The Personal Liability of Sports Officials" (1997)) 4 *Sports Lawyers Journal*, 213. For a suggestion that a referee may still be successfully sued by a club in respect of negligent decision making see Kevan *et al*, *op. cit.* at p.145

could not successfully sue a supporter or a player for assault (as, for example in cases where he has been hit by a projectile thrown from the crowd[156] or following an altercation with a player[157]) or any other party including a journalist for defamation relating, *inter alia*, to his handling of the game.[158]

5.5 DUTY OF COACHES

Coaches like referees and players will attract liability where, in the operation of the coaching process, they have a duty of care to those under their charge and have failed to adhere to the standard of care that was appropriate in the circumstances.[159] The extent of the duty owed will vary from case to case. Equally it seems clear that a coach is not a guarantor of the safety nor of the playing success of an athlete under his or her tuition, save where it is reasonable for this to be the case.[160] Thus in *Brady v. Sunderland FC*,[161] the plaintiff,

---

[156] In August 2002, Irish rugby referee David McHugh was assaulted by a fan who had scaled the perimeter fence and climbed onto the field during a match between New Zealand and South Africa in Durban. The fan, Pieter van Zyl, was convicted of assault. See Laurence, "Fan Fined for Assault", *Irish Times*, October 29, 2002. Mr. McHugh intimated that he would be taking a civil action against van Zyl, but at the time of writing it is unclear whether such an action will be going ahead. See "Sports Law Current Survey", 11 (1) *Sport and The Law Journal* (2003) 19 and 70.

[157] See Troy Cross, "Assaults on Sports Officials", 8 *Marquette Sports Law Journal* (1998) 429, Chaifullo, "From Personal Foul To Personal Attack; How Sports Officials Are The Target Of Physical Abuse From Players, Coaches And Fans Alike", 8 *Seton Hall Journal of Sports Law* (1998) 201 and Wallace, "The Men in Black and Blue", 6 *Seton Hall Journal of Sports Law* (1996) 341. Wallace says that the most effective way of dealing with players who assault officials is not to bring civil or criminal actions against them but rather to impose hefty internal suspensions.

[158] By analogy, in *Fullam v. Associated Newspapers Limited* [1953–54] Ir. Jur. Rep. 79 (H.C.) it was held to be defamatory of a football player to say that he was unable to kick the ball with his right foot, and the fact that crowds habitually used to chant "carpet slipper" at the plaintiff (a phrase used in the article intimating that he trained in a carpet slipper to build up his weak right foot) was admitted in evidence against the defendant newspaper. See Lewis, "Defamation of Sports Officials", 38 *Washburn Law Journal* (1999) 780. It is notable again by analogy, that following an English Premiership soccer match in March 2002 between Leicester City and Leeds United, during which supporters of the latter chanted racist abuse at Leicester players, police announced that they would study CCTV footage of the game and if they could identify perpetrators would take criminal action against them. See "Leeds Fans Face Arrest over Chants", *Irish Times*, March 26, 2002.

[159] Beloff, *op. cit.*, at p.118ff., Gardiner "Should Coaches Take Care?", 1 (1) *Sport and the Law Journal* (1993) 11, Stuart and Silver, "Rugby – Catastrophic Injuries, Claims and Insurance", 2 (1) *Sport and the Law Journal* (1994) 15, Kevan *et al, op. cit.* at Chap.12. See also the report of a Forum on Safety in Sport, at 6 (1) *Sport and the Law Journal* (1998) 41.

[160] McComiskey & Biedzynski, "A Guide to the Legal Liability of Coaches for a Sports Participant's Injuries", 6 *Seton Hall Journal of Sports Law* (1996) 7, Labuschagne &

Kieron Brady, a young Irish soccer player developed vascular problems in his right leg that required surgery and eventually brought about his premature retirement from the game. He sued his employers Sunderland FC claiming breach of contract and negligence, on the basis, *inter alia,* that he had been experiencing such pains for a while but the manager and coach had done nothing to help. Indeed at one training session when he was complaining of pain, the manager Malcolm Crosby had told him to continue running, ran along with him lecturing him for having a bad attitude, and only after the run allowed him to see the physiotherapist. Buckley J. (whose judgement was upheld by the Court of Appeal) ruled that Crosby's attitude was "robust" but not thereby negligent.

There will, however, be cases where it is reasonable for the athlete to rely on the coach for his safety. So in inherently dangerous sports such as rugby or swimming, athletes should be instructed in both the techniques necessary to play the sport safely (for example how to dive,[162] or how to tackle in a rugby match[163]), and also in basic "injury avoidance" principles[164] On the other hand, less concern for the safety of participants is needed in cases involving less inherently dangerous sports such as, for example, aerobics.[165] Moreover, no matter how important the game, the coach should not field a player whose participation may be of inestimable benefit to the team on the day but which could result in real long term harm to him in the future.[166] A player should be fit to play, and to play in the position in which he is picked.[167] Coaches should also be responsible enough to ensure that there are proper warm up procedures prior to a game,[168] to avoid overly excessive or dangerous training regimes, and obviously not to recommend or require use of dietary or nutritional supplements or even banned substances which are not clinically demonstrated not to have negative side-effects.[169] Similarly in dealing with equipment, if it

---

Skea, "The Liability Of A Coach for a Sport Participant's Injury" (1999) 2 *Stellenbosch Law Review* 158.

[161] Unreported, High Court, April 2, 1998, unreported, Court of Appeal, November 17, 1998 (C.A.). See note at 1 (5) *Sports Law Bulletin* (1998) 3.

[162] *Gannon v. Rotherham MBC, Halsburys Monthly Review* (1991) 91/1717.

[163] *Van Oppen v. Clerk to the Bedford Charity Trustees* [1989] 1 All E.R. 273 (Q.B.) [1989] 3 All E.R. 389 (C.A.). See Griffith Jones at 21 for the conclusion that whereas this case failed on its facts, it is authority for the proposition that a coach may be liable both in misfeasance and nonfeasance.

[164] *Fowles v. Bedfordshire County Council, Times,* May 22, 1995 (C.A.) and *Roddie v. Ski Llandudno Limited,* unreported, Court of Appeal, July 31, 2000.

[165] *McDermott v. Sports Management,* unreported, Supreme Court, January 12, 1988.

[166] McComiskey & Biedzynski, "A Guide to the Legal Liability of Coaches for a Sports Participant's Injuries", 6 *Seton Hall Journal of Sports Law* (1996) 33.

[167] Stuart and Silver, "Rugby, Catastrophic Injuries, Claims and Insurance", 2 (1) *Sport and the Law Journal* (1994) 15.

[168] *Hill v. Durham County Council,* unreported, Court of Appeal, January 31, 2000.

[169] See Chap.3 at pp.86 *et seq.*

is reasonable for a player to rely on the assertion of a coach that a particular piece of equipment is safe to use, then this will generate a duty of care on the part of the coach.[170] Finally, the coaching session itself should be run in a manner that does not expose participants to unreasonable risks of injury, where such risks could be avoided by conducting the session in a different manner.[171] On the other hand, this does not mean that *all* risks are to be avoided, in that accidents will happen and the risk thereof is an inevitable concomitant of participation in sport.[172]

A dramatic case where a player relied on a coach for safety is that of *Woodroffe-Hedley v. Cuthbertson*.[173] Here, the deceased Gerald Hedley had hired C as an expert guide on an ice-climbing holiday. On one stretch of ice, C noticed that there had been an unexpected amount of heat from the morning sun, so he decided that it would be a good idea to move towards a shady rocky outcrop, because there was otherwise the risk of ice melting and a consequent danger of rock falls. Universal mountain practice where two climbers are connected is to (a) hammer two ice screws into the ice to act as an anchor, and (b) to set up an intermediary point between the two called a running belay to lesson the strain. Because of what C saw as the imminent risk of a rock fall, he only hammered in one screw and did not set up a running belay. He then fell as an ice sheet gave way, and dragged Mr. H who was connected to him, to his death (C landed on snow and suffered minor injuries). Had there been two screws or a running belay, the line would have held and H would not have been killed.

The basic question for the English High Court was whether C acted reasonably in departing from universal mountaineering procedure because of what he saw as the imminent risk of rock falls. It concluded that whereas it would not say that an alpine leader could *never* depart from such procedures, here the risk of an ice sheet giving way (as happened) *was* foreseeable, and the risk of rocks falling during the two minutes it would have taken to secure and remove the ice screws were negligible, hence C's action was not that of a reasonable instructor in the circumstances. The duty of the coach/instructor was to act reasonably in the circumstances, and whereas all mountain climbers ·

---

[170] See Clancy, "Judo Mats, Climbing Walls, Trampolines and Pole Vaulters", 3 (1) *Sport and the Law Journal* (1995) 28
[171] *Whelan v. Mowlds* [2000] I.E.H.C. 73, High Court, October 12, 2000.
[172] *McDermott v. Sports Management*, unreported, Supreme Court, January 12, 1988.
[173] Unreported, Queen's Bench, June 20, 1997 *per* Dyson J. For comment see Helen Lloyd Davies, "Liability issues in Outdoor Pursuits", 4 (6) *Sports Law Administration and Practice* (September/October 1997) 1. See also Duff, "Medico-Legal Aspects of High Altitude Mountaineering", 8 (3) *Sport and the Law Journal* (2000) 85 and Pickford, "Playing Dangerous Games" (1998) 6 *Tort Law Review* 221 at p.228 *et seq*. See also *Pawlak v. Doucette & Reinks* [1985] 2 W.W.R. 588, *Bacon v. White*, unreported, Queen's Bench, May 21, 1998.

are taken to assume the risk of the normal hazards of mountain climbing, they are not taken to assume the risk of their instructor acting negligently.[174]

On the other hand in *Affiong-Day v. High Performance Sports Ltd*,[175] the plaintiff had taken part in an indoor wall climbing exercise at the defendant's sports centre. She had got into difficulties some thirty feet up the climbing wall. Rescue attempts by another climber in the vicinity – acting both of his own volition and subsequently under instruction of the sports centre's duty manager – failed to assist her, and she fell some twenty five feet to the floor and suffered brain damage. In this case the court found that although the defendant owed a duty of care to the plaintiff, the extent of this duty, as well as the reasonableness of his conduct would have to be gauged in light of his view of the urgency of the situation. In hindsight, his efforts to secure the claimant were perhaps doomed to failure, and it might have been better if the centre had provided a harnessed floorwalker, however, the defendants were entitled not to be judged by reference to hindsight. In the immediate circumstances of the case, they had acted reasonably even if such actions did not have the desired affect of rescuing the claimant.

Beyond such safety concerns, the extent of a coach's duty to athletes under his or her tuition is uncertain, and raises issues under both contract and tort law, including questions of liability for negligent misstatement under the principle in *Hedley Byrne v. Heller.*[176] From the standpoint of tort law, the coach must of course act reasonably in the circumstances, hence the level of duty owed by a coach will differ from case to case depending on factors such as the age, skill, size and experience of the participant, and the nature of the sport.[177] Generally, duties will exist in areas such as supervision,[178] training and instruction,[179] ensuring proper use of safety equipment, ensuring that "sub-coaches" are reasonably competent, providing appropriate medical care should

---

[174] In similar vein see Maxlow-Tomlinson, "Skiing and the Law", 3 (1) *Sport and the Law Journal* (1995) 18.

[175] [2003] E.W.C.A. Civ. 197, February 26, 2003, noted at (March/April 2003) *Sports Law Bulletin* 4.

[176] [1964] A.C. 465. See Gardiner, "Should Coaches Take Care", 1 (1) *Sport and the Law Journal* (1993) 11 and Kevan *et al*, p.130ff. It is questionable whether a senior player or captain might incur liability for negligent advice given to a junior player in situations where it was reasonable for the junior player to rely on the same.

[177] For example see *Morrell v. Owen*, unreported, Queen's Bench, December 14, 1993. For analysis see case note by Ray Farrell, 1 (2) *Sports Law Journal* (1995) 3.

[178] This may well, in the circumstances, cover both the field of play/training and also related settings such as locker rooms. See McComiskey & Biedzynski, "A Guide to the Legal Liability of Coaches for a Sports Participant's Injuries", 6 *Seton Hall Journal of Sports Law* (1996) 21–22.

[179] Gardiner, "Should Coaches Take Care", 1 (1) *Sport and the Law Journal* (1993) 11, appreciates that it will be difficult to translate potential into result and hence to prove the extent of damage in such a case. See also Stuart and Silver, "Rugby, Catastrophic Injuries, Claims and Insurance", 2 (1) *Sport and the Law Journal* (1994) 15.

the need arise,[180] preventing injured athletes from competing, ensuring, where appropriate, that necessary forms have been filled in by the athlete,[181] and matching athletes of similar competitive levels.[182] Most player/coach contracts will not contain clauses whereby the coach guarantees tangible results in terms of playing success, and hence a breach of contract action will be unlikely to exist where an athlete claims that poor coaching has stunted his playing potential. On the other hand, a negligence action might be sustained in such a case, subject to the rule at English and now probably at Irish law against recovery of damages for pure economic loss.[183] Ideally a coach should endeavour to keep up to scratch with latest developments in respect of coaching, because by doing so and by incorporating such developments in his coaching, he or she will be fulfilling any duty owed to athletes.[184] Ideally also, coaches and indeed sports teachers in schools should seek to attend courses in sports coaching run by the governing bodies of the relevant supports (of for example the IRFU youth and schools coaching scheme) and to act on the basis of the instruction received at such courses, both as a way of ensuring best practice and also as a defence in the event of a negligence action being taken against him or her. The reality of the situation, of course is that especially for school teachers, this may be simply impossible, having regard to resources of time and money.

Finally, there is also the possibility of civil liability arising where the coach of one side has 'over-psyched' his players causing them to be too aggressive, or has in any sense condoned play that is in breach of the safety rules of sport, as a result of which an opponent gets injured.[185] Indeed the UK Law

---

[180] Stuart and Silver, "Rugby, Catastrophic Injuries, Claims and Insurance", 2 (1) *Sport and the Law Journal* (1994) 15.

[181] This would include for example the situation where a minor athlete who is permitted to avail of a therapeutic use exemption in respect of a banned substance is obliged to inform the relevant authorities of this fact. Typically, however, athletes should be expected to make the relevant communications themselves.

[182] *Affutu-Nartoy v. Clarke*, *Times*, February 9, 1984. See also McComiskey & Biedzynski, "A Guide to the Legal Liability of Coaches for a Sports Participant's Injuries", 6 *Seton Hall Journal of Sports Law* (1996) 7 at p.34.

[183] *D&F Estates Ltd v. Church Commissioners for England* [1988] 2 All E.R. 992. *McShane Wholesale Fruit and Vegetables Ltd v. Johnston Haulage Company Limited* [1997] 1 I.L.R.M. 86 (H.C.), *Glencar Communications v. Mayo County Council*, cited *supra*. Generally see Beloff, *op. cit.* at p.118.

[184] Gardiner, 1(1) *Sports Law Journal* (1993) 18. An analogy may be drawn with the duty at tort law of a doctor to keep up to pace with what is standard practice by doctors provided that such practice has no patent inherent defects. See *Dunne v. National Maternity Hospital* [1989] I.R. 91.

[185] See Drowatzky, "Assumption of Risk in Sport", 2 (1) *Journal of Legal Aspects of Sport* (1992) 92 at p.99 and Stuart and Silver, "Rugby, Catastrophic Injuries, Claims and Insurance", 2 (1) *Sport and the Law Journal* (1994) 15. See also McArdle, *Football, Society and the Law*, p.168. For the American experience in this regard see *Tomjanovich v. California Sports Inc*, No. H–78–243 (S.D. Tex. 1979).

Commission had suggested that coaches who habitually selected or who failed to exercise reasonable care over players who were known to be violent might even incur criminal liability.[186]

5.6 DUTIES OF SPORTS TEACHERS AND SCHOOLS[187]

The extent of the duty of the sports teacher in any case, will depend on a number of factors, most pressingly the vulnerability of the pupils – usually though not always dictated by their age – and the nature of the sport in question. In assessing whether a course of action taken by the teacher is reasonable, the courts will assess both the foreseeability and the seriousness of the risk that it presents, and also the extent to which it is reasonable to deem the injured party to have assumed that risk. In practice this means that the more dangerous the sport and the younger the children participating, the more foreseeable the risk of injury and the less reasonable it is to expect the children to have assumed the same, and hence the more onerous the duty on the part of the teacher.[188] In Ireland, "the standard of care imposed on a schoolteacher is to take such care of the pupils as a careful parent would take of her own children,"[189] and in practice this will mean acting in accordance with what may be termed informed common sense.

The approach of both law and policy to school sports involves a balance between various competing realities. Public policy sees school sport as a good thing, promoting health and fitness, and emotional and psychological development, and recognises that schools have limited resources with which to provide sports facilities and equipment and indeed expert instructors. On the other hand, the inherent risks in all sport are exacerbated in the school setting in that the resource implications mentioned may well mean that facilities and equipment are sub-standard, and the instruction (including instruction in injury avoidance principles) given by non-experts – typically teachers who happen to have an interest in sport and who are prepared to give up their free time for their students – may be inadequate,[190] and where a child is seriously injured as a result, then it may seem intuitively desirable that he receive compensation in respect of such injuries. We will consider the duties in respect of school sports under five headings namely:

---

[186] See Farrell at 2 (1) *Sport and the Law Journal* (1994) 1 & 5ff.
[187] Generally, see Grayson, *op. cit.* at p.190ff and Grayson, *School Sports and the Law* (Coroner CCH, London, 2001), Kevan, *et al*, *op. cit.* at Chap.14, McMahon & Binchy, *op. cit.* at Chap.16.
[188] Beloff, *op. cit.* at p.119.
[189] *Kane v. Kennedy*, unreported, High Court, March 25, 1999. See also *Thornton v. Board of School Trustees of School District No.* 57 (1976) 73 D.L.R. 3d 35.
[190] For the comparable position in the UK see Brierly, "School Sports and the Law", 1 (1) *Sports Law Journal* (1995) 19.

– The rules relating to mandatory participation in sport.

– Duties in respect of coaching.

– Duties in respect of equipment.

– Duties in respect of supervision.

– Duties in respect of facilities.

5.6.1 Mandatory participation in school sport

It is important that schools have a considered policy in respect of a child who does not want to take part in physical education or sporting lessons. As we have seen, a major reason why there is relatively little litigation arising out of sport generally is the fact that, by consenting to play sport, a player may be taken to have assumed the inherent risks thereof, and this will reduce the duty of care owed by other participants as well as coaches and teachers. But if the participant (here the schoolchild) does not consent to such participation, but despite having intimated this lack of consent to the school is still forced to play sport by his school, then presumably he cannot be taken to have assumed any of the said risks.

Again this presents a conundrum for schools, because as against these concerns, there is obvious merit in requiring that students participate in school sport (just as there is merit in requiring unwilling students to study, for example, science), especially given that the unwilling children may be those who by reason of their habitually sedentary nature most need the exercise. It is suggested here that a policy of mandatory participation in school sport is legally acceptable provided that it admits of two provisos.[191] First no student should be required to participate in a sport that has strong inherent risks – for example a contact sport or swimming, nor indeed should they be permitted to play in a sport or a sporting position of which they are physically incapable.[192] Thus ideally a

---

[191] *Law Commission Consultation Paper No.139* at pp.173ff. For analysis see Farrell, "Consent to Violence in Sport", 4 (1) *Sport and the Law Journal* (1998) 5. For US analysis see Drowatsky, "Assumption of Risk in Sport", 2 (1) *Journal of Legal Aspects of Sport* (1992) 92. See also the Belgian case in which a heavily built girl fell and suffered injuries as a result of her participation in a gymnastics class that was beyond her capabilities. The teacher had been participating in the class and hence was not able to give all of his attention to the student. He was found liable for negligence both by reason of the inadequate supervision of the class and also by reason of the fact that he had required this girl to take part in the activity despite the fact that she was incapable of doing so. *Current Law Survey* at 6 (3) *Sport and the Law Journal* (1998) 64.

[192] See for example *Watson v. Haines*, unreported, Allen J, Supreme Court of New South Wales, April 10, 1987, where a schoolboy with a long thin neck was permitted to play as hooker on the school rugby team – a position for which (according to the medical

school should offer students who do not wish to participate in such contact sport an alternative – for example jogging around the sports field, or some other form of light workout. Secondly, no student should be required to participate in sport if he or she is physically incapable of doing so. Thus in *Williams v. Rotherham LEA*,[193] where a pupil was required to join a PE class despite having previously injured his ankle, and his participation in the class aggravated the pre-existing condition, the teacher was deemed to be negligent for requiring participation in circumstances where there was a patent risk of injury.

Having said this, it is not the case that a teacher is negligent in *allowing* a child to take part in an endeavour, which turns out to have a dangerous result, provided that the activity in question is suited to the child's age and level of experience.[194] In *Delaney v. O'Dowd*,[195] the teacher had organised a handball exercise, in the course of which children had to run parallel to each other and about three metres apart. Two of the children collided and the claimant was injured. Carroll J. concluded that this was a safe exercise and the teacher was not negligent for failing to keep his eyes focused on the children at all time. Similarly in *Murphy v. Jackson*,[196] a teacher was held not to be negligent in organizing a perfectly supervised piggy back race.[197]

5.6.2 Duties in respect of coaching school sports

The issue of coaching has already been dealt with, and the principles mentioned above apply in a school context. Equally a school sports coach should of course be aware that because he or she is dealing with younger and probably less strong players, he should make allowances accordingly. For example, it may be necessary when dealing with school children and with dangerous sports to ensure that the player has sufficient basic instruction in the game that he is able for the level of coaching that he is currently receiving.[198] It is unclear

---

experts) he was plainly unsuited. Generally see Millane, "Neighbours in Law", 4 (2) *Sporting Traditions* (May 1988) 1.

[193] *Times*, August 6, 1998.

[194] *McCabe v. Westlock* (1998) 226 A.R. 1 (Q.B.).

[195] [1997] I.R. L. Log W. 157 (C.C.).

[196] D.P.I.J. Trinity and Michaelmas Terms 1993 (H.C.) 146. See McMahon & Binchy, *op. cit.* at p.444.

[197] On the other hand in *Moore v. Hampshire County Council*, 80 L.G.R. 481 (C.A.), November 4, 1981, a twelve year old pupil with two dislocated hips was injured while participating in a gymnastics class, having told her teacher (untruthfully) that her doctor had given permission for her to do so. The teacher was found to be negligent by reason of his failure to investigate the matter fully.

[198] This obligation does not appear to apply in the case of an adult participating in a sport that is not inherently dangerous: *McDermott v. Sports Management*, unreported, Supreme Court, January 12, 1988.

whether a teacher must ensure that players in school sports are evenly matched, in terms of size, skill and experience. In *Ward v. Donegal Vocational Committee*,[199] the claimant and a much larger boy were competing in a Gaelic football match. The two boys challenged together for a ball and the claimant was injured. He argued that the school was negligent in allowing pupils of different sizes to compete together in a contact sport of this nature. Keane J. (as he then was) rejected this claim, holding that the risk of such injury was an inherent hazard of the sport. It is submitted, however, that the simple fact that a sport carries inherent risks does not adequately answer the question whether in *school sports* (where the participants are unusually susceptible to the risk of injuries), there should be particular precautions taken in terms of matching players, where failure to do so poses a foreseeable risk to such players, and where such risk could have been avoided without any particular cost to the playing of sport in the school.

A teacher should also take reasonable precautions for the well being of students if he himself chooses to participate in for example, a training match – a useful and widely practiced coaching tactic. Thus in *Affutu-Nartoy v. Clarke*,[200] a local club rugby player was coaching an under 15 team, and decided that he would himself play in a practice game. Tragically in the course of tackling one of the players on the opposing team he broke the young boy's back. The court held that he was negligent, not because he played in the training session, but because he failed to take account of the foreseeable consequences of the fact that he was considerably heavier than the boys on the other team.[201]

5.6.3 Duties in respect of sports equipment in schools

Generally as we have seen if it is reasonable for a player to rely on the assertion of a coach that a particular piece of equipment is safe to use, then this should generate a duty on the part of the coach,[202] and should there be some latent defect in the equipment then the coach should be liable for the same. In the case of school sport, because of the almost inevitable nature of such reliance, the school will incur liability for injuries caused by defective sports equipment, insufficient safety equipment and inadequate instruction in the use of the same. It is thus necessary for schools to have routine checks (both before lessons and also ideally in the form of a regular independent audit) to ensure that there is

---

[199] D.P.I.J. Hilary and Easter Terms 1993 (H.C.) 116. See McMahon & Binchy, *op. cit.* at p.444.
[200] *Times*, February 9, 1984.
[201] Generally see Narol, "Sports Participant Litigation: The Emerging Reckless Disregard Standard", 1 *Seton Hall Journal of Sports Law* (1991) 29.
[202] See Clancy, "Judo Mats, Climbing Walls, Trampolines and Pole Vaulters", 3 (1) *Sport and the Law Journal* (1995) 28.

adequate sporting equipment for the activities offered, and that it is in non-defective condition.

It should also be noted that the adequacy of the equipment should be gauged by reference to the fact that it is being used by children. In other words, a level of safety equipment that would be appropriate for adults may not be adequate for children. In *Harrison v. Shields*,[203] the claimant was a schoolgirl who was injured during a high jump competition. On the facts, the court concluded that her injuries were caused by her inexperience and lack of knowledge as to landing technique (and this might go to the question of inadequate instruction) rather than the inadequate protection afforded by the landing mats, *but*, had the injury been caused by such inadequate protection, then liability would have been imposed irrespective of the fact that the positioning of the said mats complied with the International Athletics Federation rules in this regard.

5.6.4 Duties in respect of supervision of school sports

As a rule of thumb it may be said that the younger the pupil, and the more dangerous the sport, the higher is the necessary level of supervision by the teacher. Moreover, such supervision will not be confined to the field of play at the school. Rather it will include supervision of (for instance) peripheral areas where injury might occur, possibly before or after the actual sporting activity.[204] It will extend to situations where the sporting event occurs in a different school or in a different country, and to the process of travelling to that other school or other country.[205] It will extend also to the "unofficial kickabout" on school premises before lessons begin, during break time or at the end of the school day.[206] Again resource issues come to the fore, in that the sports teacher may need to operate as both a supervisor and (for instance) a match referee, and in fulfilling his role as the latter he may be unable to attend adequately to the former.[207] A related question arises as to the extent of the duty of a school to

---

[203] Unreported, High Court, November 15, 1996.

[204] In *Alexander (A Minor) v. King Edward School Bath Governors*, unreported, Circuit Court, May 9, 2000, a school was held liable for negligent supervision in circumstances where one schoolboy accidentally hit another in the mouth with a hockey stick as a group of boys were leaving the hockey pitch in unruly fashion following a match. See Kevan *et al*, *op. cit.* at p.154.

[205] *Chittock v. Woodbridge School, Times*, July 15, 2002.

[206] *Kearn-Price v. Kent County Council* [2002] E.W.C.A. Civ. 193.

[207] In *Barfoot v. East Sussex CC*, unreported, August 16, 1939, see Grayson, *School Sports and the Law*, p.14) the defendant, a school cricket teacher, was also umpiring the match and hence didn't notice that one of his pupils who was fielding had moved to within nine yards of the batsman, who struck the ball into the young boy's face. The court held that, in the circumstances, the teacher's duties as umpire prevented him from exercising the requisite supervisory attention.

pupils, in cases where responsibility for sports tuition has been transferred to an outside agency – for example when children receive tuition at equestrian centres, adventure centres or swimming pools from persons employed by those institutions.[208] It is submitted that where a school endorses such an agency or where part of the curriculum (for example a swimming class) occurs on that agency's premises, then provided that the school has taken reasonable steps to ensure that such bodies are suitable for the children (in terms of the institution itself, the nature of the activity offered and the staff whom it employs), responsibility in respect of tuition and indeed supervision will pass to the outside agency, unless it is understood that the teacher retains a responsibility to supervise the children.

· From the outset, it should be pointed out that if inadequate supervision is to form the basis of a successful negligence action, then it must cause the harm complained of. Thus in *Clark v. Bethnal Green Corporation*,[209] a child at a swimming bath let go suddenly of a springboard that she had been holding, thereby causing another child who had been preparing to jump from the same to fall and suffer injury. Here the court held that the action of the first child was unpredictable and incapable of being anticipated, and would have occurred irrespective of the adequacy of supervision. A recent controversial case in this area is *Chittock v. Woodbridge*.[210] Here the 17 year old claimant (who was a keen sportsman) was left in a wheelchair following a skiing accident in Austria. For two successive days prior to the fateful accident he had skied "off piste" and had been reprimanded for doing so. However, his "ski pass" was not removed by the teachers on the trip on the basis that they were trying to treat the boys as adults. The next day he duly went off piste again, and this time suffered the horrific injuries mentioned. At first instance the judge found the teachers 50% responsible, concluding that the inadequacy of their disciplinary measures in the face of evidence that the boys could not be trusted constituted unreasonable supervision. In the circumstances, it is understandable why the court would want to balance out the financial cost to the unfortunate victim. Equally, it is submitted that the decision does not take adequate account of the nature of such trips, and indeed of the significance of allowing teachers a discretion on the question of how to apply disciplinary sanctions. Indeed it was on this basis that the Court of Appeal upheld the appeal by the school, concluding that the reaction of the teachers was a reasonable response to the situation.[211]

The conclusion in one recent Irish case seems to suggest that all sporting

---

[208] See Kevan, *et al*, *op. cit.* at chaps 15 and 16 and Grayson, *School Sports and the Law*, at pp.35ff. Ireland has no equivalent of the English Activity Centres (Young Persons Safety) Act of 1995.

[209] 55 T.L.R. 519 (1939).

[210] *Woodbridge v. Chittock* [2002] E.W.C.A. Civ. 915.

[211] [2002] E.W.C.A. Civ. 915 (2002) E.L.R. 735, [2003] P.I.Q.R. P6.

activity involving young persons should be supervised. In *Doyle v. Little*,[212] the plaintiff schoolboy was playing unsupervised indoor football in a parish hall. He apparently tripped while playing the ball and fell backwards onto the ground. He then stood up and walked to the wall of the hall where he fell again, this time as a result of dizziness or fainting. In falling he knocked two teeth out and sprained his neck. The plaintiffs alleged that the absence of supervision of this game constituted negligence, whereas the defence argued that any such supervision could not have prevented the first fall, and that it was the shock engendered by the same that caused the second fall. The court however, found for the plaintiff, concluding that whereas the presence of a supervisor would not have prevented the first fall, it could have prevented the second fall and hence the negligent failure to provide a supervisor or referee could be seen as the cause of the young boy's injuries. It is submitted that this is a somewhat harsh decision, and perhaps does not appreciate the limited extent of what a supervisor of such a game can actually achieve. More particularly, any requirement of mandatory supervision goes against all relevant case law from Ireland and England which requires merely that there be reasonable supervision *in the circumstances*. Three of the most significant such circumstances will now be considered, namely the vulnerability of the participants, the nature of the sport and the location in which the activity takes place.

5.6.4.1 Circumstance one: the vulnerability of the injured party

This goes not just to the question of the age of the pupils (although this is highly significant) but also to other related factors. Thus in *Morrell v. Owen*,[213] Mr. Justice Mitchell in the English High Court ruled that a higher level of supervision was required for a training session for disabled athletes than would be required for a training session for athletes who would perhaps be better able to take care of themselves. The point is that the older and less vulnerable the pupil, the less foreseeable it is that participation in sport will generate a serious risk of injury, and the more reasonable it is to expect the pupils to assume such risks for themselves. In *Smith v. Jolly*[214] a High Court jury refused to find negligent supervision on the part of a teacher who allowed a group of 15 year olds to compete in a shot putt event (which included marking the distance of a throw with a peg) when one of the girls managed to throw the shot at another girl's head while the latter was close by and bending down to measure a third girl's throw. Viewed from the standpoint of what might be

---

[212] Unreported, Circuit Court, August 2, 2002.

[213] *The Times*, December 14, 1993. See case note by Farrell, 1(2) *Sport and the Law Journal* (1993) 5.

[214] Unreported, High Court, O'Hanlon J., May 17–18, 1984. See McMahon & Binchy, *op. cit.* at p.443.

expected from a 15 year old in the circumstances, the action of the shot putter was so unreasonable that it was objectively unforeseeable by a teacher.

Similarly in *Mulligan v. Doherty*[215] a gymnastics teacher of 17 year old girls had demonstrated a particular exercise (involving a descent down wall bars) for students and had then supervised one girl in the exercise, before moving to another part of the gym to instruct another class. The claimant attempted the exercise, but claimed that she did not remember what the teacher had done in the demonstration and managed to let go of the bars and fell, injuring her back. She alleged that the teacher was negligent in that she should have supervised the entire class, so that all students would know the correct means of descent. The Supreme Court found for the defendants, concluding that the exercise in question was an easy one, and the technique needed to complete it successfully was obvious. Hence there was no need to supervise 17 year olds engaged in such activity. However, the Supreme Court expressly stated that had it been dealing with "young children," it might well have required such supervision.

On the other hand in *A (A Minor) v. Leeds City Council*,[216] the plaintiff was one of twenty five 11 year old girls taking part in her first PE class in her new school's sports hall. Having been given a safety talk, the girls were brought into the hall and told to move around the hall and to touch its four walls. The exercise was unstructured in that the girls were not told the order in which they were to touch the walls, nor were they told not to run. It was also somewhat competitive, as twenty-five children, (who were keen to please a new teacher and were in unfamiliar circumstances and with peers whom they barely knew) ran extremely vigorously in a variety of directions. During the course of the exercise, the plaintiff collided with another girl and fell on her wrist breaking a bone. She successfully sued the school for negligence, with the court concluding that in as much as it was entirely foreseeable that injury would flow from the mêlée in question, the teacher was negligent in allowing it to proceed.

Finally in *Comer v. Governors of St Patrick's Roman Catholic Primary School*,[217] the adult plaintiff took part in the 'father's race' at a school sports day – a race in which he had competed on several previous occasions. This race was a sprint over approximately thirty yards, however only five feet beyond the finish line there was a brick wall. Mr. Comer had previously warned the relevant teachers of the dangerousness of the course in question and had suggested that there should be a longer course allowing more of a stretch for deceleration. On this occasion, Mr. Comer competed with such vigour in the race that he was unable to stop in time, and so he collided with the wall seriously injuring his wrists and elbows. He sued the school in negligence, claiming

---

[215] Unreported, Supreme Court, May 17, 1966.

[216] Unreported, Leeds County Court, March 2, 1999. For comment, see 2 (3) *Sports Law Bulletin* (1999) 5.

[217] Unreported, Court of Appeal, November 13, 1997.

that it had exposed him to a foreseeable risk. The Court of Appeal, however, rejected this claim on the grounds *inter alia* that the plaintiff was well aware of the existence of the wall, and hence should have taken steps to avoid colliding with it and it was legitimate for the teachers to expect the fathers competing in the race to do so taking into account the obvious danger at the end of the track.

5.6.4.2 Circumstance two: the nature of the activity

Put simply, the more dangerous the activity the greater the need for complete supervision. In *Wright v. Cheshire County Council*,[218] during a school gymnastics class, students were participating in a range of various exercises, with the teacher moving from group to group giving supervision. One exercise involved the vaulting horse, where the students took it in turns to vault aided by a group of standbys whose job was to ensure that the vaulter landed safely. Unhappily, one such standby ran off upon hearing the school bell, and the student who was in mid vault was unable to land properly as a result and suffered injuries. Legal action was taken against the school but was unsuccessful on the grounds that the procedure followed – namely allowing 11 and 12 year old boys who were fairly well trained in the area to look after each other – had been approved for years and had operated safely. Similarly in *Lennon v. McCarthy*,[219] two pupils were playing "tag" in a hollow below a schoolyard where a number of trees and hawthorn bushes were growing. A branch of one tree projected out horizontally for seven feet from one of the hawthorn bushes. As one boy ran along, he brushed against the said branch and it rebounded hitting the chasing boy in the eye. The school was sued *inter alia* for negligent supervision. The court rejected this claim, holding that a reasonably prudent parent would not deem it necessary to have children in a playground routinely supervised at every moment.[220]

On the other hand in *Gibbs v. Barking Corporation*,[221] a pupil suffered injury during gymnastic training when he jumped off a vaulting horse "in a stumble," but the teacher had not made any efforts to have anyone assist him in the landing. Here the teacher was deemed to be negligent, in that the activity was sufficiently dangerous that the absence of an assistant posed a foreseeable risk to the plaintiff. Similarly in the United States in *Carabba v. School District*,[222] the defendants were organizing a wrestling competition and had hired a referee to supervise the competition. During the contest, the referee

[218] [1952] 2 All E.R. 789. For analysis see Brierly, "School Sports and the Law", 1(1) *Sports Law Journal* (1993) 19.
[219] Unreported, Supreme Court, July 13, 1966.
[220] See also *Wilson v. Governors of the Sacred Heart Roman Catholic School* [1998] 1 F.L.R. 663.
[221] [1936] All E.R. 115.
[222] See on this Drowatsky, "Assumption of Risk in Sport", 2 (1) *Journal of Legal Aspects of Sport* (1992) 92.

went to close a gap between mats and allowed the students to continue wrestling while his back was turned. During this time an illegal hold was applied on one of the students by the other, and as a result the former suffered a broken neck. The court held that the defendants owed a duty of care to the students, and were liable in negligence for the inadequate supervision of the contest. The point here was that immediate and intense supervision of every moment of the match was necessary to protect the safety of the contestants, and it was eminently foreseeable that a failure to supervise the event *at all stages* could lead to risk. Finally in Canada, in *MacCabe v. Westlock*,[223] during a gymnastics class, a student failed to complete an exercise properly and as a result sustained a spinal cord fracture and quadriplegia. At the time the teacher was supervising another exercise. The student was awarded $4m in damages, with the court concluding that the duty to provide adequate supervision was not met when a teacher sent students off to their own areas, thereby encouraging and not restricting dangerous activity.[224]

5.6.4.3 Circumstance three: the location of the activity

Finally, the responsibilities of the teacher in supervision will depend on the nature of the location in which the sporting activity takes place. It is necessary for a teacher to exercise due caution in determining whether a venue (including an indoor venue) is safe for a sporting event as it is likely to be played by the children in question, and also what precautions are necessary to ensure such safety. In *Kane v. Kennedy*,[225] a class had been timetabled to have an outdoor game of rounders. The weather rendered this impossible so the teacher decided that the game would be held inside in the sports hall. The plaintiff was injured during the game, when in an attempt to reach "home base," she had collided with a wall, being unable to stop. Budd J. accepted the plaintiff's version of events, which was that the teacher had placed the final base cone very close to the wall. After an extensive analysis of the history and nature of the game of rounders, he concluded that whereas it was not necessarily negligent for a PE teacher to organise an indoor game of rounders, nonetheless she was negligent in placing the home base cone so close to a wall that it was foreseeable that an accident of the type at issue in this case would occur.[226] Significantly, the

---

[223] [1998] 226 A.R. 1 (Q.B.).

[224] See also *Thornton v. Board of School Trustees of School District No.* 57 (1976) 73 D.L.R. 3d 35 (school liable when a student vaulted off a vaulting horse in somersault fashion and overshot the landing mat, landing on his head and as a result became quadriplegic), and also *Lunenburg (County) Dist. School Board v. Peircy* (1998) 41 C.C.L.T. (2d) 60 (N.S.C.A.) where a school was ordered to pay $2.3m in damages for not having supervised students properly at an adventure camp as a result of which one student was rendered quadriplegic when he fell head first from a rope line. For analysis see 2 (4) *Sports Law Bulletin* (1999)14.

[225] Unreported, High Court, March 25, 1999.

ruling in this case does not strike at the notion of indoor school sport – but it does require that where sport is being played inside, then necessary remedial measures be taken to make the playing thereof safe.[227]

5.6.5 Duties in respect of facilities[228]

In the next chapter we will be considering the responsibilities under Irish law for the occupiers of sports premises. From a schools perspective, two additional points over and above those made at this later juncture should now be made.

First, in recognition of the limited resources available to schools, Irish courts have maintained that school sports premises need not be perfect. Thus in *Lennon v. McCarthy*, which has already been considered, the court refused to accept that the field in question was unsuitable for the game of tig that the pupils were playing (or that a reasonably prudent parent would look into it and deem it to be so). To do so according to the court would be to proscribe the playing of "ordinary simple games like tig in rural Ireland." Similarly in *Flynn v. O'Reilly*,[229] the claimant was an 11 year old girl who had been competing in her school Sports Day. The event included a "running backwards race," and the girl in question in running backwards caught her foot in some kind of hole or depression, fell on her wrist and fractured it. She claimed that the field was unsuitable for the event in question, and hence that the school was negligent in allowing the event to take place. The Supreme Court refused to make this finding, concluding instead that the field in question was not: "Wimbledon, or Lansdowne Road, or Wembley or some place like that." Rather in the circumstances of the sports day, the playing surface was adequate for simple games and sports, as was evidenced by the fact that there had been no previously recorded incidents of injuries of this nature. A rule that required that on a pitch of this nature there be no difficult events like running backwards would, according to the Supreme Court, be excessively harsh and would overly restrict

---

[226] Similarly in *Ralph v. London County Council*, unreported, Kings Bench, February 11, 1947, the defendant teacher conducted a supervised indoor game of "tag." The plaintiff in an endeavour not to be "tagged" put his hand through a glass panel of a partition door and was injured. The court found that in not acting in contemplation of the possibility of such an accident (by for example keeping the children away from the glass door) the teacher was negligent. Equally in *Cahill v. West Ham Corporation* (81 Sol. J. 630 (1932)) the court found no negligence where a teacher organised a relay race in a classroom with a glass partition and where one pupil's arm went through the partition and was severely cut.
[227] In similar vein in *Petersen v. School District No. 36* (1993) 104 D.L.R. 334 (BCCA), a teacher was deemed negligent when during a baseball game he positioned the plaintiff too close to the batter.
[228] Generally see Grayson, *School Sports and the Law*, p.41ff.
[229] [1999] 1 I.L.R.M. 458.

the freedom of children to engage in sports.

Secondly, as with equipment, it is necessary for schools and indeed clubs to ensure that facilities are checked routinely by teachers or club officers (for instance to ensure that tiled areas in the vicinity of changing facilities or swimming pools are not dangerously slippy)[230] and it is advisable that such bodies would also commission regular independent checks on their sports facilities – both indoor and outdoor – and to act on any recommendations that might be forthcoming.

5.6.6 Litigation avoidance strategies

It goes without saying that a school, like a sports club, can and must avoid many of the problems mentioned above by taking out appropriate insurance policies, particularly in the areas of public liability insurance, personal accident insurance, professional indemnity insurance, possibly legal expenses insurance and directors and officers insurance[231] Plainly in doing so the school should ensure that it has disclosed the full nature of the activities on school premises to the insurer (and also mentioned issues such as school trips, the fact that the school team played "away" matches and so on), and has checked the policy to ensure both that cover is sufficient and also that pupils are not engaged in any activity that is expressly not covered on the policy.[232] Beyond this, it is necessary to ensure that actions by the school fit within the said policy – that for example a decision to appoint a sports coach, or indeed to appoint a 'regular' teacher as a coach of a particular sport is reasonable.

Finally, in seeking out best practice, schools would be well advised, in consultation with a solicitor, to draw up a policy document in respect of all areas of sports tuition and then to stick rigidly to that framework.[233] The document should deal, *inter alia,* with:

– Qualifications necessary for coaches/teachers of sport in that school.

– The extent to which individual pupils can be alone with individual teachers,

---

[230] Thus in *Taylor v. Bath & NE Somerset District Council*, unreported, Queen's Bench, January 27, 1999, the claimant sued successfully when she fell on an excessively slippery tiled floor having dropped her daughter off at swimming baths. She suggested that the excessively slippery nature of the tiles was caused by the fact that, not being properly cleaned, there had been an accumulation of body fats thereon. The court accepted this proposition, noting that despite instructions from the manufacturer of the tiles, they had not been properly chemically cleaned and this caused the build up of fats, which led to the injury.

[231] Generally see Grayson, *School Sports and the Law*, p.71ff.

[232] Equally, it does not seem that there is a legal obligation on the school to advise its pupils to take out personal insurance policies. See *Van Oppen v. Bedford Charity Trustees* [1990] 1 W.L.R. 235, *Sweeney v. Duggan* [1997] 2 I.L.R.M. 211.

[233] Brierly, "School Sports and the Law", 1 (1) *Sports Law Journal* (1995) 19.

and other matters mentioned in the Code of ethics and good practice.

– The extent to which sport is compulsory.

– The degree and extent to which sporting activities will be supervised.

– The availability of medical assistance in the event of injury or illness.[234]

– The existence and extent of safety checks on equipment and premises.

– The extent to which (if at all) a younger player may be selected for an older team.

– A clear statement on the use of performance enhancing substances, and also on whether the school will test for such substances.

– General safety precautions.

If a school can ensure a good policy on these issues and also adherence thereto by staff, then it will ensure that it avoids unwanted litigation, and more importantly protects the needs of its pupils.

5.6.7 The Irish Sports Council Code of Good Practice for Children's Sport

Finally, as we look to the responsibilities of those involved with children's sport, it is important to mention the *Code of Ethics and Good Practice for Children's Sport in Ireland*, published jointly by the Irish Sports Council and the Sports Council for Northern Ireland in 2001. The stated objective of the Code is: "to ensure that sport in the island of Ireland is as safe as it can be for children." In this respect, whereas most of the Code can be construed as "non-legal" (focusing as it does on providing advice to parents and schools as well as clubs for the purposes of ensuring that children enjoy sport), equally in as much as it can be seen to constitute best practice, the fact that a sporting body has failed to comply with the guidelines contained therein will be evidence that it has acted in breach of its duty of care to the child.

The Code covers such areas as the organisation of children's sport and the proper motivations behind children's competitions – concluding that the focus should be on competing and taking part rather than on winning. Importantly, the club or sporting organisation should always prioritise the interests of the child. To assist in this, the Code recommends that all clubs appoint children's officers,[235] and that each governing body for sport should appoint a national children's officer[236] Moreover, clubs and governing bodies should endeavour to ensure that the interests of children are heard strongly at committee level,

---

[234] Generally see Millane, "Neighbours in Law", 4 (2) *Sporting Traditions* (May 1988) 1.
[235] Para.2.6.1.
[236] Para.2.6.2.

and that the terms of the Code are well known and widely implemented. Beyond this, the Code contains recommendations on proper procedure for disciplinary matters,[237] recruitment, education and training of sports leaders,[238] and the training and supervision of children's sport, including supervision of away trips.[239] This includes for instance guidelines for coaches as to when it is appropriate to take a "hands on" approach to sports tuition, for instance where this is necessary to demonstrate a particular sporting technique[240] envisaging separate but complimentary roles for parents, guardians and coaches. Finally, the Code deals with probably the seminal issue relating to children's sport, namely the protection of the child from forces such as substance abuse,[241] psychological stress and burnout caused by excessive participation,[242] bullying,[243] and child abuse[244] in the forms of neglect, physical, emotional and sexual abuse.[245] This includes matters such as appropriate reporting procedures and especially where there are allegations made by a child against a sports coach or teacher.

5.7 DUTIES OF GOVERNING BODIES TO PARTICIPANTS

There are two separate contexts in which a governing body may owe a duty to participants in a sport over which it has control.[246] First, as we have seen, a governing body may also be vicariously liable for injury to a participant caused by one of its employees.[247] Secondly, in as much as its rules will tend to govern the operation of its sport, the governing body may owe a duty of care in the creation of its rules, to ensure that they provide adequately for the safety of participants. Moreover, because such rules are created calmly and dispassionately and with time for thought (unlike the split second decisions taken by a participant in a contact sport for example), governing bodies will not benefit from the same concession to circumstances, which the other sporting bodies discussed above, enjoy.

The most important case in this area, certainly at English law, is *Watson v. British Boxing Board of Control.*[248] In 1991 Michael Watson fought Chris

---

[237] Paras 3.4 and 4.9ff.
[238] Paras 3.5 and 3.6.
[239] Para.4.5.
[240] Para.4.2.
[241] Para.5.2.
[242] Para.5.3.
[243] Para.5.4.
[244] Generally para.5.5ff.
[245] Para.5.9.
[246] Generally, see Kevan *et al*, *op. cit.* at Chap.10.
[247] *Vowles v. Evans & WRU, op. cit.*
[248] [2001] 2 W.L.R. 1256.

Eubank for the WBO Super Middleweight Championship belt.[249] The match was stopped in the 12th Round having been fiercely contested. Disorder ensued between rival supporters and there was chaos in the ring for some time. During this time, Watson's trainer realised that Watson was slipping into unconsciousness. It took roughly seven minutes for a doctor to be summoned, and some 25–30 minutes before Watson arrived in hospital and was given the benefit of necessary medical equipment. As a result, he suffered a subdural haemorrhage and was paralysed down his left side, having lost half his brain function. He claimed that the British Boxing Board of Control (BBBC) owed him a duty of care to provide appropriate medical assistance – in particular resuscitation equipment and a person or persons qualified to use such equipment present at ringside – and that it was the absence of such equipment which caused a remediable injury to become irremediable.[250]

The BBBC claimed that it did not owe the plaintiff the said duty, and that even if the aforementioned equipment had been present it would not have saved him. Their safety rules – guidelines under which all promoters of boxing in Britain had to operate – required that three doctors be present at ringside (as they were on the fateful night) but not that resuscitation equipment or experts in this area be present. On the other hand, expert evidence was adduced suggesting that the importance of timely resuscitation for the treatment of sporting injuries had been accepted since the 1970s. In a case of this nature, the standard response to subdural bleeding is to intubate, ventilate, sedate, and paralyse the patient and then to administer drugs. Had the equipment been present at ringside, he would have been treated within three minutes of collapsing, rather than some half an hour later when he arrived at hospital. It was also pointed out that as a result of reform prompted by concerns for participant safety, the rules authorized by the governing bodies of other dangerous sports (for example motor racing and horse racing), contain requirements that resuscitation equipment and trained medical experts be present at sporting events conducted under their auspices.

In the High Court,[251] it was held that even though BBBC had no contractual involvement in the fight, it nevertheless gave its blessing to the contest, which took place under its auspices, and this was enough to establish a nexus between the BBBC and any professional boxer who fought in such a contest. Here, there was a breach of the duty owed to the plaintiff, in that the medical facilities on the evening in question were inadequate for the nature of the event. Indeed, Kennedy J. intimated that the BBBC had been very complacent in not looking beyond its own domain to other dangerous sports where the presence of such

---

[249] For analysis see 2 (6) *Sports Law Bulletin* (1999) 1 & 3ff.

[250] Michael Watson has made a spectacular recovery from his injuries, and in 2003 completed the London Marathon.

[251] September 24, 1999. See 2 (6) *Sports Law Bulletin* (1999) 1 & 3ff.

resuscitation equipment was mandatory. In its defence, the BBBC had claimed
that the plaintiff had voluntarily assumed the risks of the injury suffered. The
court rejected this argument, however, holding that the plaintiff might have
consented to the inherent risks of boxing, but not to the consequences of the
BBBC's failure to provide adequate safety arrangements.

Perhaps most controversially, the court found a causal link between the
negligence of the BBBC and the injury suffered, in that Watson would have
got treatment much quicker had the relevant equipment been present at ringside.
It recognised that it was impossible to say exactly how improved his condition
would have been had he received such treatment but said that on the balance
of probabilities, Watson's state of health would have been much better than it
was at the time the case was litigated, and that he would have recovered from
the haemorrhage and would have been able to lead a normal life, although he
would never have boxed again.

On appeal,[252] the Court of Appeal held that since the board set out by its
rules, directions and guidance to make provision for the protection of
professional boxers from the risks inherent in competing in an intrinsically
dangerous sport,[253] and since all participants in professional boxing matches
were bound to accept and comply with the board's requirements, there was
sufficient proximity between the board and the claimant to give rise to a duty
of care.[254] Moreover in the circumstances, it was fair, just and reasonable that
such a duty should be imposed.[255] In the fulfilment of that duty, the Court of
Appeal held that it was necessary for the board to be prospective in its thinking
and to seek competent advice as to how to proceed, particularly in respect of
the risk of something like brain damage to a participant which was at once one
of the most obvious and most catastrophic risks involved in the sport.[256] By
failing to do so, the Board was in breach of its duty to Mr Watson (and by
extension to all boxers in the United Kingdom).

The overall impact of the decision in *Watson* remains uncertain.[257] It has

---

[252] [2001] 2 W.L.R. 1256. See Mackay, *"Michael Watson v. British Boxing Board of Control"*
(2000) 1 *International Sports Law Review* 7, Block, *"Michael Watson v. British Boxing
Board of Control"* [2001] *International Sports Law Review*, 168, Thompson, "Will
Watson open the Floodgates?", 8 (1) *Sport and the Law Journal* (2000) 4, Grayson,
"Denial of Justice – Part Three – A Tale of Two Watsons", 8 (3) *Sport and the Law
Journal* (2000) 50, Manning, *"Michael Watson v. British Boxing Board of Control"*,
Sports Law Administration and Practice (February 2000) 8.
[253] It is submitted that the sports governing bodies' guidelines for safety should be seen
merely as setting minimum standards. See Maxlow-Tomlinson, "Skiing and the Law",
3 (1) *Sport and the Law Journal* (1995) 18.
[254] [2001] 2 W.L.R. 1256 at p.1265ff.
[255] *Ibid.* at p.1281.
[256] *Ibid.* at p.1289.
[257] See Manning, "The Implications for Other Sports of the Court of Appeal's *Michael
Watson* Judgment", *Sports Law Administration and Practice* (February 2001) 9.

been argued that it means that all boards of control or national governing bodies must now reassess their roles, and see whether they may now also legitimately be regarded as *safety* bodies, and if so, they will have to review their safety policies, address the most pressing risks attaching to participants and above all, get insurance.[258] Most importantly, in the creation of rules, which may affect the well being of those who will compete under such rules, sports governing bodies must be alive to developments in other sports and in the wider world, which could contribute to what is "best practice" in the area. Otherwise they may find themselves liable on any occasion when a player is injured competing in an event, which is planned, and run according to the governing body rules.[259]

A different approach to this issue was taken by the Australian High Court in the joined cases *Agar v. Hyde* and *Worsley v. Australian Rugby Football Union*.[260] In these cases the plaintiffs were both former rugby players who had suffered significant spinal injuries as a result of collapsing scrums. Having already sued co-participants and the referee, they now sued the individual members of the International Rugby Football Board (IRFB) (who were responsible *inter alia* for rule changes within Rugby Union) claiming that the rules of the game at the time at which the plaintiffs suffered their injuries did not provide adequate protection for players.

The High Court of Australia overturned the decision of the Court of Appeal and refused to find for the plaintiffs. This was largely because of the minimalist nature of the control which each individual member of the board had over the creation of new rules for rugby football. Moreover, there is a clear implication from the Australian High Court with its characteristically incrementalist approach to the development of duty of care principles, that it would not favour the possibility of hundreds of thousands of rugby players throughout the world being afforded the opportunity of suing individual members of the board in the event of injury, on the basis of general principle. Finally, the court rightly asserted that in assessing the duty of care owed to competitors in sport, the court should have regard to the fact that competitors may legitimately be taken

---

[258] Thompson, "Will *Watson*, Open The Floodgates? Lessons To Be Learnt", 8 (1) *Sport and the Law Journal* (2000) 3 at 8.

[259] For an Irish comparison, see *O'Reilly v. Nolan & Irish Amateur Boxing Association*, unreported, Galway Circuit Court, May 2, 2003 (Generally see "Boxer who Suffered Broken Jaw in the Ring Fails in Compensation Claim", *Connaught Tribune*, May 7, 2003) a case in which the plaintiff who had been injured in a boxing match unsuccessfully sued the governing body in negligence. It is submitted that in this case there was very little evidence demonstrating negligence on the part of the governing body, and no evidence at all to suggest that the governing body was in any sense responsible for the harm suffered by the plaintiff.

[260] [2000] H.C.A. 41.

to know the rules of the game, and to have assumed the risks of playing within the framework of those rules.[261]

The points of similarity between *Watson v. BBBC* and this case are striking. In the former case the Court of Appeal decided that the governing body owed a duty to persons competing under its auspices, to act in accordance with best practice when matters of safety were at issue.[262] It is arguable that nowhere is this duty more crucially exercised than in the creation of the safety rules by which the sport will operate. On the other hand there were also three important points of distinction between the cases. First, in *Agar* unlike in *Watson*, the individual appellants had a very remote level of control over the rules in question. Secondly, it was accepted in *Agar* that rugby players consent to engaging in a dangerous activity, and the only responsibility of the IRFB was not to create "unnecessarily dangerous' rules, yet it was far from clear whether the rules in question were 'unnecessarily dangerous," given that the risk factor in rugby is an aspect of its attractiveness. On the other hand in *Watson* the rules in respect of medical facilities were patently unnecessarily dangerous, nor were there any factors militating in its favour. Finally, in *Watson*, there was an established causal link between the negligence on the part of the defendants and the extent of harm suffered by the plaintiff. On the other hand in *Agar* and *Worsley*, the plaintiffs had actually been injured by an action that was in violation of the (allegedly defective) rules that were in place at the time. In other words, even if the governing body had revised safety rules in place, it is likely that the plaintiffs would still have suffered the injuries complained of.

Finally, it should be stressed that the mere fact that someone is injured as a result of a particular rule is not sufficient for liability to be imposed. Rather there must be genuine negligence on the part of the governing body in creating the rule. Thus in *Wertheim v. United States Tennis Association*,[263] the court held that the organisers of the US Open tennis tournament would only be found liable if it could be demonstrated that they acted recklessly. In this case, during a match, Swedish champion Stefan Edberg served an ace, which on bouncing, swerved and hit linesman Richard Wertheim in the groin, causing him to have a stroke and die. Mr. Wertheim was in a new "ready" position (as required by the USTA) crouched forward with his hands on his knees, and his estate claimed that the USTA were negligent in requiring this stance in light of the risks to linesmen which occurred in this case. The court rejected the claim

---

Manning & Taylor, "Liability of Sports Governing Bodies for Injuries to Players", 7 (6) *Sports Law Administration and Practice* (November/December 2000) 1.

[262] Generally on this point see Opie, "Negligence Liability of Rulemaking Bodies in Sport" [2002] *International Sports Law Review* 60.

[263] See Mel Narol, "Sports Participation Litigation: The Emerging Reckless Disregard Standard", 1 *Seton Hall Journal of Sports Law* (1991) 29.

holding that there was not proof of a sufficient level of negligence to justify imposing liability.[264]

5.8 CONCLUSION: REPLACING THE LAW ON THE SPORTS FIELD – ALTERNATIVE DISPUTE RESOLUTION AND NO FAULT INSURANCE

In conclusion we should note that there is of course persistent argument that the civil law, no more than the criminal law, should have at best a very restricted role to play in this area.[265] Thus commentators argue that it would be more effective for all concerned if issues of this nature were dealt with by the relevant sporting federations, who know the sport and the culture thereof as experts, who will be able to work more quickly and more effectively than the law courts, and whose punishments – especially in the context of major professional sport – in terms of suspensions for infringers will be more effective deterrents than any fine a court could impose.[266] Thus, it is felt, it would be preferable for sporting bodies to operate their own disciplinary tribunals and appeal bodies and, if it is absolutely necessary to resort to non-sporting methods of resolving such disputes, mediation or arbitration rather than litigation should be used.[267]

Linked in with this there are calls for sport simply to establish a no fault insurance scheme, whereby injured parties could be compensated without the need to litigate.[268] This is for instance the approach in New Zealand both

---

[264] *Ibid.* at p.40.

[265] Thus Gardiner and Felix comment that: "The appeal of contact sports such as football comes from their unrestrained qualities, unpredictability, exploitation and sheer physicality. The involvement of the law and courts put these all at risk and would create a climate where players would shy away from physical contact." See Gardiner and Felix, "*Elliott v. Saunders*: Drama in Court 14", 2 (2) *Sport and the Law Journal* (1994) 1 at 3. On the other hand, it is argued that because of the financial impact of a damages award, it will strike at the reason why much sports field violence is committed – i.e. the money fuelled obsession with winning. See also Hanson and Dernis, "Revisiting Excessive Violence in the Professional Sports Arena", 6 *Seton Hall Journal of Sports Law* (1996) 127.

[266] See Hanson and Dernis, "Revisiting Excessive Violence in the Professional Sports Arena; Changes in the Past Twenty Years", 6 *Seton Hall Journal of Sports Law* (1996) 127 at 151.

[267] See Gardiner and Felix, "*Elliott v. Saunders*: Drama in Court 14", 2 (2) *Sport and the Law Journal* (1994) 1, for the view that: "The football authorities need to seriously consider appropriate alternative dispute resolution mechanisms. Until this occurs there will be continued support for the use of the civil law."

[268] See for example Mark James, "Sports Injuries: No Fault Insurance – Kill or Cure for Sport", 2 (1) *Sports Law Bulletin* (1999) 10, Stuart and Silver, "Rugby, Catastrophic Injuries, Claims and Insurance", 2 (1) *Sport and the Law Journal* (1994) 15, O'Brien, "Liability Insurance and the Needs of Sport", 2 (1) *Sports Law Journal* (1994) 22, Miller, "A Sporting Chance Personal Injury Compensation in a No-Fault System", 7(2) *Sport and the Law Journal* (1999) 33 and Wolohan, "Sports Injuries; Risk Management Developments in the United States", 1 (6) *Sports Law Bulletin* (1998) 10.

through individual sporting federations and under the Sporting Injuries Insurance Act 1978, which created a state sponsored insurance scheme to which all clubs and players are affiliated.[269]

---

[269] See Levinson, "Foul! Tackling the Problem of Violence in Sport", *Sports Law Administration and Practice* (November/December 1998) 7, Felix, "Sports Injuries: Risk Management and the Role of Insurance", 1 (4) *Sports Law Bulletin* (1998) 10. The importance of such an approach was highlighted by the facts of *Cubbins v. Minnis*, *London Independent*, October 12, 2000. For analysis see Harvey, "Amateur Football and the Law", 9(1) *Sport and the Law Journal* (2001) 103.) An amateur Sunday league player whose leg was broken by another player as a result of a non-malicious tackle, was awarded £18,500 plus costs (estimated at £7,000). The reason why this was significant was that Mr. Minnis was not insured for this either personally or on his team's insurance, nor was Mr. Cubbins covered on *his* team's insurance, not being officially registered as a player. Mr. Minnis summed up the gravity of the situation saying: "I really think that this might open the floodgates for claims from footballers ... this could happen to anyone going out on a Sunday to play a game of football ... I wonder if people realize what risks they are taking when they put on their kit on a Sunday morning." Mr. Minnis claimed that he was facing financial ruin and would have to sell his house.

CHAPTER SIX

Occupiers, Organisers and Crowd Control

INTRODUCTION

In this chapter, we consider the duties of organisers of sporting events and occupiers of sporting venues. In many cases, of course, the organiser and the occupier will in fact be the same person, as where, for instance, a GAA organised All-Ireland final is staged at the GAA owned Croke Park. On other occasions, however the two parties may be different as for instance where the FAI organises a soccer match at the IRFU owned Lansdowne Road. The occupier only incurs liability for damage arising from the state of the premises (as distinct from damage arising out of an activity conducted thereon) and the distinction between the two types of damage is important both in determining *who* should be the proper defendant in any legal action, and also whether such action should be taken under common law principles of negligence or under the terms of the Occupiers' Liability Act. In reality, of course a claimant would be advised to take his or her claim against both the organiser and the occupier, and both in negligence and under the terms of the Occupiers' Liability Act.

Within this chapter we consider three broad categories of duty namely:

– the duties of the occupier of the stadium in which a sporting event is taking place;

– the duties of the organiser of a sporting event to persons inside the stadium;

– the duty of the organiser of the event to persons outside the stadium.

Finally, and on a related matter, we consider the approaches taken on a legal and quasi-legal basis to the problem of spectator violence within sport.

6.1 THE DUTIES OF OCCUPIERS OF SPORTS STADIA

As has been mentioned, whereas organisers of sporting events may incur liability under the tort of negligence for injuries to participants and non-participants arising out of activities on the field of play, the obligations of occupiers of stadia or other locations where sport is played, (including local authorities who own public sports facilities) relate to the state of the premises and arise under the Occupiers' Liability Act of 1995. The relevant terms of this legislation will now be considered.

6.1.1 The Occupiers' Liability Act 1995

The Occupiers' Liability Act of 1995[1] replaced all common law rules governing the duties, liabilities and rights attaching to occupiers in respect of entrants onto their property.[2] The 1995 Act deals with the circumstances in which an entrant onto land may sue the occupier of that land (defined by the Act as someone in sufficient control of the premises that it is reasonable to impose a duty towards the entrant upon him)[3] for injury occasioned on the premises. Obviously the concept of premises covers sports stadia, but because of the wide definition of the term "premises" given in the 1995 Act, it could also apply to a racing car or other means of transport.[4]

The 1995 Act classifies three categories of entrant[5] who receive differing levels of protection depending on the benefit that they bring to the occupier.[6]

6.1.1.1 *Visitors*

First there are visitors, including entrants as of right, entrants by virtue of contract, entrants present at the invitation or with the permission of the occupier (excluding recreational users), members of the occupier's family, entrants present at the express invitation of a member of the occupier's family, and entrants present for social purposes connected with the occupier or a family member. To these persons the occupier owes a "common duty of care," that is to say a duty of reasonable care to ensure that the premises are in a safe state and that injury is not suffered by reason of the state of the premises or of structures thereon.[7]

---

[1] Generally see McMahon & Binchy, *Law of Torts* (3rd ed., Butterworths, Dublin, 2000), Chap.12 and Quill, *Torts in Ireland* (Gill & MacMillan, Dublin, 1999), pp.137–146, Byrne & Binchy, *Annual Review of Irish Law 1995* (Roundhall Sweet & Maxwell, Dublin, 1996), pp.493–518 and Hall, "The Occupiers' Liability Act 1995: Codification of Occupiers' Duty to Entrants", 89 *Incorp. L. Soc of Ireland Gazette* (1998) 189.

[2] S.2.

[3] S.1.

[4] S.1. See McMahon & Binchy, *op. cit.*, p.319. Thus for example if the plaintiff in a post–1995 version of a case like *McComiskey v. McDermott* was injured by reason of the state of the car he or she could seek to recover under the Act.

[5] These three categories replaced the former common law categories of contractual entrant, invitee, licensee and trespasser. See McMahon & Binchy, *op. cit.*, pp.300–309.

[6] McMahon & Binchy, *op. cit.*, p.300.

[7] S.3. See McMahon & Binchy, *op. cit.*, pp.319–321. In s.3(2) two factors are expressly listed as relevant for determining what is reasonable in the circumstances. First, the level of care that visitors can be expected to take in respect of their own safety and

6.1.1.2 Recreational users and trespassers

The next category of entrant is recreational users – persons who are not visitors as defined, but whose presence is tolerated if not desired by the occupier, and who are there for recreational activity. It is not clear whether such recreational activity must be organised and hence whether a group of youths playing with a football in an unorganised fashion would fit within the terms of this definition.[8] Equally under section 1 of the 1995 Act, sporting activity is expressly deemed to come within the definition of recreational activity. Recreational users may not be charged an entrance fee (for then they would be contractual entrants/visitors) but may be charged a reasonable parking fee.[9] Finally there are trespassers – persons whose presence is undesired and not tolerated by the occupier.

The occupier owes a duty not to act with reckless or intentional disregard for the person or property of both of these categories of entrant.[10] Generally in determining whether the occupier is guilty of such reckless disregard, all relevant circumstances should be taken into account and in particular the following questions should be addressed;

– Did the occupier know or have reasonable grounds for believing that a danger existed on the premises?

– Did the occupier know or have reasonable grounds for believing that the entrant was likely to be on the premises?

– Did the occupier know or have reasonable grounds for believing that the entrant was likely to be in the vicinity of the danger?

---

secondly the level of supervision and control that others can be expected to exercise over the visitors. These are only factors that the courts may consider and do not fetter the discretion of the courts but they may serve to shift some onus of responsibility on to the visitor.

[8] McMahon & Binchy, p.324. It is submitted that the definition of recreational activity given in s.1 is sufficiently broad that any sporting activity however disorganized would be involved. In *Byrne v. Dun Laoghaire County Council* 20 Ir. L. T. (ns) 16, Circuit Court, Smyth P., November 13, 2001), however, the plaintiff fell over an indentation in the ground while training an under–15 soccer team in July. Despite the fact that these were public playing fields, the court found that the plaintiff was a recreational user (and hence that the defendants were not liable) on the grounds that it was "off season" when the event occurred and hence that the plaintiff did not have permission to use the playing fields at the time.

[9] S.1.

[10] S.4. In this sense the use of the term "act" in the statute is interesting and contrasts sharply with the focus on the state of the premises when dealing with visitors. Equally if, for instance, a golfer strikes a golf ball and hits a spectator, then it is the activity of the participant and not the occupier that has caused the injury and hence the Occupiers' Liability Act would not come into play.

– Was the danger one against which the occupier should in all the circumstances, reasonably be required to provide protection?

– How onerous was the burden of eliminating the danger or providing protection against it, taking into account the cost, the character of neighbourhood, and the impracticability of such renovation?

– What was the character of the premises (for example was there a tradition of open access)?

– What was the nature of the conduct of the entrant and what level of care could reasonably be expected of entrants in relation to their own safety?

– What was the nature of any warnings given by any person in respect of the danger?

– What level of supervision could be expected of persons accompanying the entrant?

It is not clear whether priority will be given to any one of these factors, nor indeed whether there is a precise definition of reckless disregard, as a standard of behaviour compared to, for instance, negligence or gross negligence.

So how do these rules affect the occupier of premises in which a sporting event is taking place? Clearly in the context of an organised game to which the occupier of the premises has consented, players, paying spectators and others inside the stadium at the invitation of the occupier (for example vendors of food) as well as persons entitled to be on the premises (for instance a rambler walking across a portion of a golf course over which there is a public or private right of way) will be classed as visitors and are owed a common duty of care in respect of dangers accruing from the state of the premises, as is a golfer visiting another club to play a match.[11] Players of organised and possibly unorganised games, present on the premises of an occupier (be it a sports field or simply any premises) without his/her invitation and with or without his/her consent, as well as non paying spectators[12] or persons present on the property for unrelated purposes (for example someone who is taking a short cut through a private golf course) will be classed as recreational users or possible trespassers. Such persons will only be protected against intentional and reckless harm caused by the occupier. Finally, a person who enters the ground for criminal purposes – including someone who knowingly avoids paying a mandatory entrance fee

---

[11] *Heaves v. Westmeath County Council* (May 2002) *Law Society Gazette* 38. See Murdoch, "Tigerland" (May 2003) *Law Society Gazette* 8.
[12] But see *Donaldson v. Irish Motor Racing Club*, unreported, Supreme Court, February 1, 1957, for discussion as to whether such non paying supporters were invitees or licensees under the pre 1995 law.

will be deemed a criminal entrant – and hence can only recover for harm caused intentionally by the occupier.[13]

6.1.1.3 *Injury resulting from the state of the premises*

As has been mentioned, the Act only covers harm occasioned "due to the state of the premises."[14] In other words, liability for injuries caused by *activities on the premises* is still gauged by reference to common law principles and the tort of negligence. Thus if a stadium wall collapses on a spectator then he may recover under the terms of the 1995 Act,[15] but if the same spectator suffers harm having been hit by a football that emerges from the field of play, then he can recover under traditional principles of negligence. Equally, the distinction between the two types of harm may not always be easy to draw.[16] It may, after all, be possible to view the injury to the spectator hit by the football as being caused by the fact that the grandstand in which he was sitting was built too close to the pitch or did not have adequate protection (in the form of screening) from what is an obvious and foreseeable risk.[17] Even more starkly, in the case of a spectator on a golf course who is struck by a golf ball, we may see his injury as being caused by an activity (the golf) or by the state of the course (as where the course is designed in such a way that a golfer playing a shot is unable to see whether there are spectators (or other golfers) in his intended line of play). The significance of this distinction lies in the fact that as we have seen, an occupier owes a lesser duty to non-visitors on his property under the terms of the Occupiers' Liability Act than he would at common law. If therefore, a non-paying spectator (who may probably be classified as a recreational user) is injured at a sporting event, it will be in his interests to claim that the injury derived from an activity on the premises. Equally it will be in the interests of the defendant to claim that it was the result of the state of the premises.

For now we would submit that in the situation of a spectator (or indeed player) injured as a result of an on field activity, the Occupiers' Liability Act will only apply where the design of the stadium or course is so negligent in the face of foreseeable risk that it can be seen as genuinely causative of the plaintiff's injuries. Generally, however, such design will amount merely to a condition in which another cause is played out.[18]

---

[13] S.4(3). See McMahon & Binchy, *op. cit.*, pp.327–328.

[14] S.1. See McMahon & Binchy, *op. cit.*, p.318.

[15] See generally *Cowan v. O'Freaghaile* [1991] 1 I.R. 389

[16] See for instance *Smith v. CIE* [1991] I.R. 1.

[17] *Murray v. Harringay Arena* [1951] 2 K.B. 529, *Hall v. Brooklands Auto Racing Club* [1993] 1 K.B. 205, *Callaghan v. Killarney Race Course* [1958] I.R. 366 and *Donaldson v. Irish Motor Racing Club*, unreported, Supreme Court, February 1, 1957.

[18] Generally, see McMahon & Binchy, *op. cit.* at Chap.2.

6.1.1.4 Exclusion notices

Finally, as we look at the general nature of Irish occupiers' liability rules, the question of the extent to which duties under the 1995 Act may be limited – for instance by a notice at a golf club disclaiming any responsibility for injury caused on the premises – should be addressed.

Under the Act, the duty owed by an occupier to a visitor may be restricted or extended by express agreement or by notice given by the occupier,[19] but may be reduced only to the level of the duty owed to a recreational user or trespasser (reckless disregard). Any express agreement purporting to restrict or exclude the duty towards visitors must be reasonable and is not binding on strangers to a contract in which it is contained. Moreover reasonable steps must be taken to bring it to the attention of the visitor.[20] Under section 5(2)(c) of the Act, prominent display at the normal entrance to the premises is deemed to be reasonable notice although this presumption is rebuttable. Finally, under section 5(5), if injury or damage is caused to any person by reason of a danger of which they have been warned in an exclusion notice, the occupier will only be absolved from liability if the notice could have enabled the visitor to avoid the injury or damage caused.

The concept of exclusion clauses has clear potential for sports clubs and stadium operators, not just because of the terms of the Occupiers' Liability Act, but also because it may be possible for such clause to be drafted in wide terms and to be deemed to constitute a *contractual condition* for admission to the relevant property, and in such circumstances it may be possible for an occupier or an organiser to absolve himself absolutely from any duty for the safety of the entrant. In *Regan v. The Irish Automobile Club*,[21] the plaintiff, was employed by the defendants as a flag marshal at a motor race held in the Phoenix Park. Prior to the race she had signed a form that contained an extremely wide exclusion clause whereby she agreed to absolve the organisers for "… liability arising out of accidents howsoever caused, resulting in damage and/or personal injury to my person and/or property." She was injured during the race, allegedly owing to negligent design of the course on the part of the defendants. In the High Court, however, Lynch J. held that the exclusion clause in question was wide enough to cover injury caused by the negligence of the defendants.

The decision in *Regan v. IAC* was perhaps unsurprising given the explicit nature of the form signed by the plaintiff, and also the fact that she had signed the form for valuable consideration – namely the effecting by the defendants of a personal accident policy on her behalf. None of these factors were present, however, in the English case *White v. Blackmore*.[22] Here, a competitor at a

---

[19] S.5.
[20] S.5(2)(b)(ii).
[21] [1990] 1 I.R. 278.
[22] [1972] 2 Q.B. 651. See Gardiner, *op. cit.*, p.758.

jalopy race was killed when, as he was standing beside safety ropes watching another race, a car became entangled in the ropes at another part of the course and the stakes holding the ropes were violently pulled up (the result, *inter alia,* of negligent planning on the part of the defendants) causing him to be catapulted some twenty feet in the air as a result of which he died. An exclusion clause was printed on a notice at the entrance to the field (and on other documents including the programme) and couched in extremely wide terms. Under section 2 of the UK Occupiers' Liability Act of 1957, this clause was deemed to apply to the deceased even though it was directed at spectators, in that at the time of the accident he was a spectator rather than a competitor. Moreover, although it is unlikely that the warning in the clause would have enabled any spectator to have protected him or herself against the risks inherent in such activity, nonetheless the Court of Appeal felt that the clause laid down conditions subject to which the deceased had entered the premises, including the condition that the defendants would not be liable in the event of his death. In England this result would probably be reversed by the terms of the Unfair Contract Terms Act 1977. If a similar case were to occur in Ireland, the exclusion clause in issue would probably be struck down as void under the terms of the European Communities (Unfair Terms in Consumer Contracts) Regulations 1995, secondary legislation which is dealt with in greater detail in chapter seven of this book.

Finally, it should be noted that an exclusion notice published *inside* a stadium will not bind an entrant on his first visit to a stadium, but, provided that, having attended the stadium, he is aware or ought reasonably to be aware of the notice, it will bind him in respect of all subsequent visits thereto.

6.1.2 The duty of the occupier to the sporting participant

The duty of the occupier to the sporting participant will depend on whether the latter is seen as a visitor, or recreational user.[23] Assuming that the player *is* a "visitor" then the occupier will be required to ensure that the premises are reasonably safe for the activity in question. A number of general guiding principles emerge from the case law in this area. These guiding principles lead to an overall statement of principle, namely that the question of whether an occupier of a sports stadium should be liable to an injured participant will be decided by balancing the extent to which the risk was foreseeable and probable against the extent to which the sportsperson can be taken to have assumed the same.

First, whatever the status of the entrant, the courts will not impose liability for injury to a participant deriving from a risk that was obvious and foreseeable

---

[23] Generally, see Lewis & Taylor, *op. cit.,* pp.619ff.

to him. Thus in *Comer v. Governors of St Patrick's RC Primary School*,[24] the plaintiff, who was competing in a father's race at a school sports day, had injured his hands in colliding with a wall that was located five feet beyond the finish line of the race. Mr. Comer had previously warned the school of the dangerousness of the course in question and had suggested that there be a longer course allowing more of a stretch for deceleration. The Court of Appeal, however, rejected his claim against the school, on the grounds *inter alia* that the plaintiff was well aware of the existence of the wall, and hence should have taken steps to avoid colliding with it and it was legitimate for the teachers to expect the fathers competing in the race to do so taking into account the obvious danger at the end of the track.[25]

On the other hand the courts *will* impose liability where the risks to the participant are serious and latent.[26] Thus in *Dibble v. Carmarthern Town*,[27] the defendant soccer club had drawn its pitch markings with hydrated lime. The plaintiff, a goalkeeper had on a number of occasions dived to make saves. When he removed his shirt after the game, he noticed that the pitch markings had burnt a four-inch wide strip of flesh on his body from his shoulder to his hip. He recovered £20,000 in damages.[28] On the other hand, it is less clear how negligent an occupier of a sports stadium must be to be guilty of reckless disregard for the safety of a participant who is deemed to be a recreational user of the property. Similarly in *Farrant v. Thames District Council*,[29] a 17 year old was playing on a beach near what was termed a tidal pool, which was used for activities ranging from diving to rowing to swimming. The plaintiff and his friends had been diving in at the deep end of the pool, but he then dived into the middle of the pool, hit his head off the bottom and suffered serious spinal injuries. The court found that the occupier was negligent (with contributory negligence assessed at 20%), in that he had allowed the pool to fill up with silt, thereby making the depth levels of the pool uncertain, nor had he erected any signs warning people not to dive outside of the deep end. Because

---

[24] Unreported , Court of Appeal, November 13, 1997.

[25] See also *Jones v. Northampton BC, The Times*, May 2, 1990, where the plaintiff who had slipped on a wet floor while playing soccer in the defendant's sports hall was unsuccessful in his claim, on the basis that he had been given due warning of the fact that the floor was wet.

[26] In *Cook v. Doncaster Borough Council, The Sporting Life*, July 16, 1993, a local authority was found liable in respect of a race track it owned, when a defect in the track caused horses and riders to fall.

[27] See Kevan *et al, Sports Personal Injury: Law and Practice* (Sweet & Maxwell, 2002), p.164 and 9(2) *Sport and the Law Journal* (2001) 37.

[28] See Gardiner, *op. cit.*, p.767 for comment on an unreported case, *The Times*, July 10, 1996, in which an athlete – who suffered a knee injury when he jumped into a long jump pit in which the sand was wet – successfully sued the local authority which owned the stadium in which the accident occurred.

[29] Unreported, Queens' Bench, June 11, 1996.

of this failure, it was foreseeable that people would suffer injuries of the type suffered by the plaintiff, and hence the defendant should be liable.[30] In the same way, in *Glenie v. Slack*,[31] the occupier of a race track and the organiser of a race meeting were held liable for serious injury to a participant which occurred when the car he was driving at the race meeting collided with a fence that ran around the inside of the race track, on the grounds that the presence of such fence with no unobstructed run off area meant that the track was unsafe for the activity for which it was being used.[32]

On the other hand in *Tomlinson v. Congleton Borough Council*,[33] the House of Lords imposed some limits on the extent of the duty of the occupier in this regard. Here the plaintiff was swimming in a lake in a public park owned and occupied by the defendants. Ignoring a sign that warned against swimming in what was a dangerous lake, (a sign which, according to evidence was habitually ignored by local people) the plaintiff ran into the lake and dived, striking his head off the bottom of the lake and causing paralysis from the neck downwards. The House of Lords rejected the plaintiff's claim that the defendant's warning signs were inadequate and that they should have landscaped the shores and planted over the beaches from which people swam. According to their Lordships the duty on the part of the defendants did not include a duty to do what was necessary to prevent all foreseeable risks. Rather the extent of such duty would depend not only on the likelihood of injury but also on the social value of the activity that gave rise to the risk and the cost of taking preventative measures. In this case, whereas the defendants would be entitled to take measures to prevent people from taking risks that were inherent in an activity in which they voluntarily chose to participate, they would not be obliged to incur costs to protect people who, like the plaintiff, had chosen to ignore a clearly visible warning sign.

---

[30] Other 'latent risks' accepted by the courts include a slippery oiled bowling lane (*Thomas v. Osprey Leisure Ltd* (December 8, 2000, Whitehaven County Court, Case No. 213212), a poorly defined tiled edging indicating the perimeter of a swimming pool (*Greening v. Stockton-on-Tees BC*, unreported, Court of Appeal, November 6, 1998), swimming pool at which the depth of the shallow end was inadequately indicated (*Banks v. Bury Borough Council* [1990] C.L.Y. 384, *O'Shea v. Royal Borough of Kingston Upon Thames Council* [1995] P.I.Q.R. 208, but see also *Ratcliffe v. McConnell, The Times*, December 3, 1998), and a highly polished floor unsuitable for dance classes *Gilmore v. LCC* [1938] 4 All E.R. 331.

[31] [2000] E.W.C.A. (Civ.) 145.

[32] See also *Harrison v. Vincent* [1982] R.T.R. 8, and *Latchford v. Spedeworth International, The Times*, October 11, 1983, where a claimant successfully sued a race organiser having been injured when his car crashed as a result of an unprotected flower bed running alongside the track.

[33] [2003] U.K.H.L. 5 [2003] All E.R. 1122. See also *Rhind v. Astbury Waterpark* [2004] E.W.C.A. (Civ.) 756 (June 16, 2004) and *Gorringe v. Calderdale Metropolitan Borough Council* [2004] 1 W.L.R. 1057 (April 1, 2004).

Following on from this, the courts tend to the view that participants may be taken to have assumed the risk that led to the injury in question, (typically where such risk is inherent in the sport), but not the risk of negligence on the part of the occupier.[34]

Just as the fact that a participant is acting within the rules of a sport will be a strong defence to a civil action taken against him, so also if the state of the premises is in line with standards for sports stadia set by the relevant governing body, the occupier will be unlikely to be liable for injuries resulting from such premises. In *Simms v. Leigh*,[35] a rugby league player was tackled off the pitch by three opponents, collided at speed with a concrete wall that was only just over seven feet from the touchline, and suffered a broken leg. The positioning of the wall was within the standards laid down by the rugby league governing body, nor was there any previously recorded incidences of such accidents. The court concluded that the injury in question was not caused by the collision with the wall but rather by the fact that the plaintiff had been heavily tackled by an opponent, but that even if it *had been* caused by the collision the club would not have been in breach of its duty to the player. This conclusion was based largely on the fact that the court was unprepared to oblige an individual club to live up to standards higher than those required by the relevant governing body – *inter alia* on the basis that players can be taken to have assumed the risks inherent in playing in a competition organised within the rules of the relevant governing body.[36] Equally since the case *Watson v. BBBC*,[37] it may be that the governing body could *itself* have been sued for setting standards that did not adequately protect the athlete.

It seems that stadium owners and occupiers are not required to guard against *all* foreseeable risks. Thus in *Simms v. Leigh*, Wrangham J. held that the injury in the case, while foreseeable, was so improbable that the club were not under an obligation to guard against it.[38]

---

[34] In *Jason Green (A Minor) v. Dublin Corporation*, 19 *Irish Law Times* (2001) 212, a nine year old boy was awarded £7,500 in general damages having cut his foot on a broken tile at a swimming pool.

[35] [1969] 2 All E.R. 923. See Gardiner, *op. cit.*, p.766ff. In a similar case in Ireland, a soccer player whose momentum carried him beyond the goal during an indoor soccer match, and who injured himself when his hand went through the window behind the goal was awarded €6,500 in damages against the occupier of the sports hall. See "€6,500 award for soccer player", *Irish Times*, February 11, 2004.

[36] On the other hand, liability will follow as a matter of course where an organiser acts in violation of a governing body safety rule. See *Davis v. Feasy*, unreported, Court of Appeal, May 14, 1998.

[37] [2001] 2 W.L.R. 1256.

[38] See *Bolton v. Stone* [1951] A.C. 850.

6.1.3 The duty of the occupier to the non-participant – stadium and crowd safety

The duty owed by the occupier to the non-participant will depend on the status of that person for the purposes of the Occupiers' Liability Act 1995. If he is a visitor, then he is owed a common duty of care. This will arise, most obviously, where a spectator has paid an entry fee into the event. On the other hand, if he is to be classed as a recreational user (for example, where he is a non-paying participant), then the occupier merely owes him a duty not to harm him intentionally or as a result of showing reckless disregard for his safety. Equally, irrespective of the status of the event, occupiers of sporting venues also have obligations imposed on them under the terms of legislation.

The notion of sporting disasters, where participants and non-participants are injured or killed as a result of inadequacies in the stadium in which a sporting event is taking place, is not a new one. The first occasion at which a problem with stadium safety resulted in legal action was in *Francis v. Cockrell*.[39] A stand had collapsed at the Cheltenham National Hunt Festival and an injured spectator sued for breach of contract. Despite the fact that it was the builder of the stand rather than the owner thereof who was negligent, the owner was deemed to be bound by an implicit contractual term of safety with the spectator. In *Brown v. Lewis*[40] – a case decided in the era before the doctrine of separate legal personality of companies came to the fore – the individual members of a club committee were deemed liable when a stand collapsed at Blackburn Rovers Football Club. In 1902, 26 people were killed at an England v. Scotland soccer game in Ibrox Park, Glasgow.[41] In 1946, 33 people died in Burnden Park, Bolton as a result of overcrowding and the collapse of two protective barriers.

It is more recently, however, that the scale of disaster involved has tended to make such issues front-page news. In 1971, 66 people died owing to poor stairways and handrails in Ibrox Park in Glasgow, leading to successful litigation.[42] In 1985, a fire at Bradford City FC killed 56 spectators,[43] and in the same year a combination of football hooliganism and the defective state of the Heysel Stadium in Brussels during the European Cup Final between Liverpool FC and Juventus left 38 people dead and more than one hundred injured. Most notably, in 1989, in an event witnessed live on national television, severe overcrowding and the collapse of crush barriers during an FA cup semi-final between Liverpool and Nottingham Forest at Hillsborough in Sheffield,

---

[39] (1870) 5 L.R. 5 Q.B. 501. See Gardiner, *op. cit.*, p.756.
[40] (1896) 12 T.L.R. 455.
[41] Gardiner,. *op. cit.*, p.734ff.
[42] *Dougan v. Glasgow Rangers Football Club, Daily Telegraph*, October 24, 1974.
[43] *Fletcher v. Britton v. Bradford City AFC, The Times*, February 24, 1987.

led to the deaths of 95 Liverpool fans, a disaster that would later be attributed to poor crowd management by the police.[44]

A couple of brief points should be made at this juncture. First, the official response to many of these events was to draw a direct link between the issue of stadium safety and the issue of football hooliganism and, in legislative terms, to tackle the latter – seen as the great cancer in British sport. In reality, the two issues are conceptually different and should be dealt with as such.[45] Secondly the Hillsborough disaster shows us that a stadium may be defective (or put another way, the occupier may be in breach of his duty of care) not just because it might collapse, but also it cannot cope with a foreseeable and related problem – for instance poor crowd management or hooliganism. It should also be noted that at the time that Lord Taylor wrote a series of reports on the Hillsborough disaster, there had been eight previous official reports concerning crowd safety at football grounds. Indeed in writing his report, Lord Taylor expressed disbelief that given what had gone before, the tragic events of that day could have happened.[46]

Our principal concern, however, is with the extent to which an occupier can be liable for poor stadium safety and more specifically, with the question of what an occupier must do to make his stadium reasonably safe and hence to avoid liability.[47] Many of the obligations considered attach both to occupiers of sporting venues *and* organisers of sporting events, and should be understood as such.[48]

6.1.3.1 Statutory obligations

In Ireland the Fire Services Act of 1981 imposes an obligation on persons having control of premises used, *inter alia*, for purposes of entertainment, recreation or instruction or for the purpose of any club, society or association,

---

[44] For analysis of the Hillsborough disaster see Hartley, "Hillsborough – A Disaster Unfolds", 5(2) *Sport and the Law Journal* (1997) 65, and by the same author *Exploring Sport and Leisure Disasters: A Social-Legal Perspective* (Cavendish, 2002).

[45] Gardiner, *op. cit.*, p.735.

[46] In terms of the legal action flowing from Hillsborough (and bearing in mind that most personal injury cases resulting from this were settled), in *Hicks v. Chief Constable of South Yorkshire Police* [1992] 2 All E.R. 65, a father unsuccessfully sued for personal injuries suffered by his two daughters in the lead up to their death at Hillsborough. Beyond this, there were a number of cases (*Alcock v. Chief Constable of South Yorkshire* [1992] 1 A.C. 310, *Frost v. Chief Constable of South Yorkshire* [1999] 2 A.C. 455) dealing with the question of whether victims' families or police officers on duty could recover for nervous shock. Equally, none of these cases are specifically relevant for present purposes.

[47] We will not consider the issue of liability of stadium owners to members of the rescue services as a specific topic. For analysis of this see Kevan *et al*, *op. cit.* at Chap.8.

[48] Generally see Partington, "A Study of Football Stadium Safety; Are We Safe Yet?", 8(2) *Sport and the Law Journal* (2000) 63.

or for any purposes involving access to the premises by members of the public, to guard against the outbreak of fire therein and to ensure as far as is reasonably practicable the safety of persons on the premises in the event of an outbreak of fire. Under the 1981 Act, a fire authority can serve a fire safety notice on an occupier of a building, which is particularly dangerous for fire prevention purposes, which may prohibit use of the building or a part thereof until specified precautions are taken to the satisfaction of the fire authority.[49]

This Act has been amended by the Licensing of Indoor Events Act of 2003. Under this Act, it is necessary for someone who organizes an indoor event that falls within a class of events prescribed by the Minister for the Environment and Local Government,[50] to apply to his or her local fire authority for a license to hold the said event.[51] It is an offence to hold or organize such an event, or for an occupier of a premises to permit it to occur, unless a licence has been attained for the same.[52] In determining whether or not to proscribe a class or classes of indoor event, the Minister should bear in mind factors such as the number of people likely to attend the event, whether the level of supervision for such persons that is available is conducive to ensuring their safety, whether there is a need to provide seating for such persons, the place or area at or in which the event shall take place and other matters relevant to the safety and security of attendees.[53] It is unclear, however, whether this Act will actually apply to sporting events. Under section 2 of the Act, an indoor event for its purposes is defined as "a performance which takes place wholly or mainly in a building and comprises music, singing, dancing, displays of entertainment or any similar activity and in respect of which members of the public may or may not attend." On the face of it, and through application of the *eiusdem generis* maxim of statutory interpretation,[54] this seems to exclude sporting (or indeed any non-musical) events. On the other hand, under section 4 (2) of the Act, the Minister retains a residual power to proscribe any indoor class of activity, having regard both to the factors listed above, and also to the type of indoor event under discussion.

In terms of the general condition of the premises, section 37 of the Public Health Acts (Amendment) Act of 1890 requires that any temporarily constructed structures where people are likely to assemble for any show

---

[49] Linked with this there are Ease of Escape Regulations 1985 created under the terms of the 1981 Act.
[50] Under s.5(2) of the Act.
[51] S.5(4).
[52] Ss 11 and 12.
[53] S.5 (2).
[54] Under this maxim, where a general word is preceded by a list of specific words that create a genus, then the general word shall be interpreted consistently with the specific words. Thus under this section, the interpretation of the general phrase "similar activity" will be informed by the specific words preceding it which give the impression of a musical event.

entertainment, public procession, open-air meeting, or other like occasion, should be safely constructed or secured to the satisfaction of the local authority. Moreover the Safety, Health and Welfare at Work Act of 1989 requires that a place of employment (for example a stadium in which professional sport is being played) should be safe, and that employers should draw up a safety statement in respect of the premises and appoint a safety officer therefor.[55] Finally, under the Building Control Act, 1990 and the Building Regulations of 1991 and 1994, technical standards are set both for new buildings and also in respect of material alterations to old ones, dealing with matters such as structure, fire, site preparation, materials and workmanship, ventilation, hygiene, sound, drainage and waste disposal, heat producing appliances, stairways, ramps, guards, conservation of fuel and energy and access for those with disability. Needless to say such standards must be complied with by the owner of the relevant structure.

6.1.3.2 *The approach of the courts*

The most significant Irish case in this area is *Cowan v. Freaghaile (representing the GAA) and McInerney & Sons Ltd.*[56] During half time in the 1985 All-Ireland hurling final, in Croke Park, Dublin, a screen wall outside one of the Hogan Stand toilets collapsed on the plaintiff. This part of the wall had no strengthening bars nor dowel rods, whereas the rest of the wall had three inch long strengthening bars. Equally expert witnesses claimed that the whole wall should have contained bars/rods of about 3–4 feet in length. O'Flaherty J. found that the wall was unsafe. Indeed the fact that part of the wall contained rods implied that the original specifications for the wall required rods. Accordingly, he deemed the original builders to have been negligent. Equally, however, he also found that the GAA were 20% responsible. The case was heard in 1985 and O'Flaherty J. looked to the other infamous events of 1985 – those at Bradford and Heysel – and concluded that these events should have prompted the GAA to review its practices and to have undertaken a general structural examination of Croke Park before the All-Ireland finals of that year. This conclusion – that the standards to be expected from an occupier may be gauged by reference to external factors and developments that don't directly pertain to him – is a salutary one, in that it imposes an obligation on the occupier to familiarize himself both with the standards laid down by statute (with which he *must* obviously comply) and also with standards laid down elsewhere which are not binding in nature, in that adherence to these standards may well be used as a yardstick for assessing whether the preparations of the occupier are or are not negligent. Accordingly we shall shortly consider not only statutory

---

[55] On this point see Gardiner, *op. cit.*, p.769.
[56] [1991] 1 I.R. 389.

obligations for occupiers of stadiums but also the non-binding recommendations in this area that may constitute best practice, by which the reasonableness of the occupiers' efforts will be gauged.

The issue of stadium safety arose more recently in the Circuit Court in *Healy v. Fleming*.[57] In this case the plaintiff was a contractual entrant to the defendant's point-to-point race meeting.[58] During a shower of rain, she made her way to a tent to shelter via a steep incline behind the bookmakers' ring. This was not the only way to the tent, however, as there was a longer but safer route. Equally, all the patrons were going the way she chose. On the way, she slipped and was injured.[59] Judge McMahon acquitted the defendants of negligence. He held that such race meetings conferred significant benefit on the community, and to impose a duty requiring that all risks however unforeseeable should be obviated, would impose an enormous cost, insofar as the race committee would find it next to impossible to fulfil such standard, and hence its imposition "... might sound the death knell for such occasions and this ...[in his view] would be a sad social loss." It is submitted that this is a correct approach under the terms of the Occupiers' Liability Act 1995. After all, the standard of care imposed on persons by the tort of negligence is that they must act reasonably *in the circumstances*, and it is an accepted principle of Irish law that reasonableness in the circumstances is to be assessed by reference, *inter alia* to the social utility of the impugned action and the cost of eliminating any risk that flows from it.[60]

6.1.3.3 Non-binding recommendations and codes of practice

There are three important sources of extra-legal recommendations in respect of stadium safety.

UEFA Guidelines Governing bodies may themselves lay down certain criteria for stadia, and given that soccer has been the sport that has attracted most notoriety as far as the question of the safety of spectators is concerned, it is important to consider the UEFA Guidelines for Safety and Security in the Stadium For All UEFA Competition Matches.[61] These regulations are binding for all matches played in any UEFA competition and breach thereof will lead to disciplinary sanction. Equally, it is stressed that such requirements are not exhaustive in terms of the responsibilities of match organisers and participating

---

[57] 19 Ir. L .Times (ns) 241 (Circuit Court, Kanturk, June 2, 2001).
[58] This case was decided on pre-1995 principles but proceeded on the basis that these represented the same test as that prescribed by the 1995 Act in respect of the occupiers' duty to visitors.
[59] This was the first injury at this point-to-point since 1954.
[60] See McMahon & Binchy, *Law of Torts* (3rd ed., Butterworths, Dublin, 2000), pp.154ff.
[61] The 2000 UEFA guidelines are available at www.uefa.com.

organisations and clubs, and that ultimate responsibility for determining what is necessary to ensure stadium safety and security lies with such organisations and clubs.

The recommendations begin by requiring that certain matches – namely all UEFA Champions League, UEFA Cup, European Championships and UEFA Super Cup matches – be played exclusively before seated spectators,[62] that certain other less high-profile matches be played in stadia where at least 80% of total capacity is seated, and that all other matches be played in stadia whose seating capacity is determined by relevant local authorities. Moreover, seats should be fixed to the floor, and must, *inter alia,* be made from unbreakable, inflammable material.

Obligations also exist in respect of matters other than the state of the premises. Thus the need for strict control of the sale of tickets is stressed.[63] Responsibility for distributing tickets belongs to each association or club, as also does responsibility for ensuring that none of its ticket allocation is passed either onto the black-market or into the hands of unauthorised individuals.[64] The guidelines stress the value of local authorities operating in tandem with supporters' clubs to ensure that, *inter alia*, ticket distribution runs smoothly.[65] Moreover there should be co-ordination with police to try to alleviate problems connected with the black market,[66] and with authorization for match day sales[67] and counterfeit tickets.[68]

UEFA guidelines require that, no more than two years prior to the date of the UEFA game, the stadium has been thoroughly inspected by competent local safety authorities and that a certificate testifying to its safety and suitability has been issued thereby.[69] Moreover, the day before the game, the stadium must be guarded against unauthorised intrusion, and before any spectators are admitted, there must be an efficient security sweep of the stadium to search for unauthorised persons or dangerous objects.[70] In order to achieve these objectives efficiently and to ensure that appropriate security precautions are in place, a liaison group should be appointed comprising the police commander, and a senior representative of the safety security, medical and fire services, the competing teams, stadium authorities, match organisers and UEFA.[71]

---

[62] See Moore, *Sports Law and Litigation* (2nd ed., CLT Professional Publishing, 2000), p.91 for how the *Taylor Report* recommended the phased introduction of all-seater stadia for designated grounds under the 1975 Act.
[63] Instruction 1.01.
[64] Instruction 1.04.
[65] Instruction 3.04.
[66] Instruction 1.07.
[67] Instruction 1.09.
[68] Instructions 1.10–1.11.
[69] Instruction 2.02.
[70] Instruction 2.05.
[71] Instruction 2.04.

Moreover, the police officer or stadium security officer who will be in overall command of safety or security matters must be clearly identified.[72] There must also be a stadium control room affording the police an appropriate view of the stadium,[73] a television surveillance room that can be used for spectator control[74] and a functioning public address system.[75] There must also be adequate first aid and other facilities.[76] Finally, the sale or distribution of alcohol is prohibited within the stadium or its private environs.[77]

In terms of dealing with spectators, the instructions require that spectators be screened initially at an outer cordon/perimeter fence, to ensure that only ticket holders approach the turnstiles, and a preliminary check is made to prevent alcohol, fireworks or other dangerous objects from entering the stadium. Moreover, immediately outside the stadium a final screening process should be undertaken to achieve these objectives and also to forbid access to known or potential trouble makers, and persons under the influence of alcohol or drugs. Equally UEFA seeks to ensure that common sense will be used in this regard, to prevent excessive screening and to ensure that searches do not excessively delay matters or create unnecessary tension.[78] In similar vein emphasis is laid on the need for an effective stewarding process within the stadium.[79] As with all documents in this area, there is a requirement that there should be an effective segregation process for spectators,[80] including a process for restricting spectator movement within the stadium.[81] There must also be an effective pre-determined crowd dispersal strategy.[82]

Match organisers are also charged with taking action to prevent provocative or racist actions or behaviour by supporters within or in the immediate vicinity of the stadium, and to inform police in the event of such activities occurring.[83] Furthermore, and in order that the tendencies of any set of spectators might become better known, each association or club should appoint a security officer who should liaise with supporters and also should compile a list of known trouble makers.[84]

---

[72] Instruction 2.03.
[73] Instruction 2.20.
[74] Instruction 2.21. This requirement only pertains to UEFA Champions League group matches, and European Championships final matches
[75] Instruction 2.22. Moreover, announcers using such systems must operate in neutral fashion.
[76] Instructions 2.27–2.28.
[77] Instruction 2.19.
[78] Instruction 2.08.
[79] Instruction 2.10.
[80] Instruction 2.11.
[81] Instruction 2.13.
[82] Instruction 2.26.
[83] Instruction 2.31.
[84] Instruction 3.01.

Finally, and in a theme that recurs throughout most recommendations in this area, UEFA emphasises the importance of co-ordination of efforts in this area. Thus associations and clubs are urged to co-operate with match organisers.[85] In similar vein, match organisers should co-operate with public authorities, to ensure that there are adequate police forces present at any event to deal with problems that might arise,[86] and to facilitate the exchange of information both nationally and internationally.[87] This would also be necessary for matters as simple as ensuring that where someone has been refused entry to a sporting event, he is not then later admitted by another person.[88] To this end, all involved parties should be able to communicate freely with each other through radio-telephone link.[89]

The Council of Europe   The Council of Europe has been at the forefront of efforts to deal both with spectator violence at sporting events (and in particular at soccer matches) and also with the issue of stadium safety, particularly through the creation of the *European Convention on Spectator Violence and Misbehaviour at Sports Events and in Particular at Football Matches*, of 1985.[90] This document deals primarily with issues of crowd control rather than stadium safety but a number of themes emerge from it which impact on all the subsequent Council of Europe documents on the subject.[91] Most notable is the view that there is a link between stadium safety and supporter violence, in that both pose risks for spectators. Thus in Article 4 of the Convention, concepts like segregation of supporters, control of ticket sales, control of alcohol, preventing dangerous objects from being brought into stadia, effective communication between all parties and the appointment of liaison and safety officers are introduced, which are important themes in this area, and pervade virtually all proposals for improvement of stadium safety from various different bodies. The Convention also creates a Standing Committee, which monitors its application[92] in consultation with the relevant sports organisations, and keeps the whole issue of stadium safety and crowd control under continuous review.

---

[85] Instruction 3.07.
[86] Instruction 4.01.
[87] Instruction 4.02.
[88] Instruction 4.03.
[89] Instruction 4.04.
[90] European Treaty Series – No. 120.
[91] See for instance the Recommendation on the Promotion of Safety at Stadia (91/1), Recommendation on Measures to be Taken by the Organisers of Football Matches (93/1), Recommendation on Measures to be Taken by Organisers and Public Authorities Concerning High Risk Indoor Sports Events (94/1), Statement on Fences and Barriers (adopted June 5–6, 1997), Recommendation on Removal of Fences in Stadiums (99/2).
[92] Art.8.

The Department of Education Code of Practice Finally, in 1996, the Irish Department of Education created a *Code of Practice for Safety at Sports Grounds*, which applies to all grounds with a holding capacity of 20,000 spectators or more. In common with the Council of Europe resolutions and recommendations, the contents of the Code of Practice are non-binding. Equally they may be seen as constituting "best practice" and it is against such standards that the behaviour of any particular club will be assessed in a negligence action. We now consider what such "best practice" entails.

6.1.4 Best practice for stadium and crowd safety

In its 1991 *Recommendation on the Promotion of Safety at Stadia*, the Council of Europe concluded that there were three main categories of risk as regards safety in stadia, namely danger from fire, danger from structural failures and problems inherent in the presence of large crowds. This is not dissimilar to the approach taken in the Department of Education Code of Practice, although the latter also refers to problems deriving from underfoot conditions and distinguishes between crowd pressures *per se* and problems connected with emergency evacuations.[93]

6.1.4.1 Fire safety

In respect of fire safety, it is recommended, *inter alia*, that there be responsible control of any flammable substances at football matches, that the design of the stadium and the materials used in the construction thereof should be conducive to good fire safety and that there be adequate fire-fighting equipment at the match.[94]

6.1.4.2 Structural matters

In respect of structural matters, it is recommended that there be a maximum capacity laid down for each stadium and indeed for each sector of a stadium, bearing in mind factors such as the dynamics of crowd effects, the minimum size of seats and the type of partitioning between sectors.[95] In addition, there should be clear access to, and egress from stadiums,[96] especially in cases of

---

[93] *Code of Practice*, p.10.
[94] See Section B of Appendix to the Recommendation on the Promotion of Safety at Stadia (91/1). See also the *Code of Practice*, pp.93ff. See also *Code of Practice for the Management of Fire Safety in Places of Assembly* (1991), *Code of Practice for the Safety of Furnishings and Fittings in Places of Assembly* (1989) and *Code of Practice for Fire Detection and Alarm Systems for Buildings* (1989).
[95] *Ibid*. See also *Code of Practice*, pp.43–55.
[96] *Ibid*., pp.43–55.

emergency, and clearly demarcated parking areas for emergency vehicles. Finally, the state of the relevant structure should be the object of regular checks and especially prior to matches, to identify weaknesses and damage.[97] Article 6 of the European Convention had recommended a system of licensing of stadiums that conformed to safety standards. Following on from this, the Standing Committee set up under the Convention, called for such pre-match checks to be a "condition *sine qua non* for the grant of such a safety certificate."[98] Similarly the Department of Education Code of Practice suggests methods for assessing the safe holding capacity of grounds, by reference to entrance and exit capacity (including emergency capacity), the holding capacity in either a seating or standing area, and the recommended flow rates from stands, stairways and terraces.[99]

6.1.4.3 Crowd management

In respect of crowd management, the standing committee called for the provision of spaces inside stadiums conducive to the free movement of large numbers of persons.[100] It also emphasised the role of a strong ticketing policy to ensure adequate segregation where necessary, and to prevent overcrowding in sections of stadia. Finally there is a call for safety features such as perimeter fences and crush barriers to be designed in a fashion that would prohibit unauthorized entry onto the field of play but would not prevent access in the event of a crisis, for example by ensuring that perimeter fences could be opened to allow access onto the field of play in the event of an emergency.[101] Moreover, there is a suggestion that associations and clubs work to phase out the existence of perimeter fences.[102]

6.1.4.4 Co-Ordination of efforts

All recommendations in this area stress the need for co-ordination between all parties involved in stadium safety[103] – police, health authorities, stewards and

---

[97] *Ibid.*, p.37ff.
[98] Recommendation XII of Appendix B to the Council of Europe Recommendation on the promotion of safety at stadia (91/1).
[99] It is recommended that there be a rate of 40 persons per minute per unit of exit width (550mm) from stands and stairways and 60 persons per minute per unit of exit width from terraces. See *Code of Practice*, pp.127–140.
[100] Recommendation XIII of Appendix B to the Council of Europe *Recommendation on the Promotion of Safety at Stadia* (91/1).
[101] *Code of Practice*, pp.123–126. The Council of Europe Standing Committee later recommended that fences be removed. See *Recommendation on Removal of Fences in Stadiums* (99/2).
[102] Instruction 2.15.
[103] *Code of Practice*, pp.3ff and 103ff.

spectators. This would include ensuring that there was a suitable office for police at a game with a proper view of the field,[104] and that there was some effective means of communicating with the spectators. The Code of Practice, moreover, stresses the need to ensure that civil authorities be given appropriate notice of major sporting events,[105] and that Health Authorities be notified in advance of major events, in order to enable hospitals to make whatever prior arrangements are deemed necessary.

6.1.4.5 Best practice checklists

Most helpful in determining best practice, however, is the fact that both the Code of Practice and also the Council of Europe in subsequent recommendations on *Measures to be Taken by the Organisers of Football Matches and Public Authorities* (1993),[106] and *Measures to be Taken by Organisers and Public Authorities Concerning High-Risk Indoor Sports Events* (1994)[107] create specific checklists for sports organisers and public authorities for improving stadium safety.[108] For a club or stadium or governing body wishing to operate in compliance with these safety recommendations, the following requirements should be fulfilled:

– the stadium's safety should be verified by the granting of a public authority safety certificate. Moreover, there should be verification of the fact that there has been a correct application by the club or National Football Association of UEFA guidelines;

– the facilities used for matches should be carefully maintained and the structural suitability and conformity with regulations checked regularly and especially in good time before any match. Of particular concern are items such as stairs, terraces, viewing slopes, crush barriers, guard rails and other guarding, covered standing and seating accommodation, temporary stands and other structures;

– before the match there should be searches for and removal of dangerous objects, including building materials, rubble, lose seats and glass both inside and in the vicinity of the stadium;[109]

– there should be a thorough check on the morning of the match for bombs, smoke grenades, fireworks and other dangerous objects;

---

[104] See for instance the Recommendation on Measures to be Taken by the Organisers of Football Matches and Public Authorities (93/1).
[105] See *Code of Practice*, pp.23 and 144.
[106] (93/1).
[107] (94/1).
[108] *Code of Practice*, pp.18–20.
[109] *Cunningham v. Reading FC* [1991] P.I.Q.R. 141.

– there should also be a check of safety barriers, fencing and so on to ensure that they prevent unwanted spectator movement, facilitate spectator separation and prevent unauthorized access to the playing field (and, through use of netting, preventing projectiles from being hurled onto the pitch) while simultaneously facilitating emergency evacuation of the stadium and emergency access onto the pitch;

– police forces should be provided with the facilities necessary to ensure that they are able to do their jobs, including CCTV systems, public address system and control posts;

– moreover there should be arrangements in consultation with police for security within the ground, including the provision of adequate stewards within the ground to control movement of spectators;

– where necessary, it should be ensured that rival supporters are segregated. Ticket sales should be properly monitored, to prevent counterfeit tickets from being sold and to prevent ticket touts from selling outside the game. Where necessary, organisers should be prepared to reduce the number of tickets on sale, to ensure crowd safety;

– there should be adequate entrances and exits to facilities with doors opening to the exterior;

– as far as possible efforts should be made to improve the quality of spectators areas – on the basis that the poor quality of sports grounds is a causative factor in crowd violence;

– there should be liaisons between organisers, including nominated safety officers, and public authorities and police in good time in respect of planned matches, and especially those matches that may require extra police resources;

– there should be entry controls on spectators, if necessary by controlling approaches to the stadium by removable barriers.[110] Particularly, known troublemakers, and persons with dangerous objects, alcoholic drinks (and those who are intoxicated), or who are carrying offensive or racist banners or signs should be denied entry;

– there should be a control on the sale of drinks in glass bottles and preferably of any alcoholic beverages in and in the vicinity of the stadium;

– there should be adequate medical facilities present, with the Code of Practice suggesting that an ambulance be present at any ground where a crowd of more than five thousand persons is expected, and that there should be one first aid worker present per 2,500 spectators. Moreover there should be appropriate facilities in which such persons can operate;

---

[110] This is the effect of s.21 of the Irish Criminal Justice (Public Order) Act 1994.

– particular care should be taken in checking fire safety mechanisms and electrical installations;

– in the case of an indoor stadium there should be efforts made to ensure that spectators and players are protected from objects flying out of or into the stadium respectively.

Plainly these recommendations go beyond the requirements of the Occupiers' Liability Act, and attach both to occupiers of stadia and also to organisers of events. Nor is it to be understood that the above guidelines are an infallible guide to the legal obligations of an event organiser in any circumstances. A prudent occupier or organiser, while appreciative of any particular concerns attaching to his or her event, should, in general, seek to ensure that his premises or his event is run according to the standards listed above, both to avoid civil liability and, more importantly, to prevent disasters of the type witnessed most notably at Hillsborough in 1989 from ever re-occurring.

6.2 DUTIES OF ORGANISERS OF SPORTING EVENTS

6.2.1 The duty of the organiser to participants

Organisers of sporting events owe a duty to participants to guard against foreseeable risks inherent in the staging of such events. Precisely what this requires in specific cases is unclear.[111] It does not require the organizer of the event to be a guarantor or insurer of the safety of all participants.[112] It will include, however, the following matters:

– ensuring that there are no hidden threats to the safety of the participant;[113]

– ensuring that the event is not likely to be beyond the reasonable capabilities of the participants – an issue of special concern when the participants are children;

---

[111] See Greenberg and Gray, "Designing and Implementing a Sports Based Risk Management Programme", 5(2) *Sport and the Law Journal* (1997) 49, "An Ounce of Prevention is Better than a Pound of Cure", (May/June 2002) *Sports Law Bulletin* 12 and Kevan *et al*, *Sports Personal Injury: Law And Practice* (Sweet & Maxwell, London, 2002), Chap.6.

[112] *Affiong-Day v. High Performance Sports Ltd* [2003] E.W.C.A Civ., 197 (February 26, 2003) noted at (March/April 2003) *Sports Law Bulletin* 4.

[113] See *Harrison v. Vincent* [1982] R.T.R. 8 where the organizers of a motor rally were deemed to be negligent in not keeping a slip road off the track clear of obstructions, on the basis that it was foreseeable that competitors might accidentally drive off the track and onto the slip road.

– ensuring that the equipment used is safe,[114] or that unsafe equipment is clearly marked as such;[115]

– ensuring that appropriate medical facilities are present;[116]

– ensuring that the standard of refereeing (where this is an important safety element of the game) is adequate;

– ensuring that all necessary safety and security precautions are taken (and, since September 11, 2001, this increasingly includes precautions against terrorist attack);[117]

– determining whether the event should go ahead in the relevant weather conditions;

– it may also be that organisers of contact sport competitions, should also be obliged to undertake mandatory testing for HIV and Hepatitis B & C of all competitors and – because of the risk to the other competitors – to ensure that there are strict guidelines in respect of blood related incidents in place, or in extreme circumstances to prohibit anyone with an infectious or blood based disease from competing.[118] Equally this raises issues pertaining to anti-discrimination laws that will be dealt with in a subsequent chapter.

---

[114] See also Tonner, Sawyer and Hypes, "Legal Issues in Golf; A 25 year Litigation History 1973–1998", 9(2) *Journal of Legal Aspects of Sport* (1999) 125 at 135.

[115] Greenberg and Gray, "Designing and Implementing a Sports Based Risk Management Programme", 5(2) *Sport and the Law Journal* (1997) 49 at 57.

[116] *Watson v. BBBC* [2001] 2 W.L.R. 1256. See also Millane, "Neighbours in Law", 4(2) *Sporting Traditions* (May, 1988) 1.

[117] See Hurst, Zoubek and Pratsinakis, "American Sports as a Target of Terrorism: The Duty of Care After September 11th", 10(1) *Sport and the Law Journal* (2002) 134 and "Security at Major Sporting Events and the Role of Governments", (February 2002) *Sports Law Administration and Practice* 6. Moreover, in sports where spectators and participants are within touching distance of each other, and where it is foreseeable, that a player might suffer damage as a result of an intentional assault perpetrated by a spectator (as happened for instance to tennis player Monica Seles) it may be necessary for the organiser to guard against such occurrence.

[118] The argument here is that whereas the risk of infection is negligible, the consequences are astronomical, and that other persons (e.g. health care workers) are more likely to spread such diseases accidentally than athletes. See Anderson, "The Punch that Landed: The Professional Boxing Safety Act of 1996",9 *Marquette Sports Law Journal* (1998) 191, Flannery & O'Brien, "Mandatory HIV testing of Professional Boxers", 31 *University of California Davis Law Review* (1998) 409, Hums, "AIDS in the Sports Arena; After Magic Johnson, Where do We go From Here", 4(1) *Journal of Legal Aspects of Sport* (1994) 59, Claussen, "HIV Positive Athletes and the Disclosure Dilemma for Athletic Trainers", 3(2) *Journal of Legal Aspects of Sport* (1993) 25, Anderson, "Cautious Defence: Should I be Afraid to Guard You? Mandatory AIDS Testing in Professional Team Sports", 5 *Marquette Sports law Journal* (1995) 279, Mitten, "AIDS and Athletics", 3 *Seton Hall Journal of Sports Law* (1993) 5, Wolohan, "An Ethical and Legal Dilemma; Participation in Spots by HIV Infected Athletes', 7 *Marquette Sports Law Review* (1997)

Importantly the foreseeability of a risk is not the same as the regularity with which that risk eventuates. Thus an organiser will be negligent if he ignores a substantial risk, merely on the grounds that it does not often come to fruition. On the other hand the fact that a risk is so small as to be negligible will be evidence that it was not foreseeable.[119] Equally, organisers of sporting events are not guarantors of the safety of athletes and in order for liability to arise, they must act in genuinely negligent fashion.[120]

6.2.2 The duty of the organiser to non-participants

There is uncertainty as to whether the Occupiers' Liability Act applies to a scenario in which a non-participant is injured within a stadium as a direct result of activity on the field of play. We have concluded, however, that the Occupier's Liability Act would only come into play where the negligent construction of the stadium is a significant cause (as distinct from a condition in which a cause operates) of the plaintiff's injury. In other cases, (and apart from the possibility that the injured spectator might sue a participant), the spectator will sue the organiser of the sporting event under basic principles of the tort of negligence.[121]

Once again, case law indicates that the extent of the common law duty owed by an organiser to any person present at a sporting event under its auspices will be measured by reference to a balance between the risks which it is reasonable to have deemed the entrant to have assumed and the extent to which the organiser or occupier has taken reasonable steps to guard against serious and latent risks.[122] Thus in *Callaghan v. Killarney Race Company Limited*,[123]

---

at 373, di Maggio, 'Suffering in Silence; Should They be Cheered or Feared? Mandatory HIV Testing of Athletes as a Health and Safety Issue", 8 *Seton Hall Journal of Sports Law* (1996) 663, Magnusson & Opie, "HIV and Hepatitis in Sports; An Australian Legal Framework for Resolving Hard Cases", 5 *Seton Hall Journal of Sports Law* (1995) 69 and Webber, "When the Magic Rubs Off; The Legal Implications of AIDS in Professional Sports", 2 *Sports Lawyers Journal* (1995) 1. See also *Doe v. Dolton Elementary School District No. 48*, 649 F. Supp. 440 ND Ill, 1988, where the courts in America allowed a school to prevent a child with HIV from taking part in contact sports.

[119] *Bolton v. Stone, Stratton v. Hughes*, unreported, Court of Appeal, March 17, 1998. See generally Griffith-Jones, *op. cit.*, pp.20–21.

[120] See Beloff, *op. cit.*, pp.131–132 for discussion of the case *Griffith v. Barbados*, where one team unsuccessfully sued the cricket association in respect of the outcome of a cricket match, seeking to overturn the decision on the result of a game.

[121] See Gardiner *op. cit.*, p.752. This will apply where the organiser is negligent in respect of a risk that jeopardizes the safety of the spectator. Thus in *MacDonald v. FIFA/SFA*, unreported Court of Session, Outer House, 1999, it was held that organisers of a soccer match did not owe a duty of care to spectators in deciding to cancel the match.

[122] Gardiner, *op. cit.*, p.755.

[123] [1958] I.R. 366.

the plaintiff, who was a regular visitor to the race course owned and controlled by the defendants, was injured when a horse involved in a race jumped into the crowd of spectators. The Supreme Court held that because the risk in question was inherent in racing, it was one which the plaintiff could be held to have accepted, and accordingly there was no evidence of any breach of duty on the part of the defendant. Ó Dálaigh C.J. also pointed out that whereas the risk was inherent in racing, nonetheless it was also unusual and unexpected and hence the defendants were not negligent in having failed to anticipate it. On the other hand in *Coleman v. Kelly*,[124] the plaintiff, a paying spectator at an agricultural show, had been injured when a horse that had thrown its rider and was galloping furiously back to the paddock, collided with him. The Supreme Court upheld the verdict of the jury in finding the defendant organisers liable in negligence, on the grounds that the risk in question was a foreseeable one, which it would not have been overly expensive for the promoters to guard against.

Perhaps the clearest statement of the duty of organisers of sporting events to spectators (albeit one made prior to the 1995 Act) is given in *Donaldson v. Irish Motor Racing Club & Thompson*.[125] Here some spectators had been killed and others injured when a racing car swerved off the track at the Curragh race circuit and into the crowd. The plaintiff – the father of one of the dead spectators – sued, *inter alia,* the organisers, claiming negligence in the failure to take proper precautions to ensure both that the venue was suitable and also that there was proper protection for the safety of spectators. In the Supreme Court Kingsmill Moore J. rejected the plaintiff's claim. First, he noted that the organisers were not bound to protect the plaintiffs against every danger however improbable, nor could they be seen as insurers of the safety of the spectators. Rather they had to act reasonably in the circumstances, which circumstances included the facts that most fast moving sport has an overspill element to it, and yet to remove spectators to a place where they were insured against all risks would be to mean that the view enjoyed by spectators would be so poor that the entertainment of the sport would be lost:

"Yet it is in the public interest, alike from the point of view of players, competitors and spectators that games and sports should be carried on. Moreover it corresponds to common sense and reality to suppose that the spectators appreciate and take the risk of certain accidents inherent in the nature of the game or sport."

Hence the position as between organisers and spectators was clear:

---

[124] (1951) 85 I.L.T.R 48.
[125] Unreported, Supreme Court, February 1, 1957. See McMahon & Binchy, *Casebook on the Irish Law of Torts* (1st ed., Professional Books) 221.

"The promoters of the sport or game are bound to take normal, reasonable and practicable precautions to protect spectators from the risk of injuries the occurrence of which is not improbable and the result of which would be likely to be serious, but the spectator accepts the risk of occurrences which though inherent in the nature of the activity are either unlikely to happen or, though not unlikely to happen, are unlikely to cause injuries of any seriousness."

On this logic, the Supreme Court found that the risk in this case was a remote one, and that spectators could be taken to have assumed it (in that it was inherent in the sport in question). Furthermore, the Supreme Court concluded that the organisers had exercised sufficient precautions to protect spectators and had not breached the duty of care, which they owed to such spectators.

A similar balance between foreseeability and assumption of risk is drawn in English case law on the topic. In England, the two leading cases *Hall v. Brooklands*[126] and *Murray v. Harringay*,[127] both proceeded on the basis of an alleged breach of a contractual term that the organiser would take care of the spectator subject to an implicit contractual responsibility on the part of the spectator to take care of him or herself. In *Hall*, the defendants owned a car racing track open to the public, many of whom preferred to stand in the vicinity of the track rather than in the more secure environment of the stands. On the occasion in question, a collision at speed between two cars led to one being propelled into the air, over the railing separating the track from the spectators and into the crowd, killing two spectators and injuring others. One injured spectator sued the club and was successful at first instance. In the Court of Appeal, however, the decision of the jury was reversed, with the court holding that whereas the owners of the stadium had a duty to use reasonable care and skill to make the course as free from danger as was possible, equally they were not insurers of the safety of spectators. In particular, they did not have an obligation to prevent accidents that were either inherent in a sport and therefore foreseeable by the spectator, or alternatively so unusual that they were unforeseeable by the organiser. Similarly in *Murray* – where an infant spectator seated in the front row of an arena during an ice hockey match was injured when a puck left the arena and struck him in the eye – the Court of Appeal concluded that the implied term in the contract between the parties as to the safety of the plaintiff required only that the occupiers of the stadium took reasonable care and not that all risks would be obviated. Especially, the defendants would not have to protect against those dangers that were inherent to the sport in question.[128]

---

[126] [1933] 1 K.B. 205.

[127] [1951] W.N. 38 [1951] 2 K.B. 529.

[128] See also *Piddington v. Hastings*, *The Times*, March 12, 1932 and *Wilkins v. Smith* (1976) 73 Law Society Gazette, 938. For a similar analysis in respect of baseball and ice hockey

In *Gillon v. Chief Constable of Strathclyde Police*,[129] the plaintiff was a police sergeant responsible for policing a Scottish Premier League soccer match between Airdrie and Celtic. She was in charge of 10 officers and had sent two in to intervene in crowd trouble. She was standing with her back to the pitch watching events in the crowd unfold, when a Celtic player left the field of play at great speed, cannoned into her and knocked her across a track beside the pitch and into a barrier, as a result of which she suffered injury. She sued both the police and the club for negligence. The court found that there was no negligence on the basis that the risk of injury occurring was so small that no reasonable person would have guarded against it, but had they found negligence then liability would have been apportioned on a 50-50 basis between club and police. The plaintiff had claimed that a safety barrier should have been erected, but this claim was rejected by the court. On the other hand in *Cunningham v. Reading FC*,[130] spectators at a local derby match between Reading FC and Bristol City FC threw pieces of concrete that had been loosened from the terraces at police, causing injury. The police successfully sued the club both for negligence and under English occupiers' liability legislation, on the grounds that the stadium was in a very poor state, and it was easy for spectators to loosen concrete by kicking it and jumping on it – indeed four months previously similar events had happened yet the club had done nothing to remedy the situation. The negligence of the club was compounded by the fact that the violent nature of the visiting fans and the hostility evoked by these derby matches were known in advance of the match, and hence it was eminently foreseeable that the spectators would use the poor state of the terraces to dislodge concrete blocks that could be used as missiles.[131]

---

in the US see *Yates v. Chicago National League Ball Club*, 595 N.E. 2d. 570 (Ill. 1992), *Gilchrist v. City of Troy*, 495 N.Y.S. 781 (N.Y. App., 1985), *Rosa v. County of Nasseau*, 544 N.Y.S. 2d. 652 (N.Y. Ct App. 1989), *Pestalozzi v. Philadelphia Plyers*, 595 A. 2d. 1269 (Pa. Super. 1991) and generally, Kastenberg, "A Three Dimensional Model of Stadium Owner Liability in Spectator Injury Cases", 7 *Marquette Sports Law Review* (1996) 187. See however, *Klyne v. Bellegarde* (1978) 6 W.W.R. 743, where a plaintiff ice hockey spectator, injured by an ice hockey stick, successfully sued the organizers of the event on the basis that there was no protection whatsoever for him at the venue in that there were no protective guards above the side boards.

[129] *The Times*, November 22, 1996. For analysis see Stoner, "An Assessment of Risk", (January/February 1997) *Sports Law Administration and Practice* 8.

[130] [1991] P.I.Q.R. 141.

[131] More recently, British police considered taking civil actions against Milwall FC after 47 officers were hurt in clashes with up to 900 hooligans outside the ground in London. Injuries to officers included broken legs, arms and feet, facial lacerations as well as injuries to 26 of the 34 horses on duty that night. See "UK Police May Sue Soccer Club after Riots", *Irish Times*, May 3, 2002.

6.3 Case Study – Occupier and Organiser Liability on the Golf Course

Having looked at the basic duties of occupiers and organisers, we now consider how these duties play out in a specific fact situation, namely in the context of a golf tournament.

As we have seen earlier, the game of golf presents a unique set of circumstances as far as application of legal principle is concerned, in that it is reasonably foreseeable that no matter how a course is designed, nor how a golf tournament is organised, there is a risk of injury to other players and spectators on the course every time any player, (no matter how skilful) swings a club at a ball.[132] As we saw in chapter five, a spectator may be taken to have assumed the inherent risks of attending a sporting event.[133] Moreover, the only way to obviate all foreseeable risks connected with a golf course is to close the course, or at least to prohibit the staging of tournaments on it – a move that would entail excessive cost in social terms. Hence in designing a course or staging a tournament, the occupier or organiser is not required to act as guarantor of anyone's safety, but merely to ensure that there are no unreasonable risks for player or spectator, which the latter can not be taken to have assumed.[134]

---

[132] McMahon & Binchy, *op. cit.*, p.56. See generally *Carey v. Albany Golf Club*, 4 S.R.W.A. 168 (D.C.), *Potter v. Carlisle and Cliftonville Golf Club* [1939] N.I. 114. See Murdoch, "Tigerland" (May 2003) *Law Society Gazette* 8, Kastenberg, "A Three Dimensional Model of Stadium Owners' Liability in Spectator Injury Cases", 7 *Marquette Sports Law Review* (1996) 187 and Vieira, "Fore may be just par for the course", 4 *Seton Hall Journal of Sports Law* (1994) 181 at p.192ff.

[133] In *Potter v. Carlisle and Cliftonville Golf Club* [1939] N.I. 114, the injured golfer was deemed to assume all inherent risks deriving from the game and from the course on which he played, provided that it was free from unusual dangers or traps. See also *Knittle v. Miller*, 09 P. 2d. 32 (1985) for the view that in as much as it is foreseeable that any spectator on a golf course may get hit by a ball, this is a risk assumed (at least to some extent) by the spectator, who should be careful to watch when players are playing. See generally Tonner, Sawyer and Hypes, "Legal Issues in Golf; A 25 year Litigation History 1973–1998", 9(2) *Journal of Legal Aspects of Sport* (1999) 125. See *Grisim v. Tapemark Charity Pro-Am Golf Tournament*, 394 N.W. 2d. 261 (Minn. Ct App., 1986).

[134] For an analogous approach taken in the context of automobile racing see *Capitol Raceway Promotions Inc v. Smith*, 332 A.2d. 238 (Mo. App. 1974) *Richoux v. Herbert*, 449n So. 2d. 491 (La. Ct App., 1983), *Lane v. Eastern Carolina Drivers Assoc.*, 117 S.E. 2d. 737 (N.C., 1961). Generally see Kastenberg, "A Three Dimensional Model of Stadium Owners' Liability In Spectator Injury Cases", 7 *Marquette Sports Law Review* (1996) 187.

6.3.1 Unreasonable risks in course design

The most obvious such risk is caused by the design of the course. In other words, a person – be it a player, a spectator or another person – injured on the golf course may argue that the risk of his being hit was greatly exacerbated by the design of the course – for instance because the course is constructed in such a fashion that a person playing off a tee is unable to follow the precise line of flight of his ball, because an area of the course is "clustered" in that tees and greens are located too close to each other, leading to a substantially increased risk of injury, or because there is an absence of protective fencing or netting on the course. Thus in *Gray v. Leopardstown Golf Centre*,[135] a golfer recovered £5,250 having been injured by a golf ball in circumstances where, according to the Circuit Court, the club was negligent in not erecting a protective fence or netting to guard against the risk of an injury of this kind arising.

On the other hand, in *Horton v. Jackson*,[136] the plaintiff was playing on the 6th hole of a particular golf course. The 9th tee on this course was located only ten yards from the 6th green. A substantial screen of fencing and trees separated the green from all but the front of the 9th tee. Moreover, a sign beside the 9th tee bore the words "Players putting on the 6th/15th green have priority," indicating that players teeing off the 9th tee should wait until players playing the 6th or 15th holes had reached the safety of the green. In this case, the plaintiff, who had mislaid his ball, finally found it on the 9th fairway and played it to the 6th green. He was struck in the eye by the first defendant who had played off the 9th tee without checking whether there was anyone in his line (to the amazement of his playing partners). Having successfully sued the player, the plaintiff also sued the club claiming that this area of the course was known to be dangerous and that there had been a history of accidents there. That being the case, the club should either have screened off the whole of the 9th tee with fencing or trees, or should have indicated by a clearly worded sign the dangers to players near or on the 6th green. Moreover, the club should also have ensured compliance with the terms of the sign.

The Court of Appeal refused to find the golf club liable in this case. The Court noted that the duty under section 2 of the (English) Occupiers' Liability Act 1957 was to provide a common duty of care in the circumstances (the same standard as applies under the terms of the Irish Occupiers' Liability Act). Here the court adjudged the relevant circumstances to be the fact that in the history of the club there had only been two accidents as compared to numerous safe rounds of golf played. In other words, whereas the risk of injury was inherently foreseeable, it was legitimate for the club to regard it as being improbable. Moreover, it had taken measures to obviate such risk by the building

---

[135] Unreported, Circuit Court, July 20, 1999. See Murdoch, "Tigerland" (May 2003) *Law Society Gazette* 8.
[136] Unreported, Court of Appeal, February 28, 1996.

of the screen of fencing and trees and by the creation of the warning sign. Especially, the mere fact that this part of the course was potentially dangerous did not impose an obligation on the club to prevent players like the first defendant from behaving in what was a patently foolish manner, nor could any steps, which it might have taken, have prevented such idiocy. Thus in legal terms:

> "It is not reasonable to require a golf club to erect a sign to tell a golfer that he must not aim a drive at a person standing or walking 25 yards away from him who is in plain view."

A similar judgment was handed down by the Ontario High Court in *Ellison v. Rogers*.[137] Here the plaintiff had been struck by the first named defendant while the two were playing separate holes, which had parallel fairways. The parties were playing in opposite directions and at all material times, the plaintiff and defendant were clearly visible to each other. The plaintiff also sued the club claiming that it had failed to provide him with a safe place to play and should have had a sign on each tee urging players to be careful of players on parallel fairways. The court refused to find the club (or indeed the player) liable. Rather it said that the duty of the occupier of the club was merely to guard against unusual dangers or traps. Parallel contiguous holes were common on golf clubs as were incidences of balls crossing fairways. Moreover, having a sign as suggested by the plaintiff would have been no more than a statement of the obvious. The Ontario High Court accordingly concluded that the actions of other golfers will not comprise risks in respect of which a golf club will be liable provided that such actions constitute normal risks of the game.

6.3.2 Unreasonable risks in the organisation of a tournament

Beyond ensuring safe course design, it is necessary to ensure that precautions are taken to protect players and spectators in the specific circumstances of any golfing event. Thus for example, if an organiser is in charge of a pro-am tournament, it should be borne in mind that, whereas most spectators are there to watch the professional, who will most likely hit the ball in a straight line, they are also going to be in the vicinity of his amateur playing partner – who may be a 'wild' player (in the sense of not hitting the ball straight), and such spectators will need to be protected from the heightened risk of being hit by such a player.[138] In other words it may be necessary that spectator galleries are

---

[137] 67 D.L.R. (2d.) 21 (1967).

[138] Equally, it is not the duty of the amateur golfer to ensure that spectators are standing in a position where they would not be hit by his shots – despite the fact that, apart from when he is actually on the tee, it will be he who will dictate where the spectators will

kept further away from the fairway at a pro-am than at a normal professional tournament, or are given specific warnings of such risks.[139]

It may also be necessary to ensure that people who are not actually in the "sporting arena" are protected from badly aimed or mis-hit golf balls. In the American case of *Duffy v. Midlothian*,[140] a golf tournament organiser was successfully sued by a woman who was standing in line at a concession stand when she was hit by a golf ball. The court's point was that in such a circumstance the woman could legitimately have concluded that she was no longer in the "danger zone." In other words, at this point, the defendant's negligence in placing the concession stand too close to the zone of play overtook her assumption of the risks inherent in being in the vicinity of a golfer.

6.3.3 Lightening on the golf course

Finally, as we consider the potential for legal liabilities on the golf course, it is necessary to consider the legal position of a participant/spectator who is struck by lightening on a golf course *vis-à-vis* the golf club[141] or the organiser of any tournament during which he was struck.[142]

American courts have stressed that lightening strikes must be considered to be "Acts of God" and hence cannot *per se* ground legal action.[143] If liability

---

stand, in that each shot that he plays will dictate the angle of his next shot to the target and hence the line at which spectators will stand. See *Grisim v. Tapemark Pro-Am Golf Tournament*, 394 N.W. 2d. 261 (Minn. Ct App., 1986) and generally, Tonner, Sawyer and Hypes, "Legal Issues in Golf; A 25 Year Litigation History 1973–1998", 9(2) *Journal of Legal Aspects of Sport* (1999) 125.

[139] See *Baker v. Mid Maine Medical Centre*, 499 A. 2d. 464 (1985) and generally, Tonner, Sawyer and Hypes, "Legal Issues in Golf; A 25 Year Litigation History. 1973–1998", 9(2) *Journal of Legal Aspects of Sport* (1999) 125.

[140] 481 N.E. 2d. (Ill. Ct. App., 1985). See Kastenberg, "A Three Dimensional Model of Stadium Owners' Liability in Spectator Injury Cases", 7 *Marquette Sports Law Review* (1996) 187. See also *Grisim v. Tapemark Pro-Am Golf Tournament*, 394 N.W. 2d. 261 (Minn. Ct App., 1986) and Tonner, Sawyer and Hypes, "Legal Issues in Golf; A 25 Year Litigation History 1973–1998", 9(2) *Journal of Legal Aspects of Sport* (1999) 125.

[141] See *Muehlfelder v. Crystal Woods Golf* Club, No. 851–27954 (1993) W.L. 456111 Cir. Ct Ill., Ruth Alexander, "Lightening Strikes and Negligence in Sport", 9(2) *Journal of Legal Aspects of Sport* (1999) 63 and Tonner, Sawyer and Hypes, "Legal Issues in Golf; A 25 Year Litigation History 1973–1998", 9(2) *Journal of Legal Aspects of Sport* (1999) 125 at p.130ff.

[142] Flynn, "Lightening: A Double Hit for Golf Course Operators", 6 *Marquette Sports Law Journal* (1995) 133, Shadiack, "Does a Golf Course Owner and/or Operator Owe A Duty of care to their Patrons to Protect Them from Lightening Strikes?", 8 *Seton Hall Sports Law Journal* (1998) 301, Kastenberg, "A Three Dimensional Model of Stadium Owner Liability in Spectator Injury Cases", 7 *Marquette Sports Law Review* (1996), 187.

[143] *Hames v. State*, 808 S.W. 2d. 41 (Tenn, 1991), *Estate of Fisher v. City of South Portland*, No. CV–92–714 (1994) Super Ct Me.).

is to arise then there must be some quantifiable act of negligence on the part of the golf course operator in failing to deal with a foreseeable risk.[144] Such negligence could exist in inadequate provision of shelters,[145] but in areas where lightening is an extremely regular phenomenon, it may be found where the club/tournament director has failed to install a lightening detection system.[146] On the other hand, courts have said that it is unnecessary to construct warning signs on the golf course outlining the dangers of playing golf in lightening on the basis that the risks inherent in such activity should be obvious to anyone.[147] Similarly organisers of tournaments should be cognisant of the fact that if the meteorological conditions are not conducive to the safe playing of sport, then the event which they are organizing should be cancelled, or else that they should attempt to persuade all competing athletes to sign waiver forms.

6.4 DUTIES TO PERSONS OUTSIDE THE STADIUM

The occupier of a stadium/organiser of a sporting event may also incur liability where the interests of those *outside* the stadium are affected by the activities that go on *inside* it, although the Occupiers' Liability Act has no application in such a situation.[148] This can range from cases where cricket balls fly from the cricket field into someone else's property,[149] to situations where a person passing by[150] or living near[151] a golf club is hit by an escaping golf ball,[152] to cases where the simple operation of a sport is oppressive to those living in the vicinity, who may be subject to excessive noise,[153] or to traffic restrictions or to other limitations on their capacity to live a normal life.

Two grounds for legal action may arise in such a circumstance, namely

---

[144] *Davis v. Country Club*, 381 S.W. 2d. 41 (Tenn. 1991), *Maussner v. Atlantic City Country Club*, 691 A. 2d. 826 (N.J. Super. Ct. App. Div. 1997), Alexander, "Lightening Strikes and Negligence in Sport", 9(2) *Journal of Legal Aspects of Sport* (1999) 63.

[145] *Davis v. Country Club*, 381 S.W. 2d. 41 (Tenn, 1991).

[146] Flynn, "Lightening: A Double Hit for Golf Course Operators", 6 *Marquette Sports Law Journal* (1995) 133 at p.147.

[147] *Hames v. State*, 808 S.W. 2d 41 (Tenn., 1991), *Estate of Fisher v. City of South Portland*, No CV–92–714 (1994 M.E.). Generally see Alexander, "Lightening Strikes and Negligence in Sport", 9(2) *Journal of Legal Aspects of Sport* (1999) 63.

[148] See Gardiner, *op. cit.*, p.740, Kevan *et al*, *op. cit.* at Chap.7.

[149] *Miller v. Jackson* [1977] Q.B. 966.

[150] *Castle v. St Augustine's Links* (1922) 38 T.L.R. 615, *Bolton v. Stone* [1951] A.C. 850.

[151] *Hennessey v. Pyne* [1997] 694 A.2d. 691.

[152] *Spray v. Mayor Alderman and Burgess of Ellesmere Port*, unreported [1997] E.W.C.A. (Civ.) 2883. See Tonner, Sawyer and Hypes, "Legal Issues in Golf; A 25 Year Litigation History 1973–1998", 9(2) *Journal of Legal Aspects of Sport* (1999) 125 at pp.136–137.

[153] *Kennaway v. Thompson* [1980] 3 W.L.R. 361 and *Tetley v. Chitty* [1986] 1 All E.R. 663.

negligence and nuisance. As a rule of thumb, it may be said that a nuisance action is more likely to follow an ongoing situation (as for example where cricket balls are persistently threatening a neighbour's garden by reason of the design of the cricket field) whereas a negligence action is likely to arise in a "once off situation," and especially where the injured party has no proprietorial interest in the land on which he is injured (although in such circumstances it may be possible to take an action in public nuisance).[154] In both cases the court's analysis proceeds on a reasonableness standard. However, whereas in a negligence action the court focuses on the reasonableness of the defendant's conduct, and in particular, on the measures he has taken to alleviate foreseeable risks, a nuisance action is different insofar as the court looks at the reasonableness of the situation from the plaintiff's standpoint.[155] Hence if a situation is utterly intolerable for the plaintiff, then the court will find the defendant liable irrespective of his or her efforts to reduce its impact.[156] Finally, whereas a negligence action will only result in a claim for damages, injunctions may also be granted in the event of a finding of actionable nuisance.[157]

6.4.1 Negligence

The most obvious instances where sporting activity causing damage to persons outside the stadia can ground negligence actions, are cases where balls or other projectiles fly out of the ground causing harm to another party. Again the primary factors used by the courts in determining whether there should be liability will be the foreseeability of the risk and the extent (if at all) to which the plaintiff can be taken to have assumed the said risk. In *Bolton v. Stone*,[158] a cricket match was being played on a ground that had been used as a cricket field for the previous ninety years. Records from the previous thirty years indicated that on only six previous occasions had cricket balls escaped from the enclosed ground, and on no previous occasion had there been any damage caused. On this occasion, however, a visiting cricketer hit a "six" which cleared a seventeen foot fence at the boundary (which was some seventy five yards from the wicket), and then travelled a further hundred yards before striking the plaintiff who was standing on the highway.

---

[154] Generally see McMahon & Binchy, *op. cit.* at Chap.24. It is possible (albeit unlikely) that an action could be taken under the rule in *Rylands v. Fletcher* (1868) L.R. 3 H.L. 330 (McMahon & Binchy, *op. cit.* at Chap.25) where as a result of non natural user of land the defendant has accumulated for his own purposes dangerous substances likely to cause damage should they escape.

[155] McMahon & Binchy, *op. cit.*, p.690.

[156] *Mullen v. Hynes*, unreported, Supreme Court, November 13, 1972.

[157] *Bellew v. Cement Ltd* [1948] I.R. 61.

[158] [1951] 1 All E.R. 1078. See Gardiner, *op. cit.*, p.740.

The House of Lords refused to find the occupiers of the ground to be liable on the grounds that the likelihood of injury occurring was so slight that a reasonable person would be justified in ignoring it. Even though the risk of injury being caused in this fashion was foreseeable (as was evidenced from the fact that the club had erected fencing to prevent it from happening), the risk was so minuscule that it was legitimate for the appellants to ignore it. On the other hand in *Castle v. St Augustine's Links Ltd*[159] and *Whitefield v. Barton*,[160] where (in both cases) the risk of golf balls landing on a public road was relatively high, the defendant golf course owners were deemed to be negligent for failing to guard against a foreseeable and probable risk.

From these cases, it seems clear that the courts in determining whether there should be liability will afford significance both to the foreseeability and likelihood of the risk eventuating and the severity of the consequences if it does, in fact, materialise.[161] In *Hilder v. Associated Portland Cement Manufacturers*,[162] the defendants owned a piece of grassland upon which, to the knowledge of the defendants, children habitually played football. The children used to play towards a goal constructed out of a tree and a stick stuck in the ground, in the direction of the highway with the only barrier between the "goal" and the highway being a wall of between three and four feet in height. On the occasion in question a ball went over the wall and onto the highway (a not unusual occurrence) causing a passing motor cyclist to swerve. In doing so he fell, fractured his skull and died. The High Court, finding for his widow in a negligence action taken against the defendants, held that a reasonable occupier of the green would have realized that as a result of the children playing in such fashion, there was a risk of harm to road users and as the risk was significant, he should have taken steps to remedy it and his failure to do so constituted negligence.

Finally, it should be noted that what may be seen as reasonable conduct in the past may be rendered unreasonable in the present or future by developments in technology. Thus to take the most obvious example, developments in the technology associated with designing graphite shafted golf clubs mean that players can hit the ball considerably further now than in the past. Accordingly, a protection of a course boundary that would have been reasonably capable of preventing balls from straying from the course in the past may be ineffective and hence unreasonable in the present era.[163]

---

[159] (1922) 38 T.L.R. 615.
[160] [1987] S.C.L.R. 259.
[161] Gardiner, *op. cit.* at 744.
[162] [1961] 1 W.L.R. 1434. For criticism of this case, especially in its purported acceptance of the decision in *Bolton v. Stone*, see Gardiner, *op. cit.* at 743.
[163] See Kevan *et al*, *op. cit.*, pp.83–84.

6.4.2 Nuisance

In general as far as Irish rules on private nuisance are concerned, it is possible to distinguish two classes of disruption of interests.[164] As regards the first – where the action causes actual damage to property – the courts tend to impose liability without any particular regard to the context of the defendant's action – for example whether it is of social utility.[165] As regards the second – where the impugned activity causes a substantial interference with the plaintiff's use or enjoyment of his land – the courts will balance the harm suffered[166] against the reasonableness of the actor's conduct, looking at such factors as the utility of the conduct,[167] the character of the neighbourhood in which it occurred,[168] the motive behind the nuisance and the reasonableness of the use of the property which caused the nuisance.[169] Typically the defendant in such an action will be the creator of the nuisance,[170] although an occupier/owner of property who is not the creator of the nuisance may be liable therefor where he or she is in a position to alleviate the risk of a nuisance yet fails to take reasonable measures to do so.[171] Traditionally in Ireland as in England, because nuisance was seen as an offence against one person's proprietorial interests in land, it was the owner of property who was the exclusive plaintiff in such a case.[172] Recent developments in Ireland, however, have meant that a nuisance action may also be taken by the occupier of land or someone present on land.[173]

The application of nuisance principles to the sporting situation again tends to focus primarily on injury caused by objects escaping from sports stadia. Thus in *Miller v. Jackson*,[174] a couple had bought a newly built house in the vicinity of a cricket pitch where cricket had been played since 1905. Cricket balls landed in the plaintiffs' garden damaging brickwork and tiles, and following complaints the cricket club erected a fence on top of the wall at the end of the plaintiff's garden. Even still, in the following seasons, five balls

---

[164] McMahon & Binchy, *op. cit.*, p.685ff. See also *Patterson v. Murphy* [1978] I.L.R.M. 85.

[165] McMahon & Binchy, *op. cit.*, p.686ff.

[166] *Mullen v. Hynes*, unreported, Supreme Court, November 13, 1972; *O'Kane v. Campbell* [1985] I.R. 115.

[167] McMahon & Binchy, *op. cit.*, p.690 and *Bellew v. Irish Cement Limited* [1948] I.R. 61.

[168] *Dewar v. City and Suburban Racecourse* [1899] 1 I.R. 345, *O'Kane v. Campbell* [1985] I.R. 115 and *Molumby v. Kearns* [1999] I.E.H.C. 86.

[169] *Christie v. Davey* [1893] 1 Ch 316, *Hollywood Silver Fox Farm v. Emmet* [1936] 2 K.B. 468.

[170] McMahon & Binchy, *op. cit.*, p.702 and *Royal Dublin Society v. Yates* [1997] I.E.H.C. 144.

[171] *Goldfarb v. Williams* [1945] I.R. 433, *Leakey v. National Trust* [1980] 2 W.L.R. 65.

[172] McMahon & Binchy, *op. cit.*, p.699 and *Hunter v. Canary Wharf* [1997] A.C. 655.

[173] *Hanrahan v. Merck Sharpe & Dohme* [1988] I.L.R.M. 629.

[174] [1977] Q.B. 966. See Parpworth, "Lord Denning and the Other Cricket Ball Case", 2(2) *Sport and the Law Journal* (1994) 4.

landed in the plaintiffs' garden one of which just missed breaking the window of a room in which the plaintiffs' son was sitting. The plaintiff was so upset that she and her husband took to going out whenever cricket was being played. Rejecting offers from the club to pay for any breakages and indeed to construct a net over the plaintiffs' garden when cricket was being played, the plaintiffs sued in negligence and nuisance and despite an extraordinary dissent from Lord Denning the Master of the Rolls, they were successful on both counts. Against this, however, the Court of Appeal refused to grant an injunction restraining the activities of the club on the grounds that the social utility of their action had to be balanced against the interests of the plaintiffs.[175] There is, however, a significant argument that in light of the risks faced by the plaintiffs as well as the dominant legal authority in the area, such injunction should have been granted.[176] Moreover, it should be noted that there is authority in Ireland for the proposition that just as an organiser of an event may be liable for a nuisance caused by the escape of inanimate objects escaping from his stadium, so also he may be responsible for nuisance caused by the escape of living objects – namely spectators,[177] and indeed in England, clubs have been held liable for the actions of spectators.[178]

In the Canadian case *Segal v. Derrick Golf & Winter Club*,[179] the plaintiffs lived in a house with a back yard some 45 feet behind the 14th green of the defendant golf club. During the period between 1972 and 1976, hundreds of golf balls landed in their back garden, occasionally striking the house and nearly injuring persons on the property. On occasion, the errant golf balls would be followed by their owners who would invade the plaintiff's property in a bid to retrieve their balls. The situation had become so bad that, despite efforts by the golf club to construct some form of protection for the plaintiff's house, the plaintiff's children were not allowed out to play in the back garden during the golf season. Belzil J. had no hesitation in granting both an injunction and damages to the plaintiff, on the basis that the construction of the 14th hole (where players would play a long approach shot to the green over a pond) meant that there was a plainly foreseeable risk to the plaintiffs. Similarly in the Australian case *Lester Travers v. City of Frankston*,[180] where the plaintiff lived adjacent to a golf course and had her property regularly invaded by golf balls, the court granted an injunction restraining the operators of the course

---

[175] See also *Lacey v. Parker*, *The Times*, May 15, 1994.
[176] See also Parpworth, "A Further Cricket Ball Case: *Lacey v. Parker & Bingle*", 2(3) *Sport and the Law Journal* (1994) 9.
[177] In *O'Kane v. Campbell* [1985] I.R. 115, a shopkeeper was held liable for nuisance caused by late night customers at his shop.
[178] *Cunningham v. Reading FC* [1991] P.I.Q.R. 141 and *Hosie v. Arbroath FC* [1978] S.L.T. 122.
[179] (1977) 76 D.L.R. (3d.) 746.
[180] [1970] V.R. 2.

from permitting players to play on that part of the golf course which posed a risk to the plaintiff's property.

Nuisance from a sporting event is of course not confined to situations where balls land in neighbouring property. In *Kennaway v. Thompson*[181] and *Tetley v. Chitty*,[182] injunctions were granted to restrain organised power boat racing and go-karting activities respectively, because of the degree of nuisance involved related to the noisy nature of such activities. The courts in both cases concluded that excessive noise was a concomitant of such activities and that in the circumstances, damages would be an insufficient remedy. Similarly, in *Stretch v. Romford Football Club Ltd*,[183] an injunction was granted (but suspended until that season had ended) restraining the operation of speedway racing at a former football club because of the excessive noise levels involved.[184]

Miller v. Jackson is, however, authority for the proposition that where a nuisance is being committed, the fact that the victim has 'come to the nuisance,' that is to say that the nuisance was in operation when the victim moved into the locality, is not a defence to a tort action.[185] Indeed in *Kennaway v. Thompson* the plaintiff was granted a partial injunction restraining the defendant's power boating activities despite the fact that she was aware of the existence of such activities when she built her house in the vicinity of the lake where the power boating occurred. Equally, the fact that the impugned action is in operation before the commission of the tort would go to the question of the character of the neighbourhood, which the court will bear in mind when assessing whether an actionable nuisance has occurred at all.

Finally, the organiser of a sporting event should bear in mind that the mere fact that he may have planning permission to build a stadium or stage an event does not preclude the possibility that a civil action in nuisance or negligence will be taken against him. Equally, provided that no physical damage is caused to the plaintiff or his property, the social utility inherent in the staging of an event (especially if such event is not inconsistent with the character of the neighbourhood) will tend to reduce the likelihood of a successful nuisance action being taken against him, especially if he has taken reasonable steps to dilute the extent and impact of any interference with the rights of the plaintiff. Moreover, the fact that planning permission has been granted would be evidence that the activity is not inconsistent with the character of the neighbourhood, and hence that it should not be regarded as creating an actionable nuisance.[186]

---

[181] [1981] Q.B. 88 (CA). See Gardiner at 751.
[182] [1986] 1 All E.R. 663.
[183] [1971] E.G.D. 763.
[184] Such decisions do not sit easily with the refusal of the Court of Appeal to grant the injunction sought in *Miller v. Jackson*, and it is tempting to suggest that this is because the latter was wrongly decided in light of existing authority.
[185] *Sturges v. Bridgman* (1879) 11 Ch. D. 852. Generally see McMahon & Binchy, *op. cit.*, pp.711–713.
[186] *Molumby v. Kearns* [1999] I.E.H.C. 86.

6.5 THE PROBLEM OF SPECTATOR VIOLENCE

In the 1980s, events at football matches in Europe, and in particular in England, led to a growing public concern with the threat of spectator violence at sports matches, and in particular with what has become known as football hooliganism. Anecdotal evidence suggests that violence between soccer fans had been common for decades,[187] but in 1985 the Heysel stadium disaster, which followed hot on the heels of the Bradford stadium disaster which itself occurred on the same day as a pitched battle between rival supporters of Birmingham City and Leeds United, was the catalyst for major change. First and foremost, English soccer clubs were banned from competing in European competitions for five years. Secondly, in England, legislation was enacted to deal specifically with soccer hooliganism. Nonetheless, the behaviour of certain soccer supporters – in particular German, Dutch and especially English fans – at home and more significantly abroad continued to cause alarm on a number of occasions. Notable amongst such occasions were the World Cup finals in France in 1998, where English fans fought pitched battles with rival supporters on the streets of Marseille,[188] and German fans did the same in Lens,[189] and in 2000, when two Leeds United supporters were killed in Turkey before the European Cup-Winners Cup semi-final game between Leeds United and Turkish soccer club Galatasaray.[190]

Ireland has not known anything like the degree of spectator violence witnessed in the UK. This is for a number of reasons, most notably the fact that its national sport is amateur, and also the fact that its domestic soccer league does not attract the level of support enjoyed by its English counterpart.[191] Moreover, soccer fans supporting the Irish team abroad are celebrated for their good behaviour.[192] Accordingly, the only legislation of significance in this area is the Criminal Justice (Public Order) Act of 1994, which deals with large public events including sporting events. Under section 21 of this Act, Gardaí are entitled to erect a barrier on any road, street, lane or alley not more than one mile from the event, and can divert persons at this point. Moreover, if the event is an "all ticket" affair, Gardaí can prohibit people from passing the barrier without a ticket. Under section 22 of the Act, Gardaí can seize

---

[187] For one of the greatest books ever written about the life of a football supporter in the "bad old days", see Hornby, *Fever Pitch* (Victor Gollancz, 1992).

[188] See "Marseille Violence seen as worst since 1982", *Irish Times*, June 16, 1998, and "Nerves Taut as Towns Await Thugs' *Irish Times*, June 20, 1998.

[189] See Staunton, "Germans want Tough Actions on Hooligans", *Irish Times*, June 25, 1998.

[190] See "Football Fans Stabbed to Death in Riot", *The Times*, April 6, 2000.

[191] This is not to say that crowd violence is unknown at League of Ireland soccer matches. See "Trouble Mars Derby Clash", *Irish Times*, March 11, 2000.

[192] See "Ireland have the Best Fans says [*sic*] World Cup Organisers", *Irish Times*, June 21, 2002 and McNally, "Tough Job being a Fan", *Irish Times*, June 15, 2002.

intoxicating liquor or any disposable container or other article, which could be used to cause injury.[193]

6.5.1 The Lansdowne Road riots

The most significant incident of football hooliganism in Ireland occurred on 15 February 15, 1995.[194] On this day, Ireland and England were scheduled to play in a friendly soccer match at Lansdowne Road, Dublin. In the lead up to the game, sporadic incidents of violence involving English fans had arisen, both inside and outside the stadium. After Ireland took the lead in the 27th minute, however, serious violence broke out in the upper and to a lesser extent the lower deck of the West Stand. Such violence consisted of throwing of portions of the seating in the upper deck, including planks, metal supports and on occasion the seats themselves, at fans seated below in the lower deck. Roughly 100 seats were broken up and destroyed on the upper deck and roughly 90 on the lower deck. The violence was coordinated by some 50 to 80 people, and it seemed (from a scrutiny of the literature found at the scene) that extreme racist and far right groups such as Combat 17 were involved.[195]

Following the events at Lansdowne Road outlined above, the former Chief Justice Finlay was commissioned to investigate the events of the evening of February 15, 1995 and to make recommendations with a view to preventing any recurrence of such events. This report in fact followed on from the report of the Committee on Public Safety and Crowd Control (1990) under the chairmanship of Mr. Justice Hamilton as he then was.

The first point of consideration in the report was the fact that undoubted trouble-makers had gained access to the stadium on the evening in question. As was noted above, under the terms of the Criminal Justice (Public Order) Act of 1994, police are entitled to erect a barrier in the vicinity of a location where a major public event is being held, (and this was done on the evening in question) and may, *inter alia*, prohibit a person from passing that barrier without a ticket where the event is one for which a ticket is required, and indicate to a person in possession of alcoholic drink, disposable drink containers or other offensive articles that such objects will be liable to confiscation. Moreover, the Garda may, on suspicion that someone is in possession of such an article, search that person and if he *is* in possession of such an article, require him to

---

[193] It is possible that racist chanting could lead to prosecution under the terms of the Prohibition of Incitement to Hatred Act, 1991, although past experience shows that it is notoriously difficult to obtain a conviction under the somewhat unwieldy terms of the Act.

[194] See generally the *Finlay Report into Violence at Lansdowne Road, Ireland v. England, 15 February, 1995* (Government of Ireland, 1995) [hereafter the *"Finlay Report"*].

[195] *Ibid.*, pp.35–36.

surrender it or, in the alternative, direct him away from the vicinity of the barrier. Equally, Finlay C.J. noted that the terms of the 1994 Act would not permit the Garda to deny access to a person in possession of a ticket merely on suspicion that such person had a reputation or even a previous conviction for disorderly conduct.[196]

It was true moreover that in a contractual condition printed on the back of the ticket, the FAI had reserved to itself the right to refuse admission even to a ticket holder in the interests of public safety, "or otherwise." Equally Finlay C.J. recognised that in practice, such a provision would be virtually unenforceable in the context of an event attended by a great number of persons. Moreover, entry by such a person following a refusal of permission by the FAI would constitute a breach of contract but *not* a criminal offence.

The *Finlay Report* concluded that a limited number of English fans had forced their way into the ground without tickets at the turnstiles – and plainly in order to do so, they must have avoided the barriers erected in the vicinity of the stadium.[197] On the other hand, in a collection of the missiles that were thrown, there were relatively few bottles and other containers, indicating that police may have been successful in preventing fans from entering the stadium with such items in their possession.

As far as problems connected with the management of the situation were concerned, Finlay C.J. concluded that there was no evidence of serious overcrowding at the match, nor of significant problems caused by forged tickets.[198] Indeed, the exclusive cause of the violence was the targeted and intentional actions of certain English fans. However, there were three contributory factors that could have been avoided. First, there was insufficient co-ordination of security efforts as between Gardaí, stewards, the FAI and the English National Criminal Intelligence Service. Secondly, there was insufficient segregation of English fans, as a result of both the FA method of selling tickets and of FAI re-sale of returned tickets, which was not aimed at ensuring complete segregation. Finally, it was felt that the uniformed Gardaí to be used as a reserve in the stadium were insufficient in number and in availability and in the speed with which they could be brought into action.[199]

For the purposes of dealing with these problems, Finlay C.J. argued that remedial legislation might target areas such as:

"– permitting courts on conviction of an individual for offences of this nature to make an order prohibiting him from attending certain categories of public events for a certain period of time;
  – outlawing the actions of ticket touts;

---

[196] *Finlay Report*, p.44.
[197] *Ibid.*, pp.43–44.
[198] *Ibid.*, p.49.
[199] *Ibid.*, pp.50–52.

     – entering into reciprocal arrangements with the English authorities
       concerning mutual enforcement of prohibition orders under the UK
       Football Spectators Act, 1989."

In the end, however, he doubted whether such remedial legislation would be
effective as a means of preventing similar acts of violence on the part of visiting
fans.[200] Instead, he made certain recommendations for controlling spectator
violence and in particular for avoiding a recurrence of the violence of February
15, 1995, which recommendations apply to what might be called top priority
games from a security standpoint.[201]

    First, he recommended that at such games (be they 'friendly' or competitive)
all spectators should be seated. Secondly, tickets allocated to visiting fans
should be completely different in appearance to those afforded to home fans.
Moreover, for such top security games, negotiation should be undertaken with
the rival football association to allow less than the suggested 10% of tickets to
be allotted to visiting fans. Thirdly, as regards co-ordination of efforts, any
offer of assistance, especially in the form of an intelligence co-coordinator or
police observers from the visiting country should be utilized. Moreover, a formal
liaison committee should be established comprising representatives from the
FAI, IRFU (in the case of matches being staged at Lansdowne Road), Gardaí,
transport authority, fire services and ambulance services. Similarly, there should
be increased liaison between senior stewards for the match and members of
the Gardaí, and a system should be created whereby Gardaí could co-operate
in the training of a specialised body of stewards or security men – an initiative
which could apply not only to the FAI but also to the IRFU and GAA. Finally,
stewards should be easily identifiable through wearing a distinguishing apron.

    In terms of the game itself, it was recommended that the Gardaí should be
given the right to veto any suggested kick off time for a match, but that as a
matter of preference there should be agreement on this matter following
consultation between the FAI and the police. During the game the Gardaí and
the FAI should have adequate communications systems safeguarded against
disturbance from noise in the stadium (a major problem on the night in
question). Segregation should be ensured by a cordon of stewards and Gardaí
between rival fans and also by a sufficient vacant area between blocks of rival
fans. A reserve force of uniformed Gardaí should be present in the ground
from the time that the gates opened, as also should a public order unit with riot
equipment, which could be activated with immediate effect. Furthermore there
should be a special entrance at each end of the stadium for use by emergency
services and the Gardaí. Moreover plans should be made to allow such entrances

---

[200] *Finlay Report*, pp.45–46.
[201] Generally on such recommendations see *Finlay Report*, pp.54–60.

to be used both for the entry of emergency services and also, simultaneously for the evacuation of crowds of people in the event of an emergency.

6.5.2 The legislative response to spectator violence in England

As has been mentioned, English sport and particularly soccer creates a factual context very different to that in Ireland, and unsurprisingly England has a number of very specific laws targeting crowd behaviour at sporting fixtures.[202] We now briefly consider the nature of this, arguably rather draconian legislation.[203]

The Football Spectators Act 1989 requires those convicted of crowd trouble to attend at a police station on match days – thereby obviously ensuring that they could not attend at matches.[204] It also prevents such persons from leaving the country when English teams are playing aboard. The Football (Offences and Disorder) Act, 1999 introduced domestic and international football banning orders, [205] preventing people from attending matches either at home or abroad, and the Football (Disorder) Act 2000 (as amended by the Football (Disorder) Amendment Act, 2002), permits a magistrate, on complaint by the police, where he or she is satisfied that someone has caused or contributed to violence at soccer matches in the UK or aboard, to grant a banning order for up to 10

---

[202] The two elements of the issue appear to be linked by reason of the fact that it is the responsibility of the stadium owner or event organiser to look after all aspects of stadium safety including spectator misbehaviour. Thus in *Harris v. Sheffield United*, unreported, March 26, 1986, the court concluded that in policing a game, the police were doing more than was required of them under their functions as police, and hence that the club was liable to pay for special police services under the terms of the Police Act of 1964. See Gardiner, *op. cit.*, pp.758–759. This conclusion was re-emphasised in the Taylor Report, however there was a recommendation that a written document be produced outlining the respective functions of club and police in respect of crowd safety. Moreover the fifth paragraph of the preamble to the 1985 *European Convention on Spectator Violence and Misbehaviour at Sports Events and in particular at Football Matches* declares that 'both public authorities and independent sports organisations have separate but complimentary responsibilities to combat violence and misbehaviour by spectators, bearing in mind that the sports organisations also have responsibilities in matters of safety. ..." See Moore, *op. cit.*, pp.85ff, McArdle, *op. cit.*, pp.61ff, Gardiner, *op. cit.*, p.763, and Pearson, "Legislating for the Football Hooligan: A Case for Reform", p.182 in Greenfield and Osborn eds., *Law and Sport in Contemporary Society* (Frank Cass Publishing, 2000).

[203] See Pearson, "Legislating for the Football Hooligan: A Case for Reform", p.182 in Greenfield and Osborn eds. *Law and Sport in Contemporary Society*, p.187ff. In *Gough v. Chief Constable of the Derbyshire Constabulary* [2002] 2 All E.R. 985; [2002] 2 W.L.R. 289, it was held that the operation of such barring orders was not in conflict with EC law.

[204] Pt II of the Act.

[205] See Gardiner, *op. cit.*, p.763 and McArdle, *op. cit.*, pp.83ff.

years.[206] Such order can be granted even in the absence of any conviction for such behaviour, and permits the subject's passport to be confiscated save where there are exceptional circumstances. Finally the Football Offences Act 1991 criminalised three separate activities namely the throwing of projectiles onto the playing area or any area in which spectators or other persons might be present,[207] the taking part in chanting of an indecent or racist nature even where there is no violation of public order legislation,[208] and the going onto the playing area or an adjacent area without lawful excuse.[209]

There has been much criticism of this legislation, but more generally a question arises as to why anti-social activities should be defined in terms of sport.[210] If throwing projectiles at another person, or engaging in racist or indecent chanting or gesticulation is to be an offence then so be it. It is simply unclear why the fact that it occurs at a soccer match should render it sufficiently different that specific legislation is enacted to target it.[211] This problem is exacerbated by the fact that because sport is a form of theatre, certain actions by spectators, which seem appalling when taken out of context are actually quite harmless within this 'theatre'. Alcohol is consumed by many people who enter sports grounds on a weekly basis yet who never cause harm.[212] Indecent (as distinct from racist) chanting is part of the culture of attending sports games but it is also meaningless hot air, nor is there evidence to suggest that it might lead to violence.[213] This is perhaps why this legislation is unenforced and unenforceable. People are simply *not* stopped from entering a ground drunk, nor from chanting indecent or racist songs, because with scarce resources, it is impossible to monitor the situation completely, nor is there any particular need to do so until such actions create a real risk of harm to other people.

The Sporting Events (Control of Alcohol) Act of 1985, as amended by section 40 of the Public Order Act 1986,[214] made it a criminal offence to;

---

[206] Sch.1.

[207] S.2.

[208] S.3.

[209] S.4. On November 18, 2002, Michael Harper, a Birmingham City fan, was sentenced to four months in prison under the terms of the Act for invading the pitch during a match between Birmingham and local rivals Aston Villa, in order to taunt the Aston Villa goalkeeper Peter Enckelman. He was also banned from attending at designated football matches for six years.

[210] McArdle, *op. cit.*, p.62 and Pearson, *op. cit.*, pp.189–193.

[211] There may also be difficulty in defining precisely what is meant by "chanting" under the terms of the Act, and specifically, what constitutes "indecent" chanting. See *Brutus v. Cozens* [1973] A.C. 854.

[212] Moreover, it is bizarre that whereas alcohol cannot be brought into a ground, it may be sold therein out of sight of the pitch.

[213] McArdle, *op. cit.*, pp.74–75.

[214] Moore, *op. cit.*, p.87.

"– cause or permit intoxicating liquor to be carried on public transport carrying passengers to and from designated sporting events, to possess intoxicating liquor on such vehicles or, most alarmingly, to be drunk on such a vehicle;

– possess intoxicating liquor or certain articles capable of causing injury (a bottle or other container) at or while entering a designated sports ground during a designated sports event, or to consume alcohol within sight of the pitch;

– to possess (within a stadium) any article or substance whose main purpose is the emission of a flare, smoke, or visible gas (Not including matches, cigarette lighters or heaters) also fireworks as introduced by Schedule One to the Public Order Act, 1986."

The 1985 Act also regulates the opening hours for licensed premises situated within designated sports grounds, including private facilities such as corporate hospitality boxes. Moreover, a police constable in uniform can close a bar if it appears to him that the sale of intoxicating liquor is detrimental to the orderly conduct or safety of spectators at the event.

This Act has been criticized as being cumbersome and unenforceable.[215] It is seen as notoriously difficult to enforce (and hence is unenforced). Moreover, it is far from certain that alcohol is a causative factor in spectator violence.[216] Indeed the control on alcohol in stadia may have had some negative effects, in that because fans are not permitted to bring alcohol onto sporting premises, there is evidence that they are staying longer in pubs before games and turning up late for matches, and that there are problems stemming from the presence of long queues outside the ground just before kick-off.[217]

Finally and on a slightly different issue, the *Taylor Report* had concluded that the actions of ticket touts, apart from being anti-social, could thwart the operation of segregation policies and could lead directly or indirectly to disorder and hence that such actions should be banned. Accordingly, section 166 of the Criminal Justice and Public Order Act of 1994 makes it an offence for an unauthorized person (someone other than a person authorized in writing by a club or by the match organizers) to sell, offer to sell or expose for sale a ticket for a designated football match in any public place to which the public has access or in the course of a trade or business in any other place.[218] Police are

---

[215] Pearson, "Legislating for the Football Hooligan: A Case for Reform", p.182 in Greenfield and Osborn, *Law and Sport in Contemporary Society*, p.184 and Healey, "Licensing at Football Grounds", 2(3) *Sport and the Law Journal* 17.

[216] See Pearson, "Legislating for the Football Hooligan: A Case for Reform", p.182 in Greenfield and Osborn eds. *Law and Sport in Contemporary Society*, p. 184.

[217] On the other hand see McArdle p.77 for the view that delays outside grounds (as for instance happened at Hillsborough in 1989) are more likely to be the result of roadworks.

[218] Moore, *op. cit.*, p.93 and Greenfield and Osborn, "Criminalising Supporters: Ticket

given power under the Act to arrest and search persons and vehicles, on suspicion that an offence under the section has been or is being committed.

6.5.3 The Council of Europe and spectator violence

In the *Convention on Spectator Violence and Misbehaviour at Sports Events and in Particular at Football Matches* (1985), the signatory states committed to taking measures aimed at preventing and controlling violence within football matches. This would be done:

> "– through co-ordination of domestic efforts (Article 2) and of the efforts of police forces in the different localities involved (Article 3 (1) b);
> – through provision of resources to ensure effective reaction to such violence;
> – through the creation and operation of legislation aimed at penalizing those found guilty of spectator violence;
> – through liaison with supporter's clubs to ensure good management of visiting supporters;
> – through co-ordination of efforts from all parties involved to ensure that potential trouble makers do not travel to matches;
> – through the enactment of legislation where necessary to ensure that responsible bodies including stadium owners take practical measures to help reduce spectator misbehaviour (Article 3), including improved stadium design, segregation of rival supporters, exclusion of known trouble makers or persons under the influence of alcohol or drugs, provision of an effective public address system, and appointment of liaison officers to prevent alcohol or dangerous objects from being brought onto the stadium."

Moreover, all such efforts should be underpinned by educational measures aimed at diluting the culture of spectator misbehaviour. Finally, the Convention recommended that states co-operate with each other on matters contained in the Convention, notably through effective communication and liaison in the lead up to international matches, (Article 4) as well as in the identification and treatment of offenders, through either prosecution or extradition. (Article 5) Since the adoption of the Convention, the Standing Committee created thereunder has adopted a variety of recommendations dealing with matters relating to spectator violence. In 1987 it adopted a *Recommendation on Alcohol Sales and Consumption*,[219] which concluded that restricting the dissemination

---

Touts and the Criminal Justice and Public Order Act, 1994", 3(3) *Sport and the Law Journal* (1995) 36.

[219] (87/1).

of alcohol at sports events was an important measure in controlling spectator violence, and called on contracting parties to ensure (as far as legally possible) both that the general provisions concerning the non-introduction of alcohol into sports events would be extended to include the travel arrangements of groups of visiting supporters, and also that local authorities would use any powers that they might have to prohibit or restrict the sale of alcohol in the neighbourhood of a stadium for a predetermined period, before, during or after such matches.

In 1987, the Standing Committee adopted a *Recommendation on Crowd Searches,*[220] calling on contracting parties to ensure that the relevant authorities both sporting and civil, have the necessary powers to search entrants to sports stadiums to ensure that dangerous objects are not brought in to such stadia – a recommendation given force in Ireland by the Criminal Justice (Public Order) Act of 1994. And in 1988, it adopted a *Recommendation On Police Co-Operation*[221] which provided that where an international sports event is planned, at which it is feared that there might be outbreaks of spectator violence, plain clothes policemen from countries of participating teams should be deployed to help to deal with the issue, *inter alia*, by identifying known trouble makers.

In 1988, the Sports Ministers of the European Community asked the Standing Committee to produce a practical report on a comprehensive list of measures to counter hooliganism.[222] This was adopted by the Standing Committee in 1989.[223] The Recommendation was divided into five sub-sections covering permanent measures to deal with spectator violence, measures to be taken before, during and after high-risk matches, and long term measures. In the main, these measures relate to themes brought up in earlier recommendations and in the Convention, and are expressed in "checklist form." In other words, clubs are asked whether they have fulfilled 70 different tasks ranging from the regular review of a list of undesirable spectators, to the provision of adequate medical care staff at games to the somewhat more nebulous question: "Do Clubs develop ways of making their fans important for them?" In as much as it is undoubtedly extremely comprehensive, the checklist should be a useful yardstick by which a club can assess both its safety precautions and also its "counter-hooligan" measures.

The Standing Committee has also considered the issue of ticket sales in its *Recommendation on Guidelines for Ticket Sales.*[224] The measures listed in

---

[220] (87/2).

[221] R (88/1).

[222] Resolution on Spectator Violence (89/3) drawn up by the European Sports Ministers in May/June 1989.

[223] *Recommendation on Comprehensive Report on Measures to Counter Hooliganism* (89/2).

[224] (89/1).

the latter included suggestions relating to the numbering and colouring of tickets to ensure that spectator movement can be controlled and supervised, ensuring that at various points of passage spectators will be stopped unless they have an appropriate ticket, restricting the amount of tickets any individual could buy, and where necessary, reducing the quantity of tickets which might be sold for any sector of a ground. Equally, in its Explanatory Memorandum to the Recommendation, the Standing Committee recognised that the problem in this area was less likely to be solved by new legislation than by improved operational supervision and practical management of existing rules. These objectives were re-emphasised in 2002 in a new *Recommendation on Guidelines for Ticket Sales at International Football Matches (Teams and Nations)*.[225] The recommendation stressed that a successful ticketing policy should focus on:

– ensuring an effective and efficient separation of fans;

– preventing black market sales and ticket fraud (by for example use of bar-coding, UV precautions and other means of detecting fraud);

– giving support to the policy of stadium bans by sharing data on banned spectators;

– ensuring that there is a clear demarcation of responsibilities between the various parties involved – organizers, ticket distributors, and ticket holders;

– the identification of fans, essentially by recording the entitled ticket holder's name on the ticket.

Beyond this, the Standing Committee has adopted recommendations on *Identification and Treatment (Under the National Criminal Law of a Contracting Party) of Offenders (1990)*,[226] (and specifically on the treatment of offenders at the 2000 European Football Championships in Holland and Belgium),[227] *Furthering of International Co-Operation and Co-Ordination of Policing of International Football Matches According to Listed Guidelines*,[228] and *Stewarding*.[229] In this last recommendation, a list of suggested tasks for stewards is given, ranging from searching the stadium before, during and after the match, responding to spectator complaints, keeping spectators out of parts of the stadium to which they are denied access, responding to emergencies and assisting the police and emergency services and generally dealing with the needs of spectators. To this extent the Standing Committee recommended that stewards be trained both as to their legal status, and also in the basic require-

---

[225] (2002/1).
[226] (90/1).
[227] (T–RV/99/3).
[228] (91/2).
[229] (99/1).

ments of their job including the particular requirements of the stadium in which they will work and also the procedures which they should follow in a 'normal' as well as an emergency situation. It also stressed that stewards should be polite and courteous and should attempt to show no support (in actions or in dress) for either of the competing sides.

Finally, in May 2000, the European Ministers responsible for Sport called on the Committee of Ministers to publish a draft text on measures to be adopted (legislative, administrative, policing and educational), to eliminate racist and xenophobic propaganda and behaviour of all kinds at sports events, stressing the respective and joint responsibilities in this regard, for both governmental and non-governmental organisations.[230]

6.6 CONCLUSION

In the increasingly litigious world of professional sport, the duties imposed on occupiers and organisers may be characterised as increasingly onerous. It is arguable, however, that this is no bad thing. It should be remembered that the courts have consistently stressed that organisers and occupiers are *not* insurers of the safety of competitors or spectators. Nonetheless the popularity of sport is such that millions of people are involved at sporting events annually as spectators and participants, and the tragedies of the 1980s and before indicate that it is incumbent on organisers and occupiers to ensure that their treatment of such persons conforms to "best practice" standards. Adherence to the guidelines outlined above should have the dual effects of avoiding hefty damages awards and, more importantly, of saving lives.

---

[230] Resolution on Preventing Racism, Xenophobia and Intolerance in Sport (2000/4).

CHAPTER SEVEN

The Business of Sport

INTRODUCTION

As has been stressed throughout this book, sport is a multi-billion dollar business globally.[1] The bulk of this money, moreover, is earned not through prize money nor gate receipts, but through the vast sponsorship and broadcasting revenue that sportspersons, sports clubs, sports governing bodies and the organisers of sporting events can attract. So much is obvious. Equally obvious, however, is the fact that in order to gain money from sponsorship and other sources, the sporting body (be it an individual, a club or a federation) must keenly protect its product from unauthorised exploitation. In simple terms, if any company or business could, with legal impunity use for example a sportsperson's image, or a team name or the logo connected with a sporting event in its advertising campaign without the consent of that other party, then there would be no point in any particular company or business paying large sums of money for the privilege of doing so. Thus the law is invoked to regulate the business of sport, and to protect sports bodies (sportspersons, teams and federations for example) as they involve themselves with such business. Equally, it will also protect other commercial players in the sports business arena such as event organisers and broadcasters. In this chapter we consider the nature of such legal regulation and protection.

7.1 THE RIGHTS INVOLVED

As we shall see, the sports body faces a problem in this regard in that, at Irish law there is no property right in one's image[2] nor in a sporting event.[3] Hence it must rely on peripheral rights and strong contractual arrangements to protect the valuable product. So for example when safeguarding exclusivity in respect of the broadcasting of an event, the event organiser cannot rely on any property rights in the event itself, but can use property rights in the venue in which the event is taking place to restrict access, and to impose conditions on persons gaining access thereto – including obviously the condition that the event not

---

[1] See Blackshaw, "Regulating Sport Globally" (2000) 150 *New Law Journal* 617.
[2] *Irvine v. Talksport* [2002] 2 All E.R. 414.
[3] *Victoria Park Racing & Recreation Grounds v. Taylor* (1937) 58 C.L.R. 479.

be broadcast by an unauthorised broadcaster.[4] Similarly whereas an individual or a club does not have any ownership rights in respect of its image, it may well have intellectual property protection through trademark and copyright law and under the tort of passing off (and possibly as a result of constitutional and other rights to privacy), sufficient to control most, if not all, unauthorised use of its image. Indeed as we shall see, events over the last five years may have greatly strengthened the level of control, which the sporting body will enjoy in this regard.

7.2 SPORTS BUSINESS AND THE OWNERSHIP OF SPORT

We should note at this juncture that a deeper question exists as to the ownership of sport. Specifically, and as we noted in Chapter One, it remains a matter of dispute as to whether sport is capable of being owned by any one body. In July 2002, the Football Association of Ireland (as it was perfectly entitled to do) sold the exclusive live broadcasting rights for the competitive "home" internationals of the Irish soccer team to the Sky television network and away from the large bulk of Irish people who do not subscribe to the Sky Sports channel. The vitriolic reaction of large numbers of Irish people to this move[5] (which, as far as the FAI was concerned was taken in the best interests of Irish soccer) suggested a sense of disenfranchisement as if, despite its role in the organisation of soccer in Ireland, the FAI did not have the right to sell any portion of Irish soccer in a manner that would restrict their ability to view it (which, incidentally, is of course exactly what happens every time Irish soccer matches are "ticket only" affairs, as they virtually always are). In response to this, as we shall see, the Irish government enacted legislation designed to reclaim these events for the Irish people, thereby suggesting that *it* was entitled to exercise some ownership rights over the endeavours of the national team as a kind of grand steward of Irish sport acting in the nation's sporting interests.

The inference that can be drawn from this controversy, however, is that a large body of public opinion took an intuitive view that sport in all its dimensions – and especially when played by the national team – is not the property of an individual, or a club or a governing body, but is so closely tied up with society, and public policy and other important community interests

---

[4] *Sports & General Press Agency Ltd v. Our Dogs Publishing Company Limited* [1917] 2 K.B. 125.
[5] Generally see McNally, "FAI defends €7m Sky deal for soccer ties", *Irish Times*, July 6, 2002; Ruane, "The FAI would seem greedier for money than for goals", *Irish Times*, July 12, 2002; Oliver, "Green Army being asked to tune in, turn on and pay up", *Irish Times*, July 6, 2002; Hannigan, "Supporters are sold down the river to Sky", *Irish Times*, July 6, 2002; Hannigan, "Sky's the limit as the fallout continues", *Irish Times*, July 9, 2002 and "FAI/Sky: 1 Supporters: 0", *Irish Times*, July 6, 2002

that it simply transcends ownership.[6] If this view is correct then this leads to an important conclusion, namely that the exploitation of what are regarded as sports rights by bodies other than the individual sportsperson may be merely a form of stewardship of something owned in perpetuity by those who follow sport.

7.3 THE SIGNIFICANCE OF INTELLECTUAL PROPERTY RIGHTS

In considering the legal mechanisms available to the sportsperson, the club and the federation to protect their stake in the revenue earning potential of sport, we focus *inter alia* on the connection between intellectual property rights and sport and in this regard two introductory points should be made. First, we do not consider the totality of intellectual property law as it may impinge on sport. Thus, for example, whereas the inventor of a particular sports product may seek to obtain a patent in his invention[7] (and indeed whereas there may be confidential information involved[8]) this is sufficiently peripheral to our analysis that we shall not consider it. Secondly, whereas the three major intellectual property protections under discussion – trademarks, copyright and under the tort of passing off – are all available in appropriate contexts to sports persons, clubs and organisers of sport, for ease of exposition we shall assess the nature of such protections in the context of the instances in which they have applied most significantly. Thus we shall look at passing off in our assessment of an individual's image rights, trademarks in our analysis of the position of sports clubs and copyright in our consideration of governing bodies, and shall only briefly look at such protections outside of these contexts.

7.4 THE IMPACT OF CONTRACT LAW

As we have said, any rights that arise within the business of sport must be underpinned by a strong contractual arrangement or arrangements if they are to be effective. So, for example, many League of Ireland soccer players have

---

[6] Generally see Holden, "Sporting Treasures: Do you have any TV rights?", *Irish Times*, September 25, 2002; "Governing Bodies and the Ownership of Television Rights" (July/August 1998) *Sports Law Administration and Practice* 9, Abramson; "Whose Rights are they Anyway?", 4 (3) *Sport and the Law Journal* (1996) 100 and Bitel, "Redefining the Ownership of Sport", 6 (3) *Sport and the Law Journal* (1998) 88.

[7] *Windsurfing Inc v. Tabur Marine* [1985] R.P.C. 59. See Griffith Jones *Law and the Business of Sport* (Butterworths, 1997), p.189ff and Lewis & Taylor *Sport: Law And Practice* (Lexis-Nexis, London, 2003), p.611.

[8] For a suggestion that a particularly secret "move", planned for e.g. a rugby match might constitute confidential information, see Griffith Jones, *Law and the Business of Sport* (Butterworths, London, 1997), p.225ff.

written contracts of employment with their respective clubs, and professional rugby players in Ireland have contracts of employment with the IRFU. Similarly, high profile sportspeople will often enter into contractual negotiations in order to sell their image rights to a wide range of interested parties, including clubs, governing bodies, event organisers and promoters. Moreover, the organisers of specific sporting events will, for example, enter into contractual agreements to sell the broadcasting rights to the event, and indeed will use contractual terms and conditions (generally printed in a minuscule typeface on the backs of tickets) to regulate the activities of spectators at such events. Given the pivotal role played by the law of contract in this area of business, it is necessary briefly to identify the key contractual concepts which are of significance in a sporting context. In particular, we focus on the nature of employment contracts, the role of exclusion clauses in contracts and the importance of having a written contract. It should be stressed, however, that this is not a textbook on contract law, and hence the analysis of these concepts is by no means exhaustive.

7.4.1 Employment contracts and sport

In Chapter One we noted that one of the (perhaps under-appreciated) consequences of the professionalisation of sport, is that it turns sport into a business which, like any other business, is subject to basic rules of employment law. The participants in sport may be categorised as amateurs, self-employed professionals and employed professionals. Although most amateurs[9] participate in sport without the protection of written contracts, the converse is true in respect of professionals. In this connection, self-employed professionals engaged to participate in an individual event or series of events are classified as independent contractors operating under a contract to provide services. In contrast, employed professionals, in common with workers in general, may be employed under a standard contract of service. The best example is where a football club engages the services of a player for a term of fixed duration and

---

[9] The distinction between amateur sport and professional sport is not as clear cut as it was in the past. In Case C–51 & 191/97, *Deliege v. Ligue Francophone de Judo et Disciplines Associees ASBL* [2000] E.C.R. I–2549, [2002] 2 C.M.L.R. 1574, the European Court of Justice confirmed that the activities of athletes (even amateur athletes) were governed by Article 49 EC which enables self-employed solo sportsmen and sportswomen of EU nationality to provide their services without being discriminated against in all of the Member States of the Union. It was recognised by the Court that even amateur events have an economic dimension insofar as the successful promulgation of amateur contests of a high sporting calibre involves the organisers in the commercial exploitation of the secondary features of the contest such as broadcasting and sponsorship rights. More importantly, however, the Court acknowledged that many amateurs received payment in kind for their services, *viz.*, generous grants to train and compete. The freedom to provide services is analysed in greater depth in Chap. Eight of this book.

the contractual relationship between the two parties is classifiable as that of employer and employee respectively.[10]

There is a wide range of employment legislation governing the contracts and activities of sportsmen and sportswomen in this jurisdiction. The major sources of statutory employment law in Ireland are the Unfair Dismissals Acts 1977–1993, the Anti-Discrimination (Pay) Act 1974, the Employment Equality Act 1977, the European Communities (Safeguarding of Employees' Rights on Transfer of Undertakings) Regulations, 1980, the Safety, Health and Welfare at Work Act 1989, the Payment of Wages Act 1991, the Terms of Employment (Information) Act 1994, the Organisation of Working Time Act 1997, the Employment Equality Act 1998 and the Parental Leave Act 1998. But this is not a book on employment law and lawyers advising sportsmen and sportswomen as to their statutory rights would do well to consult the most up-to-date textbooks in this area.[11]

It is necessary, as a preliminary to examine the legal tests which identify whether a participant in sport is an employee and therefore governed by the aforementioned common law and statutory rules. The employer/employee relationship was in the past often characterised by the element of control that the former exercised over the latter,[12] although the current approach of the Irish courts focuses on the extent to which the individual worker is part of the overall enterprise, and especially the extent to which that worker can act independently of the enterprise.[13] Thus despite the unique skills possessed by many footballers (for example) they are not able to act independently of the clubs that pay their wages. In *Walker v. Crystal Palace Football Club*,[14] Cozens-Hardy M.R. refused to differentiate between an ordinary workman and a skilful footballer whose employer would have no right to dictate how he should play the game. He explained that the footballer in question would be obliged "under the express terms of his contract to obey all general directions of the club"

---

[10] Up until recently, much of the case-law in contractual disputes involving sportsmen and sportswomen and their respective clubs has focused on the issue of whether they had been wrongfully dismissed. There have also been several decisions which have examined the question of whether the sportsman or sportswoman in question has been culpable of the gross misconduct necessary to justify his/her dismissal. The statutory action for unfair dismissal (as opposed to the contractual action for wrongful dismissal) has yet to be prayed in aid in a sporting context.

[11] Recent publications in this area include: Byrne, Kennedy, Shannon & Ní Longáin, *Employment Law* (Law Society of Ireland/Oxford University Press, Dublin/Oxford, 2003); Meenan, *Working Within the Law* (Oak Tree Press, Dublin, 1999) and Kerr & Madden, *Unfair Dismissal – Cases and Commentary* (IBEC, Dublin, 1996).

[12] *Roche v. Kelly* [1969] I.R. 100.

[13] *O'Coindealbhain v. Mooney*, High Court, Barr J., March, 12, 1992; *Denny v. Minister for Social Welfare* [1988] 1 I.R. 34; *Tierney v. An Post* [2000] 1 I.R. 536; *McAuliffe v. Minister for Social Welfare* [1995] 2 I.R. 238. Generally see Gardiner et al, *Sports Law* (Cavendish Publishing, London, 2001), p.528.

[14] [1910] 1 K.B. 87.

and, in any particular game, he would also be bound by the specific instructions of the captain or whoever it was the club had chosen as its "delegate of authority" for the purpose of conveying those instructions.

In general, professional tennis players, athletes and golfers all possess the requisite degree of economic independence and control over their respective destinies to characterise themselves as self-employed professionals.[15] Boxers (and especially those with nascent careers) on the other hand, do not enjoy the same freedom of action. So, for example, a professional boxer will usually employ a manager even though the latter, viewed from a business perspective, is the stronger of the two parties. The manager usually operates as the agent of the boxer and the terms of the contract will not preclude him from entering similar contracts with other boxers. Paradoxically, the manager is the one pulling the strings even though he is employed by the different boxers in his stable. The boxer – who is technically under the *de facto* control of his manager – is "self-employed" in a narrow, legalistic sense of the term. Indeed, the legal nature of the arrangement is often unfavourable to the boxer insofar as it will preclude him from relying on the employment statutes cited above and he may have to rely for protection on the common law principles of contract.[16]

7.4.2 The express terms of the employment contract

Professional players engaged by teams as members of their squads almost invariably conclude written agreements which define the rights and obligations of the respective parties. Although most of these involve the conclusion of a written contract as between the player and the team for whom he agrees to play, this is not always the case. Let us take for example the issue of professional rugby in Ireland. In Ireland, the Irish Rugby Football Union ("IRFU") regulates and exercises overall control over the game of rugby at both an international and a provincial level. So, for example, rugby players engaged by any of the four provincial Irish teams (Munster, Leinster, Ulster and Connaught) conclude Full Time Provincial Player Contracts "with the IRFU". These contracts deal with a host of matters and impose a wide-ranging series of obligations on the player including:

- to play the game in a sportsmanlike manner and to the best of his ability and skill;

- to observe the rules of both the International Rugby Board ("IRB") and the IRFU;

---

[15] See *Hendry, Williams and Sportmasters Network Ltd v. World Professional Billiard and Snooker Association Ltd* [2002] European Commercial Cases 8.

[16] See *Hearn and Matchroom Boxing v. Collins*, unreported, High Court, O'Sullivan J., February 3, 1998.

- not to engage in any activity which involves unnecessary danger or participate in any other sport save those in which the chances of injury are unlikely;

- to make himself available for the promotion of the game through attending at schools and youth clubs and providing coaching services;

- to maintain the level of health and fitness necessary to enable him to play the game;

- to undergo any fitness examination or medical treatment when required to do so.

The IRFU, for its part, is obliged to pay the player a retainer fee and a fee per match played (together with (where applicable) an Inter-provincial Championship, European Cup, European Shield or Celtic League match win bonus).

The player is also subject to the overriding obligation (contained in the *Full Time Provincial Player Contract*) not to bring the game into disrepute nor to engage in any activity which would diminish its integrity. Any serious breach of the contract by the player may result in the termination of the agreement, although any such decision by the IRFU Contracts Sub-Committee is subject to a right of appeal to the IRFU Disciplinary Committee (and it is, of course, also open to the player concerned, in appropriate cases, to pursue his right of recourse to the courts if he is dissatisfied with either the conduct or the outcome of the disciplinary proceedings). Examples of serious breaches include:

- the acceptance of a bribe by a player;

- a criminal conviction (other than an offence under the Road Traffic legislation);

- a finding by a competent authority to the effect that a player has taken or used any drugs or dope on a prohibited list, or a refusal by a player to undergo a test or provide a sample when required to do so by the competent authority.

Breaches of the agreement of a less serious nature can be punished by a fine or suspension.

The issue of a finding by a relevant authority that the player has committed a doping offence thereby constituting a breach of contract is a particularly interesting one. When Manchester United defender Rio Ferdinand was suspended in 2003[17] for eight months and fined £50,000 sterling on account

---

[17] Generally on this case see Warner, "Ferdinand Given an Hour's Notice", *Evening Standard*, October 7, 2003; Winter, "FA Take Tough Line on Rio", *Daily Telegraph*, October 30, 2003; Warner, "Anti-Doping Chief: Forgetting is No Excuse", *Evening Standard*, October 8, 2003; Kelso, "I'd Never Used Drugs – Ferdinand", *Guardian*, October 8, 2003; Winter, "Furious United and FA on Ugly Collision Course", *Daily Telegraph*, October 8, 2003 and McCarra, "Ferdinand Test Case Exposes Palios to FA's Failings", *Guardian*, December 2, 2003.

of his failure to submit to drug testing, this constituted evidence of serious misconduct which would probably have entitled his club (and as we shall see, his personal sponsors) to terminate their agreement with him.[18] But it is not always in the interests of clubs to insist on their strict contractual rights and the Manchester United board and manager supported Rio Ferdinand *inter alia* because they felt that the sanction was excessive, given that (they submitted) his failure to attend the test was attributable to his forgetfulness and all the evidence indicated that he had not actually used drugs. Moreover, it would have been counter-productive to dismiss a 25 year old player who is central to the cohesiveness of the team's defence and has a lengthy career ahead of him. Not surprisingly, the club provided him with full legal assistance when he (unsuccessfully) appealed the Football Association ("FA") ruling to an Independent Appeal Board.[19] Equally, the fact that a finding that a player has committed a doping offence could lead to the cancellation of multi-million euro contracts means that (as we saw in Chapter Two) the level of fair procedures to which such a player is entitled in the processing of his case by the relevant sports federation is very high indeed.

7.4.3 The implied terms of the employment contract

If there is a lacuna in the express terms of an employment contract, the courts will often correct an intrinsic failure of expression on the part of the contracting parties by implying terms into an agreement in order to make it workable. Examples of such terms are as follows:

> "... an employee is obliged faithfully to serve his employer, to obey reasonable orders, to work with reasonable skill and care, honestly and in good faith and not to abuse his employer's confidential information; the employer, for his part, is, above all, obliged to pay his employee his salary or wages. Moreover, because the relationship between an employer and his employees is a personal one, the courts have in recent times been prepared to imply a general obligation on both parties not to act in such

---

[18] Under the terms of the standard form *FA Premier League and Football League Contract*, a club employing a player culpable of either "serious" or "persistent" misconduct is entitled to terminate its contract with the player concerned provided that it affords him fourteen days written notice of such termination.

[19] As matters transpired, however, the Board dismissed his appeal on March 19, 2004 and upheld the eight month suspension (which had initially been handed down on December 19, 2003). This decision to uphold the suspension effectively precluded him from playing for England at Euro 2004 and delayed his return for Manchester United until September 20, 2004. See Brodkin, "Ferdinand Verdict a Relief for English FA", *Guardian*, March 19, 2004.

a way as to be likely to undermine the underlying 'relationship of trust and confidence' between them."[20]

Perhaps most importantly, as we saw in Chapter Two, all contracts contain an implied term that the employer will observe standards of fair procedures in respect of the contract.[21]

7.4.4 Termination of contracts of employment in sport

Prior to the enactment of the unfair dismissals legislation in Ireland, an employee who contended that he had been unfairly dismissed could only pursue a common law action through the courts for wrongful dismissal – a more cumbersome and expensive process than that afforded litigants under the current legislation. Moreover, the remedies afforded him were also more limited than those available to him today. When the Unfair Dismissals Act was enacted in 1977, it improved the lot of employees in substantial measure insofar as it endowed them with three different statutory remedies where there was found to be an unfair dismissal, namely, reinstatement, re-engagement or a maximum of 104 weeks' remuneration. The legislation is based on two fundamental principles. First of all, substantial grounds must exist to justify the termination of a contract of employment. Secondly, the employer must abide by fair procedures in effecting the termination.[22]

Not all sportsmen and sportswomen employed by clubs are covered by the legislation. To fall within the scope of the Unfair Dismissals Acts 1977–1993, the employee must have the requisite one year's continuous service with the employer. This is interpreted strictly and it means fifty-two weeks of unbroken service as defined by the rules of continuity embodied in the Minimum Notice and Terms of Employment Act 1973, Schedule 1. The Unfair Dismissals (Amendment) Act 1993 operates in ease of employees insofar as it provides that the dismissal of an employee followed by their re-employment by the same employer within twenty-six weeks will not break their continuity of service if the dismissal was effected in order to avoid liability under the legislation.

---

[20] See Griffith-Jones in *Law and the Business of Sport* (Butterworths, London, 1997) at p.172.
[21] *O'Reilly v. Minister for Industry and Commerce*, unreported, High Court, Carroll J., March 4, 1993; *Mooney v. An Post* [1998] 4 I.R. 288.
[22] There are three main forms of dismissal comprising: (i) the termination of a contract of employment with or without notice; (ii) the resignation of the employee as a result of the conduct of the employer (constructive dismissal); and (iii) non-renewal of a fixed term or specified purpose contract.

There are a number of forms of dismissal which are automatically deemed to be unfair under the legislation:[23]

- dismissal on the grounds of an employee's membership (or proposed membership) or activity on behalf of a trade union provided that such activity takes place either outside his hours of work or, at permitted times, during his hours of work;

- dismissal on the grounds of the employee's religious or political opinions;

- dismissal on the grounds of the involvement of the employee in actual, threatened or proposed civil or criminal proceedings against the employer, or where the employee has made any complaint or statement to the prosecuting authority connected to the case ;

- dismissal on the grounds of the employee's race, colour, sexual orientation or membership of the travelling community

- dismissal on the grounds of the employee's age;

- dismissal on the grounds of the pregnancy of the employee and related matters. The actionability of the latter form of unfair dismissal is subject to the proviso that the employee is capable of adequately performing the work for which she was employed. For virtually all sportswomen, pregnancy will effectively signal the temporary ending of their careers and their employers are not obliged to keep their contracts open for them in such circumstances (unless there is an express stipulation in the contract to this effect).

The non-renewal of fixed term and specified purpose contracts can constitute unfair dismissal. It is important to point out, however, that it is possible to secure an exclusion (from the consequences of the Unfair Dismissals Acts 1977–1993) in respect of dismissals resulting from the ending of a fixed term contract, (or dismissals resulting from the cessation of the purpose of a specified purpose contract). To secure an exclusion, the employer must comply with the following conditions:

- the contract must be in writing;

- the contract must specifically exclude the legislation; and

- the contract must be signed by both parties.

In Ireland, most of the *fixed term* contracts concluded between clubs and the players contain clauses designed to exclude the operation of the Unfair Dismissals legislation. The wording of such clauses is generally clear and

---

[23] Unfair Dismissals Act 1977, s.6(2) (as amended by Unfair Dismissals (Amendment) Act 1993, s.5).

unequivocal: "The Unfair Dismissals Acts 1977–1993 shall not apply to a termination of this agreement consisting only of the expiry of the agreement without its being renewed."

In general, however, a fixed term contract can be terminated without cause if due notice is given. Although a contract of fixed duration normally ends on the date scheduled for its expiry, there is nothing to prevent the parties from relying on an express clause in the agreement which provides for termination on notice. A fixed term contract can also be terminated summarily. But this form of termination normally carries financial consequences for the club responsible for the summary execution. So, for example, at the end of May, 2004, Chelsea Football Club dismissed their manager Claudio Ranieri without notice even though his contract still had another three years to run. But there is speculation at the time of writing that it will cost Chelsea in excess of £6 million sterling in an out of court settlement to compensate Ranieri for the lost years of his contract.[24]

If the Ranieri case had been litigated, there is strong probability that a summary termination of that nature would have been treated by the English courts as an unfair dismissal) unless the former manager of Chelsea was himself culpable of gross misconduct. But such misconduct is often difficult to establish, especially in the absence of evidence that the employee concerned broke an express or implied term which formed part of the core of the contract or that he himself wrongfully repudiated the contract. If, for example, the manager of a leading football club started tinkering with the composition of his team in a vital Champions League tie and this cost his side the match (as arguably happened during the first leg of the European Champions League semi-final match between Monaco and Chelsea in 2004[25]), such behaviour would fall decidedly short of the gross misconduct necessary to justify his summary dismissal.

The notion of gross misconduct has been examined in a number of cases (primarily focusing on *wrongful* as distinct from *unfair* dismissal) and it is more or less settled law that the refusal to obey a lawful and reasonable instruction by an employer will, in most instances, constitute gross misconduct. If, however, the employee finds himself in a conflict of interest situation, a single act of disobedience on his part may not necessarily indicate that he is repudiating the contract or one of its essential conditions. In *Laws v. London Chronicle*,[26] the plaintiff had accompanied her immediate superior to a meeting with the managing director of the company. A row erupted as between her superior and the managing director. Her superior requested her to leave the meeting and she acceded to this request notwithstanding a verbal directive

---

[24] See Stewart, "Chelsea's axe finally falls on Ranieri", *The Scotsman*, June 1, 2004 and Brodkin, "Mourinho on Standby as Ranieri finally Goes", *Guardian*, June 1, 2004.
[25] See "Tinker Tailor – Made to Fail", *Irish Times*, April 21, 2004.
[26] [1959] 2 All E.R. 285.

from the managing director that she should stay. He subsequently dismissed her summarily for wilful disobedience. Although Lord Evershed MR explained that wilful disobedience can justify summary dismissal insofar as it amounts to a complete disregard of a condition essential to the contract of service, namely the requirement that a servant must obey the proper orders of her master. In this case, however, the single act of disobedience did not fall within this category because it was an isolated occurrence and the employee had been placed under undue pressure by her immediate superior.

If an employee is culpable of gross misconduct, the employer is entitled to treat the breach on the employee's part as one which has discharged the employer from his obligations under the contract. This also entitles the employer to elect to treat the contract as terminated. In more recent cases, the courts have tended to eschew the "master/servant" language which was used by Lord Evershed in the *Laws* case in favour of the "employer/employee" terminology. This has been matched by an increasing unwillingness on the part of the courts to categorise all forms of disobedient behaviour as wilful misconduct. In *Wilson v. Racher*,[27] a gardener was unfairly accused of shirking his work by his employer. The unfairness of this accusation needled him and he told his employer to "Get stuffed" and "Go and shit yourself". This outburst occurred in the presence of his employer's wife, Mrs. Racher. The Court of Appeal refused to categorise the gardener's response to provocation as gross misconduct and adopted a more enlightened approach to the employer/employee relationship. As pointed out by Lord Edmund Davies, the older cases treated employees as if they were in a Czar-serf relationship and this probably explained why dismissed employees usually failed to recover damages. Finding in favour of the gardener, Lord Edmund Davies explained that "a contract of service imposes upon the parties a duty of mutual respect."

Even before the above duty was first identified, the courts were interested in the motivations which induced employers to terminate their contracts with employees. In one case, in particular, the Scottish Sheriffs Court upheld a claim by a professional footballer, who appeared to have been the victim of sharp commercial practice at the hands of his club. In *Shankland v. Airdrieonians*[28] the pursuer[29] was a professional football player who had been employed by and played for the defenders during the five playing seasons 1949–50, 1950–51, 1951–52, 1952–53 and 1953–54. He had held a series of written contracts for each season. In April 1953, the directors of the club decided to retain the pursuer's services for the 1953–54 season. The pursuer refused to sign unless he was guaranteed a lump sum benefit of £750 sterling during the same season. At a meeting on April 30, 1953, the directors decided to pay the

---

[27] [1974] I.R.L.R. 114.
[28] (1956) Scots Law Times ("S.L.T.") 69.
[29] The Scots law equivalent of the plaintiff; the defendant is known as the defender in Scotland.

pursuer the sum of £500 sterling on completion of five years service at the end of the 1953–54 season (on April 30, 1954) and this promise induced the pursuer to sign a contract with the club for the forthcoming season.

Towards the end of the 1953–54 season, on April 26, 1954, the defenders wrote to the pursuer to inform him that they would not be retaining his services for the 1954–55 season and that his appointment would be terminated as of April 30, 1954. The club contended that only players who had completed five calendar years of service were entitled to claim a lump sum benefit from their employers. Since the first of the pursuer's five consecutive contracts had not commenced until November 4, 1949, the lateness of that date effectively precluded him from having served the requisite five calendar years by the end of the 1953–54 season. The club only sought to make an issue of the fact that he had not played for five calendar years after they dispensed with his services and they sought to rely on Scottish Football League practice in relation to lump sum payments by clubs. Sheriff-Substitute Young was unimpressed with this argument, given that the club was unable to produce a single witness to corroborate their averments in relation to the practice of the Scottish Football League. In the final analysis, the pursuer secured a decree for £500 sterling on the basis that the club had promised to pay him this sum of money at the end of the 1953–54 season.

The implied duty of trust and confidence, referred to earlier, is mutual and it binds both employers and employees in equal measure. It means that an employer should not, without justification, behave in a manner calculated or likely to destroy or seriously undermine the relationship of trust and confidence with its employee. In *Macari v. Celtic Football and Athletic Co. Ltd.*,[30] the defenders, Glasgow Celtic FC, were arguably in breach of this duty when Fergus McCann, the head of the consortium which had taken over the club in March 1994, peremptorily notified the pursuer, Lou Macari, that he did not want him as manager (without taking more active steps to dismiss him) and excluded him from meetings of the Board (which Macari had attended under the previous regime). At that point in time, the pursuer would have been entitled to accept the breach, treat the contract as repudiated and claim damages for constructive dismissal.

However, he did not choose this option, preferring instead to remain on at the club and drawing his salary under his contract. He was therefore obliged to comply with the directions issued to him by Fergus McCann to reside within 45 miles of George Square in Glasgow. The pursuer, however, continued to reside in Stoke where he had his family home. The pursuer also failed to attend more regularly at Celtic Park and to report to Fergus McCann on a weekly basis. In June 1994, in response to a letter from McCann, the pursuer sent a defiant fax, followed by a phone call, to make it clear to McCann that he did

---

[30] [1999] I.R.L.R. 787, (2000) S.L.T. 80.

not intend to be bound by his directions and that he was opposing his lawful authority. Macari was subsequently dismissed by McCann and he instituted an action for alleged wrongful dismissal against Glasgow Celtic Football Club. The Lord Ordinary concluded that McCann was entitled to treat the pursuer's conduct as indicative of an intention to flout his obligations under the contract and as an intimation of repudiation of it thereby justifying his dismissal by McCann. The moral of the story is plain; even if an employer has breached his duty to maintain mutual trust and confidence, this will not avail an employee who has chosen to affirm the breach of his contract by continuing to work under it. In such circumstances, the employee must continue to comply with any instructions given by the employer which are, in themselves, reasonable.

In *Hearn and Matchroom Boxing v. Collins*,[31] Barry Hearn, the promoter and manager of professional sportsmen, claimed 25% of the defendant's earnings in respect of the management services which he had allegedly provided him with during the calendar year ending on May 10, 1996. Towards the end of his relationship with the first named plaintiff, the defendant, Steve Collins, became the World Boxing Organisation ("WBO") Super Middleweight Champion of the World when he defeated Chris Eubank at Millstreet, County Cork on March 18, 1995. The relationship between the first named plaintiff and the defendant had deteriorated before the Millstreet fight when Barry Hearn became aware that Collins was talking to another promoter and manager, Frank Warren. There was a preliminary issue in this case as to which, if any, of a number of contracts governed the relationship between the parties and as to whether a contract concluded between the second named plaintiff and the defendant could be the subject of enforcement by a third party in the absence of the requisite privity of contract. O'Sullivan J. decided that the third party. (and first named plaintiff), Barry Hearn, could take the benefit of the contract in question[32] and that, in addition, there was a binding management agreement in force between Hearn and Collins up until June 6, 1995.

The main issue in the proceedings was whether, by virtue of his conduct two months after the Millstreet fight, Barry Hearn had committed a fundamental breach of contract which would have justified the defendant in treating it as repudiated and in terminating the contract without any further liability on his part. O'Sullivan J. found that the first named plaintiff *had* breached his contract with the defendant by corresponding with Francisco Valcarcel, the then President of the WBO, seeking to persuade him to favour another one of Hearn's clients, Chris Eubank, by allowing him to fight against another boxer for an interim boxing championship in advance of his scheduled title re-match with Collins. Such an arrangement would have been hugely detrimental to Collins insofar as it would have caused him to sustain a substantial loss of earnings in

[31] Unreported, High Court, O'Sullivan J., February 3, 1998.
[32] The privity of contract issue is discussed by Clark in *Contract Law in Ireland* (Roundhall Sweet & Maxwell, Dublin, 1998), p.403.

relation to his eventual title defence against Chris Eubank.[33] Given that the plaintiffs enjoyed a contractual relationship with both Eubank and Collins, O'Sullivan J. ruled that their behaviour in attempting to favour Eubank over Collins amounted to a fundamental breach of their contract with the latter.

In addition O' Sullivan J. found that, a fortnight before Barry Hearn had initiated his correspondence with the WBO, he had also conducted himself in a manner that was detrimental to his client's interests at the purse bid ceremony (for the Collins/Eubank rematch) in New York on May 29, 1995. He had attempted to undermine the efficacy of the purse bid by attacking the credibility of the Frank Warren and the Sports Network organisation in order to question the financial viability of the Collins/Eubank rematch. Once again, this behaviour had the potential to hurt Stephen Collins in his pocket.

O'Sullivan J. concluded that *both* the correspondence between Barry Hearn and the WBO and his behaviour at the purse bid ceremony in New York amounted to fundamental breaches of his management contract with Stephen Collins. This repudiation of the management contract by Hearn was accepted by Stephen Collins on June 6, 1995 when he sent him a letter which terminated their contractual relationship. In the light of this finding that June 6, 1995 was the operative date of the termination of the contract, O'Sullivan J. dismissed Hearn's claim for a 25% cut of the defendant's earnings in the calendar year ended May 10, 1996.

In conclusion, it is salutary to point out that *Hearn and Matchroom Boxing* differs from *Macari* insofar as a contract for the supply of services was at issue in the former case whereas the latter case involved a contract of employment. But the fundamental lesson which emanates from both of these cases is that when relationships begin to deteriorate as between the various players in the world of sport, it is very important to keep a cool head. Macari had been mistreated in the wake of the takeover of Celtic; but he chose to continue in the employ of the club and, having elected to stay, he erred fundamentally in disobeying the instructions of Fergus McCann, his superior. Barry Hearn had concluded a potentially lucrative contract to manage Stephen Collins. If, instead of attempting to stymie both Collins and Frank Warren, he had concentrated instead on safeguarding the financial welfare of his fighter, the circumstances giving rise to the litigation might never have arisen (or – if the relationship between Collins and himself had still fractured on account of the arrival on the scene of Frank Warren – the outcome of the High Court litigation might have been completely different if Hearn had acted with greater circumspection in May and June of 1995).

---

[33] In his correspondence with Valcarcel, Hearn had suggested that the winner of the interim championship should go on to fight Collins for the World Championship on a 50/50 basis. This requirement if accepted, would have meant that Collins' entitlement to a 75% share of the purse as champion would have been reduced to a 50% share.

7.4.5 Exclusion clauses

Onerous terms in a contract must be drawn to the attention of a party on whom they are imposed. If for example, therefore, a spectator purchases a ticket for a rugby match and subsequently discovers that there are terms and conditions on the back of the ticket which attempt to exclude the legal liability of the organiser in respect of injuries sustained by spectators at the match, the spectator will not be bound by this term if it was not drawn to his attention beforehand (unless, through a consistent course of dealings with the organiser, he is fixed with knowledge of the term). In this electronic age, many of the sports federations refer to "ticket terms and conditions" on their respective WebPages, thereby alerting potential purchasers of tickets to the terms of the contract prior to purchase. Often, the purchaser of the ticket will have to click on an icon to the effect that he has read the terms and conditions before concluding the contract by giving his credit card details.

There is a stark contrast between the more consumer oriented terms and conditions as to the exclusion of liability used by the Rugby Football Union at Twickenham and the rather more antiquated terms used by the Irish Rugby Football Union. Clause 3 of the Twickenham Ground Rules provides as follows:

"The RFU, its servants or agents will not be liable for any loss, injury or damage, including of or to any vehicle or its contents in any car park or to any person who enters the ground caused by the RFU or its servant or agents:

(i) in circumstances where there is no breach of a legal duty of care owed by the RFU or any of its servants or agents; or

(ii) in circumstances where such loss or damage is not a reasonably foreseeable result of any such breach (save for death or personal injury as a result of a breach of a legal duty of care owed by the RFU, its servants or agents); or

(iv) to the extent that any increase in loss or damage results from breach by you of any of the terms of admission of these rules."

In other words, the RFU is not attempting to exclude liability in respect of death or personal injury arising from its own breach of a legal duty of care or that of its servants or agents. This is scarcely surprising given that exemption clauses or notices purporting to exclude liability in respect of breach of contract, negligence or a breach of statutory duty occasioning death or personal injury are void in their entirety under the Unfair Contract Terms Act 1977. Indeed the Office of Fair Trading in the United Kingdom has been especially vigilant – ever since the enactment of the legislation in 1977 – to intervene in the marketplace and to compel the withdrawal of such clauses.

In Ireland, on the other hand, the tradition of regulating unfair contract terms is much more recent. Perhaps this explains, at least partially, why an organisation such as the Irish Rugby Football Union ("IRFU") continues to insert the following clause (Clause 3) on the back of its tickets for RBS Six Nations Championship matches held at Lansdowne Road:

> "The Union, its servants or agents, shall have no liability for loss, injury or damage to the ticket holder or his or her property while in the ground or any part thereof or entering or leaving the ground whether caused by negligence or breach of contract of the Union or any of its servants or agent or otherwise."[34]

Although there is nothing illegal in this practice and the IRFU are fully entitled to limit their liability in this regard, it is highly questionable whether such a clause would survive scrutiny under existing Irish and European Community law on the notification and fairness of contractual terms. Under section 40 (1) of the Sale of Goods and Supply of Services Act, 1980, exclusion clauses in respect of the provision of services must be specifically drawn to the attention of consumers and must be both "fair and reasonable". It is probably safe to say that – given the manner in which tickets for the Six Nations Championship are distributed in Ireland - the vast majority of ticket holders are unaware of such exclusion clauses on the back of their tickets (unless a prominent icon or symbol on the website for the sale of the tickets has alerted the lucky few who have managed to purchase their tickets online) and that such clauses are therefore non-binding because the ticket containing the exclusion clause is issued after completion of the contractual bargain. In any event, even if such exclusion clauses were "specifically drawn" to the attention of ticket holders, they would be unlikely to survive scrutiny under the "fair and reasonable" criterion given that spectators who pay full value for match tickets should not be expected to insure themselves against injuries caused to them by the breach of contract or the negligence of the IRFU.

Furthermore, the European Communities (Unfair Terms in Consumer Contracts) Regulations, 1995 contain an indicative grey list of terms, which are *prima facie* classifiable as unfair and unreasonable and therefore void. Prominent at the top of the list are those terms which "have the object or effect" of excluding or limiting legal liability in respect of the death or personal injury of the consumers of goods and services. More importantly, however, Regulation 8 of the 1995 Regulations empowers the Director of Consumer Affairs to apply to the High Court for an order prohibiting the use or, if appropriate, the continued use of any term in a contract adjudged by the Court

---

[34] A similar practice, of exempting from liability in respect of death or injury attributable to the organiser of international rugby matches, also obtains in South Africa. Clause 5 of the ticket used for the South Africa v. Ireland match in Cape Town on June 19, 2004 provided that "The company will not be liable for any loss, injury or damage, howsoever caused, to the holder of this ticket."

to be an unfair term. Clause 3 of the IRFU terms and conditions seems ripe for challenge under this particular provision of the 1995 Regulations.

Finally, as we saw in Chapter Six, outside of a situation where a contract may be said to exist, under section 5 of the Occupiers' Liability Act 1995, the effect of exclusion clauses when contained in prominent signs at the premises merely reduces the duty owed by the occupier to a *visitor* to his premises (and paying spectators would be classed as visitors) to the level owed by that occupier to the *recreational user* or *trespasser* – in other words from the level of a common duty of care to the level of a duty not to injure the entrant intentionally or to act with reckless disregard for his or her well being.

7.4.6 The importance of a written contract

As a general rule, there is no requirement that a contract is written or that it should take a particular form. Griffith-Jones notes, however, that a "contrary belief appears to be prevalent, especially in the football world where club managers in particular are regularly described as working "without a contract" simply because they have not yet signed a written contract (usually for a fixed term)."[35] But managers of this ilk are nevertheless employed by their clubs under an oral contract and "owe and are owed the ordinary obligations which arise as between an employer and an employee."[36] In common with managers who possess written contracts of fixed duration, managers employed on a more tenuous verbal basis "must generally give due notice if they decide to leave and are entitled to similar notice in the event that their club decides to dispense with their services."[37]

But, in most instances, it makes sense for sportspersons to commit their business contracts to writing. This is borne out by three recent high profile pieces of litigation, which have highlighted the dangers inherent in failing to define the parameters of commercial relationships in writing in a meticulous and clearly defined fashion. In *Ferguson v. Coolmore*,[38] a dispute arose over the ownership and breeding rights in respect of *Rock of Gibraltar*, one of the leading flat horses of his generation. According to Sir Alex Ferguson (the Manchester United manager and recent horseracing devotee), John Magnier (a major shareholder in Manchester United and the co-owner of the horse) and he had a verbal agreement whereby Magnier had offered him either 50% of the prize money or 50% of the breeding rights (and hence the stud earnings) in the horse. Magnier on the other hand, insisted that Sir Alex had been offered

---

[35] Griffith-Jones, *op. cit.*, p.36.
[36] *Ibid.*
[37] *Ibid.*
[38] See the description of the background to this litigation in "A Horse's Tail", *Sunday Times*, February 1, 2004.

merely 5% of the prize money or one stud fee per year. The case was settled in March 2004 and a deal was brokered whereby Sir Alex Ferguson would receive a £2.5 million sterling settlement tax-free, a concession that effectively translated into a settlement of £3.5 million sterling in real terms. The lump sum was calculated on the basis that Sir Alex would be offered the equivalent of four "covers" a year by Rock of Gibraltar for the projected duration of the horse's life at stud and that any putative rights to ownership of the horse would be terminated immediately.[39]

The importance of ensuring clear contractual protection in sponsorship contracts was borne out in *Jordan Grand Prix Limited v. Vodaphone Group Plc.*[40] The case involved the well known Formula One team owner Eddie Jordan. He claimed that in the course of a phone conversation between himself and the global brand director of the Vodafone company, the latter agreed to be the Formula One title sponsor for the Jordan team for three seasons for a total cost of $150million. When Vodafone refused to go ahead with the alleged agreement, Jordan sued them for breach of contract and/or misrepresentation. The defendants on the other hand, claimed that no contract had been made because there had been no agreement between the parties and that even if such agreement had been made it was plainly incomplete, in particular because Mr Jordan was well aware that the global brand director in this case did not have the authority to commit the defendant to such a contract. In the event the Queen's Bench Division of the High Court held that there was no sponsorship contract in existence in this case.[41] The Court found that the claimant's case was demonstrably without foundation. It simply did not make sense to suggest that - as the result of a telephone conversation held shortly after 6.00 p.m. and lasting some 10 to 15 minutes – a complex sponsorship contract had come into existence. Langley J. questioned the credibility of this aspect of Jordan's case in a key passage of his judgment:

"At 22 March no one could have deduced what were the terms of any contract which [the parties] were supposedly making. It was the understanding of both Vodafone and Jordan that any agreement would have to be in writing. Not even Heads of Agreement (which might or might not have been drafted as to be legally binding) had been established. At this stage there was nothing, which could sensibly even have been said to be 'subject to contract'. There was no agreement on livery, no agreement on bonuses, no agreement on intellectual property matters or joint ventures and no agreement on a renewal option which, it is agreed,

---

[39] *Daily Telegraph*, March 6, 2003 and March 8, 2003.
[40] [2003] E.W.H.C. 1956 (Queens Bench, August 4, 2003). See also *Glolite Ltd v. Jasper Conran Limited*, Times Law Reports, 28 January, 1998.
[41] Para.190.

was a provision it was in the interests of the sponsor to secure in order to safeguard and benefit from the investment the sponsor was making in the team. Mr Boyle [Jordan's QC] submitted that the 'deal' was for those few matters, which had been argued, and those, which could not be ignored or had been rejected. That submission disguises an impermissible form of cherry-picking when on any view of the facts a comprehensive agreement and certainly agreement on the key factors to which I have referred was both expected and required."[42]

Put bluntly, the Court felt that the gross implausibility of an absolutely enormous contract of this kind being made in such an unofficial way was obvious and indeed was completely borne out by the body of the evidence, which it had heard during the course of the trial.[43]

A similar logic emerges from the decision of the English High Court in *Carlton Communications plc v. The Football League*.[44] The ITV Digital company (in which the Carlton and Granada companies each had 50% shareholdings) had gone into liquidation on March 27, 2002 with massive debts. A sizeable proportion of this debt was owed to the Football League, which, in a contract dating from June 2000 had agreed to sell the broadcasting rights to the Nationwide League games for three seasons to ITV Digital for Stg£89.25 million. In this case the Football League sought to recover payment due under the terms of this agreement from Carlton and Granada. It is of course trite law that a company has separate legal personality from its shareholders, thus Carlton and Granada would not be liable for the debts of ITV Digital in the normal course of events.[45] The Football League, however, claimed that it was entitled to recovery of such payments because Carlton and Granada had agreed under the terms of the June 2000 contract to act as guarantors of any losses that ITV Digital might make under the terms of the June 2000 contract. In the claim that was at the centre of this case, the claimants sought a declaration that they were not liable for any payments due under the June 2000 contract and the defendant's counterclaimed a declaration that they were.

Ultimately the case turned on a relatively simple issue of contract law. The Football League contended that in an Initial Bid document of June 7, 2000, the claimants had made a unilateral offer to guarantee the obligations of ITV Digital. The claimants on the other hand, contended that this document represented a "subject to contract" proposal and was not a document that could

---

[42] Para.191.

[43] Para.189.

[44] [2002] E.W.H.C. 1650 (August 1, 2002). See "ITV Digital Teeters on the Brink", *Irish Times*, March, 28, 2002 and "Football League Loses ITV Digital Case", *Irish Times*, July 25, 2002.

[45] *Salomon v Salomon & Co* [1897] A.C. 22. See [2002] E.W.H.C. 1650 at para.68.

be accepted by conduct, nor did the Football League purport to accept it.[46] The High Court refused to accept the argument of the defendants, pointing out that it was simply unthinkable that obligations as massive as those that Carlton and Granada were supposed to be making (and indeed benefits as massive as those that the Football League was supposed to be receiving) would not be referred to in more express terms within the actual contract itself, rather than in a mere accompanying document.[47] Thus the judge noted rather sardonically that:

> "It is an unpromising start for a party who seeks to rely on a guarantee by third parties of obligations involving £315m entered into by another party that the only reference to a guarantee is to be found in one short sentence of a document produced by the supposed primary obligor in the course of a negotiating process which was 'subject to contract' and the only subsequent effective or binding contract is one agreed by the primary obligor which is on different terms and contains no guarantee nor a reference to one save in the overt oblique terms of [one clause] of the June Contract. It is all the more unpromising when the relevant negotiations are conducted in a major commercial context between two companies with the benefit of the professional advice of experienced management and lawyers. In my judgement the Football League's case remains just as unpromising at the finish as it looked at the start."[48]

Indeed even if the Initial Bid document had been intended to constitute an offer, the court held that it would have been insufficient to satisfy the terms of the Statute of Frauds.[49] Like the Jordan case then, the ITV Digital case is indicative of the importance of ensuring that the terms of any agreement – particularly one involving significant sums of money – are clearly expressed within the terms of a written contract.

7.5 THE RIGHTS OF THE INDIVIDUAL SPORTSPERSON

Our first substantive concern in this chapter is with the legal protections available to individual sportspersons as they engage in the business of sport. Top sportspersons are of course also role models and heroes for people of all ages and many people desire to associate themselves with the sportsperson's image, be it through using a golf club endorsed by Tiger Woods, or a soccer replica shirt with Roy Keane's name on the back of it, or simply by having a

---

[46] Paras 10 and 11.
[47] Para.59.
[48] Para.49.
[49] Para.81.

poster with David Beckham's face on it on their bedroom wall.[50] From the perspective of businesses wishing to advertise their products, this fact, coupled with the fact that most sports fans will demonstrate unswerving loyalty to their heroes, means that it can be assumed that use of sports people's images will help to sell products. In this section, we consider two issues, namely the nature of an image rights agreement and the legal remedies available to the sportsperson whose image is being used without his authorisation.

7.5.1 Image rights agreements

When David Beckham left Manchester United in the summer of 2003 and signed for Spanish giants Real Madrid for some €25m, there was a good deal of speculation that Real Madrid were more interested in the arguably unique merchandising and marketing potential that Beckham possesses than in his undoubted playing skills.[51] There was also speculation that one reason why Manchester United was rather glad to sell him (apart from the media circus that inevitably follows Mr and Mrs Beckham) was that his contract with the club saw him earn a huge sum of money weekly in exchange for the club being allowed to exploit his image, but the club's main kit manufacturer Nike had recently bought out the club's replica short business for 13 years for a cost of £300m, thereby negating many of the benefits accruing to the club from the right to use Beckham's image (which was costing them some £20,000 per week).

In any event, Beckham did something that was pioneered by one of his Real Madrid team-mates – Portuguese superstar Luis Figo – and is now commonplace, and earned a large amount of money by ceding exclusive control of his image rights to his new club when signing for it.[52] This reflects a contemporary reality for high profile professional athletes of significant contractual negotiations with clubs,[53] governing bodies, event organisers[54] and private

---

[50] See Bond, "Sports Personalities: Sponsorship and Endorsement Deals" [2004] *Entertainment Law Review* 51.

[51] See for example. Taylor, "Beckham becomes Real Asset", *Guardian*, June 18, 2003 and "Beckham joins Real Madrid for €35 million", *Irish Times*, June 18, 2003.

[52] See Blood, "Footballers' Image Rights in the UK", 15 *Sports and Character Licensing* (April 2001) 23. Interestingly at the time, Figo was contracted to Nike, yet sold his image rights to Real Madrid which is sponsored by rivals Adidas.

[53] Lewis & Taylor, pp.635–636. Thus under the standard FA Premier League and Football League contract a player will have image rights clauses in his contract with his club and (if he is an international player) with his governing body. See Lewis and Taylor, *op. cit.*, p.658.

[54] The organisers of the Wimbledon tennis tournament obtain the right from all competing players to use their names, likenesses, voices and biographical information in promotional material connected with the tournament. Couchman, "Image Rights – The State of Play", 15 *Sports and Character Licensing* (April 2001) 11.

sponsors in respect of their ability to use his image for their purposes.[55] More-over, in practice, the player may well have assigned his image rights to an image rights company, and it is that company which will contract with the club[56] – an approach that may be beneficial for the sportsperson as far as tax obligations are concerned.[57] This is less usual in Irish sport, but will undoubt-edly become more prominent as sport becomes more professionalised.[58]

Naturally therefore, contractual negotiations in this regard need to be conducted with increasing sophistication. Apart from standard contractual clauses, including for example those outlining the amount of money that the sponsor will pay to use the player's image, a number of other issues should be clarified.

– First, it should be clear as to the circumstances in which the player's image will be used. These would typically include (but not be restricted to) television appearances, audio recording, video or computer images including images for computer games purposes, merchandising, personal appearances, use of images on posters, specific occasions on which the sportsperson will be present at the club or at another promotional event and so on.

– Secondly, the sponsor would be advised to insert a clause, allowing it to be free from obligations should the sportsperson act in a way, either on or off the field, that would tarnish his reputation to the point that the sponsor would no longer wish his goods to be connected with him (especially given the level of media interest in the moral indiscretions of sportspersons),[59] or if

---

[55] The 2003–2004 FA Premier League contract obliges players to support the activities of their club sponsor and the league sponsor. See Couchman, "Recent Developments in Image Rights, Copyright, Trademarks, Domain Name and Patent Protection Law" (August 2003) *Sports Law Administration and Practice* 6.

[56] See Teves and Plesman, "Maximising the Revenue, Minimising the Risks: Licensing Image Rights", 7 *Sports and Character Licensing* (July 2000) 22; Korman, "Football Merchandising – Theory and Practice", 3 *Sports and Character Licensing* (February 2000) 8 and Odendaal, "Taxation of Sportsperson's (sic) Image Rights; Company Schemes and Potential Application of IR35", 9(2) *Sport and the Law Journal* (2001) 105.

[57] Lewis and Taylor, *op. cit.*, p.658, Blood, "Footballers' Image Rights in the UK", 15 *Sports and Character Licensing* (April 2001) 23 at p.24. See *Sports Club Evelyn and Jocelyn v. Inspector of Taxes* [2000] S.T.C. (SCD) 443.

[58] See McNeill & Daly, "Image and Personality Rights in Ireland – A Brief Overview", 15 *Sports and Character Licensing* (April 2001) 21 and Whelan, "The Rights and Wrongs of Image Rights", *Irish Times*, October 18, 2003.

[59] See Korman, "Moral Dilemmas" Issue 11 *Sports and Character Licensing* (December 2000) 20. See Bond, "Sports Personalities: Sponsorship and Endorsement Deals" [2004] *Entertainment Law Review* 51 at p.52 and Smith, "Commercial Exploitation of Sport", 6(2) *Sport and Law Journal* (1998) 59 at p.75. So for example, the Diadora company withdrew their £2.5 million sponsorship of soccer player Stan Collymore following newspaper reports that he had beaten up his then girlfriend in a Paris nightclub. See "Sports Sponsorship – the Role of the Disrepute Clause", 6(2) *Sports Law Administration and Practice* (March/April 1999) 9.

owing either to injury or loss of form or some other reason, the player is not getting the exposure that was anticipated when the contract was originally signed.

– Similarly, however, the sportsperson might wish to insert a clause expressly permitting him to refuse to endorse a product that would disgrace or degrade him or that would bring his sport into disrepute.[60]

– Above all, from the point of view of the sponsor, it is vital to ensure some element of exclusivity over the use of the sportsperson's image in the particular context in which it is to be used.[61]

– Finally, such contracts should include a standard clause covering duration, termination and an option to renew.

7.5.2 Protecting image rights under the tort of passing off

As we have mentioned, there is no such thing at either Irish or English law as a property right in one's image,[62] despite the fact that for a sportsperson his or her image is such a potential source of revenue.[63] On the other hand such a concept is by no means unknown in other jurisdictions,[64] where courts have recognised both that a sportsperson should be entitled to make money from his image without having the potential in this regard diluted by unauthorised use of that image, and also that that sportsperson has what is akin to a privacy interest in choosing the products or services with which he is to be associated.

---

[60] See Blackshaw, "Exploiting Sports Image Rights" 4(6) *Sports Law Bulletin* 2002 4.

[61] In *Magic Merchandising v. Lomu*, unreported, High Court of New Zealand, Barker J., March 3, 1997, Auckland CP 38/96, the plaintiffs contracted with the management of world famous rugby player Jonah Lomu for the right to sell high quality prints of a painting of him. They did not, however, demand the inclusion of an exclusivity clause and hence Lomu's management made a similar contract with another company. In the final analysis, the plaintiffs were unable to prevent this, because their contract did not give them exclusivity in the matter. See Brown, "Character Merchandising Down Under", 15 *Sports and Character Licensing* (April 2001) 16.

[62] On the other hand, in Ireland under s.10 (4) of the Trade Marks Act 1996, one of the grounds for refusal of registration of a trademark is where it would infringe a *right to a name or a right of personal portrayal*, a concession which may seem to envisage the concept of an image right. Such a possibility is as yet unexplored. See McNeill & Daly, "Image and Personality Rights in Ireland – A Brief Overview", 15 *Sports and Character Licensing* (April, 2001) 21.

[63] See Jones, "Manipulating the Law Against Misleading Imagery" [1999] *European Intellectual Property Review* 28, Boyd, "Does English Law Recognise the Concept of an 'Image' or 'Personality' Right", 9(2) *Sport and the Law Journal* (2001) 134 and Harrington, "Image Rights" (July 2002) *Sports Law Administration and Practice* 11.

[64] See Harrington, "Unauthorised Commercial Use of A Sports Star's Image in the UK and Internationally", 1 *Sports & Character Licensing* (October–November, 1999) 1.

Thus European Union nations such as France, Germany,[65] Spain, Italy, Sweden[66] and the Netherlands afford protection to athletes in respect of their image rights.[67] In the United States, where, unsurprisingly there is a major concern with the capacity of the athlete to make money through use of his image, the athlete benefits both from a "right of publicity"[68] (essentially a right to control the extent to which one's image is publicised) which will descend to one's estate when one dies,[69] and also from a tort of unfair competition.[70] Similarly in Canada, where the exclusive right of a person to market for gain his personality, image and name is recognised,[71] the athlete can avail of a tort of appropriation of personality.[72] Most significantly as far as the developments in English and by extension Irish law are concerned, Australian law has long afforded protection to the athlete through a development of the common law rule against passing off,[73] to cover situations where there

---

[65] Poeck, "Use of Athlete's (sic) Images in Games – the German Perspective", 2 *Sports and Character Licensing* (December 1999–January 2000) 20 and Schlindwein, "Marketing National Team Image Rights in Germany", 15 *Sports and Character Licensing* (April 2001) 27.

[66] See Hober and Nilsson, "Sports Personality Rights in Sweden'" 15 *Sports and Character Licensing* (April 2001) 25.

[67] Lewis & Taylor, *op. cit.*, p.643.

[68] *Haelan Laboratories Inc v. Topps Chewing Gum Inc*, 202 F.2d 866 (2d Cir, 1953), 346 US 816 (1953). Generally see Goodenough, "The Price of Fame, the Development of the Right of Publicity in the US – Parts 1 & 2" [1992] 2 *European Intellectual Property Review* 55 and [1992] 3 *European Intellectual Property Review* 90. For an argument that England should adopt a US style "publicity right", see Porter, "Character Merchandising: Does English Law Recognise a Property Right in Name and Likeness ?" [1999] Ent. L.R. 180.

[69] *Price v. Hal Roach Studios*, 400 F. Supp. 836 (1975), *Lugosi v. Universal Pictures*, 25 Cal 3d 813 (1979).

[70] *International News Service v. Associated Press*, 248 US 215 (1919), Lewis & Taylor, *op. cit.*, p.640ff; Devitt, "Protecting Personal Names in the USA", 3 *Sports and Character Licensing* (February 2000) 20 and McMahon & Binchy, *Law of Torts* (3rd ed., Butterworths, Dublin, 2000), para.31:76.

[71] Lewis & Taylor *op. cit.*, p.641.

[72] *Athens v. Canadian Adventure Camps Limited* (1977) 17 O.R. 2d 425, *Krouse v. Chrysler Canada Ltd* (1973) 40 D.L.R. (3d) 15, *Horton v. Tim Donut Ltd* (1997) 75 C.P.R. (3d) 451. Courts in South Africa, Hong Kong and New Zealand have also granted relief in such circumstances. See Griffith–Jones, *op. cit.*, p.249.

[73] See, *inter alia, Paracidal Pty v. Herctum Pty Ltd* (1983) 4 I.P.R. 201 (professional horse rider successfully sued to prevent unauthorised use of his picture in a riding school's advertisements), *Hutchence v. South Sea Bubble* (1986) 64 A.L.R. 330 (members of the band INXS successfully sued in respect of t-shirts with their images on them). See Fewell, "Character Merchandising beyond Characters: The Duff Beer Case", 3 *Sports and Character Licensing* (February 2000) 22; Brown, "Character Merchandising Down Under", 15 *Sports and Character Licensing* (April 2001) 16; Terry, "Image Filching and Passing Off in Australia" [1990] 6 *European Intellectual Property Review* 219 and Burley, "Passing Off and Character Merchandising: Should England lean towards Australia" [1991] 7 *European Intellectual Property Review* 227.

is a suggestion that the person (or product)[74] whose image is being portrayed is connected with the subject of the advertisement,[75] even where there is no suggestion that a licensing agreement existed.[76] Thus in *Talamax Pty v. Telstra*,[77] swimmer Kieran Perkins successfully sued the sponsors of his former club team (who were also a major sponsor of the Australian National Team) who used his photograph in an article about the upcoming Australian Swimming Championships, in circumstances that suggested that Perkins was endorsing their products.[78] Perkins was awarded $15,000 – which represented the extent to which his commercial potential had been disadvantaged and the loss of chance that he had suffered.[79]

In England and Ireland, the traditional view was that the tort of passing off involved some element of misrepresentation by the defendant (whether intentional or not)[80] which might lead a consumer, who is in fact buying A's goods to be under the impression that he is buying B's goods.[81] Application of this principle led to a settled judicial view that for the tort to come into play, there must be a common field of activity between the plaintiff and the defendant.[82] Accordingly the tort of passing off was seen as providing no redress for a celebrity whose image was being used to further the sale of products with which he had no connection in his primary career.[83]

---

[74] *Twentieth Century Fox v. South Australian Brewing* (1996) 34 I.P.R. 225. What is interesting about this case is that here the goodwill in the fictional product of Duff Beer was itself created in the realms of fiction.

[75] Lewis & Taylor, *op. cit.*, p.643, Griffith Jones, *op. cit.*, p.246ff. Moreover under ss.53 and 54 of the Trade Practices Act 1974 a corporation is prohibited from engaging in trade practices that are deceptive or from falsely implying that it or its goods have approval, sponsorship or affiliation that they do not in fact possess.

[76] *Hogan v. Koala Dundee Pty Ltd*, September 23, 1988, 12 I.P.R. 508.

[77] Unreported, Supreme Court of Queensland, Byrne J., March 14, 1996.

[78] See Fewell, "Protection of Personality Rights in Australia", 1 *Sports and Character Licensing* (December 1999) 29.

[79] Nettleton & Hyde, "Postcard from Australia" (July/August 1997) *Sports Law Administration and Practice* 7.

[80] *Grange Marketing v. M&Q Products*, unreported, High Court, June 17, 1976, *C&A Modes v. C&A Waterford Ltd* [1976] I.R. 198 and *Warnink v. Townend & Sons Hull Ltd* [1979] A.C. 731.

[81] *Private Research Ltd v. Brosnan* [1996] 1 I.L.R.M. 27, *C & A Modes v. C & A (Waterford) Ltd* [1976] I.R. 198 and *Adidas v. O'Neills* [1983] 1 I.L.R.M. 27

[82] McMahon & Binchy, *op. cit.*, Chap.31 and Clark & Smith, *Intellectual Property Law in Ireland* (Butterworths, Dublin, 1997), Chap.24. *Polycell Products Ltd v. O'Carroll* [1959] Ir. Jur. Rep. 34; *Player & Wills (Irl) Ltd v. Gallagher*, unreported, High Court April 30, 1997; *An Bord Trachtala v. Waterford Foods* [1994] F.S.R. 316 and *Smithkline Beecham v. Antigen Pharmaceuticals* [1999] 2 I.L.R.M. 190

[83] *McCullough v. Lewis A May* [1947] 2 All E.R. 845; *Lyngstad v. Aanabas Products* [1977] F.S.R. 62, *Tavaner Routledge v. Trexaplam* [1977] R.P.C. 275; *Wombles Ltd v. Wombles Skips* [1975] F.S.R. 488, but see *IPC Magazines v. Black and White Music Corporation* [1983] F.S.R. 348 and *Harrods v. Harrodian School of Law* [1996] R.P.C. 697; *Nice &*

By the beginning of the twenty first century, however, it was clear that the commercial realities of the celebrity's situation had altered radically, such that it can now be expected that many, if not most, well known celebrities are making money through agreements whereby they endorse products that have nothing to do with the field of activity in which they have gained celebrity.[84] Put another way, if one is a celebrity then there are now few conceivable areas of business with which one cannot potentially have a common field of activity. This was recognised by the English courts in *Mirage Studios v. Counter Feat Clothing*[85] (a challenge to the use on t-shirts of characters resembling the (thankfully fictitious) Teenage Mutant Ninja Turtles), where Brown-Wilkinson VC found for the plaintiffs, concluding that the use of such images on t-shirts or other memorabilia would generate an inference in the minds of the general public that a licensing agreement existed, and that such activity therefore constituted passing off – not in the sense that the defendants passed off their goods as being those of the plaintiff, but rather that the goods were passed off as being endorsed by the plaintiff.[86] Equally, the courts have continued to distinguish between situations where there is such an implication of an endorsement (where the tort of passing off might apply) and those in which no such implication arises (in which case it would not).[87]

In Ireland there has been no decided case law on this issue as it applies to sportspeople.[88] Similarly, in England, prior to 2002, there was no clear judicial

---

Safe Attitude v. Piers Flook [1997] F.S.R. 14 and *Halliwell v. Panini*, unreported, High Court, June 6, 1997. For application of these cases to the sporting situation see Lewis & Taylor, *op. cit.*, p.651, Griffith-Jones, *op. cit.*, pp.249–252 and King, "Sport and Personality Rights", 5 (5) *Sports Law Administration and Practice* (September/October 1998) 1.

[84] For suggestion that sportspersons should attempt to set up companies to market themselves in order to demonstrate that they are in the business of merchandising and endorsement see "Personality Merchandising, Licensing Rights and the March of the Turtle", 5(2) *Sport and the Law Journal* (1997)14.

[85] [1991] F.S.R. 145.

[86] See Elmslie and Lewis, "Passing Off and Image Marketing in the UK" [1992] 8 *European Intellectual Property Review* ("E.I.P.R.") 270; Burley, "Passing Off and Character Merchandising; Should England lean towards Australia" [1991] 7 E.I.P.R. 227 and Chong and Maniatis, "The Teenage Mutant Hero turtles case: Zapping English Law on Character Merchandising Past the Embryonic Stage" [1991] 7 E.I.P.R. 253. It has been suggested that in both the UK and Australia, it is easier to win a case of this nature if one is representing a fictional rather than a living character. See Clark and Smith, *op. cit.*, Chap.24, para.46.

[87] *Elvis Presley Enterprises v. Sid Shaw, Elvisly Yours* [1999] R.P.C. 567. See Lewis and Taylor, *op. cit.*, pp.652–653. See also Lyons, "Elvis All Shook up by the High Court" [1997] 10 E.I.P.R. 613; Porter, "Character Merchandising: Does English Law Recognise a Property Right in Name and Likeness" [1999] *Entertainment Law Review* ("Ent. L.R.") 180 and Cordery & Watts, "Character Merchandising – All shook up?" (Court of Appeal re-mix)" [1999] Ent. L.R. 155.

[88] Former Olympian Mary Peters took a legal action in respect of the unauthorised use of

pronouncement on the issue, although former soccer player Eric Cantona had secured a settlement with a wine company that had marketed a range of wines, brandies and aftershaves entitled "Cantona" which referred to the Manchester United Premiership and FA Cup "double" of 1996, and used phrases associated with Cantona such as "ooh aah" and the number 7.[89] The decision of the English courts in *Irvine v. Talksport*,[90] however appears to have solidified the approach taken in the "Turtles" case above, such that there seems to be a significant legal protection now available to sportspeople who would wish to have their image rights protected.

The facts of the *Irvine* case are as follows. As part of an advertising promotion sent to various businesses (and not the general public) the defendants had acquired a photograph of the well-known motor racing driver Eddie Irvine from the owner of the copyright in the same photograph. Using computer technology, the defendants had altered the photograph,[91] so that the original photograph in which Mr Irvine was holding a mobile telephone was transformed, in their advertisement, into a photograph in which he was carrying a portable radio bearing the word "Talksport". Mr Irvine objected to the photograph being used without his authorisation and took a passing off action against the defendants.

In the High Court Laddie J. insisted that the tort of passing off should reflect contemporary commercial realities.[92] It was evident, he argued, that many celebrities augmented their incomes through endorsement deals and indeed judicial notice could be taken of that fact.[93] That being the case, the requirement of the existence of a common field of activity between the plaintiffs and the defendants no longer stood[94] – or perhaps more accurately, because the widespread nature of celebrity endorsement commitments meant that the general public would naturally be confused as to the existence or otherwise of an endorsement agreement, there were no limits to the commercial activity of the celebrity for the purposes of the tort of passing off. Nor indeed was there any need to demonstrate tangible damage in economic terms to the plaintiff.[95]

---

her image in an advertising campaign but the case was settled. See McNeill & Daly, "Image and Personality Rights in Ireland", 15 *Sport and Character Licensing* (April 2001) 21 at p.22.

[89] See Gannon, "Sporting Glory" (1996) 146 *New Law Journal* 1160 and Nash, "Image Contracts and Rights", 2(3) *Sport Law Bulletin* (1999) 1.

[90] [2002] 2 All E.R. 414, [2002] E.W.H.C. 539 (HC), [2003] 2 All E.R. 881, [2003] 1 W.L.R. 1576 (CA).

[91] It has been noted that the owner of the copyright in the photograph (i.e. the photographer) might have had a copyright claim in respect of such alteration if he did not consent to it. See Lewis & Taylor, *op. cit.*, p.737.

[92] Paras 13 & 43. Generally see 5(2) *Sports Law Bulletin* (2002) 4.

[93] Para.39.

[94] Paras 29–34.

[95] Para.34.

Rather the tort of passing off would apply in all cases where there was a false suggestion of endorsement, in that it existed to protect an individual's exclusive right to goodwill and to prevent unlicensed actions that could reduce, blur or diminish its exclusive nature.[96] All that the plaintiff would have to show in order to succeed was that he had goodwill in his name and image at the time of the infringement,[97] and that a not insignificant section of the public would infer that the plaintiff was endorsing the defendant's goods.[98] In the instant case it was clear that both requirements were made out and that on this basis Mr Irvine should win his case.

Laddie J. also made two significant *obiter dicta* points. First (and in keeping with the decision in the *Elvisly Yours* case) he drew a sharp distinction between cases of product endorsement where people would assume the existence of a commercial link between the celebrity and the goods advertised, and character merchandising *per se*, where the celebrity's image is used in circumstances where there is no suggestion of licensing or endorsement. The tort of passing off would have no application in this latter category of cases.[99] It is perhaps somewhat difficult to understand this distinction, in that in all cases where a celebrity's image is used on a product or on promotional literature during the course of an advertising campaign, the earning power of such image is diluted.[100] Indeed it is not entirely clear as to the precise factual circumstances in which a situation of character merchandising can be regarded as one carrying the implication of an endorsement agreement. Presumably there are a range of variable factors which would affect consumer perception as to the existence of a link between the celebrity and the product – factors such as the quality of the item, where it is sold, its cost, and so on. In the modern commercial reality it is certainly at least arguable that whenever the image of a living sportsperson is being used as part of an advertising campaign or on a company product then it would be reasonable for the general public to assume the existence of a licensing arrangement.[101]

Secondly, the plaintiff had also claimed relief for a breach of his right to privacy under the Human Rights Act, 2000. It would have been extremely interesting to see how the judge would have dealt with this issue, which has enormous potential for sporting celebrities, and particularly from an Irish perspective with the existing constitutional protection of the right to privacy

---

[96] See 10(2) *Sports Law Journal* (2002) 86.
[97] And there was significant evidence to show that Mr Irvine possessed such goodwill at the time. See para.47ff.
[98] Paras 38 & 46.
[99] Paras 9 and 44.
[100] Porter, "Character Merchandising: Does English Law Recognise a Property Right in Name and Likeness" [1999] Ent. L.R 180.
[101] See Farnsworth, "Does English Law Lack Personality?" [2001] *International Sports Law Review* 210.

under Article 40.3 of the Constitution. The precise application of the right to these circumstances is, however uncertain. In *Kaye v. Robertson*,[102] reporters from the *Sunday Sport* "newspaper" had gained access to a hospital bedroom in which the plaintiff actor was recovering from brain surgery and conducted an interview with him when he was in a semi delirious state. The plaintiff obtained an injunction preventing publication of any aspect of the interview that implied that he had consented to the interview under the tort of malicious falsehood. Equally the court (despite clearly favouring the plaintiff's claim) felt unable to grant an injunction restraining the publication as a whole on the basis of a right to privacy on the grounds that, in its view, there was no legal mechanism available to do so. Moreover, this judicial reticence was mirrored in the judgements of the Court of Appeal in the "post Human Rights Act" case *Douglas v. Hello!*[103] where the plaintiffs sought damages against *Hello!* magazine for the unauthorised publication of photographs taken at their wedding. Here the court granted the relief sought on the grounds that the defendants' actions constituted an interference with confidential information, and having decided the case on this basis, it felt it unnecessary to consider the privacy claim.

A similar approach was taken in *Irvine v. Talksport* where the judge ruled that because Mr Irvine's case was amply made out on a passing off basis, there was no need for him to rule on the privacy question.[104] Equally it is submitted that the court's reluctance to allow relief in the so called "character merchandising" situations would suggest that had the judge been required to answer the point, it is unlikely that he would have allowed a broad privacy right to dominate the situation, in that such a right would surely cover all unauthorised use of a plaintiff's image and not just that that implied endorsement. Moreover the House of Lords' subsequent decision in *Wainwright v. Home Office*,[105] in which the existence of a common law tort of invasion of privacy was rejected, appeared to have sounded something of a death knell for this line of reasoning, particularly given that in this case their Lordships held that nothing in the jurisprudence of the European Court of Human Rights in respect of Article 8 of the Convention demanded that English law adopt some "high level principle" of privacy to bring its law into line with the Convention.[106]

On the other hand in the more recent case *Campbell v. Mirror Group Newspapers*[107] the House of Lords, while continuing to accept that there was "no overarching, all-embracing cause of action for "invasion of privacy" did accept that "... protection of various aspects of privacy is a fast developing

---

[102] [1991] F.S.R. 62.
[103] [2001] 2 All E.R. 289.
[104] Para.77.
[105] [2003] All E.R. (D) 279.
[106] Para.32.
[107] [2004] U.K.H.L. 22, May 6, 2004.

area of the law."[108] Thus for example, this case was decided (in favour of the appellant) on the basis of a breach of confidence deriving from the wrongful disclosure of *private* information, rather than on the basis of a more general privacy right.[109] Similarly whereas the right to privacy more generally in Article 8 of the Human Rights Act would only apply against public bodies, nonetheless the terms of Article 8 like the terms of Article 10 (freedom of expression) and the values enshrined therein could be used to inform the development of the common law in a number of areas.[110] Thus for example, according to Lord Hoffman, in the context of the law relating to breach of confidence, "What Human Rights law has done is to identify private information as something worth protecting as an aspect of human autonomy and dignity."[111] Indeed Lord Hoffmann went on to imply that insofar as the values underpinning the approach to law had been altered by the terms of the Human Rights Act, this might lead to more tangible changes in the operation of the law.[112] Whether or not this has implications for the sportsman seeking to prevent use of his image in circumstances outside the parameters of the *Irvine* case remains to be seen.

All that remained to be addressed for Mr. Irvine was the issue of damages.[113] Mr Irvine who colourfully alleged that he would not get out of bed for less than £25,000 sought at least this sum in damages. In the High Court the level of damages was assessed by reference to what would be a "reasonable fee" for the endorsement.[114] Rather strangely, given the overall tenor of the judgement, Laddie J. assessed the question of reasonableness from the standpoint of the defendants (what they would reasonably pay for such endorsement) and fixed damages at £2,000 – a figure falling significantly shy of the defendant's lodgment in the case.[115] On appeal, the Court of Appeal decided that a reasonable fee would in fact be that which the defendant would have to have paid to obtain lawfully that which it had obtained unlawfully, and fixed damage at £25,000 – a figure that did beat the lodgment.[116] Equally the fact that Mr Irvine was merely paid that which he would have received for a voluntary promotion may in fact prove dangerous for celebrities, in that no attempt was made to impose damages for what was a fairly flagrant abuse of the plaintiff's intellectual property rights.[117] In other words, the logic from this case seems to be that if a celebrity declines to endorse a product, then the relevant company

---

[108] Para.11.
[109] Para.15.
[110] Paras 16ff and 43.
[111] Para.50.
[112] Para.52.
[113] [2002] E.W.H.C. 539 (Ch.).
[114] *General Tyre & Rubber Co. v. Firestone Tyre & Rubber Co.* [1975] 2 ALL E.R. 173.
[115] Para.30.
[116] [2003] E.W.C.A. Civ. 423 [2003] 2 All E.R. 881. Para.106.
[117] See Amanda Michaels, "Passing off by False Endorsement – But what's the damage?" [2002] E.I.P.R. 448.

might just as well use his image anyway, content that it will merely have to pay the relevant image fee, should the action be challenged in court. Nonetheless, the case can generally be seen as affording a new and important protection to the sportsperson in England (and in all probability in Ireland) who seeks to defend his or her image rights from unauthorised exploitation.[118]

7.5.3 Protection of image rights beyond the tort of passing off

Beyond the tort of passing off there are other potential mechanisms available to the individual sportsperson who would wish to prevent unauthorised use of his image.[119] First, it may be possible for the individual to register his name, nickname or a derivative thereof as a trademark. Thus for example in England, a number of famous sportspersons have registered trademarks in their name, or nickname and image, such as Ryan Giggs (GIGGS11), Paul Gascoigne (GAZZA), Eric Cantona (CANTONA7) and Eddie Irvine (an image of Irvine's eyes peering through his visor).[120] Equally, in order for a trademark to be registered as such, it should be non-descriptive[121] and distinctive,[122] and from the perspective of the individual, it should attach to all merchandised goods so

---

[118] Since the *Irvine* decision, cricketer Ian Botham secured a settlement with the Guinness company for unauthorised use of his image (in television footage of the 1981 Ashes series) in an advertising campaign. See 11 (1) *Sport and the Law Journal* (2003) 91 and Veysey, "It's just not Cricket" (2002) 152 *New Law Journal* 1391. Interestingly in this case there was no suggestion that Botham was actually endorsing the product, and hence he may have fallen into the "character merchandising" category referred to by Laddie J. in *Irvine*.

[119] See Harrington, "Image Rights" (July 2002) *Sports Law Administration and Practice* 11, Jones, "Manipulating the Law Against Misleading Imagery" [1999] E.I.P.R. 28, Farnsworth, "Character Merchandising: Does English Law Recognise a Property Right in Name and Likeness?" [1999] Ent. L.R. 180 and Farnsworth, "Does English Law Lack Personality?" [2001] *International Sports Law Review* 210.

[120] See Moore, *Sports Law and Litigation* (2nd ed., CLT Publishing, 2000) 49. From an Australian perspective see Dwyer and Yates, "Court Action to Protect the BRADMAN Name", 11 *Sports and Character Licensing* (November 2000) 17 and Lee, "Thorpedo Wins Trade Mark Court Battle" [2004] Ent. L.R. 59. For a superb analysis of trade mark law in general, see Phillips, *Trade Mark Law – A Practical Anatomy* (Oxford University Press, 2003). Copyright law, on the other hand, offers the individual sportsperson little protection in that there is no copyright in a sporting performance nor in a name or a face, and unless the sportsperson is involved in a specific contractual agreement with a photographer, then the copyright in any photograph taken of the sportsperson will inhere in the person who took the photograph

[121] In other words, if a soccer player registers his name as a trademark, its use (for instance) in a match programme will not breach that trademark in that there is no suggestion that it is being used in a trademark sense. See Lewis & Taylor, *op. cit.*, p.648.

[122] Thus for instance, Welsh soccer manager Mark Hughes was unable to register his name as a trademark on the grounds that it was not sufficiently distinctive. See Lewis & Taylor, *op. cit.*, p.649.

as to be instantly linked in the consumer perception with the player.[123] Furthermore the trademark should be regarded as a badge of origin,[124] although as we shall see in the next section, the rigidity of this rule may have been significantly ameliorated since the decision of the European Court of Justice in *Arsenal v. Reed*.[125] Finally, whereas it is possible to register one's name as a trade mark it may still be used by another person of the same name provided that such use is honest and not intended to exploit commercial possibilities.[126]

A sportsperson may also seek to rely on the tort of defamation to protect unauthorised use of his image. Thus in *Tolley v. Fry*,[127] a well known amateur golfer successfully sued for defamation in respect of an advertisement by Fry's Chocolate which featured a caricature of himself with a cartet of Fry's chocolate protruding from his pocket, accompanied by a Limerick comparing a bar of Fry's chocolate to the plaintiff's golf shot. The defamation here lay in the implication that the plaintiff had foregone his amateur status to endorse the defendant's product. Alternatively defamation may exist in a situation where the plaintiff's image is used to advertise products that are sub-standard or morally questionable, in that the plaintiff might feel lowered by the implication that he would lend his name to such goods. Equally the tort of defamation is probably unlikely to have any great impact here given the competing demands of fair competition, free speech and right to a good name.[128] A celebrity litigant might also seek to have recourse to the tort of malicious falsehood,[129] and/or the tort of unlawful interference with business relations.[130]

Finally, an athlete may rely on the (non-binding) Code of Sales Promotion Practice of the Advertising Standards Authority of Ireland. Under this code advertisers are required to seek written permission in advance from anyone portrayed or referred to in an advertisement. Moreover, advertisers are not permitted to exploit the public reputation of another person in a manner that is humiliating, offensive or that implies the existence of an endorsement, where none in fact exists. Eoin MacNeill argues that failure to comply with this code

---

[123] See Harrington, "Unauthorised use of a Sports Star's Image in the UK and Internationally – A Level Playing Field", 1 *Sports and Character Licensing* (December 1999) 1.

[124] Davidson, "Fresh Hope for the Famous – Personality rights in the UK Settle Down in the Wake of the *Elvis* Case", 9 *Sports and Character Licensing* (September 2000) 24.

[125] [2003] All E.R. (EC) 1, [2003] R.P.C. 144.

[126] See McNeill & Daly, "Image and Personality Rights in Ireland – A Brief Overview", 15 *Sports and Character Licensing* (April 2001) 21.

[127] [1931] A.C. 333. For a similar case involving Welsh rugby legend JPR Williams see *Williams v. Reason* [1988] 1 W.L.R. 96.

[128] McMahon & Binchy, *op. cit.*, para.31:82, Lewis & Taylor, *op. cit.*, p.645ff. But see also Clark & Smith, *op. cit.*, para.24: 47.

[129] *White v. Mellin* [1895] A.C. 154, see Clark & Smith, *op. cit.*, para 24:49 and Lewis & Taylor, *op. cit.*, p.646.

[130] *O'Neills v. Adidas*, unreported, Supreme Court, March 25, 1992. See Clark & Smith, *op. cit.*, para 24:51.

may lead to a judgement that the actions of the advertiser constitute misleading advertising.[131]

7.5.4 A property right in one's image?

Finally, it is arguable that the law is fundamentally out of touch with modern commercial practice.[132] Although the extent of merchandising using images of sportspeople (and indeed actors, TV characters - both human and animated – and pop stars) is obvious, to the point that judicial notice has been taken of the fact[133] (and indeed it has also been accepted that as far as tax law is concerned, monies paid to players for promotional services are not disguised payments, but are for something of independent value, over and above the player's contribution on the field of play),[134] there is still no such thing in English or Irish law as a specific property right in one's image.[135] The law in this regard appears to be rooted in the view that if someone is in the public eye, then he or she can expect publicity with or without his or her consent.[136]

There is, it is submitted a strong argument that the position in America or Canada should be adopted in Ireland and England, in light both of the constitutional and European Convention protection of privacy. This issue gains a new urgency in Ireland given both the progressive professionalisation of Irish sport and also the increasing number of Irish people who could be classed as sports stars whose image might be valuable from the point of view of sponsors.[137]

---

[131] McNeill & Daly, "Image and Personality Rights in Ireland", 15 *Sports and Character Licensing* (April 2001) 21 at p.22.

[132] See Farnsworth, "Does English Law Lack Personality" [2001] *International Sports Law Review* 218. It is notable that in *Irvine v. Talksport*, Laddie J. insisted that the law of passing off should always strive to be consistent with the reality of contemporary commercial practice.

[133] *Irvine v. Talksport* [2002] All E.R. 414, para 39.

[134] *Sports Club, Evelyn & Jocelyn v. Inspector of Taxes* [2002] S.T.C. (STD) 443.

[135] Lewis & Taylor, *op. cit.*, p.635. It has been questioned whether there is such a thing as a property right in one's goodwill under Art.1 of Protocol 1 of the European Convention on Human Rights. See *ibid.*, pp.656–657. See also Griffith-Jones, *op. cit.*, p.245, Couchman, "Image Rights – The State of Play", 15 *Sports and Character Licensing* (April 2001) 11; Harrington, "Image Rights" (July 2002) *Sports Law Administration and Practice* 11 and Jones, "Manipulating the Law Against Misleading Imagery" [1999] *European Intellectual Property Review* 28.

[136] *Tolley v. Fry, Elvis Presley Enterprises v. Sid Shaw, Elvisly Yours* [1999] R.P.C. 567.

[137] See McNeill & Daly, "Image and Personality Rights in Ireland – A Brief Overview", 15 *Sports and Character Licensing* (April 2001) 21 where it is argued that the notion of the marketable Irish "sports star", only really became significant since the success of the Irish soccer team in Germany in 1988. See also Whelan, "The Rights and Wrongs of Image Rights", *Irish Times*, October 18, 2003. Currently any number of Irish soccer

As mentioned, there are two conceptually distinct arguments as to why any citizen (but in practice a celebrity) *should* have a legal right to control marketing that uses his image.[138] First, an argument from privacy – that is to say that one should be entitled to decide whether and when one's image appears publicly. Secondly an argument from economics – that is to say that in as much as an athlete's livelihood is increasingly dependent upon money received from sponsorship, he should be able to earn as much as he can from his image, rather than having his earning potential diluted by unauthorised use thereof, which will cost him in terms of unpaid royalties, potential over-exposure to the public and loss of goodwill should his image be affixed to inferior quality goods.[139]

Finally, it has been suggested that athletes should have the right not only to protect their image *per se*, but also to obtain royalty fees whenever celebrated moments in sport, in which they are the central figure occur.[140]

7.6 THE RIGHTS OF THE SPORTS CLUB AND THE GOVERNING BODY

The other major categories of sporting body on which we will focus are the sporting club and the governing body or federation, both of which may also need to seek to invoke legal protection in respect of their involvement in the business of sport.[141] Like the sportsperson, such bodies will seek to protect their interests both through reliance on intellectual property rights, and also through contractual negotiations with sponsors, event organisers, broadcasters and players.[142]

---

players and rugby players as well as other sports people like Padraig Harrington, Darren Clarke, Paul McGinley (golf) Ken Doherty (snooker) Sonia O'Sullivan (athletics) would be useful in the promotion and advertising of goods and services.

[138] See Harrington, "Unauthorised use of a Sports Star's image in the UK and internationally – a Level Playing Field", 1 *Sports and Character Licensing* (December 1999) 1.

[139] See Lewis and Taylor, *op. cit.*, p.639.

[140] See Rush and Reeve, "They think it's all over – it isn't yet", *Times*, February 8, 1990. Two graphic examples of such moments are Packie Bonner's penalty save during the quarter finals of the 1990 World Cup and Dennis Taylor's black ball pot during the final of the 1985 Embassy Snooker World Championships, both of which are used for advertising purposes.

[141] A recent case involving intellectual property rights and governing bodies involved the World Wildlife Fund successfully taking an action against the World Wrestling Federation for use of the initials WWF. Since this case WWF wrestling has been known as WWE wrestling. See 5(2) *Sports Law Bulletin* (2002) 8. Readers may feel that a reference to either WWF or WWE wrestling is out of place in a book on sports law.

[142] The point has been made that players tend not to be permitted to use their clubs logos to assist in their own merchandising of themselves. See Korman, "Football Merchandising – Theory and Practice", 3 *Sports and Character Licensing* (February 2000) 8.

7.6.1 The sports club

The club, like the individual, is an ideal focus for corporate sponsorship in that "Football clubs enjoy the kind of loyalty from their fans which companies can only dream about from their consumers."[143] I am, after all completely unable to explain my affinity to a particular English Premiership soccer club, especially given that the same club has, over the twenty seven years since I started supporting it, caused me considerably more pain than joy! Nonetheless I am unable simply to stop supporting that club, and I have a terrifying suspicion that if I live until I am one hundred, I will still have an almost obsessive devotion to its well-being. There is simply no product, and no company that would inspire such unthinking devotion in me or in millions of other people globally.[144] Needless to say, it is a very good thing for any business to link itself with an entity, which can generate such phenomenal product loyalty in the minds of its consumers.[145] Once again, however, the only manner in which a sports club can make money out of its image is to limit its usage in order that it can guarantee authorised sponsors some degree of exclusivity in its use. Recent developments in England appear greatly to have strengthened the protection available to sports clubs in this regard.

7.6.1.1 Arsenal FC v. Reed

In order to protect their revenue earning potential, clubs, like individual sportspersons, will be able to avail of the passing off action should an appropriate defendant market his goods in circumstances where an inference of endorsement can be drawn. Moreover, the case of *FA Premier League v. Panini*,[146] considered below, suggests that a club may be able to establish a copyright in for example a club crest or indeed any club emblem – a possibility that will also be considered later in the context of the protection afforded to

---

[143] See Korman, "Football Merchandising – Theory and Practice", 3 *Sports and Character Licensing* (February 2000) 8 at p.16.

[144] In this respect, a club's merchandising becomes an essential way not only of earning money, but also of ensuring that its identity becomes well known in new financial and geographical markets, thereby boosting the support base of the club, see Lewis and Taylor, *op. cit.*, p.734. See also *ibid.*, p.746ff for the principal elements of a merchandising or licensing agreement.

[145] Moreover, this obsession appears to be a recognisable aspect of culture. Thus increasingly sports clubs are designing the colour schemes for their club strips based on whether people will want to wear it as leisure wear – whether for example it looks good with jeans. See Korman, "Football Merchandising – Theory and Practice", 3 *Sports and Character Licensing* (February 2000) 8 at p.12 and Williams, "The Shirt off your Back? Football Supporters and Merchandising", 9 *Sport and Character Licensing* (September 2000) 18.

[146] [2002] E.W.H.C. 2779, [2002] All E.R. (D) 260, (2002) S.L.J.R. 8 (HC), [2003] E.W.C.A. Civ. 995, [2003] All E.R. (D) 201, (July) (CA).

governing bodies.[147] The most significant English case in which a club sought to protect intellectual property rights connected with its money making potential, however, is *Arsenal v. Reed*, a case that focused primarily on the use of trademarks and the protection afforded thereby.[148] It is to this issue that we now turn.

At this point it is necessary briefly to set out the nature of trademark protection in Ireland, which, in substantial measure, is the same as its English counterpart.[149] Protection for trademarks is afforded under the 1996 Trade Marks Act.[150] Traditionally, a trademark was a sign that could be graphically displayed on goods, (and now also on services), which was capable of distinguishing the owner's goods[151] and could be used by a consumer to determine the origin of the goods to which the mark was attached.[152] This in turn would enable that consumer to return to a source of goods with which he or she was satisfied in the past.[153] Registration of such a mark can be refused on a number of absolute[154] and relative[155] grounds, for example where the mark is non-distinctive, descriptive, contrary to public policy or public morality, or where there is an earlier identical or similar mark.

To be actionable, unauthorised use of a registered mark must arise "in the course of trade",[156] and can occur when an identical mark is used on goods for which the trade mark has been registered[157] (in which case there is a presumption of confusion on the part of consumers),[158] when an identical mark is used on similar goods, or when a similar mark is used on identical goods[159] (in which case confusion on the part of consumers must be shown),[160]

---

[147] It may also be possible for, for example, a golf club to establish a copyright in the design on paper of a particularly distinctive hole or holes. See Ruskin and Clark, "Letter from America" (March-April 1997) *Sports Law Administration and Practice* 6.

[148] See generally, Whittaker and Rudgard, "An Own Goal or Merely Extra Time?", 9(1) *Sport and the Law Journal* (2001) 107.

[149] See Clark and Smyth, *op. cit.*, p.479ff.

[150] Which implements the terms of the Trade Mark Harmonisation Directive (89/104/EEC). The rights to a trademark are also governed by the Community Trade Mark Regulation (40/94/EEC). Generally see Woulfe, "The Republic of Ireland Trade Mark Act, 1996" [1996] 6 *Entertainment Law Review* 238.

[151] *WATERFORD Trademark, re* [1984] F.S.R. 390.

[152] S.6(1) of the Trade Marks Act 1996, see Clark & Smyth, *op. cit.*, pp.480–481. See also *American Greetings Corporation's Application* [1984] R.P.C. 329 and *Bristol-Myers Squibb v. Paranova, Euri-Pharm v. Beiersdorf, MPA Pharma v. Rhone-Poulenc* [1997] F.S.R. 102.

[153] *SA CNL-Sucal NV v. Hag GF AG* [1990] 3 C.M.L.R. 571.

[154] S.8 of the Trade Marks Act 1996.

[155] Ss.10–12 of the Trade Marks Act 1996.

[156] S.4 of the Trade Marks Act 1996.

[157] S.14(1).

[158] [2003] All E.R. (EC) 1, [2003] R.P.C. 144.

[159] S.14(2).

and even where an identical or similar sign is used on dissimilar goods, in situations where such goods have a particular reputation and the use of the sign takes unfair advantage of or is detrimental to the distinctive character of the mark[161] (in which case there is no requirement to prove confusion). In the event of infringement the owner may seek an injunction and/or damages[162] as well as an order for delivery up of infringing goods and materials, and for disposal thereof.[163] Moreover such infringements may leave the perpetrator open to criminal prosecution.[164] The duration of a trade mark registration is ten years from the filing date, and it is renewable for successive ten-year periods.[165]

In *Arsenal v. Reed*, the defendant, Matthew Reed, had for a number of years sold merchandise relating to Arsenal football club outside Arsenal's home ground, Highbury. The merchandise in question carried, *inter alia*, the Arsenal name, the club crest and Arsenal's nickname, "the Gunners", all of which Arsenal football club had registered as trade marks. The defendant had a sign beside his stall indicating that this was not official Arsenal merchandise and that such official merchandise carried a specific tag.[166] In addition, match programmes circulated by Arsenal contained warnings about pirated merchandise and also indicated that official merchandise was tagged. Arsenal apparently sold official goods to merchandisers located outside of the stadium for the purpose of resale, but Mr Reed was allegedly blacklisted by the club in this respect.[167] Arsenal took an action against Mr. Reed seeking an injunction against his activities, claiming infringement of trademarks and passing off as well as a breach of copyright – although by the time of the hearing the copyright claim had been dropped.[168]

In the High Court,[169] Laddie J. rejected the passing off claim because of the absence of any significant evidence indicating that consumers had been confused as to the unofficial status of Mr Reed's merchandise. Indeed, beyond the evidence provided to the court and as a matter of commonsense, Laddie J.

---

[160] It has been noted that where such confusion exists, a passing off action may also be sustained. See *C & A Modes v. C & A (Waterford) Limited* [1976] I.R. 198.

[161] S.14(3).

[162] S.18 of the Trade Marks Act 1996.

[163] Ss 20, 22 and 23 of the Trade Marks Act 1996.

[164] Ss 92–94 and 97 of the Trade Marks Act 1996.

[165] S.47 of the Trade Marks Act 1996.

[166] See Couchman, "Sports Merchandising Paradise Lost and Regained?", 9(4) *Sports Law Administration and Practice* (2002) 1.

[167] Robinson [2003] *Entertainment Law Review* 112.

[168] It is not clear why this aspect of the case was dropped. See Farnsworth, "An Own Goal for Arsenal", 6 *Sport and Character Licensing* (May/June 2001) 7.

[169] See Farnsworth, "An Own Goal for Arsenal", *op. cit.*, p.7 or Couchman, "Sports Merchandising Paradise Lost and Regained", 9[4] *Sports Law Administration and Practice* (2002) 1, Miles, [2002] E.I.P.R. 543.

found that such confusion was entirely unlikely.[170] Moreover, in the language used in *Irvine v. Talksport* Laddie J. felt that a reasonable consumer would not consider the possibility that Arsenal football club had endorsed Mr Reed's merchandise.

A stronger point in Arsenal's favour was that Mr Reed had undoubtedly used Arsenal trademarks. Under Article 5 of the European Trade Mark Directive, however, the protection afforded to trade mark owners extends only to cases where use of the mark takes unfair advantage of or is detrimental to the distinctive character of the trade mark. Hence, in order for the protection under the Directive to come into play, the offending use of the trade mark should be "trade mark use." According to Laddie J., the only essential function of a trade mark is to distinguish goods or services *by indicating their origin*.[171] In this case, however, Laddie J. felt that most consumers who bought the defendant's merchandise would do so not because they thought it emanated from the club but simply because the goods in question with the trade marks on them constituted badges of affiliation to the club.[172] In other words the significance of the badges, logos and names on Mr Reed's merchandise did not derive from their status as indicators of origin. This being the case, Laddie J. felt that there was no trade mark infringement in this case. Equally, he was uncertain as to the correctness of his conclusion under European Community law and therefore referred the case to the European Court of Justice asking the question whether under the European Trade Marks Directive infringing use must be trademark use.[173]

In his opinion in the case,[174] the Advocate General held that whereas infringing use under the terms of the Directive must indeed be trademark use, equally in establishing trade mark use, two factors must be borne in mind. First, the protection of trade marks is important to the European Community because it fosters competition.[175] Secondly, a trade mark is capable of acquiring a life of its own and becoming an indicator of quality and reputation as well as origin.[176] Therefore, a trade mark owner is entitled to protection whenever any of the functions of the trade mark are being compromised – and not merely the function of indicating origin, but also the functions of indicating proven

---

[170] [2001] European Trade Mark Reports ("E.T.M.R.") 860, para.36.
[171] Existing Court of Appeal case law seemed to suggest that under English Law a trade mark could be violated by non trade mark use. See *British Sugar PLC v. James Robertson & Sons* [1996] R.P.C. 281 and *Phillips Electronics Ltd v. Remington Consumer Products* [1999] R.P.C. 809.
[172] Para.58.
[173] Para.65.
[174] [2002] European Trade Mark Reports ("E.T.M.R.") 975. See also Couchman, "Sports Merchandising Paradise Lost and Regained?", 9(4) *Sports Law Administration and Practice* (2002) 1 and Blackshaw, 5(4) *Sports Law Bulletin* (2002) 7.
[175] Para.42.
[176] Para.46.

quality or reputation.[177] On that basis, infringing use under the directive is that "... which occurs in the world of business, in trade, the subject of which is precisely the distribution of goods and services in the market. In short, use in trade."[178]

Moreover, for the purposes of the instant case, the Advocate General also pointed out that in the case of an identical sign being used in an identical context there is a presumption that the functions of the trade mark are being compromised.[179]

The central point made by the Advocate General was that whatever the motivations of Mr. Reed's consumers, Mr. Reed himself used the Arsenal trade marks on his goods *because of their revenue earning potential*, and this fact of itself meant that his acts constituted trade mark use.[180] Thus, whether a purchaser was an Arsenal fan buying the goods out of loyalty to Arsenal or a rival fan buying the goods for the purpose of burning them, the common factor was still the connection with the club both as a playing and commercial empire which the trademark betokened. Put simply, a red and white, or blue and yellow shirt would not satisfy the consumer's needs unless it had the club crest on it.[181] The clear message from the Advocate General's opinion is that registration of a trade mark gives the trade mark owner an exclusive entitlement to exploit the commercial potential of that mark, and such exclusivity is threatened whenever another person dilutes the effect of the mark by using it to sell his products or for any other commercial purpose.

The European Court of Justice, in its judgment in the case, took a similar approach to the issue. Again the ECJ accepted that "use" for the purposes of the Trade Mark Directive meant trade mark use, however, like the Advocate General, the ECJ accepted that trade mark use meant more than simply use as an indicator of origin. Rather, a trademark represented a guarantee to the consumer that all goods bearing it came from a common source that was responsible for their quality[182] – something that would be important to a company wishing to retain customers. In other words, a trademark was a *guarantee of origin* and not merely an *indicator of origin*, and the protection afforded to the owner of the trademark should operate on this basis.[183] In this case, because Mr. Reed's use of the trade mark clearly implied a connection between him and Arsenal – an implication not corrected by Reed's disclaimer notice, which of course would not be read by post-sale consumers (for example consumers who purchased unofficial Arsenal shirts from traders who, at an

---

[177] Para.48.
[178] Para.62.
[179] Para.52.
[180] Para.63.
[181] Paras 67–68.
[182] [2003] E.T.M.R. 227, para 46.
[183] Para.48.

earlier stage, had purchased them directly from the stallholders near Highbury) – there was a trade mark infringement.[184] Equally, the logic of the Court leads to the conclusion that whenever a trademark is used without authorisation on a product that is to be sold (that is to say where the goods being sold do not derive from the source guaranteed by the mark) there will be infringement. On this basis, the ECJ remitted the case to the High Court, having found that whereas infringing use under the Trade Mark Directive must constitute trademark use, equally, in this case, there had been such trademark use.

The High Court[185] accepted the ECJ finding on the question of law (that infringing use under the Directive must be trade mark use), but interpreted it as meaning that infringing use was confined to use where the mark could be taken as indicating the origin of the goods[186] – an interpretation which, it may be argued, is somewhat at variance with what the ECJ actually said, given that it had clearly spoken of the *functions* of the trade mark.[187] More significantly, Laddie J. also held that the ECJ had exceeded its jurisdiction by reaching a conclusion of fact different to that reached in the High Court – namely that people purchasing Mr. Reed's goods would associate them with the Arsenal club in terms of source and origin.[188] He therefore applied what he saw as the ECJ's interpretation of the law (that infringing use must be trade mark use and trade mark use was use indicating origin) to his view of the facts – that there was no likelihood of confusion as to origin – and on this basis found that in this case there was no infringement.[189] Laddie J. did not deal with the clear implication from the ECJ's judgment that the sight of a trade mark on goods should entitle a consumer to draw a connection between the mark and the owner – and hence that any unauthorised use of a trade mark in a commercial context, (whether or not such a connection is in fact drawn), constitutes an infringement.[190]

Laddie J.'s judgment was reversed by the Court of Appeal,[191] which found that the ECJ did not exceed its jurisdiction, nor had it reached a different conclusion of fact from that reached by the High Court, but rather, that it was

---

[184] Para.57.
[185] [2003] 1 All E.R. 137. See 5(6) *Sports Law Bulletin* (2002) 3, Lewis & Taylor, *op. cit.*, p.737ff, 11(1) *Sport and the Law Journal* (2003) 95–96, Dyrberg & Skylv, "Does Trade Mark Infringement Require that the Infringing Use be Trade Mark Use and if so what is Trade Mark Use?" [2003] *European Intellectual Property Review* 229, Robinson [2003] *Entertainment Law Review* 112.
[186] Paras 18–20.
[187] It is perhaps notable that under Art.10 of the Paris Convention it is recognised that one of the functions of a trade mark is to protect against unfair competition.
[188] Para.27.
[189] Para.29.
[190] Para.50 of the judgment of the European Court of Justice.
[191] [2003] 3 All E.R. 865, [2003] E.T.M.R. 895, see (June 2003) *Sports Law Administration and Practice* 8.

an inevitable conclusion given the ECJ's interpretation of the Directive that there had, in fact been trade mark use in this case.[192] The Court of Appeal felt that the view of the ECJ was that there was infringement of a trademark whenever the impugned use was likely to affect the function of the mark as a *guarantee* rather than an *indicator* of origin, and that this had clearly happened in the instant case.[193] Finally, the Court of Appeal also indicated that it was possible to see Mr. Reed's actions as constituting passing off even in the absence of any confusion in that it posed a threat to the distinctiveness of the official Arsenal product.[194]

The impact of this judgment for sports clubs is significant. It affords clubs and indeed governing bodies the power to crack down on unauthorised sales of memorabilia connected with themselves and thus to run an unfettered and potentially extensive merchandising campaign. Clearly it is also very bad news for unofficial traders. Nonetheless, in as much as clubs will invest heavily in merchandising, and their trademarks constitute the means whereby such investment can be protected, the judgment of the Court of Appeal is arguably to be welcomed.

7.6.2 The governing body

In Ireland, the governing bodies of sport, such as for example the FAI or the IRFU, (charged as they are with responsibility for furthering the playing of their respective sports domestically, at professional, amateur and underage level), find it necessary to raise finance from exploiting the commercial possibilities connected with their respective domestic leagues, and especially in relation to games played by the national teams involved in the different sports.[195] It is not unusual for such bodies to invest substantial time and effort into protecting their interests in this way, as three recent English cases demonstrate.

In *Trebor Bassett v. FA*,[196] the plaintiffs manufactured candy sticks in packets. Also contained in such packets were collectable cards, which depicted English soccer players in England jerseys, bearing the FA logo (a registered

---

[192] Para.48.
[193] *Ibid*. Indeed, the Court of Appeal also concluded that, on the evidence, many supporters who had complained to Arsenal football club about having bought unofficial merchandise regarded the trade marks in question as indicators of origin rather than merely badges of loyalty. See paras 67–69.
[194] Para.70. See also *Vine Products Limited v MacKenzie* [1969] R.P.C. 1.
[195] Generally see Baldwin, "The Business Development of Sport" (September/October 1997) *Sports Law Administration and Practice* 8.
[196] [1997] F.S.R. 211. See Clark & Smyth, *op. cit.*, para.31.05, Harrington, "Trade Marks and Sports Marketing in the UK", 9 (March-April 1997) *Sports Law Administration and Practice* 1.

trade mark). The FA sought to prevent the plaintiffs from engaging in this activity. However, the plaintiffs, pre-emptively sought and were granted a declaration that in as much as there was no suggestion of consumer confusion as to origin, nor any sense that the use of the trade mark in the stickers constituted "trade mark use" (even under the broad definition of trade mark use given by the ECJ in *Arsenal v. Reed*), the use in question did not constitute infringement.[197] It should be noted, of course, that since *Irvine v. Talksport* an action in passing off would be available to the players whose images were used in such stickers provided that the circumstances of the sticker offer indicated endorsement by players.

At issue in *RFU & Nike v. Cotton Traders*,[198] was the rose emblem that appears on English rugby jerseys. Prior to 1997, the defendant company had had the licence to produce English rugby jerseys, and hence, obviously it had permission to use the rose. It appears that since the 1980s when the RFU started to sell official English rugby tops to the public there had been unauthorised use of the rose on unofficial jerseys, but that the RFU had taken no steps to prevent this. In 1997 the RFU signed a new exclusive agreement with Nike to produce English jerseys. Nonetheless the defendants continued to manufacture unofficial jerseys and to use the rose thereon. The RFU sought to prevent such use claiming that it represented an infringement of its rights in respect of the trademark. In response, the defendants while admitting that they had engaged in trademark use, claimed that the trademark had in fact been invalidly registered, on the grounds of absence of distinctiveness.[199]

The High Court held that whereas the rose was the emblem associated with English rugby jerseys, it had a wider significance beyond this.[200] Put simply, for many people the rose was associated with English rugby *as a concept* (and indeed – in the context of rugby football – with *England* as a concept). In the terms used by Laddie J. in the *Arsenal* case, the rose was a badge of

---

[197] On the other hand in a similar case in Italy it was held that reproduction of trade marks on stickers of this kind *did* constitute infringement: *Milan A.C. and Juventus A.C. v. Topps Italia*, Appeal Court of Milan, May 25, 1998, [1999] *European Trade Mark Review* 128 noted in 8(2) *Sport and the Law Journal* (2000) 35. See also *Halliwell v. Panini*, unreported, High Court, June 6, 1997 in which the Spice Girls lost a claim against a sticker company for unauthorised use of their images on stickers on the basis that they had no reputation in the area of sticker manufacturing that therefore the question of infringement simply did not arise. It is strongly arguable that this precedent has been effectively overruled by the decision in *Irvine v. Talksport*.

[198] [2002] 2 All E.R. (d) 417 [2002] E.W.H.C. 467 (Ch.). See Lewis & Taylor, *op. cit.*, p.603, Miles,[2002] *European Intellectual Property Review* 543, Blackshaw (May/June 2002) *Sports Law Bulletin* 4.

[199] For a similar case involving alleged unauthorised use of the fern leaf on the New Zealand rugby jersey see *New Zealand Rugby Football Union v. Canterbury International Limited*, noted in Morris, "The Future for the Silver Fern is not All Black", 19 *Sports and Character Licensing* (September/October 2001) 9.

[200] Para.37.

allegiance neither to the RFU nor necessarily to the England team, but to the ideal of English rugby.[201] Certainly, in the mind of the average supporter, it did not denote trade origin – especially as it had for years been used on unofficial jerseys – but rather was a generic and descriptive emblem. Accordingly the Court held that the rose was invalidly registered as a trademark. In this respect, it distinguished the *Arsenal* case, concluding that the link in the public mind between the team and the money making industry behind it is far clearer in the case of a Premiership soccer club than it is in the case of a national rugby team.[202] Moreover, it concluded that for the same reason, the RFU did not own any goodwill in the English rose and hence its passing off claim would also fail.[203]

In *FA Premier League v. Panini*,[204] the defendants had unsuccessfully bid for the rights to use the images of Premiership players on collectable stickers and an album into which such stickers could be inserted. Nevertheless they continued to create such stickers, first displaying just the names and faces and shoulders of players, but later also their badges and team logos – a development which the Court of Appeal felt was aimed at making the stickers more attractive to potential consumers.[205] The *Trebor Bassett* precedent meant that there was little point in the FA taking a trademark action in this case. Therefore the plaintiffs sought and obtained an injunction on the basis that, whatever about the issue of unauthorised use of trademarks, the defendants had violated the copyright, which the clubs had in the design of their badges and logos.[206]

Finally, the governing body may be able to avail of database protection under the Copyright and Related Rights Act 2000 in respect of any statistical data compiled by the governing body.[207] Although the 2000 Act is a piece of Irish legislation, a similar position also applies in England. So, for example, in

---

[201] Para.38ff. See Miles [2002] *European Intellectual Property Review* 543 at p.546.

[202] For a criticism of this conclusion see Miles, *op. cit.*, p.546. Miles also wonders whether the decision stands in light of the Court of Appeal conclusion in *Arsenal v. Reed* that the reason why the mark is displayed on the jersey (whether as indicator of trade origin or as badge of allegiance) is irrelevant, provided that use affects the *functions* of the trademark as a guarantee of origin. It may be argued in response that the two cases are about different things. Thus *Arsenal* is about infringement, whereas *Cotton Traders* is about whether a mark was invalidly registered. Interestingly in Ireland the ubiquitous shamrock which appears on rugby jerseys is a registered trade mark and is protected as a national emblem under Art. 6 of the Paris Convention of 1883. See Clark & Smyth, *op. cit.*, p.489ff.

[203] Para.60.

[204] [2002] E.W.H.C. 2779, [2002] All E.R. (D) 260, (2002) S.L.J.R. 8 (HC), [2003] E.W.C.A. Civ. 995, [2003] All E.R. (D) 201 (July) (CA). See (June 2003) *Sports Law Administration and Practice* 7, 11(2) *Sport and the Law Journal* (2003) 8.

[205] [2003] E.W.C.A. Civ. 995, [2003] All E.R. (D) 201 (July) (CA) para.27.

[206] Governing bodies may also seek to protect copyright in any music written as a theme tune to a major event. See Lewis & Taylor, *op. cit.*, pp.594–595.

[207] See Pt V of the Copyright and Related Rights Act 2000.

Football League v. Littlewoods Pools Ltd,[208] such protection was afforded under general copyright law to fixture lists for the forthcoming season, such that persons wishing to reproduce such lists would have to enter into a royalty based licence agreement for the right to do so. Equally the nature of copyright protection meant that it would apply only to the design of the data and not to the data itself.

Of particular significance in this context is the protection afforded under the EC Directive on the Legal Protection of Databases,[209] which was implemented into Irish law by the Copyright and Related Rights Act 2000. The Directive applies whenever there is unauthorised extraction, utilisation or reutilisation of a substantial part of a database. The implications of this Directive for sports governing bodies were explored by Laddie J. in *British Horseracing Board v. William Hill Ltd*.[210]

In this case the plaintiff governing body had, at considerable expense, compiled a comprehensive database on the horseracing industry, including lists of upcoming races with full details of the runners and riders. The plaintiffs entered into licensing agreements with various entities including the defendants whereby, in exchange for royalties, it would release lists of horses and jockeys involved in each race to newspapers and other licensed users the day beforehand, on condition that the users did not publish such information before noon on the day of the race itself. The defendant company was authorised to use such information in the betting offices it owned and as part of its telephone betting business. It then started an Internet betting business and used the plaintiffs' data on its Internet site. The plaintiff body claimed that the defendants were not authorised to do so and sought relief for a violation of its database rights.

The defendants claimed first that database rights only protected the database *per se* and not the component parts thereof – a claim rejected by Laddie J. who said that the database was comprised of its component parts, and was protected in its entirety as an overall entity.[211] In other words, there was no need to use

---

[208] [1959] 2 All E.R. 546.

[209] Directive 96/99. See Lewis & Taylor, p.599ff .

[210] [2001] R.P.C. 612. See Savvides, "Database Rights a Powerful New Monopoly", 15 *Sports and Character Licensing* (April 2001) 30; Reid and Roy, *"British Horseracing Board v. William Hill"*, 9(2) *Sport and the Law Journal* (2001) 105 and Duthie, "Database Rights – The Form Guide", 8(2) *Sports Law Administration and Practice* (April 2001) 1, and 4(4) *Sports Law Bulletin* (2001) 4. For similar situations in other jurisdictions see "Sports Statistics and Personality Rights in the USA", 15 *Sports and Character Licensing* (April 2001) 13 and for a similar case in Sweden in which it was held that unauthorised use of items from a database did not infringe copyright protection see Case T 99–99, *Fixtures Marketing Limited v. AB Svenska Spel*, Gotland City Court [2001] European Copyright and Designs Reports p.406ff noted at 9(3) *Sport and the Law Journal* (2001) 77.

[211] Para.47.

the material as systematically and methodically as it was used in the database. More significantly, Laddie J. rejected the defendant's claim that in as much as it was using a fraction of the plaintiff's material, this did not constitute extraction of a substantial part of the database. Laddie J. held that the "substantial part" test was both quantitative and qualitative.[212] The importance of the database lay in the fact that it was complete and accurate as a result of the plaintiff's efforts. Indeed this was the reason why it was being used by the defendant. Accordingly, use of any section of the material inevitably involved the defendant company in dipping into the fruit of the totality of the plaintiff's efforts and therefore constituted use of a substantial part thereof.[213] Finally, Laddie J. held that there was a breach of the rights of the database owner despite the fact that all the material involved was already in the public domain[214] – a point of great significance for database holders whose database contents have been raised essentially to the status of confidential information even though it is in the public domain. Furthermore, the Court of Appeal referred certain questions pertaining to the correct interpretation of the Directive to the ECJ[215] and in June 2004, Advocate General Stix-Hackl gave her opinion in the case.[216]

The Court of Appeal had referred various questions to the ECJ, focusing, *inter alia*, on

- whether the terms of the European Database Protection Directive[217] applied to materials that were derived from a database but which did not have the same systematic or methodical arrangement of and individual accessibility to be found in the database;

- what was meant by the prohibition in the directive on uses of "a substantial part evaluated qualitatively..." and "a substantial part established quantitatively ..." of the contents of the database; and

- what was the proper meaning of those actions that infringed the rights of the database owner, that is to say "extraction" and "re-utilisation" of the contents of the database, and acts "which conflict with a normal exploitation of that database" or "unreasonably prejudice the legitimate interests of the maker of the database".[218]

Advocate General Stix-Hackl found, first that the directive did apply to materials that were derived from a database but which did not have the same systematic or methodical arrangement of and individual accessibility to be

---

[212] Para.51.
[213] Para.53.
[214] Para.59.
[215] [2001] E.W.C.A. 1268.
[216] Case C–203/02, June 8, 2004. See also cases C–46/02, C–338/02 and C–444/02 all of June 8, 2004. Press Release 46/04/EN.
[217] Directive 96/9/EC, March 11, 1996.
[218] Para.27.

found in the database.[219] Moreover, she noted that there were two alternative
contexts in which prohibited acts could occur, namely where the part of the
database that was being used was substantial in *qualitative* terms and where it
was substantial in *quantitative* terms. In other words, there was no force in the
argument that there must always be a minimum in quantity of the part of the
database being used.[220] Where the allegation was that the part of the database
being used was substantial in *quantitative* terms, then the amount of the affected
part was relevant (although it is not solely the relative amount of the affected
. part as a proportion of the overall contents that is relevant).[221] Moreover, the
question of whether in any case there was use of a quantitatively substantial
part would be one for the domestic court.[222] Similarly when assessing whether
there had been use of a qualitatively substantial part of the database, regard
should be paid to the technical or commercial value of the affected part and
the extent to which its unauthorised use causes detriment to the rights holder,
having regard to the investment [s]he has made in the database.[223] Again, this
would be a question for the domestic court.

In terms of the definition of the abusive actions Advocate General Stix
Hackl felt first that there was no need under the terms of the directive, that
such actions be repeated or systematic.[224] "Extraction" covered only the transfer
of the contents of the database directly from the database to another data
medium, either on a temporary or a permanent basis, "by any means or in any
form".[225] "Re-utilisation" covered not only the making available to the public
of the contents of the database directly from the database, but also the making
available to the public of works, data or other materials which are derived
indirectly from the database without having direct access to the database.[226]
Acts that conflict with the normal exploitation of the database rights were
those that prevented such exploitation even on potential markets.[227] Finally,
acts that unreasonably prejudice the legitimate interests of the maker of the
database are those that damage the legitimate economic interests of the database
maker to a degree which exceeds a certain threshold.[228] Equally, according to
the Advocate General, interpretation of the term "unreasonably" in this context
must not be too strict, in that if this were intended to be the case, the Community
legislature would have been more explicit in requiring damage (or even

---

[219] Para.70.
[220] Para.73.
[221] Para.75.
[222] Para.81.
[223] Paras 77ff.
[224] Para.89.
[225] Paras 97–99.
[226] Paras 105ff.
[227] Paras 125ff.
[228] Paras 132ff.

significant damage) to the database maker.[229] Once again, the question of whether the relevant threshold of damage had been crossed would be one for the domestic court to decide.[230] Finally, the Advocate General stressed that where (as in the instant case) the database was a constantly changing one, then the spirit of the directive meant that it would always be the new rather than the old database that would be protected.[231]

It is submitted that this opinion upholds in substantial measure the approach of Laddie J. in the High Court, and provides companies like the plaintiff with a significant protection for the potentially enormous investment represented in databases of this nature. Naturally the decision of the European Court of Justice in this case is awaited with interest.

7.6.3 The sportswear company

Finally, and as a somewhat peripheral issue, we should note that of course manufacturers of sporting goods will be able to avail of basic intellectual property right protections in their goods. Thus an invention might be patented, a particular design may be copyrighted and indeed a logo or a design may be registered as a trademark, and if another company were to sell goods that were confusingly similar to the goods of this company, then it could seek relief under the tort of passing off[232] – especially if its design or mark is particularly distinctive. Thus most famously, courts around the world have heard cases brought by the Adidas company in an effort to protect the goodwill inherent in its famous "three stripe" design.[233]

---

[229] Para.134.

[230] Para.138.

[231] Para.152.

[232] *O'Neills Irish International Sports Co Ltd v. O'Neills Footwear Dryer*, unreported, High Court, April 30, 1997, *Adidas v. O'Neills* [1983] 1 I.L.R.M. 112 and *O'Neills v. Adidas*, unreported, Supreme Court, March 25, 1992.

[233] Generally see Couchman, "Recent Developments in Image Rights, Copyright, Domain Name, and Patent Protection Law", *Sports Law Administration and Practice* (August 2003) 6. Cases involving the Adidas stripes include *Adidas v. Charles O'Neill* [1983] F.S.R. 76, Bundesgerichtsof Case IZR 21/98 (July 6, 2000) [2000] *European Trade Mark Review* 325, *Marca Mode v. Adidas*, ECJ Case C–425/98 (June 22, 2000), noted in Turner Kerr, "Confusion or Association under the European Trade Marks Directive" [2001] *European Intellectual Property Review* 49. See also Case 251/95, *SABEL v. Puma* [1997] E.C.R. 1–6191.

7.7 THE RIGHTS OF THE EVENT ORGANISER

We move now to consider the position of the organiser of a sporting event. Such events, after all, offer the potential to generate substantial amounts of revenue through sponsorship, merchandising and most significantly through the sale of broadcasting rights. Once again, it is vital that the event organiser be able to deliver some element of exclusivity to prospective sponsors and indeed broadcasters, and, like the sportsperson who enjoys no property right in his or her image, the event organiser faces a major stumbling block in the fact that there is no such thing at common law as a property right in a sporting event.[234] Thus in *Victoria Park Racing and Recreation Grounds v. Taylor*,[235] the defendants entered into an agreement with persons living in the vicinity of a stadium in which a major horseracing event was to take place, whereby they erected a scaffolding on their premises and then broadcast a commentary of the event on the radio, without paying any fee to the event organisers. The plaintiff organiser sued the defendants alleging that his property rights in the event were being interfered with, but the Australian High Court rejected this claim, holding that the organiser did not possess a property right in the event by virtue of the money that he had spent in respect of it. Moreover, not only is there no property right in a sporting event, but neither does it constitute a performance, and therefore there is no copyright inherent in it.[236] There will of course be copyright in the broadcast thereof, but in the absence of an agreement such copyright will vest in the broadcaster.

In the absence of a property right *per se* in a sporting event, the event organiser will need to have recourse to other legal vehicles for his protection.[237] First, as we have seen, the organiser may enjoy certain intellectual property (or indeed statutory) rights in elements of the event.[238] So for example elements of the Olympic Games, such as the oath and the rings are trademarks – indeed in England their use is protected under the Olympic Symbol (Protection) Act, 1995.[239] Similarly the FIFA World Cup is trademarked[240] and indeed there is

---

[234] *Victoria Park Racing and Recreation Grounds v. Taylor* (1937) 58 C.L.R. 479. See Lewis & Taylor, *op. cit.*, pp.581 *et seq.*

[235] (1937) 58 C.L.R. 479.

[236] Griffith Jones, *op. cit.*, p.236.

[237] Lewis and Taylor, *op. cit.*, p.583 *et seq.*

[238] For an analysis of the registration by the Scottish Rugby Union of the "Calcutta Cup", as a trademark see Finn, "The Calcutta Cup – a Trademark Case Study", 9 *Sport and Character Licensing* (September 2000) 26.

[239] See Mellstrom, "Statutory Protection for Olympic Merchandise", 4 (3) *Sport and the Law Journal* (1996) 23.

[240] On the other hand, in 1999 the French Cour d'Appel ruled that the words *Coupe du Monde* could not be registered as a trademark being too generic a term. See 7(1) *Sport and the Law Journal* (1999) 19. Equally in 2000, the IOC successfully objected to inclusion of the word "Olympic", in a trademark. See [2000] *European Trade Marks Reports* 919, 9(1) *Sport and the Law Journal* (2001) 47.

a copyright in its design.[241] Finally, it is not inconceivable that the precedent in *Irvine v. Talksport* could be used by an event organiser in situations where a business uses the logo, name or image of the event in a context that suggests that its product is endorsed by or connected with the event.

More importantly, the organiser will need to ensure that his or her control over the relevant event is firmly protected by the terms of his contractual relationships with venue owners,[242] commercial partners, participating teams and players and spectators.[243] We have already considered the basic intellectual property rights which a team or governing body and, by extension, an event organiser will enjoy in respect of merchandising. Accordingly for the rest of this section we will consider the primary concerns of the event organiser as they apply to the two great moneymakers in sport, namely sponsorship and broadcasting.

7.7.1 Sponsorship

It is estimated that by the end of 2005 the amount of money spent annually on sports sponsorship will reach $16.8bn of which $4.9bn will be spent in Europe.[244] The reason for this is that the return on sports sponsorship is obvious. Sport and especially televised sport attracts huge viewing figures and having one's name or logo associated with major sporting events means that it is constantly being brought into millions of homes worldwide.[245] Moreover the sponsor's name and image, whether it be on advertising hoardings in the stadium, on a participant's clothing, on the pitch or anywhere else in sight, is reaching people at the height of their concentration –that is to say during the main event, rather than when they are on a "concentration break," as happens whenever advertisements are shown during breaks or intervals in television programmes.[246] It is also targeting huge numbers of people very quickly indeed.

---

[241] Bragiel, "Intellectual Property Rights and the World Cup" (1998) 148 *New Law Journal* 884, Wall, "The Game behind the Games" [2002] *Marquette Sports Law Review* 557, Mellstrom, "Statutory Protection for Olympic Merchandise", 4(3) *Sport and the Law Journal* (1996) 93, Stupp, "Marketing the Olympic Games – Some Legal Aspects", 5(1) *Sports Law Bulletin* (2002) 10, Jacob, "Trade Marks and the Olympic Games Throughout The Years" [2001] *European Intellectual Property Review* 1.

[242] Lewis and Taylor, *op. cit.*, pp.585 and 619 *et seq.*

[243] *Sports and General Press Agency Ltd v. Our Dogs Publishing Company Ltd* [1917] 2 KB 125, *McCutcheon v. David Mac Brayne* [1964] 1 All E.R. 430. See "Confidence, Privacy and a Place to Play" (June 2003) *Sports Law Administration and Practice* 4.

[244] See Lewis and Taylor *op. cit.*, p.705. Generally see Smith, "Commercial Exploitation of Sport", 6 (2) *Sport and Law Journal* (1998) 59 at p.75.

[245] For a general analysis of the impact of sponsorship, see "Switching on and Tuning in to Money in Sport" (proceedings of the 1996 BASAL Annual Conference) 4 (3) *Sport and the Law Journal* (1996) 19.

[246] Lewis and Taylor, *op. cit.*, p.706ff.

Most importantly, one is associating one's product with an entity that attracts generally positive emotions in people.[247]

7.7.1.1 The sponsorship contract

There is much within sport that can be sponsored and many different roles that a sponsor may take.[248] Let us consider briefly any major sports event. Such an event will have a primary or title or event sponsor (for example Guinness as the sponsors of the All-Ireland hurling championships). The venue in which the event occurs may be sponsored and indeed it is possible that individual component parts of the venue may have individual sponsors – for example individual holes on a golf course, or individual lanes in a bowling alley. There may also be secondary sponsorship – as where each of the six or seven races at a horseracing event is individually sponsored. If the event is covered on live television, then the broadcast may be sponsored either by the event sponsor or some other organisation. The event may have any number of persons contracted as "official suppliers" of various products, ranging from games to soft drinks to beer.[249] Finally, the teams taking part in the event may be sponsored as may the individual players of such teams, and even the team mascots.[250] Given that there is no such thing as a "sponsorship right" or "sponsorship law",[251] all the various parties are utterly reliant on the terms of their sponsorship contracts to protect their interests. More specifically they are reliant on lawyers who will ensure that whatever contract they enter into will ensure that they get good value for the potentially vast amounts of money that they will be paying to be recognised as a sponsor.

A sponsorship contract is therefore obviously necessary, and it is also vital for both parties to ensure that the contract contains all the elements that they wish it to contain. The following are some such basic elements.[252]

Guarantee of capacity   First and foremost the sponsor should demand the insertion of a clause whereby the organiser agrees to guarantee both his right

---

[247] See e.g., Smith, "The Commercial Exploitation of Sport", 6(2) *Sport and the Law Journal* (1998) 59 at 62.

[248] Lewis & Taylor *op. cit.*, p.709ff, Griffith Jones, *op. cit.*, p.261.

[249] In *Danish Tennis Federation Commission* OJ 1996, C 138/6 [1996] 4 C.M.L.R. 885 the ECJ said that unless the "official sponsor" label could be justified on technical grounds, its use would mislead consumers as to the qualitative characteristics of the product, and hence it would be necessary for the event organiser to clarify that the description in question was sponsorship based.

[250] Generally see Griffith Jones, *op. cit.*, p.263ff

[251] Smith, "The Commercial Exploitation of Sport", 6 ((2) *Sport and the Law Journal* (1998) 59 at 69.

[252] *Ibid.*, p.75.

and his capacity to grant the rights that he is granting.[253] Similarly, he will seek to be indemnified against any claims that might arise from the event in question.[254]

Exclusivity   From a sponsor's perspective, there are two primary concerns, namely exposure and exclusivity.[255] As regards the latter, the sponsor (who will be aware that the commercial reality of the situation is such that it can never hope to be the only business connected with a major event), will want to ensure that rival businesses are either not permitted to be co-sponsors of the event, or else that their exposure is appreciably less than that which it enjoys, and it will seek to ensure that its sponsorship contract with the event organiser reflects this aspiration. Thus it may negotiate for the insertion of a clause in the sponsorship contract which affords it some power of veto over other businesses associated with the event as co-sponsors or official suppliers to the event, and also to ensure that where teams and individuals participating in the event are themselves sponsored by rival businesses that they are not permitted to display the images of their own sponsors before, during or after the event.[256] Beyond this the sponsor may seek to have a say in the overall organisation and management of the event being sponsored including the merchandising thereof,[257] and also to be involved in negotiations with the broadcaster of the event. Finally, the sponsor will want control over elements of the merchandising and advertising in the venue in which the event is being held, and will, for example, demand a "clean" venue – that is to say one in which there is no sign

---

[253] Steele, *op. cit.*, p.27, See also "Aspects of Sports Marketing: Event Sponsorship Contracts", 6(1) *Sport and the Law Journal* (1998) 10.

[254] Steele, *op. cit.*, p.27.

[255] See Steele, "Sponsorship Contracts – The Full Monty", 5(3) *Sport and the Law Journal* (1997) 25, Nadler, "Successful Sponsorship", 20 *Sports and Character Licensing* (November 2001) 4, Smith, "The Commercial Exploitation of Sport", 6(2) *Sport and the Law Journal* (1998) 59, Lewis and Taylor, *op. cit.*, pp.208 and 270ff, Moore, *op. cit.*, p.59, Vero, Lawrence and McCormick, *Sport, Business and the Law* (Jordan, 1999) 343 and Griffith Jones, *op. cit.*, p.270.

[256] Thus during the 1996 Coca Cola Cup final in England problems arose when both the title sponsors and Lucozade (the official drinks suppliers to both finalists) claimed exclusive rights to have bottles with their logos on them present on the field of play. Vero, Lawrence and McCormick, *op. cit.*, p.721ff. This issue also came to the fore in April 2004, when, just two days before a National League semi-final match, the Mayo Women's Gaelic Football team successfully appealed a competition ban imposed on them by the Women's Football Association, arising out of their refusal to obey a directive from GAA Headquarters in October 2003 preventing them from wearing their own gear (sponsored by their own sponsors, Azzurri) as opposed to the official O'Neill's sponsored gear. See "Mayo Cleared to Play in Semi-Final After Appeal", *Irish Times*, April 17, 2004 and O'Riordan, "Appeal Sets Ban Aside", *Irish Times*, April 17, 2004.

[257] Steele, *op. cit.*, p.26 and Lewis and Taylor, *op. cit.*, p.272–276.

of the image of any of his competitors.[258] This issue will be returned to later in our consideration of the problem of ambush marketing.

Exposure . Whatever the category of sponsor that is involved, it will want to receive as much exposure as possible both at the event itself and at all accompanying promotional events.[259] From the standpoint of the event organiser, accommodation of such sponsor needs must be met again through intense contractual negotiations with all the relevant bodies (venue owners, commercial partners and so on) connected with the event. Thus the title sponsor will demand that its name be mentioned whenever the event is mentioned – in all broadcasting and advertising, on programmes, on tickets and even on the tournament trophy.[260] In this way names such as the Eircom Football League, the Heineken European Rugby Cup, and the Embassy World Snooker Championships have become part of contemporary sporting language.

Beyond this, sponsors will want to have their advertising logos used in all promotional literature surrounding the event and, to have press conferences and post-match interviews conducted in front of a board with all the sponsors' logos on it. Similarly, all sponsors will seek to have their images displayed on advertising hoardings within the venue where the event is taking place. Here once again the concept of a clean stadium becomes important.[261] Indeed the sponsor may seek in his sponsorship contract to ensure that the stadium owner takes some responsibility for control of advertising sites in the vicinity of the sporting venue. The sponsor may also want to use the event logo in connection with its products in an advertising or merchandising campaign.[262] Indeed it may also seek to secure the right to use the image of players who competed in the event in an advertising campaign, or indeed to require such players to engage in promotional activities in respect of the event.[263] The sponsor may also demand filming rights – that is the right to film the event and to use footage as part of an advertising or promotional campaign. Again the sponsor may seek to be involved in the negotiations between the event organiser and the broadcasters thereof, and to secure maximum exposure of its name and image during the broadcast.[264] Finally, the sponsor may also seek presentation rights (the right to present the trophy to the winning team[265]) as well as more

---

[258] Griffith Jones, *op. cit.*, p.280 and Vero, Lawrence and McCormick, *op. cit.*, p.343ff.
[259] Vero, Lawrence and McCormick, *op. cit.*, p.208 *et seq.*
[260] Lewis and Taylor, *op. cit.*, p.712.
[261] *Ibid.*, p.716.
[262] Moore, *op. cit.*, p.56. So for example, as part of its sponsorship deal with the Brazilian national soccer team, Nike is permitted to organize 50 friendly games in which the Brazilian team will participate. See "Sports Sponsorship – the Role of Disrepute Clause", 6(2) *Sports Law Administration and Practice* (March/April 1999) 9 at p.10.
[263] Steele, *op. cit.*, p.27.
[264] Griffith Jones, *op. cit.*, p.273.
[265] *Ibid.*, p.717.

obvious hospitality rights – free tickets for the event and other in-stadium hospitality entitlements.

Providing against unforeseen circumstances We have already mentioned that where a business is sponsoring an individual or indeed a team, it is advisable to insert a clause in the contract providing either that the sponsor may walk away from the contract where the individual does something that would mean that a connection with him would bring the business into disrepute, or else linking sponsorship payments to the level of exposure that a sponsor company receives, which of course will be considerably diminished if the player is suspended for a long period, or if a team is knocked out in the early stages of a particular competition.[266] In similar vein, when sponsoring an event the sponsor will want to provide against unforeseen circumstances – for example the cancellation of the event (a vista that becomes increasingly predominant in the era of global terrorist threats)[267] – that will diminish his return from the same. Finally, the sponsor may wish to ensure that his interests are protected against unforeseen changes in the law – thus for example a company manufacturing alcoholic beverages might be advised, if it decides to sponsor sports events, to insert a clause into the contract allowing it to get out of its contractual obligations in the event of such sponsorship becoming illegal.[268] This is of particular concern in Ireland, where, in June 2004, there was a strong suggestion that the Joint Oireachtas Committee on Health and Children would be recommending to the Government that it should ban all sponsorship of sporting events by drinks companies.[269]

---

[266] *Ibid.*, p.186.

[267] See Rudgard, "Controlling the risk – Who Pays When an Event is Cancelled?", 10(1) *Sport and the Law Journal* (2002) 130.

[268] Steele, *op. cit.*, p.28. There may also be a need to guard against a situation where a team sponsored by a company that manufactures alcoholic beverages will be playing an important match in a country in which such sponsorship is not permitted. See Korman, "Sponsorship and Branding of Football Teams" (July/August 1997), *Sports Law Administration and Practice* 8 at p.9.

[269] See Beasley, "Drink Firms Face Call for Sports Sponsorship Ban", *Irish Times*, June 12, 2004. A similar concern exists in respect of the sponsorship of sporting events by tobacco companies. The EU had originally sought to prohibit tobacco advertising and sponsorship through the terms of Directive 98/43/EC, but this directive was struck down in its entirety by the ECJ for lack of EU competence: *Federal Republic of Germany v. European Parliament and Council of the EU*, Case C–376/98, [2000] E.C.R. I–2247. See Pearl, "Kicking the Habit: The Battle to Rid Sport of Tobacco", 4(1) *Sports Law Bulletin* (2001) 15. The issue has, however, been dealt with in a new directive, Directive 2003/33/EC (May 26, 2003) under the terms of Article 5 of which, "Sponsorship of events or activities involving or taking place in several Member States or otherwise having cross border effects shall be prohibited".

Miscellaneous contractual clauses   Apart from standard boiler plate clauses, there are a couple of other matters that should be contained in the sponsorship contract. First, and from the standpoint of the event organiser, it will be necessary to ensure that a suitable sponsorship fee is paid and also that the event organiser (or where appropriate the relevant sporting body) retains full trademark and copyright protection in respect of any logos being used.[270] Secondly, and from the standpoint of the sponsor, it would be advisable to ensure that there are clear dates for termination of the sponsorship agreement, and if desired, an option to renew the same.[271] Thirdly, the sponsor should insist that a clause be contained in the contract whereby he is absolved from any responsibility or liability arising in whatever fashion from the staging of the event. Finally, the sponsor will need some measure of protection against the most insidious contemporary threat to sports sponsorship, namely ambush marketing.

7.8 AMBUSH MARKETING

The fact that there is no such thing as a property right in a sporting event means that a major concern for both the event organiser and the sponsor is the increasingly prevalent concept of ambush marketing.[272] This can occur in a number of ways, but the principle is the same in all cases, namely, that someone who has not paid the sponsorship fee nonetheless seeks to associate its image with that of the club or player or event and thereby to avail of its goodwill. For some, ambush marketing is no more than sound commercial practice. For others it is no less than theft.[273] As far as an organiser of an event or a governing body is concerned, ambush marketing presents serious risks in terms of loss of sponsorship revenue both immediately and in the future,[274] not to mention, the loss of goodwill which might stem from the sale of substandard merchandise. Moreover, if a prospective "event staging city" is unable to demonstrate that it can control ambush marketing, and provide a "clean city" in which the event can take place, it will be unlikely to succeed in its bid to

---

[270] Lewis & Taylor, *op. cit.*, p.721ff.

[271] Steele, *op. cit.*, p.27.

[272] See Griffith Jones, *op. cit.*, p.277ff, and Vero, Lawrence and McCormick, *op. cit.*, p.276, Bartman, "Live Events and Illegal Merchandise", 12 *Sports and Character Licensing* (December 2000-January 2001) 33, Bitel, "Ambush Marketing", 5(1) *Sport and the Law Journal* (1997) 12. For an analysis of ambush marketing as it affected the London Marathon, see Bitel, 4 *Sports and Character Licensing* (March 2000) 18.

[273] See Garrigues, "Ambush Marketing: Robbery or Smart Advertising" [2002] 11 *European Intellectual Property Review* 505.

[274] So for example, during the Euro 1996 Football Championships 23% of those surveyed thought Nike was a sponsor, even though it wasn't, and only 28% thought that Umbro was a sponsor, which it was. See Smith, "The Commercial Exploitation of Sport", 6(2) *Sport and the Law Journal* (1998) 59 at 83.

host a major sporting event.[275] Finally, from the perspective of the sponsor, it makes little sense to invest millions of dollars or euros in an event if a rival company, through strategic ambush marketing, will manage to connect its name and image with the event in the minds of the general public, either in the vicinity of the event or through the medium of television coverage of the event.

Examples of ambush marketing include the following:[276]

– intentional conflict marketing – that is to say where a business, aware that a rival is sponsoring a sporting event, sponsors a team competing in that event in order to have its image and logo present thereat;[277]

– giveaways – for example where a company hands out free t-shirts with its image on them in the vicinity of a venue where an event is to take place, in the hope that spectators will wear such t-shirts in the venue and will be televised doing so;

– misleading advertising – for example in the run up to a major soccer event such as the World Cup, running a television advertising campaign with a clear football theme running through it;[278]

– advertising on billboards or bus shelters or other prominent public places in the vicinity of the stadium in which an event is to take place, or indeed advertising anywhere in a city in which, for instance, a major marathon is being run;

– offering tickets to the sporting event as prizes in a competition associated with one's product;

– driving a vehicle (or vehicles) with one's business image on it up and down the streets in the vicinity of the stadium;[279] alternatively, ambushers have flown aircraft over the stadium or indeed have hired private property nearby and tethered a blimp carrying an advertisement of this kind to the same property so that the message is visible to spectators inside the stadium;

– cyber squatting – where the name of a sporting event or a sports team or

---

[275] Couchman and Harrington, "Tackling the Ambush Marketers Head On", 4 *Sports and Character Licensing* (March 2000) 17

[276] Reid, "Combating Traditional and 'New Age' Ambush Marketing", 4(4) *Sports Law Bulletin* (2001) 10, Lewis and Taylor, *op. cit.*, p.612 and Garrigues, "Ambush Marketing: Robbery or Smart Advertising" (2002) 11 *European Intellectual Property Review* 505.

[277] Couchman and Harrington "Tackling the Ambush Marketers Head On", 4 *Sports and Character Licensing* (March 2000) 17.

[278] So for example at the time of the Barcelona Olympic Games Benetton took out a two page advertisement in newspapers depicting five coloured condoms made up to look like the Olympic rings, which suggested that there was a link between Benetton and the Olympic Games. See Lewis & Taylor, *op. cit.*, p.613.

[279] Whitehead, "Ambushing the Ambushers" (April 2000) *Sports Law Administration and Practice* 8 at p.9.

sports person is registered as a domain name by a third party so that when an internet user seeks such sport entity s/he will in fact be routed to the offending company;[280]

– typo squatting – where the name of a sports entity slightly misspelled is registered as a domain name in order to take advantage of inadvertent misspellings.[281]

7.8.1 Targeting ambush marketing

Provided that the "ambusher" does not engage in the expanded form of passing off recognised in *Irvine v. Talksport*, or use images that contain either a trade mark or a design protected by copyright law, then he/she is acting within the law, in the sense that, as we have noted, there are no property rights in a sporting event *per se*.[282] Moreover, where attempts are made to prohibit ambush marketing, these may prove abortive – given the strictures of both national and EC competition law, especially in cases in which it can be established that the ambush advertisement is neither false nor misleading.[283] Accordingly, as a practice it is both damaging to the sponsor/organiser relationship and also very difficult to prevent.[284] There are, however, two different types of ways in which ambush marketing may be countered, either through reliance on the law, or through shrewd forward planning and good contractual negotiation.

In terms of legal protection, the organiser may of course first rely on intellectual property rights – in the event of such rights being breached – and possibly (although it is submitted improbably) under defamation law. In the context of a major event, such as for example the Olympic Games, the organiser may seek to persuade the relevant local authorities to enact ordinances controlling the types of advertising that can be practiced in the area around a stadium.[285] Beyond this, more radical measures have been taken against ambush

---

[280] See Edgar & McArdle, "Selling Your Sole: e-Europe, EU Law and Sports Marketing", 141 in Caiger & Gardiner eds., *Professional Sport in the European Union: Regulation and Re-regulation* (TMC Asser Press, 2000).

[281] Generally, on the subject of online ambush marketing see Reid, "Combating Traditional and "New Age", Ambush Marketing", 4(4) *Sports Law Bulletin* (2001) 10, Harrington, "Intellectual Property – Sport and the Internet", 6(2) *Sports Law Administration and Practice* (March-April 1999) 1, Harrington, "E-Commerce and Sports Marketing; Legal Issues", 7(1) *Sports Law Administration and Practice* (February 2000) 1 and 7(2) *Sports Law Administration and Practice* (April 2000) 1.

[282] Lewis and Taylor, *op. cit.*, p.613.

[283] See Griffith Jones, *op. cit.*, p.279.

[284] Whitehead, "Ambushing the Ambushers" (April 2000) *Sports Law Administration and Practice* 8.

[285] The Organising Committee of the 2002 Winter Olympic Games reached agreement with the local authority in Salt Lake City that the streets around the major Olympic

marketing in the context of the hosting of a major sporting event.[286] Thus, in advance of the Cricket World Cup in 2003, South African authorities amended the Trade Practices Act of 1976 to prohibit the making of statements or advertisements that falsely imply a connection between the person making a statement and a sponsored event. They also amended the 1941 Merchandise Marks Act to create a criminal offence of using the ambusher's mark in circumstances where such use is not authorised by the event organiser yet is calculated to achieve publicity for the mark and to derive goodwill from the sponsored event.[287]

"Non-Legal" approaches to counter ambush marketing will in practice, however, be likely to be the more effective means of targeting the practice. First and foremost it is necessary to have control over the area in which an event is being staged, including both the particular venue where the event will take place (which of course becomes hugely difficult where the venue in question is the course of the Dublin City Marathon or the Circuit of Ireland rally) and also the area around that venue.[288] Thus the event organiser should, as early as possible,[289] seek to enter into contractual negotiations with both the owner of the venue in which the event is being staged and also with businesses in the vicinity of the stadium with the aim of buying up advertising space and thereby ensuring that the venue and indeed its environs are "clean" for the purposes of sponsors.[290] This expansion of the concept of a "clean venue" has become particularly prevalent in the context of the Olympic Games, such that cities bidding for the rights to host the Olympic games are now

---

venues would be closed down. See Naidoo, "Ambush Marketing – Innovative Ideas for Salt Lake City, 2002", 5(1) *Sports Law Bulletin* (2002) 9.

[286] See, for example, Duthie, "It's Just Not Cricket: Ambushing the Ambushers in South Africa", 11(1) *Sport and the Law Journal* (2003) 171, Roper Drimie, "Sydney 2000 Olympic Games – A Case Study on How to Combat Ambush Marketing", 7(7) *Sports Law Administration and Practice* (February 2001) 1, Naidoo, "Ambush Marketing: Innovative Ideas for Salt Lake City 2002" (January/February 2002) 5(1) *Sports Law Bulletin* (2002) 9, Reid "Combating Traditional and New Age Ambush Marketing", 4(4) *Sports Law Bulletin* (2001)10 and Naidoo "Salt Lake City Brand Protection Program – Ambush Marketing and Its Repercussions", 4(4) *Sports Law Bulletin* (2001) 13.

[287] See Duthie, "It's Just Not Cricket: Ambushing the Ambushers in South Africa", 11(1) *Sport and the Law Journal* (2003) 171 at 172 for analysis of the Australian approaches in this regard.

[288] Lewis & Taylor, *op. cit.*, p.615.

[289] Whitehead, "Ambushing the Ambushers" (April 2000) *Sports Law Administration and Practice* 8. The organisers of the Sydney Olympic Games acquired all advertising space around the centre of Sydney some four years before the event took place. See Reid, "Combating Traditional and 'New Age' Ambush Marketing", 4 (4) *Sports Law Bulletin* (2001) 10.

[290] Thus in 2002, the Salt Lake City Olympic organising committee persuaded local builders to ensure that Neon signs advertising competitor goods would be turned off during the games. See Naidoo, "Ambush Marketing – Innovative Ideas for Salt Lake City, 2002", 5(1) *Sports Law Bulletin* (2002) 9.

required to guarantee a "clean city" free from ambush marketing both on the ground and also in the airspace above the ground.[291]

Secondly, it is necessary to control (again through the use of contracts) the actions of participants, commercial partners (including broadcasters) and spectators at such events.[292] Thus for example, participants may be required to wear clothes and indeed other sporting equipment produced by sponsor companies (and to refrain from wearing the logos and images of rival companies)[293] when competing at the event and when appearing at all related events – for example, press conferences.[294] Indeed, under Rule 45 of the Olympic Charter, athletes are precluded from making commercial appearances during the Olympics (and from acting as journalists during this period) without first obtaining a waiver from their National Olympic Committee.[295] Similarly, where unauthorised businesses *have* managed to advertise their products in the vicinity of the stadium, the broadcaster should be required to avoid broadcasting any footage of such advertisements.[296] Spectators too may be targeted by contractual obligations contained on the backs of tickets, and may be prohibited from wearing clothes with rival sponsors names on them both inside the venue and at all times that they might be caught on camera, in order to prevent them from acting as tools for the ambush marketer.[297]

---

[291] Thus, during the staging of the 1996 Olympic Games in Atlanta there were restrictions on air traffic in the vicinity of the Olympic Stadium in order to prevent unauthorised advertising. See Couchman and Harrington, "Tackling the Ambush Marketers Head On", 4 *Sports and Character Licensing* (March 2000) 18.

[292] Lewis & Taylor, *op. cit.*, pp.588 and 617, Couchman and Harrington, "Tackling the Ambush Marketers Head On", 4 *Sports and Character Licensing* (March 2000) 18.

[293] The controversy over the gear that Irish Olympic track and field athletes should wear has been a source of much tension because the Olympic Council of Ireland and the Irish governing body for athletics (BLE) have different sponsors, and both wish to see the interests of their sponsors being protected. The issue came to a head in 1996 when Irish track star Sonia O'Sullivan was forced to strip in the tunnel minutes before the Olympic 5,000 metres final, in order to change from the OCI's Reebok uniform into BLE's Asics uniform. Generally see O'Riordan, "Chronology of Gear Fiasco", *Irish Times*, March 25, 2000, Byrne, "McDaid may Mediate in Sponsorship Dispute", *Irish Times*, March 25, 2000. More recently (December 2003) tennis star Kim Clijsters announced that she would not be competing at the Athens Olympic Games because she was not allowed to wear clothes bearing the logos of her sponsor company Fila.

[294] Bitel, "Ambush Marketing", 5(1) *Sport and the Law Journal* (1997) 12.

[295] Wall, "The Game behind the Games" ([2002) 12 *Marquette Sports Law Review* 557.

[296] Bitel, *op. cit.*

[297] Duthie, "It's Just Not Cricket: Ambushing the Ambushers in South Africa", 11(1) *Sport and the Law Journal* (2003) 171 at 173–174, Whitehead, "Ambushing the Ambushers" (April 2000) *Sports Law Administration and Practice* 8, Roper-Drimie, "Sydney 2000 Olympic Games – A Case Study on How to Combat Ambush Marketing", 7(7) *Sports Law Administration and Practice* (February 2001) 1. Thus at the 2003 Cricket World Cup in South Africa (where Pepsi were the major sponsors) spectators were evicted from the stadia for drinking Coke. See 11(2) *Sport and the Law Journal* (2003) 88

7.9 BROADCASTING OF SPORTS' EVENTS

Whereas there is suggestion that the massive financial outlay connected with the broadcasting of sporting events in the late 1990s has waned somewhat, it is undoubtedly true that television coverage of sporting events is still huge business.[298] Equally much of professional sport is now dependent on revenue received from broadcasting companies. Thus as we have seen many football clubs in the English Nationwide League suffered serious financial loss following the collapse of the ill-fated ITV digital network, in as much as they had budgeted on the basis that the payments from that company would come through.[299]

For our purposes, three major questions arise in respect of the broadcasting of sporting events. First, what is meant by the notion of broadcasting rights, and what issues should be considered in a broadcasting contract? Secondly, to what extent may a national government seek to restrict the sale of broadcasting rights, in order to ensure that sporting events of major national importance are accessible to the majority of sports fans in any country. Finally, what role does domestic or European competition law play in regulating the sale and purchase of broadcasting rights? This last question will be addressed in Chapter Nine. For now, we will focus on the first two questions raised above.

7.9.1 What are broadcasting rights?

Unlike its American,[300] French or Australian counterparts,[301] English and by extension Irish law recognises a property right neither in the sports event itself (as we have seen) nor in news emanating from the sporting event. Accordingly the notion of "broadcasting rights" is something of a fiction and ultimately refers to the entitlements granted by the event organiser to the broadcaster or broadcasters under contract.[302] Once again, the only way in which the event owner, or the governing body as the case may be, can secure any degree of exclusivity for the broadcaster, is by ensuring, through contractual agreement

---

[298] Harvey, "New Opportunities for Media Rights Exploitation", 9(3) *Sport and the Law Journal* (2001) 150.

[299] Lewis & Taylor, *op. cit.*, pp.675–678.

[300] *Pittsburgh Athletic Co v. KQV Broadcasting*, 24 F.Supp 490 (WD Pa 1937).

[301] Thus France recognises a property right in a sports event and in Australia it is an offence for anyone with a broadcasting licence to transmit an unauthorised broadcast from any event held in a place entry into which is dependent on the payment of an admission charge. Harrington, "Sports Rights and the Media" (December 2001) *Sports Law Administration and Practice* 9 and (February 2003) *Sports Law Administration and Practice* 8. See also Beloff *et al*, *Sports Law* (Hart Publishing, 1999), p.134.

[302] See Vero, Lawrence and McCormick, *op. cit.*, p.387.

with the venue owner and spectators, that the official broadcaster and only the official broadcaster gains access to the venue[303] for the purpose of broadcasting footage of the event in question.[304] Obviously this will be far more difficult to achieve when the event takes place outside of an enclosed venue, (as for instance with the English "boat race" or a marathon), in which case any guarantee of broadcasting exclusivity may be dependent on regulation by local ordinances.[305]

Having said that there is no such thing as a "broadcasting right" *per se*, equally the broadcaster will own a copyright in any broadcasts that are produced.[306] On the other hand, there are two significant limitations on this right. First, it is considered fair dealing for extracts from the copyrighted material to be used for the purpose not only of general news programmes, but also items of genuine sporting news.[307] Thus in *BBC v. British Satellite Broadcasting Limited*,[308] the use on Sky news of 14–37 second snippets from BBC's coverage of the Italia '90 World Cup soccer tournament in its news bulletins was deemed to constitute fair dealing for the purposes of reporting current events.[309]

Secondly, there does not appear to be any good ground for preventing "off tube" coverage, that is to say a company broadcasting a radio commentary of a sporting event where the commentator is looking at the pictures from the television broadcast thereof. Thus in *BBC v. Talksport*[310] the BBC had acquired the exclusive radio broadcast rights to the Euro 2000 football championships from UEFA. The Talksport channel broadcast radio commentary of the games from commentators watching the TV coverage in hotel rooms in Belgium, and spiced up the broadcast of the games by advertising them as "live" and accompanying the commentary with simulated crowd noises. The High Court, despite disapproving of what Talksport was doing, decided that it had no grounds for granting the interlocutory injunction on the commentary sought by the BBC. Indeed the only possible manner in which Talksport had acted otherwise than lawfully was in its suggestion that the commentary was "live" – a suggestion which might have constituted passing off. Thus in a subsequent

---

[303] Given that most broadcasting rights are sold by the governing body of the sport, it is usual that the controller of access to the venue will not be the same entity as the controller of the broadcasting rights. See Lewis & Taylor, *op. cit.*, p.685, see also Griffith Jones, *op. cit.*, pp.303–305.

[304] *Sports & General Press Agency Ltd v. Our Dogs Publishing Co Ltd* [1917] 2 K.B. 125, *McCutcheon v. David Mac Brayne* [1964] 1 All E.R. 430. Generally see Lewis & Taylor, *op. cit.*, p.585.

[305] Lewis & Taylor, *op. cit.*, pp.680ff.

[306] *Ibid.*, pp.682ff.

[307] Fair dealing in respect of the reporting of current events is covered by s.51(2) of the Irish Copyright Related Rights Act 2000.

[308] [1992] Ch. 141. Generally see Simpson, "Exclusive Sports Broadcast Rights and Fair Dealing" [2001] 7 Ent.L.R. 207.

[309] Beloff, *op. cit.*, p.137 and Griffith Jones, *op. cit.*, p.311.

[310] [2001] F.S.R. 53.

settlement, Talksport agreed that in the future it would make it clear that its broadcasts were not live.[311]

From the position of the event organiser, whereas previously all that happened was a simple sale of broadcasting rights to a single company, now it is possible to have a far more sophisticated exploitation of the potential in an event, by dividing up the overall broadcasting package into a number of smaller sub packages, with consequently far more revenue earning potential for the event organiser.[312] Thus in relation to most major sporting events there will be:

- live TV coverage,

- live radio coverage,

- "as live" rights (that is to say the right to show the game in its entirety but with a slight delay, beginning perhaps half an hour after the event begins),

- extended highlights coverage,

- mobile telephone rights,

- news footage rights,

- magazine programme rights,

- "new technology" rights.

From the event organiser's perspective, the objective is both to gain the highest possible revenue from all of these complimentary rights packages, as well as working out the precise means by which it can be achieved – for example the question of whether one broadcasting company can get a feed from another company and other such issues.[313] It is imperative that issues of this kind be resolved within a broadcasting contract.

Amongst the other issues (apart from the standard contractual clauses covering payment, termination, options to renew and so on) to be contained in a broadcasting contract are:

- issues of rights ownership;

- the nature of the coverage (is it live, deferred, highlights or other?);

- promotional and advertising obligations;

---

[311] See Lewis & Taylor, *op. cit.*, p.683. See also 10(1) *Sports Law Journal* (2002) 68–69 and Harrington, "Sports Rights and the Media" (December 2001) *Sports Law Administration and Practice* 9 and (February 2003) *Sports Law Administration and Practice* 8.

[312] See Vero, Lawrence & McCormick, *op. cit.*, p.388 and Lewis & Taylor *op. cit.*, pp.685–689.

[313] Lewis & Taylor, *op. cit.*, p.701ff.

– obligations to event sponsors;

– the timetabling and content of advertising breaks in the coverage of the event;

– obligations in respect of the quality of the broadcast;

– issues pertaining to copyright and future use (*inter alia* by sponsors) of broadcast – material

– territorial licenses (licenses to broadcast outside of the country in which the event takes place – something of enormous importance where the event in question is a major international event);

– capacity to sub licence;[314]

– insurance against cancellation of the event;

– measures to be taken to combat ambush marketing.[315]

7.9.2 Article 3A of the *Television Without Frontiers Directive*[316] and the protection of "listed" events

As the broadcasting of sporting events became more lucrative and as the notion of subscriber channels and pay-per-view events became more prominent in the 1980s, a strong view emerged within Europe that there was a need to ensure that some sporting and cultural events which were of particular importance should be protected against exclusive broadcasting that was not freely available to all people in Europe who had access to normal terrestrial television stations.[317] To this end, the *Television Without Frontiers Directive* was amended

---

[314] See Harris, "Transfrontier Broadcasting of World Cup Qualifying Games", 9(2) *Sport and the Law Journal* 100. Interestingly in 2001 the Kirch Group who had been sold the rights to the 2002 Soccer World Cup by FIFA was under significant pressure from the World Cup sponsors to sell national broadcasting rights of the event to as many countries as possible in order that the sponsors' material would be very widely viewed. See Barr-Smith, "Listed Events and the Sale of World Cup TV Rights", 9(3) *Sport and the Law Journal* (2001) 135.

[315] Generally see Griffith-Jones, *op. cit.*, p.306ff.

[316] Directive 89/552/EEC, OJ 1989, L 298/23 as amended by Directive 97/36/EC, OJ 1997, L 202/60.

[317] See for example the Council of Europe European Convention on Transfrontier Television (ETS: No 132 as amended by the Protocol to the Convention (ETS: NO 171)), Art.9 of which authorises Member States, having regard to their obligations under the European Convention on Human Rights to list events of major cultural and sporting importance that must be shown on a free to air basis. Generally see Barr-Smith, "Listed Events and the Sale of World Cup TV Rights", 9(3) *Sport and the Law Journal* (2001) 135 and Ferragu, "Anti-Syphoning Legislation" (July-August 1999), *Sports Law Administration and Practice* 3.

in 1996, in order to further two major objectives; first, that in the interests of fair competition, broadcasting packages should be split – that is to say that the entity that had live broadcasting rights should not also be awarded the highlights package, and secondly that Member States should be entitled, irrespective of the impact on fair competition, to ring-fence certain sporting events by requiring that they be shown on a free to air basis, thereby guaranteeing the widest possible access to same.[318]

For present purposes, the major impact of the amendment to the Directive lies in the cumulative effect of Articles 3(a)1 and 3(a)3 of the Directive.[319] Under the new regime, a Member State is entitled, *in accordance with Community law*, to draw up a list of events that are of major national importance (and the directive cites, by way of example, events such as the Olympic Games, the FIFA World Cup and the UEFA European Championships) and to require by law that such events are broadcast on a free to air basis. Interestingly, the obligations in this regard fall on the broadcaster, such that it is obliged either to broadcast the material on a free to air basis, or else to share its broadcasting entitlements with a free to air channel for a fair market price – a prospect that is obviously highly unattractive for sports subscriber channels whose popularity is largely based on the exclusive nature of their broadcasts. The directive also imposes responsibility on member states for broadcasters operating within their territory. Thus if a company based in France sought to broadcast transmission into Ireland of a listed sporting event, it would be subject to control by the French government.[320] Importantly, the spirit of the directive prioritises the interests of all would be viewers of sport in the European Union over the rights of a company that might have paid significant sums of money for exclusive broadcasting rights.

The House of Lords considered this aspect of the Directive in *R v. Independent Television Commission ex parte TV Danmark 1 Ltd*.[321] The UK had by this stage enacted the Broadcasting Act of 1996, which contains two categories of listed events. Events in the first category could not be broadcast exclusively by subscriber channels, unless such broadcast was sanctioned by the Independent Television Commission (ITC). Events in the second category could be broadcast by subscriber channels, but delayed broadcast of the event

---

[318] Griffith Jones, *op. cit.*, p.297ff, Beloff, *op. cit.*, p.138–139 and Lewis & Taylor, *op. cit.*, p.32ff.

[319] See "'Sport and Policy' or 'Sports' Policy'; The broadcasting of Sporting Events in the European Union", 6(3) *Sport and the Law Journal* (1998) 73 for suggestion that the post-Amsterdam co-decision legislative process is manifest in this amendment which is so plainly in the interests of the public, rather than European competition policy.

[320] Griffith-Jones, *op. cit.*, p.298 and Lewis & Taylor, *op. cit.*, p.701

[321] [2001] 1 W.L.R. 1604. Generally see Harrington, "Fans 2 – Pay TV 1. Shock Result in House of Lords Final", 19 *Sports and Character Licensing* (September/October 2001) 7.

would have to be permitted on a free-to-air basis. The ITC was also charged with the granting or refusing of permission to companies located in the UK to broadcast sporting events into other European Union countries. In deciding whether or not to grant permission in either instance, the ITC code of practice required it to have regard to a list of criteria, including the question of whether terrestrial channels in the other Member State had had a reasonable opportunity to purchase such rights, and the nature of the regulatory system in place in the country into which signals are to be broadcast.[322]

In the *TV Danmark* case, the applicants were a newly formed UK based company whose transmissions reached approximately 60% of the Danish population. It had purchased (in an open public auction) the exclusive broadcasting rights for Denmark's five "away" qualifying matches for the 2002 World Cup, which were listed events in Denmark. Under the regulatory system in place there, such listed events would have to be broadcast by companies with coverage reaching in excess of 90% of the population. In line with the requirements under the Broadcasting Act of 1996, TV Danmark applied to the ITC for permission to broadcast such games into Denmark, pointing out that under its own Code of Practice, the ITC was bound to have regard to the question whether terrestrial broadcasters had had a chance to purchase the rights to such events, and in this case they had had such a chance – in that the auction for such events was a free public auction.[323]

It should be noted, however, that the Code of Practice also required the ITC to consider the Danish regulatory system, under which a Pay TV broadcaster who had access to less than 90% of the population would be required to share its exclusive rights to a listed event with terrestrial broadcasters on a non-exclusive basis and at a reasonable price. On this basis, the ITC then asked TV Danmark to share its rights on such a basis, and when TV Danmark refused, the ITC refused to sanction the broadcasts, asserting that free to air stations had not had a fair chance to acquire the rights in question. TV Danmark then sought a judicial review of this decision, and were successful in the Court of Appeal, where Kennedy L.J. accepted the contention that the broadcasting rights in this case were acquired in the context of fair competition and at a price that the ITC accepted was fair and reasonable, and that for the ITC to refuse to sanction a broadcast acquired in such circumstances would involve an excessive interference with competition policy.[324] Indeed it was also held that once the ITC found that the bidding process had been fair, it was not permitted to have regard to post-acquisition matters, such as TV Danmark's failure to share the rights with terrestrial broadcasters. Walker L.J. concluded that if a substantial proportion of the Danish public was being denied access

[322] Griffith-Jones, *op. cit.*, p.290ff.
[323] Lewis & Taylor, *op. cit.*, p.32ff.
[324] [2001] 1 W.L.R. 74, para.26 of Kennedy L.J.'s judgment.

to these events then "they were deprived by the refusal of the public broadcasters to pay the price in a fair auction process."[325]

The House of Lords reversed the Court of Appeal ruling.[326] It held that the clear spirit of the amendment to the Television Without Frontiers directive was to ensure that broadcasters would be prevented from exercising exclusive rights in such a way that a substantial proportion of the public in another Member State was deprived of the possibility of following a designated event on television. Hence the principal question to be addressed was whether such exclusive rights *were* being exercised in such a way in this case.[327] The House of Lords unanimously concluded that they were. It rejected emphatically the contention that the ITC's decision must be based exclusively on the question whether a fair public auction of the viewing rights had taken place. Rather, regard would have to be paid to the reality of the situation – in this case, the reality that public service broadcasters would in general be simply unable to compete with the subscriber channels,[328] in that what would be a reasonable price to one company would be unreasonable to another.[329] Indeed such a situation was essentially what the amendment to the Directive – created to protect the public against the operation of market forces – was designed to prevent.[330] Hence the Broadcasting Act 1996 and the regulatory scheme created thereunder did not mean that the ITC was bound to sanction the broadcasting intentions of the highest bidder in such an auction situation, nor did it create a legitimate expectation in the mind of the bidder that this would be the case.[331] Instead, the ITC could legitimately look to post acquisition matters, where such were relevant in the context of the regulatory scheme of the country into which the broadcast would be made.[332] In this respect, whereas the ITC was not bound by the Danish regulatory scheme, it was appropriate that it should pay serious regard thereto, in that the spirit of Article 3A envisaged a system of reciprocal enforcement and even harmonisation of the approaches taken in

---

[325] *Ibid.*, para.8 of Walker L.J.'s judgment.

[326] [2001] 1 W.L.R. 1604, [2001] U.K.H.L. 42 (July 25, 2001), Lewis & Taylor, *op. cit.*, p.32, "Listed Events Legislation – Identifying A Rationale", 8(5) *Sports Law Administration and Practice* (2001) 1, Harrington, "Fans 2 – Pay TV 1. Shock Result in House of Lords Final", 19 *Sports and Character Licensing* (September/October 2001) 7, Harris, "Transfrontier Broadcasting of World Cup Qualifying Games", 9(2) *Sport and the Law Journal* (2001) 100 and Casenote, 4(4) *Sports Law Bulletin* (2001) 1.

[327] Paras 33–34.

[328] Paras 35–36.

[329] Harris, "Transfrontier Broadcasting of World Cup Qualifying Games", 9(2) *Sport and the Law Journal* (2001) 100. Harris suggests (p.104) that an independent body be set up to determine the notion of a reasonable price – particularly in respect of the question of what a public service broadcaster should have to pay a pay-TV channel in order to share in its broadcast rights.

[330] Para.37.

[331] Para.38.

[332] Para.39.

the Member States,[333] where all entities seeking to broadcast in or into (for example) Denmark would operate under the same regulatory system.[334] The House of Lords accepted that the notion of requiring pay-TV companies to share such rights with public service broadcasters would seriously depress the value of the broadcasting rights in such events:

> "But that is a consequence which inevitably follows from the protection which the Directive was intended to confer upon the public right of access to such events."[335]

7.9.3 The FAI/Sky Television deal, July 2002

The significance of Article 3A of the Directive was brought into sharp focus from an Irish perspective in July 2002 when the FAI announced that it had sold the exclusive live broadcasting rights to the home competitive (European Championship and World Cup qualifiers) matches of the Republic of Ireland soccer team for the next four years to the SKY Television network. The deal was worth €7m and was said by the FAI to constitute good business that would secure the future of Irish soccer.[336] Public reaction, however, was vociferously against the move, which was seen as preventing the majority of Irish soccer supporters from having live access to such games.[337]

Reacting to the news, the Minister for Communications, Dermot Ahern promised to draw up a list pursuant to the Broadcasting (Major Events Television Coverage) Act 1999 of major sporting events which would have to be shown on terrestrial television and on a free to air basis, and he stated that the list would operate retrospectively to invalidate exclusivity aspects of the FAI/SKY contract.[338] Under section 2 of this Act, the Minister is entitled to

---

[333] Paras 41–45.

[334] Para.45.

[335] Para.40.

[336] See Menton, "Television Deal Will Get Ball Rolling At All Levels", *Irish Times*, July 13, 2002, O'Sullivan, "RTE Bid not in Ballpark Say FAI", *Irish Times*, July 10, 2002 and McNally, "FAI defends €7m Sky Deal for Soccer Ties", *Irish Times*, July 6, 2002.

[337] Ruane, "The FAI would seem greedier for Money than for Goals", *Irish Times*, July 12, 2002, Oliver, "Green Army Being Asked to Tune In, Turn On and Pay Up", *Irish Times*, July 6, 2002, Hannigan, "Supporters are Sold Down the River to Sky", *Irish Times*, July 6, 2002, Hannigan, "Sky's the Limit as the Fallout Continues", *Irish Times*, July 9, 2002 and Hennessy, "FAI/Sky: 1 Supporters: 0", *Irish Times*, July 6, 2002.

[338] See Cullen, "List of Protected Events to be Drawn Up", *Irish Times*, July 9, 2002, Hennessy, "EU Official says Sky Deal an Be Bypassed", *Irish Times*, July 11, 2002, Cullen and Donohoe, "Legal Battle now looming in TV soccer dispute", *Irish Times*, July 15, 2002, Donohoe, "Sky May Challenge TV Move", *Irish Times*, October 16, 2002, Hennessy, "Ahern to push for changes in FAI deal with Sky", *Irish Times*, July 12, 2002.

designate events as being of major importance to society which a qualifying broadcaster should have the right to broadcast,[339] on a live, deferred (or both) basis and in whole, or in part, or both.[340] In determining whether the event is of major national importance, the Minister should have regard to the twin questions of whether and to what extent it had a "special general resonance" for the Irish people,[341] and whether and to what extent it had "a generally recognised distinct cultural importance" for the Irish people.[342] Moreover, in addressing these questions within the framework of the Major Events Television Coverage Act 1999, the Minister is expressly entitled to take into account factors such as past experience of such an event, and whether it involved participation by the Irish national team, or Irish players.[343] The drawing up of such a list is also ideally to be carried out following consultation with both the broadcasters and the organisers of sporting events,[344] and in this regard, the three most powerful sports organisations in the country, namely the GAA (which already had an exclusive agreement with Setanta Sport as regards broadcasting of GAA games to England) the IRFU and the FAI had previously indicated to the Minister that they would oppose the existence of such a list in that it would represent an unreasonable interference with their bargaining power.[345]

Under the terms of the Act, where such a list *is* drawn up, and where a broadcaster acquires exclusive rights to broadcast a designated event, then it can not be broadcast unless it has been made available to a qualifying broadcaster on request and subject to payment of "reasonable market rates,"[346] which, in the event of a dispute, would be determined by the High Court.[347] If the broadcaster failed to make the event available in this manner, then the qualifying broadcaster could apply to the High Court for relief, including injunctive relief and a declaration that the contract under which the broadcaster received the exclusive rights was void.[348] In other words, in the case of a deal such as that reached between the FAI and Sky, the legislation targets the

---

[339] Under s.1(2) of the Act, a qualifying broadcaster, prior to December 31, 2001, was one who provided free television coverage to which at least 85% of the population had access, and since that date, one who provided 'near universal coverage of a designated event'. Under s.1(4), the Minister could, at the request of the broadcaster, resolve any disputes as to the meaning of "near universal coverage."

[340] S.2(1)(b).

[341] S.2(2)(a).

[342] S.2(2)(b).

[343] S.2(3).

[344] S.3. See also McNally, "Submissions Sought on TV Sport", *Irish Times*, July 20, 2002; Healy, "Forum Hears Case for Free Viewing of Big Matches", *Irish Times*, August 27, 2002 and Brennock, "FAI to tell Ahern of Sports Rights Concerns", *Irish Times*, August 13, 2002.

[345] See Moran, 'GAA does not want to be 'protected" *Irish Times*, 9 July, 2002.

[346] S.4.

[347] S.7.

[348] S.6.

broadcaster rather than the governing body. Finally, under section 5 of the Act, broadcasters under the jurisdiction of the state are prohibited from broadcasting events – designated by legislation in another state – into that state in a manner which deprives a substantial proportion of the public of the possibility of following such events.

Insofar as the Act is created pursuant to Article 3(a) of the Television Without Frontiers Directive, the legislation is unlikely to fall foul of either Irish or EC competition law and hence the Minister's decision, in August 2002, to draw up a list was also valid – albeit arguably a fairly spectacular case of closing the stable door after the horse had bolted.[349] It is, however, salutary to point out that there were four difficulties with what the Minister was planning to do in the immediate circumstances of the FAI/Sky TV deal.

– First, and given that the notion of designation of events is an exception to the spirit of EC competition policy, it is perhaps doubtful whether all qualifying matches for a major soccer competition could constitute "events of major importance to Irish society" even if they involved participation by the national team. Against this, however, the procedure for designation under the Directive involved submission of the proposed list to the European Commission, who in April 2003 announced its approval of the list of designated events, which included the soccer matches under discussion.[350]

– Secondly, it may be argued that the deal made by the FAI was in fact within the terms of both the Television Without Frontiers Directive and the Broadcasting (Major Events Television Coverage) Act, in that apart from selling the rights to live coverage to SKY, it had also sold the right to show deferred coverage of the games (one hour after they ended) to the terrestrial TV3 station.

– Thirdly, and most importantly, however, section 4 of the Act refers to a situation "Where a broadcaster ... acquires exclusive rights to broadcast *a designated event*", a provision which, it is submitted, implies that the restriction on the actions of the governing body cannot apply retrospectively

---

[349] Much criticism was levelled at the Irish government for what was perceived as its failure to protect major sporting events in Ireland by drawing up a "protected" list *before* a contract of this nature was concluded between a sports governing body and a TV Network. See Hennessy, "Tough Stance in FAI Deal only Comes During Extra Time", *Irish Times*, July 15, 2002 and Donohoe, "Taoiseach Criticised over Sky Agreement", *Irish Times*, October 17, 2002. In fact within the EU only five states – Austria, Denmark, Britain, Germany and Italy – had at this stage drawn up lists of this kind.

[350] See Beesly, "Minister Acts on Live Irish Soccer Coverage", *Irish Times*, February 28, 2003. Moreover, under the Directive, the Irish government was obliged – even before transferring the matter to the EU – to publish in national newspapers the names of the events it was designating and to invite submissions from the public in respect of the same.

from the date of the designation, or put another way, that the event acquired by the broadcaster must at the time of acquisition be a designated event.

– Finally, it is entirely arguable that even if the retrospective effect of the list were accepted, it still ought not to have affected the July 2002 deal in that BskyB is not a broadcaster based in Ireland, and hence would not be subject to regulation by the Irish authorities.[351] On the other hand the House of Lords precedent in *TV Danmark*, would surely suggest that should such a list have been in place, the ITC would have been unlikely to sanction any broadcast made by Sky TV into Ireland of a designated event.

In any event, following a consultation process in August 2002, the Minister produced a list of events that were to be designated under the Act. More generally, and in response to issues that had arisen during the consultation process, the Broadcasting (Major Events Television Coverage) (Amendment) Act 2003 was enacted and had the effect of strengthening the protection afforded under the 1999 act as well as introducing one important innovation.

Under section 4 of the 2003 Act, where an event has been designated under section 2 of the 1999 Act and if within 56 days (or any greater or lesser period determined by the Minister) before the event, the event organiser has not made an agreement with a qualifying broadcaster to televise the event on a free to air basis, then a qualifying broadcaster may apply to the High Court for an order obliging the event organiser to give rights to the qualifying broadcaster to provide such coverage on terms fixed by the High Court (which would appear to equate to reasonable market rates)[352] or, if appropriate, by an arbitrator.[353] Nor is there anything in the Act to suggest that such an application may not be made where the event organiser has already come to an agreement with a non-qualified broadcaster. Alternatively in such a situation, where a qualifying broadcaster makes no such application, the event organiser may himself apply to the High Court for an order inviting qualifying broadcasters to make such an application. Should more than one qualifying broadcaster · make such an application, then the event organiser may decide to which of them it will give the rights.[354]

Importantly in respect of the FAI/SKY TV contract, the Act provides both for the possibility of a High Court order being made adjusting the terms of an

---

[351] The Minister for Communications has intimated that during the Irish Presidency of the European Union (from January 2004) the Television Without Frontiers Directive will be amended to enable foreign satellite broadcasters to be brought within the parameters of the Irish broadcasting rules. See Smyth, "Government to Regulate BskyB from Next July", *Irish Times*, March 14, 2003 and "Ahern Pledges Regulation of Satellite Broadcasters", *Irish Times*, August 20, 2003.

[352] S.4(1)(a).

[353] S.4(4).

[354] S.4(8).

existing agreement or arrangement between the event organiser and a non-qualifying broadcaster,[355] and also in such circumstances, for the High Court to decide to whom and in what proportion the revenue gained from the sale of the broadcasting rights at reasonable market rates to a designated broadcaster should be paid.[356] We would submit, however, that these provisions do not necessarily validate what happened in this case. The language of section 4 (10), which permits the High Court to "adjust an existing agreement or arrangement ...". should be taken as referring to a situation where the agreement existed prior to the application to the High Court under section 4(1) of the Act, and not to a situation where the agreement existed prior to the designation of the events in question (or indeed prior to the enactment of this legislation). The alternative would arguably fall foul of the constitutional prohibition on legislation with retrospective effect.

Significantly, section 5 of the Act provides for the possibility, where an event organiser has agreed to sell an event to a qualifying broadcaster, that an arbitrator be appointed for the purpose of fixing reasonable market rates for the acquisition of the relevant broadcasting rights in the event. In determining such reasonable market rates the arbitrator (or where appropriate the High Court) should consider *inter alia*:

– the previous fees for the event or similar events;

– the time of day at which the event will be covered live;

– the period for which rights are offered;

– the revenue potential of live or deferred coverage of the event;

– the purposes and spirit of Article 3(a) of the Television Without Frontiers Directive;

– other relevant matters.[357]

Finally under section 9 of the Act, the Minister is required to undertake a periodic review of the list of designated events. The first such review should occur within three years of the passing of the Act and all subsequent reviews should occur within three years of the preceding review. As to the present situation, the current list of designated events is contained in the Broadcasting (Major Events Television Coverage) Act 1999 (Designation of Major Events) Order 2003.[358] Under this Order, the following events are designated as being required to be shown live by a qualifying broadcaster:

---

[355] S.4(10).
[356] S.4(11).
[357] S.6.
[358] S.I. No. 99 of 2003 (March 13, 2003).

- The Summer Olympic Games.

- The All Ireland senior hurling and football finals.

- Ireland's home and away qualifying games in the European Football Championships and FIFA World Cup tournaments and also Ireland's games (if any) in the finals of such tournaments. In addition, the opening games, semi-finals and finals of such tournaments.

- Ireland's games in the Rugby World Cup finals tournament.

- The Irish Grand National and the Irish Derby.

- The Nations' Cup at the Dublin Horse Show.

Surprisingly in this list there is no mention of the Irish Open Golf Championship, any League of Ireland football matches, any rugby matches involving Irish rugby teams in the Celtic league or the Heineken European Cup, the Dublin City Marathon, the Irish Masters snooker championship and so on. Under the Order, Ireland's games in the Six Nations Rugby Football Championships are, however, listed as events for which a qualifying broadcaster must be given the right (at least) to provide coverage on a deferred basis.

As a postscript to the events surrounding the FAI/Sky contract, it should be noted that the agreement between Sky and the FAI was eventually amended (with the issue being settled before RTÉ's application to the High Court under section 4 of the 2003 Act was heard). Under the amended contract Sky was awarded joint rights (with RTÉ) to show all of Ireland's remaining European Championship games, (in an overall deal worth €5.5m to the FAI) and an ongoing exclusive right to Irish friendly internationals.[359]

7.9.4 The Broadcasting Commission of Ireland Codes of Practice

Finally, it is necessary for us to consider the Broadcasting Commission of Ireland Codes of Practice in respect of advertising and sponsorship. These codes, were created by the Minister for Arts, Culture and the Gaeltacht in 1995 and amended in 1999, pursuant to section 4(1) of the Broadcasting Act 1990 and cover all advertisements and sponsorship on Television and Radio. For present purposes, whereas they only cover these media, nonetheless they have the potential to impact strongly in the areas already discussed in this chapter.

---

[359] See Hennessy, "RTE deal worth €5.5m to FAI", *Irish Times*, May 28, 2003, Hannigan, "RTE Secures Deal to Show Irish Games Live", *Irish Times*, May 28, 2003, Beesly, "No Compensation for FAI over Broadcast Deal, says Minister", *Irish Times*, May 24, 2003. The FAI was unwilling to reveal how much of the €5.5 million was paid by RTÉ.

Under the terms of the codes, all broadcast advertising should be "legal, honest, decent and truthful"[360] and the terms of the codes are to be applied in the spirit as well as in the letter.[361] Importantly, from the perspective of the individual sportsperson who does not authorise his image or name to be used in connection with a product, the code prohibits situations where living individuals are portrayed or referred to in advertisements without their permission.[362] Indeed more generally it is provided that "Advertisements shall not be misleading or shall not prejudice the interests of the consumer."[363]

Finally in terms of the impact of advertising and sponsorship, the codes insist that the editorial autonomy in respect of any television or radio programme should not be compromised by the presence of sponsorship[364] or advertisements.[365] Thus in the case of sports programmes, whereas sponsors should be identified as such by their names and logos at the beginning and end of the programme, equally product placement and the display of advertising material in the studio during the programme is prohibited.[366] Moreover, broadcasters should ensure that neither the decision to cover sporting events nor the manner in which they are covered is in any way influenced by the presence of a sponsor or sponsorship.[367]

---

[360] S.4(1).
[361] S.4(2).
[362] S.16.
[363] S.6(1).
[364] S.20(2).
[365] S.7.
[366] S.23(4).
[367] S.23(5).

CHAPTER EIGHT

European Community Law Freedoms and the Business of Sport

INTRODUCTION

Of all the cases that have ever been decided in courts throughout the length and breadth of the European Union, perhaps the one whose name is used most prominently within the language of popular culture generally (let alone the language of sport), is *Union Royale Belge des Societes de Football Association ASBL v. Jean Marc Bosman.*[1] This case, which, generated what is colloquially known as the "*Bosman* ruling" may be regarded as marking the starting point of modern European sports law, but more importantly it transformed the manner in which professional sport is organised, not just in Europe but globally. It also represents the first major statement in European Community law to the effect that if sport is to receive the benefits of professionalisation, it must also accept that it is a business and is subject to the controls of what may loosely be termed "business law." In particular, sports bodies must regard sportsmen and women as employees or service providers (depending on the context), rather than as commodities.

Bosman is the most important in a series of cases in which a drama is played out, as European sport – organised on national lines, with national leagues and national teams, and governed by institutions that prioritised the interests of the sports industry above the interests of the sportsperson – clashed with European Community law – which exists to create a single European market in which classification of any industry on national rather than European lines is frowned upon and which affords both substantial and far-reaching protections to workers and providers of services. In particular, this law protects the freedom of individuals to provide services[2] and to establish one's business

---

[1] Case C–415/93, [1995] E.C.R. I–4921; [1996] 1 C.M.L.R. 645; [1996] All E.R. (EC) 97. Generally see Lewis & Taylor, *Sport: Law And Practice* (Butterworths Lexis-Nexis, 2003) [hereafter Lewis & Taylor], p.431ff.

[2] Art.49 EC provides that: "Within the Framework of the provisions set out below, restrictions on freedom to provide services within the Community shall be prohibited in

in another Member State,[3] and the freedom for workers to move without obstacles throughout the territory of the Union in order to engage in lawful employment.[4] Thus the cases, which form the focal point of this drama, are cases where workers and service providers seek both to have their status in this regard confirmed, and also to avail of the benefits that EC law provides to such categories of person. Moreover, the drama is played out against the backdrop of an organisational structure, which, in many cases, regarded itself as being somehow above the law.

On the other hand, and perhaps surprisingly, the judgments of the European Court of Justice (ECJ) in these cases do not assess whether another major plank of EU economic policy – namely the competition law provisions in Articles 81 and 82 of the EC Treaty – are applicable to this area. This issue is addressed in the next chapter.

The cases we consider deal with the factual issues of nationality quotas, transfer rules, selection policies, and equivalency of coaching qualifications. Yet in a broader sense, they involve far more than these specific concerns. In this broader sense they deal with the fundamental question of the status of professional sport, and whether the vestiges of cultural significance that it retains are sufficient for the law to regard it as being somehow special –

---

respect of nationals of Member States who are established in a State of the Community other than that of the person for whom the services are intended."

[3] Art.43 EC provides that: "Within the framework of the provisions set out below, restrictions on the freedom of establishment of nationals of a Member State in the territory of another Member State shall be prohibited. Such prohibition shall also apply to restrictions on the setting-up of agencies, branches or subsidiaries by nationals of any Member State established in the territory of any Member State.

Freedom of establishment shall include the right to take up and pursue activities as self-employed persons and to set up and manage undertakings, in particular companies or firms within the meaning of the second paragraph of article 48, under the conditions laid down for its own nationals by the law of the country where such establishment is effected subject to the provisions of the Chapter relating to capital."

[4] Art.39 EC provides that:

"1. Freedom of movement for workers shall be secured within the Community

2. Such freedom of movement shall entail the abolition of any discrimination based on nationality between workers of the Member States as regards employment, remuneration and other conditions of work and employment

3. It shall entail the right subject to limitations justified on grounds of public policy, public security or public health–
   (a) to accept offers of employment actually made,
   (b) to move freely within the territory of the Member States for this purpose,
   (c) to stay in a Member State for the purpose of employment in accordance with the provisions governing the employment of nationals of that state laid down by law, regulation or administrative action,
   (d) to remain in the territory of a Member State after having been employed in that State subject to conditions which shall be embodied in implementing regulations to be drawn up by the Commission.

4. The provisions of this Article shall not apply to employment in the public service."

somehow above or outside the law, and if so, to what extent is this to be the case. This is a question that is at the heart of sports law whenever and wherever it is developed. But it is in the ECJ, in the cases that follow that it has received most significant consideration. The result has changed European and global sport forever.

8.1 *Walalrave and Koch v. Union Cycliste Internationale (UCI)*[5]

The first case in which the European Court of Justice (ECJ) had to consider its relationship with sport was in *Walrave & Koch v. UCI*. The two applicants in this case were Dutch pacemakers who worked for professional cyclists. The job of the pacemaker in this context is to use "pedal-powered" cycles to create a vacuum through which individual cyclists travel, thereby enabling them to go faster in major championship races. In 1973 the UCI – the world governing body for cycling - introduced a rule saying that in World Championship races, the pacemakers had to be of the same nationality as the riders they were assisting. The reason for this ruling was that the UCI regarded the World Championships essentially, as being competitions between national teams, and argued that there should be no legal principle, which prevented a governing body from demanding that someone representing a country in such an event be a national of that country. On the other hand, considered objectively, if these cyclists were deemed to be "workers" for the purposes of the EC Treaty, then their freedom to work in the geographical territory of what is now the European Union was being restricted (admittedly by the rules of a private body that was *not* based in the EU) on the basis of their nationality – a practice that is anathema to EC law.

The pacemakers took their case to a Dutch court, where they obtained both declaratory relief and an injunction restraining the application of the UCI rule, with the court deciding that the rule in question violated Article 39 of the EC Treaty.[6] This decision was successfully appealed by the UCI, but on further appeal the domestic court made a request for a preliminary ruling, asking the ECJ to determine, *inter alia*, whether sporting rules of this nature were immune from the impact of EC law.

The ECJ, (largely following the opinion of Advocate General Warner),

---

[5] Case 36/74, [1974] E.C.R. 1405, [1974] 1 C.M.L.R. 320. Generally see McArdle *From Boot Money to Bosman: Football Society and the Law* (Cavendish, 2000), p.35ff, Parrish *Sports Law and Policy in the EU*, (Manchester University Press, 2003), p.85ff, Griffith-Jones *Law and the Business of Sport* (Butterworths, 1997), p.123ff, Gardiner *et al, Sports Law* (2nd ed., Cavendish, 2001), p.241ff.
[6] For convenience we will refer to the relevant Treaty provisions by their new (post-Treaty of Amsterdam) titles, despite the fact that many of the cases we will consider occurred prior to these changes to the Treaty numbering system.

found that the rule in question violated EC law, in as much as it restricted the free movement of the workers in this case on the basis of their nationality. In doing so, the Court made a number of points of critical importance to the development of a still embryonic European sports policy. First, and most importantly, it made it clear that sport *is* subject to EC law *when it is an economic activity.*[7] In other words, the business of sport can be divorced from the cultural phenomenon that is sport, and whereas the cultural importance of sport will, in practice, be a factor to be taken into account in determining the extent to which the law should apply to the business of sport, nonetheless in principle the latter is subject to governance by EC law just as is any other business. Needless to say, this is a most important statement and one which would have a marked impact in the years to come.

Secondly, the Court confirmed that organisations like the UCI, which were not based in what is now the European Union, would still be subject to the full force of EC law when their rules impacted within the geographical territory of the Union.[8] This is again of enormous importance. The UCI like many international governing bodies is based in Switzerland, and, being the international federation for the sport, it has membership from organisations based throughout the world. The ECJ determination in theory means that such federations need only ensure that their rules comply with EC law when they apply in the European Union, but the nature of international sport means that it is not possible for a federation to divide its rules in such fashion, and hence that the ECJ ruling applies to the governance of sport globally.

One final aspect of the decision in *Walrave & Koch* deserves a mention. Given that the ECJ had struck down rules restricting the capacity to compete in professional sport on the grounds of nationality, it had then to explain whether this meant that the principle that one must be of a certain nationality to compete for one's national team in international competition was thereby also invalid, and if not, why not? In other words, could, for example, the management of the Irish soccer team be found to be in violation of EC law if it refused to select an excellent French or German soccer player, purely on the basis of his nationality (i.e. because he was not Irish).[9]

Were such a fundamental principle of international team selection to be struck down, then this would render the nature of international sports competitions unrecognisable, and would considerably lessen the degree of popular interest in the same. Nor was there any real prospect that such rules would be struck down. What was important, however, was that the rule be

---

[7] Para.4.

[8] Para.28.

[9] For an excellent analysis of the ECJ treatment of this issue see McCutcheon, "National Eligibility Rules after *Bosman*", p.127 in Caiger & Gardiner (eds.), *Professional Sport in the European Union: Regulation and Re-regulation* (TMC Asser Press, 2000).

upheld on a basis that was sound and consistent, yet it is arguable that this did not happen in this case. The Advocate General took the approach that the rule in question was so patently not in violation of EC law that nothing further needed to be said on the subject. The Court, in attempting to find a more satisfactory basis for such an approach took the rather dangerous step of saying that international representative sport was not part of the business of sport – in other words that it involved the more esoteric concerns that we have considered – glory, patriotism, love of the game and so on – and could not be classified as economic activity, and thus the rule that required national teams to be composed of players from that nation was an exclusively sporting rule, and hence was not covered by EC law.[10]

Such an approach, it is submitted, is fundamentally inaccurate.[11] The point is that in professional sport, one is paid to represent one's country, and whereas the remuneration is not at the level one would expect if one was a major club player, equally the ECJ in *Bosman* emphasized that the mere fact that one is dealing with a comparatively small amount of money does not render the issue a "non-economic" one. Moreover, there was no need for the Court to have come to this conclusion. It would have been perfectly legitimate for it to have said that whereas the rule was economic in nature, nonetheless it was sufficiently fundamental to the organisation of sport that it could be upheld as a proportionate restriction on the protection of the free movement of workers. Indeed, as we shall see, later case law does take this approach, and further deems the proper organisation of sport to be a public interest concern, for which restrictions on the free movement of workers are justified.

Two final points to emerge from *Walrave* are of importance. First, the ECJ said that the rules in respect of free movement of workers had horizontal effect – that is to say that they applied not merely to public authorities, but also to private bodies such as sports federations[12] – a point of obvious importance in the sporting context, and which has been endorsed by the ECJ in all later cases. Moreover these rules were directly effective in the Member States.[13] Secondly, and despite the fact that the case had an obvious competition law component to it, the ECJ started a trend – which it has again continued in later

---

[10] Para. 8.

[11] See on this Griffith-Jones, *op. cit.*, p.125, Beloff et al *Sports Law* (Hart Publishing, 1999), p.87ff and Weatherill, "Resisting the Pressures of 'Americanisation': The Influence of European Community Law on the 'European Sport Model'", p.157 in Greenfield and Osborn, *Law and Sport in Contemporary Society* (Frank Cass, 2000), p.173. It should, however, be borne in mind that *Walrave* was decided thirty years ago, at a time when the commercial value of representing one's country was not writ as large in either the public or judicial consciousness as it is today.

[12] Paras 15–22. Parrish, *op. cit.*, p.84, Beloff *et al*, *op. cit.*, p.74 and Lewis & Taylor, *op. cit.*, p.433.

[13] Paras 30–34.

cases – of not addressing the competition law elements of the case, preferring to decide it purely on the basis of Article 39 of the EC Treaty.

8.2 *Donà v. Mantero*[14]

This second case in which the ECJ ruled on the legitimacy of an aspect of the organisation of sport, concerned a rule of the Italian Football Federation, which required players who wished to play professional soccer in Italy to have a membership card issued by the Federation. Such a card was normally only issued to Italians, with an exception being made in the case of foreign players who were resident in Italy, who wanted to come through the youth system there and who had never been a member of a foreign federation. The Federation had total discretion as to whether to grant a licence in respect of all other foreign players.

The applicant in this case was an agent who, as part of a scouting expedition for a small Italian club, had placed an advertisement in a Belgian newspaper seeking the services of Belgian players. When he sought reimbursement for the money he spent on this advertisement, the Italian club refused to pay him on the basis that the placing of the advertisement was a pointless waste of money, given that any interested players would be unable to play in Italy in the absence of the grant of a licence from the Federation. He then sued for reimbursement, and the case was referred to the ECJ, *inter alia*, on the question of whether the nationality requirements for playing football professionally in Italy were consistent with the Treaty. Specifically the domestic court asked for clarification on the following questions:

- Did the Treaty afford all the nationals of the Member States the right to provide services throughout the community for financial reward, and was such a right directly effective?

- If so, did this invalidate a rule of the kind drawn up by the Italian Federation that was at issue in this case[15] ?

In this case, both Advocate General Trabucchi and the ECJ endorsed many of the propositions put forward by the Court in *Walrave & Koch*, most notably the propositions that sport was subject to EC law when it constituted an economic activity,[16] and that rules which limited the capacity to take part in

---

[14] C13/76, [1976] E.C.R. 1333, [1976] 2 C.M.L.R. 578. See McArdle, *op. cit.*, p.36ff.
[15] See Parrish, *op. cit.*, p.88 for the view that these questions were disproportionate to the issues at hand and were formulated in a manner which would.suggest that the case may have been a set up for the purposes of admitting foreigners into Italian soccer.
[16] Para.12.

sport on the grounds of nationality were incompatible with the Treaty.[17] In this respect it was stressed that sportspersons are workers. Moreover this description would cover not merely professional sportspersons, but also semi-professionals and even amateurs, in circumstances where such amateurs provided services for remuneration.[18] Again the Court upheld the principled legality of a rule that permits nationality to be taken into account in respect of certain matches where this is for non-economic reasons[19] (including but not limited to situations where a national team is being selected) provided that it does not go further than is necessary to achieve the desired aim.[20] On the other hand, it seems clear that the ECJ will not rely on a governing body's assertion that a rule is of sporting interest only, but rather will analyse the rule carefully to see if it is genuinely inherent in the organisation of the sport, and whether it is necessary to achieve the desired aim.[21] Moreover, in this regard, the ECJ will look not merely to the purpose of the impugned rule, but also to its effects.[22]

8.3 *UNCTEF v. HEYLENS*[23]

The somewhat gentle approach by which the ECJ informed governing bodies that their actions were subject to control by EC law continued in the next sports related case to come before the court, *UNCTEF v. Heylens*. The defendant in this case was a Belgian national who worked as a coach for a French football club, Lille Olympic Sporting Club. He had a Belgian coaching diploma, but

---

[17] Para. 9.

[18] Para.12. Moreover, it would be for the national court to determine whether in any individual case there was sufficient economic activity at stake that EC law could legitimately be invoked; see para.16 of the judgment. Parrish, *op. cit.*, p.90 suggests that players who are not remunerated but can make money indirectly *viz*, through sponsorship, are not regarded as workers, nor are solo players who are not employed by a club. Such persons would, however, probably benefit from the protection under the Treaty of the freedom to provide services. See also Beloff *et al*, *op. cit.*, p.73 and Lewis & Taylor, *op. cit.*, p.434. This was the basis for the Court's involvement in joined cases C–51/96 and C–191/197, *Deliège v. Ligue Francophone de Judo et Disciplines Associees ASBL* [2000] E.C.R. I–2549.

[19] Equally it may be said that one of the weaknesses of the Court's reasoning in both *Walrave* and *Donà* is that it does not adequately explain why international representative sport may be regarded in purely non-economic or sporting terms when there are so many economic elements to this kind of sport.

[20] Paras 14–15. See Beloff et al p.86, Weatherill, "Do Sporting Associations Make 'Law' or are They Merely Subject to it?" (July/August 1998) *European Business Law Review* 217.

[21] Beloff *et al*, *op. cit.*, p.69.

[22] *Ibid.*, p.71.

[23] Case 222/86, [1987] E.C.R. 4097. See Parrish, *op. cit.*, p.89, Beloff et al, *op. cit.*, pp.88–89 and Griffith-Jones, *op. cit.*, p.133.

under the rules of the French football federation, in order to operate as such, it was necessary to have either a French coaching diploma, or a foreign diploma recognised by the French government as being equivalent to the French diploma. The defendant applied to the French authorities for recognition of his diploma, but this was rejected and, despite his requests, no reasons were given for this rejection. The French football trainers trade union then prosecuted both the defendant and his club for continuing to work as a football coach in France despite not possessing the requisite diploma. During the case, the French court referred the question of whether the French rule was compatible with EC law to the ECJ.

The ECJ accepted in principle the notion that the free movement of workers could be restricted in the interests of ensuring that workers were properly qualified to do the job for which they were employed. In other words, the requirement that workers from one EU state have a particular qualification which can be recognised by another Member State before they work in a specific field in that other state is a legitimate one. In cases in which the rules in respect of reciprocity of qualifications have been harmonised at EC level, workers with the requisite qualifications enjoy an immediate entitlement to work. Where this is not the case, however, the Court held that Member States are entitled to specify the level of knowledge and qualifications that are needed in order to pursue a career in that State.[24] In other words, the principle underpinning the French rules was valid. What was invalid, however, was the fact that there was no mechanism by which such rules could be reviewed, and in particular the fact that the unsuccessful applicant was not provided with reasons for his refusal.[25] This offended against the basic principle that restrictions on Article 39 must be objective, transparent and non-discriminatory, and must be capable of being tested to ensure that this is the case. Moreover, national law must provide a mechanism by which such testing can occur.[26]

Prior to the seminal decision in *Bosman* then, it was firmly established that sport is not above Community law, if and when it constitutes an economic activity. Sportspersons are not just celebrities or heroes but are also workers (if playing for a club) or providers of services (if not).[27] And the basic protections of Articles 39, 43 and 49 of the EC Treaty attach to these individuals. It is also entirely possible that the competition law provisions in Articles 81 and 82 of the Treaty apply to sport, although in the three cases discussed above the ECJ quite deliberately avoided considering this possibility.

---

[24] Para.10; see Parrish *op. cit.*, p.89. See also Case 222/84, *Johnston v. Chief Constable of the RUC* [1986] E.C.R. 1651, [1986] 3 C.M.L.R. 240.

[25] Paras 14–16.

[26] See Beloff *et al*, *op. cit.*, p.89 for the view that where a Community law right is at stake, the most appropriate mechanism to be made available may well be an application by way of judicial review – an issue considered earlier in Chap. Two.

[27] Generally see "The Impact of European Union Activities on Sport" 17 *Loyola of Los Angeles International and Comparative Law Journal* (February 1995) 245.

The point is worth making, however, that this new vista of sport as a business with workers and service providers was so radical, that it is unsurprising that the effects of these cases was not really felt within European sport especially given the comparative reluctance of the Commission to enforce the principles that emerge from these cases.[28] There was still a marked view that sport was sufficiently 'special' that it could and should be allowed to be effectively entirely self-regulatory. Thus, for example, in the English courts, the legitimacy of aspects of anti-doping policy (specifically of suspensions for doping offences) was upheld as entirely sporting in nature, despite the fact that such suspensions of professional athletes were plainly going to have a significant economic effect on them.[29] Moreover, it was clear that prior to *Bosman*, certain governing bodies, most notably UEFA, (the European governing body for soccer), regarded themselves as operating above the law.[30] Yet in *Bosman* – by far the most significant of all its cases on sport – the ECJ made its point in far stronger terms, and in doing so completely altered the manner in which sport is organised in Europe.

8.4 *UNION ROYAL BELGE DES SOCIÈTÈS DE FOOTBALL ASSOCIATION ASBL v. BOSMAN*[31]

Given the cataclysmic effect that the ruling in *Bosman* had on European sport, it is arguable that the case could have been avoided altogether, had UEFA displayed a little foresight in the 1980s and early 1990s in the creation and

---

[28] Parrish, *op. cit.*, p.92.

[29] *Wilander v. Tobin (No.2)*, [1997] 2 C.M.L.R. 346, [1997] 2 Lloyd's Rep. 296, [1997] Eu L.R. 265, *Edwards v. British Athletic Federation* [1998] 2 C.M.L.R. 363, [1997] Eu L.R. 721. See Griffith Jones, *op. cit.*, p.134–135, Beloff *et al*, *op. cit.*, pp.70–71, Lewis & Taylor, *op. cit.*, p.437, McCutcheon, "National Eligibility Rules after *Bosman*", pp.134ff in Caiger & Gardiner eds., *Professional Sport in the European Union: Regulation and Re-regulation* (TMC Asser Press, 2000).

[30] McArdle, *op. cit.*, pp.34–35.

[31] Case 415/93, [1995] E.C.R. I–4921, [1996] 1 C.M.L.R. 645, [1996] All E.R. (EC) 97. See Beloff *et al*, *op. cit.*, p.75ff, Lewis & Taylor, *op. cit.*, p.853ff, Ulhom, "The *Bosman* Case: Freedom of Movement and its Implications" (October 1998) *European Current Law*, Blanpain and Inston, *The Bosman Case: The End of the Transfer System?* (Peeters, Sweet & Maxwell, London, 1996), Weatherill, "Resisting the Pressures of 'Americanization': The Influence of European Community Law on the 'European Sport Model'", p.157 in Greenfield and Osborn, *Law and Sport in Contemporary Society* (Frank Cass, 2000), p.159ff, Vieweg, "The Restrictions of European Law", pp.85–89 in Caiger & Gardiner eds., *Professional Sport in the European Union: Regulation and Re-regulation* (TMC Asser Press, 2000), Morris, Morrow and Spink, "EU Law and Professional Football: *Bosman* and its Implications" 59 *Modern Law Review* (1996) 893, Blanpain, *The Legal Status of Sportsmen and Sportswomen under International, European and Belgian National and Regional Law* (Kluwer Law International, 2003), pp.9ff.

operation of its rules, and in particular of its rules relating to transfer fees for out of contract players and its rules setting a quota on the number of foreign players that could play for a club in a particular national league.[32] That it failed to display such foresight is entirely its own fault.

8.4.1 UEFA Rules prior to *Bosman*

UEFA and the Europe Commission had had disagreements on various matters since as far back as 1978.[33] There had been a number of different meetings on the above-mentioned issues and the Commission also threatened legal action. Eventually UEFA promised to make minor changes for the 1990-1 season and more wholesale changes thereafter. Nonetheless in 1989 the "Van Raay" Report was published, intimating that there was wholesale anti-competitive activity within European soccer.[34]

As mentioned, the focus was predominantly on two issues. First, the practice within European soccer that when a player's contract with his club expired, he remained the property of that club, to the extent that they could demand a transfer fee for him, and refuse to sell him to a club that was interested in him but would not pay the sum demanded. This had a detrimental impact on the player insofar as it restricted his choice of the clubs for which he wished to play, and also because the payment of such a fee meant that a club would be unlikely to be able to pay the player a substantial signing on fee. Equally the justification for such rules proffered, *inter alia*, by UEFA was that they provided smaller clubs both with an incentive to invest in the training of young players, and also with much needed revenue when a valuable player stopped playing for them and moved to a bigger club.

Secondly there was a concern over UEFA's rules insofar as they restricted the number of foreign players who could play for a particular team in a national league. Following a succession of proposals and gentlemen's agreements from UEFA and threatened legal action in response from the Commission, UEFA finally adopted a rule (known as a "gentleman's agreement") in 1991, which stipulated that from July 1992, whereas there would be no restriction on the number of foreign players that a side could *employ*, as far as European competitions were concerned (and in practice the rule filtered down so that it also applied within domestic leagues as well), a club could have a maximum

---

[32] McArdle, *op. cit.*, p.31.

[33] *Ibid.*, p.34, Parrish, *op. cit.*, pp.91–92. See also Miller, "Free Market Football" 1 *Sport and The Law Journal* (1993) 13.

[34] See Van Raay *Report on the Free Movement of Professional Footballers, 1989*, European Parliament Committee on Legal Affairs and Citizens' Rights. DocA–0415/88. See McArdle, *op. cit.*, p.35.

of four foreigners per squad for any game but could only play three at any one time.[35] In addition a club could field two 'assimilated players' that is to say, players who had played in the country for five years, including three years in junior teams. This rule became colloquially referred to as the "3+2" rule. The Commission appears to have given some level of endorsement to these rules – a fact which, as Parrish notes, may have furthered the confusion that existed as to the precise nature of the relationship between EC law and sport.[36]

8.4.2 The facts of Bosman[37]

In 1986 Jean Marc Bosman – a Belgian soccer player – signed terms with the well-known Belgian soccer team, Standard Liege. In 1988 he joined a smaller club SA Royal Club Liegois for two years on a salary of BFr120,000. In 1990 just before this deal was due to expire he was offered a one-year deal on BFr30,000 – the lowest wages legal in Belgium. He refused to sign this deal and was placed on a transfer list. Under existing Belgian rules, he had a month at the end of the domestic season in which he could move to another club against the wishes of his existing club. In such cases the Belgian FA would determine the fee to be paid, thereby preventing a player's club from effectively stymieing the deal by asking for a ridiculous transfer fee. In his case, the fee was calculated at BFr12 million – a figure that no Belgian club would pay for the services of a player who was by no means one of the stars of Belgian, let alone European football.

Eventually, Bosman negotiated a deal with a small French club, US Dunkerque, under which they would pay in the region of one and a quarter million Belgian francs for him for a one-year deal, or six million Belgian francs for a permanent deal. His old club – Liegois – doubted that the French club could raise the necessary cash, so they did not apply for the necessary clearance certificate to allow Bosman to move countries. On this basis, the deal collapsed and Bosman was suspended in accordance with Belgian FA rules. He then went to the Belgian courts and sought an order compelling his club to pay him his salary while he sought a new club, and also prohibiting the club from seeking a transfer fee for him. Various hearings of the matter took place in which Bosman sought an array of reliefs, and also petitioned the courts to make an Article 234 reference to the ECJ to check the compatibility with the EC Treaty of the UEFA rules under discussion. Finally, in June 1992 the Belgian

---

[35] See McArdle, *op. cit.*, p.35 for an instance of a match where a team started with three foreigners and then brought on a further foreign player as a substitute thereby contravening UEFA rules.

[36] Parrish, *op. cit.*, p.92.

[37] See paras 6–24 inclusive of the ECJ judgment. See also Parrish, *op. cit.*, pp.92–94 and McArdle, *op. cit.*, p.39ff.

Court of Appeal made an Article 234 reference asking the court to rule on the legitimacy both of the nationality quota rules and also the rules whereby a club could seek a transfer fee for a player who was out of contract.

8.4.3 The judgment of the European Court of Justice in *Bosman*

8.4.3.1 The application of Article 39 to this case

Unsurprisingly, UEFA's defence hinged, *inter alia*, on a claim that this was not a case to which EC law applied. There were a number of aspects to this defence. First, UEFA claimed that the EU institutions had always respected the autonomy of sport,[38] and for the Court to find against UEFA in respect of its transfer rules would severely affect the whole organisation of sport in Europe.[39] Thus the Court should show restraint by refusing to apply EC law in this context. The Court rejected this, (and also the German government's claim that sport was a matter of culture rather than a business)[40] invoking the *Walrave/Donà* logic that, however self-regulating, sport as an economic activity would come under the jurisdiction of the EU.[41] Moreover, it reiterated the point that the EC law rules that would apply would have horizontal effect, such that they could be invoked against a body other than a state body.[42] The Court stressed that if its decision would have significant effects on the organisation of football in Europe, then whereas this might at best be relevant in determining whether the temporal effect of its judgment should be limited, it was not capable of diminishing the objective character of the law, or restricting its application.[43]

The Court also rejected the argument that the impugned rules should be deemed to be legitimate under EC law insofar as they specifically provided that the relationship between two clubs under such rules could not be used to exercise an economic influence over the player concerned. The Court made the point that – whatever about the theory behind such rules – the reality was that they would generate such an economic influence.[44] In the present case, moreover, this economic activity severely restricted a Belgian worker's capacity

---

[38] Para.71.
[39] Similarly the German Government (para.72) argued that because of subsidiarity, the Court should limit its findings to what was strictly necessary in the case.
[40] Paras 72 and 78.
[41] Para.73.
[42] Para.82.
[43] Para.77.
[44] Para.101. See Griffith Jones, *op. cit.*, p.126ff. The ECJ also rejected an argument that the rules were necessary to protect the rights of the clubs to freedom of association, paras 79–80. See Griffith-Jones, *op. cit.*, p.128.

to pursue his trade.[45] Similarly, the Court rejected the argument that this was not properly a free movement of workers issue in that the transfer rules involved merely a relationship between clubs. As it pointed out the transfer rules also impinged on the relationship between club and player – in that here they were preventing Mr. Bosman from changing clubs.[46]

UEFA further argued that even if sport was to be seen as subject to EU law, this should only apply when big business was at stake. Put simply, and in the football context, EU law should only apply in the case of major European soccer clubs and not to small clubs like Liegois. Quite rightly, the ECJ rejected this claim pointing out that once sport was deemed to be an economic activity, the level of profit to be made from such activity was immaterial.[47] On all these bases, the ECJ accordingly found that Article 39 did apply to this case. It then proceeded to consider whether the rules under discussion were in conflict with this provision.

8.4.3.2 The transfer fee rule

The ECJ felt that any rules that would preclude or deter an out of contract professional footballer and national of one Member State from leaving his country of origin to play in another Member State constituted an obstacle to the free movement of that worker.[48] The Court reached this conclusion despite the fact that the transfer rules at issue were non-discriminatory and did not make it any more difficult for a player to move between clubs in different Member States as opposed to clubs in the same Member State. Much more important, so far as the Court was concerned, was the fact that the Belgian transfer rules operated to restrict access to the French marketplace for professional footballers. On this basis, the ECJ found that the rule in respect of transfer fees violated Article 39, in that it allowed a vendor club to restrain the actions of a former employee with whom it no longer had a contractual relationship.[49]

It was then necessary for the Court to determine whether this (admittedly non-discriminatory) obstacle to free movement of workers could be justified. In other words, the Court had to assess whether it amounted to a proportionate restriction that served a mandatory requirement of the common good as this concept is understood in a sporting sense.[50] URBSFA, UEFA and the French and Italian governments had sought to argue that such rules could be justified

---

[45] Para.5.
[46] Para.75.
[47] Para.70.
[48] Para.96. See also Case C–10/90, *Masgio v. Bundesknappschaft* [1991] E.C.R. I–1119 paras 18 and 19.
[49] Paras 100, 104 and 114.
[50] See Lewis & Taylor, *op. cit.*, p.443ff.

both by the need to preserve a balance between richer and poorer clubs throughout Europe, and also by the need to support the search for young talent and the training of young players.[51] The Court accepted the principled legitimacy of such arguments, but nonetheless rejected them as they applied in this case. It pointed out that the existence of transfer fees did not improve the situation in terms of the imbalance between richer and poorer clubs, in that in reality, it would be the bigger clubs only that would be able to afford to pay the transfer fees for the better players.[52] Thus the bigger clubs would still attract the best players, and the gulf between bigger and smaller teams would actually increase. Nor did such rules promote the training of young talent, in that it is impossible to know for certain whether a good young player will turn out to be a top senior professional, and hence the prospect of receiving transfer fees would not, in practice, amount to an incentive to teams (and especially smaller teams) to train young players.[53] Thus the ECJ deemed the rule in respect of transfer fees to be an unjustified infringement of Article 39 of the EC Treaty.

8.4.3.3 *The nationality quota rules*

The ECJ also decided that the nationality rules[54] constituted a fairly obvious *prima facie* violation of EC law, in as much as they decreased the chances of one EC national finding work in another EC State. Nor was it relevant that the rules did not relate to the *employment* of a player, but rather to the *fielding* of a player, in that the reality of the situation was that a club would only employ someone if there were a chance that he would play for it.[55]

The attention of the Court then turned to the question of whether this rule could be justified, and again URSBFA, UEFA and the German, French and Italian governments argued that the nationality clauses could be justified on non-economic or "sporting" grounds which had a connection to the common good.[56]

First, it was argued that the rules were necessary to ensure that spectators would identify with their local teams (especially when those teams represented

---

[51] Para.105.

[52] Para.107.

[53] Paras 108–9.

[54] The ECJ (Para.64) accepted that Bosman himself was not affected by the nationality rules in this case, but considered the rules on the basis that they could impede his career by reducing his chances of being employed or fielded by a club from another Member State.

[55] Para.120. For analysis see Gardiner & Welch, "Show Me the Money: Regulation of the Migration of Professional Sportsmen in Post *Bosman* Europe", p.110 in Caiger & Gardiner eds., *Professional Sport in the European Union: Regulation and Re-regulation* (TMC Asser Press, 2000).

[56] Para.122.

their national leagues in European competitions) and hence that the support for such teams and such sport would be bolstered, and also that such teams would effectively represent their countries in international competitions.[57] The Court rejected this argument[58] pointing out that there was no rule requiring a link between players and the locality in which the club was based. Yet if the UEFA justification were to be accepted, then surely a link between the player and the locality (being one reason why people would be drawn to support the club) would also be required by UEFA rules.

Secondly, it was argued that the nationality quotas were necessary to ensure that the international teams of the particular Member States, whose domestic leagues operated in accordance with such quotas, would have a ready supply of home grown talent coming through.[59] The Court rejected this argument pointing out that, in reality, most clubs throughout Europe were not focusing on training youngsters but rather were buying established domestic players. Moreover, the Court noted that, if the nationality rules were struck down, then the Belgian soccer team, for example, could be drawn from Belgian soccer players competing freely in all the leagues in Europe and this would serve to increase (as opposed to decrease) the breadth and depth of the talent on which Belgium would be able to draw in its international matches. The Court therefore used the argument put forward by the governing bodies as a double-edged sword with which to wound them insofar as it ultimately worked in favour of Bosman.

Finally, it was argued that the nationality rules were necessary to ensure that within domestic football leagues there is a workable balance between teams and to prevent the bigger teams from being able to attract all the top stars.[60] The Court pointed out that this justification was not particularly convincing, given that there were no similar rules in existence that would prevent the bigger clubs from recruiting the top domestic stars.[61] Interestingly, in his dealings with the case, Advocate General Lenz had accepted that there was a certain validity in the argument for the need to support the competitive balance between smaller and bigger clubs, but had said that the football authorities had not satisfied the burden of proving that the restrictions on foreigners represented a proportionate response to the perceived problems. Collective wage capping or re-distribution of funds might represent a more proportionate response in this regard. In other words the fact that the purpose of the rules might have been sporting in nature was not relevant when the rules had a significant economic impact and represented an overly restrictive means

---

[57] Para.123.
[58] Paras 131–132.
[59] Para.124.
[60] Para.125.
[61] Para.136.

of achieving the desired (sporting) objective.[62] The ECJ appeared to endorse this view.[63]

Finally, it is notable that whereas Advocate General Lenz found in the UEFA rules a violation both of Article 39 and also of Article 81 (dealing with competition law),[64] the ECJ, having found that the rules fell foul of Article 39, felt that it was unnecessary to go further and consider whether they also contravened Articles 81 and 82.[65] Equally, there is a strong probability that such rules do violate Articles 81 and 82:[66] indeed Advocate General Stix Hackl suggested that this would be the case in relation to Article 81 in *Tibor Balog v. Charleroi Sporting Club*[67] – a case which, somewhat unfortunately so far as the evolution of the jurisprudence in this area is concerned, settled before the ECJ was able to give judgment in it. The impact of this is discussed in the next chapter.

8.4.4 Conclusions on the *Bosman* case

8.4.4.1 Introducing the consequences of professionalisation

Thus the ECJ struck down two central planks of the transfer rules of a governing body that had long regarded itself as being above EC law (although as it had done in previous case law, it upheld the validity of rules imposing nationality restrictions where selection for national teams was concerned).[68] In reality,

---

[62] Point 262 of the Advocate General's opinion. See Weatherill, "Resisting the Pressures of 'Americanization': The Influence of European Community Law on the 'European Sport Model", p.157 in Greenfield and Osborn, *Law and Sport in Contemporary Society* (Frank Cass, 2000), p.164ff.

[63] Para.110.

[64] Advocate General Lenz was of the view (at para.262) that the nationality rules restricted the "possibilities for the individual clubs to compete with each other by engaging players." With regard to the transfer rules, he opined that they effectively replaced the normal situation of supply and demand, thereby preserving an anti-competitive environment in respect of the market for players and depriving the clubs of the possibility of "making use of the chances, with respect to the engagement of players, which would be available to them under normal competitive conditions." Although such rules might conceivably have been justified under Art.81(3) EC, they were *prima facie* in breach of Art.81(1). For analysis of Advocate General Lenz's opinion see "The *Bosman* Case", 3(2) *Sport and the Law Journal* (1995) 3, Farrell, "Bosman Opinion – What Does it Mean?", 3(3) *Sport and The Law Journal* (1995) 17 and McArdle, *op. cit.*, p.40ff.

[65] Para.138. See Parrish, "The *Bosman* Case and European Competition Policy" 1(5) *Sports Law Bulletin* (1998) 11.

[66] See Beloff *et al*, *op. cit.*, p.80–83 and Lewis & Taylor, *op. cit.*, p.859ff. Alternatively such rules might be seen as constituting an unreasonable restraint of trade. See Beloff *et al*, *op. cit.*, p.83ff.

[67] C–264/98, Opinion of March 29, 2001.

[68] Para.127. Generally see Arnedt, "European Union Law and Football Nationality

however, it did more than this. The reason why *Bosman* is so fundamental as far as European sports law is concerned is arguably due to its symbolic rather than its practical effect. Not only did the Court in *Bosman* confirm that many, if not most, aspects of professional sport (aside from the actual playing of the game) constituted economic activity, it also for the first time showed that it would be unafraid to regulate such economic activity – even in the face of pressure from the relevant governing body that the rule in question was a sporting one or was fundamental to the organisation of sport. The message from the ECJ was clear. Even if the rule *is* fundamental to the organisation of sport it will still be struck down if it represents a disproportionate interference with the provisions of the EC Treaty. In other words, there is a need for sport in Europe to re-organise itself in a manner that evolves into an appreciation of the consequences of its professionalisation.

It is important to bear in mind that, as McArdle points out,[69] the shockwaves caused by the decision in *Bosman* were not the fault of Jean Marc Bosman nor of the ECJ. Rather it was the fault of European sport, which sought the best of both worlds – the money that went with professionalisation and the autonomy that went with amateurism. *Bosman* is a message to European sport that in this respect it is not possible to have one's cake and eat it.

8.4.4.2 The effects on the football transfer system

In practical terms, the *Bosman* decision caused shock waves throughout the European transfer system,[70] in that it ensured that two planks of the UEFA

Restrictions: The Economics and Politics of the *Bosman* Decision" 12 *Emory International Law Review* (1998) 1091.

[69] McArdle, *op. cit.*, p.58.

[70] See Miller, "Beyond Bosman", 4 (3) *Sports Law Bulletin* (1996) 49. One response of clubs was to try to persuade their young players to sign long contracts in order that the clubs would get value from them. For a view that this might itself violate the young players' freedom of movement or constitute an unreasonable restraint of trade, see Beloff *et al*, p.94ff and McCutcheon, "Negative Enforcement of Employment Contracts in the Sports Industries" (1997) *Legal Studies* 65 and Caiger & O'Leary, "The End of the Affair: The '*Anelka* Doctrine' – the Problem of Contract Stability in English Professional Football", p.205 in Caiger & Gardiner eds., *Professional Sport in the European Union: Regulation and Re-regulation* (TMC Asser Press, 2000). See also *Schroeder Music Publishing Co. Ltd v Macaulay* [1974] 3 All E.R. 616. On the other hand if a player was induced by another club to breach his existing contract this might activate the tort of direct inducement to act in breach of contract. *Liverpool FC v. Middlesborough* FC, unreported Queen's Bench, May 21, 2002, see Lewis & Taylor, *op. cit.*, p.887 and *Crystal Palace v. Steve Bruce*, November 22, 2001, see [2002] 2 *International Sports Law Review* 81. Generally see *Lumley v. Gye* (1853) 2 E&B 216, *Talbot (Ireland) Ltd v. ATGWU*, unreported Supreme Court, April 30, 1981. Generally for analysis of the impact of *Bosman* on the movement of players throughout the EU see Gardiner & Welch, "Show Me the Money: Regulation of the Migration of Professional Sportsmen in Post *Bosman* Europe", p.107 in Caiger & Gardiner eds., *Professional Sport in the European Union: Regulation*

approach to transfers (namely nationality quotas and transfer fees) were abolished – albeit with great reluctance by UEFA and following a threat of further legal action from the Commission.[71]

8.4.4.3 Application to "in-contract" players

It is true that the *Bosman* decision only extended to out of contract players – that is to say it did not rule on the question of whether it was legitimate to demand payment of a transfer fee where a player was still in-contract. Equally there is a strong argument that if a player breaches the terms of his contract by moving to another club, then, whereas he should be required to pay compensation for the breach of contract, there should still be no question of his club treating him like a piece of property and selling him to a competitor.[72] This argument was nearly brought to a legal head in 1999 when the then Arsenal FC striker Nicolas Anelka insisted that he wished to breach his contract with Arsenal to join another club, and was entitled to do so if he wished.[73] Ultimately the issue was settled when Arsenal agreed to sell Anelka to Real Madrid[74] and replaced him with another young French striker named Thierry Henry – a decision of which, it is tempting to suggest, they are now most proud.

8.4.4.4 Application to domestic transfers

Similarly, the *Bosman* decision did not seem to impact on transfers *within* one country.[75] In other words, where there was no cross border element to the

---

and *Re-regulation* (TMC Asser Press, 2000). Thus they report that by 1999 – in the wake of *Bosman* – there was a 1,800% increase in the number of foreign players playing in the Premiership.

[71] McArdle, *op. cit.*, pp.46–47, "In the Footsteps of Bosman", 4(1) *Sports Law Bulletin* (2001) 2, Welch, "The *Bosman* Ruling and its Ongoing Implications for Professional Sport", 1(5) *Sports Law Bulletin* (1998) 8, Kranz, "Have German Courts Finally Learned from *Bosman*?", 8(1) *Sport and the Law Journal* (2000) 66, Rose *et al*, "Solicitors on the Ball", Vol. 95 No. 23 *Law Society Gazette* (June 10, 1998) 18.

[72] McArdle, *op. cit.*, p.56, Beloff *et al, op. cit.*, p.78. See also Caiger & O'Leary, "Whither the Transfer System?", 3(1) *Sports Law Bulletin* (2000) 13, Gardiner & Welch, "Show Me the Money: Regulation of the Migration of Professional Sportsmen in Post *Bosman* Europe", p.122 in Caiger & Gardiner eds., *Professional Sport in the European Union: Regulation and Re-regulation* (TMC Asser Press, 2000).

[73] See Caiger & O'Leary, "The End of the Affair: The '*Anelka* Doctrine' – the Problem of Contract Stability in English Professional Football", p.197 in Caiger & Gardiner eds., *Professional Sport in the European Union: Regulation and Re-regulation* (TMC Asser Press, 2000) and Tsatsas, "Anelka's Costly Walk Out Case Has A Hole In It", *Guardian*, July 23, 1999, Humphries, "Evils That Soccer Can Do Without", *Irish Times*, July 26, 1999, Brodkin, "Anelka Saga Unresolved as Sides Dig In", *Guardian*, July 28, 1999.

[74] Brodkin, "Anelka Saga Nears The End", *Guardian*, August 2, 1999.

[75] See Griffith-Jones, *op. cit.*, pp.131–132 for the view that even internal transfer dealings have a cross border element to them.

transfer deal, then it appears that it was legitimate under the *Bosman* ruling to continue to demand the payment of transfer fees. On the other hand, as we shall see in the next chapter, the European Commission steadfastly maintained that whether or not such "internal" transfers had a "free movement" aspect to them, they were undoubtedly anti-competitive for the purposes of Articles 81 and 82 and should be struck down on that basis. Indeed the point is made that one major difference between *Bosman* and the cases that preceded it, is the strength of the Commission's response to the decision.[76] In this respect, the previous attitude of UEFA, whereby it saw itself as being somehow above EU law became plainly untenable.[77] Thus as McArdle puts it:[78]

> "Since the Commission so obviously has the law on its side, the governing bodies have to do all the running if they are to persuade the Commission to treat football nicely."

As we shall see in the next chapter, by 2001, FIFA's transfer rules were substantially altered to address the concerns of the European Commission.[79]

8.4.4.5 *Application to non-EU nationals*

Whereas the decision in *Bosman* only applies to transfers from one EU /Member State to another,[80] equally it also applies to the transfers of non-EU nationals from a non-EU State into the EU where that state has concluded an agreement with the EU prohibiting discrimination on the grounds of nationality.[81] In *Deutscher Handballbund v. Kolpak*,[82] the ECJ considered a rule of the German Handball Federation (DHB) that required non-EU players to have the letter A

---

[76] Parrish, *op. cit.*, p.101.
[77] McCutcheon, "National Eligibility Rules after *Bosman*", pp.137 in Caiger & Gardiner eds., *Professional Sport in the European Union: Regulation and Re-regulation* (TMC Asser Press, 2000).
[78] McArdle, *op. cit.*, p.55.
[79] See Caiger, "Changing the Transfer System in Professional Football: Towards Contract Stability", 3(6) *Sports Law Bulletin* (2000) 1, Welch, "From Self-Regulation to *Bosman* – There and Back Again", 4(4) *Sports Law Bulletin* (2001) 14 and Miller, "Beyond *Bosman*", 4(3) *Sport and the Law Journal* (1996) 45.
[80] Beloff *et al*, p.77.
[81] *Malaja v. French Basketball Foundation* (2000) 3 (2) *Sports Law Bulletin* 1. See Parrish, *op. cit.*, p.98 for a list of non-EU states to sign such agreements. Parrish makes the point that *Bosman* also does not cover transfers of non-EU nationals from one EU state to another. See also Lewis & Taylor, *op. cit.*, p.439, Bailey, "Bosman 2" (March/April 1999) *Sports Law Administration and Practice* 11, Gardiner & Welch, "Show Me the Money: Regulation of the Migration of Professional Sportsmen in Post *Bosman* Europe", p.119 in Caiger & Gardiner eds., *Professional Sport in the European Union: Regulation and Re-regulation* (TMC Asser Press, 2000).
[82] Case C–438/00, (May 8, 2003).

after their licence number, and under which, no more than two players so described could play in a league or cup match. Kolpak, was a Slovak national employed as a goalkeeper on a handball team in Germany. As a Slovak national, his status as a worker in the EU was governed by the Association Agreement between Slovakia and the EC, establishing economic and political ties between the two entities. Under Article 38(1) of this agreement (which the Court noted, was directly effective[83] and also had horizontal effect – that is to say that it covered a decision of an organisation like the DHB[84]), discrimination on grounds of nationality against Slovakian nationals employed in the EC was prohibited, in respect of pay, working conditions, remuneration and dismissal.

The ECJ found that the rule in question violated Article 39 of the Treaty. In doing so, it applied the *Bosman* ruling to this case[85] because it involved a national of a country with whom the EU had signed a non-discrimination agreement.[86] Thus, for example, the arguments raised by the DHB in support of its rules were similar to those raised by UEFA in support of the nationality quotas in *Bosman*, and were struck down on the same grounds as those used in *Bosman*.[87]

Three final points should be made about the decision in *Bosman*. First, as Parrish notes[88] it is interesting that the court in *Bosman* struck down UEFA rules which were plainly non-discriminatory and apply across national barriers throughout the Community, despite the fact that, at this time, it had deemed the non-discriminatory "selling arrangements" of Member States to be legitimate under the Treaty protection of free movement of goods.[89] It would have been easy – had the Court wished to avoid the central issue in *Bosman* - for it to have upheld the legitimacy of the UEFA rules by analogy with these developments, yet it expressly chose not to do so.[90]

Secondly, it is significant that the ECJ dealt with these rules, and particularly

---

[83] Para.24.

[84] Para.37.

[85] Para.49ff.

[86] It should be noted that this Agreement only extends to workers who have been given permission to work in a Member State. In other words, Member States retain a discretion as to whether to grant work permits to such nationals. Paras 42–43. See Cox "Sports Law", p.461 in Byrne & Binchy, *Annual Review of Irish Law 2002* (Roundhall Sweet & Maxwell, Dublin, 2003). In any event, the Agreement which underpinned the ruling in *Kolpak* is no longer important given that Slovakia became a fully fledged Member of the European Union on May 1,2004.

[87] Para.53ff.

[88] Parrish, *op. cit.*, p.100 and Beloff *et al*, *op. cit.*, pp.76–77.

[89] Joined Cases C–267 and 268/91, *Keck* and *Mithouard* [1993] E.C.R. I–6097, [1995] 1 C.M.L.R. 101.

[90] Paras 102–103. Analogy was instead made with the decision in Case C–384/93 *Alpine Investments v. Minister van Financien* [1995] E.C.R. I–1141 paras 36–38, a case on freedom to provide services.

the nationality quota rules, not on the basis that they constituted discrimination, but on the much broader basis that they violated the free movement of workers,[91] thereby ensuring that a far more substantial number of rules could be covered, and hence that the reforms that UEFA would need to introduce would need to be considerably more far reaching than would have been the case if the only concern was discrimination.

Finally, despite the fact that it brought about a fundamental change in UEFA transfer rules (and the Court did not follow the suggestion of the Advocate General that the rules in question could be retained but reformed),[92] the decision is still appreciative of the fact that sport is special and deserves some element of leniency under EU law.[93] Thus for example, the Advocate General in suggesting a proportionate response to UEFA's concerns for the smaller clubs that were dependent on transfer fees, had intimated that a salary cap (an otherwise anti-competitive measure) might be a legitimate approach.[94] Similarly, the ECJ – foreshadowing the approach of the Commission in subsequent years – accepted that it might be legitimate for governing bodies to impose *some* transfer rules that promote competitiveness within the sporting market, including rules that lead to smaller clubs being financially compensated for their work in training young players,[95] provided, of course, that such rules are proportionate to the objective.[96]

Despite the fact that the Court did offer this limited degree of comfort to the sports world (and it should be noted that whereas the decision in *Bosman* directly covered only professional soccer, equally and obviously it applied to all professional sport (and indeed all professional activity in Europe), the case is still seen as one that is somehow "anti-sport," in as much as it strikes at the capacity of a governing body to have unfettered regulatory control over the governance of its sport, in a manner of which doctrines like restraint of trade

---

[91] Griffith-Jones, *op. cit.*, p.129, Parrish, *op. cit.*, p.99 and Lewis & Taylor, *op. cit.*, p.441ff. See also O'Keeffe and Osbourne, "The European Court Scores a Goal", 12(2) *International Journal of Comparative Labour Law and Industrial Relations* (1996) 111 at p.119.

[92] Para.239. See Weatherill, "Resisting the Pressures of 'Americanization': The Influence of European Community Law on the 'European Sport Model", p.157 in Greenfield and Osborn, *Law and Sport in Contemporary Society* (Frank Cass, 2000).

[93] Para.106. Foster sees this approach, whereby the ECJ would play a firm role in regulating the business of sport, whilst conceding its special nature marks the "genesis of the Court's attempt to formulate a policy of non-intervention in sport." See Foster, "Can Sport be Regulated by Europe?", p.43 in Caiger and Gardiner, *Professional Sport in the EU: Regulation and Re-Regulation* (TMC Asser Press, 2000), p.47.

[94] Weatherill, "Resisting the Pressures of 'Americanization': The Influence of European Community Law on the 'European Sport Model", p.157 in Greenfield and Osborn, *Law and Sport in Contemporary Society* (Frank Cass, 2000), p.164ff.

[95] Griffith-Jones p.130.

[96] Para.104.

had never been capable.[97] What is less well known is that subsequent decisions of the ECJ have been rather more sensitive to the concerns of sports governing bodies and (admittedly in cases where the rules in question were perhaps more intuitively acceptable than those under discussion in *Bosman*) have endorsed governing body rules that clearly restrict the free movement of sports workers in the community.

The reason for this slight shift in approach is arguably related to the era in which these cases were decided. *Bosman* was decided in the post-Maastricht Treaty era, where the regulatory machinery of the EU was engaging with practices that had never concerned it in the past.[98] On the other hand, the more recent cases were decided in the post-Amsterdam Treaty era. As we noted in Chapter One, the cumulative effect of the declarations on sport in both the Treaty of Amsterdam and the Treaty of Nice, as well as the Helsinki Declaration on Sport, is that sport is afforded a special place in the European Union, such that, whereas it will not be exempt from EU law, equally there is a commitment that in the application of this law the EU institutions will listen to and take on board the concerns of the sporting bodies. Moreover, as we shall see, in the sports cases since *Bosman* the European Court of Justice has attributed a new importance to the connection between sport and the public interest, such that actions taken purely in the interests of sport (the so-called "sporting rules") may also be seen as actions in the public interest.[99] In other words, these cases, decided in this dispensation, may well mark the beginning of a new and different EU policy in regard to sport.

8.5 THE *DELIEGE* AND *LEHTONEN* CASES

8.5.1 *Deliège v. Ligue Francophone de Judo ASBL*[100]

The plaintiff in this case was a very talented Belgian judoka (and former Belgian

---

[97] For the view that the decision is in fact supportive of the special place of sport within European culture, see Weatherill, "Resisting the Pressures of 'Americanization': The Influence of European Community Law on the 'European Sport Model'", p.157 in Greenfield and Osborn, *Law and Sport in Contemporary Society* (Frank Cass, 2000).

[98] Parrish, *op. cit.*, p.106.

[99] *Ibid.* p.103.

[100] Joined Cases C–51/96 and C–191/97, [2000] E.C.R. I–2549, [2002] 2 C.M.L.R. 1574. For an analysis of the Advocate Generals' opinions in these two joined cases see 2(5) *Sports Law Bulletin* (1999) 11. See also Foster, "Can Sport be Regulated by Europe?", p.49 in Caiger & Gardiner eds., *Professional Sport in the European Union: Regulation and Re-regulation* (TMC Asser Press, 2000) and at p.89 in the same book, Vieweg, "The Restrictions of European Law" Blanpain, *The Legal Status of Sportsmen and Sportswomen under International, European and Belgian National and Regional Law* (Kluwer Law International, 2003), p.19.

under 52kg judo champion) who had not, however reached Belgian Olympic qualification standards, and hence was not selected for the 1992 and 1996 Summer Olympic Games, the 1993 World Championships and the 1994 European Championships.[101] Obviously this seriously inhibited her career (or, in EC Treaty terms, her freedom to provide services),[102] and so she challenged this decision, and in the course of her case, the Belgian courts made an Article 234 reference to ECJ on the question of whether the concept of having such qualification rules as a pre-requisite to competing in an international competition, (which didn't involve national teams competing against each other) violated Articles 49, 81 and 82 respectively of the EC Treaty. Once again the ECJ ignored the potential competition law aspects of the case – this time on the basis that it did not have sufficient information before it to make a complete evaluation of whether the rules were anti-competitive,[103] but instead focused exclusively on the question whether such rules amounted to an invalid interference with the plaintiff's freedom to provide services throughout the community.

The ECJ, endorsed many of the principles emerging from the preceding line of case law including, importantly, the proposition that the free movement provisions of the EC Treaty applied both to public bodies and private bodies.[104] It also accepted that even amateur athletes could be regarded as providing services for the purposes of Article 49 depending on all the circumstances of the case (and this was a question for the domestic courts).[105] In other words in principle, Article 49 would have application to this case. The Court decided, however to uphold the impugned rules, deeming them to be inherent in the organisation of the sport and in particular of the relevant sporting event, in the sense that without some level of qualitative entry criteria, anyone could take part in the event, and this would render high level international sports competitions, such as the European Championships, World Championships and Olympic Games, completely unworkable.[106]

This result is not, perhaps, surprising, in that the plaintiff's case was surely one of the weakest imaginable. First, the rules were plainly non-discriminatory on the basis of nationality.[107] Secondly, the rules were demonstrably integral to the nature of sporting competition, in which it is necessary to attain the highest standards if one is to be genuinely successful. After all, if the claim in this case were to be accepted, would an athlete equally be able to claim, if she did not finish first in a competition, that the decision not to award her a gold

---

[101] Para.7.
[102] Para.14.
[103] Para.37.
[104] Para.47.
[105] Paras 28 and 59.
[106] Paras 64 and 69.
[107] Para.62.

medal would restrict her career and hence that the practice of awarding medals on the basis of relative merit in the event should be deemed to violate the EC Treaty? The proposition is a ridiculous one yet it is not all that far removed from the claim made by Ms Dèliege.

What is interesting about the case is that the ECJ – which made copious reference to the Amsterdam Treaty Declaration on Sport[108] – showed considerably more deference to the needs and concerns of sport than it had done in *Bosman*. Its sole caveat in upholding the selection rules was to require that the relevant national body must be able to demonstrate that it had objectively justifiable selection criteria and was applying them fairly.[109] Moreover, as Lewis & Taylor point out, the Court's approach is somewhat unorthodox in that it did not find that these rules restricted the freedom to provide services (which they undoubtedly did) and then assess whether they were justified (which they undoubtedly were) but rather used the fact that these rules were justified as a reason why they did not constitute an obstacle to free movement in the first place.[110]

8.5.2 *Lehtonen and Castors Canada dry Namur-Braine v. Fédération Royale des Sociétés de Basketball and Ligue Belge-Belgische Liga*[111]

The decision in *Dèliege* was swiftly followed by the Court in the *Lehtonen* case. This case concerned the legitimacy of having specific transfer periods in sport, during which players could move from one club to another and outside of which no such activity could take place.

---

[108] Paras 41 and 42.

[109] See Parrish, *op. cit.*, p.105 for the view that the notion of "objectively justifiable selection criteria" is perhaps open to interpretation. It might be asked, for instance, whether it is objectively justifiable for a team to refuse to select a player to travel to a sporting event, not because of his or her performance in qualifying heats, but because that player was known to be disruptive to team morale. Indeed it is interesting to note that Ms Dèliege herself enjoyed an unhappy relationship with the relevant Belgian governing bodies, representatives of which felt that she was undisciplined. See para.8. Generally on this issue see Foster, "Can Sport be Regulated by Europe?", p.51 in Caiger & Gardiner eds., *Professional Sport in the European Union: Regulation and Re-regulation* (TMC Asser Press, 2000).

[110] Lewis & Taylor, *op. cit.*, p.442. These authors suggest that the approach is akin to the "rule of reason" doctrine in competition law which is considered in the next chapter.

[111] Case C–176/96, [2000] E.C.R. I–2681, [2000] 3 C.M.L.R. 409, [2001] All E.R. (EC) 97. See Cox & Costello, "Sports Law", p.548–550 in Byrne & Binchy ed., *Annual Review of Irish Law 2001* (Roundhall Sweet & Maxwell, Dublin, 2002) and Foster, "Can Sport be Regulated by Europe?", p.47 in Caiger & Gardiner eds., *Professional Sport in the European Union: Regulation and Re-regulation* (TMC Asser Press, 2000), Blanpain, *The Legal Status of Sportsmen and Sportswomen under International, European and Belgian National and Regional Law* (Kluwer Law International, 2003) p.20ff.

Under the rules of the Belgian Basketball federation (FRBSB) there were three different transfer periods for the 1995–1996 season. First, players could be transferred from one Belgian club to another only before the start of the season (i.e. the period from April 15 to May 15, 1995). Secondly, under the rules of the international basketball federation (FIBA) players from the European zone could transfer from one club to another club (*i.e.* across national borders) until February 28, 1996. Finally, under FIBA rules players from outside the European zone could transfer to a European club until March 31, 1996. The express purpose of having limited transfer periods was to prevent the league being distorted by a situation where, during an end-of-season title battle, one team bought a number of strong players to cover perceived weaknesses in its play during the season, thereby giving itself a major competitive advantage against its opponents – especially if those opponents were not as wealthy as it was. Under FIBA and FRBSB rules, sanctions would be imposed on any team that fielded a player signed outside the transfer window.

In this case, the first named plaintiff, a professional basketball player had played for a Finnish team, which took part in the Finnish National Championships during the 1995–1996 season. He was then transferred to a club affiliated to the Belgian league on April 3, 1996 and was essentially signed in order to take part in the final matches of the 1995-6 season. On April 5, 1996 the FRBSB (who refused to register Lehtonen for the season) informed his team that he was not properly licensed and that they would be penalised should he be played in a match during the rest of the season. Undeterred, the club played Lehtonen in a match on April 6, 1996, and as a sanction, the FRBSB awarded the game to the opposing side. In the next game, Lehtonen was picked for the team but did not play in the match, but the game was again awarded to the opposing club.

Lehtonen and his team challenged the decision of the FRBSB, and during the course of the case, the Court made an Article 234 reference, asking the ECJ to rule on the compatibility of the rule on transfer periods with Articles 12, 39, 81 and 82 of the EC Treaty (although once again, the court resolved the issue exclusively on a free movement of workers basis). The ECJ, whilst accepting that its previous case law clearly demonstrates that EU law *does* apply to sport,[112] and that the free movement provisions that are relevant in this regard are also directly and horizontally effective,[113] again took cognisance of the Amsterdam Declaration on Sport[114] and spoke of the need to have regard to the concerns of sport as expressed by sports governing bodies.

---

[112] Para.32. The Court once again endorsed the proposition that nationality rules as they apply to the selection of national teams would be acceptable under the Treaty. See para.34.
[113] Para.35.
[114] Paras 32 and 33.

The impugned rules represented a clear restriction on free movement of workers,[115] but equally the Court felt that they represented a justifiable restriction, bearing in mind the need to protect sporting competition from being distorted.[116] Moreover, the ECJ agreed with submissions from the European Basketball Federation that its rules on transfer windows were sporting rather than primarily economic rules and were necessary for the running of the game.[117] Importantly, however, this does not give a green light to all transfer window periods – merely those that are necessary to ensure that the competitive nature of the league can be maintained. Thus as we shall see in the next chapter, the Commission approved FIFA transfer rules in 2001 which had made provision for the setting of restrictive transfer window periods.

The Court was, however, concerned with one particular aspect of the transfer rules at issue in this case. The Court stressed that rules of this nature must be proportionate, in the sense that they must not go beyond what was necessary for the achieving of the desired aim. Here the fact that the transfer window was greater for players outside the European Zone than inside it, appeared not to have any objective justification deriving from the needs of sport.[118] Equally, the Court held that it was for the national court to ascertain the extent to which there were objective reasons justifying the different treatment of European Zone and other players in this case.[119] Thus, says Parrish, this decision 'brings a degree of respite for sport without undermining previous sports case law.[120]

8.6 ALCOHOL ADVERTISING AND FREEDOM TO PROVIDE SERVICES

The precise impact of the *Bosman* line of decisions is, perhaps, still uncertain. The decision in *Arsenal v. Reed*, considered in Chapter VII, clearly involved an individual being prohibited from providing services, yet the Court held that intellectual property rights could be invoked to restrict such freedoms. It might also be argued that the proposed ban on tobacco advertising in sport, again considered in Chapter VII, is also a restriction on the freedom to provide services (and indeed is anti-competitive), but it is likely that any challenge to

---

[115] Para.50.
[116] Paras 54–55; see also Parrish, *op. cit.*, p.103.
[117] Para.53.
[118] Paras 57–58. See Parrish, *op. cit.*, p.105. It is notable that the Court did not assess whether it was legitimate that the transfer windows for players moving from one Belgian club to another were considerably more restricted even than this. See Foster, "Can Sport be Regulated by Europe?", p.49 in Caiger & Gardiner eds., *Professional Sport in the European Union: Regulation and Re-regulation* (TMC Asser Press, 2000).
[119] Para.9.
[120] Parrish, *op. cit.*, p.103, Bell and Turner Kerr, "The Place of Sport within the Rules of Community Law" [2002] 5 E.C.L.R. 256.

such a law would be justified by the Court by reference to public health concerns.

This question of acceptable restrictions on Treaty freedoms has arisen in the context of a challenge to a law that restricted advertising of alcoholic drinks at sporting events. At issue in *Bacardi-Martini SAS, Cellier des Dauphins v. Newcastle United Football Company Ltd*,[121] was a French law (Loi No 91/ 32). This law effectively prohibited the advertising of alcohol on French television. Moreover, under a (non-binding) code of conduct created by the Conseil Superior de l'Audiovisuel (CSA), broadcasters are instructed to take a non-indulgent approach to alcohol advertising at sporting events, whether those events take place in France or abroad. Thus where the law of a host country allows the advertising of alcoholic drinks at sporting venues but the transmission is aimed at a French audience, it is the responsibility of all parties negotiating contracts with the holders of transmission rights to use all available means to prevent brand names relating to alcoholic drinks from appearing on the screen. No such prohibition on alcohol advertising is to be found in the British Code of Advertising.

The well-known Premiership soccer club Newcastle United had agreed a contract with an advertising company DORNA whereby the latter was appointed to sell and display advertisements on the hoardings around the touchline at Newcastle home games. Under the terms of this contract, DORNA had agreed to provide the claimants with advertising time on an electronic revolving display system during a UEFA cup third round game between Newcastle and the French side Metz in December 1996. Shortly before the game, however, Newcastle became aware of these arrangements, and, feeling that they violated the French legislation (because the French station Canal Plus had bought the rights to show the game live on French television), they instructed DORNA to remove the claimant's advertisements from the system. This was impossible because of the closeness of the game, but the display system was instead programmed so that the claimant's advertisements appeared for only two seconds at a time rather than for the thirty seconds arranged. The claimants sued the defendants under the tort of inducing a breach of contract, but the defendants claimed that this inducement was justified in order to ensure that there was not a breach of French law, to which the claimants counter-argued that this was not an acceptable justification, in that the French law was in violation of Article 49 of the Treaty. On this basis, the English High Court referred the case to the ECJ asking whether, indeed, the French rule violated Article 49 of the Treaty.

The French Government (and the Commission) had argued that the questions referred to the Court were inadmissible, in that there was no extra-territorial application of French law affecting Newcastle United. Rather it was

---

[121] Case C–318/00 (January 21, 2003).

the French channel (Canal Plus) that would have had to answer for any breach of French law, and the appropriate jurisdiction in which such litigation would occur would of course be France.[122] Ultimately the Court agreed with this position,[123] pointing out that whereas generally the question of whether a case should be referred to the ECJ was one for the national court,[124] equally the Court was entitled to refuse jurisdiction over a case where it is asked to give an interpretation to a piece of Community law that does not directly impinge on the facts of the case,[125] especially where, in reality, the Court was being asked to assess the validity of a piece of law of another Member State.[126] Here there was nothing in the High Court's analysis of the matter to suggest whether or why Newcastle was obliged to comply with the relevant French legislation (as a matter of contract or otherwise),[127] and hence the Court did not feel that it had any evidence before it to show that it was necessary to rule on the compatibility with the Treaty of the relevant French legislation.[128]

A more substantive analysis of the compatibility of this French Law with Article 49 was provided in the opinion of Advocate General Tizzano in the joined cases *Commission v France, Bacardi France SAS v. Television Française TF1, Groupe Jean-Clàude Darmon SA Girosport Sarl.*[129] Again the question was asked whether these rules violated Article 49, but this time in the context both of a Commission investigation, and also of claims by Bacardi that the French TV Channel TF1 had obliged the Groupe Jean-Clàude Darmon and Girosport companies (both of whom negotiated television broadcasting rights for football matches) to ensure that the brand names of alcoholic drinks did not appear on television screens where matches aimed at the French public were concerned. This practice had meant that a number of foreign football clubs had refused to supply Bacardi with advertising space around their grounds. A case was taken to the French Cour de Cassation, which referred to the ECJ the question whether the French rules were in violation both of Article 49 of the Treaty and of the provisions of the Television without Frontiers Directive.

Advocate General Tizzano agreed that the rule was *prima facie* in breach of the Treaty, but also accepted that there was a Treaty based justification for it – namely to secure the protection of public health. The important question therefore was whether the rules in question were a proportionate response to this justification. The Advocate General noted that excessive consumption of alcohol could generate health risks and that the ban on alcohol advertising

---

[122] Para.33.
[123] Para.54.
[124] Para.41.
[125] Para.43.
[126] Para.45.
[127] Paras 49–50.
[128] Para.53.
[129] Cases C–262/02 and C–429/02, Reference CJE/04/15 (March 12, 2004).

could potentially reduce the level of consumption thereof. He further noted that French law did not seek to ban the sale or consumption of alcohol (in other words, the restriction at stake was a comparatively minimalist one), and, because of the expensive nature of image masking techniques, it would have been exceptionally difficult for television broadcasts to secure this objective through other means (for example by obscuring hoardings advertising alcoholic beverages). In other words, in all the circumstances the French measure represented a proportionate response to the problem as perceived. At the time of writing, the case is under consideration by the European Court of Justice.

8.7 Sports Betting and the Freedom To Provide Services

A further area in which the European Courts have had to consider the legitimacy of practices relating to sport where there is a clear restriction on some of the freedoms guaranteed by the Treaty, but yet where the restriction involved is arguably justified is in the area of sports betting. In *Questore di Verona v. Zenatti*,[130] the ECJ upheld the legitimacy of an Italian rule whereby there was a strict reservation of the power to organise betting on sporting events, such that it could only be exercised by certain bodies and under certain circumstances. Importantly the rule was (according to the Court) non-discriminatory in nature, and the Court (following its approach in the area of lotteries)[131] held that Member States would enjoy a significant margin of appreciation in determining the extent to which gambling and betting would be lawful and licensed in their territory. Thus the fact that Italy had adopted a licensing system different to that adopted in other states did not mean that the system was invalid. Rather the validity of the system would have to be addressed in the light of the objectives pursued by the national authorities of the Member State concerned.[132]

On the other hand in the more recent case *Criminal Proceedings against Piergiorgio Gambelli and others*,[133] Advocate General Alber opined that the Italian rules were in fact in violation of the terms of the EC Treaty. Although this was not a case about establishment (in that the defendants owned data transfer centres in Italy but were effectively collecting bets that would be transferred over the internet to an *English* bookmaker), the Advocate General felt that had this been a case involving an English bookmaker seeking to set up business in Italy, the Italian rules would still have been invalid, being framed in an openly discriminatory manner and not being necessary for the protection

---

[130] Case C–67/98 , [1999] E.C.R. I–7289.
[131] Case C–275/92, *Schindler* [1994] ECR I–1039.
[132] Para.33ff.
[133] Case C–243/01 (March 13, 2003).

of consumers and social order in Italy. The case was, however, about the freedom to provide services, and the Advocate General noted that whereas this rule was *prima facie* in violation of the Treaty, nonetheless it might possibly be justifiable by reference to an imperative requirement of the public interest (again related to the protection of consumers and social order). In this case, however, the Advocate General found that such an approach did not justify the impugned rules, both because English legislation already satisfied the concerns of the Italian authorities as to the need to ensure the integrity of the organiser of such betting, and also because there had been an increase in recent years in the availability of what were termed "games of chance," facilitated by the Italian legislature. In other words, whatever had been the situation in the past, there was now no longer a coherent policy of opposition to betting in Italy. Thus the draconian nature of the Italian rules, while possibly acceptable when there was a strong and focused policy of opposition to betting, could no longer be deemed to be proportionate, particularly in light of the level of restriction on the freedom to provide services that was involved.

Finally, on this issue, in March 2004, the Commission sent Denmark an official letter seeking information in respect of its legislation prohibiting companies with a gambling licence in a Member State other than Denmark from advertising, supplying, facilitating participation in gambling services in or into Denmark. The Commission expressed concern that this measure might violate Articles 43 and 49 of the Treaty, although somewhat surprisingly, the Commission did not make any reference to its competition policy.[134]

8.8 CONCLUSION

The impact of the free movement provisions of the Treaty on sport has thus been significant and high profile. Equally significant (if perhaps somewhat less well known) have been the provisions in respect of competition policy, as policed by the European Commission, and more recently, in Ireland by the Irish Competition Authority. It is to these rules that we now turn.

---

[134] DN: UP/04/401 (March 30, 2004).

CHAPTER 9

Competition Law and Sport

INTRODUCTION

It is arguable that the surprising thing about the relationship between competition law (in particular European Community competition law) and sport is that the former has not had more of a marked impact on the latter. Thus as we have seen, cases like *Bosman*[1] and its progeny were decided on the basis of the protection of the free movement of workers, even though they had clear competition law dimensions to them. Yet there is no doubt that sport throws up situations that may be classed as quite clearly anti-competitive. Put bluntly, sport, like any other business, is a market place, and the economic approach of the EU as well as individual Member States is to demand that there be fair, free and effective competition within this marketplace. Any attempt by a club, a government or a governing body to restrict these core tenets of competition will be a legitimate target of competition law, whether it operates exclusively within one state (in which case it is the target of domestic competition legislation to be monitored by domestic competition authorities) or whether it has a "cross-border" element to it, (in which case it comes under the jurisdiction of EC competition law to be monitored, for the most part, by the European Commission).[2] In this respect, the increased internationalisation of sport in Europe means that it is virtually inconceivable that an issue in respect of (for example) the broadcasting of sports events would ever be deemed not to have cross-border effects.[3]

In this chapter we consider both the nature of European Community and Irish competition law, and, more importantly, the principal contexts in which these laws will interact with sport. Before doing so, however, three introductory points should be made:

- First, this chapter is not intended to provide the reader with an exhaustive account of the nature and scope of either Irish or European Community

---

[1] Case 415/93, *Union Royale Belge des Sociètès de Football Association ASBL v. Bosman* [1995] E.C.R. I–4921; [1996] 1 C.M.L.R. 645; [1996] All E.R. (EC) 97.
[2] As we shall see, the European Commission in an attempt to "modernise" competition law has decentralised the bulk of its anti-trust work to national competition authorities, see Regulation 1/2003 (2003) O.J. L.1/1.
[3] See Beloff *et al*, *op. cit.*, p.143.

competition law. There are many books, which are available in this regard, and the reader who wishes to have a fuller understanding of the nature and likely future developments of these laws should consult these books.[4]

- Secondly, in as much as the majority of Irish sport is amateur in nature, it is arguable that competition law will have less impact on Irish sport than on other European sport. Against this, however, those aspects even of *amateur* sport which have a professional component to them (ticketing and television coverage for example) are still subject to competition law. Nonetheless, from an Irish standpoint, the development of competition law principles in the sports area has, in practice been an EU thing, and hence it is on this that we concentrate.

- Thirdly, what makes this area interesting from the standpoint of the sports lawyer, is the fact that sport presents unique business challenges and opportunities from a competition policy standpoint, *inter alia* because sport constitutes both a business and an important social possession throughout Europe. This means, as we shall see, that where the EC has applied competition law to sport, it has done so in a somewhat watered down fashion, cognisant (and perhaps excessively so) of the special needs of sport. On May 1, 2004, however, the Commission yielded up its monopoly over the granting of individual exemptions under Article 81(3) of the EC Treaty (in accordance with the provisions of Council Regulation 1/2003.[5] From that date, the enforcement of Articles 81 and 82 of the EC Treaty has been entrusted to both the Commission and national-level bodies. Deals between undertakings will be valid from the date of conclusion if they satisfy the Article 81(3) criteria (without the need for prior notification to the Commission) and the requirement of an administrative decision confirming exemption has been jettisoned. Whether the Irish Competition Authority (which is now entitled to apply the directly effective Article 81(3) to cases with an EC element which it is examining) will continue this tradition of applying competition law to sport in a diluted form is a matter of conjecture. But given the high degree of co-operation which will obtain as between the Competition Authority and the Commission under the new regime, there is

---

[4] See generally Goyder, *EC Competition Law* (Oxford University Press, 2003), Whish, *Competition Law* (Butterworths, London, 2003), Power, *Competition Law and Practice* (Butterworths, London, 2001), McCarthy & Power, *Irish Competition Law – The Competition Act 2002* (Lexis Nexis Butterworths, 2003) and Motta, *Competition Policy – Theory and Practice* (Cambridge University Press, 2004).

[5] O.J. 2003, L. 1/1. For an analysis of Regulation 1/2003, see Weatherill, *Cases and Materials on EU Law* (Oxford University Press, 2003). For a critique of Irish implementation of the Regulation, see Mackey, "Which Hat Should I Wear Today? – *Reflections on the Courts as Competition Authorities: Ireland's Implementation of Regulation 1/2003*" (Paper delivered to Irish Centre for European Law Conference on May 8, 2004).

no reason to anticipate any seismic changes in the way in which the business of sport is regulated by EC competition law.

9.1 INTRODUCTION TO COMPETITION LAW

For present purposes, there are two basic elements of both Irish and European competition law that are particularly relevant to sport,[6] namely the prohibition of anti-competitive agreements between undertakings and of abuse by a single dominant undertaking of its dominant position. We will now briefly consider the Irish and European Community laws targeting these two practices. Before we do so, however, some introductory points should again be made.

First, it may be difficult on occasion to determine whether what is at stake is an agreement between undertakings or an abuse of a dominant position by a single undertaking (or, in rare cases, the abuse of a collectively dominant position by a number of undertakings). So, for example, in the context of the collective sale of broadcasting rights by a single sports federation or organisation – dealt with in detail later in this chapter – it may be legitimate to classify such activity either as the actions of a single dominant undertaking (the federation) or, alternatively, as an agreement between various separate undertakings (the clubs affiliated to the organisation).[7] Although the separate undertakings involved in a collective sale agreement might also find themselves categorised as collectively dominant under Article 82 of the EC Treaty, this is an as yet unresolved issue which awaits exploration in the future jurisprudence of the European Court of Justice.

Secondly, the bodies that are subject to the competition laws in both legal orders are what are termed "undertakings". In this respect it is clear that an undertaking is any party engaged, even indirectly or tangentially, in economic activity.[8] Thus, for example, a non-profit making organization, which will normally not be targeted by competition law, will constitute an undertaking whenever it is engaged in economic activity.[9] Clearly therefore, given the amount of money involved in professional sport in Europe, there will be a myriad of occasions in which a sports body can be regarded as an undertaking for competition law purposes, be it a club or a governing body.[10]

---

[6] The prohibition on State Aid to undertakings which has the effect of distorting competition is considered briefly at p.434.

[7] See Beloff *et al*, pp.142–143.

[8] Joined Cases 209–215 and 218/78, *Heintz van Landewyck Sarl v Commission* [1980] E.C.R. 1325 [1981] 3 C.M.L.R. 134

[9] Case 41/90, *Hofner and Elser v. Macrotron GmBH* [1991] E.C.R. I–1979 [1993] 4 C.M.L.R. 306, Joined Cases 159–160/91, *Pourcet and Pistre v. Assurances Generales de France* [1993] E.C.R. I–637.

[10] See Parrish, *Sports Law and Policy in the EU* (Manchester University Press, 2003) [hereafter Parrish], p.117. See also Brinckman and Voloebregt, "The Marketing of Sport

Thirdly, at EC level, it was predominantly the Commission which both investigated and decided on the legitimacy of certain practices under competition law and which could, where appropriate, grant exemptions. As explained shortly, however, the Commission recently abdicated its exclusive competence in this area. It is also important to point out that decisions of the Commission may be appealed to the Court of First Instance and the European Court of Justice. In Ireland, the investigation and enforcement of competition law is entrusted to the Competition Authority established under the Competition Act of 1991. All Irish statutory competition law is currently embodied in a single consolidating statute, the Competition Act 2002.

9.1.1 Anti-competitive agreements between undertakings

Under Article 81 of the EC Treaty, all:

> "agreements between undertakings, decisions by associations of undertakings, and concerted practices, which may affect trade between Member States and which have as their object or effect the prevention, restriction, or distortion of competition within the common market"

are deemed to be prohibited. A similar position is reached in Ireland under the terms of Section 4 of the Competition Act 2002. Thus for example, the Commission has looked suspiciously – in the context of an evaluation under Article 81 – at agreements between public service broadcasters under which they offer a joint bid to purchase the rights to broadcast major sporting events.[11] Equally, there may be certain agreements between undertakings, which, while *prima facie* anti-competitive, nonetheless present no significant threat to competition within the relevant jurisdiction, and the ECJ, applying a *de minimis* approach, has held that agreements of this kind do not violate the terms of Article 81.[12]

Reflecting the fact that competition law is as much designed to protect the market and consumers as it is to protect competitors, both Article 81(3) of the EC Treaty and section 4(3) of the Competition Act 2002 recognise the

---

and Its Relation to EC Competition Law" (1998) *European Competition Law Review* (hereinafter E.C.L.R.) 28. On the other hand, as we shall see, if a rule is purely of sporting interest and has no significant economic repercussions, it tends not to attract the attention of the competition authorities. See Beloff, "The Sporting Exception in EC Competition Law" [1999] *European Current Law Yearbook*, p.vi.

[11] See later at p.451 for consideration of the Commission's analysis of joint purchasing agreements entered into by the European Broadcasting Union.

[12] Case 5/69 *Volk v. Vervaecke* [1969] E.C.R. 295, [1969] C.M.L.R. 273; Case 19/77, *Miller v. Commission* [1978] E.C.R. 13, [1978] 2 C.M.L.R. 334.

possibility of the Commission granting exemptions or the Competition Authority issuing declarations in respect of otherwise anti-competitive practices if there is justification for doing so and if the level of anti-competitive behaviour is not overly significant.[13] Under Article 81(3), the Commission was empowered to grant an exemption to an agreement, decision or concerted practice,

> "which contributes to improving the production or distribution of goods or to promoting technical or economic progress, while allowing consumers a fair share of the resulting benefit, and which does not—
>
> (a) impose on the undertakings concerned restrictions, which are not indispensable to the attainment of these objectives;
> (b) afford such undertakings the possibility of eliminating competition in respect of a substantial part of the products in question."

Similar powers are afforded to the Competition Authority under Irish law to grant declarations in respect of agreements or decisions or concerted practices in the same situation.[14]

It is salutary to point out, however, that the Commission's power to grant exemptions has been eroded in substantial measure as a result of the coming into force of Council Regulation 1/2003. The whole of Article 81 was endowed with direct effect from May 1, 2004 onwards (thereby placing it on an equal footing with Article 82 which the European Court of Justice declared directly effective thirty years ago) and no "prior decision" of the Commission is required

---

[13] In practice, when a notification for an exemption in a case with an EC element (as opposed to an exclusively domestic case) was pending, domestic courts tended to stay proceedings taken by domestic competition authorities and indeed, the European institutions recommended this policy. See O.J. C. 313 (October 15, 1997) and also Case C–234/89, *Stergios Delimitis v. Henninger Brau* [1991] E.C.R. I–935; [1992] 5 C.M.L.R. 210. Generally see Lewis and Taylor, p.339. Given, however, that the competition authorities and courts of the Member States are now empowered to apply Art. 81(3) of the EC Treaty (under the provisions of Council Regulation 1/2003 (2003) O.J. L.1/1), the need to afford priority to the European Commission will be obviated in most cases. It is important to point out, however, that when national courts or competition authorities rule on agreements or practices under Art. 81 or Art. 82 of the Treaty which are already the subject of a Commission decision, they cannot takes decision running counter to the decision adopted by the Commission (see Regulation 1/2003, Art. 16).

[14] S.4(3) of the Competition Act 2002. The practice of the European Commission – before the coming in to force on May 1, 2004 of Council Regulation 1/2003 – was for undertakings to apply for both a negative clearance (a decision confirming the provision does not fall foul of Art. 81 either because it had no impact on the market because of the rule of reason, or, in the sporting situation, because the rule in question was purely a sporting rule) and also an exemption (a statement that even if it did violate Art. 81 was still legitimate).

for an exemption under Article 81(3). Both the national competition authorities and the national courts can now apply Articles 81 and 82 in their entirety, including cases with an inter-state trade element arising under Article 81(3). Under the new regime, both the Commission and the competition authorities and courts of the Member States are obliged to apply the competition rules of the Community in close co-operation. Under Article 11(6) of Council Regulation 1/2003, the Commission has the reserve power to take over a case from a national competition authority, a power which is likely to be exercised sparingly and only when – in the wake of a full consultation – there is a danger that the competition authority in question will produce a result contrary to the well established principles of EC competition law. The Commission also retains the power to carry out its own investigations in accordance with Articles 17–21 respectively of the new Regulation.

In practice, what tended to happen over the last number of years, certainly within the context of EC competition law, was that the Commission favoured informal settlements of disputes whereby, for example, Commission officials issued undertakings with non-binding "comfort letters," which intimated that the agreement would not be found to be anti-competitive, but which were not binding on the Commission. These undertakings then proceeded with such agreements, secure in the knowledge that they were underpinned by such "comfort letters".[15] The point has been made, however, that the frequency with which the Commission resorted to informal settlements meant that there was a lack of any clear line of authority emerging from the its treatment of this aspect of competition law.[16] It will be interesting to see whether the landscape changes again in the wake of the coming into operation of Council Regulation 1/2003.

Linked with this, the Commission has also endorsed what is known as "the rule of reason" approach[17] to competition law, whereby certain measures that appear on their face to be anti-competitive will nonetheless be upheld on the basis that paradoxically they will operate in the long term in pro-competitive fashion. So for example, as we shall see, when dealing with the collective sale by a centralised sports body of the broadcasting rights to games played in a league competition, the Commission has intimated that despite the apparently anti-competitive nature of such activity, it does allow the centralised body to use the revenue gained to help finance smaller clubs, thereby ensuring that the gap between richer and poorer clubs is not so wide that there is in reality no genuinely competitive league. In other words, the measure, while anti-competitive in theory, may in the long term serve to guarantee that there is a competition at all, and hence is acceptable as far as competition law is concerned.

---

[15] Lewis and Taylor, *op. cit.*, p.344
[16] Kinsella and Daly, "European Competition Law and Sports", 4(6) *Sports Law Bulletin* (November/December 2001) 7.
[17] Lewis and Taylor, *op. cit.*, p.190.

9.1.2 Abuse of a dominant position

Under Article 82 of the EC Treaty, "Any abuse by one or more undertakings of a dominant position within the common market or in a substantial part of it shall be prohibited as incompatible with the common market insofar as it may affect trade between Member States." Similar provision is made in section 5 of the Irish Competition Act 2002. Under these rules therefore, two criteria must be established before there can be said to be a breach of the rules. First, there must be dominance and, secondly, there must be abuse.

9.1.2.1 Dominance

Dominance arises, according to the European Court of Justice, where an undertaking can act independently of the rest of the market and, thereby, has the power to hinder competition.[18] In this respect it is important first and briefly to consider the notion of markets.[19] Thus, the undertaking must be dominant, not from the perspective of the overall economic situation of the Community, but rather within the particular product and geographical (and, to a lesser extent, seasonal) markets in which it operates. So, for example, the GAA, which is not at all dominant in respect of the totality of sport within the European Community, is clearly in monopolistic control of Gaelic games in a "substantial part of the common market," namely, the island of Ireland, and it is within this product and geographical market that its position should be assessed.

In this respect, it will be argued (and has largely been accepted by the Commission) that because of their enormous and near universal popularity within Europe, certain sports, such as Formula One motor racing and Association Football, operate in a geographical market that is the whole of the European Union, but within a product market that is narrowly confined to their own sports. In other words, to take the example of an English Premiership soccer match, from the consumer's point of view, there is no effective substitute for this event (in that he would not be equally satisfied if the broadcaster replaced the match with, for example, a golf tournament or indeed a soccer match in another European league). Thus the relevant product market for Premiership soccer, is merely Premiership soccer. Equally, Premiership soccer is popular throughout the whole of the Community, hence the geographical

---

[18] Case 27/76 *United Brands v. Commission* [1978] E.C.R. 207; [1978] 1 C.M.L.R. 429.
[19] See the Commission Notice on Definition of Relevant Markets [1997] (O.J. C. 372/5, December 9, 1997) [1998] 4 C.M.L.R. 177. Under this Notice, the relevant product market comprises all products which are regarded as being interchangeable or substitutable by the consumer having regard to the products' characteristics, prices, and intended use. The geographic market comprises the area in which the undertakings are involved in the supply or demand of products or services and in which there is sufficient similarity between the conditions of competition.

market is the whole of the EC. And it is within *these* markets that the alleged dominance of the English Football Association will be gauged. On the other hand, it is possible that certain minority sports would have a more limited geographical market (in the sense that the two sports mentioned above are the only sports which enjoy consistent popularity in all areas of the European Community),[20] yet because of the greater likelihood of demand substitutability (i.e. an average consumer watching one minority sport might be equally happy to watch another minority sport) the product market may be greater than the single sport. This issue is considered in detail in relation to the broadcasting of sports events later in this chapter.

9.1.2.2 Abuse

The notion of abuse under Article 81 relates fundamentally to anti-competitive practices – in other words a practice will be abusive if it is also anti-competitive.[21] We shall shortly consider instances of such abuse. There is, however, one possible instance of anti-competitive abuse which may be of great significance to Irish sport and which will be considered at this juncture.

European Court of Justice (ECJ) case law has endorsed the notion that a dominant undertaking may be acting anti-competitively if it refuses to supply competitors with what are termed *essential facilities*, without which the competitor will not be able to compete effectively – for example where a company that owns a ferry terminal will not allow certain ferry companies to dock there.[22] By far the most high profile case in Irish sport of a sporting body

---

[20] See Lewis and Taylor, *op. cit.*, p.357. See, however, Parrish, *op. cit.*, pp.119–20 for the view that when dealing with ticketing, broadcasting and transfer regulation the relevant geographical market should be the whole of the European Union. Certainly the notion that viewers are only interested in the sports leagues operating in their own country (which never had any application in Ireland where the majority of soccer fans would be more interested in English Premiership than in the League of Ireland) is now outdated. See Van den Brinck, "EC Competition Law and the Regulation of Football Part 1" (2000) E.C.L.R. 359.

[21] Thus, for example, in the investigation into the control of Formula One motor racing by the FIA, the Commission found that there had been significant efforts by the governing body to use its regulatory powers to restrict access to the market of competitors. See also Craig and de Burca, *EU Law – Texts, Cases and Materials* (Oxford University Press, 2003), p.1006.

[22] See, for example, Case C–241/91P, *Magill v. Radio Telefís Éireann RTE* [1995] E.C.R. I–743; [1995] 4 C.M.L.R. 718. See also Commission Decision IV/34.689, *Sea Containers Limited v. Stena Sealink Ports & Stena Sealink Line* (1994) O.J. L. 15/8; [1995] 4 C.M.L.R. 84. Generally see Goyder, *EC Competition Law* (Oxford University Press, 2003), pp.305–308 and 316–320, Temple Lang, "Defining Legitimate Competition: Companies Duties to Supply Competitors in Access to Essential Facilities" (1994) 18 Fordham International L.J. 437, Dougherty, "Just What are Essential Facilities?" (2001) 38 C.M.L.R.ev. 397, Stothers, "Refusal to Supply as Abuse of a Dominant Position: Essential Facilities in the European Union" (2001) E.C.L.R.. 256.

refusing in principle to allow competitors to use its facilities is the GAA's refusal under Rule 42 of its Rulebook to allow certain sports, and specifically soccer and rugby, to be played in Croke Park, the headquarters of the GAA and the only stadium in Ireland that is capable of hosting the kinds of numbers of people who wish to attend major matches in these sports.[23] It is also unquestionably the case that, as far as the Irish television market is concerned, Gaelic games, rugby and soccer are the major competitors both for participants and for television audiences (although it is accepted that for long periods of the year the highest profile games in these sports are not played at the same time). Moreover, it seems certain that the FAI and IRFU would like the opportunity to have major international soccer or rugby matches played in Croke Park – a desire that will take on a new urgency in the near future with the announcement in January 2004 by the Minister for Sport that Lansdowne Road – the major home stadium for both these sports – is to be redeveloped and, hence, that a new location capable (in the context of soccer) of *seating* large numbers of supporters must temporarily be found for international rugby and soccer matches.[24]

In this respect, it is submitted that there is a strong argument that, if the IRFU and FAI formally requested permission from the GAA to use Croke Park as a venue for their respective sports, express reliance by the GAA on Rule 42 might well be construed as an active refusal of the use of a essential facility and hence, an abuse of a dominant position which violates Article 82 of EC Treaty (because of the cross-border nature of sports broadcasting) and also section 5 of the Competition Act 2002. It also arguable that the existence of Rule 42 would, in itself, suffice to trigger the operation of the essential facilities doctrine. After all, it is unlikely that the FAI and the IRFU would be prepared to go "cap in hand" to the GAA to ask it to repeal Rule 42. Whether a challenge to Rule 42 will be brought on the basis that its presence alone in the Rulebook would suffice to trigger Article 86 EC or section 5 of the 2002 Act is a matter for the future. It is, however, salutary to point out that both the IRFU and the FAI are on the threshold of embracing a new era at Lansdowne Road and, notwithstanding any short term difficulties they may encounter in finding stadia with the requisite capacity, their pride in ultimately carving out

---

[23] Generally see Duggan, "Maybe the GAA is Stuck With Rule 42", *Irish Times*, March 13, 2004, Humphries, "Ignorance the Rule in Pious Rants", *Irish Times*, March 10, 2004, Moran, "Congress Move on Rule 42 is Defeated", *Irish Times*, April 17, 2004, O'Riordan, "Rule 42 Attitude Still Hard to Call", *Irish Times*, December 13, 2001, Duggan, "Worth Opening Gates for Windfalls", *Irish Times*, 5 April 2001.

[24] McNally, "Lansdowne Stadium Plans Unveiled", *Irish Times*, January 22, 2004, Hennessy, "Lansdowne Selected for New €300million Stadium", *Irish Times*, January 28, 2004, Thornley, "Rugby Union Welcomes Decision But Admits Practical Difficulties Lie Ahead", *Irish Times*, January 28, 2004, Malone, "'A Home for Irish Soccer' is Welcomed by FAI", *Irish Times*, January 28, 2004, Moran, "Rule 42 Remains Sole Obstacle to Soccer Qualifiers", *Irish Times*, February 6, 2004.

a new identity for themselves in a state of the art stadium at Landsdowne Road may outweigh their desire to make use of Croke Park over a brief time span by litigating the essential facilities issue with the GAA.

Finally, it should be noted that there is no procedure under Article 82 of the EC Treaty or section 5 of the Competition Act 1991 whereby exemptions can be granted for anti-competitive practices, nor is this particularly surprising in that one of the hallmarks of these provisions is the fact that there has been anti-competitive abuse.

9.2 COMPETITION LAW AND SPORT

In a 1999 speech, the Deputy Director General of the DG Comp (the Competition Directorate) of the European Commission, Jean Francois Pons highlighted two reasons for the increased EU involvement in sport.[25] First, the impact of the *Bosman*,[26] *Deliege*[27] and *Lehtonen*[28] line of case law, and secondly, the fact that because of various factors, most notably the growth of sports broadcasting, sport is now a thriving business with huge economic repercussions for the internal market, and with for example many sports clubs now listed on the Stock Exchange.[29] In reality, however, these two factors are classifiable as two sides of the one coin. After all, the reason that the ECJ decided to deal with sport at all in *Bosman* was because of its status as a business, and it is only when sport operates as a business that it comes under

---

[25] Pons, "Sport and European Competition Policy", Fordham Corporate Law Institute, 26th Annual Conference on International Anti-Trust Law and Policy, NY, October 14–15, 1999 (published in B. Hawk, (ed.), *International Antitrust Law and Policy* (Juric Publications, New York, 1999). See also *Preliminary Guidelines on the Application of the Competition Rules to Sport* (February, 1999) IP/99/133. Gardiner *et al*, *op. cit.*, p.386 and Ratliff, "EC Competition Law and Sport", 6(3) *Sport and the Law Journal* (1998) 4. Generally for an Irish slant see Massey & Daly, *Competition and Regulation in Ireland, The Law and Economics* (Oak Tree Press, Dublin, 2003), Chap.11, Blackshaw, "European Competition Law and Sport – Recent Developments", 9(3) *Sport and the Law Journal* (2001) 116, Foster, "Can Sport be Regulated by Europe?", p.56 in Caiger & Gardiner (eds.), *Professional Sport in the European Union: Regulation and Re-regulation* (TMC Asser Press, 2000) and at p.100 in the same book, Vieweg, "The Restrictions of European Law"; Parrish, "European Union Competition Law and Sport: Recent Developments", 1(3) *Sports Law Bulletin* (1998) 9 and Parrish, "A Framework for Applying EU Competition Law to Sport", 2(6) *Sports Law Bulletin* (1999) 13.
[26] Case 415/93, *Union Royale Belge des Sociètes de Football Association ASBL v. Bosman* [1995] E.C.R. I–4921 [1996] 1 C.M.L.R. 645 [1996] All E.R. (EC) 97.
[27] Cases 51, 191/97, *Deliege v. Ligue Francophone de Judo et Disciplines Associèes ASBL* [2000] E.C.R. I–2549 [2002] 2 C.M.L.R. 1574.
[28] Case 176/96, *Lehtonen and Ors v. Fèdèration Royal Belge des Sociètès de Basket-Ball ASBL (FRBSB)* [2000] E.C.R. I–2681 [2000] 3 C.M.L.R. 409; [2001] All E.R. (EC) 97.
[29] See also Commissioner Monti, DN: Speech/00/152 (April 17, 2000).

the jurisdiction of "hard" EC law.[30] On this basis, the European Community institutions, and in particular the Commission, have become more interested in sport – an interest backed up by the heightened level of activity of the Commission in the general competition sphere since the 1980s.[31]

Having said this, it is also fair to say that the efforts of the EU institutions in regulating the competition law aspects of sport have been somewhat piecemeal. Moreover, as mentioned earlier, the manner in which the Commission in the past approached the question of exemptions with recourse to unofficial comfort letters tending to be more usual than complete official decisions, effectively stunted the emergence of any clear line of authority in this regard, as also did the fact that the ECJ, in cases like *Bosman*, preferred to deal with sporting issues on a "free movement of workers" rather than a competition law basis – despite the fact that the cases in question clearly had some competition law dimensions to them.[32] It is true that in *Bosman* Advocate General Lenz expressed the opinion that the transfer rules at issue violated the competition law provisions of the Treaty as also did Advocate General Stix-Hackl in the case of *Tibor Balog v. Royal Charleroi Sporting Club ASBL* (at least in relation to Article 81 EC)[33] – a case which, somewhat regrettably, settled before it came before the ECJ. It is also true (as we shall see) that the Commission has subsequently had a major role to play in reforms to FIFA's transfer rules, but the absence of a clear court ruling on the nature of EC competition law and sport, is perhaps, a matter of regret. It is too early to speculate on how the involvement of national competition authorities and courts in the application of EC competition law under the backdrop of Regulation 1/2003 will affect the business of sport.

9.2.1 The balance to be drawn

In attempting to provide an overview of the relationship between competition law and sport, it is perhaps helpful to assess this relationship as involving a tension between two competing factors.[34]

---

[30] It has also been suggested that the increased application of the competition law provisions of the Treaty to sport derives not from the increased commercialisation of sport so much as the fact that sports "workers" have noticed how differently they are treated *vis a vis* other workers throughout Europe. See Caiger, "Regulating Sport: Can Competition Policy Have a Role?", 4 (3) *Sports Law Bulletin* (May/June 2000) 10.

[31] Parrish, *op. cit.*, p.120. For the view that the Commission's interest in sport predated the decision in *Bosman,* see Ratliff, "EC Competition Law and Sport", 6(3) *Sport and the Law Journal* (1998) 4.

[32] For a discussion of the problems that have flown from this failure of the ECJ in *Bosman* and its progeny to consider the competition law dimensions to these cases see "The Bosman Case and European Competition Policy", 1(5), *Sports Law Bulletin* (1998) 2.

[33] Case C–264/98 (Opinion of March 29, 2001).

[34] See Parrish, *op. cit.*, p.109.

9.2.1.1 Sport as big business

First, it is undoubtedly true that many aspects of sport have major economic effects, and hence it would be foolhardy for the Commission to ignore this.[35] Indeed it is estimated that sport accounts for 1% of the pre-May 2004 GNP of the 15 pre-enlargement EU Member States.[36] This is particularly the case in the area of sports broadcasting, for, as has often been pointed out, the ability to claim exclusive broadcasting rights to major sports events can be a great driver for pay televisions.[37] Put bluntly, if it were not for its exclusive rights over sports events, (and to a lesser extent over comparatively recently released movies), Sky television would be nothing like the force that it currently is in the United Kingdom and in Ireland. Sky's dominance affords it the potential to operate abusively and to restrict competition, and in as much as sport is the source of this dominance, it is a legitimate target for the competition authorities.

9.2.1.2 Sport as "something special"

As against this, it may be argued that sport is somehow different to other business, and the Commission, while refusing to create an "exemption for sport"[38] from the impact of competition law, has consistently said that in applying such rules it will consider the special needs and special nature of sport,[39] and will listen to the concerns of sports governing bodies.[40] Indeed in this regard it is simply echoing the broader sentiments of the whole European Union, as reflected in the comments on sport attached to the Amsterdam and Nice Treaties, and within the Helsinki Declaration on Sport.[41]

---

[35] See Brinckman and Voloebregt, "The Marketing of Sport and its Relation to EC Competition Law" [1998] E.C.L.R. 281.

[36] Blackshaw, "European Competition Law and Sport – Recent Developments", 9(3) *Sport and the Law Journal* (2001) 116 at 118.

[37] Ungerer, "Commercialising Sport: Understanding the TV Rights debate" (Speech presented in Barcelona, October 2, 2003, p.7, Gardiner *et al*, *op. cit.*, p.401, Lewis & Taylor, *op. cit.*, p.399ff and Harbord and Szymanski, "Football Trials" [2004] E.C.L.R. 117 at p.119.

[38] See for example the comments of Director General Schaub, "EC Competition Policy and its Implications for the Sports Sector", Speech to the World Sports Forum, March 8, 1998.

[39] Sport is regarded as being special in as much as it enjoys an educational function, a public health function, a social function, a cultural function and a recreational function – as well, of course, as an economic function. See Blanpain, *The Legal Status of Sportsmen and Sportswomen under International, European and Belgian National and Regional Law* (Kluwer Law International, 2003), p.35.

[40] Gardiner, *op. cit.*, 400, Lewis & Taylor, *op. cit.*, p. 336 and Pons, "Sport and European Competition Policy", Fordham Corporate Law Institute, 26th Annual Conference on International Anti-Trust Law and Policy, NY, October 14–15, 1999, p.6.

[41] COM (99) 644 (10 December 1999) *Report From the Commission to the European Council with a View to Safeguarding Current Sports Structures and Maintaining the*

First and foremost, sport has a huge social and cultural importance throughout the Community – not least in its contribution to public health[42] – and it is arguable that this social and cultural claim is better served by allowing sport, as far as is reasonable, to be self-governing (while appreciating that there may be problems where a governing body not only regulates the playing of sport but also the commercial aspects thereof).[43]

Secondly, as far as competition law is concerned, there is something unusual about the manner in which sports clubs and indeed sports federations (though not television companies) do business.[44] After all, the typical ambition for an anti-competitive undertaking or undertakings is that rival companies would be put out of business, and hence that the market share of the former would increase. Such an approach to business, however, makes no sense for a sporting club, which (if it is to attract interest from the viewing public, sponsors and broadcasters) depends on rival clubs continuing to exist, and existing in a sufficiently stable manner that the unpredictability of sporting results may be guaranteed. Put bluntly, Liverpool FC and Everton FC are bitter rivals, and each would wish beyond measure to beat the other in a competitive football fixture, yet it is in the interests of neither that the other would actually go out of business. Indeed should one team reach dire financial straits, it is actually in the interest of its rival that it would be financially supported. Moreover, given that the overall appeal of a sporting contest is based on the fact that the result is not completely predictable before the game starts (and indeed the more uncertain the game, the higher the level of interest in it),[45] it is important for sport to ensure that there is not such a gulf in financial and other terms between the various clubs competing, for example, in a league, that such unpredictability of results is lost.[46]

Social Function of Sport Within the Community Framework. Generally see Gardiner *et al*, p.388 and Commission Memo/02/127 (June 5, 2002),Commissioner Monti, DN: Speech/00/152 (17 April 2000). See also Lewis & Taylor, *op. cit.*, p.347 who make the point that whereas such declarations do not constitute binding law, it is nonetheless inconceivable that the Community institutions would ignore them. See also Kinsella and Daly, "European Competition Law and Sports" (November/December 2001) *Sports Law Bulletin* 7 at p.8.

[42] Pons, *op. cit.* See also Commissioner Monti, DN: Speech/00/152 (17 April 17, 2000), Kinsella and Daly, "European Competition Law and Sports", 4 (6) *Sports Law Bulletin* (2001) 7.

[43] Pons, *op. cit.*, p.6.

[44] See Parrish, *op. cit.*, p.118, Kinsella and Daly, "European Competition Law and Sports", 4(6) *Sports Law Bulletin* (2001) 7, Szymanski, "Collective Selling of Broadcast Rights to Sporting Events", 1/02 *International Sports Law Review* (2002) 3, Neale "The Peculiar Economics of Professional Sports" (1964) LXXVII *Quarterly Journal of Economics* 1 and Veljanovski, "Is Sport Broadcasting a Public Utility?", Paper presented at the IEA, October 18, 2000.

[45] "Collective Selling of Broadcast Rights to Sporting Events", 1/02 *International Sports Law Review* (2002) 3.

[46] For the suggestion that sports fans (i.e. the most prominent consumers) are not normal

The combination of these concerns means that the normally anti-competitive nature of many agreements in sport may be deemed to be justified by the demands of solidarity – that is to say a concern with enabling smaller clubs to be afforded sufficient financial security that their survival is guaranteed, and that the gulf between richer and smaller clubs remains manageable.[47] Such a concern with solidarity has been accepted by the ECJ in analogous cases (involving co-operatives), as justifying *prima facie* anti-competitive agreements.[48] Indeed this is classic application of the rule of reason doctrine. Having said this, it has also been suggested that the claims of solidarity do not justify the level of anti-competitive practices which are permitted, especially in light of the lack of evidence of any concerted attempt throughout European sport to channel necessary revenue to smaller clubs or to clubs in financial difficulty, and in fact such practices are simply examples of situations in which consumers are being exploited.[49] Indeed it may also be argued that these factors are indicative of the fact that competition rules are not drafted with sport in mind, and it is perhaps doubtful whether they are capable of managing professional sport.[50]

9.2.2 Drawing the balance

In balancing these objectives,[51] the EU institutions have tended to say that whereas inherently and unjustifiably anti-competitive rules of sports organisations will continue to be targeted, on the other hand, rules that are inherent in the organisation of sport or that otherwise give rise to positive

---

actors in the free market sense being 'consumers of adhesion' who will support their team irrespective of results see Foster, "Can Sport be Regulated by Europe?", p.54 in Caiger & Gardiner (eds.), *Professional Sport in the European Union: Regulation and Re-regulation* (TMC Asser Press, 2000).

[47] Gardiner, pp.399–400, See also Commissioner Monti, DN: Speech/00/152 (April 17, 2000), and DN: Speech 01/84 (February 26, 2001) and Blanpain, *The Legal Status of Sportsmen and Sportswomen under International, European and Belgian National and Regional Law* (Kluwer Law International, 2003), p.35.

[48] See for example Case T–61/89, *Dansk Pelsdyravlerforening v. Commission*, T–61/89 [1992] E.C.R. II–1931. See generally Bell & Turner Kerr, "The Place of Sport within the Rules of Community Law" [2002] E.C.L.R. 256 at p.283.

[49] See for example Szymanski, "Sport and Broadcasting", paper presented at the IEA, October 18, 2000, and by the same author "Collective Selling of Broadcast Rights to Sporting Events", 1/02 *International Sports Law Review* (2002) 3 at p.5. See also Bell & Turner Kerr, "The Place of Sport within the Rules of Community Law" [2002] E.C.L.R. 256 at p.283, Brinckman and Vollebregt, "The Marketing of Sport and its relation to EC Competition Law" [1998] E.C.L.R. 281 and Parrish, "Sports Broadcasting and European Competition Policy", 3(1) *Sports Law Bulletin* (1999)11.

[50] Lewis & Taylor, *op. cit.*, p.346.

[51] *Ibid.*, p.335.

benefits for sport, are acceptable.[52] Equally, however, the Commission appreciates the fact that "a cartel remains a cartel even if it works on the commercialisation of sports rights", and moreover that anti-competitive behaviour, which looks to have positive benefits for sports, may have long term drawbacks in that it can lead to short term benefits that are based on shaky foundations that can easily collapse – (as for example was the case when the collapse of the ITV Digital network led to great financial trauma for the Nationwide league clubs whose financial stability was based on receiving payments from ITV digital for broadcast rights to its games).[53]

9.2.3 Categories of rules

In practice the Commission has divided its consideration of sporting rules and competition law into three categories. Thus there are certain rules that are inherently acceptable as far as competition law is concerned, certain rules that are inherently unacceptable and certain rules that raise questions as far as competition law is concerned, but are nonetheless likely to benefit from exemptions.[54]

9.2.3.1 *Inherently acceptable "sporting" rules*

There are certain rules of sport that are so inherently caught up with the effective organisation and playing of the game that there has never been a question of their violating the competition law provisions of the EC Treaty.[55] Traditionally there was an acceptance that where the regulation of the playing of sport (and only the playing of sport) was concerned, the regulatory authority of the relevant sports body should be accepted.[56] Such inherently acceptable rules – including for example the rules of the game, basic selection rules (provided that they are applied in an objective, transparent and non-discriminatory fashion) and anti-doping rules,[57] were traditionally categorized as "sporting rules."[58] On this

---

[52] Pons, "Sport and European Competition Policy", Fordham Corporate Law Institute, 26th Annual Conference on International Anti-Trust Law and Policy NY, October 14–15, 1999, p.7.

[53] See "ITV Digital Teeters on the Brink", *Irish Times*, March 28, 2002 and "Football League Loses ITV Digital Case", *Irish Times*, July 25, 2002. Generally see Ungerer, "Commercialising Sport; Understanding the TV Rights Debate", Barcelona, October 2, 2003.

[54] See "Commission Debates Application of its Competition Rules to Sport", DN: IP/99/133 (February 24, 1999).

[55] Blackshaw, "European Competition Law and Sport – Recent Developments", 9(3) *Sport and the Law Journal* (2001) 116 at 118.

[56] Monti, DN: Speech/00/152 (April 17, 2000) 2.

[57] The Commission has rejected a complaint from an athlete suspended for doping that

basis the notion of a "sporting exception" grew up, whereby rules that were genuinely sporting rather than economic in nature would be seen as exempt from competition law.[59] It is arguable, however, that in the era of professionalised sport it is increasingly difficult to distinguish sporting from non-sporting rules,[60] especially as there may be certain regulatory rules that have economic effects if not economic objectives.[61] Even the most basic rules (for example a rule that if a player is sent off in a soccer match then he will be suspended, or a rule that says that non-nationals may not represent a country in an international competition – a rule which, as we saw in Chapter Eight, has been upheld in all the ECJ case law in this area) that would traditionally have been seen as "sporting" in nature, now have a significant economic dimension.[62]

The Commission, however, (partially though not completely on "rule of reason" grounds), appears to accept that even rules with an economic dimension that are necessary to achieve sporting objectives and that will benefit sporting teams and participants (and whose impact is proportionate to such objectives) should not be seen as violating the competition law provisions of the Treaty.[63] Thus for example in 2001 the Commission cleared aspects of UEFA's new broadcasting regulations which allowed national football associations to restrict live broadcasting of sporting events for a two and a half hour period on either a Saturday or a Sunday depending on its main domestic schedule in order to further the twin ideals of promoting amateur participation in sport and stadium attendance at games. The Commission made the point that the regulations in question did not fall within Article 81, in that albeit there was an economic dimension to the rules, they involved no appreciable impact on competition.[64] In similar vein, the Commission has always accepted the legitimacy of

---

such suspension amounted to a violation of Art 82 EC. For analysis see Cox, "Sports Law", p.455 in Byrne & Binchy, *Annual Review of Irish Law 2002* (Roundhall Sweet & Maxwell, Dublin 2003).

[58] Kinsella and Daly, "European Competition Law and Sports", 4 (6) *Sports Law Bulletin* (2001) 7.

[59] See Beloff, "The Sporting Exception in EC Competition Law" (1999) *European Current Law Year Book* vi.

[60] Lewis & Taylor, *op. cit.*, p.348.

[61] Parrish, *Sports Law and Policy in the EU* (Manchester University Press, 2003), p.118

[62] Bell & Turner-Kerr, "The Place of Sport within the Rules of Community Law" [2002] E.C.L.R. 256, McCutcheon "National Eligibility Rules after *Bosman*", p.134ff in Caiger & Gardiner (eds.), *Professional Sport in the European Union: Regulation and Re-regulation* (TMC Asser Press, 2000).

[63] Gardiner, *op. cit.*, p.400. It should be noted that this is different to the sporting exception which, says Beloff, should be construed narrowly and continues to apply only to rules that have an exclusively sporting focus. See Beloff, "The Sporting Exception in EC Competition Law" [1999] *European Current Law Year Book* vi at pp.x-xi.

[64] Commission Decision of April 19, 2001, Case 37.576 (*UEFA's Broadcasting Regulations*) O.J. L. 171/12, June 27, 2001. See also Press Release IP/01/583 (April 20, 2001) See also Gardiner, *op. cit.*, p.389, Parrish, *op. cit.*, pp.127–128 and Lewis & Taylor, *op. cit.*, p.418.

individual national league structures irrespective of their seeming incompatibility with the notion of a single European market, pointing to the importance of sport in expressing and preserving national identity.[65]

In this respect the precise decision as to whether a rule of a sports organisation will or will not fall foul of Community competition law will be decided on a case by case basis and having regard to the precise nature of the rule. Having said that, Commission officials have indicated that certain rules will almost certainly *not* violate competition law.[66] These would include rules of the game, nationality clauses in respect of national team selection, nationality quotas in respect of the number of teams or persons that may represent a country in an international competition, rules for selection of individuals based on objective and non-discriminatory criteria, rules setting transfer periods and transfer windows if they are necessary to achieve balance in the general structure of the particular sport, and rules necessary to ensure uncertainty of results.[67]

9.2.3.2 Inherently unacceptable rules

In this category we find rules that are commercial in nature, that restrict competition and that do not have any of the redeeming features of the acceptable rules. Commission officials have suggested that rules and practices that would be inherently unacceptable would include restrictions on parallel imports of sports products, sale of entrance tickets to matches based on criteria that discriminate on the basis of the nationality of the purchaser, overtly restrictive sponsorship agreements, rules in respect of equipment that favour one supplier on the basis of criteria unconnected to the goods themselves, and broadcasting contracts that afford the purchaser power to foreclose the market to rival companies.[68] The bulk of this chapter is devoted to a consideration of such unacceptable rules and practices.

9.2.3.3 Rules in violation of Article 81(1) but exempted under Article 81(3)

Certain commercial rules of sport that violated the terms of EC competition law have nonetheless received either official exemptions, or in many instances, unofficial comfort letters granted on the basis that such rules were conducive

---

[65] Lewis & Taylor, *op. cit.*, p.363.
[66] Pons, "Sport and European Competition Policy, Fordham Corporate Law Institute, 26th Annual Conference on International Anti-Trust Law and Policy, NY, October 14–15, 1999, 7.
[67] See also the comments of Commissioner Monti (IP/99/965) and Kinsella and Daly, "European Competition Law and Sports" (November/December 2001) *Sports Law Bulletin* 7 at p.9.
[68] Kinsella and Daly, "European Competition Law and Sports", 4(6) *Sports Law Bulletin* (2001) 7 at p.12.

to the good governance of sport.[69] This included rules which the Commission deemed necessary to preserve the important social and cultural forces connected with sport and indeed to foster solidarity between sporting clubs – although as has been noted elsewhere, nothing in Article 81(3) actually authorised the grant of an exemption on such bases.[70] In order for such rules to be exempt, the undertaking seeking an exemption was obliged to adduce a clear sporting purpose for their existence, and evidence that their impact on competition would be neither prolonged nor excessive. As stated earlier, Article 81(3) now produces direct effects in the legal systems of the Member States and it will be interesting to see how the national competition authorities and courts eventually apply it in exempting sporting activities with a commercial bias which are *prima facie* anti-competitive from the prohibition embodied in Article 81(1) of the EC Treaty.

9.2.4 When will the Commission intervene in sport?

There are three broad categories of sporting context in which competition law issues are likely to arise.[71] First, where the sports body enters into economic arrangements to exploit the commercial possibilities connected with sport, in terms of sponsorship, sporting equipment, ticket sales[72] and, most significantly, broadcasting.[73] Secondly, where a single body is in charge of the operation of sport in a particular place (for example a national governing body) and seeks to prevent other persons from organising rival competitions by imposing restrictions on players who compete in its own competitions or – in some other way – abuses its dominant position in that sport and in that place. Thirdly, where a governing body creates and imposes rules, which by their nature restrict the capacity of participants or clubs to take part in professional sport. In this last respect competition policy, as well as covering rules relating to the transfer of players in sport, will also provide competitors with a remedy, which along with the contractual and constitutional remedies considered in Chapter Two, and the common law doctrine of restraint of trade,[74] can be used to challenge

---

[69] See Kinsella and Daly, "European Competition Law and Sports", 4(6) *Sports Law Bulletin* (2001) 7 at p.8 for the view that such informality has meant that there is no consistent line of authority demarcating clearly what Commission policy in this area actually is.

[70] Lewis & Taylor, *op. cit.*, p.359.

[71] Generally see Lewis & Taylor, *op. cit.*, pp.192ff, Commissioner Monti, DN: Speech/00/152 (April 17, 2000).

[72] *Italia 90* (1992) O.J. L. 326/31 [1994] 5 C.M.L.R. 252, Case IV/16.888 (1998) *Football World Cup, 1998* (2000) O.J. L. 5, analysed by Weatherill, "Fining the Organisers of the 1998 Football World Cup" [2000] E.C.L.R. 275.

[73] *An Agreement Between the FA Premier League and BskyB, re* [2000] E.M.L.R. 78, [1999] U.K.C.L.R. 258.

[74] See Lewis and Taylor, *op. cit.*, p.334 for the view that to some extent the competition rules actually supplant the old restraint of trade doctrine.

rules that prevent an athlete from taking part in a competition either by denying initial access to participation or by imposing a suspension.[75]

For the remainder of this chapter, we consider how the European Commission has approached these categories of cases, and in particular how it has dealt with eight specific issues, namely:

– The dominant position of governing bodies within their particular sports.

– Sponsorship and equipment.

– Ticketing.

– Salary caps in sport.

– State aid.

– Ownership by a single party of more than one club in a competition.

– Transfer rules.

– Broadcasting.

9.3 EXCESSIVE DOMINATION OF A SPORT BY A GOVERNING BODY

The first area of concern both for the Commission and for various national competition authorities within Europe has been the traditional structure of sports governance within Europe. As we have seen throughout this book, the vast majority of sports have a single International Federation, a single European federation and a single National federation. Obvious exceptions to this rule include boxing and darts, but the more usual view is that having a single federation in each of the three aforementioned regions is logistically preferable, ensuring both that a unitary professional or semi-professional or amateur league can operate, and also that the "solidarity" claims mentioned above can be addressed, and resources channelled to smaller and more needy clubs.[76]

---

[75] Thus in *Stevenage Borough FC v Football League* [1997] 9 Admin L.R. 109, the plaintiff club challenged the rules of the governing body which prevented it from competing in the football league despite having earned the right to do so having been promoted from the conference league. The case was primarily taken on restraint of trade grounds, but the plaintiffs also alleged that the rules violated EC competition rules in that it was possible that Stevenage might win promotion through the leagues up to the Premiership and might eventually qualify to compete in a European competition. The court rejected this claim finding that there was no genuine cross border impact. It is notable, however, that the case was decided before the coming into being of the new UK Competition Act which mirrors Arts 81 and 82 of the EC Treaty in relevant part. Hence should an equivalent case arise today, it is arguable that the plaintiff club, not having to prove cross border impact would have a strong competition law claim. See Beloff *et al*, *op. cit.*, p.150 and Parrish, *op. cit.*, p.118.

[76] Generally see Parrish, *op. cit.*, p.132.

Equally, the dominance that such a position affords the relevant governing body is substantial, and hence the actions of such bodies will come under the spotlight of Article 82 of the EC Treaty (or possibly, if the federation is regarded as an association of clubs) under Article 81). The important question therefore is whether the actions of these dominant bodies amount to abuse(s) of a dominant position, in which case(s) their action(s)' will also violate the terms of the EC Treaty. So for example, it may be argued that, given the degree of control exercised by these bodies over their respective sports, whenever they act otherwise than in accordance with fair procedures, they are also violating Article 82 of the EC Treaty.

9.3.1 Use of a dominant position to restrict activities of competitors

The European competition law agencies have dealt with the nature of control exercised by sports governing bodies in two principal contexts. The first is where the governing body, in attempting to solidify its control over the sport, takes measures aimed at preventing rival organisations from setting up sports leagues or competitions.[77] In restricting the power of the governing body to act in this fashion, competition law, to a certain extent, mirrors the common law doctrine of restraint of trade.[78] Thus in 1998 an organisation named Media Partners filed a complaint against UEFA claiming that it was using its dominant position within European soccer to block the creation (by it) of a European "super league" for soccer.[79] The complaint was eventually dropped – largely because of reforms by UEFA, which ensured that the top European soccer clubs (in other words those which would have participated in such a super league) would gain more from European soccer than would have been the case in the past. Equally, in its dealings with the membership of co-operatives, the ECJ has refused to accept a rule, which prevented one from being a member of two co-operatives simultaneously in order to protect the stability of both.[80] By analogy it might be argued that a rule that prevented a club that participated in such a super league from also participating in UEFA competitions is invalid. Having said this, it is arguable that the notion of a closed European super league with only 18 participating teams and no promotion or relegation for three years was itself anti-competitive, especially given that, because there was no question of resources being reserved for smaller clubs in need of

---

[77] Lewis & Taylor, *op. cit.*, p.367ff.

[78] *Greig v. Insole* [1978] 3 All E.R. 449.

[79] Lewis & Taylor, *op. cit.*, p.368, Parrish, *op. cit.*, pp.132–133 and Van den Brink, "EC Competition Law and the Regulation of Football Part I" [2000] E.C.L.R. 359 at p.364.

[80] Case C–250/92, *Gottrub-Klim e.a. Grovvareforeninger v. Dansk Landbrugs Grovvareselskab AMbA* [1994] E.C.R. I–5641. See Lewis and Taylor, *op. cit.*, pp.368–9.

solidarity, the usual justifications for a lenient competition law analysis for sport were absent.[81]

In *Hendry v. World Professional Billiards and Snooker Association (WPBSA)*,[82] Lloyd J. applied the new English competition law (as well as the doctrine of restraint of trade) to a challenge to the control exercised by the WBPSA over professional snooker.[83] Several aspects of this control were challenged, with some (for example the rule restricting the numbers of logos that players could wear on their waistcoats during competitions) being upheld.[84] However, the High Court found that the WBPSA *had* abused its dominant position by adopting a rule requiring all players to obtain its permission before playing in snooker matches – a rule that effectively prevented rival federations from setting up and organising tournaments in which the top 64 professional snooker players would compete. Lloyd J. noted the WBPSA "rule of reason" argument that it was necessary and actually pro-competitive for it to have some level of financial control (including control of the broadcasting revenue that snooker could attract) in order that it could plough resources back into grassroots snooker, and to players who were not at the time in the world "top sixty-four." Equally he felt that, in this case, this requirement did not justify the draconian rules under discussion.

The point has been made, however, that the decision does not explain how a professional sport like snooker which has a far less widespread interest than, for example, soccer or motor racing, could survive if there were not a single controlling body able to defend its interests against rival tours. In other words, whereas Lloyd J. found the restrictions in question to be disproportionate, it is questionable whether there was in fact a less restrictive means of achieving the desired result.[85]

Finally, it is notable that whereas the court felt that there was an abuse of a dominant position in this instance, it did not rule on the question whether a governing body which dominated not only the regulation of the sport, but also its commercial exploitation, would be inherently anti-competitive. This is, however, the second of the two elements of dominance which has attracted the interest of the European Commission, and it will be considered next.

---

[81] Lewis & Taylor, *op. cit.*, pp.374–5, Parrish, *op. cit.*, p.133 and Hornsby, "'Closed Leagues': A Prime Candidate for the 'Sporting Exception' in European Competition Law?", 1(2) *International Sports Law Review* (2001) 161.

[82] [2002] U.K.C.L.R. 5, [2002] E.C.C. 8, [2002] I.S.L.R. 1.

[83] It should be noted of course, that whereas this case was brought under UK competition law, professional snooker is sufficiently internationalised that it could also have legitimately been brought under EC law.

[84] Lewis & Taylor, *op. cit.*, p.197.

[85] *Ibid.*, p.373.

9.3.2 Separating regulatory and commercial dominance

In 2003 the European Commission finally announced that it had finished its investigation into the activities of the *Federation Internationale de l'Automobile* ("FIA")[86] – the governing body for Formula One motor sport. The Commission had had many concerns with the manner in which Formula One was run, all of which stemmed from the fact that the FIA (like most governing bodies) had both regulatory and commercial authority over the sport, which it governed.[87] Moreover, there was clear evidence that the FIA was acting abusively. Thus it used its regulatory authority to prevent competitors from entering the market, by ensuring that drivers would not compete in rival races and that venues selected to host FIA events would not host competitor events for ten years after the FIA event took place there. If rival organisers wished to hold motor racing events, the reality of the situation was that (a) they would need to join the FIA to obtain FIA sanction for the event and (b) they would have to cede the broadcasting rights to the event to the FIA.[88] Moreover, broadcasters were offered incentives not to broadcast events that were in competition with the FIA, and indeed the broadcasting contracts of the FIA afforded the relevant broadcaster excessively long periods of exclusivity.[89]

Following a lengthy period of negotiation with the Commission, the FIA altered its rules. Under these changes there would be increased access to motor sport competition, reduced duration of broadcasting contracts, and increased transparency of decision making procedures.[90] More pertinently the FIA announced that it would be splitting the regulatory and commercial functions of the organisation, transferring all the commercial rights associated with Formula One for 100 years to Mr. Bernie Ecclestone, then a vice-president of the FIA and arguably the most powerful individual associated with motor sport. Despite the closeness of the link between the FIA and Mr. Ecclestone, the Commission announced that these modifications (which meant that the FIA would no longer use its regulatory powers to ensure commercial dominance) satisfied the demands of EC competition law (at least as far as the Commission was concerned).[91] Equally, it is not clear from the Commission comments

---

[86] Commission press release DN: IP/03/1491 (October 31, 2003). The Commission had closed its investigation into Formula One as a whole in 2001, Commission press release, DN: IP/01/1523, October 30, 2001.

[87] See Gardiner *et al*, *op. cit.*, p.400ff, Foster, "Can Sport be Regulated by Europe?", p.59 in Caiger & Gardiner (eds.), *Professional Sport in the European Union: Regulation and Re-regulation* (TMC Asser Press, 2000).

[88] Lewis & Taylor, *op. cit.*, p.370.

[89] See 4 (6) *Sports Law Bulletin* (November-December 2001) 14 for an evaluation of these rules.

[90] See Gardiner, *op. cit.*, p.410ff.

[91] DN: IP/01/1523 (October 30, 2001), See 4 (6) *Sports Law Bulletin* (November/December 2001) 14.

whether it requires in principle that the regulatory and commercial functions of a governing body be split (which would affect many governing bodies) or whether its concern is simply with the level of abuse which it felt existed within the running of Formula One. Indeed in this latter respect, the point has been made that it is difficult to see how the erstwhile abusive situation at the heart of Formula One could be saved by transferring responsibility for the commercial aspects of the sport to someone so intimately connected with the FIA.[92]

9.4 SPONSORSHIP AND EQUIPMENT

Two types of rule that come under this heading have attracted the interest of competition authorities. First, is the type of sporting rule that regulates the use of equipment within a particular sport, but for sporting purposes. Thus for example, there are regular calls within the world of golf for restrictions on the level of technology that can be used in manufacturing golfing equipment, in order to ensure that the game remains a test for the player rather than for the manufacturer. Similarly there may be reasons connected with safety or spectator enjoyment why there may need to be restrictions on equipment. The Commission has upheld such rules provided that they are genuinely sporting in nature, and are neither arbitrary nor discriminatory.[93]

Of far more concern for the Commission are rules that regulate use of equipment on commercial rather than playing grounds – an issue intimately tied up with the sorts of sponsorship concerns considered in Chapter Seven. The classic case in this regard is the *Danish Tennis Federation* case.[94] Here the federation in question had entered into a sponsorship agreement with a particular company whereby that company would manufacture tennis balls for it for a period of time, and these balls would be deemed to be "official" balls

---

[92] See Lewis & Taylor, *op. cit.*, p.371. See also Beloff *et al*, *op. cit.*, pp.161–162 and Parrish, *op. cit.*, pp.135–137. On the other hand, Competition Commissioner Mario Monti has made the point that as far as the Commission is concerned, the fact that the regulatory and commercial functions of the FIA are split is all that matters, nor is it relevant that the new power to regulate the commercial exploitation of Formula One has passed to someone who was once intimately connected with the governance of the FIA. See DN: Speech/01/84 (February 26, 2001) 3.

[93] See Lewis & Taylor, *op. cit.*, p.389, Griffith Jones, *op. cit.*, p.91, Pons "Sport and European Competition Policy", Fordham Corporate Law Institute, 26th Annual Conference on International Anti-Trust Law and Policy, NY, October 14–15, 1999, pp.9–10, Parrish, *op. cit.*, pp.131–132 and Kinsella and Daly, "European Competition Law and Sports", 4(6) *Sports Law Bulletin* (2001) 7 at pp.131–132.

[94] Case Nos IV/F–1/33.055 and 35.759 [1996] 4 C.M.L.R. 885. Lewis & Taylor p.392, Parrish p.131, Kinsella & Daly pp.8ff. For a similar decision, see the *FIFA 'Denominations Scheme' case*, Case No IV/F–1/35.266, and for analysis, Lewis & Taylor, *op. cit.*, pp.390–391.

(and the company an "official supplier" of such balls). No other tennis ball would be allowed to use the Danish Tennis Federation logo. A complaint was made to the Commission that the use of the term "official" in this regard carried a clear implication that the balls in question were superior to other balls, and by granting one company the exclusive right to use this term, the Danish tennis federation was impeding access to the market of other manufacturers.

The Commission upheld the complaint, both because it felt that the duration of the sponsorship agreement was sufficiently long that it ran the risk of foreclosing the market, and also because – by affording the particular balls the status of "official" – the federation had imbued them with an aura of superiority without having any good qualitative reason for doing so.[95] Thus when the Danish tennis federation engaged in new sponsorship arrangements (which received negative clearance from the Commission),[96] the word "official" in respect of the balls was replaced with the word "sponsor", a new and more open tendering process was provided for, the duration of the agreements was reduced and any ball that had reached a certain standard could use the Danish Federation logo.[97]

Importantly the decision in this case does not diminish the rights of sports bodies, including teams and individuals as well as governing bodies, to enter into sponsorship agreements, or otherwise to market and exploit their intellectual property rights. Equally, the governing body (as in this case) has more power to dominate the whole of its sport within its area of control than does a club, and hence in this case the measure emanating from such a body represented a disproportionately anti-competitive way of engaging in sponsorship deals.

9.5 TICKETING

The European Commission has, on two occasions, considered the compatibility of particular arrangements for selling tickets to major sporting events with competition law. Again there is a tension between two competing goals at play in any analysis of ticketing policy.[98] On the one hand, there may be good

---

[95] It should be noted that it is not illegitimate to use the word "official" in the context of a sponsor, where the sponsor manufactures goods unconnected with the playing of the event – for example in the designation of an "official beer". See Lewis & Taylor, *op. cit.*, p.422.

[96] Commission Press Release DN: IP/98/355 (April 15, 1998).

[97] Lewis & Taylor, *op. cit.*, pp.392–393, Parrish, *op. cit.*, p.131 and Kinsella & Daly, *op. cit.*, p.8.

[98] Lewis & Taylor, *op. cit.*, p.393. Generally see Lewis, "Ticket Distribution: The Aims and Methods of Event Organisers and the Competition Policy of the European Commission", 1(2) *International Sports Law Review* (2000) 56, Massey & Daly, *Competition and Regulation in Ireland* (Oak Tree Press, Dublin, 2003) 239.

reasons why a sports organisation would want to control the flow of tickets, ranging from a need to ensure that supporters of all participating teams or players have a chance to be represented, to facilitating grassroots supporters of various teams, to ensuring that in sports like soccer, rival supporters are properly segregated. Equally, attempts to limit channels of distribution are also inherently anti-competitive. Therefore, the relevant competition authority must balance these competing concerns.

In assessing the legitimacy of such ticketing arrangements under Community competition law, an initial question presents itself as to the relevant product market in which the allegedly anti-competitive activity is taking place.[99] After all, a sports federation with exclusive distribution channels for tickets to its events may claim that the relevant product market for assessing dominance is in fact the market in sports events generally, and hence the fact that it has exclusive control over its particular event does not make it dominant in the grander scheme of things. Thus in the *Wimbledon* case,[100] where the UK Office of Fair Trading (OFT) investigated the fact that only two operators were permitted to sell hospitality type packages that included tickets for the Wimbledon tennis tournament, it was concluded that the relevant market here was for hospitality packages generally and the organizers of the Wimbledon tournament could not be seen as dominant in respect of this. In this particular context, the Wimbledon tickets represented access to a major sporting event as part of a broader package, and could therefore be regarded as interchangeable with tickets to another major sporting event, such as a Premiership soccer match or an important horse racing event.

On the other hand in the *Italia 90* decision[101] – an investigation of ticket distribution for the 1990 soccer World Cup, the European Commission accepted, almost without any need for analysis, the proposition that the relevant product market here was limited to that particular event. This is, it is submitted, an inescapable conclusion. Whereas a company wishing to reward clients by providing them with an attractive hospitality package including tickets to a sporting event will not necessarily care what the event is, there is simply no possible way that someone who wishes to attend the soccer World Cup would be equally or in any way satisfied if, instead of obtaining tickets to that event, [s]he received tickets to an alternative event.[102]

---

[99] *Ibid.*, p.394.

[100] OFT Press Release No.20/93 (March 23, 1993). See *ibid.*, p.395.

[101] In *Distribution of Package Tours During the 1990 World Cup* (1992) O.J. L.326/31, [1994] 5 C.M.L.R. 253.

[102] In *Hospitality Group Ltd v. FA*, unreported, January 24, 1996 (case stayed pending a determination from the Commission) – a challenge to the UEFA policy on the provision of hospitality packages for the Euro 96 soccer tournament in England – the Commission appeared to intimate that the relevant market in this case was the whole hospitality market. See Lewis & Taylor, *op. cit.*, pp.395–396.

In the *Italia 90* case, FIFA had appointed a single tour operator per country as the sole supplier of travel packages to the 1990 World Cup, which included tickets to the event. Thus other operators were restricted to providing transport to the World Cup, without having match tickets to provide as part of the deal.[103] A Belgian company who wished to provide an overall World Cup package sought to acquire tickets through alternative channels, and was met with legal action taken by the only Belgian company authorised to sell ticket packages by FIFA, requiring it to cease and desist. This company then challenged that aspect of the FIFA ticketing policy, which provided for the exclusive sale of tickets to one tour operator in each country.

The Commission upheld this complaint deeming the impugned arrangement to constitute an overly excessive restriction on competition between tour operators, and indeed on the choice of travel agents as to the operator from whom they could secure their supply of tickets. Importantly, the Commission did not condemn the notion of having a limited number of tour operators, provided that the process for appointing such operators was conducted transparently and based on objective criteria.[104]

The second context in which the Commission has considered ticketing arrangements of this nature concerned the ticketing arrangement for the 1998 soccer World Cup, held in France. Here the organizers operated a system in respect of those World Cup tickets that would be sold directly to the public rather than through sports clubs, which as a matter of fact made it much easier for French residents to buy tickets for the event than other would-be spectators. So, for example, the organisers required tickets to be sent to a mailing address in France and offered French residents a quicker purchasing scheme than that available to non-residents and it took no real steps to inform non-residents of their entitlements to purchase tickets. The Commission found that there was *de facto* discrimination in this case and hence that the competition rules (and specifically Article 82) were being violated. Interestingly, the French World Cup organisation had, in 1997, received Commission approval for its distribution policy, but the Commission claimed that it had only granted such approval in ignorance of the nationality restrictions that would apply – although this claim is perhaps belied by the fact that at the time the French organisation's website was active and carried explicit details of its policy.[105]

---

[103] See Gardiner, *op. cit.*, pp.402–403, Griffith Jones, *op. cit.*, p.89, Parrish, *op. cit.*, pp.128ff, Beloff *et al*, *op. cit.*, pp.142–3 and Pons "Sport and European Competition Policy", Fordham Corporate Law Institute, 26th Annual Conference on International Anti-Trust Law and Policy, NY, October 14–15, 1999, 5.

[104] In similar vein the Commission struck down a rule requiring all entrance tickets to the 1996 Atlanta Summer Olympic Games to be sold as part of a broader tour package. Unreported Competition Report (1996) p.144. See Lewis & Taylor, *op. cit.*, p.398 for the view that some tying arrangements of this kind may be justified, provided that they are a proportionate response to a legitimate purpose.

[105] Decision of July 20, 1999 (Press Release IP/99/541) (2000) O.J. L. 5, January 8, 2000.

9.6 SALARY CAPS

Various sports (most notably English club rugby)[106] apply official salary caps
– that is to say that there is a fixed maximum salary that players can earn.[107]
Such salary caps serve two reasonable objectives – first to protect clubs from
going out of business as a result of spiralling wage bills[108] and secondly to
ensure that the unpredictability of results is maintained by not facilitating a
system whereby the top clubs are able to attract *all* the top players simply by
offering them wages which smaller clubs could not afford to pay.[109] Equally
such rules raise obvious questions as far as both the doctrine of restraint of
trade and competition law is concerned. Indeed this may be one reason why
professional soccer has considered but never implemented such salary caps.[110]
It is uncertain how the European Commission would deal with such salary
caps if asked to adjudicate on their legitimacy under Community competition
law. If, for example, the caps effectively conferred wider benefits on consumers/
spectators (in terms of increasing the outcome uncertainty of games or, less
likely, decreasing admission prices to matches), it might fit within the
parameters of Article 81(3) and escape the rigors of paragraph (1) of the same
Article. Against this, however, in a situation in which clubs were making vast
profits, and caps were introduced to increase profits even further at the expense
of the player, such a system would be unlikely to survive scrutiny under either
the restraint of trade doctrine or Article 81 of the EC Treaty. It should be borne

---

For analysis see Parrish, *op. cit.*, p.128ff, and Weatherill, "Fining the Organisers of the 1998 Football World Cup" [2000] 6 E.C.L.T. 275. In May 2003, the Commission cleared the ticketing arrangements for the Athens Olympic Games. See IP/03/738 (May 23, 2003).

[106] Irish rugby does not operate an official salary cap. In any event, there is only one employer in the Irish rugby market with all players being contracted to the IRFU and then loaned out to, for example provinces.

[107] See Parrish, *op. cit.*, p.156 and Harris, "The Benefits of the Team Salary Cap in English Rugby League", 8(1) *Sport and the Law Journal* (2000) 3, Hornsby, "The Harder the Cap, the Softer the Law?", 10(2) *Sport and the Law Journal* (2002) 142, Taylor and Newton, "Salary Caps – The Legal Analysis", 11(2) *Sport and the Law Journal* (2003) 158, Harris, "Salary Caps", 10(1) *Sport and the Law Journal* (2002) 120, Boon, "A Time for Salary Caps", 10(1) *Sport and the Law Journal* (2002) 118 and Tsatsas, "Is It Time for English Football to Adopt A Salary Cap", 9(2) *Sport and the Law Journal* (2001) 126.

[100] See Lewis & Taylor p.386–387.

[109] Boyes, "Salary Caps in Sport: Objectives, Problems and the Law", 3(1) *Sports Law Bulletin* (January/February 2000) 12, Gardiner & Gray, "Are Salary Caps the Answer to Player Power?", 5(2) *Sports Law Bulletin* (2002) 16.

[110] Generally see McAuley, "Windows, Caps, Football and the European Commission; Confused? You Will Be" [2003] E.C.L.R. 394, Gardiner & Gray, "Will Salary Caps Fit European Professional Football?", 4(3) *Sports Law Bulletin* (2001) 14 and Tsatsas, "Is It Time for English Football to Adopt A Salary Cap?", 9(2) *Sport and the Law Journal* (2001) 126.

in mind, however, that consumers may not be the only beneficiaries of such caps and it is submitted that outcome uncertainty – which goes to the question of the unusual economics of sport – may protect the imposition of such caps (insofar as they ensure that smaller clubs will be able to exist as serious competitors to the bigger clubs) provided that they are applied reasonably, equally and proportionately.

9.7 STATE AID

Under Article 87 of the EC Treaty, Member States are prohibited from granting aid to undertakings where this would distort or threaten to distort competition.[111] Pursuant to this general prohibition on State Aid, under Article 88 Member States are obliged to inform the Commission of any plans to grant or alter aid. The Commission may deem the aid either to be compatible or incompatible with the common market, and if the latter, then the aid is deemed to be illegal.

Thus far, the State Aid provisions of the Treaty have had little application in the sporting sphere.[112] Equally the suspicion remains that in as much as government sponsored sports bodies throughout Europe (for example the Irish Sports Council) are providing large amounts of financial aid to bodies connected with sport, it may be only a matter of time before Article 87 is used to strike down some such aid.[113] This may cover situations where clubs and sports bodies receive Sports Council or National Lottery funding,[114] or where governments or local authorities give tax breaks or other assistance to clubs, including assistance in the building of stadia. It may also cover situations where state television companies (such as RTE or the BBC) can use licence fee revenue to help them bid for the rights to broadcast major sporting events.[115]

Finally, Article 87 might be used to challenge the controversial planning agreement, which was entered into in May 2001 by Real Madrid and both the Madrid City Council and the Community of Madrid respectively. Under the agreement, land that currently houses the club's training fields may, in the future, be used to construct four skyscrapers, a sports centre and other sports facilities in order to develop a "sports city" (and ultimately in order to boost Madrid's bid to host the 2012 Olympic Games). In return for participating in

---

[111] Generally see Quigley & Collins, *EC State Aid: Law and Practice* (Hart Publishing, Oxford, 2002), Evans, *EC Law of State Aid* (Oxford University Press, 1997) and Craig & de Burca, *EU Law – Text, Cases and Materials* (3rd ed., Oxford University Press, 2003), p.1141ff.

[112] See Lewis & Taylor, *op. cit.*, p.423ff.

[113] In PE Doc A3–0326/94 (April 27, 1994) "Report on the EC and Sport", the European Parliament highlighted the potential significance of the State Aid provisions for sport. See Parrish, *op. cit.*, p.137.

[114] Lewis & Taylor, *op. cit.*, p.425.

[115] *Ibid.*, p.425.

the agreement (which of course would work substantially to its benefit), Real Madrid (which in 1986 nearly sold the land for €3 million) received €420 million – thereby enabling it to pay off its debts of €280 million – and to afford to purchase (and pay) its Galacticos – foreign stars such as Zinedine Zidane (bought from Juventus for in excess of €75 million) and Luis Figo (bought from Barcelona for in excess of €60 million). It is strongly arguable that this cash injection to an ailing club represented State Aid, and moreover that in as much as Real Madrid won the Champions League in 2002, and have arguably been the best team in Europe at least since 2001 (and are known as a club with the financial resources to buy whatever players the President of the club wants), that this State Aid has massively distorted competition within the European football market.[116]

Thus far, apart from one decision in which the Court of First Instance[117] upheld a Commission decision[118] to uphold aid granted by a Member State to a ski equipment company that was in financial difficulty, the major statement of principle given by the EC institutions in this area came in an analysis by the Commission of the legitimacy of an official French government programme to grant financial aid to soccer, basketball, rugby and volleyball clubs. The stated objective of such aid was to improve the organisation and promotion of sport and physical activity in France. Equally because such clubs might also take part in European club competitions, such aid raised serious questions for the purposes of Article 87 of the Treaty. In the event the Commission ruled that in as much as the aid in question was granted to clubs with state approved youth training facilities, and hence provided a social benefit (*inter alia* by encouraging the combination of sports training and education for young people), the aid was compatible with the internal market.[119] Equally, the Commission insisted that the aid was only compatible with the common market to the extent that it *did* assist in provision of facilities for young people and that any aid not connected with this purpose should be recovered.

9.8 OWNERSHIP OF MULTIPLE CLUBS

Both the European Commission and the Court of Arbitration for Sport have been called on to evaluate the legitimacy of the UEFA rule that restricts the possibility of a single body having ownership stakes in more than one soccer

---

[116] For an excellent account of the planning agreement between Real Madrid and the Madrid Council and Community of Madrid see Montana-Mora, "The Financing of Professional Football and EC Competition Law: Is the Zidane Deal in an Offside Position", 9(3) *Sport and the Law Journal* (2001) 159.

[117] Case T–123/97, *Salomon SA v. Commission* [1999] E.C.R. II–2925.

[118] (1997) O.J. L. 25.

[119] Commission press release IP/01/599 (April 25, 2001), (2001) O.J. C. 333 (November 28, 2001), See also Lewis & Taylor , *op. cit.*, p.426ff.

club competing in competitions run under its (UEFA's) auspices.[120] The specific rule dating from 1998 prohibited two clubs with the same owners from competing in the same UEFA competition,[121] and was underpinned by a concern that in the absence of such a rule there might be an appearance of collusion between clubs with the same owners, and particularly a view that such collusion could affect the unpredictability of results where such clubs were drawn to play each other in such a competition.

The factual context in which the rule attracted the interest of CAS and the Commission focused on the business group ENIC that had ownership rights in clubs including Glasgow Rangers and also Slavia Prague and AEK Athens. The problem arose in 1998 when both of the latter two clubs qualified to play in the UEFA cup. Under the 1998 UEFA rule AEK Athens was prohibited from competing in the competition on the basis that Slavia Prague had already qualified for it.[122] When the issue was appealed to CAS, it originally granted an interim injunction preventing UEFA from introducing the rule for the 1998–9 season on the basis that the clubs did not have prior notice of the rule, and hence would have had a legitimate expectation that they would both be able to play in the Champions' League. On the full hearing,[123] however, it was held that by application of a "rule of reason" approach, the UEFA rule would not be regarded as being anti-competitive. Rather, the rule was absolutely necessary to preserve the integrity of the UEFA competitions, and hence was necessary to ensure genuine competition within the European soccer market.

In similar vein the Commission (to whom the CAS verdict was appealed) rejected the complaint from ENIC saying that any effect on competition that the rule might have was more than outweighed by the valid objective sought to be achieved and that the rule was a proportionate response to this objective.[124]

Finally it is salutary to note the decision of the UK Monopoly and Mergers Commission recommending the rejection of the proposed acquisition by BSkyB of Manchester United Football Club.[125] The concern with this proposed

---

[120] Gardiner, *op. cit.*, p.397, Lewis & Taylor, *op. cit.*, p.376, Parrish, *op. cit.*, p.134, Van den Brink, "EC Competition Law and the Regulation of Football Part I" [2000] E.C.L.R. 39, Broome, "Advice on Dual Ownership of Football Clubs", 8(2) *Sport and the Law Journal* (2000) 83.

[121] The full text of the rule is available on the UEFA website at www.uefa.com.

[122] See Lewis & Taylor p.376, Grey, "Where Broadcasting and Football Collide: Conflicting Approaches to Football Club Ownership" [2004] *Entertainment Law Review*, 42 at 44.

[123] *AEK PAE and SK Slavia Praha v. UEFA*, CAS 98/2000, August 20, 1999, the interim ruling was delivered on July 17, 1998.

[124] DN:IP/02/941 Case COMP/37.806 (June 27, 2002).

[125] See Caiger, "Murdoch loses out in BskyB/Manchester United Merger", 2(2) *Sports Law Bulletin* (1999) 1, Welsh, "BSkyB. MMC: Policy 1 Law 0", 7(3) *Sport and the Law Journal* (1999) 44, Van den Brinck, "EC Competition Law and The Regulation of Football Part 1" [2000] E.C.L.R. 359 at p.363. See also Lewis & Taylor, *op. cit.*, p.428. For a general analysis of the potential impact of the EC Merger Regulation in Sport, see

takeover was twofold. First, there was the possibility that such a deal which would afford enormous financial power to Manchester United – already the richest football club in the world – could lead to a widening of the gap between richer and poorer clubs. More importantly, the Commission was concerned with the impact of the deal on future broadcast contract negotiations between the Premier League and Sky. After all, the proposed takeover would mean that the Sky group would effectively have representation on both sides of the negotiation table in such discussions. Moreover, it might enable the broadcasting company to obtain confidential information in respect of other bids for such TV rights, thereby enabling it to cement its position as the major supplier of live televised soccer in the UK.

9.9 TRANSFER RULES

As has been mentioned, one of the surprising aspects of the relationship between European Community competition law and sport is that is has not had more of an impact in the area of transfer rules, particularly given that this is the area in which European Community law *per se* has impacted in the most high profile and spectacular fashion.[126] Thus the ECJ in *Bosman* was happy to base its condemnation of the existing soccer transfer rules on Treaty provisions relating to free movement of workers and did not see the need to go further and apply the admittedly rather complicated competition rules to this area.[127] On the other hand, Advocate General Lenz in his opinion in *Bosman*, did intimate that the transfer rules in question violated Article 81[128] as also did Advocate General Stix Hackl in *Tibor Balog v. Royal Charleroi Sporting Club ASBL*.[129] In subsequent cases like *Deliege*[130] and *Lehtonen*[131] the ECJ followed the lead given in *Bosman*, by not resolving the particular questions which arose under competition law principles. Nonetheless, the Commission has continued

---

Ungerer, "Commercialising Sport; Understanding the TV Rights Debate" (Barcelona , October 2, 2003) 5.

[126] See Griffith Jones, *op. cit.*, p.92ff, Pons, "Sport and European Competition Policy", Fordham Corporate Law Institute, 26th Annual Conference on International Anti-Trust Law and Policy, NY, October 14–15, 1999, 14, Beloff, *op. cit.*, p.152 and Parrish, *op. cit.*, p.12. See Lewis & Taylor, *op. cit.*, p.841ff for a general analysis of the nature of transfer rules in sport.

[127] See Parrish, "The *Bosman* Case and European Competition Policy", 1(5) *Sports Law Bulletin* (1998) 11.

[128] [1996] 1 C.M.L.R. 645, para.262.

[129] Case C–264/98 (Opinion of March 29, 2001). See "Balog: The New Bosman Case", 4(3) *Sports Law Bulletin* (May/June 2001) 1.

[130] Cases 51 and 191/97, *Deliege v. Ligue Francophone de Judo et Disciplines Associèes ASBL* C–51 191/97 [2000] E.C.R. I–2549, [2002] 2 C.M.L.R. 1574.

[131] Case 176/96, *Lehtonen v. Fèdèration Royale Belge des Sociètès de Basket-Ball ASBL (FRBSB)* [2000] E.C.R. I–2681, [2000] 3 C.M.L.R. 409, [2001] All E.R. (EC) 97.

to have difficulties with aspects of the FIFA transfer rules that did not come under the impact of the decision in *Bosman* and has applied competition principles in its analysis of these rules.[132]

In December 1998, the Commission sent FIFA a statement of objections to its transfer rules. Such objections focused on a number of concerns:[133]

- the fact that in the event of unilateral termination of a contract, where the party in breach of contract paid whatever damages were necessary for breach of contract, he would still not be permitted to register with his new club;

- where transfer fees were agreed they tended to bear no relationship to the actual costs that the selling club had invested in training the player, leading to potentially excessive costs, which could be anti-competitive;

- the rule that obliged national associations to organize domestic transfer regimes in accordance with the FIFA international system;

- the rule that prohibited clubs and players from taking transfer disputes to the courts.

Following a protracted period of discussion involving FIFA and the Commission (though generally not FIFPRO, the world players organisation) with significant intervention from national governments,[134] an agreement was reached in 2001.[135]

---

[132] See Egger and Stix Hackl, "Sports and Competition Law: A Never Ending Story" [2002] E.C.L.R. 81 and Parker, Lane and Gibson, "Football Transfer Fees", 1(2) *International Sports Law Review* 156, Caiger, "Changing the Transfer System in Professional Football: Towards Contract Stability", 3 (6) *Sports Law Bulletin* (2000) 1, Welch, "From Self-Regulation to Bosman – There and Back Again", 4 (4) *Sports Law Bulletin*, (2001) 14.

[133] See Lewis & Taylor, *op. cit.*, p.380 and Parrish, *op. cit.*, p.138ff.

[134] For the view that the acceptance of this new FIFA transfer policy represented the Commission "… [giving] in under pressure from European government leaders", see Blanpain, *The Legal Status of Sportsmen and Sportswomen under International, European and Belgian National and Regional Law* (Kluwer Law International, 2003), p.30. Blanpain's point (see *ibid.,* p.34ff) is that the acceptance of these rules was motivated *inter alia* by a feeling that *Bosman* had overly distorted the manner in which sport is governed in Europe.

[135] IP/01/314 (March 6, 2001) See Parrish, *op. cit.*, pp.139–149, Gardiner, *op. cit.*, p.408, Lewis & Taylor, *op. cit.*, p.862ff, McAuley, "They Think It's All Over…it Might Just Be Now: Unravelling the Ramifications for the European Football Transfer System post-*Bosman*" [2002] E.C.L.R. 331, Egger and Stix Hackl, "Sports and Competition Law: A Never Ending Story" [2002] E.C.L.R. 81, McAuley, 'Windows, Caps, Footballs and the European Commission: Confused? You will Be' [2003] E.C.L.R. 394, Bennett, "'They Think it's All Over … It is Now!' – how Extra Time was Required to Finally Settle Football's Transfer Saga", 9(3) *Sport and the Law Journal* 180, Reding, "The Reform of FIFA Rules Governing International Transfers", 9(1) *Sport and the Law Journal* (2001) 80. In June 2002 the Commission closed its investigation into FIFA transfer rules. See Commission Press Release IP/02/824.

Under the new rules,[136] the following changes – all of which were subsequently implemented – were made:[137]

– the international transfer of under-18s was deemed to be acceptable subject to conditions including the creation of a code of conduct for dealing with such young players;

– it was agreed that a scheme should be designed for the purposes of compensating clubs which have trained players when those players are transferred and re-transferred in order to encourage small clubs to assist in the training of such young players.[138] Thus for example, if a young league of Ireland soccer player signs terms with a Premiership club and is then sold to another club, the League of Ireland club is entitled to be compensated for its training of that young player, depending on the amount of years that it has trained that player and the category of club involved;

– contracts of players up to the age of 29 were to be protected for three years, and for two years thereafter. Sporting sanctions would apply where there was a unilateral breach of such contracts, including the requirement that injured parties be paid financial compensation;

– solidarity mechanisms, based on a proportion of compensation payments, were to be enforced in order to redistribute income to smaller clubs who helped in the training;

– transfer windows were to operate for the sale of players, i.e. clubs would only be able to sign players during one period in the season and during a small mid season window. Moreover an individual player would only be permitted to transfer once annually;

– a dispute resolution body was to be established to deal with grievances.

As a result of these changes, the Commission has dropped its investigation into the FIFA rules.[139] Equally, the criticism is made that these rules lead to a practical situation where exorbitant transfer fees *are* charged for players – albeit when they are still in contract with their clubs – and that this is inappropriate, *inter alia* because the protection of free movement of workers should permit players to breach their contracts on payment of appropriate

---

[136] See "FIFA Circular – Status and Transfer of Players", 9(3) *Sport and The Law Journal* (2001) 185.

[137] See Parrish, *op. cit.*, p.148–149 and Kinsella and Daly, *op. cit.*, p.12.

[138] For the process of calculating the training and development fee due to a club, see Lewis & Taylor, *op. cit.*, p.871.

[139] Generally for analysis (in light of the proposed European Model for Sport) see Blanpain, *The Legal Status of Sportsmen and Sportswomen under International, European and Belgian National and Regional Law* (Kluwer Law International, 2003), p.46.

compensatory damages to their employers.[140] In other words, it may be suggested that the endorsement by the Commission of these rules is a significant victory for the Governing Bodies. It is, however, salutary to point out that the experience in *Bosman* is indicative of the fact that the endorsement by the Commission of particular rules does not mean that they will withstand scrutiny by the European Court of Justice.

In this respect it is notable that at the time of going to print an Irish case is ongoing in which the legitimacy of one aspect of these rules is being challenged. The plaintiff in the case is Alan Cawley, a 23-year-old former Leeds United and Sheffield Wednesday player. Having returned from England, Mr. Cawley played for two seasons at UCD, and when his contract expired (and UCD were relegated from the Eircom Premier League), Cawley was approached by Shelbourne FC – one of the top League of Ireland clubs – and offered €500 per week to play for them. Cawley wished to play for Shelbourne but, because he was 23, under FAI rules (which derived from the FIFA rules) UCD were entitled to compensation for training him. They demanded €50,000, which was later reduced by an FAI tribunal to €20,000. Shelbourne refused to pay this figure and repudiated its agreement with Cawley.[141] As a result, Cawley issued High Court proceedings against the refusal of the National League to register him as a player, claiming that the imposition of the €20,000 fee, which now, effectively accompanied him wherever he sought work, constituted a severe restraint on trade and a breach of EU employment law.[142] In late April 2004 an interim deal was reached with the FAI allowing Cawley to register with Shelbourne pending a full hearing of the action which will take place in the autumn of 2004 and which has the capacity to throw the validity of the new transfer system into jeopardy.[143]

There are other aspects of the rules relating to "sports workers" that have also attracted the interest of the Commission to sport. Chief among these was the FIFA rule prohibiting players and clubs from using unlicensed agents.[144]

---

[140] McArdle, *op. cit.*, p.56, Beloff *et al, op. cit.*, p.78. See also Caiger & O'Leary, "Whither the Transfer System?", 3(1) *Sports Law Bulletin* (2000) 13, Gardiner & Welch, "Show Me the Money: Regulation of the Migration of Professional Sportsmen in Post *Bosman* Europe", p.122 in Caiger & Gardiner (eds.), *Professional Sport in the European Union: Regulation and Re-regulation* (TMC Asser Press, 2000). For a suggestion that the new transfer rule permit a system that is tantamount to human trafficking see Blanpain, *The Legal Status of Sportsmen and Sportswomen under International, European and Belgian National and Regional Law* (Kluwer Law International, 2003), p.59ff.

[141] See "Club Disputes Fee for ex-UCD Player", *Irish Times*, April 15, 2004.

[142] Malone, "Cawley Plans Test Case", *Irish Times*, April 9, 2004. This press report refers to the alleged illegality of the compensation system in the light of EU employment legislation. Given that the proceedings are still *sub judice*, the authors will not analyse the ramifications of this litigation from either a restraint of trade or an EC perspective until after the case has been resolved.

[143] See "Interim Deal Reached on Cawley Action", *Irish Times*, April 24, 2004.

[144] Lewis & Taylor, *op. cit.*, p.385.

In October 1999 the Commission had issued a statement of objections to the FIFA rules, focusing on the fact that in order to receive such a licence an agent was required to pay a substantial sum of money as a deposit. The Commission objected that this was a disproportionate way of achieving the FIFA aims of preventing unscrupulous persons from becoming sports agents. Accordingly the FIFA rules were changed, such that instead of having to pay a deposit, prospective agents are now required to pass an exam and to sign a code of professional conduct. In April 2002 the Commission said that these changes had achieved the desired results, such that any remaining restrictions on agents could be justified by the need to protect players and clubs from unscrupulous agents.[145]

A further aspect of the rules relating (in a broad sense) to the free movement of workers, which has also attracted concern from a competition law perspective, is that which prevents a team that takes part in a national league run by a national governing body from basing itself in another state. Thus for example there is ongoing concern over whether the "big two" Scottish soccer teams (Glasgow Celtic and Glasgow Rangers) could ever play in the lucrative English Premiership, assuming that both of them were good enough to do so.[146] It will also be remembered that there was at one stage a question as to whether the then Premiership team Wimbledon would be allowed to relocate to Dublin.[147]

The European Commission had occasion to consider the validity of this rule in a case called *Mouscron*.[148] The case concerned a small Belgian club, which had qualified for a UEFA run competition to be played over two legs on a "home and away" basis. The Belgian club wished to play its home leg in a nearby French stadium, because the stadium was bigger than its own and hence would have met the demand for attendance at this major event in the club's history. UEFA, however, had a rule under which a club was required to play its "home" games in its own national territory. When the Belgian club challenged this rule under EC competition law, the Commission found that the UEFA rule represented a legitimate regulatory power. By extension, it may be argued that

---

[145] Commission press release IP/02/585 (April 18, 2002) See also Parrish, *op. cit.*, p.149.
[146] See "Old Firm Switch to England Gathering Pace", *Irish Times*, May 6, 2002.
[147] Vieweg, "The Restrictions of European Law", p.95 in Caiger & Gardiner (eds.), *Professional Sport in the European Union: Regulation and Re-regulation* (TMC Asser Press, 2000), Bates & Thorpe, "Wimbledon gets *Bosman* Lawyers on Their Side", *Guardian*, January 24, 1998, "Dublin's Premier Ambitions", September 7, 1996, Thornley, "A Fresh Sense of Direction Required", *Irish Times*, September 10, 1996 and "Wimbledon Try to Sell A Dummy with EU Laws", *Irish Times*, November 26, 1997, Ratliff, "EC Competition Law and Sport", 6(3) *Sport and the Law Journal* (1998) 4 at 5, Massey & Daly, *Competition and Regulation in Ireland – The Law and Economics* (Oak Tree Press, Dublin, 2003), p.243.
[148] Commission Press Release IP/99/965, December 9, 1999. See Parrish, *op. cit.*, p.135 and Lewis & Taylor, *op. cit.*, p.364.

any rules requiring clubs participating in national leagues to be resident in the jurisdiction of that league are justified by the need to preserve the integrity of the national league structure, and hence will not fall foul of EC competition law.

9.10 TELEVISION AND BROADCASTING

Of all the issues that have concerned the competition authorities in their relationship with sport, the area that has attracted by far the most concern is that of the sale and purchase and operation of rights to broadcast sporting events.[149] Nor is this particularly surprising in light of the impact that sport can have as a "driver" and an image enhancer for a television station. Thus in a recent survey in the UK, some 65% of those polled said that sport programmes would be their main reason for subscribing to pay television. Indeed in the same survey, the figure in Spain was as high as 85%.[150] Moreover, between 30–70% of the revenue of football clubs throughout Europe comes from television revenues.[151] Finally from an EC perspective, the broadcasting of sports events is increasingly cross border in nature.[152]

There are many reasons why existing rules pertaining to the sale of TV rights for major sports events might be anti-competitive. First, the impact of the Commission's involvement with the FIA, discussed above, raises a question over whether the regulatory body for a particular sport should be permitted also to have the commercial control necessary to conclude broadcasting

---

[149] Griffith Jones, *op. cit.*, p.87, Weatherill, "Resisting the Pressures of 'Americanisation': The Influence of European Community Law on the 'European Sport Model'", p.157 in Greenfield and Osborn, *Law and Sport in Contemporary Society* (Frank Cass, 2000), p.175ff, Ungerer, "Commercialising Sport: Understanding the TV Rights Debate" (Speech presented in Barcelona, October 2, 2003), Wachtmeister, "Broadcasting of Sports Events and Competition Law" (1998) 2 *Competition Policy Newsletter* (June 1998), Parrish, "Sports Broadcasting and European Competition Policy", 3(1) *Sports Law Bulletin* (1999) 11, Parrish, "A Framework for Applying EU Competition Policy to Sport", 3(6) *Sports Law Bulletin* (1999) 13, "European Competition Law and Sport; Recent Developments", 2(3) *Sports Law Bulletin* (1998) 9, Mario Monti, DN: Speech/00/152 (April 17, 2000), Massey & Daly, *Competition and Regulation in Ireland* (Oak Tree Press, Dublin, 2003), p.234ff, Spink & Morris, "The Battle for TV Rights in Professional Football", p.165 in Caiger & Gardiner (eds.), *Professional Sport in the European Union: Regulation and Re-regulation* (TMC Asser Press, 2000) and Torben, "Football: Joint Selling of Media Rights" [2003] 3 *Competition Policy Newsletter* 47.
[150] Ungerer, "Commercialising Sport: Understanding the TV Rights Debate" (Speech presented in Barcelona, October, 2, 2003, 7).
[151] *Ibid.*
[152] Wachtmeister, "Broadcasting of Sports Events and Competition Law", 1998 2 *Competition Policy Newsletter* (June 1998) 2.

contracts.[153] Secondly, and whereas the European Commission has always decided that this is a matter of national law,[154] there must be some concern from the Irish and British perspectives as to what precisely a television station is buying when it buys broadcast rights from a governing body given that, as we have seen in Chapter Seven *supra*, the governing body does not itself own the rights to a sporting event, as there are no such things as rights in a sporting event. This becomes relevant in that, (as we shall see shortly), where a challenge is made to a governing body's collective sale of the broadcasting rights in, for example, a league, it is uncertain whether the proper grounds for challenge should lie within Article 81 or Article 82 of the EC Treaty – in other words whether the decision represents a decision of a single dominant undertaking, namely the federation (which would be the case if the governing body is deemed to own the rights in the event) or whether it represents a concerted practice or agreement involving many separate undertakings, namely the clubs, (which would be the case if the clubs own the individual rights to their own home games).[155] The sale of broadcasting rights raises questions under five headings:

– the relevant markets under discussion;

– the exclusivity and duration of broadcasting rights;

– the extent to which rights, and especially "new media" rights are underexploited in existing deals;

– the practice of collective selling of broadcasting rights;

– the practice of collective purchase of broadcasting rights.

Naturally many broadcasting contracts investigated by national competition authorities or by the European Commission (and the nature of sports broadcasting means that it will nearly always have *some* cross border element to it) will raise concerns under all or many of the above headings. We will consider them in turn and will conclude with an assessment of the treatment by the Commission of two recent broadcast agreements whereby rights were sold to the UEFA Champions League and the English (soccer) Premiership.

9.10.1 Assessment of markets

A number of points should be made in respect of the relevant markets for television in which allegedly anti-competitive practices will be gauged.

---

[153] Brinckman & Vollebregt, "The Marketing of Sport and its Relation to EC Competition Law" [1985] E.C.L.R. 281 at p.285.
[154] *Ibid.*, p.284.
[155] *Ibid.* See also Beloff *et al, op. cit.*, pp.142–143.

Firstly in terms of the relevant geographical market for sport, it is true that certain sports are somewhat regionalised in Europe, with the only sports that enjoy widespread interest throughout the whole of the community being soccer and Formula One motor racing. Nonetheless, the market in televised sport is increasingly internationalised.[156] Equally, depending on the sport, there may need to be an assessment of limited geographical markets based on regional interests in the sports in question.

The authorities have repeatedly endorsed the proposition that the type of sports broadcast that is by far the most valuable is the broadcast of live sport.[157] In other words there is a completely different product market for live sport and for any other delayed or highlights coverage.

In assessing interchangeability of product, there may be some sports coverages, which are interchangeable. In other words it is possible that some minor sports may be lumped together into the same product market. Premium content sports, such as soccer, Formula One, major rugby matches and so on are not interchangeable with any other event.[158] In other words, a television station seeking to break into the sports market in any concerted way will need some such premium content. Thus in assessing relevant product markets it is almost certain that such premium content items will have an individualised product market for themselves.[159] So therefore for example, Sky Television with its formerly exclusive rights to broadcast Premiership soccer could not claim that it was not dominant in its market because the relevant product market was the whole of televised sport in Europe (or even in the UK). The relevant product market is top class football matches in Europe, and in respect of this, there is no question but that Sky is dominant.

In addition there is general acceptance[160] that there is a distinct market for the various different kinds of television stations that broadcast sport. In other

---

[156] Gardiner, *op. cit.*, p.418ff.

[157] Pons, "Sport and European Competition Policy", Fordham Corporate Law Institute, 26th Annual Conference on International Anti-Trust Law and Policy, NY, October 14–15, 1999, 14 (full text published in Hawk (ed.), *International Anti-Trust Law and Policy*, Juric Publications, New York, 1999), Beloff, *op. cit.*, p.152, Parrish, *op. cit.*, p.121, Wachtmeister, "Broadcasting of Sports Events and Competition Law" (1998) 2 *Competition Policy Newsletter* (June 1998) 6, Commissioner Monti, DN: Speech/00/152 (April 17, 2000) 5.

[158] Pons, "Sport and European Competition Policy", Fordham Corporate Law Institute, 26th Annual Conference on International Anti-Trust Law and Policy, NY, October 14–15 (1999) 6 at p.14, Beloff, *op. cit.*, p.151, Wachtmeister, "Broadcasting of Sports Events and Competition Law" (1998) 2 *Competition Policy Newsletter* (June 1998) 6, Commissioner Monti, DN: Speech/00/152 (April 17, 2000) 5.

[159] Generally see Lewis & Taylor, *op. cit.*, p.403ff and Di Mauro, "Defining the Retail Markets for Audiovisual Products" [2003] E.C.L.R. 384.

[160] See Lewis & Taylor, *op. cit.*, pp.400–401, Beloff, *op. cit.*, p.151ff and Wachtmeister, "Broadcasting of Sports Events and Competition Law" (1998) 2 *Competition Policy Newsletter* (June 1998) 6.

words, there is a separate market for pay television, for commercial television financed by advertisements and for free to air public broadcasting television. This is largely because all these different kinds of television stations involve different categories of relationships; the pay TV station is involved only with its clients (and in reality will have more financial clout than its competitors),[161] the advertisement financed station also has a relationship with the businesses which it is advertising and the public broadcaster also has a relationship with the state.

9.10.2 Exclusive broadcasting contracts

As we have seen in Chapter Seven, whenever the marketing of sport is at issue the one thing that the sports body must be able to guarantee is exclusivity. Thus, if it is to justify spending vast sums of money in acquiring the broadcast rights to sporting events, the television company will want to ensure that it can attract viewers (and thereby drive its overall programming schedule) by being the only television station able to broadcast the relevant event.[162]

The Commission has consistently recognised the legitimacy of this claim, and does not appear to have any difficulty with exclusivity *per se*.[163] What it *is* concerned with is the manner in which such exclusive contracts operate, and particularly with the possibility that they will be used by a dominant firm to foreclose the relevant market.[164] So for example in the *Screensport* case, the Commission found a violation of Article 81 in a deal between the European Broadcasting Union (EBU) (a conglomeration of various public service broadcasters throughout the European Union) and the sports channel Eurosport,

---

[161] Case IV/M 469, *MSG Media Service*, O.J. L. 364/1 December 31, 1994.

[162] Ungerer, "Commercialising Sport: Understanding the TV Rights Debate" (Speech presented in Barcelona, October 2, 2003) 7. See www.europa.eu.int/comm/sport/key_files/comp/a_comp_en.html. See also Gardiner *et al*, *op. cit.*, p.401 and Lewis & Taylor, *op. cit.*, pp.399 and 412.

[163] Case 262/81, *Coditel v. Cinè Vog Films SA* [1982] E.C.R. 3381. See Parrish, *op. cit.*, p.125ff, Spink & Morris, "The Battle for TV Rights in Professional Football", p.165 in Caiger & Gardiner (eds.), *Professional Sport in the EU: Regulation and Re-regulation* (TMC Asser Press, 2000) and Brinckman and Vollebregt, "The Marketing of Sport and its Relation to EC Competition Law" [1998] E.C.L.R. 281 at p.285. See also Wachtmeister, "Broadcasting of Sports Events and Competition Law" (1998) 2 *Competition Policy Newsletter* (June 1998) 3, and Commissioner Monti DN: Speech / 00//152 (April 17, 2000).

[164] Pons, "Sport and European Competition Policy", Fordham Corporate Law Institute, 26th Annual Conference on International Anti-Trust Law and Policy', NY, October 14–15, 1999, 14, Lage and Alonso, "Access to Spanish Football Stadia for TV Networks not Holding Exclusive Broadcasting Rights" [1996] 6 *Entertainment Law Review* 247 and by the same authors "The Law on Sports Broadcasts: One More Battle in the Spanish Digital Television War" [1998] 8 *Entertainment Law Review* (hereafter Ent. L.R.) 115.

under which Eurosport had exclusive access to all programmes to which the EBU had exclusive rights and indeed had exclusive free access to the signal transmitting these programmes. Screensport – a rival broadcasting company to Eurosport – claimed successfully that in as much as it had to pay for such signals, and in any event could only obtain rights to such programmes through a sub-licensing arrangement, the relevant market was being foreclosed. It is notable that in this case the Commission refused to give Eurosport an exemption under Article 81(3) of the EC Treaty, despite its claim that it had invested heavily in upfront technology and hence that the exclusivity granted to it was justifiable.[165]

Thus the Commission will seek to ensure that any such exclusive rights are awarded on an objective basis, that they are for a fixed and limited period of time, and that the buyer does not have an automatic right to renew his contract. There do not appear to be any hard and fast rules as to the maximum acceptable length of an exclusive rights contract – rather this will be decided in all the circumstances and on a case-by-case basis.[166] Thus the Commission has recognised that longer than usual periods of exclusivity may be necessary in certain circumstances – for example where an operator is new to the market and is having to invest substantially in equipment or infrastructure, or is trying to make an initial bid to attract new subscribers.[167] This approach was taken

---

[165] Fleming, "Exclusive rights to Broadcast Sport in Europe" [1999] E.C.L.R. 143 at p.144, Pons, "Sport and European Competition Policy", Fordham Corporate Law Institute, 26th Annual Conference on International Anti-Trust Law and Policy, NY, October 14–15, 1999, p.15.

[166] Wachtmeister, "Broadcasting of Sports Events and Competition Law" (1998) 2 *Competition Policy Newsletter* (June 1998) 8. For an assessment of those factors that the Commission deems relevant in such an analysis see Fleming, "Exclusive Rights to Broadcast Sport in Europe" [1999] E.C.L.R. 143 at p.147. In *KNVB/Sport 7*, Case IV/36.033 (1996) O.J. C.228/4, a seven year deal giving exclusive rights to Dutch soccer was deemed to be excessive. See Pons, "Sport and European Competition Policy", Fordham Corporate Law Institute, 26th Annual Conference on International Anti-Trust Law and Policy, NY, October 14–15, 1999, 14 and Fleming, *op. cit.*, p.146. On the other hand, the Commission in dealing with the UEFA Champions League broadcasting agreement in 2002, considered below, was happy to uphold a three year deal. Lewis & Taylor, *op. cit.*, p.414 suggest that contracts of up to three years even for premium events will probably be acceptable as far as the Commission is concerned. Thus in January 2004 the Commission cleared a deal between Telenor and Canal Plus regarding satellite and pay television distribution, after the original deal was shortened in its duration. See Commission press release DN: IP/04/2. Once again, however, there is an absence of clear Commission guidance on this which will probably be exacerbated from May 2004 when the bulk of responsibility for enforcing EC anti-trust law passes to the Member States.

[167] Lewis & Taylor, *op. cit.*, p.413, Pons, "Sport and European Competition Policy", Fordham Corporate Law Institute, 26th Annual Conference on International Anti-Trust Law and Policy, NY, October 14–15, 1999, 15, Wachtmeister, "Broadcasting of Sports Events and Competition Law" (1998) 2 *Competition Policy Newsletter* (June 1998) 9.

by the Commission when it issued a comfort letter upholding the first deal between the Premier League and Sky Television, under which the latter had exclusive rights to all FA Cup, Charity Shield and English international matches for five years. The Commission concluded that in light of the start up costs experienced by Sky, and indeed the fact that in its view the presence of Sky in the market sharpened rather than blunted competition, the deal which was *prima facie* anti-competitive would nonetheless be upheld.[168] On the other hand this does not afford the broadcaster in question the right to foreclose the market.[169]

Finally, where a deal does present significant anti-competitive effects stemming from its exclusive nature, the Commission has intimated that this may possibly (albeit not necessarily) be offset by an *adequate* sub-licensing arrangement.[170] Furthermore the problematic nature of exclusivity may also be diluted by affording a different broadcaster a different package (e.g. a highlights or new media package) in the same event.[171] On the other hand, it has been suggested that the only way genuinely to improve the position of the consumer is to require that the rights to major events are not sold exclusively to a single broadcaster but rather are licensed "non-exclusively to multiple broadcasters".[172]

---

[168] See Lewis & Taylor, *op. cit.*, p.413, Beloff, *op. cit.*, p.161 and Fleming, "Exclusive Rights to Broadcast Sport in Europe" [1999] E.C.L.R. 143 at p.145. See Gardiner *et al*, *op. cit.*, p.427 for suggestion that this may not constitute good law under the new competition regime in the United Kingdom (and by extension in the EC). Finally it is notable that in 1997 former Competition Commissioner Van Miert suggested that the five year exclusive deal given to Sky in 1990 was in fact unnecessarily long in hindsight in that the technology bedded n quicker than expected. *Le Monde*, October 27, 1998. See Parrish, *op. cit.*, p.126 and Lewis & Taylor, *op. cit.*, p.413.

[169] Case IV/32.524, *WH Smith & Son Ltd v. Screensport and the European Broadcasting Union* (1991) O.J. L.63/32 [1992] 5 C.M.L.R. 273. See Fleming, *op. cit.*, 144.

[170] Lewis & Taylor, *op. cit.*, p.415, Wachtmeister, "Broadcasting of Sports Events and Competition Law" (1998) 2 *Competition Policy Newsletter* (June 1998)11–12, Parrish, *op. cit.*, p.125. See however, Harbord and Szymanski "Football Trials" [2004] E.C.L.R. 117 at p.120 for the view that whenever such sub licensing arrangements operate on the basis that the sub-licensee pays the licensor a fee per subscriber (rather than a lump sum) the sub-licensing arrangement will not alleviate competition problems in that the original rights holder can raise the sub-license fee to the point where the sub-licensee's fee to subscribers is inflated above the level charged by the original rights holder. The original rights holder can then increase its own subscriber fees and outmanoeuvre the market by pitching its prices at levels just below or exactly equal to those of the sub-licensees so that the consumers of its services have no incentive to switch supplier.

[171] Wachtmeister, "Broadcasting of Sports Events and Competition Law" (1998) 2 *Competition Policy Newsletter* (June 1998) 8.

[172] Harbord and Szymanski, "Football Trials" [2004] E.C.L.R. 117 at 122.

9.10.3 Maximum possible exploitation of broadcast rights and the use of "new technology"

It is one of the objectives of competition policy that economic activity should be stimulated. Therefore from the perspective of competition authorities, it is a particularly undesirable state of affairs if the rights to an event are underexploited. This problem arises particularly in the context of "new media" rights – for example internet rights and mobile phone rights[173] – and, as we shall see, it was one of the concerns of the Commission in its analysis of the most recent broadcasting arrangements for the UEFA Champions League. Holding back such rights, according to Ungerer represents "a blatant output restriction that blocks technical and social progress, and is the direct route into market stagnation." The same author makes the point that whereas such new media rights only account for 1% of total revenue from sport, that figure still corresponds to the total global revenue earned by football clubs from broadcasting in 1993.[174] The clear implication is that this is an area that will increasingly attract the attention of the Commission. Thus in January 2004 the Commission launched an inquiry into the sale of sports rights to Internet and 3g Mobile Operators. The Commission expressed concern at the possibility of anti-competitive practices in terms of refusal to supply unbundled rights packages or otherwise favouring TV coverage over new media.[175]

9.10.4 Collective selling of broadcast rights

The collective sale of broadcasting rights (e.g. where the rights to all the games in a competition are sold collectively by the competition organiser rather than individually by participating teams) is plainly an area that has the potential to generate significant discussion as far as competition law is concerned, not least because it throws up certain nice questions as to the proper ownership of sport.[176] In general, the indications are that the legitimacy of collective selling *per se*, (as distinct from abusive practices connected with collective selling) will remain a matter for national courts rather than for the European Commission.[177] Thus for example, whereas courts in Germany[178] and the

---

[173] Generally see Harvey, "New Opportunities for Media Rights Exploitation", 9(3) *Sport and the Law Journal* (2001) 150.

[174] Ungerer, "Commercialising Sport; Understanding the TV Rights Debate", Barcelona, October 2, 2003, 8.

[175] Commission Press Release DN: IP/04/134.

[176] Foster, "Can Sport be Regulated by Europe?", p.58 in Caiger & Gardiner (eds.), *Professional Sport in the European Union: Regulation and Re-regulation* (TMC Asser Press, 2000).

[177] Wachtmeister, "Broadcasting of Sports Events and Competition Law" (1998) 2 *Competition Policy Newsletter* (June 1998) 10.

Netherlands[179] have held that the obligations of competition law mean that individual clubs should have the right to seek individual deals for the matches played at their venues, the Office of Fair Trading in England has upheld a high profile example of collective bargaining in the case of the deal that afforded Sky Television the right to show live coverage of Premier League soccer matches.[180]

The debate on this issue reflects, once again, two competing tensions. On the one hand, as we saw in Chapter Seven, the only basis by which exclusive broadcasting can be guaranteed, is by the venue owner exercising his capacity to exclude other broadcasters from his property. Thus it may be argued, that the venue owner (typically the club hosting the relevant game) should be the person entitled to exploit this ability.[181] The counter argument to this sees the league as representing a single entity rather than a collection of sub-entities.[182] What is being sold to the broadcasting company is the right to broadcast the real life soap opera that is the league campaign or cup campaign and of which each game is a component part and not a stand alone attraction (after all the viewing figures for a friendly rugby match involving Ireland and England would be considerably less than if that game were a competitive one with a grand slam resting on it). The view that it is the league organiser that is the rightful possessor of the rights in the event, is supported by the fact that, in all likelihood,

---

[178] For analysis see Lentze, "Collective Marketing of Football Television Rights" (January/February 1998) *Sports Law Administration and Practice* 7, Schmike, "Legal Principles Applicable to the Centralised Marketing of TV Broadcasting Rights in Germany" (2003) (3) *International Sports Law Journal* 15, Brautigam and Schmitz, "German Football Broadcasting at a Turning Point: The Supreme Court's Decision on the Central Marketing of Television Rights" [1998] Ent. L.R. 122, Von Wallwitz, "Sports between Politics and Competition Law – The Central Marketing of TV Rights to Sports Events in Light of German and European Competition Law" [1998] Ent L.R. 216.

[179] *KNVB v. Feynoord.* See Gardiner *et al, op. cit.,* pp.428–429.

[180] *An Agreement between the FA Premier League, re* [2000] E.M.L.R. 78, [1999] U.K.C.L.R. 258 (Restrictive Trade Practices Court, 1999). See Spink & Morris, "The Battle for TV Rights in Professional Football", p.165 in Caiger & Gardiner (eds.), *Professional Sport in the EU: Regulation and Re-regulation* (TMC Asser Press, 2000), Caiger, "Premier League Football: A Question of Broadcasting Rights", 2(1) *Sports Law Bulletin* 9 and by the same author, "BSkyB/BBC Deal with the Premier League Upheld", 2(5) *Sports Law Bulletin* (September/October 1999) 1. Lewis & Taylor, *op. cit.,* p.194, note that whereas the decision in this case predated the 1998 Competition Act, nonetheless insofar as the case involved discussion of broader competition law principles, it may still be relevant as far as the interpretation of the new Act is concerned.

[181] Lewis & Taylor, *op. cit.,* pp.404–406.

[182] See Roberts, "The Single Entity Status of Sports Leagues Under Section 1 of the Sherman Act: An Alternative View" (1986) 60 *Tulane Law Review* 562. See also Massey & Daly, *Competition and Regulation in Ireland – The Law and Economics* (Oak Tree Press, Dublin, 2003), p.231 and Foster, "Can Sport be Regulated by Europe?", p.56 in Caiger & Gardiner (eds.), *Professional Sport in the European Union: Regulation and Re-regulation* (TMC Asser Press, 2000).

it will be this body, which has contributed most significantly to the creation and organisation of the event.[183] Equally this 'single entity' theory has not enjoyed much popularity in European Commission analysis of the situation.[184] Moreover of course, even if the single entity theory can be accepted, this merely means that the issue falls to be considered under Article 82 as opposed to Article 81 of the Treaty.[185]

The potential anti-competitiveness of the collective sale of rights is multi-faceted. It is felt that it can lead to price fixing, it can lead to a limited availability of rights to sporting events including new media rights with a concomitant slow down in the development of technology, it can generate other anti-competitive practices such as long periods of exclusivity, and it will, in practice, favour the richer broadcasters who will come out on top in any bidding war.[186] Most significant, perhaps is the fact that it prevents the more popular teams with huge independent support from exploiting their own popularity to the maximum possible level.[187] Thus, to take the example of the English Premiership, the reality of the situation is that high profile teams like Manchester United, Liverpool, Chelsea, Newcastle United and Arsenal are the main attraction, and would probably be able to get a better deal through individual negotiation of television rights than they currently receive under the collective deal.

As against this the claims in support of the principle of solidarity discussed earlier would militate in favour of the notion of collective marketing (as indeed would pragmatic arguments in respect of efficient selling and reduced costs for the ultimate broadcaster)[188] which ensures that a significant proportion of the revenue gained from the attractive fixtures involving the big clubs is channelled to the smaller clubs who would not attract such revenue if they were left individually to sell their own matches, and who, without such revenue would suffer, possibly to the extent that they could not survive, and certainly to the extent that the gulf between richer and poorer clubs would increase dramatically.[189] Therefore if a rule of reason approach were to apply, it is

---

[183] Lewis & Taylor, *op. cit.*, p.403.
[184] See Gardiner, *op. cit.*, p.425, "Collective Selling of Broadcast Rights to Sporting Events", 1/02 *International Sports Law Review* (2002) 3 at p.4.
[185] See Beloff *et al*, *op. cit.*, p.153ff.
[186] Pons, "Sport and European Competition Policy", Fordham Corporate Law Institute, 26th Annual Conference on International Anti-Trust Law and Policy, NY, October 14–15, 1999, 17, Beloff *et al*, *op. cit.*, p.154, Parrish, *op. cit.*, p.122 and Wachtmeister, "Broadcasting of Sports Events and Competition Law" (1998) 2 *Competition Policy Newsletter* (June 1998) 11.
[187] Gardiner *et al*, *op. cit.*, p.425.
[188] Lewis & Taylor, *op. cit.*, p.403, "Collective Selling of Broadcast Rights to Sporting Events", 1/02 *International Sports Law Review* (2002) 3 at p.4ff.
[189] Gardiner, *op. cit.*, p.425. See also "Collective Selling of Broadcast Rights to Sporting Events", 1/02 *International Sports Law Review* (2002) 3 at p.5 and Lewis & Taylor, *op. cit.*, p.403.

possible to regard the collective selling of such rights as being paradoxically pro-competitive.[190]

As we shall see in our consideration of the UEFA and FA deals, the view within the Commission appears to be that collective selling *per se* is acceptable, provided that it does not result in a situation where either the full extent of the rights in an event is underexploited, or where, for any other reason, (notably where there is a sale of exclusive rights to a single bidder) there is a foreclosure of the relevant markets.[191] Once again, the key concern is that the sale operates in transparent and non-discriminatory fashion, and that any impact on competition is proportionate to a legitimate objective, in that that objective could not be achieved by a less anti-competitive formula.[192] The Commission has also suggested that whereas the main rights to the event could be sold collectively, it would prefer if other rights (for example delayed rights and new media rights) could be sold individually.[193]

9.10.5 Collective purchasing

The other side of the coin which has also attracted the interest of the European Commission (albeit to a much lesser extent) concerns the collective *purchasing* of the broadcast rights to sporting events. Typically this occurs where a group of broadcasters band together to offer a joint bid for an event or events that they would not be able to afford individually. The extent to which this will attract the attention of the competition authorities depends on the circumstances, including the position in the market of the relevant undertakings[194] and the duration, exclusivity and scope of any agreement.[195]

---

[190] Lewis & Taylor, *op. cit.*, p.406. In its analysis of the deal between Sky Television and the Premier League, the Restrictive Practices Court referred to the fact that without such a collective sale, all parties, i.e. the purchaser of the rights, the league and the clubs would be in a less advantageous position. The RPC also felt that a strong solidarity argument would apply in this case. On the other hand see Pons, "Sport and European Competition Policy", Fordham Corporate Law Institute, 26th Annual Conference on International Anti-Trust Law and Policy, NY, October 14–15, 1999, p.17 for the view that claims of solidarity cannot be used to justify the abuse of a dominant position.

[191] Gardiner, *op. cit.*, p.434 and Beloff *et al*, *op. cit.*, p.155.

[192] Pons, "Sport and European Competition Policy', Fordham Corporate Law Institute, 26th Annual Conference on International Anti-Trust Law and Policy, NY, October 14–15, 1999, 17.

[193] See for example the decision in the challenge to the new UEFA broadcasting arrangements. COMP/37.398 (July 23, 2003).

[194] The Commission has suggested that there is a presumption in favour of collective purchasing arrangements where the individual members of the purchasing group would not by themselves be financially capable of buying the relevant rights. See Wachtmeister, "Broadcasting of Sports Events and Competition Law" (1998) 2 *Competition Policy Newsletter* (June 1998) 12, Commissioner Monti, DN: Speech/00/152, 6.

[195] Beloff *et al*, *op. cit.*, p.156ff, Pons, "Sport and European Competition Policy", Fordham

On the one hand it may be said that such arrangements represent collusion between various undertakings which prevents competitors from entering the market. On the other, and especially where the purchasing group consists of smaller undertakings who would not, of themselves, be able to afford to purchase the rights to the relevant events, the impact of such agreements may actually be pro-competitive in that they ensure that smaller competitors have the chance to enter the relevant market and compete against the large European broadcasters such as BSkyB, Canal Plus and Bertelsmann,[196] and also that consumers have access to the greatest possible number of events at the cheapest possible prices.[197]

The Commission has considered this in the context of the European Broadcasting Union (EBU), a group of mainly public service broadcasters throughout Europe who, *inter alia*, seek jointly to acquire the rights to major sporting events. In a 1993 decision,[198] the Commission decided that the EBU actions were (in principle) acceptable, provided that provision was made for a reasonable sub-licensing system. This decision was appealed to the Court of First Instance, which struck down the exemption granted to the EBU, on the basis that the Commission had not considered adequately whether the particular activities of the EBU represented a reasonable, proportionate and non-discriminatory restriction on competition.[199] So in 2000, the Commission again granted an exemption to the activities of the EBU. Again its principal basis for granting the exemption was the sub-licensing provisions of the agreement, but on this occasion, the Commission focused on how the joint purchasing agreement was indispensable if the relevant public service broadcasters were to have any access to the markets, and also on how the agreement improved the capacity of the consumer to have access to events of this nature.[200] From an Irish perspective, the impact of the sub-licensing saver to the EBU deal has meant, for example, that RTE (a member of the EBU) is required to sub-license some rights to major tournaments (for example the Euro 2004 soccer

---

Corporate Law Institute, 26th Annual Conference on International Anti-Trust Law and Policy, NY, October 14–15, 1999, 17.
[196] Wachtmeister, "Broadcasting of Sports Events and Competition Law" (1998) 2 *Competition Policy Newsletter* (June 1998) 13.
[197] Lewis & Taylor, *op. cit.*, p.415ff.
[198] Decision of June 11, 1993, 93/403/EEC (IV/32.150 (1993) O.J. L.179, 23). See Lewis & Taylor, *op. cit.*, p.416, and Beloff *et al*, *op. cit.*, pp.157–158 and Parrish, *op. cit.*, p.126ff.
[199] Joined Cases T–528/93 and T–542–543/93, *Mètropole Tèlèvision SA, Reti Televisive Italiane SpA, Gestevision Telecinco*, Case T–546/93 *Antena 3 de Television* [1996] E.C.R. II–649. See Pons, "Sport and European Competition Policy', Fordham Corporate Law Institute, 26th Annual Conference on International Anti-Trust Law and Policy, NY, October 14–15, 1999, 18.
[200] Commission Decision of May 10, 2000, Case IV/32.150.

tournament, sold by UEFA to the EBU, and the Athens Olympic Games) to
other stations such as TV3 and Sky Television.[201]

9.10.6 The approach of the European Commission to major broadcasting deals

To conclude this section on broadcasting, we consider the approach of the
European Commission to two recent "broadcasting deals," namely the sale by
UEFA of the broadcasting rights to the European Football Champions League
and the sale in England of the broadcasting rights to the FA Premier League.
Both are instructive in their statement of the contemporary concerns of the
Commission in relation to this issue.

9.10.6.1 The UEFA Broadcasting Rights Deal 2003[202]

In 2001 the Commission opened proceedings into the sale by UEFA of the
broadcast rights to the Champions League.[203] Under the previous arrangements[204] UEFA sold the TV rights to one broadcaster per Member State, with
the minimalist condition that the broadcaster was required to televise a Tues-
day night game live either on free to air television or on pay television, and a
Wednesday night game live on free to air television, with highlights to be
broadcast on both nights on free to air television. The Commission, while
accepting both the impact of the Nice Treaty Declaration on Sport, and also
the acceptability in principle of the practice of collective selling, nonetheless
expressed its concern with this arrangement, *inter alia* because of the undis-
puted impact of a major tournament like the Champions League, as a driver
for commercial television stations. In the case of the existing Champions League
arrangements, moreover, there were a number of unused rights – particularly
in the area of new media broadcasting – suggesting output restriction, and
there were no rights available for exploitation by individual competing clubs
that might mitigate against the harshness of the collective selling rule.[205]

   In July 2003, an agreement was reached between the Commission and
UEFA, under which the Commission approved new and substantially modified

---

[201] Under the 2000 agreement with the Commission, if the parties cannot agree on the
games to be sub-licensed then the matter is transferred to arbitration. See Oliver, "RTE
forced to sell Euro Soccer Rights to Sky, TV3", *Irish Times*, February 24, 2004.

[202] Generally see Torben, "Football: Joint Selling of Media Rights" [2003] 3 *Competition
Policy Newsletter* 47.

[203] Commission press release, DN: IP/01/1043 (20 July, 2001). See Parrish, *op. cit.*, p.123.

[204] Generally see the Commission background note to this case, Press Release DN: Memo/
01/271 (July 20, 2001).

[205] Ungerer, "Commercialising Sport; Understanding the TV Rights, Debate Barcelona,
October 2, 2003, p.8.

selling agreements for the Champions' League.[206] Under the new arrangements, the scheme has an open tender procedure with fourteen separate rights packages including three live packages and the possibility for individual clubs and individual leagues co-exploiting certain TV rights as well as new media rights and archive rights – a process which, it is felt, will ensure that there are no unused rights.[207] The deal is strongly indicative of the approach of the European Commission to this issue whereby the bidding process for such rights must be open, and the rights to such events must be unbundled and thereby fully exploited. Finally, the Commission does not approve of excessive periods of exclusive rights (although three years would seem to be, in most circumstances, acceptable), nor will it permit a rights holder to be automatically entitled to a renewal of his contract.

9.10.6.2 The Sky/FA Premier League Broadcasting Rights Deal 2003

The second deal which we shall consider concerns the sale by the FA Premier League (FAPL) of broadcast rights to Premiership soccer matches to Sky Television. In fact the Commission had been interested in this arrangement ever since the Restrictive Practices Court in the UK had given it the green light in 2002. In December 2002 the Commission opened proceedings into the FA Premier League's joint selling arrangements.[208] The Commission was concerned with the arrangements on the basis that (a) only 25% of matches were broadcast live, (b) the FAPL approach necessarily favoured the bigger media groups, (c) the arrangements would lead to higher prices and (d) there was limited exploitation of new media rights. The Commission accepted that there was a potential justification based on the solidarity claims discussed earlier, but felt that the FAPL approach to selling did not represent a proportionate method of securing this objective.

In order to address these concerns, the FAPL altered its arrangements such that in June 2003 the new tendering process increased the number of matches to be broadcast on TV from 106–138 in the UK and split the overall TV rights into three packages – a gold and silver package with the rights to thirty eight top games each and a bronze package with sixty two less valuable games (and in July 2002 the bronze package was itself split into two equal sized packages following pressure from the Commission).[209] It also provided for a limited number of matches to be shown live on Irish television on Saturday afternoons,

---

[206] For the analysis by the Commission of the issues in this case, see COM/37.398 (July 23, 2003) and at www.europa.ed.int/comm/competition/antitrust/cases/decision/37398/en.pdf .

[207] Ungerer, "Commercialising Sport; Understanding the TV Rights Debate", Barcelona, October 2, 2003, p.9.

[200] Commission Press Release DN: IP/02/1951 (December 20, 2002).

[209] See Harbord and Szymanski, "Football Trials" [2004] E.C.L.R. 117 at p.118.

and for a significant upgrade of highlights packages. In terms of the exploitation of new media rights, under the new deal, video clips could be sent to mobile telephones as soon as the action occurred in the match and not (as had been the case previously) hours or days later. Finally, club internet and television rights were increased under the deal. On August 8, 2003 it was announced that Sky had again secured all the live rights to Premiership soccer with a bid worth over £1 billion, and that there had been no competition at all for the gold and silver packages and very little for the bronze packages – a state of affairs arguably flowing from the fact that the Sky offer had been pre-announced.[210] By the Autumn of 2003 it was clear, however, that the Commission was still unhappy with the Sky/FAPL deal, (in that, as Syzmanski and Harbord point out, the fact that formerly exclusive rights packages are split into multiple packages makes no discernible difference if a single bidder buys all the packages[211]) and despite claims from representatives of the FA that the deal could be saved by requiring more money to be paid into a solidarity fund to assist smaller clubs, it appeared that the Commission was poised to strike down the deal in its entirety – which would have been financially ruinous for many Premiership clubs.[212]

Eventually, in December 2003 the FA reached an agreement with the Commission thereby saving its broadcast arrangements.[213] Under this agreement, the FAPL agreed that after 2006 the tendering process would be opened up so that there would be at least two broadcasters entitled to broadcast live Premiership matches. The general rights packages under such broadcasting arrangements would be unbundled, nor could any one broadcaster buy all the packages. Indeed the Commission would undertake a rigorous scrutiny of the tendering process to ensure that it is not anti-competitive. As regards the existing deal, (which would run from 2004 until 2006), BskyB agreed to sub-license up to eight top quality Premiership matches annually to another broadcaster to be shown live on free to air television.

The worry, from the perspective of the Premiership clubs is that BSkyB will of course demand to pay significantly less than the £1.024 billion which it had paid for the rights that it had acquired under the original deal, thereby opening up the vista that Premiership clubs would be exposed to the same pressures as those felt by Nationwide League clubs following the collapse of ITV digital. In all probability, however, the agreement between the FA and the

---

[210] Harbord and Szymanski, "Football Trials" [2004] E.C.L.R. 117 at p.118.
[211] *Ibid.*, p.119.
[212] Halland Chaudhary, "Sky TV Deal May Be Ruled Unlawful", *Guardian*, November 8, 2003. See also Whittaker, McDonnell and Singh, "United We Stand: Collective Media Rights Sales under Challenge in England" (2003) (3) *International Sports Law Journal* 15.
[213] "Commission Reaches Provisional Agreement with FAPL and BskyB over Football Rights", DN: IP/03/1748 (December 16, 2003).

Commission will not spell financial disaster for clubs.[214] It also means that for the first time in its history, live Premiership matches will be available on free to air television.

Finally, from an Irish perspective a deal agreed in October 2003 between FAPL/Setanta Television and RTE means that 15 live matches[215] could be shown on RTE television for three years starting in 2004–2005. Also Setanta is entitled to show 15 pay per view games at times when RTE is not showing live games.

9.11 Conclusion

As has been mentioned earlier, it is difficult to predict how the post-May 2004, "decentralised" EC competition law will develop, both generally and in its application to sport. It may be suggested, for example, that controls on the advertising of alcohol at sporting events, or indeed of any sponsorship by alcohol companies of sporting events run the risk of being anti-competitive, although, as we have seen, thus far, the challenges to such laws are taken on the basis of Article 49 EC and the freedom to provide services.[216] From an Irish perspective it will, in particular be interesting to see whether Rule 42 of the GAA Rulebook could be challenged as a refusal to supply competitors with an essential facility.

Perhaps the most salutary lesson to be drawn from the application of competition law to this area, however, is that the institutions of the EU, in attempting to provide some legal regulation over sport, are caught between a vision of sport as a somewhat idealistic "social possession for Europeans" and the rather cruder reality of sport as a business. In keeping with the overall development of sports policy within the EU framework the institutions attempt to resolve this "double-vision" by applying law to sport, but in a rather strained fashion, with perhaps undue deference being paid to the claims of sport that it is, somehow above the law. It is entirely arguable that such a 'kid gloves' approach to sporting bodies reflects not just the approach of the EU institutions, but also that of national courts throughout Europe, including the Irish courts. Moreover, it reflects their approach in respect of all the various different contexts in which sport and the law interact that we have considered in this book. The result is sports law.

---

[214] Chaudhary, Milmo and Osborn, "Deal Saves Clubs From Financial Meltdown", *Guardian*, December 17, 2003.

[215] All the live games are to have 5.15 p.m. kick offs.

[216] See Opinion of Advocate General Tizzano in Cases C–262/02 and C–429/02 *Commission v. France Bicardi France SAS v. Television Française TF1*, March 11, 2004 (DN: CJE/ 04/15).

CHAPTER TEN

Sport and Equality

INTRODUCTION

The world of sport is highly segregated – men and women play and compete separately; seniors have separate tennis and golf tours; the fully-abled and the disabled have separate sporting events; national teams exclude foreigners. Application of equality law in this segregated universe poses particular conceptual and practical challenges.[1] Such segregation is often justified in order to preserve the competitive ethos of sport and its commitment to excellence. For example, it is argued that as men are on average faster and stronger than women, competitive sport requires that the sexes be segregated in order to ensure a level playing field. Similarly, certain sporting activities are deemed to be distinctly "unfeminine." Sport initially appears to be an arena where difference is exemplified and equality a misplaced value. However, other types of discrimination appear to be as pernicious in the sporting context as in any other – distinctly "unsporting" in fact. There is no "level playing field" justification for discrimination on the basis of race, religion, sexual orientation or membership of the Traveller Community.

The chapter argues that equality law in the sporting context faces four particular challenges. First, the weight of history is particularly heavy in the sporting context – stereotypes long rendered taboo in other areas of public discourse are routinely invoked in the sporting arena. In fact, sport is not only the medium, but also the means by which gender, sexual orientation and racial stereotypes are constructed. Secondly, the segregated nature of sport means that it is often regarded, in the words of a US court, as "at least one island in the sea of life reserved for man ... impregnable to the assault of woman."[2] This leads to the attempts to exclude women not only from competing against men, but also from sharing leisure facilities such as golf-clubs. Similar

---

[1] Indeed, some sports lawyers appear to be under the misapprehension that segregation is not discrimination at all. Thus Moore states, "Sport is segregated along two distinct lines: firstly, according to gender and, secondly, between the able-bodied and the disabled. The fact that men and women participate separately means that racially discriminatory behaviour is encountered more regularly than sex discrimination." Craig Moore *Sports Law and Litigation* (2nd ed., CLT Professional Publishing London, 2000) 189–190.

[2] *State v. Hunter*, 300 P2d 455, 457. Cited in Amy Bauer, "If You Build It, They Will Come: Establishing Title IX Compliance in Interscholastic Sports as a Foundation for Achieving Gender Equality" (2001) *Wm & Mary J. of Women & L.* 983, 933.

observations may be made about racial, religious and national segregation. In addition, the comparator requirement in Irish and EC equality law makes its application particularly difficult in segregated fields. Thirdly, sport has collective and cultural dimensions, such that freedom of association and expression may be raised to attempt to justify exclusionary practices. Fourthly, sport trades on its apparent frivolity to trivialise equality concerns while at the same time, relies on its internal integrity and seriousness in order to preserve its current features.

Of course, although sport may be inherently trivial, this does not mean it is without serious consequence. A finding in a recent study on women lawyers in Ireland was that men and women had different experiences of the impact of sport on the workplace, with many women reporting exclusion from networking opportunities, which were linked to sport. This led the authors to suggest that: "Golf appears to be such a major cause of social exclusion of women in the legal professions that one might well query whether women should be trained to play golf as students. It appears that this might well be more useful to them than academic qualifications in obtaining work."[3]

On closer examination, it becomes apparent that sport is not a unique domain, but that its construction along segregated, exclusionary and stereotypical lines is the result of historical choices.

"Competitive sport evolved in the mid Victorian era when men were men and women stayed at home. Sport was designed for men, with the nature of most sports reflecting predominantly male traits of strength, size and shape. Indeed, many sports evolved from the celebration of the physical attributes of the successful soldier in battle. But, while the world has changed, sport has remained in times past and although we see increasing opportunities for women in sport, these simply reflect extensions of male sports rather than the introduction of sport to which women would be particularly suited. The rules, regulations and values of sport thus remain rooted in a different era and can cause conflict between our idealised female role model and the demands of top sport."[4]

How does equality law apply to such a resolutely conservative domain, constructed on the stereotypes of times past? One lesson from the application of equality law in other areas is that commonplace distinctions, which may at first glance appear natural, often mask prejudicial treatment. Thus equality law serves as a rationality filter, providing a basis to scrutinise the stereotyping that is commonplace in sport. However, equality law can do far more than

---

[3] Ivana Bacik, Cathryn Costello and Eileen Drew, *Gender Injustice: Feminising the Legal Professions* (Trinity College Dublin, Law School, 2003) 297.

[4] Domhnall Macauley, "Editorial" (1999) *British Journal of Sports Medicine* 225, cited by Edward Grayson, *Sport and the Law* (3rd ed., Butterworths London, 2000) 326.

simply provide a basic rationality test to root out the worst stereotyping. It can also develop the conceptual tools to challenge institutional discrimination, inequitable resource allocation and even the composition and methods of decision-makers.

Christopher McCrudden refers to "equality as mere rationality" as just one of five meanings attaching to the concept of equality in equality law and discourse. The others are equality as individualised justice, equality as group justice, equality as recognition of cultural diversity and equality as participation.[5] "Equality as individualised justice" allows individuals to challenge official decisions based on characteristics deemed irrelevant (e.g. gender, race, age etc), allowing them to point to their true ability and merit. However, its individualised focus means that "the apparent commitment to neutrality masks an insistence on a particular set of values, based on those of the dominant culture."[6] The "group justice model" therefore attempts to overcome these limitations, by recognising the different positions of groups and attempting to achieve substantive equality in order to overcome disadvantage. "Equality as recognition" refers to the importance of securing recognition of diversity, be it in life-style choices, ethnic, religious or sexual identity. "Equality as participation"[7] focuses on the importance of political voice for the marginalised. McCrudden argues "no *one* model can or should claim to represent *the* central or best case of equality in interpreting and explaining European equality law... All of these conceptions of equality are necessary for us to capture the full richness of the legal meanings we give to equality ...".[8]

What these models do have in common is that they reflect attempts to address equality concerns in a manner sensitive to difference, acknowledging that equality should not be predicated on sameness. In addition, they take equality beyond considerations of sameness and difference, to issues of disadvantage. Furthermore, unlike individualist approaches to equality, group and diversity based models can accommodate asymmetrical outcomes. For example, while we may abhor homophobia in mainstream sport, should the discrimination against heterosexual athletes inherent in the Gay Games be seen in the same way?[9] Or in the Bingham Cup, a rugby tournament "predominantly for gay and bisexual men", with over 350 international amateur rugby players?[10] Our response depends very much on the model of equality to which we adhere. "Equality as recognition" would clearly support events such

---

[5] Christopher McCrudden, "Theorising European Equality Law" in Cathryn Costello & Eilis Barry (eds.), *Equality in Diversity: The New Equality Directives* (ICEL/Equality Authority 2003), pp.1, 19–34.

[6] Sandra Fredman, "Equality, A New Generation" (2001) *I.L.J.* 145 at 154.

[7] See Ann Philips, *The Politics of Presence* (OUP Oxford, 1995).

[8] McCrudden, *op. cit.*, n.5 at p.33.

[9] See discussion below in para.10.5 below.

[10] For a history of the tournament, see www.binghamcup.com/BinghamCupHistory.htm.

as the Gay Games, which aim to "bring a global community together in friendship, to experience participation, to elevate consciousness and self-esteem and to achieve a form of cultural and intellectual synergy."[11]

Various models of equality thus may have particular application to sport, in light of sport's range of forms, purposes and contexts. However, when we examine equality law as currently applied to sport, particularly in Ireland, it is apparent that not only has there been a failure to articulate the underlying concepts of equality, but also a distinct tendency towards the avoidance of any clear conceptual foundation. The Irish statutory regime adopts a somewhat contradictory and piecemeal approach. In order to illustrate the current legal frameworks, the chapter begins with an overview of equality law in Ireland (para.10.1). It then provides an examination of various grounds of discrimination, namely gender (para.10.2), nationality, race, ethnicity, and religion (para.10.3), disability (para.10.4), sexual orientation (para.10.5), and age (para.10.6). The final section deals with the special statutory regime for private clubs (para.10.7). Some comparative material from the UK and US is referred to in order to illustrate different ways to improve opportunities in sport. The chapter follows a rigid separation of types of discrimination, in keeping with the legal typology. Of course, this ignores problems of intersectionality. For example, lesbian athletes may be doubly discriminated against, as may disabled athletes from minority ethnic backgrounds. In following the law's classifications, we should bear in mind the need for equality law to develop more refined approaches to these problems.[12] In addition, the chapter devotes unequal attention to the different grounds of discrimination, focusing on gender equality. This is not to suggest that other forms of inequality are any less serious. In fact "the different forms of discrimination cannot be ranked; all are equally intolerable".[13] The unequal attention simply reflects the greater legal attention afforded to gender equality in sport to date, and admittedly, biases in the author's own interests.

---

[11] Excerpt from "White Paper" by Dr. Tom Waddell, founder of the Gay Games, answering a question, "Why a Gay Games?" (1982). He writes:
"The Gay Games are not separatist, they are not exclusive, they are not oriented to victory, and they are not for commercial gain. They ARE, however, intended to bring a global community together in friendship, to experience participation, to elevate consciousness and self-esteem and to achieve a form of cultural and intellectual synergy." Available at <www.gaygames.com/en/games/waddell_text.htm>. The sixth Gay Games were held in Sydney in 2002.
[12] There is a substantial literature on multi-ground discrimination or intersectionality. See, for example, Sandra Fredman and Erica Szyszczak, "The Interaction of Race and Gender" in Bob Hepple & Erica Szyszczak (eds.), *Discrimination: The Limits of Law* (Mansell, London, 1992) 221. In the sports context, see Patricia Cain, "Women, Race & Sports – Life Before Title IX" (2001) *J. Gender Race & Justice* 337.
[13] Recital 5 of Council Decision establishing a Community Action Plan to combat discrimination (2001 to 2006) [2000] O.J. L303/23.

10.1 OVERVIEW OF THE RELATIONSHIP BETWEEN IRISH EQUALITY LAW AND SPORT

The purpose of this section is to highlight the provisions of Irish equality law, which are of particular relevance to the sporting context. Until relatively recently Ireland's equality law was chiefly of EU origin and focused on employment discrimination on gender and nationality grounds. The Constitutional equality guarantee in Article 40 has yet to be explored in the sports context. This is in large part due to the fact that that guarantee had for some time been rendered inert by the "human personality doctrine"[14] which provides that equality only applies to the "essential attributes of the human person" rather than her activities and interests. Accordingly it cannot be invoked, for example, in the commercial context.[15] Although there appears to be a move away from the more restrictive aspects of this approach,[16] the judiciary appear to take a very limited view of the permissible legal responses to inequalities, and even partly struck down the original Employment Equality Bill in order to protect the commercial freedom of the employer.[17]

Since the late 1990s equality law has been extended to cover new grounds and new contexts. Prohibited grounds of discrimination now include gender, marital status, family status, sexual orientation, religion, age, disability, race and membership of the Traveller Community. The Employment Equality Act 1998 ("EEA") prohibits each of these grounds of discrimination in the employment context. Given that much professional sporting activity involves employment relationships, the EEA is of course of relevance.

In addition, the Equal Status Act 2000 ("ESA") prohibits discrimination on the same grounds in a range of other situations. These include the disposal of goods "to the public generally or a section of the public" and the provision of services "whether the disposal or provision is for consideration or otherwise and whether the service provided can be availed of only by a section of the public."[18] Thus, for example, the organisers of a sporting tournament provide services not only to the viewing public but also to the participants in the tournament, and must respect equality law as regards both categories of persons.[19] The ESA also applies to the provision of accommodation and the

---

[14] For a detailed discussion see Oran Doyle, "The Human Personality Doctrine in Constitutional Equality Law" (2001) *Irish Student Law Review* 101.

[15] *Quinn's Supermarket v. Attorney General* [1972] IR 1.

[16] Gerard Hogan & Gerry Whyte, *JM Kelly: The Irish Constitution* (4th ed., Butterworths, Dublin, 2003) 1345–1348.

[17] *Article 26 and the Employment Equality Bill 1996, re* [1997] 2 I.R. 321. For a critique, see Gerard Quinn & Siobhan Quinlivan, "Disability Discrimination: The Need to Amend the Employment Equality Act 1998 in Light of the EU Framework Directive on Employment" in Costello & Barry (eds.) above n.5 at p.213, especially pp.224–225.

[18] S.5(1) of the ESA.

[19] This issue has important ramifications for the scope of equality law. An analogous point

disposal of property interests[20] and to educational establishments.[21] The latter term includes pre-school, primary, post-primary school, and tertiary institutions "whether or not supported by public funds."[22] The non-discrimination rule applies to admission, expulsion, "access to any course, facility or benefit provided by the establishment" and "any other term or condition of participation in the establishment by a student."[23] Thus, the ESA clearly covers sports programmes offered by educational establishments.

Section 7(4) of the EEA provides an exception for certain discrimination in the educational context. Section 7(4)(a) permits differences in treatment on grounds of gender, age and disability "to the extent that the differences are reasonably necessary having regard to the nature of the facilities or events." In addition section 7(4)(b) allows differences in treatment for disabled students if making a particular facility available to a disabled student would "by virtue of the disability, make impossible, or have a seriously detrimental effect on, the provision by an educational establishment of its services to other students." The breadth of these exemptions is regrettable and considerably weakens the EEA as an instrument to challenge segregation in educational sport. However, section 7(4) does not grant the institution carte blanche – exclusions must still be shown to be reasonable in the circumstances.

Both the EEA and ESA must comply with, and be read in light of EC law, on gender equality (mainly the "Gender Equal Treatment Directive")[24] and more recently on other grounds. In 2000, the EC adopted a framework directive on discrimination in employment, dealing with discrimination on grounds of religion or belief, disability, age and sexual orientation (hereafter "the Framework Directive")[25] and a directive prohibiting racial discrimination in employment and in relation to the provision of goods and services ("the Race & Ethnicity Directive").[26] As yet, there is no EC law governing gender discrimination in the provision of goods and services, but the Commission has proposed a Directive in this area, which may be adopted some time in 2004.[27]

---

arose in before the US Supreme Court in *Casey Martin v. PGA*, 121 S.Ct 1879 (May 20, 2001), discussed in para.10.4 below.

[20] S.6 of the ESA.

[21] S.7 of the ESA.

[22] S.7(1) of the ESA.

[23] S.7(2) of the ESA.

[24] Council Directive 76/207/EEC on Equal Treatment for Men and Women as regards access to Employment, Vocational Training and Promotion, and Working Conditions, [1976] O.J. L45/19. This Directive was amended in 2002. Parliament and Council Directive of September 23, 2002 [2002] O.J. L269/1. The new directive does not have to be implemented by the Member States until October 5, 2005.

[25] Council Directive 2000/78/EC establishing a general framework for equal treatment in employment and occupation [2000] O.J. L303/16.

[26] Council Directive 2000/43/EC implementing the principle of equal treatment between persons irrespective of racial or ethnic origin [2000] O.J. L180/22.

[27] Proposal for a Council Directive implementing the principle of equal treatment between

The Irish Government recently published the Equality Bill 2004, which purports to implement the Framework and Race & Ethnicity Directives, as well as the amendment to the Gender Equal Treatment Directive. Concerns have been expressed that it not only fails to properly implement the Directives, but also that in some areas it dilutes non-discrimination guarantees.[28]

Discrimination under Irish and EC law is defined in broadly similar terms. Direct discrimination is prohibited, unless expressly permitted. Direct discrimination refers to basing a decision or practice on the ground in question, e.g. refusing to hire a woman coach due to her gender. In addition, EC law has developed a sophisticated concept of indirect discrimination, which allows challenges to be brought to apparently neutral practices and structures, which in fact have a disproportionate impact on those belonging to one gender, ethnicity and so on. There are various definitions of indirect discrimination in EC law and Irish law.[29] The Framework and Race & Ethnicity Directives adopt a flexible approach, defining indirect discrimination as "where an apparently neutral provision, criterion or practice would put persons having … a particular [characteristic] at a particular disadvantage compared with other persons…".[30] Indirect discrimination may, however, be objectively justified, on the basis of a legitimate aim, provided that the means of achieving that aim are appropriate and necessary.[31]

In order to establish direct or indirect discrimination it is necessary to draw a comparison with a person who does not share the characteristic in question. Thus, for example, in order for a girl to argue that she is being discriminated against by her school if she is not allowed to play soccer, she must show that a boy in that school (her "comparator") is permitted to play. If she is attends an all-girls school, this will not be possible, as the law only rarely allows complainants to use a hypothetical comparator. She will not be able to draw comparisons with the sports opportunities of boys in a neighbouring school, as her comparator must attend the same institution. This considerably weakens the possibility to challenge discrimination in a segregated context. As is illustrated below, in the US specific policy tools have been developed to overcome this feature of traditional anti-discrimination law.

---

women and men in the access to and supply of goods and services COM/2003/0657 final (November 5, 2003).

[28] See Equality Coalition, *Submission on the Equality Bill 2004*, available at www.iccl.ie/minorities/bill/04eqbill_submission.pdf.

[29] For an overview, see Mary Finlay, "Indirect Discrimination and the Article 13 Directives" in Costello & Barry (eds.) *op. cit.*, n.5 at p.135. Different definitions apply in different contexts, depending on whether the discrimination is in employment legislation, social security legislation, employer practices or commercial practices. In addition, different tests of objective justification apply in these different areas. Moreover, there are differences between the treatment of gender discrimination and other types of discrimination.

[30] Art.2(2)(b) of the Framework Directive and Art.2(2)(b) Race & Ethnicity Directive.

[31] *Ibid.*

In addition to direct and indirect discrimination, harassment is now acknowledged as a form of discriminatory conduct.[32] Under the Framework Directive and the Race & Ethnicity Directive, harassment is defined as "unwanted conduct related to any of the [prohibited grounds] with the purpose or effect of violating the dignity of a person and of creating an intimidating, hostile, degrading, humiliating or offensive environment."[33] The Directives also go on to state that harassment may be "defined in accordance with the national laws and practice of the Member States."

As well as permitting discrimination in limited circumstances in derogation from the principle of equal treatment, EC law also permits a stronger group-based understanding of equality in that it allows Member States to adopt positive action with the objective of promoting equality. Positive action encompasses a range of policies and practices which aim to achieve full equality in practice, for example, by targeting disadvantaged groups, creating special programmes for those who have been historically excluded and providing preferences in selection procedures. Both the EEA and ESA contain a complex patchwork of permissive provisions in this regard.[34] Thus, once carefully tailored, sports employers and bodies may adopt such policies and still comply with equality law.

Sports employers, regulators, governing bodies, organisers, schools and public authorities all have obligations under equality law. These obligations require them not only to refrain from intentional acts of overt discrimination, but also to examine their processes to remove indirectly discriminatory and exclusionary practices. The law also requires the development of appropriate procedures in order to secure internal redress for complainants. Such procedures must also ensure that complainants are not victimised if they complain about discriminatory acts. A further feature of equality law in the employment context is vicarious liability. Employers are in principle liable for the discriminatory acts of their employees.[35]

As well as providing for an individual right of complaint and specific procedures for dealing with such complaints, Irish equality law also provides for institutional enforcement in the form of the Equality Authority.[36] The Authority's role is broadly defined as working towards the elimination of discrimination and promoting equality of opportunity in employment and matters covered by the ESA.[37] To this end it has a variety of powers, including

---

[32] For a discussion of the various EC and national definitions and approaches to harassment, see Ivana Bacik, "Harassment" in Costello & Barry (eds.), *op. cit.*, n.5 at p.151.

[33] Art.2(3) Framework Directive; Art.2(3) Race & Ethnicity Directive.

[34] For a detailed analysis, see Cathryn Costello, "Positive Action" in Costello & Barry (eds.), *op. cit.*, n.5 at p.177.

[35] S.15 of the EEA.

[36] See Eilis Barry "Different Hierarchies – Enforcing Equality Law" in Costello & Barry (eds.), *op. cit.*, n.5 at p.411.

[37] S.39 of the EEA and s.39 of the ESA.

the preparation of Codes of Practice and conducting equality reviews. Thus for example, two voluntary reviews of Irish universities, namely DCU and UCD are underway, but it is understood that these reviews did not consider the universities' sporting programmes. The Race & Ethnicity Directive and the Amendment to the Gender Equal Treatment Directive require the establishment of "bodies for the promotion of equal treatment."[38]

While some aspects of purely recreational sport may not be subject to equality law (where no service is offered to the public or a section thereof) nonetheless an equality ethos should be fostered. Mainstreaming refers to a policy technique designed to ensure that equality is taken into account in all areas by using tools such as impact assessment and participation of disadvantaged or excluded groups in decision-making.[39] In the sports context, mainstreaming could become particularly important in order to promote equality and institutional change, whilst allowing sport to maintain its self-regulatory and autonomous nature.

10.2 GENDER DISCRIMINATION IN SPORT

10.2.1 Irish law

The provisions of the EEA on gender equality, which are to be interpreted in line with the Gender Equal Treatment Directive, prohibit direct and indirect discrimination and harassment. It should be noted that gender discrimination includes discrimination on grounds of transsexuality, such that a transsexual professional athlete may insist on being treated as belonging to her true (reassigned) sex.[40] In addition, discrimination on grounds of pregnancy is direct gender discrimination.[41] However, some protective measures for pregnant women are permissible.[42]

---

[38] Art.13 of the Race & Ethnicity Directive; Art.1(7) of the Amendment to the Gender Equal Treatment Directive.

[39] Mainstreaming is most developed in the gender context. For a discussion, see Siobhán Mullally, "Beyond the Limits of Non-discrimination: Promoting Gender Equality" in Costello & Barry (eds.), *op. cit.*, n.5 at p.295, especially pp.302–311.

[40] Case C–13/94 *P v. S & Cornwall* [1996] E.C.R. I–2143. Case C–117/01 *KB v. NHS*, 7 January 7, 2004. It is notable that in 2004 the IOC has said that transsexual athletes will be permitted to compete in the Athens Olympic Games (and all future Olympic Games) against members of their true (reassigned) sex. See Duggan, "Transsexual Ruling Only Muddies Waters", *Irish Times*, May 22, 2004.

[41] Case C–177/88 *Dekker* [1990] E.C.R. I–3941. For a detailed discussion of the law on this topic see Marguerite Bolger & Clíona Kimber, *Sex Discrimination Law* (Round Hall Sweet & Maxwell Dublin 2000), Chap.9, "Pregnancy", pp.292–314 and Chap.10, "Maternity Rights and Beyond: From Motherhood to Parenting", pp.316–364.

[42] Art.2(3) of the Gender Equal Treatment Directive which states:
"The Directive shall be without prejudice to provisions concerning the protection of

Gender discrimination has been inferred by the Irish authorities where interview questions suggest gender bias.[43] This contrasts sharply with the UK case of *Saunders v. Richmond-Upon Thames BC*[44] concerning a woman professional golfer who applied for a position as a local council golf coach. She argued that the refusal to appoint her was based on gender discrimination, as evidenced by the fact that the letter of acknowledgment of her application had been addressed to "Dear Sir" and many interview questions related to her gender. The Industrial Tribunal ("IT") and Employment Appeal Tribunal ("EAT") held that there had been no discrimination. Such a finding would not be reached today, as adjudicators would quite rightly infer gender discrimination from such questioning.

Direct gender discrimination (where a decision or practice is explicitly based on gender) may only be justified on the basis of a specific exemption in the Gender Equal Treatment Directive. Exemptions must remain within the limits of what is proportionate, which allows courts to scrutinize whether the measure is necessary and appropriate to achieve the aim pursued. Of relevance to the sporting context is Article 2(2), which allows gender discrimination where the sex of the worker is a determining factor. It refers to "those occupational activities ... for which, by reason of their nature or the context in which they are carried out, the sex of the worker constitutes the determining factor." In *Sirdar*[45] the ECJ held it was permissible for the UK to reserve all positions in the Royal Marines to men, in light of its status as a front line fighting force. However a full exclusion from the armed forces would not be permissible.[46] Barnard notes "how easy it is ... to use the derogations as a shield for gender stereotyping and untested assumptions about male soldiers' attitudes to women."[47] However, justifications are usually carefully scrutinised under EC law. While challenging access to the battlefield has only been partly successful, exclusion from the sports field would certainly be subject to rigorous appraisal.

The EEA does not contain any specific provisions permitting gender differentiation in sport. However, section 25(2) provides that it is permissible to treat sex as an occupational qualification where on grounds of physiology

---

women, particularly as regards pregnancy and maternity." See also, Directive 92/85 EC on the introduction of measures to encourage improvements in the safety and health at work of pregnant workers and workers who have recently given birth or are breastfeeding [1992] O.J. L.348/1.

[43] *Rotunda Hospital & Mater Misericoridiae Hospital v. Dr. Gleeson*, ODEI Determin. No. DEE003, April 18, 2000.

[44] [1978] I.C.R. 75.

[45] Case C–273/97 *Sirdar v. Secretary of State for Defence* [1999] E.C.R. I–7403.

[46] Case C–285/98 *Kreil* [2000] E.C.R. I–69. For a discussion of both *Sirdar* and *Kreil*, see Martin Trybus, "Sisters in arms: European Community Law and Sex Equality in the Armed Forces" (2003) *E.L.J.* 631.

[47] Catherine Barnard, *EC Employment Law* (2nd ed., OUP Oxford, 2000), p.242.

or on grounds of authenticity for the purposes of entertainment, the nature of the post so requires. It is noteworthy in relation to gender discrimination, physiology is stated to *exclude* physical strength or stamina, unlike the analogous provision of section 37(3) in relation to other types of discrimination. This provision could provide much ammunition to challenge gender differentiation in sports employment. Section 25(2) must be interpreted in light of EC law, so the principle of proportionality applies. It is surprising that to date, there have been no challenges to gender discrimination in sport in Ireland on the basis of these provisions. When we turn to the UK context, we see that exclusionary practices are pervasive.

In contrast to the EEA, the ESA has several significant exemptions from the general anti-discrimination regime for sporting activities. As mentioned in the previous section, Section 7(4)(a) of the EEA permits educational establishments to treat people of different genders differently "to the extent that the differences are reasonably necessary having regard to the nature of the facilities or events." Differences in treatment on the basis of gender, age, disability, nationality or national origin in relation to the provision or organisation of a sporting event are permissible to the extent that the differences are reasonably necessary having regard to the nature of the facility or event and are relevant to the purpose of the facility or event.[48] In addition, section 5(2)(g) allows differences in the treatment of on the basis of gender where "embarrassment or infringement of privacy can reasonably be expected to result from the presence of a person of another gender."

10.2.2 The United Kingdom

10.2.2.1 Challenging discrimination

In the UK the common law provided some protection against discrimination. In *Nagle v. Feilden*[49] the Jockey Club refused the applicant a trainer's licence, on the basis that she was a woman. Lord Denning MR stated that: "the Jockey Club's unwritten rule may well be said to be arbitrary or capricious."[50] As such, the Club's decision was struck down as an unreasonable restraint of trade. However, the malleability of the common law did not promise great transformative effects. The Law Lord continued :"It is not as if the training of horses could be regarded as an unsuitable occupation for a woman like that of a jockey or speedway rider."

It was with the enactment of the Sex Discrimination Act 1975 ("SDA")

---

[48] S.5(2)(f) of the ESA.
[49] [1966] 2 Q.B. 633.
[50] *Ibid.*, p.647. Cited in Beloff *et al*, *Sports Law* (Hart Publishing, Oxford, 1999), p.97.

that gender discrimination was explicitly prohibited. Like the ESA, the SDA must be read in light of EC law. Under the Act, direct and indirect gender discrimination are prohibited. Several English cases concern overt gender discrimination.

A series of early cases secured women's access to the snooker table. In *Rice v. Chatterton*[51] a publican was found to have discriminated unlawfully by refusing to allow women to play snooker because, in his view, women ripped snooker tablecloths. Again in *Bateson v. Belfast YWCA*[52] the refusal of the YWCA to allow access to its snooker tables was held to be discriminatory. Here, it was again alleged that women were more likely to tear the cloths and in addition, that by talking and laughing, they would disturb the necessary silence. These arguments were naturally rejected. The YWCA also failed in its argument that it was a private club and hence exempt. Thirdly in *Priestly v. Stork Margarine Social and Recreational Club*[53] Sandra Priestly challenged the unwritten "men only" rule for the snooker table in her workplace. She argued that the social club was not private, and so did not fall under the exemption on section 29 SDA. This was accepted in light of the fact that it did not have a selection procedure, and all employees were entitled to join.

The Football Association's ("FA") discriminatory practices were challenged in *Hardwick v. FA*.[54] Vanessa Hardwick was refused a coaching certificate by the FA. She was deemed to have failed the FA coaching course, although she performed better on the advanced part of the course than many male counterparts who were awarded the certificate. Partly, this was due to the fact that the FA was surreptitiously running a course for retired footballers that was easier to pass. Out of the total of 1500 people that had passed, only two were women. It was inferred that Hardwick had been discriminated against on gender grounds.

The most high-profile challenge to gender discrimination was that of Jane Couch, who successfully challenged the British Boxing Board's refusal to grant her a license as a professional boxer.[55] She held the title of British Women's Welterweight Boxing Champion, although all fights took place in US.[56] The British Boxing Board refused to licence Couch on the basis that it had medical concerns about women's boxing and that licensing women would require "drastic changes to the rules" to allow the wearing of apparel above the waistband. The medical concerns included *inter alia* trauma to the breasts, hormonal changes, premenstrual tension, and the prohibition of taking

---

[51] *The Times*, June 29, 1977.
[52] [1980] N.I. 135.
[53] Unreported, Birkenhead County Court, June 24, 1988. Discussed in Edward Grayson *Sport and the Law* (3rd ed., Butterworths London 2000), pp.342–343.
[54] IT Case 2320451/96.
[55] *Couch v. BBBC* IT Case No 2304231/97.
[56] 1 (3) *Sports Law Bulletin* (1998) 1.

contraceptive pills since no drugs or medication is allowed. The IT rejected these arguments, finding that the changes required to the Board's rules could not be characterised as "drastic" nor was there evidence to support the view that it was more dangerous for women to box than for men. The IT noted that the Board had not carried out a physical examination of Couch and that women's boxing was deemed safe in other countries.

10.2.2.2 Preserving segregation

The SDA contains a specific exemption for sport. Section 44 provides:

> "Nothing in Parts II-IV shall in relation to any sport, game or other activity of a competitive nature where the physical strength, stamina or physique of the average woman puts her at a disadvantage to the average man, render unlawful any act related to the participation of a person as a competitor in events involving that activity which are confined to competitors of one sex."

The scope of the section is limited. In *GLC v. Farrar*[57] the EAT noted that:

> "In a case where it is desired to exclude, for example, a girl from a mixed team, or to exclude girls from playing in teams against other boys or men, such an exclusion would not be unlawful for the purposes of the Act of 1975. But it seems to us that this section is dealing with a situation in which men and women might both be playing the same game or taking part in the same activity [where] physical strength, stamina or physique would become a relevant matter. It does not seem to us that this section is dealing with the situation where it is desired that a girl should play a game against a girl or where teams of girls are to play teams of girls."

In addition, the section may not be relied upon where there is no evidence that physique had any role to play. An attempt to rely on the section as regards snooker therefore failed.[58] In effect, there is a three-stage test for the application of section 44:

– Is the applicant seeking to participate in a sport, game or physical activity?

– Is she seeking to participate as a competitor (as opposed to a coach, referee)?

– Is she seeking to compete in the same event as men?[59]

---

[57] [1980] I.C.R. 266.

[58] *French v. Crosby Links Hotel*, unreported, Great Yarmouth County Court, May 7, 1982.

[59] David McArdle, "Rethinking Sports Organisations" Responses to Workplace Concerns' in Steve Greenfield & Guy Osborn, *Law and Sport in Contemporary Society* (Frank Cass, London, 2000), pp.201, 208.

Unless there is a positive answer to all three questions then section 44 will not apply.

The section has prevented able women and girls from challenging their exclusion from playing sport with boys and men. This is exemplified in *Football Association and Nottinghamshire Football Association v. Bennett*,[60] which concerned whether a 12-year-old girl could be prevented from playing football with boys her age. The evidence was that she "ran rings around the boys." The trial judge held that prior to puberty there was little difference in terms of strength and stamina between girls and boys so that section 44 did not apply. The Court of Appeal reversed this decision on the basis that section 44 required a consideration of whether the average woman would be at a disadvantage in playing the sport, compared to the average man. Football was such a sport, so excluding Bennett from a boys' school team was upheld. More recently the FA did change its rules for children under 11.[61] In 2000, a minor victory was won in Wales, where a 12-year-old girl won her right to play on a boys' team. The Football Association of Wales changed its rules to allow girls to play until 16, in areas where there is no girls' junior league.[62]

In other decisions, the English courts have applied a restrictive interpretation of section 44. Thus in *Petty v. British Judo Association*[63] Petty was granted a judo referee certificate, but was not entitled to referee men's games. The Association sought to rely on section 44, arguing that a woman would not have the strength to separate two male contestants. In fact, one of the testimonies was as follows, "I would not feel happy on the mat with a woman refereeing. I think I would find the physical aspects of a woman controlling two hefty men on the mat a little degrading."[64] It was held that the word "participation" in section 44 should be given its ordinary meaning and thus only included taking part as a competitor.

Section 44 has been heavily criticised. For example, Swindell argues that it: "protects intrusion by women unto the arena of the 'real' sporting world of men, leaving women to tread a separate and often undervalued pathway of sporting achievement." She notes also that: "It is in sport and no other sphere that discrimination against women is legally validated and raises questions that an Act specifically intended to eliminate sex discrimination legitimises sexist assumptions." [65] In addition, the EOC has argued that: "there is a particular concern at the inhibiting impact of section 44 upon the development

---

[60] Unreported, Court of Appeal, July 28, 1978.
[61] Lesley Swindell, "Football is a Masculine Noun", 10(2) *Sport and the Law Journal* (2002) 126 at 127.
[62] 3(5) *Sports Law Bulletin* (2000) 5.
[63] [1981] I.C.R. 660.
[64] Cited in Edward Grayson, *Sport and the Law* (3rd ed., Butterworths, London, 2000), p.342.
[65] Swindell, *op. cit.*, n.61.

of the interest and skill of young people across a broad range of sporting activities." It urged that, "The exception in section 44 of the SDA should no longer permit the exclusion of young people of school age from competing in any sport, game or other competitive activity."

10.2.3 The United States of America

10.2.3.1 Sport and the American way

The starting point in the US is an acknowledgement of the centrality of sport to physical and psychological well-being. In addition, sport is seen as fostering American ideals – individual excellence, competitiveness and teamwork. Indeed the consensus around the importance of sport is such that it is routinely lauded as a universal panacea. Bauer's comments are typical: "Studies show that women who have the opportunity to participate in athletics acquire a greater sense of confidence, self-esteem and pride. Three studies have also shown that athletics foster personal skills and relationships in addition to promoting physical and psychological health. Further, there is a positive correlation between student participation in sports, a reduced probability of teenage pregnancy, and increased likelihood of high school graduation. Lastly, with every athletic achievement comes prestige and respect."[66] In addition, the benefits of team sports are emphasized. "Participation in sports is where boys traditionally learn about teamwork, goal-setting, and the pursuit of excellence in performance. ... Men learn the rules of human organizations and interactions from sport in their childhood and adolescent years. Women who do not know the written and unwritten rules of sport are at a significance disadvantage in the traditional, male-dominated corporate workplace."[67]

From this starting point of emphasising the seriousness and importance of sport, US policy is based, secondly, on an assumption that women's historical lack of participation is due not to lack of interest, but to lack of opportunity. As a US court stated: "interest and ability rarely develop in a vacuum; they evolve as a function of opportunity and experience .. [W]omen's lower rate of participation in athletics reflects women's historical lack of opportunities to participate in sports."[68] The third key aspect of US policy is the development of tools to ensure equality in the segregated world. Thus, "determining whether

---

[66] Amy Bauer, "If you build it, they will come: Establishing Title IX Compliance in Interscholastic Sports as a Foundation for Achieving Gender Equity" (2001) *Wm & Mary J. of Women & L.* 983, 991–992. References omitted.

[67] Rocio de Lourdes Cordoba, "In Search of a Level Playing Field: *Baca v. City of Los Angeles* as a Step Toward Gender Equity in Girls' Sports Beyond Title IX" (2001) *Harvard Women's L.J.* 139, 159. References omitted.

[68] *Cohen v. Brown University*, 101 F3d 155, 178–179 (1st Cir 1996), cert denied 520 US 1186 (1997).

discrimination exists in [sex-segregated] athletic programs *requires* gender-conscious, group-wide comparisons."[69] US policy thus entails detailed assessments of resource allocation, in order to examine whether women's sporting opportunities, while they need not be the same as men's, are proportionate thereto. The final aspect underpinning the US policy is institutional and individual enforcement, with strong incentives for compliance and monitoring of institutional changes.

10.2.3.2 Title IX – Ensuring equality in a segregated world?

The USA has the most highly developed gender equality law applicable to sport in the educational context. Congress passed Title IX of the Education Amendments in 1972. Its key provision states:

> "No person in the United States shall, on the basis of sex, be excluded from participation in, be denied the benefits of, or be subjected to discrimination under any educational programme or activity receiving Federal financial assistance."

The Title became effective in phases from 1975 to 1978. The issue of whether it should cover sports was vigorously debated during its passage.[70] The initial legislation did not refer explicitly to sports so some confusion persisted on this matter. The Supreme Court in *Grove City College v. Bell*[71] decided that the Title only applied to activities directly in receipt of federal funds. This approach was overturned by Congress with the Civil Rights Restoration Act of 1987, which adopted an "institution-wide" approach, such that "all operations of an institution … any part of which is extended federal financial assistance" were subject to Title IX.

In 1974 Regulations were passed to deal specifically with athletics, followed by a Department of Health, Education and Welfare "Policy Interpretation" in 1979. The Office for Civil Rights within that Department enforces these rules. In addition to strong institutional enforcement, Title IX may be enforced by any individual or group with standing, which can and does lead to substantial awards of punitive damages. Moreover, each organisation subject to Title IX must designate an employee to receive and investigate in house complaints.

The Policy Interpretation deals in detail with two areas where Title IX compliance is required. First, as regards sports scholarships, it requires that funds for scholarships are allocated in proportion to the number of men and

---

[69] *Neal v. Board of Trustees of the California State Universities*, 198 F3d 763,770 (9th Cir 1999).

[70] Deborah Brake & Elizabeth Catlin, "The Path of Most Resistance: The Long Road Toward Gender Equity in Intercollegiate Athletics" (1996) Duke J. Gender L. & Pol'y. 51.

[71] 465 US 555, 570 (1984).

women participating in athletic programmes. Secondly, it deals with the benefits and opportunities available to such programmes, listing ten factors to determine whether an institution is providing gender equal opportunity:

1. Whether the selection of sports and levels of competition effectively accommodate the interests and abilities of members of both sexes;

2. The provision of equipment and supplies;

3. Scheduling of games and practice time;

4. Travel and *per diem* allowance;

5. Opportunity to receive coaching and academic tutoring;

6. Assignment and compensation of coaches and tutors;

7. Provision of locker rooms, practice and competitive facilities;

8. Provision of medical and training facilities and services;

9. Provision of housing and dining facilities and services;

10. Publicity.[72]

Most litigation under Title IX has focused on the first issue, whether the institution has provided "effective accommodation." This requires a demonstration of the following:

1. Whether intercollegiate level participation opportunities for male and female are provided in numbers substantially proportionate to their respective enrolments; or

2. Where the members of one sex have been and are underrepresented among intercollegiate athletes, whether the institution can show a history and continuing practice of program expansion which is demonstrably responsive to the developing interest and abilities of that sex; or

3. Where the members of one sex are underrepresented among intercollegiate athletes, and the institution cannot show a continuing practice of programme expansion such as that cited above, where it can be demonstrated that the interests and abilities of the members of that sex have been fully and effectively accommodated by the present programme.[73]

This three-prong test has been employed in a host of cases, often requiring significant structural changes. Where institutions can demonstrate "substantial proportionality" in participation opportunities, they are deemed to be in

---

[72] 34 CFR para.106.41(c). Cordoba, *op. cit.*, n.67 at p.147.
[73] 44 Fed Reg 71, 418 (December 11, 1978).

compliance. Even if this is not the case, compliance may be demonstrated by reliance on either of the other two prongs, namely by demonstrating programme expansion or that the interests of both sexes have otherwise been effectively accommodated. The test does not challenge gender segregation, and may, in fact encourage it.[74]

The application of this three-limb test is rigorous. In *Favia v. Indiana University of Pennsylvania*[75] a 17.8% discrepancy between the percentage of female students and female athletes was found to be disproportionate. As the university had eliminated women's field hockey and gymnastics teams, it was unable to fulfil the second prong of programme expansion. Based on the plaintiffs' testimony, the court found that the third prong was not fulfilled. Similarly in *Roberts v. Colorado State University*[76] a 10.5% discrepancy between female athletes and female students was held to demonstrate lack of proportionality. The university was ordered to reinstate the women's softball programme. In *Cohen v. Brown University*,[77] due to budgetary cuts, the University eliminated four varsity level sports – men's water polo, men's golf, women's gymnastics and women's volleyball. Each team was downgraded to a club, which was thereby entitled to participate in intercollegiate sports, provided it could raise its own finances. The court found that the university had failed to demonstrate effective accommodation, applying the three pronged test strictly.

10.2.3.3 *Title IX – A victim of its own success?*

Title IX has had an enormous impact. It has been described as the impetus for a revolution that has changed the face of American sports by making room for the female athlete.[78] While fewer than 32,000 women participated in college sports prior to its enactment, today that number has increased by more than 400% to approximately 163,000 women.[79] Even more dramatic increases in participation have taken place at high school level, increasing by 847%.[80]

Such is its success that there has been a considerable political backlash against the programme, with frequent claims being made that it results in

---

[74] Dana Robinson, "A League of Their Own: Do Women Want Sex-Segregated Sports?" (1998) *J. of Contemporary Legal Issues* 321.

[75] 7 F3d 332 (3rd Cir 1993).

[76] 998 F2d 824 (10th Cir 1993).

[77] 991 F2d 888 (1st Cir 1993).

[78] Bauer, above n 66.

[79] US General Accounting Office No 01–297 *Intercollegiate Athletics: Four-Year Colleges' Experiences Adding and Discontinuing Teams*, March 2001, 7. Cited in Donna de Varona and Julie Foudy, *Minority View on the Report of the Commission on Opportunity in Athletics* (February 2003), 2.

[80] National Federation of State High School Associations (NFHS), *2001 High School Athletics Participation Survey*. Cited in de Varona & Foudy, *ibid.*

reducing men's sporting opportunities.[81] A constitutional challenge to Title IX on these grounds was dismissed, on the basis that the men's team allegedly disadvantaged could not show causal connection between their treatment and Title IX.[82] A wider backlash has also been noted, as evidenced in the media's trivialization and objectification of women athletes and external pressure on women athletes to appear sexualised in order to adhere to traditional notions of femininity.[83] In addition, the strict application of the three-prong test is seen to hamper sports administrators too severely.[84] Furthermore, it has been pointed out that in focusing predominantly on intercollegiate level sports, it has failed to foster equality at a more junior level.[85]

As a result, in June 2002, the US Secretary of Education appointed the Commission on Opportunity in Athletics to review the operation of Title IX. That Commission issued its recommendations in February 2003, which would have significantly reduced the scope of Title IX. The Secretary announced that he would not be following those recommendations, "narrowly [averting] a civil rights disaster."[86] The main recommendation was to dilute the "substantial proportionality" test for compliance and imposing an obligation on female athletes to demonstrate empirically that an interest in a particular sport exists. The Commission itself split and a minority report was issued by Donna de Varona and Julie Foudy.[87] They disputed the report's findings in relation to the disadvantaging of certain men's sports, and objected to the proposal to use interest surveys to determine the level of women's interest.

10.2.3.4 The equal protection clause

Title IX attempts to achieve equality in a segregated world. It is by no means all-embracing and is open to the accusation that it entrenches some gender

---

[81] See, for example, David Klinker, "Why Conforming with Title IX Hurts Men's Collegiate Sports" (2003) *Seton Hall J. Sport* 73. Sangree counters these claims by examining the impact of the increasing commercialisation of certain men's college sports to the detriment of others. Suzanne Sangree, "Symposium: Title IX: Women, Athletics and the Law: The Secretary's Commission on Opportunity in Athletics Squandered its Opportunity to Understand Commercial Collegiate Sports: Why they eliminate Men's Minor Sports and Prevent Title IX from Achieving Full Gender Equality" (2003) *Margins* 257.

[82] *National Wrestling Coaches Association v. United States Department of Education*, June 11, 2003. On May 14, 2004, the Federal District Court of Appeal for Washington DC affirmed the dismissal.

[83] Note, "Cheering on Women and Girls in Sports: Using Title IX to Fight Gender Role Oppression" (1997) *Harvard Law Review* 1627.

[84] Ted Riley Cheesebrough, "Case Note: Cohen v. Brown: I am Woman, Hear me Score" (1998) *Vill Sports & Ent. Law Journal* 295.

[85] Bauer, *op. cit.*, n.66.

[86] Sangree, *op. cit.*, n.81.

[87] *Ibid.*, n.79.

stereotypes. For example, it contains a sweeping exemption for contact sports.[88] When women want to challenge specific discriminatory treatment, they must have recourse to the Equal Protection Clause (be it in state or the federal Constitution). Such litigation is less common, but two cases illustrate the importance of complementing Title IX with a strong equal protection guarantee.

The first case predates Title IX and concerns women's basketball. The rules of basketball were re-written for women at the turn of the century, in order to avoid the necessity of women players running the entire court. The reason? Their sportswear rendered such exertion excessively difficult.[89] Over time, these modified rules become became passé and women in most states reverted to playing full-court five-a-side. However, some states maintained the half-court rules for high school games. This practice was constitutionally challenged in 1976. The District Court found that it did violate the Equal Protection Clause.[90] On appeal, the Court of Appeals held that as schools were entitled to segregate according to gender, they were also entitled to apply different rules to girls' and boys' games.[91] Later in *Dodson v. Arkansas Activities Association*, the district court held that half-court rules prevented girls from accessing college athletic scholarships, and so did violate the Equal Protection Clause.[92] The case illustrates the importance of an equality guarantee even in the context of single-sex sports. However, the limits of the equal protection jurisprudence in this area are also evident. It was only when full-court rules were employed for all college level sports that an equal protection case could have been made. Had the women's game been entirely run along the modified genteel rules, an equality challenge would have been more difficult to sustain.

A more recent example of an equal protection challenge arose in *Baca v. City of Los Angeles*. The case concerned a challenge to municipal allocative decisions in relation to the use of public parks for girls' softball.[93] The only girls' softball team in the area was without a regular playing area, as boys' little league baseball teams effectively monopolised the use of public spaces, due to the manner in which the city's permit system was implemented. The case was settled, part of the settlement being the establishment of a new program for girls' equity in the city's sports and recreation programs. Entitled "Raise the Bar" it affirmed the city's commitment to "achieve gender equity in youth programs" and established quantitative and qualitative goals to meet this

---

[88] For a discussion and critique, see Suzanne Sangree, "Title IX and the Contact Sports Exemption: Gender Stereotypes in a Civil Rights Statute" (2000) *Connecticut Law Review* 381.

[89] Cain, *op. cit.*, n.12 at p.341.

[90] *Cape v. Tennessee Secondary School Athletic Commission*, 424 F Supp 732 (1976).

[91] *Cape*, 563 F2d (6th Cir, 1977).

[92] 468 F Supp 394 (1979).

[93] Cordoba, *op. cit*, n.67 at pp.139, 140.

commitment.

10.3 NATIONALITY, RACE, ETHNICITY AND RELIGION

Racial and sectarian violence are often associated with sport. Racial stereotypes prevail in the sporting world. Many sports have an ignominious history of racist insult and injury, both internally and in their spectators' conduct. Nationalism and xenophobia find an outlet in competitive tournaments. How does the law respond to these many challenges? This part examines the response of equality law, revealing a largely piecemeal and incoherent approach.

10.3.1 Nationality discrimination in EC and Irish law

Sport is currently the vehicle for nationalistic impulse. National teams are typically made up of nationals of the state concerned, defined as that state sees fit. However, nationality discrimination in the economic sphere is prohibited by Community law, where Community nationals are at issue.[94] As we saw in Chapter Eight, it has been accepted that the composition of national teams is not subject to the provisions on non-discrimination on grounds of nationality. These nationality requirements may only be imposed in limited contexts. In *Dona*[95] the ECJ confined its ruling to certain matches, which for non-economic reasons relating to the particular nature and context of such matches, were "of sporting interest only." In *Bosman*, the European Football Association ("UEFA") attempted to argue that nationality discrimination should not be prohibited in relation to the composition of professional club teams. At issue was UEFA's 3+2 rule, whereby a maximum of 5 non-national players could play on any club team. The ECJ rejected the argument that the composition of such teams required a national element.[96] The impact of the *Bosman* case was dramatic and enduring. For example, it resulted in a 1,800% increase in the number of non-British players in the English Premiership.[97]

Nationality discrimination falls under the provision of the EEA dealing with race discrimination, race being defined as "race, colour, nationality or ethnic or national origins."[98] In fact, this is broader than the EC provisions, as EC law is principally concerned with discrimination against other Community nationals, the position of so-called third country nationals being in most

---

[94] Art.12 of the EC.
[95] Case 13/76 [1976] E.C.R. 1333.
[96] Case C–415/93 [1995] E.C.R. I–4921.
[97] *The Guardian*, July 18, 1999.
[98] S.6(2)(h) of the EEA.

instances outside its scope.[99] The EEA thus treats nationality discrimination just as strictly as race discrimination and does not provide any specific exemptions for sporting activities.

There is a general exemption in section 37(2) where the criterion in question is an "occupational qualification for the post in question."[100] Thus any attempt to employ only nationals or even persons from a particular locality (which may be regarded as indirect nationality discrimination) requires justification on the basis of occupation qualification. It is difficult to see how nationality requirements can be regarded as occupational requirements – players of any nationality could play equally well. Rather the requirement is related to the employment context, rather than the employment role. In addition, section 37(3) of the EEA allows discrimination on race/nationality grounds:

> "where on grounds of physiology or on grounds of authenticity for the purpose of entertainment, the nature of the post:
>
> (a) requires a person having the same [race, colour, nationality or ethnic or national origins] as [the employee], and
> (b) would be materially different if filled by a person not having that [race, colour, nationality or ethnic or national origins]."

In addition, section 37(4) allows such discrimination where nationality /national origin is an occupational qualification as "it is necessary that the post should be held by" someone with that identity "because it is likely to involve the performance of duties outside the State in a place where the laws or customs are such that those duties could not reasonably be performed by a person who does not have that" characteristic.

These provisions are not drafted with nationality discrimination in mind, applying to the range of identities embraced by the statutory definition of "race" being "race, colour, nationality or ethnic or national origins." This means that they are essentially ill-fitting to the issue of nationality, particularly in light of the detailed rules on nationality discrimination, which form part of EC law.

The EC provisions allowing nationality discrimination in the selection of national teams do not override the Irish legislation, being facilitatory rather than mandatory. Thus, it would appear that nationality criteria for Irish national teams, while permitted under EC law, may in fact be prohibited under the EEA, at least where an employment relationship is at issue. In contrast, where the participants are not employees, the ESA creates an exception for this approach. Section 5(2)(f) of the ESA permits differences in the treatment of persons "on the basis of nationality or national origin in relation to the provision

---

[99] For a discussion, see Niamh Nic Shuibhne, "Non-discrimination on Grounds of Nationality" in Costello & Barry, *op. cit.*, n.5 at p.269.
[100] S.37(2) of the EEA.

or organisation of a sporting facility or sporting event to the extent that the differences are reasonably necessary having regard to the nature of the facility or event and are relevant to the purpose of the facility or event."

10.3.2 Race, ethnicity and membership of the Traveller Community in EC and Irish law

The Race and Ethnicity Directive provides an EC framework for issues of race and ethnicity (but not nationality) discrimination. The Directive required implementation by 19 July 2003.[101] It deals not only with the employment context, but also with the provision of good and services. The Directive is broader than the EEA and ESA combined, in that it covers a wider range of state activities.[102] The Directive does not define the terms "race" and "ethnicity,", but the better view is that these terms also encompass membership of the Traveller Community, being an ethnic group.[103]

Aside from the differences in scope, the main impact of the Directive is that exemptions provided for in the EEA and ESA must be interpreted strictly, in accordance with the general feature of EC anti-discrimination law. First, as regards direct discrimination, the only exception is for genuine *occupational* requirements. No other exemptions are applicable, which suggests that race discrimination in the provision of goods and services is never permissible.

Under the EEA, race and nationality may all be regarded as occupational qualifications under section 37(2). The provisions of section 37(2), (3) and (4) as outlined in the previous section apply to discrimination on the grounds of race, colour, nationality or ethnic or national origins. However, it is difficult to see how race could ever be a genuine physiological criterion. Given that racial identity lacks any biological foundation, the provision appears to entail a basic contradiction in terms if applied in the sporting context. While there may be superficial differences between individuals of different ethnic and racial backgrounds, any biological generalisations should be regarded as inherently suspect. Thus, while recruiting an Othello of African origin may be permissible under the section, recruiting a black basketball team would not. The ESA also contains an "entertainment authenticity" exception in section 5(2)(i).

The EEA and ESA treat membership of the Traveller Community as a separate ground of prohibited discrimination. While the general "occupational requirement" exception may also be invoked to justify refusal to employ Travellers, it would be very difficult, if not impossible, to establish that

---

[101] For a detailed consideration of the changes to the Irish legislation required by the Directive, see Clíona Kimber, "The Directive on Race Discrimination in Ireland: Reform or Radical Change" in Costello & Barry (eds.), *op. cit*, n.5 at p.243.
[102] *Ibid.*, pp.252–254.
[103] *Ibid.*, pp.249–251.

membership of the Traveller Community was a genuine requirement for a particular activity. Section 33 of the EEA does however permit special programmes for Travellers in order to facilitate integration into employment provided these 'reduce or eliminate the effects of discrimination.'

10.3.3 UK Law on race discrimination

The Race Relations Act 1976 ("RRA") prohibits race discrimination in the UK in the employment context. In addition, the UK Race Relations Act 2000 imposes a general positive duty on public authorities to promote equal opportunity and good relations between ethnic groups.[104]

Cases concerning overtly racist conduct are not uncommon, revealing a disturbing lack of awareness of the basic legal requirements in this area. For example, *Hussaney v. Chester City Football Club*[105] arose out of the manager's calling the 16 year old plaintiff a "black cunt." After Hussaney made his complaint he was refused a professional contract with the club. The IT held that use of such racially abusive language was direct discrimination and that the club's handling of the matter had exacerbated the situation. However, it was found that the refusal of a contract was for purely footballing reasons. Hussaney appealed the latter finding, arguing that he had been victimised for making the complaint. The EAT expressed concern about the IT's failure to detail its findings on this matter fully.[106]

Sterling v. Leeds Rugby League Club[107] concerned a race discrimination claim brought by a rugby player of Afro-Caribbean origin. His claim was supported by the Commission for Racial Equality ("CRE"). The IT held that Sterling had been discriminated against on racial grounds, as he was treated differently from all other players in that he was told that irrespective of his performance in training and preparatory matches, he would not be selected for a place in the first team. In addition, the team manager had indicated that Afro-Caribbean players were unsuited to playing rugby, and that 'those boys' played basketball and other sports. In addition, the IT found that the club's investigation had been poorly conducted.

Singh v. FA & Others[108] concerned the only Asian referee in the English Football League. His claim of racial discrimination and unfair dismissal was upheld. Throughout his career, he had suffered persistent career disadvantage,

---

[104] For a detailed discussion, see Colm O'Cinnéide, "The Race Relations (Amendment) Act" (2001) *Public Law* 220. See also by the same author "Making Use of Positive Equality Duties: The UK Experience" in Costello & Barry (eds.), *op. cit.*, n.5 at p.75.
[105] IT 2102426/97 (unreported, November 21, 1997).
[106] *Hussaney v. Chester Football Club & Ratcliffe* (unreported, January 15, 2001).
[107] (2000) Case No. IT 1802453/00.
[108] IT 5203593/99 [2002] I.S.L.R 141.

racial slurs and discrimination, despite the fact that he had been an excellent referee. The Tribunal held that his dismissal was unfair and that he had been discriminated against.

As well as dealing with race discrimination, the RRA also prohibits discrimination on the basis of nationality and national origin. Due to the breadth of the prohibition, a specific exemption was created to allow geographically based selection of teams. This permits differentiation on the basis of nationality or place of birth or duration of residence in a particular area, where this is done in selecting members to represent a country, place or area, or any related association, in any sport or game.[109] Of course, this must be read in light of EC law on nationality and race discrimination.

As well as legislative developments, there is also a considerable move towards tacking racism in other ways. For example, racial abuse of football players[110] and other racist conduct led to the establishment in 1993 of *Let's Kick Racism Out of Football*. Established by the CRE and the Professional Footballers' Association ("PFA"), the programme works throughout the football, educational and community sectors to challenge racism and work for positive change. In 1998, the Football Task Force produced a report entitled *Eliminating Racism from Football*. In addition, the CRE published a *Charter for Racial Equality in Sport*[111] and *Achieving Racial Equality – A Standard for Sport* in 2000. The aim of the Standard is to guide sports governing bodies as to how to adopt measures to increase participation of ethnic minorities and ensure mainstreaming of racial equality. The standard is based on three "levels of achievement" each dealing with three areas of action at each level. These are the Preliminary Level, which refers to drawing up a written policy and "equity action plan" that will be monitored. The Intermediate Level deals with implementation of the plan and monitoring and consultation with ethnic minorities. The Advanced Level concerns identification of best practices.

10.3.4 Religious discrimination

The EEA, ESA and Framework Directive prohibit discrimination on grounds of religion.[112] In terms of justifying religious discrimination, there is specific provision to permit religious organisations to discriminate on grounds of religion in order to maintain their religious ethos. Section 37(1) of the EEA provides:

---

[109] S.39.

[110] The chanting of racist abuse at football players continues. See the recent incidents detailed at www.kickitout.org/index.php?id=4.

[111] For signatories, see www.cre.gov.uk/speqs/chartersigs.html.

[112] For a detailed discussion, see Marguerite Bolger, "Discrimination on Grounds of Religion" in Costello & Barry (eds.), *op. cit.*, n.5 at p.371.

"A religious, educational or medical institution which is under the direction or control of a body established for religious purposes or whose objectives include the provision of services in an environment which promotes certain religious values shall not be taken to discriminate against a person … if–

(a) it gives more favourable treatment, on the religion ground, to an employee or a prospective employee over that person where it is reasonable to do so in order to maintain the religious ethos of the institution, or
(b) it takes action which is reasonably necessary to prevent an employee or a prospective employee from undermining the religious ethos of the institution."

Under the Framework Directive, it is stated that such selection should not amount to discrimination on another ground.[113] In contrast, the EEA is more facilitatory to religious organisations. It would appear that while it under Irish law it may be permissible for a Catholic sports club to refuse to hire an openly gay coach on the basis that her presence could undermine the club's religious values, this is not permissible under the Directive, as it would amount to discrimination on grounds of sexual orientation.[114]

Religious sectarianism frequently finds an outlet in sport. The complex confluence of national, religious and sporting identity embodied in the GAA is pertinent. The GAA played a central role in forging national identity in the early 20th century, and became linked with the national struggle and the Catholic Church.[115] It chose to organise its structure on the basis of Catholic parishes. The first patron of the GAA, Roman Catholic Archbishop Croke of Cashel, introduced the rule prohibiting members from playing "foreign and fantastic games" such as tennis, polo and croquet in 1885. Also precluded from membership were members of the British security services. The former rule remained in place until 1971, the latter until 2001. Both rules were undeniably sectarian, leading to an organisation which effectively excluded non-Catholics throughout the island of Ireland.

In Northern Ireland, until November 2001, the GAA's Rule 21 excluded members of the Northern Irish security forces from participation in Gaelic games. This was clearly indirectly discriminatory on grounds of religion, given

---

[113] Art.4(2) of the Framework Directive.
[114] See Mark Bell, "Equality Dialogues: Comparing the Framework Directive with the Regulation of Sexual Orientation Discrimination in Ireland" in Costello & Barry (eds.), *op. cit.*, n.5 at pp.329, 336–337. This was confirmed recently by the UK administrative courts (Queens Bench Division) in *R (on the application of Amius v. Secretary of State for Trade and Industry and conjoined applicators* [2004] All E.R. (D) 238, April 26, 2004.

that the RUC was overwhelmingly Protestant. It was only once the Northern Irish Peace Process was well underway and the Police Service of Northern Ireland established that the rule was abolished. The Protestant community in Northern Ireland traditionally perceive the GAA as a sectarian organisation, not only because of Rule 21, but also due to the flying of the Irish Tricolour at matches and the naming of GAA grounds after republican heroes.[116] A stated aim of the GAA remains "the strengthening of the National Identity in a 32 county Ireland through the preservation and promotion of Gaelic Games and pastimes." The organisation's official guide of 2003 also refers to its primary purpose of the GAA as "the organisation of native pastimes and the promotion of athletic fitness as a means to create a disciplined, self- reliant, national-minded manhood. The overall result is the expression of a people's preference for native ways as opposed to imported ones." While such provisions are not in themselves discriminatory, they reflect an ethos that may exclude those of different political and religious backgrounds.

Religious segregation in sport in Northern Ireland goes beyond Gaelic games however, reflecting the divided society. Protestant and Catholic schoolchildren play different sports.[117] Sports such as rugby and hockey are highly segregated, with boxing being the only "working class sport that has avoided major sectarian divisions."[118] Golf is also non-sectarian, but exclusive.[119] As a result in 1998 the Northern Ireland Sports Council launched *Sport without Prejudice* in order to raise awareness of sectarianism in sport, asking supporters to refrain from using foul, abusive or sectarian language or flags and symbols that could be so regarded. It also established cross-community sports projects. In Scotland, the infamous tensions surrounding soccer matches between Glasgow Celtic and Glasgow Ranges have led to specific legislative changes in order to tackle sectarian violence and incitement to religious hatred.[120]

---

[115] For a discussion of the GAA's continuing role in relation to Irish identity, see Mike Cronin, "Ignoring Post colonialism: The Gaelic Athletic Association and the Language of the Colony" (1999) *Jouvert – A Journal of Postcolonial Studies*, available at social.chass.ncsu.edu/jouvert/v4i1/con41.htm.

[116] John Sugden, "Sports, Community Relations and Community Conflict in Northern Ireland" in Seamas Dunn (ed.), *Facets of the Conflict in Northern Ireland* (McMillan Press London 1995), p.199.

[117] See, for example, John Sugden and Scott Harvie, "Sport and Community Relations in Northern Ireland" (University of Ulster Coleraine 1995); "Northern Irish Assembly Sectarianism and Sport in Northern Ireland" (Research Paper 26/01, October 10, 2001).

[118] Northern Irish Assembly, *op. cit.*, n.117 at p.5.

[119] *Ibid.*, p.6.

[120] See discussion see 11 (2) *Sport and the Law Journal* (2003) 113.

10.4 DISABILITY

Disability discrimination is prohibited in the EEA and ESA. Under section 2 of the EEA, disability has a medical definition, encompassing:

"(a) the total or partial absence of a person's bodily or mental function including the absence of a part of a person's body,

(b) the presence in the body of organisms causing, or likely to cause, chronic disease or illness,

(c) the malfunction, malformation or disfigurement of a part of a person's body,

(d) a condition or malfunction which results in a person learning differently from a person without the condition or malfunction, or

(e) a condition, illness or disease which affects a person's thought processes, perception of reality, emotions or judgement or which results in disturbed behaviour, and shall be taken to include a disability which exists at present, or which previously existed but no longer exists, or which may exist in the future or which is imputed to a person."

Under this definition, most of us are disabled in some way. However, this is not to suggest that the provision is absurdly broad, but rather that it was drafted in order to avoid litigation on the vexed issue of the requisite seriousness of impairment. Employers may avail of various exemptions when they seek to justify differences in treatment on the basis of disability. For example, section 35(1) allows different rates of remuneration for disabled employees, if "the employee is restricted in his or her capacity to do the same amount of work (or to work the same hours) as a person who is employed to do the same work of that description but who is without a disability." This section has been criticised as a "coarse tool ... in the face of a delicate task."[121]

The EEA provisions must now be re-read, or indeed amended, in light of the Framework Directive.[122] In particular, in the EEA, there is an attempt to acknowledge that tackling exclusion of disabled persons requires not only prohibition on discrimination (direct and indirect) but also changes to structures and facilities in order to adapt to the presence of the disabled. The concept employed to facilitate such change is "reasonable accommodation." However, under the EEA, employers are required to provide reasonable accommodation for their disabled employees, only in so far as this does not entail more than a "nominal cost."[123] In contrast, under the Framework Directive, employers must

---

[121] Quinn & Quinlivan, *op. cit.*, n.17 at pp.213, 233.
[122] *Ibid.*
[123] S.16 of the EEA.

take "appropriate measures" "to enable a person with a disability to have access to, participate in, or advance in employment, or to undergo training." This positive duty applies unless it would impose a "disproportionate burden" on the employer.[124] Thus the Directive requires a higher standard than the EEA.

A further difference is that the EEA refers to the employer's entitlement to hire only those who can undertake the duties attached to the position.[125] In contrast, the Directive refers to the "essential functions" of the post, such that it would require employers to consider the centrality of the tasks in question and whether a particular post could be adapted to the particular disabled employee's range of abilities.[126]

Beyond the employment context, the ESA deals with the provision of goods and services, again in the form of a "reasonable accommodation" obligation, subject to a nominal costs cap.[127] This requires adaptation of stadia and other sports venues in order to facilitate disabled customers.

Disabled sports persons tend to be segregated from the able bodied. The Special Olympics caters for over 1 million people with intellectual disabilities in 150 countries. However, as well as running the games which are exclusively for the disabled, the organisation also runs the "Unified Program" which aims to encourage the integration of those with intellectual disabilities through sports activities with the fully able. The paralympics were established originally for World War II veterans with a spinal cord injury. Now, the paralympics describe themselves as "elite sport events for athletes from six different disability groups. They emphasise, however, the participants' athletic achievements rather than their disability."[128] According to the participation rules, a "competitor who cannot participate on reasonably equal terms in a sport for 'able-bodied' because of a functional disadvantage due to a permanent disability is eligible for that sport within the IPC programme."

Special provision for disabled sports is clearly permissible under the ESA, which contains many special needs provisions (including sections 5(2)(h) discussed in Part VI below and section 14). In addition, as regards educational establishments, Section 7(4) of the EEA allows differences in treatment between able-bodies and disabled students. Section 7(4)(a) permits differences in treatment on grounds of disability "to the extent that the differences are reasonably necessary having regard to the nature of the facilities or events." In addition section 7(4)(b) allows differences in treatment for disabled students if making a particular facility available to a disabled student would "by virtue of the disability, make impossible, or have a seriously detrimental effect on,

---

[124] Art.5 of the Framework Directive.
[125] S.16 of the EEA.
[126] Recital 17 of the Framework Directive.
[127] See Equality Authority Guidance, *Reasonable Accommodation for People with Disabilities in the Provision of Goods and Services* (Dublin December 2002).
[128] See www.paralympic.org.

the provision by an educational establishment of its services to other students."
The latter provision clearly privileges the position of able-bodied students,
and its drafting is regrettable in that it suggests no duties to provide equivalent
special facilities for the disabled students.

In some instances, disabled athletes may wish to challenge their segregation.
There has been no such litigation as yet in Ireland. However, the US Supreme
Court decision in *Casey Martin v. PGA* illustrates the powerful role of equality
law in reviewing the very rules of the game of sport, in order to allow disabled
athletes access to mainstream sport.[129]

The decision was the first time the Supreme Court considered Title III of
the Americans with Disabilities Act ("ADA"). It held that Title III required
the Profession Golfers' Association ("PGA") to allow a disabled golfer, Casey
Martin, to use a golf cart in PGA Tour events rather than walking the course as
required by PGA rules. Title III applies to places of "public accommodation."
This explicitly includes golf courses. The Supreme Court held that for both
players and spectators of the event, the PGA tournament was a "public
accommodation" and so the PGA was required to make modifications in order
to secure access to the disabled. Modifications are required if they are (i)
reasonable (ii) necessary and (iii) will not fundamentally alter the nature of
the enterprise or operation. The case turned on whether altering the walking
rules in golf would "fundamentally alter" the game. Lower courts had reached
divergent conclusions on this issue. The Supreme Court explained that
"fundamental alteration" could arise in two ways – either by altering an essential
aspect of the game, or by giving the disabled athlete not simply access, but an
advantage in the game. The Court held that the walking rule was not an essential
aspect and that Martin would not be advantaged by the use of the golf cart.

Justice Scalia (with Justice Thomas) dissented on the basis that the
tournament was not a public accommodation for the players. In addition, he
argued that the Act did not require businesses to alter their products, so that
the PGA could not be required to alter the game it offered Martin. Thirdly, he
argued that the walking rules had to be regarded as essential, as the rules of
any game were essentially arbitrary and the courts could not determine which
rules were "essential" or not.

This case allows disabled athletes to challenge their exclusion from
mainstream sports and to challenge the rules of those sports. However, it comes
to the aid of those whose disability is limited. "Someone who cannot run is not
qualified to participate in a foot race. But if a player qualifies by demonstrating
exceptional ability in the sport's essential skills, his permanent disability
unrelated to the sport should not exclude him from using that ability."[130]

---

[129] 121 S.Ct 1879 (May 20, 2001).
[130] Roy Reardon and Joseph McLaughlin, *"GA Tour Inc v. Martin*: The Decision and its
Implications" (2002) *Sport and the Law Journal* 150 at 155.

10.5 SEXUAL ORIENTATION

Discrimination on grounds of sexual orientation is prohibited under the EEA, ESA and the Framework Directive.[131] There are no specific exemptions in the Acts for direct sexual orientation discrimination, and it is difficult to see how it could be justified in practice. However, the defined gender roles in sport often foster an environment hostile to lesbian and gay athletes. Homophobia is undoubtedly prevalent in sport.

In the introduction to this chapter, we referred to the Gay Games and Bingham Cup, examples of gay sports activities, which are by their nature exclusionary. In addition, the Eurogames, the European Gay and Lesbian Sports Championships are now in their 10th year.[132]

Are these permissible under equality law? Section 5(2)(h) of the ESA is of relevance. It allows differences in treatment of persons for whom services are provided "for a *bona fide* purpose and in a *bona fide* manner to promote the special interests of persons in that category to the extent that differences in treatment are reasonably necessary to promote those special interests." An unsuccessful attempt to rely on the section was made by the defendant restaurant in *Shanahan v. One Pico*.[133] The restaurant did not allow young children to dine, in a manner that was found to be discriminatory on family status grounds. The restaurant argued that the exclusion was justified on the basis of section 5(2)(h) in that the "special interests" of its business clientele justified the exclusion. This was rejected on the basis that there was no evidence of such special interests. In contrast, it may be permissible to rely on the section in order to justify predominantly gay social sporting events as gay athletes arguably share such a "special interest". Also relevant are the special provisions on clubs, discussed in para.10.7 below.

10.6 AGE

The EEA and ESA prohibit discrimination on grounds of age, as does the Framework Directive.[134] Although the bulk of the Framework Directive

---

[131] For a comparison of the provisions of the EEA with those of the Framework Directive on sexual orientation, see Mark Bell, "Equality Dialogues: Comparing the Framework Directive with the Regulation of Sexual Orientation Discrimination in Ireland" in Costello & Barry (eds.), *op. cit.*, n.5 at p.329.

[132] www.eurogames.info.

[133] DEC–S2003–056, June 30, 2003.

[134] For a discussion of the implications in Ireland, see Peggy O'Rourke, "Age Discrimination" in Costello & Barry (eds.), *op. cit.*, n.5 at p.345. See also, in the UK context, Bob Hepple, "Age Discrimination in Employment: Implementing the Framework Directive 2000/78/EC" in Sandra Fredman & Sarah Spencer, *Age as an Equality Issue: Legal and Policy Perspectives* (Hart Publishing Oxford, 2003), p.71.

required implementation by December 2, 2003, the period for the provisions on age discrimination is extended to December 2, 2006.

The EEA only applies to those between 18 and 65.[135] Employers may generally not take decisions on the basis of age in relation to their employees between these ages. However, this is subject to the general exemption under section 16 of the EEA, which acknowledges that the Act does not require employers to recruit or retain employees "not able or no longer able to undertake the duties attached to the position" or "not fully competent and available and fully capable of undertaking the duties attached to the position." In addition, Section 34(3) of the EEA permits differentiation on the basis of age where there is clear actuarial or other evidence that significantly increased costs would result if discrimination were not permitted. These sections must now be read in light of Article 4 of the Directive on occupational qualifications and/or the specific exemption for age discrimination under Article 6. Article 4 allows decisions to be taken on the basis of age where "by reason of the nature of the particular occupations or activities concerned or of the context in which they are carried out, such a characteristic constitutes a genuine and determining occupational requirement, provided that the objective is legitimate and the requirement is proportionate."

Article 6 allows employment decisions based on age where they are objectively and reasonably justified by a legitimate aim, including legitimate employment policy, labour market or vocational training requirements, and the means employed are appropriate and necessary. Article 6 gives examples of positive action, minimum conditions of age for access to employment or certain advantages of employment and maximum ages for training. Concern has been expressed that Article 6 is ambiguous and requires detailed elaboration as part of its domestic implementation.[136] In addition, Article 6 also entails a proportionality test, which casts doubt on whether the sweeping exemption in section 34(3) is still permissible.

Age clearly affects athletic ability, so sports employers may take age into account in so far as it affects ability. However, EC equality law is based largely on an individual model, which means that rigid age limits require careful scrutiny. Even under Article 6 of the Framework Directive, measures must be shown to be "appropriate and necessary" which appears to require an individual examination of whether a particular employee is able, rather than a generalised decision based on the "normal" abilities of athletes her age.

The ESA also prohibits age discrimination, defined in the same way. However, there are many exemptions, allowing differences in treatment on grounds of age. As regards educational establishments, Section 7(4)(a) of the EEA permits differences in treatment on grounds of age "to the extent that the

---

[135] S.6(3) of the EEA.
[136] Hepple, *op. cit.*, n.134 at p.86.

differences are reasonably necessary having regard to the nature of the facilities or events."

10.7 SPECIAL PROVISIONS IN RELATION TO CLUBS

The ESA contains special provisions in relation to clubs, defined as bodies, which have applied for or hold a certificate of registration under the Registration of Clubs Act 1904–1999.[137] This registration allows clubs to sell alcohol to members and certain visitors. Unlike the provisions in relation to goods and services, the ESA does not prohibit discrimination in all circumstances in relation to clubs. A balance was struck in the legislation between the importance of non-discrimination and the value of freedom of association.

In principle, a club will be considered to be acting in a discriminatory manner where it has a rule, policy or practice, which discriminates against a member or applicant in relation to the affairs of the club. These include issues of admission, termination of membership and making reasonable accommodation for members with disabilities. However, a club will not be regarded as discriminating where the principal purpose of the club is to cater only for the needs of persons of a particular group from within the nine grounds.[138] This provision allows freedom of association to effectively trump non-discrimination where the principal purpose of the association is to cater for the needs of the group.

Whether this strikes the correct balance remains to be seen. Clearly the provision could not be availed of by, say, a tennis club, which excludes women on the basis of "tradition" or misogyny, as it would be difficult to demonstrate a link between the composition and principal purpose of the association. However, the section could have been more tightly worded, so as to require a higher threshold in relation to the nexus between the activities and the purpose of the club.

Also permitted is the practice of confining benefits or privileges to particular categories of age or gender where it is not practicable for those outside the category to enjoy the benefit or privilege at the same time as members within the category.[139] Clubs must make arrangements to offer the same or reasonably equivalent benefit or privilege to those members outside the category. This is the most troubling of the exemptions, as it appears to warrant such a low standard of justification – all that must be demonstrated is that it is not practicable to extend the benefits to all at the same time. This runs counter to the essence of anti-discrimination law, which requires equal treatment even

---

[137] S.8 of the ESA.
[138] S.9(a) of the ESA.
[139] S.9(b) of the ESA.

where scarce resources are at issue. If a club has categories of membership, which are discriminatory, and only limited availability of its resources, the solution is to redraft those categories of membership, and reallocate in a rational manner to all. All that the subsection requires is a "reasonably equivalent benefit" to be made available to all. The section is an uneasy compromise, which arguably aims to protect commonplace discrimination against women by golf clubs, in making available only inferior membership status to women. Whether it succeeds remains to be seen – the requirement of "reasonably equivalent benefit" when read in light of the object and purpose of the legislation, may allow for robust scrutiny of these measures.

It is also permissible to have different types of membership, access to which is not based on any discriminatory ground.[140] Also allowed are measures to eliminate past discrimination by offering particular fee rates or membership arrangement to persons of a particular gender, by reserving places on the management board etc.[141] Finally, there is a sports-related permissive clause which allows clubs to provide reasonably necessary different treatment to member of a particular gender, age, disability, nationality or national origin as regards sporting facilities or events.[142]

A special enforcement mechanism is available in the case of discriminating clubs. The Equality Authority may apply to the District Court in order to suspend the club's certificate, with the effect that it cannot sell alcohol for the duration of the suspension. There is an appeal to the Circuit Court, and clubs may re-apply to the District Court for a declaration that it is not longer discriminating.

This issue came to the fore in 2003 with the decision to hold the Irish Open Golf Tournament in the internationally renowned Portmarnock Golf Club in Dublin for the 13th time. Under current membership rules the club's only full female member is Irish President Mary McAleese. The National Women's Council of Ireland said it would lead protests to try to force Portmarnock Golf Club to admit women members before the tournament commenced, but eventually decided against such a strategy.[143] After months of negotiations (during which the tournament took place without any problems), the Equality Authority sought a declaration that the Club was a discriminating club within the meaning of the Act.

Proceedings were brought before the District Court in which the club captain argued strongly that the refusal to admit women members was an expression of diversity and should be just as acceptable as "... ladies' boutiques, hairdressers and even ladies' rugby teams" on the basis that equality and

---

[140] S.9(c) of the ESA.

[141] S.9(d) of the ESA.

[142] S.9(e) of the ESA.

[143] See Joe Humphries, "Women's Group Not to Boycott Open", *Irish Times*, July 19, 2003.

sameness could be separated.[144] For the purposes of section 9 of the ESA, the club argued that its principal purpose was to cater for the playing of men's golf. Having said that, the club did not actually defend the District Court proceedings in the normal manner, but rather brought a High Court application seeking a declaration that the Equal Status Act is unconstitutional,[145] which is still pending at the time of publication of this book. It is understood that the club will argue that its members' freedom of association should entail a right to exclude women.

Judge Collins in the District Court rejected the above argument, however, concluding that in fact the principal purpose of the club was to facilitate the playing of golf generally (as distinct from men's golf specifically). She pointed out that whereas women were not allowed to become full members, they were permitted to play on the course – an illogical state of affairs if the principal purpose of the club was that claimed by the Portmarnock Committee.[146] As a result, the club had its drink licence suspended for seven days. However, enforcement of this sanction was itself suspended pending the hearing of the constitutional action taken by the club.[147]

The furore here mirrored arguments over the exclusion of women members at the Augusta National Golf Club, perennial host of the US Masters tournament.[148] The political nature of the controversy was highlighted by the fact that Minister for Sports, John O'Donoghue TD defended a government grant of more than €250,000 for tourist promotion of the Irish Open[149] He said he had no role in selecting Portmarnock to be host to the 2003 Irish Open, and was opposed to Portmarnock's membership policy, but insisted that the monies were provided to assist in the staging of an international competition in Ireland, and were not a donation to the club.

---

[144] Olivia Kelly, "Portmarnock Captain says Ban on Women Expresses 'Diversity'", *Irish Times*, November 29, 2003. For a criticism of this logic see Fintan O'Toole, "Diversity" Endangers Equality", *Irish Times*, January 20, 2004.

[145] See Christine Newman, "Club to Challenge Constitutionality of Act Rather than Appeal Decision", *Irish Times*, February 21, 2004

[146] See "In the Bunker", *Irish Times*, February 21, 2004, "Golf Club Breaches Equality Law", *Irish Times*, February 21, 2004 and "Authority Greets Ruling as a 'Stimulus for Change'", *Irish Times*, February 21, 2004.

[147] See Kitty Holland, "Golf Club Sanctioned for not Admitting Women", *Irish Times*, May 19, 2004

[148] For a description of the views of the US National Organization for Women, see www.now.org/issues/wfw/111202augusta.html. Interestingly less attention centered on the fact that the Royal St George's course in Sandwich which hosted the 2003 British open tournament also refuses to admit women members. See "Not Open for Women", *The Times*, July 14, 2003

[149] See Joe Humphreys, "Ministers Clash on Golf Sponsorship", *Irish Times*, November 30, 2002, Joe Humphreys, "Women's Council Criticises Sponsor of Portmarnock Golf Event", *Irish Times*, July 24, 2003 and by the same author, "RTE says it has Declined Irish Open Marketing Opportunities", *Irish Times*, July 22, 2003.

Such challenges have been heard in the US context, and have led to a subtle, if somewhat contradictory line of authority. In one case, the US Supreme Court held that the Boys Scouts association could exclude gay men and boys.[150] In contrast, in another case, the Supreme Court held that the United States Junior Chamber ("Jaycees") was prohibited from excluding women. The Jaycees was established in 1920 to provide opportunities for young men to develop personal and leadership skills through service to others.[151] It should be noted that the US Supreme Court examines the nature of the association carefully, and it is only where the association can be linked to the expression of particular values and beliefs (referred to as "expressive association") that in rare circumstances the right to association will trump the right to equality. It is difficult to imagine that a sports club could sustain such a claim. If anything, the ESA is too deferential to freedom of association, in that it does not require a tight nexus between the purposes of the club and the exclusion in question.

In contrast, in the UK Sex Discrimination Act 1975 does not apply to private clubs. Section 34 exempts discrimination by non-profit making voluntary bodies in restricting their membership to one sex or providing benefits to one sex only in accordance with their main object. However, it appears that discriminating clubs have been refused National Lottery funding due to their exclusionary policies.[152]

10.8 CONCLUSIONS

Equality in sport is an elusive concept. However, that does not mean it should not have a central role to play. Equality law is inherently flexible, and different models of equality may be adopted. A basic individual approach to equality will serve to challenge some of the most egregious exclusions and stereotypes in sport. The drafting of section 25(2) of the EEA allows women to challenge gender based occupational requirements. In other areas, sport itself is a

---

[150] *Boy Scouts of America v. Dale* 530 US 640 (2000). For discussion of the impact of the case see Jean Hughes & Merry Moiseichik, "Expressive Association: The Right of a Congressionally Chartered Membership Organization to Discriminate" (2002–2003) *J Legal Aspects Sport* 305.

[151] *Roberts v. United States* 468 U.S. 609 (1984).

[152] See 1(5) *Sports Law Bulletin* (1998) where reference is made to the decision of Marylebone Cricket Club to admit women, noting that the club "has been turned down for National Lottery money in the recent past, largely due to this discriminatory policy." The *Bulletin* also cites two members of the MCC In the *Daily Telegraph* of September 25, 1998: "One does not need the brain of Einstein to twig that the case for admitting women is to use them as a convenient 'stalking horse' despite vehement denials, in the wider pursuit of new sponsors and Lottery money. It is all totally cynical, covered with the veneer of 'political correctness' to the detriment of many members' wishes, and much of what the MCC has stood for decades."

manifestation of the politics of identity, and as such, equality law permits say, gay and disabled sports in order to enhance equality. In yet other respects, equality law must go beyond individual and identity based approaches, to develop tools to root out inequitable resource distribution. In the disability context, the "reasonable accommodation" requirement takes on new potency in light of the Framework Directive. Similarly, Irish law warrants reform in that it lacks anything like the concept of "effective accommodation" as developed in the US to allow scrutiny of allocative decisions in segregated sports. Non-binding rules, policies and codes may well have a role to play, particularly in the context of self-regulation and amateur activities. However, for the necessary institutional change to take place, strong enforcement is required, together with commitment and leadership from within sports bodies. At present, this appears to be lacking.

The Irish Sports Council's most recent strategy statement "Sport for Life"[153] mentions neither "equality" nor "discrimination." It does however reference recent social changes in Ireland, noting recent increases in immigration and the need for policies and programmes to reflect the need to help [sports governing bodies] "reach out to and attract more people from a variety of backgrounds, interested in a greater range of sporting activities. They must also encourage and support life-long participation and take account of the new challenges and opportunities presented by ethnic diversity." While this statement is welcome, the strategy statement as a whole reflects an underdeveloped appreciation of equality issues.

There appears to be widespread lack of awareness of equality law among sports governing bodies, sports employers and organisers. Cases in the UK reveal persistent problems in this respect. While big business has internalised some of the lessons of equality law, this does not appear to be the case with the sports industry. At a minimum, the application of current statutory provisions to the sporting context should be clarified and publicised. In this respect the Australian initiative *Play by the Rules* could serve as a model. A joint initiative of the Equal Opportunity Commission of South Australia and the South Australian Office for Recreation and Sport, and produced in consultation with the main sports governing bodies, it is a basic online training and information resource for sport and recreation clubs and associations. It provides information on how to prevent and deal with inappropriate behaviour including discrimination, harassment, favouritism, bias and various forms of abuse.[154]

Equality law must address the lack of opportunities for girls and women in sport. The lack of sporting opportunities for girls is striking. In the UK, findings are that girls aged 7–11 are less than half as likely to take part in physical

---

[153] Available at www.irishsportscouncil.ie/PDF/Strategy2003.pdf. This document is discussed in Chapter One.
[154] www.playbytherules.net.au/intro.html.

education and sport compared to boys and that 40% of girls drop out of sport and physical recreation by the age of 18.[155] In schools, girls are afforded fewer sporting opportunities than boys. If other educational opportunities were distributed so unfairly, there would be a national outcry. Sport for children should be no exception. Unfortunately, section 7(4) of the EEA allows educational establishments to treat girls and boys differently "to the extent that the differences are reasonably necessary having regard to the nature of the facilities or events." The breadth of this exemption weakens the EEA's potential to act as a means to challenge the denial of sporting opportunities to girls. In addition, the comparator requirement inherent in Irish equality law means that challenging differences in treatment between institutions (for example separate boys and girls schools) poses particularly challenges.

It also appears to be time to question segregation of all kinds in sport. Even at the most elite level, it appears that rigid segregation is open to challenge. The law should allow challenges to the rigid categorisation that have evolved in sport, and to create fluid boundaries based on ability. This is not a fanciful aspiration. Hanna Ljungberg, a 25–year-old Swede, considered by some to be the world's best female soccer player will play for Italian Seria A club Perugia from the beginning of next year.[156] Perhaps most famously, between May 2003 and February 2004, four female golfers played in tournaments on the men's professional tour in America and Australia,[157] with one golfer Suzy Whaley qualifying to play in a tournament and three other golfers, Annika Sorenstam, Laura Davies and fourteen year old Michelle Wie[158] receiving sponsors' invitations to play. These women competed without much success[159] but with significant publicity and indeed debate[160] In response, Canadian golfer Brian Kontak announced in March 2003 that he would attempt to qualify for the US Women's open in July of that year.[161] Moreover in March 2004, the European Tour Players' Committee issued a statement saying that it did not wish to see any more women competing on the circuit, with committee chairman Jamie

---

[155] Source: www.sportni.net/what_we_do/community/women_in_sport.htm.
[156] See "Perugia to Open Talks with Leading Ladies", *Irish Times*, October 29, 2003.
[157] Billy Jean King, "On a Swing and a Prayer for World's Best Woman Golfer", *Irish Times*, May 22, 2003, Donald McRae, "Davies Can Cut it With the Big Boys", *Irish Times*, February 11, 2004 and "Davies to Take on the Men", *The Times*, September 12, 2003.
[158] "Wie accepts Evian's Sparkling Offer", *The Times*, January 28, 2004 and "Teenage Girl Tees it Up in Hawaii", *Irish Times*, January 14, 2004
[159] "Wie Falls Short", *The Times*, September 20, 2003.
[160] See "Battle of the Sexes does Women no Favours", *The Times*, February 18, 2004, "Norman Hits out over Promotion of Women", *The Times*, February 4, 2004, "Davies Invitation causes man-sized Consternation", *The Times*, January 29, 2004 and Tom Humphries, "Singh's Attitude to Sorenstam is Way Off Course", *Irish Times*, May 19, 2004.
[161] Shane Hegarty, "Playing the Gender Game", *Irish Times*, May 24, 2003.

Spence saying: "It was discussed in depth and it's fair to say that from the players' point of view, we don't want women in our tournaments. Some of our own players are struggling for starts."[162]

Nonetheless, equality law is the appropriate tool to challenge the rigid categorisations all too prevalent in sport, and the current statutory regime allows such challenges. In order to succeed, exemption clauses must be read appropriately narrowly.

Of course, there will still be a place for single sex, special, senior and gay sports. Participation in sport should not be dependent on conformity with the abstract ideal of the warrior male. However, segregated sports may or may not be equitable. In order to ensure equality between different groups, the dramatic impact of Title IX in the US is instructive. Strong institutional and individual enforcement leading to close scrutiny and alteration of allocative decisions brought about dramatic change in a short period of time. Thus, single-sex sports provided the locus for a flourishing of sporting achievement. However, segregation can only be justified in relation to the participation in sports themselves. Segregation at the margins of sport – in clubs and recreational facilities, requires much more careful scrutiny. Discriminating clubs and associations should not be able to hide behind the mask of privacy, but rather under the ESA must demonstrate that their exclusionary practices are closely tied to the promotion of special interests of members as embodied in the club's principal purpose. The pillars of society in Portmarnock who seek to defend prestige, privilege and patriarchy do not qualify.

Equality law allows those traditionally excluded from sporting activities to challenge discriminatory practices. It is to be hoped that as this process develops, the rules of the game, written and unwritten, will adopt to the new diversity. As exemplified by Casey Martin's case, rules should not be cast in stone. Sport itself must adapt to accommodate its diverse participants.

---

[162] "Players' Group Rules on Women", *Irish Times*, March 6, 2004.

Index

Advertising, *see also* **Business of sport**
alcohol, 402 *et seq.*, 456
  British law and, 403
  French law and, 403, 404
  restricted advertisement of, 403
billboards on, 359
British Code of Advertising, 403
Broadcasting Commission of Ireland
  code of practice and, 375, 376, *see also* **Broadcasting**
bus shelters, 359
campaigns, 331 *et seq.*, 356
Code of Sales Promotion Practice of the Advertising Standards Authority of Ireland, 336
contract obligations and, 365, 366, *see also* **Contract law**
hoardings, 353, 356, *see also* **Sponsorship**
local authorities and, 359
misleading, 359, *see also* **Ambush marketing**
programmes on, 356
revenue from Olympic Games and, 18
sites, control of, 356
tickets on, 356
Aeronautic Federation, 99
Alcohol, see **Advertising**
Ambush marketing, 358 *et seq.*, *see* **Marketing** and **Sponsorship**
examples of, 359, 360
  advertising on vehicles, 359
  advertising where event occurring, 359
  cyber squatting, 359
  giveaways, 359

Ambush marketing—*contd.*
examples of—*contd.*
  intentional conflict marketing, 359
  misleading advertising, 359
  tickets and, 359
  typo squatting, 360
protection against, 360
  legal, 360
  non-legal, 361
targeting, 360–362, 366
Anti-doping, *see also* **Doping, Irish Sports Council, Prohibited Substances, Steroids** and **World Anti-Doping Agency**
Clean Sports Guide, 17
Convention for, 17
Europack, 17
fair procedures and, 121 *et seq.*
future for, 141 *et seq.*
  development of testing and procedures for, 142 *et seq.*, *see also* **Testing**
  dietary supplements, regulation of, 148 *et seq.*
  genetics and, *see* **Genetics**
  punishment of coaches, 142
justifications for, 100 *et seq.*
  ethics of sport, 104
  health of athlete, 100
  interest of would-be-clean athlete, 103
  International bodies and, *see* **Council of Europe, International Olympic Committee, Irish Sports Council** and **World Anti-Doping Agency**

Anti-doping—*contd.*
  justifications for—*contd.*
    level paying field for all
      competitors, 103
    protecting good name of sport
      and the clean athlete,
      102
  policy, 82
    harmonisation of, 152, 153
  programmes, 10,
  strict liability basis, 57, 59, 129 *et*
    seq., *see also* **Doping**
  innocent ingestion of banned
    substances and, 133
  mitigation of severity of rules,
    131
  moral innocence, 129
  severity of sanction, 129
  therapeutic exceptions to rules of,
    135, 136
  World Anti-Doping Agency
    (WADA), *see* **World Anti-**
    Doping Agency
  World Anti-doping Code, 18, *see*
    World Anti-Doping Agency
Apartheid,
  ban on sports tours, 56
Arbitration, 19 *et seq.*, *see also* **Court**
  of Arbitration for Sport and
  International Court of
  Arbitration for Sport
  clause in rules, 20
  independence of arbitrators, 24
  role of, 19, 20
Archery Federation, 99
Arsenal FC, 339 *et seq.*
Association, freedom of, 54
Athletes, *see also* **Business of Sport**
  arbitration and, 10, *see* **Arbitration**
  clean, 102, 103
  drugs and, 83 *et seq.*, *see* **Anti-**
    doping, Doping and
    Prohibited substances
  fair procedures for, 58, 74, *see* **Fair**
    procedures
  gay, *see* **Equality**
  governing bodies and, 4, *see also*
    Governing bodies

Athletes—*contd.*
  lesbian, *see* **Equality**
  protection of the rights of, 144, 145
  pursuit of excellence by, 10
  testing of, 108, 120, *see* **Testing**
Automobile Federation, 99

Baseball Federation, 102
Betting, 405, 406
  industry, 72
  internet, 348
  restriction on power to organise,
    405
Beckham, David, 325, *see also* **Image**
  rights
Billiards' Federation, 99, *see also*
  Snooker
Body building,
  diuretics and, 99, *see also*
    Prohibited substances
Bosman case, 12, 39, 377, 385 *et seq.*,
  see also **European Union,**
  Restraint of trade and **transfer**
  rules
  consequences of professionalism
    and, 392, 393
  domestic transfers, application to,
    394
  facts of, 387, 388
  football transfer system, effect on,
    393
  impact of, 377
  in-contract players, application to,
    394
  judgment in, 388 *et seq.*
  freedom of movement for workers,
    378
  transfer fee rule, 389
  nationality quota rules, 390–392
  non-EU nationals, application to,
    395 *et seq.*
  UEFA rules prior to, 386
Boxing, 9, 99, 165, 166, *see also*
  Contact Sports
  criminal law in Ireland and, 176
  disciplinary proceedings by, 50
  diuretics and, 99, *see also*
    Prohibited substances

Boxing—*contd.*
  legality of, 169
    anti-social activity, regards as,
      170
    bare knuckle prize fighting, 172,
      173
    chronic brain damage, 170
    classification as unlawful activity,
      169
    consent, 171
    prize fighting distinguished from
      boxing, 172, 183
    punch drunk syndrome, 170
    terms of fatalities, 170
    UK Law Reform Commission
      and, 171, 175
  reform of, 176–178
    16-year career limit, 178
    centralised records of medical
      conditions of boxers, 178
    headgear, utilisation of, 177
    increased padding in gloves, 177
    thumbless gloves, 177
  Restraint of trade and, 53, *see also*
    Restraint of trade
British Athletics Federation (BAF),
  55, *see also* **Athletes**
**British Boxing Board of Control
  (BBBC),** 50, 249, 250, *see also*
  Boxing
**Broadcasting Commission of Ireland
  Codes of Practice,** 375, 376, *see
  also* **Broadcasting**
Broadcasting, 363 *et seq.*, *see also*
  Business of Sport
  Competition law and, 442, *see also*
    Competition law
  Contract clauses, 365, *see also*
    Contract law
    advertising obligations, 365
    capacity to sublicense, 366
    combating ambush marketing,
      366, *see also* **Ambush
      marketing**
    content advertising breaks,
      366
    insurance against cancellation of
      event, 366

Broadcasting—*contd.*
  Contract clauses—*contd.*
    nature of coverage, 365
    obligations to event sponsors,
      366
    options to renew, 365
    payment, 365
    promotional obligations,
      365
    quality of broadcast, 366
    rights ownership, 365
    termination, 365
    territorial licences, 366
    timetable, 366
  EC Commission and, 453 *et seq.*, *see
    also* **European Union**
  exclusivity and, 304
  FAI/SKY television deal, 370 *et seq.*,
    454 *et seq.*, *see also* **FAI** and
    Sky
    designated events to be shown
      live, 374, 375
    free to air basis, 370
    list of events on terrestrial TV,
      370 *et seq.*
    market rates, determination of,
      374
    power of minister for
      communications and, 370
      et seq.
    public reaction to, 370
  listed events, protection of, 366 *et
    seq.*
  revenue, 304
  rights, 363 *et seq.*
    as live, 365
    extended highlights coverage,
      365
    live radio coverage, 365
    live TV coverage, 365
    magazine programme, 365
    mobile telephone, 365
    new technology, 365
  television and competition law, 442
    et seq.
    assessment of markets and,
      443
    collective purchasing, 451

Broadcasting—*contd.*
  television and competition law—
    contd.
    collective selling of broadcast
      rights, 448–451
    exclusive broadcasting rights,
      445–447
    maximum possible exploitation of
      rights, 448
    UEFA broadcasting rights deal 2003,
      453, *see also* **UEFA**
Business of sport, 304 *et seq.*
  advertising and, *see* **Advertising**
  ambush marketing, *see* **Ambush**
    marketing
  broadcasting, *see* **Broadcasting**
  competition law, *see* **Competition**
    law
  contracts, *see* **Contract law**
  European Community law and, *see*
    European Union
  events organiser, *see* **Events'**
    organiser and **Sponsorship**
  governing bodies and, *see*
    Governing Bodies
  rights involved, 304
    individual sportsperson, *see*
      Individual sportsperson
    intellectual property, *see*
      Intellectual property
    ownership, 305, 306
    peripheral, 304
    property, 304
  sponsorship, *see* **Sponsorship**
  sports clubs and, *see* **Sports**
    clubs
  sportswear company, *see*
    Sportswear company

Canadian Commission of Inquiry
    into the use of Banned Drugs
    and Practices, 83, 110, *see also*
    Prohibited substances
Cantona, Eric
  trademark in name, 335
Charities, 19
Chelsea FC, 211, 229, 314, 450
Christie, Linford, 90

Civil Liability and Sport, 197 *et seq.*
  coaches, *see* **Coaches**
  governing bodies and, *see*
    Governing bodies
  negligence, 198
  no-fault insurance scheme proposal,
    253
  nuisance, tort of, 198
  public policy concerns, 198
  referees, *see* **Referees**
  regulation of persons involved in
    sport, 197, 198
  restriction of role of, 253
  school sports and, *see* **School**
    sports
  trespass to the person, 198
Coaches,
  civil liability arising, 234
  criminal liability, 235, *see also*
    Criminal Law
  duty of, 230 *et seq.*
  duty of care of, 230
    liability of, 230
    over-psyching of players,
      234
    safety issues and, 231–233
    school, *see* **School Sports** and
      Sports Teachers
Collins, Kim, 136
Collins, Steve, 317, 318, *see also*
    Boxing
  Committee for the Development of
    Sport (CDDS),
  monitoring programme of, 17
  mutual assistance programme of
    (SPRINT), 18
Committee on Public Safety and
    Crowd Control (1990), 294 *et*
    seq., see also **Crowd Control**
Competition law, 13, 39, 407 *et seq.,*
    see also **EU** and **Restraint of**
    trade
  abuse of dominant position, 409, 413
    et seq.
    abuse, 414–416
    dominance, 413
  anti-competitive agreements, 409
    between undertakings, 410 *et seq.*

Competition law—*contd.*
  broadcasting and, 442 *et seq.*, *see*
    Broadcasting
  European Commission, intervention
    of, 424, 425
  governing bodies and, 425 *et seq.*,
    see also **Governing bodies**
    excessive domination by, 425 *et
      seq.*
    regulatory and commercial
      dominance, 428
    use of dominant position to
      restrict competitors,
      426
  impact of, 53
  ownership of multiple clubs,
    435–437
  rules and, 421 *et seq.*
    inherently acceptable sporting,
      421–423
    inherently unacceptable, 423
    violation of EC law, 423
  salary caps and, 433, *see also*
    Salaries
  sport and, 416 *et seq.*, *see also*
    Business of Sport
    balance to be drawn, 417,
      420
    sport as big business, 418
    sport as something special,
      418–420
  sponsorship and equipment and,
    429
  State aid, 434 *et seq.*, *see* **State
    Aid**
  ticketing arrangements and, 430 *et
    seq.*
  transfer rules, *see* **Transfer rules**
  undertakings, 409, 410 *et seq.*
Contact sports (Lawfulness of),
    165 *et seq.*, *see also* **Non-contact
    sports**
  boxing, *see* **Boxing**
  consent of participants, 156–167
  duties of participants in, 211 *et seq.*,
    see also **Negligence**
    carelessness, 214
    error of judgement, 214

Contact sports—*contd.*
  duties of participants in—*contd.*
    momentary carelessness, 214
    oversight, 214
    reckless disregards, 214
    simple breaches of safety rules,
      213
    split second incidents and
      liability, 212
    tort of battery and, 215
  on-field violence, *see* **Violence**
  Irish position and, 167
    assault causing harm, 167
    causing serious bodily harm, 167,
      168
    Law Reform Commission
      recommendations, 168,
      187
  statutory position re assault, 167
  legality of organised sport, 166
  rugby, *see* **IRFU** and **Rugby**
  United Kingdom Law Commission
    and, 168, 169, 188
Contract law, *see also* **Business of
    Sport**
  breach of, 38, 55, 56
  broadcasting contracts, *see*
    Broadcasting
  employment, 307 *et seq.*
    breaches of contracts, 319
    employed professionals, 307
    employer/employee relationship,
      308, 316
    employer's obligations, 313
    exclusion clauses in contracts,
      319–321
    express contract terms, 309
    fixed term contracts, 313, 314
    gross misconduct, 314, 315
    implied contract terms, 311,
      312
    independent contractors, 307
    legislation governing, 308
    non-renewal of contracts of,
      313
    specified purpose contracts, 313
    Statute of Frauds, compliance
      with, 324

Contract law—*contd.*
  employment—*contd.*
    termination of contract of, 312
    unfair contract terms, 320 *et seq.*
    unfair dismissal, types of, 313,
      314
    written contracts, 321–324
  impact of, 306 *et seq.*
  rugby and, *see* **IRFU**
  Sponsorship and, 354 *et seq.*, *see*
    Sponsorship
Council of Europe, *see also* **European
  Union** and **Governing bodies**
  Antidoping Convention, 109 *et seq.*
  fair hearing, requirements for, 141,
    see also **Fair procedures**
  monitoring of, 111
  Committee for Development of
    Sport, 109
  Committee of Ministers of, 111
    recommendation to combat traffic
      of doping agents, 111, 112
  European Anti-doping Charter, 109
  fight against doping and, 105,
    109–112, *see also* **Anti-
    doping** and **Doping**
  impact of, 16
  role of, 17
  safety recommendations of, 272
  spectator violence and, 300–303, *see
    also* **Spectators**
    convention on, 300
    recommendations and, 300, 301
    alcohol consumption and, 300
    crowd searches, 301
    guidelines for ticket sales, 301,
      302
    stewards and, 302
    racist behaviour, 303, *see also*
      Racism
    xenophobic propaganda, 303
Court of Arbitration for Sport (CAS),
  20 *et seq.*, *see also* **Arbitration**
  appeals procedure, 24
  awards by, 24
  code of, 23, 24
  costs and, 24
  financial maintenance of, 21

Court of Arbitration for Sport—
  contd.
  founding of, 20
  independent status of, 21
  jurisdiction of, 22
  number of arbitrators, 22
  oral pleadings before, 24
  overhaul of, 21, *see* **International
    Court of Arbitration for
    Sport**
  taking a case to, 23
Cricket, 52
  duty of care and, 257
  English Test and County Cricket
    Board (TCCB), 52
  governing body for (ICC), 52, *see
    also* **Governing bodies**
  official matches, 52
  restraint of trade and, 52
  test series, 52
Criminal law, 165 *et seq.*, *see* **Boxing,
  Coaches, Contact sports** and
  violence (on-field)
Crowd control, 273, 274, *see*
  Spectators, Stadia and **Violence**
**Committee on Public Safety and
  Crowd Control (1990),** 294 *et
  seq.*
Cyclists,
  cycling season, 152
  drugs scrutiny of, 84
  EPO use of by, 98, *see also*
    Prohibited substances
  French Cycling Federation, 83
  International Cycling Union, 83
  Pacemakers, use of, 379
  Tour de France (1998), 83, 85, 93,
    110, 112

Darts, 8
Delgado, Pedro, 93
Department of Education, *see also*
  Stadia
  Code of Practice for Safety at Sports
    grounds, 273, 274
**Department of Tourism, Sport and
  Recreation,**
  responsibility for sport and, 10

Dietary supplements,
 regulation of, 148 *et seq.*, *see also*
  Anti-doping and **Prohibited**
  Substances
Directorate on Sport and **Youth,**
 17
Disability, 461, 484 *et seq.*, *see*
  Discrimination
 definition, 484
 employers and, 485
 reasonable accommodation
  obligation, 484, 485
 segregation and, 486
 sports and, 485, 486
Discrimination, *see* **Equality**
 age, 461,
 clubs and, 489 *et seq.*, *see* **Sports**
  clubs
 definition of, 463
 definition, 487–489
 direct, 463, 464
 disability, *see* **Disability**
 ethnicity and, 479
 family status, 461
 gender, 461
 gender, 465 *et seq.*, *see* **Gender**
  discrimination
 indirect, 463, 464
 marital status, 461
 nationality, 477
  permitted, 478
  race, definition of, 477
 permitting of, 463
 prohibited grounds of
  discrimination, 461
 prohibition on grounds of, 487
 race, 461, 479
  UK law on, 480, 481
 religious grounds, 461
  Northern Ireland, 482
  permitting, 481
  prohibition of discrimination on,
   481
  religious secretariansim, 482
 sexual orientation, 461, 487
  prohibition of, 487
 travelling community, membership
  of, 461, 479

Doping, 82 *et seq.*, *see also* **Prohibited**
  substances
 arbitration and, 22, see **Arbitration**
 blood, 95 *et seq.*
  Aranesp, 98
  blood boosting hormones, 98
  definition of, 96
  DynEPO, 98
  Erythropoietin (rEPO), 97, 98
  high altitude training and, 96
  operation of, 96
 cases of, *see also* **Anti-doping**
  burden of proof, 122, 123 *et seq.*
  definition of offence of, 122, 123
  deviations from listed rules and
   procedures, 137 *et seq.*, *see*
   also **Fair procedures**
  fairness of hearing, 122
  lawful exceptions to anti-doping
   rules, 122
  provisional suspension prior to
   hearing, 136
  provisional suspension prior to
   hearing, 136
  standard of proof in, 122, 123
  strict liability, 122, 126 *et seq.*,
   129 *et seq.*
 control of in Ireland, *see* **Ireland**
 cyclists, 83, 84, *see also* **Cyclists**
 definition of, 156
 detecting, 85
 fault based doping offences, 126
 history of, 82 *et seq.*
 international focus on, 82
 penalties for, 161–163
 scale of problem of, 85 *et seq.*
 state sponsored programmes of, 85,
  91
 steroids, *see* **Steroids**

Equality, 457 *et seq.*, *see also*
  Discrimination
 Authority, *see* **Equality Authority**
 Bingham Cup, 487
 European Lesbian and Gay Sports
  Championships, 487
 gay athletes, 487
 Gay Games, 459, 460, 487

Equality—*contd.*
  homophobia, 459
  Irish statutory regime, 460, 461 *et
    seq.*
  lesbians, 460, 487
Equality Authority, 464, *see also*
    Discrimination and **Equality**
  codes of practice, preparation of by,
    465
  equality reviews by, 465
  powers of, 464, 465
  role of, 464
Ethics,
  children's sports and, 25, 247
  Code of Sports' Ethics, 17, 247
  European Group on Ethics, 113
  Protecting, 104, 105
European Annual Sports Forum,
  16
**European Convention on Spectator
    violence and Misbehaviour at
    Sports Events,** 17
European Group on Ethics, 113, *see
    also* **Ethics**
European Sports Charter, 17
European Union, *see also*
    **Competition law and Council of
    Europe**
  broadcasting deals and, 453 *et seq.*,
    see also **Broadcasting**
  business of sport and, 377 *et seq.*,
    see also **Business of Sport**
  betting and, *see* **Betting**
  Bosman ruling case, *see* **Bosman**
  European Model of Sport
    Consultation Document,
    13
  freedom of movement of workers,
    379 *et seq.*, 398 *et seq.*
  freedom to provide services, 402
    et seq., 405, 406
  governing bodies and EC law,
    383 *et seq.*, *see* **Governing
    bodies**
  sport subject to EC law when an
    economic activity, 382
  specific transfer periods,
    legitimacy of, 400 *et seq.*

European Union—*contd.*
  doping and, 105,112–115, *see also*
    Anti-doping and **Doping**
  community support plan to
    combat doping, 113
    et seq.
  Hardop project, 112
  provision of information re dugs,
    114
  seat on WADA board, 114, *see
    also* **World Anti-Doping
    Agency**
  role of, 11
  sports policy of, 13 *et seq.*
**European Year of Education through
    Sport (2004),** 16
Events organisers, *see also* **Business
    of Sport** and **Sponsorship**
  rights of, 352 *et seq.*
  contractual relationships and,
    353
  intellectual properties, 352,
    see also **Intellectual
    property**
  protection of, 352
  trademarks, *see* **Intellectual
    property**
Everton FC, 419

FAI (Football Association of Ireland),
    5, 19, 63 *et seq.*, 345, *see also*
    Governing bodies
  Croke Park and, 415, *see also* **GAA**
  disciplinary process of, 5
  IRFU and, *see* **IRFU**
  ISC programme and, 120
  registration policy of, 62 *et seq.*
  resale of returned tickets by, 295
  rulebook of, 66, 69, 440
  Sky television deal, 370 *et seq.*, *see*
    Broadcasting
  Tribunàl, 43
Fair play, 2, 17, 178, *see* **Fair
    procedures**
Fair procedures, 27 *et seq.*, 57 *et seq.*,
    see also **Judicial review**
  acting *intra vires*, 62
  application of fair rules, 59

Fair procedures—*contd.*
  anti-doping policy and, 121 *et seq.*,
    see also **Anti-doping** and
    doping
    deviations from listed rules and
      procedures, 137 *et seq.*
  constitutional guarantee of, 73
  disciplinary hearings and, 73
    constitutional justice and,
      73
    cross-examination at, 74
    disciplinary panel, 74
    evidence, right to, 73
    legal representation at, 74
    natural justice and, 73
    oral hearings, right to, 75
    precise requirements for, 74
    procedure at, 76
    right to address, 74
  fair hearing, right to, 141, 160
    rules for, 160, 161
  fair rules, creation of, 59
  standards for, 58
FIFA, 19, *see also* **FAI**
  anti-doping programme of, 133, 152,
    see also **Anti-doping**
  governance by, 19
  rules, 23, 66, 440, 441
  trademarks and, 352, *see also*
    Intellectual property
  transfer rules, 23, *see* **Transfer**
    rules
  World cup, *see* **World Cup**
Figo, Luis, 325
FINA (world swimming body), 18,
  102
Football hooliganism, *see* **Spectators**
Footballers, *see also* **Bosman, FAI,**
    FIFA and **World Cup**
  earnings of, 4
  foul tackles by, 3, *see also* **Violence**
  gaelic, *see* **Gaelic football**
  professionalisation, 4, 5
  transfer system, 12, *see* **Transfer**
    rules
Freedom of information,
  access to records, 79
  documentation, access to, 79

GAA, *see also* **Gaelic football** and
    Hurling
  aim of, 483
  Central Council of, 70
  Croke Park, 255, 268, 415, 416
  FAI and, *see* **FAI**
  games administration council of,
    70
  IRFU and, *see* **IRFU**
  ISC programme and, 120, *see also*
    Anti-doping and **Prohibited**
    substances
  religion and, 482
  Rule 21, 482, 483
  Rule 42, 415, 456
  rules of, 55, 61, 69 *et seq.*, 163,
    456
  status of, 33
Gaelic football, 54, 181, 182, 238, 415,
    see also **GAA** and **Hurling**
  All-Ireland final, 375
  Northern Ireland and, 482, 483
  Rules of, 69, 70
  women and, 355
Gascoigne, Paul,
  trademark in name, 335
Gay athletes, *see also* **Athletes** and
    Equality
Gender discrimination, *see*
    Discrimination and **Equality**
  Irish law and, 465
    direct, 466
    pregnant women, 465
  UK position, 467 *et seq.*
    challenging discrimination on
      grounds of, 467
    preserving segregation, 469
  United States of America and,
    471
    ensuring equality in a segregated
      world, 472
    equal protection clause, 475
    gender equal opportunity factors,
      473
    sport and the American way,
      471
Genetics,
  threat posed by, 151, 152

Giggs, Ryan,
  trademark in name, 335
Golf, 216 *et seq., see also* **Negligence**
    and Non-contact sports
  golf courses, 216
    lightening on, 286
    occupiers' liability on, 283 *et
        seq., see also* **Occupiers'
        liability**
    organiser liability on, 283 *et seq.*
    unreasonable risks in course
        design, 284, 285
    unreasonable risks in organisation
        of tournament, 285
  negligence in, 216 *see also*
        Negligence
    categories of circumstances for,
        217 *et seq.*
    duty of care and, 220, 221
    foreseeable zone of danger,
        217
    reasonable behaviour, 218
    remedial actions of golfers,
        220
    wild golfer, 218, 220
  playing rules and, 216
  safety rules and, 216
Governing bodies,
  best practice, 251, 252
  business of sport and, 345 *et seq.,*
        see also **Business of sport**
    database protection for, 347 *et
        seq.*
    raising finance and, 345 *et seq.*
  competition law and, *see*
        Competition law
  duties of to participants, 248 *et seq.*
  duty of care in creation of rules,
        248
  EC law and, 383 *et seq.*
  Safety bodies as, 251
  Vicarious liability, 248

Hearn, Barry, 317, 318, *see also*
        Boxing
Hepatitis B & C,
  mandatory testing, 278, *see also*
        Testing

High Court,
  supervisory jurisdiction of, 81
HIV,
  mandatory testing, 278, *see also*
        Testing
Hockey, 143, 192, 213, 239, 474
  ice, 193, 203, 281, 282
  International Hockey Federation's
        Disciplinary Commission,
        22
  World Cup, 22
Horseracing, 71, 77
  Irish Derby, 375
  Irish Grand National, 375
  syndicate, 71
  Turf Club rules, 71, 72, 73
    Referral's Committee, 77
Human rights,
  impact of European Convention on,
        78, 79, *see also* **European
        Union**
  United Kingdom and, 78
Hunter, Alan, 9
Hurling, 179, 182, *see also* **GAA** and
        Gaelic football
  All-Ireland final, 61, 268, 354,
        375
  rules of, 61

Intellectual property, 305, *see also*
        Image rights
  copyright, 305, 306
  passing off, 305, 306
  patents, 306
  significance of, 306
  trademarks, 305, 306, 340, *see also*
        Sports clubs
Image rights, *see also* **Business of
        Sport**
  agreements, 325
    contractual negotiations and, 326,
        327
    standard contractual clauses and,
        326
  privacy,
    invasion of, 333
    right of, 332, 333
  property right in one's image,

Image rights—*contd.*
protection of, *see also* **Intellectual
property**
Code of Sales promotion practice
of Advertising Standards
Authority of Ireland, 336,
see also **Advertising**
defamation and, 336
tort of passing off and, 327
et seq.
trademarks and, 335
Individual sportspersons,
rights of, 324 *et seq.*, *see also*
Business of Sport
image rights and, *see* **Image rights**
Insurance,
cancellation of events and, 366
health, 178
legal expenses, 246
no fault insurance scheme, 253,
254
personal accident, 246
professional indemnity, 246
public liability, 246
schools and, 246
State sponsored insurance scheme,
254
vicarious liability and, 210
**International Amateur Athletics
Federation (IAAF),** 55, *see also*
Athletes
doping rules of, 49, *see* **Doping**
**International Court of Arbitration
for Sport (CAS),** 18, 20, *see also*
Arbitration and **International
Olympic Committee**
creation of, 21
divisions of, 21
appeals arbitration, 22
doping cases and, 22, *see also*
Doping
ordinary arbitration, 21
responsibility of, 21
**International Olympic Committee
(IOC),** 18, *see also* **Olympics**
arbitration and, 22, *see* **Arbitration**
and **International Court of
Arbitration for Sport**

International Olympic Committee—
contd.
drugs and,
banned list, 86 *et seq.*, 97 *et seq.*,
see **Prohibited substances**
guidelines, 127
international sports federations
and, 109
medical code, 107
funding and, 21
impact of, 106, 107
jurisdiction of, 18, 19
opposition of to doping, 106, 107,
see also **Anti-doping** and
Doping
powers of, 21
International Tennis Federation,
drug testing rules of, 49, *see*
Testing
Ireland,
doping control in, 115 *et seq.*, *see
also* **Doping**
Michelle Smith case, 115
Irish Sports Council anti-doping
unit, *see* **Irish Sports
Council**
IRFU, 255, 345, *see also* **Governing
bodies**
breaches of player's contracts, 310,
see also **Contract Law**
contract obligations on player, 309,
310
FAI and, 255, 296
GAA, 296
Lansdowne Road, 255
mobility rule of, 43
payers' contracts with, 307, 309
players' contracts, 309 *et seq.*, 319,
320
regulation of game of rugby by, 309,
see also **Rugby**
retainer fees paid by, 310
rules of, 43
youth and schools' coaching scheme,
234
**Irish Footballer's Supporters'
Association,** 9, *see also* **FAI** and
Footballers

Irish Sport's Council (ISC),
Anti-doping unit of, 87, 105, 119 *et
        seq.*, *see also* **Anti-doping** and
        Doping
    3 strand approach of, 121
    Anti-doping Committee, 119
    Anti-doping initiative for Medical
        Professionals, 121
    establishment of, 119
    functions of, 120
    Irish Anti-Doping Rules, 121
    National Anti-doping programme,
        11, 121, 120
Anti-doping rules of, 18, 155, *see
        also* **Anti-doping** and *World
        Anti-doping Code*
    Anti-doping Appeal panel, 162
    burden of proof, 157
    definition of doping, 156, *see
        also* **Doping**
    fair procedures and, 160, *see also*
        Fair procedures
    penalties for doping offences,
        161–163
    results management, 159
    standard of proof, 157
    testing and, 158, 159, *see also*
        Testing
    therapeutic use exemptions,
        157
children's sport, *see also* **School
        sports**
    Code of Good Practice, 247, 248
funding by, 19
objectives of, 10, 11
role of, 10
strategies, 10
Irvine, Eddie,
    trademark in name, 335

Johnson, Ben, 82, 92, 110, *see also*
        Doping
Judicial review, 29 *et seq.*, *see also*
        Fair Procedures
benefits of, 29
criteria for, 31
doctrine of legitimate expectations
        and, 30

Judicial review—*contd.*
doctrine of *ultra vires*, 30
irrationality, 56
sporting bodies and whether public
        or not, 32 *et seq.*, 37 *et seq.*
Juventus FC, 265, 346, 435

Keane, Roy, 5, 9, 178, 324
Krabbe, Katrin, 140

Leicester City FC, 56, 229, 230
Lewis, Lennox, 175, *see also* **Boxing**
Lesbians, *see* **Equality**
Limited liability companies, 19
Liverpool FC, 180, 211, 265, 266, 419,
        450

Manchester United FC, 178, 310, 311,
        321, 325, 331, 436, 437
Marathons, 359, 364
    Dublin City, 7, 361, 375
    London, 249
Marketing, *see also* **Sponsorship**
    ambush, 358 *et seq.*, *see* **Ambush
        marketing**
Martial arts, 99
McCarthy, Mick, 5
McGuire, Mark, 102
Motor cyclists, 289
Motor racing, 249, 427, 428
    Formula 1, 413, 444
    Irish Motor Racing Club, 258,
        280

National Olympic Committees, 19,
        362, *see also* **Olympics**
Negligence, 199 *et seq.*, *see also* **Civil
        liability**
    coaches, *see* **Coaches**
    defences, 207 *et seq.*
        contributory negligence,
            208
        volenti non fit injuria, 208,
            209
        voluntary assumption of risk,
            208
    duty of care on the sports field,
        199–202

Negligence—*contd.*
duties of participants on sports field, 211 *et seq.*
duties of participants in contact sports, *see* **Contact sports**
spectators, duty to, 221–223
non-contact sports and, 216 *et seq.*, *see also* **Golf** and **Non-contact sports**
once off situation and, 288
persons outside stadia and, 288, *see also* **Stadia**
recklessness, 205, 223
referees, *see* **Referees**
reckless disregard, 223
reasonableness, 204, 205
factors for determining, 205, 206
rules of thumb for determining, 206, 207
sports schools, *see* **School Sports**
sports teachers, *see* **School Sports**
standard of care, 202
relevant circumstances and, 203, 204
vicarious liability, 210
Newcastle United FC, 50, 51, 403, 404, 450
Non-contact sports, 206, 211, *see also* **Contact sports**
duties of participants in, 216, *see* **Golf**
Nottingham Forest FC, 180, 265
Nuisance, 290
creator of, 290
private, 290
rules for, 290
sporting events and, injury caused by, 290, 292

O'Sullivan, Ronnie, 89
O'Sullivan, Sonia, 338, 362
Occupiers' liability, 255 *et seq.*
golf course and, 283 *et seq.*, *see* **Golf**
sports stadia, duty of occupiers of, 255 *et seq.*,
Courts' approach to, 268

Occupiers liability—*contd.*
sports stadia, duty of occupiers of—*contd.*
crowd safety, 265, *see also* **Crowd control** and **Stadia**
entrants to, 256
exclusion notices, 260
injury due to state of premises, 259
non-participants, duty to, 265, 279
participants, duty to, 261–264, 277 *et seq.*
recreational users, 257, 261–263
safety, *see* **Stadia**
statutory obligations, 266–268
trespassers, 257–259
visitors to, 256, 261
Organisers (of Sporting Events),
common law duty of, 279
non-participants, duty to, 279–282
occupiers' liability and, 279, *see* **Occupiers' liability**
participants, duty to, 277 *et seq.*, *see also* **Participants**
foreseeable risks, guarding against, 277–279
matters to be considered, 277, 278
spectators and, 279, 280, *see* **Spectators**
Olympic Council of Ireland, 19, 362
Olympics, *see* **International Olympic Council**
Athens, 152
Barcelona, 185
Charter, 362
Mexico, 107
National Olympic Committees, 362
Para Olympics, 85
Special Olympics, 485
Sydney, 97, 108
trademarks and, 352
Winter, 2, 89

Participants, *see* **Civil liability, Governing bodies, Negligence** and **Organisers**

Pentathlon Federation, 99
Portmarnock Golf Club, 490 *et seq.*
Privacy, *see* **Image rights**
Private law
  challenges for decisions of sporting
    bodies, 38 *et seq.*
  principle grounds for, 38
Prohibited methods, 95, 96 *et seq.*, *see*
    also **Anti-doping** and **Prohibited**
    Substances
  blood doping, *see* **Doping**
  manipulation, 95
    chemical, 95
    methods of, 95
    pharmacological, 95
    physical, 95
Prohibited substances, 86 *et seq.*, *see*
    also **Prohibited methods**
  agents with anti-estrogenic activity,
    87
  alcohol, 99
  anabolic Agents, 87, 90
    anabolic Androgenic steroids, 89,
      see also **Steroids**
    Beta 2 agonists, 90
    Clenbuterol, 90, 140
    Erythropoietin (rEPO), 92
    Formoterol, 90
    Human growth hormone (hGH),
      92
  Banned lists, 87, *see also*
    International Olympic
    Council
  Beta-2 Agonists, 87, 93
    Salbutamol, 93
    Salmeterol, 89
    Terbutaline, 93
    Therapeutic use exceptions,
      93
  Beta-blockers, 99
  Cannabinoids, 87, 89
    Cannabis, 89
    Marijuana, 89
  Glucocorticosteroids, 87
  Masking agents (including
    Diuretics), 87, 93, 99
    Probencid, 93
    Therapeutic use exceptions, 99

Prohibited substances—*contd.*
  Narcotic analgesics, 87, 89
    Heroin, 89
    Methadone, 89
    Morphine, 98
    Pethidine, 89
  particular sports and, 99
  Peptide Hormones, 87, 94
    Andrenocoticotrophic, 94
    Erythropoietin (EPO), 94
    Human chorionic Gondatrophin
      (hCG), 94
    Human growth hormone, 94
  related substances, 88
  stimulants, 87, 88
    Amphetamines, 88
    Caffeine, 88
    Cocaine, 88
    Modafinil, 88
    pseudoephedrine, 88
  sub-divisions of, 88 *et seq.*
  testosterone,
    administration of, 91, 92
Public bodies,
  definition of, 78
  human rights and, 78, *see* **Human**
    rights

Racism, 14, 271, 303, 481
racist,
  abuse, 230, 481
    banners, 276
    chanting, 298
    groups, 294
    injury, 477
    insult, 477
    propaganda, 303
Ranieri, Claudio, 314
Real Madrid, 25
Rebagliati, Ross, 89
Referees,
  defences of, 225
  duties of, 223 *et seq.*
  duties owed to, 229
  duty of care, 223, 224
  negligence and, 224, 227, *see also*
    Negligence
  safety rules and, 229

Refugees,
sports programmes for, 18
Restraint of trade, 38, 39 *et seq., see also* **Bosman case** and **Competition law** and **Transfer rules**
circumstances of, 41, 42
criteria for successful action for, 40, 41
denial of access to the profession, 44, 50
disciplinary matters and, 48
freedom of movement, 39
Irish position and, 42–44
livelihood, constitutional right to earn, 38, 53–55
protection of, 54
restrictions on capacity to earn money, 50
salary caps and, 433, *see also* **Salaries**
suspension and, 48
unreasonable, 39 *et seq.*, 48
Rowing, 99, 262
Rugby, 165, *see also* **Contact Sports** and **IRFU**
club rules and, 62
contracts, *see* **IRFU**
doping and, 136, *see also* **Doping**
forceful contact and, 184
Heineken European cup, 375
International Rugby Football board (IRFB), 251
International Rugby Board standards, 224
safety and, 231 *et seq.*
violence and, 165, 183 *et seq., see also* **Violence**
World Cup, 136

Safety, *see* **Stadia**
Salaries, 433, *see also* **Competition law**
caps, 433
objectives of, 433
restraint of trade doctrine, 433, *see also* **Restraint of trade**

School sports,
Code of practice, 247, *see* **Irish Sports Council**
duties of, 235 *et seq., see also* **Negligence** and **Sports' teachers**
coaching in, 237, *see also* **Coaches**
facilities and, 245
public policy and, 235
sports equipment and, 238
litigation avoidance strategies, 246
policy document, 246, 247
mandatory participation in, 236
supervision of school sports and duty at, 239 *et seq.*
location of activity, 244
nature of activity, 243, 244
vulnerability of injured party, 241–243
Services,
freedom to provide, *see* **European Union**
Sheahan, Frankie, 136
Show jumping,
Nations Cup, RDS, Dublin, 375
Sky television, *see* **Broadcasting** and **FAI**
Exclusive television rights and, 9
Smith, Michele, 95, 116 *et seq., see also* **Anti-doping, Doping** and **Ireland**
Snooker, 7, 87
Irish Masters, 375
World professional Billards and SnookerAssociation (WPBSA), 427
Women and, 468
Snowboarding, 89
Soccer, *see* **Bosman, FAI, FIFA, Footballers, Transfer rules** and **UEFA**
European Chamionsgips, 367, 370, 375
World Cup, 352, 359, 367, 370, 375
1998, 293
1990, 338, 364, 431, 432
2002, 5, 366, 368

Spectators,
    duty owed to, 279–281
    violence by, 293 *et seq.*
        Birmingham City FC, 293
        Committee On Public Safety And
            Crowd Control (1990), 294
            et seq.
        Council of Europe and, *see*
            Council of Europe
        football hooliganism, 293
        Heysel Stadium disaster, 293
        Lansdowne Road riots, 294
        Leeds United FC, 293
        public order legislation and,
            293
        UK in, 293
        UK legislative response to,
            297–300
Sponsorship, 304, 353 *et seq.*
    advertising and, 353, *see*
        Advertising
    ambush marketing, *see* **Ambush**
        marketing
    competition law and, 429, *see*
        Competition law
    contract, 354 *et seq.*, *see also*
        Contract law
        exclusivity and, 355
        exposure and, 356
        guarantee of capacity and, 354
        miscellaneous terms of, 358
        unforeseen circumstances,
            provision against, 357
    corporate, 339, *see also* **Sports**
        clubs
    huge return on, 353
Sport,
    civil liability and, *see* **Civil liability**
    criminal law and, *see* **Criminal law**
    definition of, 6–9
        physical activity, 7
        competitive element, 7
        level of organisation and, 7
        criteria for (UK), 8
    discrimination and, 489 *et seq.*
        different types of membership,
            490
        penalties for, 490

Sport—*contd.*
    ethics in, *see* **Ethics**
    ownership of, 9, 10
Sports clubs, *see also* **Business of**
    Sport
    corporate sponsorship and, 339
    revenue earning potential of,
        339
        copyright in club crest, 339
        trademark protection, 340 *et seq.*,
            see also **Intellectual**
            property
    rights of, 338 *et seq.*
Sports teachers,
    coaching by, 237, *see also* **Coaches**
        and **Sports schools**
    duties of, 235 *et seq.*, *see also*
        Negligence and **Sports**
        schools
        extent of, 235
        onerous, 235
Sportswear company,
    business of sport and, 351
    intellectual property rights and, 351,
        see also **Intellectual property**
    passing off, 351
Stadia,
    crowd control, 272
    occupiers' liability and, *see*
        Occupiers' liability
    persons outside, duties to, 287 *et*
        seq.
        negligence, 288, *see also*
        Negligence
    nuisance, 290, *see also* **Nuisance**
    safety in,
        best practice checklists,
            275
        best practice for, 273
        codes of practice and, 269
        co-ordination of efforts, 274
        Council of Europe and, 272, *see*
            also **Council of Europe**
        crowd management, 274
        Department of Education Code of
            practice, 273, *see*
            Department of Education
        fire, 273

Stadia—*contd.*
  safety in—*contd.*
    guidelines (UEFA), 269
    non-binding recommendations
      and, 269
    requirements for, 275–277
    structural matters, 273
State Aid, 434, *see also* **Competition
  law**
  general provision on, 434
Steroids, *see* **Prohibited substances**
  banned, 82
  Clostebol, 90
  designer, 146, 147
  detecting, 91, 92
  Nadrolene, 90
  Nitrogen retention, 90
  road rage, 90
  side effects of, 90, 91
  Stanozolol, 82, 90
  Tetrahydrogestrinone (THG), 146
  testing procedures for, *see also*
    Testing
    gas chromatography, 91
    mass spectrometry, 91
Swimming, *see also* **FINA** and **Smith,
  Michelle**
  body suits and,
  child protection and, 25
  European Swimming Governing
    Body (LEN), 119
  safety and, 231, 240, 246, 262,
    263
Swim Ireland, 119, *see also*
  Swimming
Swiss Equestrian Federation, 21

Television broadcasting, *see*
  Broadcasting
Testing (doping), *see also* **Doping**
  constitutional rights and, 144,
    145
  development of and procedures for,
    142
  greater accreditation of laboratories,
    148
  Hepatitis, *see* **Hepatitis B & C**
  HIV, *see* **HIV**

Testing (doping)—*contd.*
  increasing the extent of testing, 142
  IOC rules and, 158, *see also*
    **International Olympic
    Council**
  mandatory, 144
  passport for athletes, 142
  research into science of, 145–147
  urine, 144
  whereabouts form and, 142
Transfer rules, 437 *et seq.*, *see also*
  Bosman case
  competition law and, 437, *see also*
    Competition law
  concerns of EC Commission and,
    438
  changes to, 439
  free movement of workers, 440,
    441
Treacy, John, 120
Tyson, Mike, 175, *see also* **Boxing**

UEFA, 19
  broadcasting Rights Deal 2003, 453,
    see **Broadcasting**
  safety guidelines of, 269 *et seq.*, *see
    also* **Stadia**
UK Law Commission, 7
UK Sports Council, 8
US Anti-doping agency (USADA),
  143

Violence (on-field), 178 *et seq.*, *see
  also* **Contact sports** and **Stadia**
  convention on, 272
  criminal law and regulation of the
    sports field, 190 *et seq.*
    player consent, 191–194
    policy to police field of play,
      194–196
  foul play, 179
  police and, 179, 180
  primary responsibility for, 188
  prosecution of, 178 *et seq.*
    instances of, 181–186
    dearth of, 183
    Director of Public Prosecutions,
      referral to, 181

Violence (on-field)—*contd.*
  prosecution of—*contd.*
    inconsistent nature of, 187
    intentional violations of safety
      rules, 188
    off the ball incidents, types of,
      184
    recommendations for reform,
      187–189
  spectator, *see* **Spectators**
Warren, Frank, 318, *see also* **Boxing**
Watson, Michael, 52, *see also* **Boxing**
Winter Olympics, *see* **Olympics**
Woods, Tiger, 324, *see also* **Golf**

World Anti-Doping Agency (WADA),
    83, 84, 87, 87, 105, 143, 144 *see
    also* **Anti-doping** and **Doping**
  development of, 152 *et seq.*
  establishment of, 107
  future of, 152
  objectives of, 107–109
World Anti-doping Code, 82, 109,
    153–155
  criteria for banning substances, 154,
    155
Wrestling, 99

Yegorova, Olga, 146